A CRITICAL
HISTORY OF ENGLISH POETRY

Other Works by Herbert J. C. Grierson

✲

MILTON AND WORDSWORTH

THE BACKGROUND OF ENGLISH LITERATURE

CROSS CURRENTS IN ENGLISH LITERATURE OF
THE SEVENTEENTH CENTURY

ESSAYS AND ADDRESSES

CRITICISM AND CREATION

✲

In collaboration with Sandys Wason

THE PERSONAL NOTE

✲

Chatto & Windus

A
CRITICAL HISTORY OF
ENGLISH POETRY

by

HERBERT J. C. GRIERSON
&
J. C. SMITH

1970
CHATTO & WINDUS
LONDON

30682

Published by
Chatto & Windus
London
*
Clarke, Irwin & Co. Ltd
Toronto

ISBN 0 7011 0727 8

First published 1944
Second (revised) edition 1947
Second impression 1950
Third impression 1955
Fourth impression 1962
Fifth impression 1965
Sixth impression 1970

Printed in Great Britain by
Lewis Reprints Limited
Port Talbot, Glamorgan

PREFATORY NOTE

ENGLISH poetry may be regarded historically as one of the ways in which the national spirit has expressed itself in successive ages; or as the work of a succession of individual poets, each expressing his own mind and spirit; or as an art with various sub-species—epic, lyric, drama, etc.—each of which has developed in accordance with its own traditions. We shall try to do such justice as our space permits to all these aspects of the subject. Considering, however, that poems are made not by influences or traditions but by men, we shall lay most stress on the second. No doubt every poet is the child of his age and the heir of a particular tradition; but the great poet helps to create the spirit of his age and to mould the tradition he has inherited. Therefore we shall dwell longest on the greatest poets, touching on the minors in so far as they supply important links in the chain of tradition or have themselves left something written which the world has refused to let die. Our plan may make this study less useful as a text-book, but it will help, we trust, to set the history of English poetry in truer perspective.

We have called this book *A Critical History of English Poetry*. But the critic, no less than the poet, is the child of his age; and we are well aware that critics like us, whose taste in poetry was formed in Victorian days, may fail to do justice to the poetry and the criticism of the present generation, between which and the Victorian Age a "shift of sensibility" has occurred comparable to that which took place between the Age of Pope and the Age of Wordsworth.

We are deeply indebted to that fine and generous scholar, Mr. John Purves, for help in preparing this book.

CONTENTS

✱

CONTENTS

Chapter One

ANGLO-SAXON POETRY

WESTERN civilisation arose in the basin of the Mediter-ranean. Greece invented science and perfected many of the arts; Rome gave law and order; and from Judæa came a religion which vanquished the old Aryan nature-worships and the orgiastic cults of the Orient. By A.D. 350 Greek culture, Roman law, and the Christian religion prevailed from the Atlas to the Solway.

But beyond this Mediterranean world, divided from it by great mountains and rivers, another world lay, very different in religion and culture and in the structure of its society, a world where men worshipped not Christ but Odin, and dwelt not in walled cities under laws but in a sort of semi-feudal order in clearings of the forest. The Romans called it by the general name of Germania. From these two worlds, the Mediterranean and the Germanic, our literature has sprung.

The Roman historian Tacitus, writing about A.D. 100, declared that Germania had been fettered for two hundred years; but presently she began to burst her chains and press upon the crumbling ramparts of the Roman Empire. In some regions the Germanic invasion was partial or gradual, infiltration rather than invasion; but on the remote province of Britain the billow of calamity broke in full force. By the middle of the sixth century all the eastern lowlands were submerged in a flood of Anglo-Saxon heathendom; at the end of it the invaders broke through to the Irish Sea and the Bristol Channel, and shattered what remained of the British realm into three fragments. Wales, the largest of these fragments, long re-mained unconquered, cherishing her sacred memories.

By A.D. 600, however, Christianity had begun to come back to Britain, from Rome and from Iona. The two missions met in Northumbria, which became, and for nearly two cen-turies remained, the greatest and most civilised of the Anglo-Saxon kingdoms, the home of famous scholars like Bede and Alcuin. When Northumbrian civilisation collapsed before the Danes, the primacy passed to Wessex, where letters re-vived for a time under Alfred the Great (c. 871 to 900). Most of the poetry composed in Northumbria has come down to us in the dialect of Wessex. In the eleventh century England was conquered, first by the Danes, and finally by the Normans. Anglo-Saxon poetry owes nothing either to the conquered Britons or to the conquering Danes: the Norman conquerors destroyed it.

The Anglo-Saxon invasion of Britain was only one episode in that Wandering of the Nations which made the Heroic Age of Germania as full of epic material as the Heroic Age of Greece mirrored in the *Iliad*. Alas! the Germans had no Homer. Still, they had some native poetry—songs with which their warriors excited themselves for battle and lays in which their scôps extolled ancient heroes—and some of this they brought with them to Britain. None of the songs survives. Alfred the Great, we are told, had many *Saxonica carmina* by heart, and Aldhelm sang songs at the bridge-end to get a hearing for his sermons; but Anglo-Saxon lyric is all lost. Of the lays, however, we have some remains. None of them has anything to do with Britain, though most, if not all, of them were written down here. *Widsith* describes Continental courts visited in imagination by a 'far-wandering' scôp; *Waldhere* should have told how Walter of Aquitaine withstood a host of foes in the passes of the Vosges; the splendid fragment called *The Fight at Finnesburgh* dealt with the same favourite theme of battle against fearful odds:

> Then cried aloud . the king young in war,
> "No dawn in the East is this . no dragon here flies;
> Nor here are the gables . of this hall aflame .
> But here is hurrying forth . Fowls of prey are singing,
> The grey-coat howls . the war-wood clangs,
> Shield rings to shaft . Now shines the moon
> Wandering through clouds . Now woeful deeds begin,
> That a folk-strife . here will frame.
> But wake now, . warriors mine,
> Don your mailcoats . deem on your prowess,
> Rush to the fore-front . be of good courage."

Finnesburgh was apparently a short lay dealing with a single episode: *Beowulf* is swollen out with three episodes to something like epic dimensions. It was composed in Britain by a Christian scribe, probably about A.D. 700; but the material from which it was composed belongs to an earlier date and to a distant and a pagan land. It tells how the King of the

Spear-Danes had his mead-hall ravaged nightly by the fen-ogre Grendel, till the champion Beowulf came from Sweden and destroyed Grendel and his fiendish dam. Returning to Sweden, he succeeded his uncle on the throne, ruled wisely for fifty years, and died at last in combat with a fire-drake that was ravaging his people. *Beowulf* is no *Iliad*. The story is mere folk-lore: Beowulf—the bees' foe, the bear—is one of those folk-tale heroes who have been suckled by a wild beast and imbibed its strength, and his three exploits are too like one another. The story, then, is a poor one, and there is not enough of it: it has to be padded out to 3000 lines with digressions and long speeches. Yet there are noble things in *Beowulf*—not only loyalty and dauntless courage but courtesy in hall and respect for ladies; the style too has a grave dignity throughout; and the figure of the old king going out to fight and, as he knows, to die for his people, is truly heroic. How much of what is noblest in the poem is due to the Christian scribe we cannot tell; but loyalty and courage at least are pagan virtues. *Beowulf*, we have said, is no *Iliad*; yet the hero's funeral—

> Men of the Weders . made thereafter
> A barrow on the sea-cliff . broad and high,
> That wave-farers . might see from far—

is not unworthy to be compared with the funeral which the Trojans held for Hector, the tamer of horses.

With these Heroic poems go a few Elegiac pieces—*The Wanderer, Deor, The Seafarer, The Wife's Complaint, The Husband's Message, The Ruin*—which, if not Continental in origin, still come from the same pagan stratum as *Beowulf*, though some of them have been touched with Christian sentiment. Most of them are laments—the lament of an exile, of a masterless scôp, a hungry sailor on the wintry seas, a wife parted from her husband. They are sombre and fatalistic in tone, but not dismayed:

> That was overcome . so may this be

is the refrain of *Deor*; and the seafarer, lashed with hailstorms, hung round with icicles, with no sound in his ears but the boom of waves and the squawk of the gannet, still feels the lure of the sea. It is a bleak world, the world of *Beowulf* and these Elegies, with its sunless meres, icy seas, and windy nesses; and the cope of doom over all.

Was it this sense of despondency and doom that made the Anglo-Saxons so ready at last to embrace Christianity? Bede tells us that when the missionaries came to King Egbert's court, one of the thanes likened man's life to the flight of a swallow through the hall, which is seen for a moment in the firelight and then vanishes again into the darkness. "If these men", he said, "can tell us aught of the whence and whither, let us hear them." Once baptised, the Anglo-Saxon poets turned away from pagan themes: "What has Ingeld to do with Christ?" said Alcuin: and applied themselves instead to paraphrases of the Bible story, as in *Genesis, Exodus, Judith*; or lives of saints like Elene and Andreas; or other religious work such as *The Phoenix* and *The Dream of the Rood*. But these sons of sea-rovers did not change their natures completely on baptism; they are still at their best when they sing of war or of the sea; their Lord is a man of war, a young hero; the apostles are his thanes, "strong men in battle", "not slow in the sword-play"; his sea-adventure and his rescue of St. Matthew from the cannibals make Andreas the most interesting of the saints.

Caedmon (*c.* 675) was the first of these Christian poets, and Bede tells us how he became one. He was a lay brother in St. Hilda's Abbey. He had no gift of song, and when singing began in the hall he would withdraw. One night as he lay asleep in the stable One appeared to him and commanded him to sing. At his visitant's bidding Caedmon sang verses that he had never heard to the glory of the Creator. In the morning he remembered what he had sung, and thenceforth devoted his life to turning into Anglo-Saxon verse such portions of Scripture as the monks translated for him from the Latin. He sang of the Creation, and the Exodus from Egypt, and the Passion of Christ; and many other parts of Holy Writ he paraphrased. So Bede tells us; but scholars no longer believe that the *Genesis* and *Exodus* which we possess are Caedmon's, if indeed we possess anything of his.

The only other Anglo-Saxon poet that we know by name is Cynewulf (*c.* 800), and Cynewulf is only a name. We cannot identify him, nor be sure that any of the poems once ascribed to him are his except the four very artificial poems—*Christ, Elene, Juliana, The Fates of the Apostles*—into which he worked his name in runes.

Judith is a brave poem, full of action and passion; but the other Scripture paraphrases are mostly very prolix, wrapping up the plain words of Scripture in clouds of metaphor, circum-locution, repetition, and pious ejaculation. *The Fall of the Angels*, though inserted in *Genesis*, is based not on the Bible but (ultimately) on Avitus. Its subject is that of *Paradise Lost*, and Milton may have read it, or had it read to him, for he may have known Junius, who published it in 1655. How-ever that may be, the Satan of the Anglo-Saxon poet is Miltonic in his unconquerable will and pride. In *The Dream of the Rood*, by a strange and touching invention, the story of the Crucifixion is told by the Cross itself in a strain of adoration unmatched in Anglo-Saxon poetry. For the first part of *The Phoenix* Lactantius's *De Ave Phoenice* provided a canvas on which the Anglo-Saxon poet embroidered his bright fancies; in the second part the self-begotten bird becomes a symbol of the resurrection of the body. The joyous piety of *The Phoenix* and its sunny, flowery Eden contrast strongly with the bleak gloom of the secular poems.

The *Riddles* in which Anglo-Saxon verse abounds seem also to be mostly paraphrases, ingenious arabesques on a borrowed ground, elaborate 'kennings' one might call them. They have not much merit as puzzles, but the vivid realism of *The Storm* recalls *The Seafarer*, and *The Badger* shows observation and imaginative sympathy.

Most of the *Riddles* apparently belong to the ninth century. In the tenth the old heroic spirit flashed up again for a moment in two poems dealing with contemporary events. *The Battle of Brunanburgh* celebrates the victory which the men of Wessex and Mercia won over the Scots King Constantine and his allies in 937. It is a savage poem, much more savage than *Beowulf*, gloating over the slaughtered foe:

> Many a carcase they left to be carrion,
> Many a livid one, many a sallow skin—
> Left for the white-tail'd eagle to tear it, and
> Left for the horny-billed raven to rend it, and
> Gave to the garbaging war-hawk to gorge it, and
> That grey beast, the wolf of the weald.[1]

Maldon, a song of defeat, is far nobler than this yell of triumph. It tells how in 991 Byrhtnoth, the aged alderman of Essex, withstood a band of Danish pirates, to whom he had granted a fair field by allowing them to cross the river. Some of the

---

[1] Tennyson's translation.

Saxons fled: the rest fought to the death around their dead leader.   Here are the words of Byrhtwold, his old companion in arms:

> Thought be the harder . heart the keener,
> Mood the more . as our might lessens.
> Here our lord lies . hewn to pieces,
> The good on the ground . Grieve may he ever
> Who now from the sword-play . weens to wend.
> I am old in years . hence will I never,
> But here beside . mine own dear lord,
> So loved a man . I mean to lie.

That is English courage, the courage never to submit or yield. We heard the note in *Beowulf*: we shall hear it again and yet again in English poetry.

Anglo-Saxon verse belongs to a type which is found in the early poetry of other Germanic peoples.   The norm is a line divided by a strong caesura into two parts, each of which carries two stresses; two or three of the stressed syllables, one or two in the first part of the line and one in the second, should be alliterated, *i.e.* should begin with the same consonant (or group of consonants) or with a vowel, *e.g.*:

> Flo'd under fóldan . nis thæt fe'or heonon.
> [Flood under fields . ne-is that far hence.]

There is nothing exactly foreign to us in all this: all English verse is stressed and much of it is embellished with alliteration. But the sledge-hammer Anglo-Saxon stress could carry so many weak syllables with it that our ears sometimes fail to catch any metrical effect; and for us metre is essential to verse, alliteration only an occasional ornament.   Moreover the language is unmelodious, clogged with harsh combinations of consonants: the raven himself sounds hoarser when you call him a 'hræfn'. There are no stanzas, except in a newly discovered poem on the Fasting Seasons.   Rhyme occurs now and then by accident or as an added embellishment, but the so-called *Rhyming Poem* is unique.

The diction of Anglo-Saxon poetry is 'poetic diction' in the fullest sense of the term.   *Beowulf*, our chief document, is not a primitive poem; on the contrary it presupposes a long stylistic tradition, in the course of which a great stock of periphrastic metaphors ('kennings') has accumulated, which however sterling when new-minted—and 'foamy-throated' is a truly imaginative epithet for ships—have become mere conventional counters. It was beneath the dignity of poetry to call a thing by its own name if there was a phrase for it in stock; the sun is "the candle of heaven", or "the jewel of the sky"; the sea is "the whale's road", or "the swan's way", or "the seal's bath", and so forth. Also it argued a poverty of invention to say a thing once when you could say it twice:

> The king bade the youths come to him. The bold young men
>   obeyed the command:
> The excellent men went as they were bidden: the young men
>   came before the heathen.

The divided line no doubt tempted to repetition, which was encouraged perhaps by the practice of Hebrew poetry: not that Hebrew parallelism is ever so childish as this specimen from the A.S. *Daniel*.

Their extant poetry shows the Anglo-Saxons a loyal, dauntless folk, serious and naturally devout, but heavy and humourless. But we must remember that much of their extant poetry was composed, and almost all of it transcribed, by monks. If any popular poetry had survived, any of those songs that Alfred knew and Aldhelm sang at the bridge-end, we might have found that England could be merry in season even in Anglo-Saxon days.

Chapter Two

EARLY MIDDLE ENGLISH POETRY

THE Norman Conquest brought England more than a change of rulers. When the *jongleur* Taillefer rode up towards Senlac ahead of the invading host tossing his sword in the air and singing the *Chanson de Roland*, he heralded the coming of a new culture, a fresh wave of Mediterranean civilisation.

After *Maldon* Anglo-Saxon poetry practically disappears for two centuries. When it reappears it is no longer Anglo-Saxon. Much had happened in these two centuries. When the millennium passed and Christ did not come again, Christendom seemed to awake from a long sleep. The Crusades, in which this awakening was first manifested on a grand scale, were in turn a main cause of its diffusion; they brought the nations of Western Europe into contact with each other and with the alien civilisation of the Saracens. All the channels of human activity were gradually flooded by a new spirit. The Church herself gained new strength and life. Great schoolmen like Albertus Magnus and St. Thomas Aquinas buttressed her dogmas afresh with arguments drawn from the Aristotelian philosophy which Europe had recovered through the Arabs. A new ardour of devotion found expression in the Orders of the Friars founded by St. Francis in Italy and St. Dominic in Spain.

But our main centre of interest is Provence. It was in this favoured region, enriched with the débris of many civilisations and shielded by the strong arm of the Counts of Toulouse, that the new poetry first came to flower. It was new both in subject and in form. It was devoted from the first to the worship of woman in a sense unknown to the Greeks and Romans. A cult of Romantic Love, love *par amours*, sprang up as it were in a night, and aped, if it did not rival, the cults of Chivalry and the Church. The speed with which this fashion spread surprises us less when we remember that in the early Middle Ages the ruling classes of Western Christendom, brought together by the Crusades, and united by a common faith and a common code of Chivalry, came nearer to forming one great society than they had ever done before or have ever done since. For all its extravagances and possibilities of sin, the code of Romantic Love did much to civilise these rough Frankish barons: manners and deportment, music, dancing, drawing, and the writing of verse became regular parts of the knightly education. Kings competed for the laurel of the troubadour and queens bestowed it.

In the form of their verse the troubadours owed much to the Latin hymns of the Church, in which accent and rhyme had displaced the quantitative prosody of classical Latin verse. This system was applied to the vernacular and worked up into a variety of metres and stanzas which have been ever since the stock-in-trade of European poets. If England held her own with the Continent in some things, in vernacular verse she lagged behind. The conquered Saxons may have kept up their old songs, but for more than a century after the Conquest there was no *written* verse in England, and by the time it came to be written the language had changed considerably. That it had shed many of its inflections was perhaps no great loss; but its vocabulary too had been sadly impoverished, especially in culture words, and had to be replenished from French. Then it had to learn a new tune, to change its native prosody of stress and alliteration for the syllabic rhymed system of France. At first it halts between the two systems, with no sure grasp on either. Layamon's *Brut* (*c.* 1205) is alliterated throughout, but the alliteration is very seldom full and is helped out with rhyme or assonance. In the *Bestiary* of somewhat later date the mixture is different; some sections are alliterated, others rhymed. On the other hand the *Ormulum* clings fast to a rigid syllabic metre without either rhyme or alliteration: happily Orm found no imitators. The early rhymed *Orison of Our Lady* (*c.* 1210) shows how hard the English poet found it to hold the iambic beat and to tell rhyme from mere assonance. The French system won first in the East and South—a decisive victory, for the capital and the Universities were there. By 1250 Nicholas of Guildford was writing very fair rhymed couplets in his *disputoison* of *The Owl and the Nightingale*. By 1300 or thereabout English lyric was beginning to run smoothly enough in the fetters of rhyme. In the second quarter of the fourteenth century Laurence Minot struck his northern lyre in celebration of Edward III's victories over the Scots and the French; his songs, though often savage in tone, are far from rude in form; he has a good command of couplet,

B

rime couée, and octet in rhyme aptly embellished with alliteration.   For while adopting the French system English verse retained some features of the Anglo-Saxon—its love of alliteration and a freedom of substitution greater than French verse allowed.   The period of experiment was well-nigh over.   How far the old system lived on elsewhere than in the East and South it is hard to say; there is scarcely any evidence of it anywhere between 1210 and 1340; but after that it enjoyed a remarkable revival in the West of England and in Scotland.   The authors of *Piers Plowman* and *William of Palerme* were both Shropshire men; farther north, probably in Lancashire, we find *Gawain and the Green Knight, Cleanness, Patience,* and *The Pearl*; while in Scotland alliterative verse survived till the end of the fifteenth century.   So much for the formal side of Middle English poetry.

But to follow the history of English literature in the Middle Ages it is necessary to remember that for the first two centuries after the Conquest England was culturally a province of France.   It was in this country as well as in France that French poets found patrons and cultivated the new poetry of courtly love and adventure.   Educated readers in England read, not English, but Latin and French.   Accordingly it will be well to survey briefly the forms and themes which were the fashion, and which, as the English language reasserted itself, passed into English.   English poetry begins again in the translation of French romance and allegory.

The trouvères of Northern France had a different kind of poetry from that of Provence and the South, in their *chansons de geste*.   The *Chanson de Roland* which Taillefer chanted was the herald of the great gift of the French conquerors, the gift of Romance.   The song tells of the defeat of the rearguard of the army of Charlemagne, a not very historical Charlemagne, in its retreat from Spain led by Roland and Oliver.   It is a romantic epic, a Christian epic, but otherwise a lineal scion of the old Germanic lay.   Its theme is still war, not love—there is little more love-interest in it than in *Beowulf*.   But in the atmosphere of the Middle Ages the love-interest was sure to invade, and in many of the lays that deal with Charlemagne, the *matière de France*, there is love as well as fighting.

But in England, perhaps in Brittany, the Normans became acquainted with another theme, one of Welsh origin, another king to match and even surpass Charlemagne in interest—

Arthur of Britain.   The historical Arthur, so far as there was
an historical Arthur, was a native of North Britain, who in the
sixth century played a part which in Roman times had been
played by the Count of the Saxon Shore, leading his mail-clad
heavy cavalry against the Saxons, in the days when the British
realm still stretched from Strathclyde to Brittany.   When that
was shattered, the memory of Arthur was still cherished in
Wales and Brittany as that of a national hero who slept an age-
long sleep in the Isle of Avalon, and would one day return to
revive the ancient glory of the British name.   And now, in a
time of peace, Welsh and Breton legends, and Gaelic legends
too brought over by Irish monks, began to swell the general
stream of Anglo-French story and poetry, bringing into it new
elements of mystery and beauty.   But in French hands the
more grotesque Celtic element diminished, and the spirit of
the whole conformed to the chivalrous fashion of the day.
Arthur became a feudal monarch and his mail-clad horse-
men feudal knights and lovers, enrolled by him in the Order
of the Round Table, vowed to repel the heathen and to
redress wrongs.   The original story of Arthur and his Queen
Guinevere and the magician Merlin and the traitor, the
Judas or Quisling, Mordred (a part played in the Charlemagne stories by Ganelon), drew into its orbit many tales
originally independent, by enrolling their heroes in the new
order.
     The well-head of the Arthurian story, which absorbed so
many diverse stories, was the work of a Welshman writing as
an historian, Geoffrey of Monmouth, anxious to link Wales
with the Norman conquerors of their old enemy the Saxon.
Just as Virgil had sought to glorify Rome by linking it with
Troy through Aeneas, so Geoffrey sought to exalt Britain by
deriving its monarchs from a grandson of Aeneas, Brutus by
name.   Geoffrey eked out his scanty monkish sources from
Welsh legends and his own imagination.   It was from
Geoffrey's *Historia Regum Britanniae* that there came what till
Milton's time figured as a part of British history, and included
many names still familiar as Cymbeline, Locrine and Sabrina,
Lear and his daughters.   Here Arthur figures not only as the
conqueror of the Saxons, but as a rival to Charlemagne in the
range of his empire, and we get the story of his Queen Guna-
mara, of Mordred and the last great battle in the West.   The
book was rendered into Norman-French verse by a certain

Wace (*c.* 1154), and from Wace into English alliterative verse in Layamon's *Brut* (*c.* 1205).

In the French romances Arthur becomes the background or centre to stories of his knights, their loves and exploits. In the earlier poems of the cycle the favourite hero is Gawain, the King's nephew—whose remoter origin is suggested by the statement that his strength in fight increased till noon and declined thereafter—and so he remained in many of the later English romances translated from the French: "Gawain with his olde courtesie", not the light-o'-love he became after he had been ousted from popularity by Lancelot, the lover of Guinevere. There be four perfect lovers, Malory tells us: Lancelot and Guinevere, Tristram and Iseult. The latter great story of passionate love, which has never lost its attraction for poet or musician, we can claim as peculiarly our own, for "it was formed in its present shape in England, a possession of our blended race before and after the Conquest, and it is localised in Britain" (Schofield). But the strangest of all accretions to the Arthurian cycle is the legend of the Holy Grail by which the Church strove to turn the passion for romance to pious ends. The story of a magic "graal" kept by a fisher king had nothing to do originally with Arthur, or even with Christianity. The man who identified it with the dish from which Christ ate at the last supper must have been a man of genius. According to the story, it was brought by Joseph of Arimathea to the Abbey at Glastonbury, whence, owing to the prevalence of sin, it disappeared, and its quest became the symbol of the quest of the beatific vision. The favourite claimant for the authorship of the story is one Robert de Boron.

The third recognised theme of romance was the "matter of Rome", which included the whole body of classical history, legend and myth, so far as known to the times. The mediaeval romancer was not strong in history or in historical perspective. He read antiquity in the light of mediaeval ideas and customs and romantic sentiment. Trojan warriors are knights fighting for their ladies' gloves and for personal honour. The two great mediaeval stories of antiquity were those of Troy and of Thebes. For the tale of Troy they relied not on Homer, whose work they did not know, and whom they thought of as a partisan, but on two forged histories attributed to a Dictys Cretensis who told the story from the Greek side, and a Dares Phrygius on that of the Trojans. But the two immediate

sources of extant English and Scottish tales of Troy were the
Roman de Troie of a French poet, Benoît de Ste. More (*c.* 1165),
and a Latin translation of this (which professed to be based on
Dares Phrygius) by a certain Guido delle Colonne (1287). It
was Benoît who devised the famous story of Troilus, the
youngest son of Priam, and his love for Cressida the daughter
of Calchas, the Trojan priest who had gone over to the Greeks.
In like manner a French romance of Thebes, deriving ultimately from the *Thebais* of the Latin poet Statius, was the
source of such later romances as the *Teseida* of the Italian poet
Boccaccio and the *Knight's Tale* of Chaucer. So also with the
story, the very romantic story, of Alexander. Of the true and
interesting history of Arrian the Middle Ages knew nothing;
but a legendary tale of Alexander had taken shape before the
Christian era in a Greek work known as the *Pseudo-Callisthenes*,
which reached the Western world through a Latin redaction,
and from this source came the *Roman d'Alixandre* of two French
poets, the source of English and Scottish romances on the
subject. Alexander's Indian campaign was an excuse for
importing a farrago of Oriental fables.

These were the main themes or cycles of French romance,
but there were independent *romans d'aventure* of knights not
attached to any of the cycles, such as *William of Palerme*, a
pleasant homely story about a werewolf, in alliterative verse.
Some of these French *romans* were English stories; the three
oldest extant English romances, the only ones which can with
probability be dated before the fourteenth century, are taken
from French originals: *Sir Tristram*, which Sir Walter Scott
edited from the Auchinleck MS. in the Advocates' Library in
Edinburgh, *Havelok the Dane*, and *King Horn*. The same is
true of the romances on the themes described above, and there
are in English examples of all of these: Carlovingian, as the
Scottish *Rauf Colyear* and the southern English *Sir Otuel*,
Roland and Ferragus, and *Sir Ferumbras*; Arthurian, as the
Breton lays contained in the Auchinleck MS., viz. *Le Freine*,
Sir Orfeo, and *Sir Degare*, the *Sir Tristram* mentioned above,
Arthour and Merlin, and *Ywain and Gawain*; Classical, as the
alliterative *Geste Hystoriale of the Destruction of Troy* and the
Scots *Troy Book*; Oriental, *King Alysaunder*. Most of these
are in the new syllabic, rhyming verse learned from the French
but used with an emphasis on accent rather than on the number
of syllables, which gives to the metre a doggerel character that

Chaucer was to parody in *Sir Thopas*.   Yet the effect is often lively and spirited.   Of young King Horn the poet writes:

> Fairer then he none was,
> He was bright as the glass,
> He was white as a flour,
> Rose red was his colour;

and there are, especially in the *King Alysaunder*, digressions of a rather charming description:

> In time of harvest merry it is enow,
> Pears and apples hang on bough,
> The hayward bloweth merry the horn;
> In every field ripe is the corn;
> The grapes hang on the vine;
> Sweet is true love and fine;

or again:

> Merry time is the wood to sere,
> The corn ripeth in the ear,
> The lady is ruddy in the cheer,
> And maid bright in the lere,
> The knight hunteth after the deer
> On foot and on destrere.

Nor are the romances wanting in interest of story and in dramatic moments.   But the most interesting and impressive of English romances is the product of that revival of the older alliterative metre which, beginning in the counties of Gloucester, Worcester, and Hereford, spread northwards, ultimately, as we shall see, affecting Scottish poets.   To this we owe also two moral poems, *Cleanness* and *Patience*, and a beautiful allegory, *The Pearl*.   The romance is *Gawain and the Green Knight*, which tells in a story with a considerable element of the marvellous of Gawain's victory in a trial of his chastity and truthfulness.   All the four poems are alliterative, but whereas the two moral poems are in straightforward verses—

> They are happen that han in hert pouerte,
> For hores is the hevenryche to holde for euer;
> They arn happen also that haunte mekenesse,
> For they schal welde this worlde and alle her wylle haue—

(so *Patience* which tells the story of Jonah), *Gawain* is in long *laisses* each tipped with the kind of rhyming tag that Guest called a bob-wheel, which we shall find again in Scottish poetry as late as Burns.   *The Pearl* is not only regularly alliterated but is rhymed in elaborate stanzas elaborately linked by rhyme and repetition.   But these poems, the work of one or more poets described as "next to Chaucer the greatest of our mediaeval poets" (Schofield), are remarkable not for language and verse alone.   Their nobility of tone may not be unique, but is not often rivalled even in that age of chivalry.   Less easy would it be to match the delicacy and tenderness of *The Pearl*, which under the similitude of a lost pearl tells of a father's grief for the death of his little Margaret, and how she came to him in a vision from her place among the blessed where all are equal; for salvation is by the grace of God alone, "unto this last".   In feeling for nature *The Pearl* is equalled, nay surpassed, by *Sir Gawain*; and the nature which the poet loves is not the trim parterre of the *Romance of the Rose*, nor Chaucer's daisied meadows, but the wild nature seen among the hills of North Wales in winter, rocks and rough woods and swollen streams rolling brown under snow-clad banks.   Here is something that we shall not find again in our poetry for centuries, except once or twice in Gavin Douglas.

The Pearl has carried us from romance to allegory and we must turn back to the great allegory of love which inspired both this and so many other allegories of the fourteenth and fifteenth centuries, the *Roman de la Rose*.   Allegory was no new thing in literature but had been used abundantly in religious literature both apologetically and for edification.   It was now taken over for the new religion of courtly love.   There were precursors which have been treated of by Neilson; but the *Roman de la Rose* so completely superseded these, and became so potent an influence for good and for ill in later poetry, that it may be well to give a brief analysis of its contents.   After a brief reference to dreams and to that favourite of the Middle Ages, Cicero's *Somnium Scipionis*, with the commentary of Macrobius on the kinds of dreams and their significance, the poet goes on to tell of a dream that he had when he was twenty years old.   He dreamed that he awoke in the month of May, when trees recover their leaves and birds begin to sing.   To hear more of the birds' songs he goes out, and coming to a stream of marvellous clearness he washes his face, and then follows the course of the stream till he comes to the high enclosing walls of a garden.   On these walls are painted in great detail the personifications of the chief enemies of life and love: the vices of Hate, Vilany (including bad manners, the opposite of Courtliness), Covetousness, Avarice, Envy, Hypocrisy ('Pope-Holy'); and with these vices such ills as Sorrow, and Old Age, and Time "that in one point dwelleth never", and that greatest enemy of love, Poverty:

> For povre thing, wherso it be
> Is shamfast and despised ay.

Wandering round the wall, the poet comes to the gate.   It is opened to him by the porter Idleness, the friend of Mirth who is Lord of the Garden.   As he roams through the garden listening to the songs of the birds, he comes on Mirth and his company—Gladness, Courtesy, and others, including Cupid and his 'bachelor' Sweet-looking, who carries a bow and in his quiver five arrows, to wit, Beauty, Simplesse, Fraunchyse, Company, and Fair Semblaunt—all the qualities that awaken love.   But in the quiver are also five other arrows—Pride, Shame, Wanhope (Despair), New Thought (Fickleness), and Vilany, the enemies of love.   On leaving the company dancing the poet comes to some wells, and sits down by one near which is a stone bearing the inscription, " Here starf Narcissus", whose story is then told.   Gazing into this well he discovers two crystals which reflect vividly everything in the garden, among them a rosary in which one particular rose catches his eye.   At that moment Cupid, drawing near, shoots through his heart the five arrows first mentioned above.   The poet becomes the lover of the rose.   The rest of Guillaume's part of the poem is an account of the quest, and the conflict between those qualities personified which promote and those which bar love's progress, a sparkling and charming elaboration in allegoric form of the philosophy, psychology, and ritual of courtly love as currently accepted by French troubadours and trouvères,—how it begins in the eye, how it refines the manners, from teaching you to keep your nails clean to unwearying fidelity, and finally the folly of love in the eyes of Reason.   So ran the first part of the *Roman de la Rose*, as Guillaume de Lorris wrote it about 1250.

The theme is continued in the second part, written by a Jean de Meun about 1290, and the poem ends with the capture of the tower in which Jealousy has imprisoned the Rose.   But the tone of the second part is very different.   To love *par amours* Jean prefers friendship and the charity which St. Paul extols.   In courtly love gifts will prevail over sonnets.   But satire of courtly love is not the sole theme of the poem.   It is as much a philosophy of life as of love, a Swift-like commentary on the evils of contemporary society, lay and clerical. Of Chaucer's translation a portion has come down to us from the part by Guillaume de Lorris; but that he also translated from the second part we know from the Prologue to the *Legende of Gode Women*. But there is more of Swift in Jean de Meun than in Chaucer, who, if satirical and occasionally cynical (*e.g.* on marriage), is never savage, is always on the side of the lover, like his disciple William Morris. Love is doubtless a folly seen *sub specie aeternitatis*, like all passions; but none so compels our interest and compassion.

Romance and Allegory originated with the knightly and clerical classes, though their passage into English confessed their popularity with all readers. But the bourgeois had their characteristic poetry too. For the fashionable Allegory they had the Fable, in which human vices and follies were satirised under the likeness of beasts, and which in *Reynard the Fox* stretched to such a length that it might be called a Beast Epic. For the Romance they had the Fabliau, a merry tale of low or middle-class life full of gross humour and often of bawdry. Nor in this wealth of narrative literature should one overlook the Saints' Legends told in English from the Latin originals as read in Church Services. They are full of the marvellous, but not wanting in interest and amusement. In the legend of St. Brandan, Celtic traditions of wonderful lands over-sea are blended with pious story of miracle, as when the Mass is celebrated on the back of a whale which refrains from diving till the service is over, and Judas is found on an iceberg enjoying his day out earned by some individual act of charity.

If we turn from romance and allegory to lyric the same fact is evident, viz. that when the English language, much changed, began to reassert itself as a medium for poetry, it took over from the French. Of Anglo-Saxon lyric we know nothing. Of Middle English lyrics we knew till lately few older than the fourteenth century. But Mr. Carleton Brown in his *English Lyrics of the Thirteenth Century* has given the text of some ninety in addition to the three allowed by Sir Edmund Chambers. He points out that, unlike those of the following century, the thirteenth-century lyrics are not seldom found in the MSS. with musical notation. They were "composed to be sung", whereas the later century is rather "the age of the literary lyric".

Of later songs preserved in MSS. many are obviously of the kind on which Miss Helen Waddell has written so charmingly in *The Wandering Scholars*, the songs of those students migratory from University to University whose primary literary medium was Latin, the *Carmina Burana*, composed in the accentual rhyming Latin verse of the Church hymns. But they could wander from one language to another—Latin, English, French—as they pleased, and could even blend them in the same song, amorous or bacchanal or pious:

> A celui que plus eyme en monde
> Of alle tho that I have found
> > *Carissima,*
> Saluz od treye amour,
> > Wit grace and joye and alle honour,
> > *Dulcissima*;

or,

> Of on that is so fayre and bright
> > *Velut maris stella,*
> Fairer than the day is light,
> > *Parens et puella*;
> Ich crie to thee, thou se to me,
> Levedy, praye thy sone for me,
> > *Tam pia,*
> That ich mote come to the,
> > *Maria.*

The favourite themes are love, the return of Spring, wine, and piety, those delightful offshoots of Catholic belief which Protestantism shore away so ruthlessly, and above all the Virgin:

> Adam lay ibounden
> > Bounden in a bond;
> Four thousand winter
> > Thoht he not too long;
> And all was for an appil,
> > An appil that he tok,
> As clerkes finden
> > Writen in a book.
> Ne had the appil take ben,
> > The appil take ben,
> Ne had never our lady
> > A ben heven quene.
> Blessed be the time
> > That appil take was.
> Therefore we moun singen
> > *Deo gracias.*

In the fourteenth century a change came over the form of the French lyric which we shall find reflected in the lyrics of Chaucer.   Romance, Allegory, Lyric, these are the main streams of the French poetry which, as the fourteenth century arrived, began to flow over into the revived English language. We have dwelt on them as our main theme is poetry and some of the didactic verses are more didactic than poetic.   As in Anglo-Saxon, so in Middle English, stories from the Bible could be told in the style and verse of the romances.   So they are in the paraphrase of Genesis and Exodus:

> For sextene yer Joseph was old
> When he was into Egypte sold:
> He was Jacobes yunkest sone
> Brictest of wasme and of witter wone—

and so on.   The *Ormulum* is a rather dreary paraphrase of the gospels for the day.   A happier effort of the thirteenth century was the *Owl and the Nightingale* of a certain Nicholas of Guildford, a 'flyting' between the owl as the voice of wisdom and the nightingale as that of "Gather ye rosebuds while ye may".   Robert of Gloucester was responsible for a long chronicle in verse of English history.   But the *Cursor Mundi* is a more important and interesting poem, as it tells in verse the history of the Bible as that was known to the mass of people and was represented in the Miracle Plays, of which later.

The author of *The Pearl* and *Gawain and the Green Knight*, if one man wrote both, was perhaps as essentially a poet as Chaucer, but in his language and verse he looked backwards. The future lay with the verse learned from the French poetry which had been the reading of all cultured persons in the first centuries after the Conquest.   As the fourteenth century drew to a close an English poet appeared who was to hold his own with the best of the French poets.

Chapter Three

CHAUCER, GOWER, AND LANGLAND

THE fourteenth century saw England become an English-speaking, English-minded nation from King to commoner. In 1340 the law of Englishry was abolished. In 1356 English became the language of the Sheriff's courts of London, in 1362 of the King's law courts and of Parliament. In 1385 Trevisa complains that boys "know no more French than their left heel". The juridical system was national: the Roman Law was "outlandish": our land laws were fixed in many principles which for centuries remained unquestioned. Learning and art had ceased to be monastic. The Oxford scholars were secular clergy. A University training was less definitely ecclesiastical: its culture extended to laymen like Chaucer and Gower. The anti-clerical spirit was felt in legislation as in literature. Our naval predominance began with the victory at Sluys in 1340; our power was felt abroad as never before or since. Over against this one has to set the Great Pestilence of 1349, and Wat Tyler's rebellion in 1381.

In poetry too the period of experiment was passing. England had learned from France a new code of manners, with new ideals of courtesy and romantic love. She was learning a new art of verse, in which the native stress prosody was wedded to the French syllabic system by making the rhetorical accent coincide with the metrical ictus; and this was achieved in the best verse without sacrificing the possibility of trisyllabic effect which our less level stress allowed. The rude and poverty-stricken vocabulary of Layamon had been enriched with words fit for courtly poetry. Moreover the East Midland dialect, which had become in the main the standard for the country, had its phonetic decay temporarily arrested at a point where the general reduction of inflections to the final -e gave it a more level, liquid, French-like flow.

But if English had established itself as the national tongue, French was still spoken and understood at court and in court circles, not the French of Stratford-atte-Bow only but the Parisian French of culture and polite use. A French poet like Froissart might visit England and find a patron in an English princess.   The new poetry represented by Chaucer and Gower was, one might say, French poetry written in English, coloured by the English temperament and character, and beginning to show the effect of another literature more mature than that of France, the literature of Italy.   "The Middle Ages", said Swinburne, "brought forth a trinity of great poets: Dante, the Italian nobleman; Chaucer, the English gentleman; Villon, the French plebeian. . . . Dante represents in its best and highest aspect the upper class of the Middle Ages as well as the Italy of that day; Chaucer represents the middle class in its best and wisest aspect; Villon the lowest class in its best and its worst aspect, even more than he represents the France of that day."   But Villon, the first great French lyrical poet, belongs to a later generation.   The French poets with whom Chaucer was familiar were of lighter build.   The age of the great romances, of Roland and Lancelot and Hector, was over, though their names and stories were familiar to poet and reader. Romance had been displaced by the Allegory of Love in that epoch-making work, the *Romance of the Rose*.   The poets of the day were Guillaume de Machault, Jean Froissart (the great prose chronicler), Eustace Deschamps and others of the like kind.   Their poems were in the main wire-drawn or filigree allegories of love, raising and answering some question of the etiquette of courtly love—"Is a cleric or a knight the better lover?"; "Whose is the harder lot, a lady's whose husband has died, or a knight's whose lady has played him false?"   The lyric too had assumed new forms in this century—the ballade, the chant royal, the lay, the virelay, the rondeau, etc.   "Earlier singers", writes Gaston Paris, "had created their own forms and varied them at will.   This age demanded fixed rule, even in its most complex forms, so that in the end a piece of verse resembled a piece of very complicated jewellery, and the poet more and more sought inspiration in a purely mechanical cleverness."

The *Romance of the Rose*, to which these French poets and Chaucer looked back for guidance, was a source not only for the allegory of love.   It was, especially in the second part by Jean de Meun, a storehouse of miscellaneous learning and moral philosophy.   The world into which Chaucer was born (about 1340) was the world of Christian tradition, with the Earth as the centre of the universe.   God was over all; but under His providence all sublunary things were subject to two mighty powers, the conception of which came to the Middle Ages from late Greek philosophy, especially through the work of a Latin writer of the sixth century, the *De Consolatione Philosophiae* of Boethius, written when that statesman and thinker was under sentence of death. These powers were Nature and Fortune, to the latter of which Boethius first gave a distinct personality. We should call them Heredity and Environment. Nature's great injunction is, "Increase and multiply". Love as a natural passion knows no law but that, as in Chaucer so in Spenser. Fortune is "God's general minister"; she distributes the good things and the evil things of this world; and the law of her being is change. She gives and she takes away, and no man may tell why. Men may curse her apparent injustice, but she, says Dante, sits aloof among the other primal creatures, turns her sphere, and is in bliss. Boethius, direct or through the medium of Jean de Meun, is the source of Chaucer's thought whenever he undertakes the direct criticism of life.

The society also into which Chaucer came was still that of the Middle Ages, though it was on the verge of disintegration. The world he knew—and he knew it well—was Western Christendom, a congeries of states with a common faith still, threatened by Islam on the south-east and on the north-east by the heathen Prussians. In all the states that composed it the structure of society was much the same; there were three main classes—the *bellatores*, the *oratores*, and the *laboratores* —knighthood, clergy, and workers, though the middle class of merchants and traders was steadily growing in power and influence. All classes held the same Catholic faith, and the knightly class had also a common code of chivalry and romance. The most brilliant focus of chivalry in Chaucer's youth was the court of Edward III. Its brilliance was in truth the brilliance of decay; but of this Chaucer shows no awareness.

That a poet should also have been a courtier and man of affairs was no unique experience. Dante, Petrarch, and Boccaccio were all at one time or another in public service, all of them as ambassadors. Chaucer's father was a wine merchant supplying the royal cellars, and the poet began life as page to Prince Lionel's wife. He became valet and armour-bearer to the King, and in the war with France was a prisoner for a year. Before 1366 he married; his wife may have been a sister-in-law of John of Gaunt; at all events they enjoyed his patronage. He served on various embassies, between 1370 and 1380, including two to Italy in 1372 and 1378 respectively. Later he held various posts, was an M.P., became Master of Works to the King, knew the vicissitudes of public life, and experienced some years of poverty. The succession of the son of John of Gaunt in 1399 brought him a larger pension, but he died in the following year, and was buried in West-minster Abbey, not as a poet but as a parishioner.

Chaucer is not only the father of English poetry, he is the first English poet except Caedmon about whom we really know anything. About him, happily, we know a great deal, not only about the events of his life but about his appearance and character. We have several portraits of him, and his own pen-portrait of himself in the Prologue to *Sir Thopas*. We see him as a good portly man, rather short in stature, with a thoughtful, almost pensive, face and downcast eyes; a shy, silent man, but shrewdly observant, with something 'elvish' in his countenance. His many and varied employments had made him acquainted with all classes from King to artisan; yet this man of the world was at heart a bookworm. When he got home from the office, he would evade his wife's demand for news, and retire to his library of sixty volumes to read and write till all hours. Only when May came round it was "Farewell my book and my devocioun": he was off at dawn to the green belt which then hugged London close, to dote on the grass and the daisies. But that was a poetic convention. English springs are not conducive to sitting on the grass, gazing at daisies. Only the opening lines of *The Canterbury Tales* indicate any love of real nature and not the gardens of the *Rose* tradition. His gusto was immense. Pleasant sights and sounds are "a heaven for to see", "a heaven for to hear"; nay, when, as the pilgrims are nearing Canterbury, the Canon gallops up perspiring profusely, the poet exclaims in rapture:

But it was joye for to see him swete!

The division of Chaucer's work into three periods, French, Italian, and English, is not a very happy one. At what date exactly he translated the *Romance of the Rose* we do not know, but it was not apparently an early work. Apart from it, only one poem of any size shows French and only French influence, namely *The Boke of the Duchesse*, called forth by the death of

Blanche, the first wife of John of Gaunt.   This is based on the
Romance of the Rose and the *Remède de Fortune* of Machault,
but has touches of Chaucer's own humour.   He has suffered
for some seven years from sleeplessness due to love.   (Early
critics took this convention rather too seriously.)   Unable to
sleep, he begins to read in Ovid or Machault the story of Ceyx
and Halcyone, and learns there for the first time of Morpheus,
the god of sleep.   He at once vows, if allowed to sleep, to
dedicate to the god a feather-bed and pillows, with the result
that he does at once fall asleep, and the rest of the poem is a
dream.   He dreams that he awakes in a beautiful room, the
glazed windows of which are adorned with the story of Troy
and of the *Romance of the Rose.·*   It is the May-morning song
of the birds which has awakened him; but he also hears the
sound of a hunting-horn, and goes on to join the hunt of the
Emperor Octavian.   The scent is lost, and while wandering
about Chaucer is guided by a little dog (as in some of the
French stories) to where a solitary knight is sitting plunged in
grief.   Pressed by the poet, the knight relates the tale of the
game which Fortune has played with him:

> My boldnesse is turned to shame,
> For Fals Fortune hath playd a game
> Atte ches with me, allas the whyle!
> The traitresse fals and ful of guile.

This leads on to the story of his love and wooing, and a detailed
description of his lady, borrowed mainly from Machault:

> And gode faire WHYTE she hete,
> That was my lady name right.

And then quite abruptly Chaucer learns of the last trick that
Fortune has played:

> "She is dead."   "Nay!"   "Yis, by my trouthe."
> "Is that your los?   By God, it is routhe!"

At this word the knight rides away, and the poet awakes to
find himself lying in bed, and the book he had been reading
in his hand; whereupon he resolves to put his dream in rhyme.
   None of Chaucer's other poems is quite so awkward and
tentative a piece of adaptation from various French sources.
But that "in the flourees of his youthe" he wrote more poems
in the French manner we know from a reference by Gower,

in which he makes Love express his special debt to Chaucer, for that

> Of Dittes and of Songes glade,
> The which he for my sake made,
> The londe fulfild is overal.

Of these early poems of Chaucer's there may be survivals in the triple roundel *Merciless Beauty*, *To Rosamunde*, and *The Compleynt of Pitee*. The *Compleynt of Venus* is a translation from the French of another poet, Oton de Granson. All Chaucer's other poems show more or less the influence of Italian poetry.

It is not, however, necessary to conclude that they must all have been written after his visits to Italy in 1372 and 1378, for there were many Italians in London, some of them in Chaucer's neighbourhood, some employed in the Mint, with which Chaucer's family had a close connection. Indeed one obvious reason for sending him to Italy may have been his knowledge of the language. Without such knowledge he could hardly have taken the interest he did in the poetry of the country when he visited it. It may be well therefore to deal shortly with other poems of the laureate, occasional character of the *Boke of the Duchesse* before going on to the longer poems which he did translate in different manners from Italian, and which led him on to his two attempts at a collection of tales, the *Legende of Gode Women* and the *Canterbury Tales*.

The earliest of these poems—though all dating of Chaucer's poems is guesswork—is probably the *Hous of Fame*. For one thing it is in the same octosyllabic verse as the *Boke*, and the only Italian influence which it shows, and that conjecturally, is that of Dante. Indeed some critics think that this is the "Daunt in English" which Lydgate ascribed to Chaucer. The poem has come down to us in an incomplete form, and as to its purpose the conjectures of critics are as varied as the rumours which it describes:

> "Thus hath he sayd", and "Thus he doth"—
> "This shal it be"—"Thus herde I say"—
> "That shal be found"—"That dar I leye".

What is clear is that, drawing on a variety of sources, with the elaborate display of learning which was the fashion, Cicero's *Somnium Scipionis*, Virgil's *Aeneid* for the story of Dido, Ovid's *Metamorphoses* for the House of Fame, Boethius, Machault,

c

and others, Chaucer has written an amusing and picturesque satire on Fame in two senses of the word—(1) Glory, Honour, dependent more on Chance than on Merit; and (2) Report, Gossip, Rumour, which is sometimes true, sometimes false, most often a mixture of the two.

The Parlement of Foules is a similar occasional, fanciful poem, perhaps a Valentine poem (a recognised kind) for the young Queen Anne, who had married Richard II after rejecting two noble suitors. For us the interest of the poem is in itself. Like the two on which we have touched, it is a dream poem. Chaucer has read Cicero's *Somnium Scipionis*, the substance of which he gives in the Proem, till he falls asleep. To him in his dream appears Scipio, and conducts him to a park over whose gate are written words of encouragement and of fear suggested by Dante's poem. This is the garden, and in it the temple, of Love:

> that blisful place
> Of hertes hele and dedly woundes cure;

but where also one must risk

> the mortal strokes of the spere,
> Of which Disdayn and Daunger is the gyde.

An elaborate description follows, taken largely from the *Teseida* of Boccaccio, of which we shall hear again. In the garden outside the temple sits Nature mating the birds, for this is St. Valentine's Day. On her hand sits a formel eagle, "the most benigne and the goodliest", which is wooed by three tercel eagles, one of them a tercel royal. To their advances the formel can reply only with a deep blush. The other fowls grow impatient, and are called on by Nature to give their opinion, which affords Chaucer an opportunity for contrasting humorously the high courtly doctrine of love with the good sense of the bourgeois as voiced by the goose:

> "I seye, I rede him, though he were my brother,
> But she wol love him, let him love another"—

a sentiment which profoundly shocks the turtle. Finally the lady is given a year to consider. The poem illustrates well the way in which by this time Chaucer could weave embroidery derived from Italian poetry into a French framework, and give to the whole a touch of his own humour and good sense.

It may be, as we have said, that Chaucer knew something of Italian before his embassies to Italy. But even as late as

the time of Drummond and Milton it was difficult to learn
much of a country's literature without a visit to gather and
bring home books.   It was therefore probably from his visits
to Italy that Chaucer brought home some real knowledge of
the three great Italian poets of the century—Dante, Petrarch,
and Boccaccio.   Dante's high seriousness was rather alien to
Chaucer's temper.   He was sceptical of descriptions of the
next world:

> A thousand times have I herd men telle
> That there is joye in Heven and payne in Helle;
> And I accorde wel that hit is so;
> But natheless, this wot I well also,
> That ther nis noon that dwelleth in this countree
> That either hath in Hell or Heven be.

Of Petrarch Chaucer translated one sonnet, making two of
the seven-line stanzas of *Troilus and Criseyde*.   It was also
Petrarch's Latin version of Boccaccio's story of Griseldis that
Chaucer used for his Clerkes Tale.   The clerk's prologue
speaking of Petrarch "that taught me this tale" has been read
as implying that Chaucer actually met the Italian poet, who at
the date of Chaucer's visit was living at Arquà near Padua.
But dates and times of coming and going have suggested
difficulties, and the prologue may well be dramatic, suggested
by Petrarch's introductory letter to Boccaccio.   Chaucer shows
that he appreciates the religious motive which had drawn
Petrarch to this story in particular:

> For sith a woman is so pacient
> Unto a mortal man, well more we oughte
> Receyven it in grace that God us sent;
> For grete skil is he preve that he wroghte.

There may or must be a motive behind God's dealings with us
which seem as arbitrary as those of her husband with Griseldis.
But at the end Chaucer's own mood breaks out, and he treats
the story as a warning to wives against excessive patience:

> O noble wives, ful of heigh prudence,
> Let noon humilitie your tongue naile.

Petrarch too moved on a higher plane of seriousness than
Chaucer cared for.   It was from another Italian poet, whose
name he never actually mentions, that he got the material for
two of his greater narrative poems.   A certain Lollius,
unknown to history, is made the source of the best of the two

long poems which he brought home and in different ways translated—(1) *Il Filostrato* (*The Lovestricken*, one might render it), the poem in which Boccaccio had elaborated from Benoît de Sainte More's *Roman de Troie* the story of the love of Troilus, Priam's youngest son, for Cressida, the daughter of the Trojan prophet who had deserted to the Greeks; and (2) *Il Teseida*, a classical epic in twelve books, which, beginning with the story of Theseus and Hippolyta, goes on to relate the rival loves of Palamon and Arcite for the fair Emilia, the younger sister of the Queen Ipolita. The whole seems to have been coloured by Boccaccio's experience as the lover of Fiammetta in Naples. It seems that Chaucer knew also *Il Filocolo*, a prose version by Boccaccio of the French *Floris et Blanchefleur*.

At what time Chaucer made his versions of the two former poems is not clear, but both were apparently known to readers before 1386, for in that year Sir Lewis Clifford brought from France a ballade addressed to Chaucer by the chief French poet of the day, Eustace Deschamps, accompanied by some other poems of that poet. Now one of these, the *Lai de Franchise*, is imitated by Chaucer in the prologue to *The Legende of Gode Women*. In his ballade Deschamps hails Chaucer as "Grant Translateur" in reference to his translation of the *Romance of the Rose*; and in the *Legende* Chaucer acknowledges himself as the author, among other works, of the translation, of *Troilus and Criseyde*, and of "al the story of Palamon and Arcite". When he made his versions is of no great importance; but his manner of treating the two stories is of the greatest interest. A close comparison of *Troilus and Criseyde* with the original affords a fascinating study of a poet's art. Chaucer translates closely, alters, omits, adds, his additions including two long insertions, and in doing so gives a fresh rendering of the principal characters. Troilus is the perfect lover, so finely drawn that even Shakespeare could only heighten the intensity of the rendering by his more powerfully dramatic language. Pandarus, who in the original was a young friend of Troilus, bound by the laws of friendship to further his friend's aims, is converted into an older man, the uncle of Criseyde, the first appearance of a type who will reappear in later fiction, the older man who makes himself an interested go-between in the amours of his younger friends, generally in later fiction with profit to himself. But Pandarus

is a not unpleasing example of the type; a good fellow according to his lights, full of a humorous, worldly, cynical wisdom
which vents itself in pithy proverbs, but with a totally dis-
illusioned view of the character of women.   Criseyde is the
boldest reconstruction, and has proved rather a puzzle to
Chaucer's critics.   Boccaccio's heroine is a light-skirts, whose
sole requirement is secrecy.   Criseyde is a more complex
character, so much so that while some critics see only the pity
of her weakness and inability to combat Troilus's passion and
the wiles of Pandarus, others will have it that she quite understands the game from the outset.   To Chaucer she is the
woman in love, with all a woman's natural weakness.   The
description of her actual falling in love, after Pandarus has a
little paved the way, when Troilus rides past and she feels as
if she had drunk a love potion, her descent to the garden where
her companion sings of love, her lying in bed, with eyes
shining like those of Anna Karenina, while the nightingale
pours its song, is one of the loveliest things of the kind in
English poetry, its closest parallel perhaps the Haidée scenes
in Byron's *Don Juan*.   But she is not a light-skirts.   She is
concerned not alone for secrecy, that others shall not know,
but that she too shall not be responsible for whatever happens.
As one critic justly says, "She is a lady who wants to yield to
destiny—and then to put the blame on destiny".   The ebb
and flow of her feelings from the first visit of Pandarus to her
final yielding are described with a subtlety of insight into the
workings of a woman's heart such as we do not find again in
literature till we come to Richardson's *Clarissa*, when another
complicating factor enters, a Puritan upbringing.   There is
something ineffably touching in her rebuke to Diomede when
he begins his insolent wooing on the very day that he brings
her from Troy.   I have been told, she says, that you are nobly
born,

> And that doth me to han so grete a wonder
> That ye wol scornen any woman so.

In truth, Chaucer has rendered the early scenes so well, has
made Criseyde so sympathetic a character, that it becomes
impossible to accept with understanding her later yielding to
Diomede.   If she yielded—and Chaucer will take no responsibility for the story—but if she did yield, it was only when his
wound had moved her compassion:

> And for to hele him of his sorwes smerte,
> Men sayn, I not, that she yaf him her herte.

And the pathos of her final vow—

> To Diomede al gate I wol be true!

It is too much for Chaucer.   He turns his head away, and in the last part of the poem the centre of interest shifts to Troilus in the anguish of his disillusionment.   Boccaccio's summing-up in a warning to young men to seek another kind of woman to love becomes in Chaucer's rendering an appeal to

> yonge, fresshe folkes, he or she,

to rise from earthly to heavenly love.   That his own feelings are entirely on that side is doubtful.   His complete recantation comes later, and is too all-inclusive to be convincing.

If Chaucer felt that he could make a more dramatic tale of *Il Filostrato*, he saw that the story of Palamon and Arcite was not the stuff of which to make a classical epic in twelve books. He seems to have used *Il Teseida* at first as a quarry to borrow from for various poems.   The fate of Arcite after death is well transferred to the more tragic Troilus.   He borrows from the same poem for the *Parlement of Foules*, as has been said.   Then at some date before 1386 he made in decasyllabic couplets, perhaps his first attempt in that measure, the charming story with which the Knight was to open the series of *The Canterbury Tales*.

But these were not to be his first attempt at a series of tales. The prologue to *The Legende of Gode Women* has come down to us in two forms.   In the earlier and fuller there are lines which suggest that the Queen had been perhaps really a little shocked by the realism of *Troilus*.   In the second and better-ordered form the passages which obviously refer to Queen Anne are omitted, she having died in the interval, leaving Richard in such grief that he destroyed the palace connected with her in his memory.   It is once more a *Romance of the Rose* prologue —the May morning, the cult of the daisy, and the dream, in which Cupid appears, followed by Queen Alcestis, who died for her husband, and nineteen other ladies, also martyrs for love.   Cupid reproaches Chaucer with treason to love in the translating of Jean de Meun and in his own *Troilus*.   The Queen pleads for mercy in lines perhaps intended to be a warning to the King, and as a penance Chaucer is ordered to write the histories of good women, beginning with Cleopatra. So he commenced, apparently meaning at first to write no fewer than twenty 'legends'. But, like others, he seems to have found good women a little boring; at all events he left his tale half told, and in the last decade of his life busied himself with his best known work, *The Canterbury Tales* with its inimitable Prologue, no longer a dream with all the abstractions of courtly love, but a picture of English society in real and recognisable types.

The Canterbury Tales is a collection of stories in a frame. The idea of framing a collection of stories was not a new one, but there was never a frame so artful as Chaucer's: it is a moving frame, a cinematograph. The tales are told by a band of pilgrims on their way to the shrine of St. Thomas at Canterbury. We amble along with them, noting our progress from time to time: now we are at Deptford, yonder is Greenwich, now we reach Broughton-under-Blee. Incidents occur in the company too, to keep us lively and link one tale to another. The miller, dry with piping the cavalcade out of town, wets his whistle so copiously that he gets roaring drunk and bursts in with a ribald story at the expense of a carpenter, which so enrages the reeve, who, we have been told, is "a wel good wrighte, a carpenter", that he retorts with such another story at a miller's expense. Later the friar and the summoner cast out, with a similar result. And so the whole machine is kept in motion. If a hitch occurs, or dulness threatens, the host intervenes as Master of the Ceremonies: he cuts Chaucer himself down peremptorily:

Myn eres aken of thy drasty speche.

But it is the knight, the *doyen* of the company, who refuses to have his feelings harrowed by any more of the monk's dreary 'tragédies'.

A mediaeval pilgrimage brought people of all ranks together in a combination of piety and holiday-making. Thus his "moving frame" enabled Chaucer to show us a cross-section, almost complete, of English life in the fourteenth century. All classes have representatives here except the highest and the lowest; and Chaucer delights in them all. As an artist, that is; morally he disapproves of many of them, but the poet, as Keats says, "lives in gusto, be it foul or fair. . . . He has as much delight in conceiving an Iago as an Imogen". One thing Chaucer does insist on: every character, good or bad, must be a perfect specimen of his class. The knight is a very perfect knight; the doctor has not his like in the world; the shipman is a smuggler, and worse,

> But of his craft . . .
> There nas noon swich from Hulle to Cartage;

the pardoner is a quack,

> But of his craft, fro Berwik into Ware,
> Ne was there swich another pardoner.

Beyond this the interest of Chaucer's picture lies in the distribution of light and shade, the depth as well as the range of the portraiture. It is not entirely satirical, nor, except in three cases, is it idealistic. There are neutrally tinted characters. The squire and the clerk, for instance, are drawn with a very friendly hand, but they are not idealised, and Chaucer permits himself a kindly smile at the squire's love-insomnia and the lean clerk's lean horse. In most of the other portraits there is a touch of satire, which grows more apparent as we descend the social scale. The lady prioress is treated with amused deference; the well-born monk is praised for accomplishments that his vows forbade. Of the professional men the man of law gets off with one little gibe:

> No-wher so bisy a man as he ther nas,
> And yet he seemed bisier than he was.

The doctor does not escape so easily; he is a bit of a humbug, grounded in astrology, hand in glove with the druggist, and making a good thing out of the plague:

> He kepte that he wan in pestilence.

The manciple and the reeve, some steps lower in the scale, are handled with an irony mordant but subtle. They belong to a class for which Mr. Belloc would reserve a special room in Hell, trusted old servants, respectful and respectable, who fleece their masters at every turn, and get thanked for their services. With the friar and the wife of Bath, the miller and the shipman, Chaucer lets himself go freely, though he shows some indulgence even to these, remembering that they are of the people, whose moral standards are not quite those of more cultured classes. The most imaginative line in the *Prologue*,

> With many a tempest hadde his berd been shake,

is given to that hardy ruffian, the shipman. The only characters whom Chaucer thoroughly detests and lashes unspar-
ingly are those vermin of the Church, the summoner and the
pardoner. Over against these rascals stand the three figures
whom he has idealised—the knight, the parson, and the
ploughman, representing the three main classes in mediaeval
society, the *bellatores*, the *oratores*, and the *laboratores*. It is
not surprising that Chaucer should idealise the knight; but
that he should invest the poor parish priest and his brother the
ploughman with haloes is indeed significant. Clerical corruption and social and economic disturbances following on war
and pestilence were driving men to question authority in
Church and State. Chaucer was no Wycliffite; but his patron,
John of Gaunt, had supported Wycliffe in his attacks on ecclesiastical abuses; the slogan of the Kentish rebels,

> When Adam delved and Eve span,
> Who was then the gentleman?

had reached his ears; and in these characters we hear an echo
of the democratic and evangelical sentiment which was
gathering strength in the fourteenth century.

Chaucer brings himself in twice in the course of the poem;
first through the mouth of the man of law to defend the
morality of his stories as compared with Gower's; later when,
challenged by the host, he begins his rhyme of Sir Thopas,
a delightful parody—perhaps the first in the language—
of the more popular of the romances recited by wandering
minstrels.

"A cross-section of English life in the fourteenth century"
we have called the *Prologue*; but it is more than that. These
characters belong, no doubt, to their own age; but they are
also of all time. Their traits are universal, the lineaments, as
Blake put it, of universal human life, beyond which Nature
never steps. They are all with us to-day, though some of
them have changed their names; the knight now commands a
line regiment, the squire is in the Guards, the shipman was a
rum-runner while prohibition lasted and is active now in the
black market, the friar is a jolly sporting publican, the pardoner
vends quack medicines or holds séances, and the prioress is
headmistress of a fashionable girls' school. Some of them
have reappeared in later literature: the poor parson was
reincarnated in the Vicar of Wakefield, the knight in Colonel

Newcome, and the monk in Archdeacon Grantly.

Of the tales themselves we can only say with Dryden, "Here is God's plenty"—romance both Classical and Oriental, moral tale and merry tale, saint's legend, Breton lay, fable and homily—they are all here, grave and gay well mingled, and nearly every tale well fitted to the teller.   Apparently Chaucer meant at first to write no fewer than a hundred and twenty tales, two for each pilgrim on the outward and two on the homeward journey, and to end where he began at the Tabard in Southwark.   Such at least is the host's proposal.   Whether or not Chaucer ever entertained so vast a project, he did not live to finish even thirty tales: when he had brought his pilgrims within sight of Canterbury, he felt the hand of death upon him, and wound up the poem, giving the last word to the parson and adding an epilogue in which he recanted all his enditings of worldly vanities and commended his soul to Christ.   There are other signs of incompleteness also.   The tales have come down to us in groups, tales and groups linked by prologues, the longest, and broadest, being the wife of Bath's on Chaucer's favourite theme of marriage.   Possibly Chaucer meant each group to correspond to a day's journey; but some of the tales are isolated and some of the links missing.   Moreover the squire's story of Cambuscan is left half told, as Milton complained, and the cook's tale breaks off abruptly with nothing to take its place, for the so-called *Cook's Tale of Gamelyn* is not Chaucer's.   There are signs too of hesitation or change of plan: the shipman's tale was clearly meant to be told by a woman, probably the wife of Bath; and the man of law's should have been in prose, possibly the *Tale of Melibeus* which Chaucer afterwards appropriated to himself.   But incomplete as they are, *The Canterbury Tales* remain an imperishable monument to one of the best and best-loved of English poets.

Chaucer had no great lyric gift, nor much invention in the narrower sense.   But give him a skeleton of plot and elbow-room, and he can tell a story with any going.   As a teller of merry tales in verse he has been equalled in our literature only by Burns, and by Burns only in *Tam o' Shanter*.   Looking back over the years that lie between him and Layamon, we may truly say that he found English poetry brick and left it marble.   His services to English metre and diction were immense.   He had a firm grasp on the true way of wedding the stressed and syllabic systems, by accommodating metrical ictus to natural accent.   Above all, he naturalised the iambic pentameter, first in stanzas of eight or of seven lines—the latter the famous rhyme royal; then in the still more famous heroic couplet.   The tetrameter is a fine measure in its way, but for variety and flexibility it is far inferior to the pentameter, how far we can scarcely realise better than by turning from Chaucer to his contemporary Gower.

John Gower (c. 1330–1408) was a gentleman of Kent, a good, rich, timid man; his Latin *Vox Clamantis* is a jeremiad over Wat Tyler's rebellion.   His chief English poem is the *Confessio Amantis*, a huge collection of stories in a peculiar frame.   An ageing lover approaches Venus, who sends him to her confessor Genius.   Genius, to prepare his penitent, discourses with him on the Seven Deadly Sins in their bearing on love, and on other matters also, such as the duties of princes, illustrating his discourse with appropriate stories.   Many of these are so good that for centuries Gower ranked with Chaucer as a prince of poets.   His frame too is interesting: at the end the lover abandons the pursuit, his fires cooled with the frost of age.   But if many of the stories are well told in a plain style, many of the others are not worth the telling; the poet's reflections are trite and prosaic; his unsure taste in relating a story of unnatural vice drew a stinging rebuke from Chaucer; and his sense of the appropriate is so erratic that he uses the story of Pyramus and Thisbe to illustrate the vice of 'contek', that is, hasty passion, as if Pyramus had killed himself in a fit of temper.   Worst of all, he cannot get out of the tetrameter couplet even the variety of which it is capable; after a time the tramp of his well-drilled iambics begins to fall on the ear like the sound of a clock striking thirty-three thousand. Nevertheless Gower did much for English culture: he provided his readers with a wealth of "storial matter" and a sort of popular encyclopaedia of mediaeval lore.

Though Chaucer recanted on his deathbed all his enditings of worldly vanities, a man of the world he had been, dwelling for choice on the variegated surface of life and retailing its braveries and humours for the delight of a courtly audience. But the world he loved, the mediaeval world of Faith, Romance, and Chivalry, was passing away.   The authority of the Church had been shaken by the failure of the Crusades and the trans-ference of the Papal chair from Rome to the sinful city of Avignon; and in England Wycliffe, having assailed its organisation, had begun to question one of its fundamental dogmas, the doctrine of transubstantiation. Feudal monarchy was tottering to its fall. As for Romance, Chaucer himself had helped to subvert it: his psychology was a corrosive to the convention of romantic love more dangerous than Boccaccio's lewdness. And what of the *laboratores*, on whom the whole fabric of society rested? Chaucer reveres the true-hearted ploughman, but he has nothing to say of the misery and discontent of the toiling masses, oppressed by the knighthood, neglected by the clergy, and scourged by recurrent pestilence and famine. These things found a voice in William Langland, whom it is still permissible to regard as the author of *The Vision of William concerning Piers the Plowman*.

Langland (*c.* 1332–1400) was probably born in Shropshire, but for most of his days he lived *in* London and *on* London, as he tells us. He was a clerk in minor orders, who earned a poor living for his wife and daughter as a cantor or a scrivener, and was sometimes reduced to beg. A tall, lean man, and country-bred—

> I have lived in londe [he says]; my name is Long Wille—

he stalked down Cornhill in the long clothes of a deacon, doing reverence to no man, gazing through the gay surface of London life to the wretchedness and corruption beneath; and all that he thought and felt he put into his poem. It was his life's work. It exists in three versions: the first appeared about 1362, the second after King Edward's death in 1377; and he went on revising and adding to it till he died.

The poem consists of eleven visions, and has something of the inconsequence of a dream. The Prologue describes how the poet fell asleep on a May morning by the side of a burn on Malvern Hills, and beheld a lofty tower, with a dungeon in a dell beneath it, and between them a fair field full of folk. The tower is Heaven, the dungeon is Hell, and the fair field is the field of the world, full of all manner of men, the mean and the rich. Here after King Edward's death the poet inserted the famous fable of Bell-the-Cat, to signify the need for a strong monarchy.

After this Prologue the dreamer sees Lady Meed (Reward) about to wed Falsehood, when Theology forbids the union, and they are had up to Westminster before the King. He proposes that she should wed Conscience, but Conscience will have none of her, and bids the King call in Reason, by whose advice he promises to abide.

In a second vision Reason harangues the people. The Seven Deadly Sins repent and set out to make confession; but on the way Gluttony is tempted into an ale-house, which gives occasion for a vivid and realistic description of low life in London. The penitents go on to seek Truth, that is, God the Father; but no one knows the way until Piers the Plowman puts out his head and offers to guide them when he has ploughed his half-acre. Meanwhile he sets them all to work: those who shirk are quelled by Hunger. God now sends Piers a pardon for kings, knights, bishops, and labourers; but a priest disputes it, and the dispute between him and Piers waxes so loud that the dreamer awakes.

Up to this point Piers has been simply the symbol of honest labour, but in the Visions of Do Wel, Do Bet, and Do Best which follow he is transfigured into the person of the Christ Himself, whose crucifixion and descent into Hell are described in language of extraordinary sublimity. The devils tremble as His coming shines far off, and at the call,

"Dukes of this dim place . anon undo these gates,"

the bars of Hell break asunder, and the King of Glory enters in, bringing light to them that sit in darkness, to lead forth His redeemed and proclaim His gospel of love:

"For I, that am lord of lyf . love is my drynke,
And for that drynke to-day . I deyde upon erthe.
I faughte so, me threstes yet . for mannes soule sake;
May no drynke me moiste . ne my thruste slake,
Til the vendage falle . in the vale of Josephath
That I drynke righte ripe must . *resurreccio mortuorum*,
And thanne shal I come as a kyng . crowned with angels,
And han out of helle . alle mennes soules."

Mercy and truth have met together; righteousness and peace have kissed each other; and the dreamer awakes in ecstasy to hear the bells ringing in Easter morning.

But the hour of triumph is not yet. It must needs be that Antichrist first come. Christ has ascended into Heaven; on Earth the powers of evil draw to a head, and the dreamer takes refuge in the citadel of Unity, which is Holy Church, whereof Conscience is castellan. As the hosts of the enemy advance, Pride bearing their standard, Conscience cries to Contrition to keep the gate. But Contrition lies asleep, drugged by a flattering friar who has gained entrance to the citadel. "Then," says Conscience, "I will go on pilgrimage, and wend through the world to seek Piers the Plowman." And so the poem ends, as it were with the cry, "Oh Lord, how long?"

The Seven Deadly Sins and the Harrowing of Hell are mediaeval commonplaces, though few poets have treated the one so realistically or the other so sublimely as Langland. Still these themes are not new; what is unique in Langland is his understanding of, and compassion for, the labouring poor— the cottars' wives who rise in winter nights to card and spin and wash and rock the cradle, and their husbands who toil and pinch to pay rent and get bread for children crying for food, and still, like true-born Englishmen, cling tragically to self-respect, and make shift, though they go hungry, "to turn the fair outward, and be abashed for to beg".

Sentiments like these made the name of Piers Plowman a catchword among the revolting peasants in 1381; but Langland himself was neither a Lollard nor a revolutionary. He was a good Catholic, who believed that the existing order of society was a thing ordained of God; the remedy for the evils that beset it lay not in its overthrow but in each order doing its duty in its appointed place, all working for the common weal in love to God and their neighbours.

Chapter Four

ENGLISH POETRY FROM CHAUCER
TO SKELTON

WITH the deaths of Chaucer, Gower, and Langland a blight fell on English poetry. The long minority of Henry VI, and the disastrous French wars, followed by the ruinous Wars of the Roses, deprived courtly poets of their natural patrons. There were literary and linguistic reasons also. Chaucer and Gower had well-nigh exhausted mediaeval themes, and no fresh ideas came from Italy to revive or replace them. The language too was changing: final -e though still written was ceasing to be pronounced; the rules for its elision were forgotten; and the English accent was beginning to prevail in French words like 'virtúé', 'liquór', 'coráge'; so that many of Chaucer's smooth pentameters were scanned as rough tetrameters, and poets who scanned them so took a similar licence. In a word, Chaucer's metrical secret was lost because poets continued to spell as he had spelt when they no longer spoke as he had spoken. Scholars have defended Lydgate's scansion; it is more than he did himself: "I took none hede," he says, "neither of short nor long." Finally, prose was beginning to annex the provinces of Chronicle and Romance, which had hitherto belonged to verse; when Malory wrote his *Morte d'Arthur* about 1470 he wrote it in prose.

In the first part of the century, however, verse was still used for romance. Chaucer's parody had not quite killed the fashion or the fashionable metre; the finest of all the fifteenth-century romances, Thomas Chestre's *Sir Launfal*, is in the sixain of *Sir Thopas* doubled. It comes from a Breton lay by Marie de France, which had already been Englished as, *Lamwell.* "Matter of Britain" also supplied the themes of Henry Lonlich's *Merlin* and *Holy Grail*. John Lydgate (c. 1370–1450) used "matter of Rome" for his long-winded *Troy Book* and *Story of Thebes*. Versions of the Orpheus and Eurydice story might be referred to either class, for they came from Greek legend through Breton lays.

But it was Allegory rather than Romance that dominated the century. We have seen how Guillaume de Lorris turned

to the service of courtly love a literary form which had previously been used for moral or religious ends.   In the fifteenth
century the moralists had their revenge, appropriating the
courtly imagery of the *Roman de la Rose* to their own didactic
purposes, religious, moral, or educational.   Thus the charming
preamble of *The Flower and the Leaf*, with its vernal pleasance
dotted with knights and ladies, seems to promise a sequel of
courtly love, but turns into a mild allegory of Honour *versus*
Idlesse.   *The Flower and the Leaf* is peculiarly interesting as
being the first English poem known to have been written by a
woman.   *The Assembly of Ladies* is also by a woman, perhaps
the same woman; it has witty feminine touches on dress and
deportment, but the point of the moral escapes us.   Lydgate's
Pilgrimage of Man and *Reason and Sensuality* are solid moral
allegories translated from the French.   Stephen Hawes (1474–
1523?) carries us well into Henry VIII's reign.   His *Pastime
of Pleasure* ends with the famous lines—

> For though the day be never so long,
> At last the bell ringeth to evensong.

Critics have sought to deprive Hawes of these lines as being
proverbial: he can ill spare them; for generally he is very dull,
dullest of all when his hero, Graund Amour, on his way to win
La Belle Pucell (romantic names!), is led through the trivium
and quadrivium of the mediaeval school curriculum.   Moral
allegory can be tedious enough, but educational allegory is
more than human nature can endure.   Yet there is something
wistful in Hawes, dreaming of *amour courtois* under Henry VIII
—the ghost of allegory sitting by the grave of chivalry.   The
puzzling *Court of Love* looks like a deliberate cast-back to love-
allegory, with no didactics about it, written by an accomplished
versifier who imitated Chaucer's early style without quite
understanding his accidence.   If it is later than *The Pastime
of Pleasure*, as it has been thought to be, it shows the extraordinary persistence of the Rose tradition.

Didacticism occupied other provinces besides allegory.
Thomas Occleve's *Regiment of Princes* (1412) is a hotch-potch
of political wisdom, translated from various originals and
designed for the instruction of Prince Hal, who needed such
instruction if ever prince did.   Lydgate's *Falls of Princes*,
translated from Boccaccio, is important as linking the
'tragedies' of Chaucer's *Monk's Tale*, stories

> Of him that stood in greet prosperitee,
> And is y-fallen out of heigh degree
> Into miserie, and endeth wrecchedly,

with the Tudor *Mirror for Magistrates*, and so, through Sackville, with the beginnings of Elizabethan tragedy. In his own day Lydgate was regularly named with Chaucer and Gower; if he pleases yet, it is not for his voluminous translations but for the personal touches in his *Teastament*, and above all for his *London Lickpenny*, if it be his, where for once he looked up from his books to describe the misadventures of a penniless wight in London. Occleve (*c.* 1368–1425) is interesting too, and even touching, when he writes about himself and tells us how, when he was a poor, prodigal clerk, drudging in the Privy Seal Office, he would take boat on the Thames for the pleasure of hearing the watermen call him 'Master'.

Two names besides that of Hawes bridge the gap between the fifteenth and sixteenth centuries. Alexander Barclay (1475–1552) deserves mention not so much for his *Ship of Fools* (a translation from the German, very popular in its day) as for his *Eclogues*. No doubt these too are only translations, but we must not ignore, as Spenser did, the fact that Barclay introduced the Pastoral into English two generations before Spenser. Its introduction at this date is significant; for the Pastoral, with its praise of the simple life, represents a reaction from the chivalric ideal. The corruption of our prosody which set in after Chaucer's death has gone very far by the time we reach Barclay. He still imitates the Chaucerian couplet and stanza, but imitates them so abominably that it is a positive relief when John Skelton (*c.* 1460–1529), after trying his hand at allegory in the old prosodic tradition, throws the syllabic system overboard altogether and falls back on a purely accentual metre, written in very short lines. 'Doggerel' his ragged rhymes may be, and ribald they often are; but they are alive. Skelton is looking at life, not at books and dead conventions. There is real passion in his onslaught on Wolsey in *Why come Ye not to Court?*, and real tenderness as well as buffoonery in *Philip Sparrow*. Even the ink-horn terms in which, like Hawes and Barclay, he indulges, show that learning has revived in England. The sap is rising again: the Renaissance is in sight.

There is little else worth noting during this period in the way of 'literate' poetry. Fifteenth-century lyric is best represented by the carol: the loveliest of all carols, "I sing of a maiden", belongs to this age.   Otherwise courtly lyric did not greatly flourish; but we have two fine examples of *disputoison* and *débat*, one from near the beginning of the century, the other just before its close.   Sir Thomas Clanvowe's sprightly *Cuckoo and Nightingale* is better mannered, though not better metred, than the early *Owl and Nightingale*.   And if one flower could make a summer, the dulness of the century would be redeemed by the exquisite *Nutbrown Maid*, a *débat* between a squire who pretends that he must flee to the greenwood as a banished man and a lady who will not forsake him for any hardship or disgrace, till, assured of her faith, he reveals that he is no outlaw but an earl's son.   This perfect poem must surely have been written by a woman.

Two forms of poetry escaped the prevailing blight, and escaped it for the same reason, that they appealed to a popular, not a courtly, audience, and were meant to be heard, not read. They were the ballad and the drama.

The ballad has been defined as a song that tells a story.   It is not found in all countries, nor in any before the Middle Ages.   For a detailed discussion of its origin, its relation to epic and romance, and the connection between the ballads of different countries, we must refer to such authorities as W. P. Ker and Professor Entwistle: here we shall only attempt to give the most generally accepted conclusions.

Some scholars have held that the ballad is simply a broken-down romance, the ballad-stave of four lines simply a curtailed sixain—the stanza of *Sir Thopas* with two lines dropped out. Now it is true that not a few ballads were made out of fragments or episodes from romances, some of them at least by professional minstrels.   But as an explanation of the origin of the ballad this theory breaks down, since it fails to account for the peculiar *form* of the primitive ballad.   A genuine primitive ballad like *Baby Lon* consists of an expanding series of stanzas which relate a single incident with variations; it is essentially dramatic; and it has a refrain.   None of these features comes from romance.   Instead they suggest that the primitive ballad was an offshoot of the *carole* or ring-dance, which originated in Provence about 1100 and spread over a great part of Western Europe as quickly as the tango did in our day.   The performers in a *carole* danced to the accompaniment of their own singing, each in turn improvising a rhymed couplet—pasquinade, riddle, or what not—with a refrain after each verse in which the whole company joined. When inspiration gave out, "storial matter" was brought in, at first simply to spin out the song. But the story, once admitted, behaved like the camel in the Arabian fable, and ousted the original occupant. Ballads, that is, began to be sung for the sake of the stories they told and not merely as dance-accompaniments, and the refrain often disappeared. In this sense, but in this sense only, the primitive ballad may be said to have had a communal origin; our mature ballads were undoubtedly made by individual poets.

Traditional ballads are often called "popular ballads". Popular they always were, in the sense that all classes enjoyed them, but not in the sense that they were made by the people for the people. On the contrary, though the ballad proved an accommodating form, admitting many kinds of matter—riddle, folk-lore, romance, legend, and history sacred and secular—it was around great individuals and families that the ballad stories gathered; and their tone is aristocratic rather than democratic as the songs are democratic, which explains why in later days the ballad appealed to Scott, the song to Burns. It was when more artistic or artificial forms of poetry became fashionable in cultivated circles, as reading took the place of reciting, that the ballad became the poetry of the populace. Then the minstrel, seeking a new audience, turned to this established form,

> And tuned to please a peasant's ear
> The harp a king had loved to hear,

singing in the village ale-house scraps or short versions of the romances he had once recited in the baron's hall. If we remember that the romances were familiar to listeners in many lands, it is not wonderful, though strange, that the story of Orpheus and Eurydice as told in mediaeval romance in which the Fairy King has taken the place of Pluto was preserved in a Shetland ballad taken down in 1878 from the singing of an old man in Unst. The body of the ballad of *King Orfeo* is in Scots; but the Norse refrain shows its origin to be older than 1750, when Norse died out in Shetland. The two lines of the refrain are said to mean "Early green's the wood" and "Where the hart goes yearly", showing that the ballad must have come from Scandinavia, since Shetland has neither woods nor harts.

Many British ballads have counterparts in other lands. Some of them may have crossed the sea, like *King Orfeo*; but remembering how many ballads were drawn from folk-lore we incline to think that in most cases only the folk-tale was common property and the actual ballads were composed independently.

Balladry goes back to 1200 or earlier, but very few mediaeval ballads have come down to us in their original form. We have only one ballad-copy, *Judas*, from the thirteenth century, and none at all from the fourteenth, though we know from Langland that "rhymes of Robin Hood and Randal, Earl of Chester" were then current. The fifteenth century, however, so poor in literate poetry, can claim some of the finest historical ballads, including that old song of Percy and Douglas which moved Sidney "more than with a trumpet", and its Scottish counterpart, *Otterburn*. Romantic ballads are harder to date, the more so because, as Professor Entwistle notes, the folk tend to give them a new setting as events within living memory. In Scotland the scene of *The Douglas Tragedy* is traditionally laid at Douglas Craig on Yarrow; but in Virginia Miss Scarborough met a nonagenarian who claimed to have been a witness. "*The Seven Sleepers* . . . was a true story. It happened way back yonder in Mutton Hollow. I was there myself. Somebody got killed over the girl. I was there soon after it happened. Another man was after the girl, and one man shot him." Despite this testimony we may still believe that the best of our romantic ballads, *The Douglas Tragedy* among them, were made in the fifteenth and sixteenth centuries. "The end of the Middle Ages comes with the practice of reading." After the invention of printing the ballad in the South of England fell into the hands of journalists like Thomas Deloney, who made it the vehicle of sensational news-items printed on one side of the paper and hawked as 'broadsides' at fairs and markets—a practice that survived till our own day. In Scotland, however, conditions were more favourable for balladry. The English ballad was always inferior to the Scottish in the capital articles of romance and gramarie, though its typical Robin Hood cycle had the good-nature and good-humour that mark the average Englishman. So the genuine old ballad lived on in the North Country after it had died out in the South: the best of the "riding ballads" are later than 1600. Indeed, the art of balladry is not yet dead: it still flourishes in the

Faroes, and Texan cowboys and Scottish ploughboys still make ballads of a kind.

Passing from mouth to mouth, the old ballads got garbled and mutilated in the course of ages, and in this form it was that many of them found their way into print. This brought with it a new temptation to which Scott and others too often succumbed, the temptation to restore the older, more romantic tone. It was left to a great American scholar, Professor Child, to collect all the known versions of all the traditional British ballads, and print them exactly as he found them.

What then is the real literary value of the genuine traditional, 'popular' ballad? Though, as we have said, it borrows not infrequently from the romance, its closest tie is with the older epic. The romances abound in digressions, story piled upon story; the common characteristics of the ballad and the epic are singleness of aim and preference for the tragic theme. "In the literature of the early Middle Ages the most important fact is the selection of tragic motives in preference to romantic adventures as the substance of heroic poetry and prose. The adventures are there, but their interest is secondary to the tragic fortune of Sigurd and Brynhild, of Hildebrand and his son, of Roland, of Grettir or Njal. The same thing is true of the ballads in the later Middle Ages, and this, quite as much as the difference of scale, is what distinguishes them from the longer stories of adventure. Not all the ballads are tragical, and tragedy is not wanting in the longer stories, in *Tristram* and the *Morte d'Arthur*. But in the longer romances there are many different policies; some authors are thinking of courtly sentiment, and some of spinning their yarn. The ballads keep to the point, and that is generally a definite tragic problem— distress like that of *Fair Annie*, or error, as in *Child Maurice*, or conflict of affections or duties, as in *The Douglas Tragedy* or in *Bewick and Graeme*—or in the simplest of them, a brave man fighting against odds, like *Johnnie of Braidislee*. In the more cheerful ballads, and those with a happy ending, like the *Gay Goss-hawk* or *Katharine Janfarie*, there is still the same definite sense of drama—something that has to be played out, rather than something that has to be continued in a string of adventures." [1]

Ker's words remind us that questions about the origin and diffusion of the ballad have more interest after all for the

[1] W. P. Ker, *Form and Style in Poetry.*

anthropologist than the lover of poetry.   For him its interest lies in the peculiar thrill of the dramatically told story, as it comes to us in the ballad composed to be sung or chanted, not printed and read.   Humble as it is in form, the ballad is a wilding from the garden of chivalry; it has a touch of race, a fugitive, often tragical beauty, that appeals to all who have hearts for romance.   By revealing something of this to the eighteenth century Percy's *Reliques of Ancient English Poetry* gave a powerful impulse to the Romantic Revival.

The other form of poetry which continued to flourish in the fifteenth century was the popular drama.   Mediaeval drama was in no sense derived from the classical drama of Greece and Rome.   Under the later Empire classical drama perished of its own bestiality, which the Church could neither utilise nor condone.   But the mimetic instinct is irrepressible, and the Church turned it to account by dramatising portions of the Christmas and Easter services so as to bring the sacred story home to simple minds in the most effective way, that is, through the eye.   Thus on Good Friday the crucifix was taken down and interred in front of the high altar—several English churches still possess stone receptacles ('sepulchres' they were called) which were used for this purpose.   At an early service on Easter Morning the cross was disinterred and replaced on the altar. Attendance by the laity at this service was discouraged or forbidden because a superstition grew up that if you were present you might count on not dying that year.   It was at a later service on the same morning that the service of the now empty tomb took place.   After the third lesson at Matins, one of the brethren sat down quietly by the sepulchre, representing an angel; then others came softly up, representing the women who came "very early in the morning" with spices; a brief Latin dialogue ensued:

Quem quaeritis in sepulcro, o Christicolae?
Jesum Nazarenum crucifixum, o Caelicolae.
Non est hic, surrexit, sicut praedixerat.
Ite, narrate quia surrexit de sepulcro.

This dialogue was the germ out of which the Liturgical Drama grew.   It was in Latin, and was performed by clerics in the church, and could be expanded by the singing of Latin hymns.

Gradually this Liturgical Drama was extended and secularised into what are known as Miracle Plays. Latin was replaced by French or English; clerical actors gave way to laymen; the performance was moved from the church first to the churchyard, then to the street or market-place; and the management passed from the hands of the Church into those of the municipalities. The municipalities entrusted the actual performance sometimes to professional actors as at Coventry, more often to the trade guilds, each of which undertook a scene. The Liturgical Drama developed, as we have said, from the Christmas and Easter services; but in 1311 the new feast of Corpus Christi, which Pope Urban had founded, was made obligatory by the Council of Vienne, and thenceforth became the favourite date for these Miracle Plays, for the simple reason that they were played in the open and Corpus Christi always fell within a few weeks of the summer solstice. (At Chester, however, they were played in Whitweek.)

We possess four complete sets or cycles of these plays, from York, Wakefield, Chester, and Coventry, besides odd scenes from other towns. The York cycle is the most elaborate, and we shall take it for illustration. It comprised forty-eight separate 'pageants', each provided by one or more of the trade guilds. Early on the morning of Corpus Christi the first pageants assembled before the Abbey gate. Each pageant was a small wooden erection mounted on wheels. It had two storeys, the lower curtained to serve as a dressing-room, the upper, or 'scaffold', open to serve as a stage. At 5 A.M. the tanners led off with the Creation of the Angels; then they moved on to the next station, where they repeated their performance, while their place at the Abbey gate was taken by the plasterers, who exhibited the Creation of Adam. And thus a long series of scenes from Holy Writ was enacted, chiefly those which dealt with man's fall and redemption. (In the York cycle there are only twelve scenes symbolic of the Fall and Redemption from the Old Testament, as against thirty-six from the New.) Every scene was repeated at every station; there might be eight to twelve stations, so that the whole performance took several days; the Chester cycle of twenty-four plays took three days to act, the York cycle with its forty-eight plays may have taken as much as a week.

The main purpose of the Miracle Play, as of the Liturgical Play, was to make common folk familiar with the sacred story, to do for spectators what *Cursor Mundi* did for readers. But mediaeval religion, though earnest, was not solemn, and, though it would not tamper with what was in the Bible, it tolerated jokes and horse-play in scenes not actually warranted by Holy Writ.   Thus Noah has a scolding wife, who refuses to leave her gossips, and has to be forcibly lifted into the Ark by her sons, where she cracks Noah over the head; in the *Second Shepherds' Play* Mak swaddles up a stolen sheep and passes it off as a baby in a cradle.   These comic episodes seem incongruous to us, but they did not jar on the simple faith of a mediaeval audience.

The next stage in the evolution of the drama was the Morality.   The Morality did not supersede the Miracle Play. On the contrary, the Miracle Play not only lived on alongside the Morality but outlived it by many years.   Moralities, even Moral Interludes, ceased to be written about the middle of the sixteenth century; Miracle Plays continued to be performed almost to the end of Elizabeth's reign; indeed one was performed in James I's reign for the entertainment of the Spanish ambassador.   The Morality was meant not to supersede the Miracle Play but to supplement it.   For though the Miracle Play sufficed to familiarise people with the *story* of man's redemption, it did not suffice to instruct them in the *means* of redemption, namely the moral and sacramental teaching of the Church.   This the Morality sought to do.   In the spirit of that didactic age, it replaced the persons of the Miracle Play by personifications: we might call it a dramatised allegory.   The earliest English Morality, the *Castle of Perséverance*, produced about 1405, is sufficiently typical.   It presents the whole spiritual history of *Humanum Genus* (mankind) from birth to the Day of Judgement; shows him between his Good and Evil Angels; beleaguered in the Castle of Perséverance by the world, the flesh, and the devil, assailed by the vices, whom the virtues repel with showers of roses; dying at last and carried before the Judgement Seat, where Mercy pleads for him and he attains salvation through Christ's atoning sacrifice.

The *Castle of Perséverance* is a very long play, and was probably acted in the open, but on a fixed stage, not like the Miracle Plays at successive stations.   For indoor performances there was a shorter type of Morality, of which *Everyman* is the best example.   Like a Greek tragedy, it starts close upon the crisis; it covers the last act, so to speak, of the drama unfolded at full length in the *Castle of Perséverance*.   God sends Death to summon Everyman; he craves a respite, which Death refuses; then he appeals to Friends and Kinsmen, but they all desert him when they learn his destination; so do Strength, Beauty, and the Five Senses; Knowledge goes with him to the brink of the grave, but no farther; none can enter that narrow room and go with him before God but Good Deeds only. This impressive play, impressive even to a modern audience, was long believed to be of Dutch origin, since the imprint of the first Dutch edition is earlier than that of any printed English version, but scholars are now disposed to think that the Dutch version was really a translation from English. In England as in other countries the Morality soon began to be used for purposes of propaganda, Catholic or Protestant, in the religious controversies of the age.

From a chamber-morality, if one may use the term, like *Everyman*, it is a short step to the Interlude. The Interlude, as its name implies, was a short play designed to entertain a company during or after a banquet. Its derivation from the Morality is shown by the fact that such a play is often described as "a Morality in the manner of an Interlude". But whereas the typical Morality was altogether serious, and its characters were all personifications, in the Interlude comedy begins to appear, and personifications begin to be mingled with and gradually replaced by types or individual characters. Our earliest Interlude is Henry Medwall's *Fulgens and Lucres* (*c.* 1494), in substance a *débat* on true nobility, but relieved by a sub-plot which parodies the serious theme. Our best-known Interlude is John Heywood's *Four P's*, which probably belongs to Henry VIII's reign. A Palmer, a Pardoner, and a Pothecary, with a Pedlar for judge, contend as to who can tell the biggest lies. The Pardoner looks like winning when he tells how he brought a woman out of Hell, whose insufferable temper made Satan glad to let her go; but the Palmer beats him on the post by averring that in all *his* travels he never saw a woman out of temper. John Bale's *King John* is remarkable among Interludes because it introduces characters from English history alongside abstract personifications, and shows King John as the champion of England against the Pope. We have reached Reformation times with the Morality used polemically on either side, and are within sight of the beginnings of the Elizabethan Drama. Here then we may conveniently leave English poetry for a time and turn to Scotland.

Chapter Five

EARLY SCOTTISH POETRY

BY Scottish poetry we mean poetry written in Scots, *i.e.* in that Northern English which remained the national language of Scotland long after it had sunk in England to the status of a provincial dialect. Scottish literature was the last of the Western vernacular literatures to flower and the first to decay. In the dawn of history we find Scotland occupied by four distinct races—Picts, Scots, Britons, and Angles. It was well into the eleventh century before these were united under one crown, and many years later before, in a time of peace, the first wave of French influence reached Scotland's shores. Thomas the Rhymer, whom tradition names as the father of Scottish poetry, seems to have lived in Alexander III's reign. If *Sir Tristram* is his, as Scott believed, then the lowest stratum of Scottish poetry rests on French romance; if it is not—and the ascription is quite uncertain—then we have nothing at all left from that brief golden age.

The earliest undoubted specimen of Scottish verse that we possess is a fragment of a *cantus* lamenting the 'perplexity' in which Scotland was bestead after Alexander III's untimely death. From this perplexity Bruce delivered her, and it was fitting that the first notable Scottish poem should be a monument to the hero-king. Between the *cantus* we have mentioned and John Barbour's *Brus* (*c.* 1375) we find nothing but three scraps of verse jeering at the English, fifteen lines in all. *The Brus* is not exactly a great poem; vivid as it is in description and shrewd in characterisation, its verse is rather unmelodious and its diction rather pedestrian. But if it is not exactly a great poem, it is a noble piece of work, animated by a chivalrous spirit worthy of its subject. The image of Bruce that Scotland still carries in her heart, the wise, patient king, high-hearted, high-minded, humorous, and kindly, is the Bruce that Barbour drew. Love of country and freedom inspired a burst of eloquence that has endeared Barbour's name to all English-speaking peoples:

> A! fredome is a nobill thing!
> Fredome mayss man to haiff liking!

Fredome all solace to man giffis:
He levys at ess that frely levys!
A noble hart may haiff nane ess,
Na ellys nocht that may him pless,
Gyff fredome failyhe: for fre liking
Is yharnyt our all othir thing.
Na he, that ay hass levyt fre,
May nocht knaw weill the propyrte,
The angyr, na the wrechyt dome,
That is cowplyt to foule thyrldome.
Bot gyff he had assayit it,
Than all perquer he suld it wyt;
And suld think fredome mar to pryss
Than all the gold in warld that is.

Barbour called his poem a romance; but though he took hints for some of his episodes from French romance and put speeches into Bruce's mouth in classic fashion, the tale he tells is substantially true—"a suthfast story", as he calls it. Apart from his singular confusion of King Robert with his grandfather and namesake the Competitor—and the confusion may be scribal, for Wyntoun quotes the two peccant lines quite differently—apart from this Barbour's sins against the Muse of History are mostly sins of omission: he ignores Wallace, and passes over Bruce's youthful errors in silence. Barbour owed nothing to Chaucer, who was his junior by a quarter of a century; his models are wholly French.

Some fifty years after *The Brus* Andrew of Wyntoun wrote his *Orygynalle Chronykil of Scotland*. Wyntoun makes no pretensions to poetry, but is a valuable chronicler once he gets past his 'origins' and comes down to the times he knew. We owe to him the story of Macbeth.

Fifty years more and we come to the *Wallace* of Henry the Minstrel, commonly called Blind Harry, the last of the Scottish chroniclers. Harry was a much better poet than Wyntoun, but a much less trustworthy chronicler. His *Wallace* is a folk-lore champion, who 'swaps' off his foes' heads like thistle-tops, and carries the war deep into England, where Queen Eleanor tries in vain to buy him off. Harry's inflamed patriotism coupled with a real gift for narrative made his *Wallace* the favourite reading of the commons of Scotland for two hundred years, and when its language grew obsolete Hamilton of Gilbertfield's modernised version (1722) gave it a new lease of life. For all his hatred of England, Harry wisely preferred Chaucer's heroic couplet to Barbour's octosyllables: though he says, "It is well knawn I am ane burel [ignorant] man", the very phrase betrays some knowledge of Chaucer. Moreover he twice breaks into Chaucerian stanzas: those at the beginning of Book VI upbraid fickle Fortune in language not unworthy of Chaucer himself.

To return to Barbour: besides *The Brus* he is credited with a *Troy Book* of which only fragments survive, and with *The Buik of Alexander the Great*. The relation of *The Brus* to *The Buik of Alexander* is obscure, but the parallels are too numerous and close to be accidental. These romances both deal with "matter of Rome"; the other Scottish romancers preferred "matter of Britain". The best of them deal in Arthurian stories, associated rather with Cumbria than with Wales; their favourite hero is not Lancelot but the peerless Gawain, Prince of Galloway. Of one of them, whom he calls "Huchoun of the Awle Ryale" (Hall Royal), Wyntoun says,

> He made the grete geste of Arthoure,
> And the Auntyrs of Gawain,
> The Pistil als of sweit Susane.

The "grete geste" has been identified with the alliterative *Morte Arthur*, and the "Auntyrs of Gawain" with the *Auntyrs of Arthur at Tarn Watheling*; the *Pistil* (epistle) *of Susane* survives under its own name. Huchoun (little Hugh) has been identified with the "Sir Hew of Eglinton" named by Dunbar in his *Lament for the Makars*, who in turn has been identified with a brother-in-law of Robert II. None of these identifications is certain, but if Huchoun wrote nothing but the *Pistil of Susane* he was a true and tender poet. The *Pistil* relates in rhymed alliterative verse the story of Susanna and the Elders: the stanza which tells how Susanna on her way to execution kneels to her husband and kisses his hand, with the words,

> " For I am dampned, I dare not disparage thy mouth,"

is one of the most touching things in our poetry. It is exceedingly doubtful if the *Pistil* is Scottish: all the extant copies are in English.

The romances so far named, to which we may add *Sir Gawain and Sir Golagros*, are all of the chivalric kind, all based on French originals, and differ in nothing but language from contemporary English romances. It is when chivalric romance begins to decay that a distinctively Scottish tone creeps in. We hear it, for instance, in *Rauf Colyear*, which, though romantic in form, is *bourgeois* in tone, rather like a *fabliau* without 'vilanye'. Rauf is a charcoal-burner, as dour and downright as any Scottish collier, who entertains Charlemagne unawares —for once we are dealing with "matter of France"—and boxes his ears to teach him manners. Later, of course, he goes to court, and discovers that he has cuffed the Emperor, is knighted, and performs knightly exploits. When the decay of romance has gone farther we get deliberate burlesque, of chivalric romance in *King Bertok*, of the romance of wonder in *The Gyre-Carling*. *Colkelbie's Sow* is a strange medley: it relates the adventures of the three pennies for which the sow was sold: the second part is an ordinary romance, the third an ordinary moral tale; but the first is a Skeltonic extravaganza, a riot of hilarious horse-play, such as we find, but much better done, in *Peblis to the Play* and *Christis Kirk on the Green*. These famous pieces both describe boisterous small-town merry-makings: a daft abandon, beyond English comprehension, made them immensely popular in Scotland. In the eighteenth century *Christis Kirk*, reprinted by Watson and Ramsay, produced a brilliant progeny in Fergusson's *Leith Races*, Burns's *Holy Fair*, and Tennant's *Anster Fair*. Both poems have been attributed, *Peblis* with some show of reason, to King James I. Certainly the metrical skill they display came from no prentice hand. But whoever wrote them, they are of the people and for the people. So is *The Wife of Auchtermuchty*, an earlier and livelier *John Grumlie*, relating the discomfiture of a goodman who attempts housekeeping; so is *The Wowing of Jok and Jinnie* with its quaint realistic details of Scottish marriage customs. In these popular poems we find Early Scots in its purest and raciest form.

Up to this point we have traced a tradition which, so far as it was not purely native, was almost wholly French in origin. In the fifteenth century a new and powerful influence came in from England: the Chaucerian tradition, withering in the South, was transplanted to Scottish soil, where it struck root and bore a rich and variegated crop. Social conditions were little more favourable to poetry in Scotland than in England; but the Scottish poets came fresh to the Chaucerian models, and they worked in a slightly different medium, and one that was for the moment fairly stable: more important than any of these reasons was the simple fact that some poets of genius happened to be born in Scotland at a time when none was born in England.   It was King James I who brought the Chaucerian tradition home from his English captivity.   In *The Kingis Quair* he tells with a lover's and a poet's licence the story of that captivity, and of how from the turret window of his prison he first caught sight of his future queen walking in the garden below:

> For quhich sodain abate anon astert
> The blude of all my body to my hert.

Then comes the inevitable dream, in which he wins a benison on his passion from the gods, and from which he wakes to bless the hour and the place that first gave him that sight,

> My hertis hale and my comfort to be.

The Kingis Quair is a new thing in love-allegory, and that in two ways: the heart of the poem is a real personal experience to which the allegory is a mere *décor*; and the love is lawful love leading to Christian marriage, not the courtly love of the Rose tradition whose end is adultery.   The poem, which is in melodious rhyme royal, was written by King James in English; the Scotticisms are due to a Scottish scribe; but as the well-head of Scottish Chaucerianism it belongs to the history of Scottish poetry.

Sir Richard Holland may be counted among the Scottish Chaucerians in so far as his allegory of *The Howlat* (1452), with its descriptions of the birds that appear in the owl's plea to the Bird-Pope (the peacock), is reminiscent of *The Parlement of Foules*.   Its style, however, and its metre—an elaborate stave of thirteen lines, rhymed and regularly alliterated—connect it rather with the Scottish romances.   Its praise of the Douglas suggests some kind of political allegory.   The story of the death of the Good Lord James is nobly told.

Of all the Scottish Chaucerians Robert Henryson (*c.* 1430–1506) is likest the master in temper.   Being only a Dunfermline dominie, he had not Chaucer's wide knowledge of the world nor his brilliant, urbane wit; but he knew men well within his narrower horizon, and he had something of Chaucer's *bonhomie*, with a keen sense of the comic and a vivid, sometimes poignant realism that is all his own.   *The Garmond of Gud Ladyes*, the romance of *Orpheus and Eurydice*, and the impressive parable of *The Bludy Serk* would have saved

Henryson's name from oblivion; but his fame rests chiefly on his *Testament of Cresseid*, *Moral Fables of Aesop*, and *Robene and Makyne*. In the *Testament of Cresseid* he carries Chaucer's *Troilus and Cryseide* on to its tragic issue. By the doom of the gods the faithless Cressida is stricken with leprosy and goes out from the homes of men, with bell and clap-dish, "to live after the law of lipper-leid". As she sits by the wayside begging among the other wretches, Troilus rides past. He does not recognise her, but something in her bearing brings to his mind

> Cresseid, sumtyme his awin darling,

and he empties his purse into her lap. She learns his name and dies. From this stern and pitiful story we turn to the *Moral Fables of Aesop*, which under the similitude of beasts and birds depict the happenings and humours of a Scottish burgh and countryside. Henryson was a born fabulist if ever there was one: his mice and 'puddocks' are at once real mice and frogs and Scottish burghers and burghers' wives to the life. His version of the Cock and the Fox will bear comparison with Chaucer's. But the gem of the *Moral Fables* is the tale of the *Uplandis Mous and the Burgess Mous*, modelled not on Aesop but on Horace. A better fable was never penned. Observe the town mouse turning up her nose at her sister's "rude dyet":

> Thir widderit peis and nuttis or thai be bored
> Will break my teith and mak my wame full sklender
> Quhilk wes befoir usit to meittis tender.

The *Fables* are much more Scots, much less Chaucerian, than the *Testament*. *Robene and Makyne* is in yet another style, a French pastourelle translated to the "holtis hair" of Scotland. Robin repulses Makyn's advances, then catches the malady of love himself, only to be told by Makyn, now heart-whole, that

> He that will not quhen he may,
> He sall not quhen he wold.
>
> . . .
>
> Makyne went hame blyth anneuche
> Attour the holtis hair;
> Robene murnit, and Makyne leuch;
> Scho sang, he sichit sair:
> And so left him baith wo and wreuch
> In dolour and in cair,
> Kepand his hird under a huche
> Amang the holtis hair.

A little masterpiece, French in its grace, Scottish in its astringent moral.

Henryson lived well into James IV's reign, but there is nothing to show that he ever came to court.   William Dunbar was a court poet first and foremost; his *Thrissil and the Rois* graced the spousals of James IV and Margaret Tudor; his religious poems no doubt found favour with the Queen and her ladies, while his merry muse beguiled the King's looser hours. This ribald priest, parasite on a rude and dissolute court, is not so estimable a character as Henryson nor so solid a poet; but he had more fire in his belly and more arrows in his quiver. His versatility and virtuosity are amazing.   Whatever vein he writes in—pious, courtly, satirical, cynical, or merely abusive, —he is always the artist, with an artist's delight in language and metre for their own sakes.   He has command of two distinct vocabularies—"aureate diction" bejewelled with French and Latin for pious and courtly work, and for satire and abuse an arsenal of the broadest, coarsest Scots, hard, concrete words that hit his victims like clods of earth.   He is master of all Chaucer's metres and some of Villon's—heroic couplet and rhyme royal, French octave, common rondeau, rime couée, and kyrielle all come alike to him; and his *Tua Mariit Wemen* is a brilliant exercise, the last of its kind, in the old alliterative verse.   Nearly a hundred of Dunbar's poems survive, but only a few of the longer pieces can be touched on here.   *The Thrissil and the Rois* is the nonpareil of courtly allegories, *The Merle and the Nightingale* the most graceful of *débats*.   *The Dance of the Seven Deadly Sins* is a macabre vision lit up by hell-fire:

> Then Yre come in with sturt and strife;
> His hand wes ay vpoun his knyfe,
> He brandeist like a beir.
>   .   .   .   .
> Syne Sweirness, at the second biddin,
> Cam like a sow out of the midden;
> Full sleepie wes his grunzie. . . .

In the famous *Lament for the Makars* the deaths of brother poets, and in the fine *Meditation in Winter* the thought of his own death, solemnise even Dunbar:

> Our pleasance heir is all vaine glory,
> This fals world is bot transitory,
> The flesche is brukle, the Fend is sle,
>   Timor mortis conturbat me.

The *Tua Mariit Wemen and the Wedo* was no doubt suggested by the Wife of Bath's prologue, but its cold obscenity would have been too much even for that veteran amourist. Many of Dunbar's other scurrilities, such as his outrageous *Flyting* with Kennedy, are half cleansed by the gale of hilarity that blows across them. The same may be said of his irreverences: we are not shocked beyond recovery when we read in *Kynd Kyttok* how God "leuch his hert sair" when he saw the old alewife slinking into Heaven, where she became Our Lady's henwife.

Two foreign influences meet in Dunbar: his pious and courtly poems are in the Chaucerian tradition, though grandiose beyond the modesty of Chaucer; from French, the contemporary French of Villon, he learned some of his metres and the clean-cut terseness that marks his shorter pieces. These influences played on a genius characteristically Scottish— fervid to excess, pungent, realistic, and strong in visual imagination. One national trait he lacked: he was a Scot, but not a kindly Scot. He has often been compared with Burns, sometimes of late to Burns's disadvantage. "Not back to Burns, back to Dunbar", our young lions roar. Certainly Dunbar was the greater virtuoso; he had more strings to his lyre than Burns. But for all his wealth of words and metres he had not Burns's gift of phrase, nor his singing voice, nor a drop of his warm humanity. The people of Scotland, clannish as they are, have never taken Dunbar to their hearts: "he wants the natural touch".

Dunbar's *Lament* names more than twenty makars, most of them apparently his contemporaries. Among these, "gude Maister Walter Kennedy" is remembered for his *Flyting* with Dunbar, whom he rivalled in scurrility if not in wit. Little is known of the rest, though sundry poems in the Bannatyne manuscript are attributed to this poet or that. The best of the *adespota* is *The Freiris of Berwick*, a merry tale about the discomfiture of an amorous abbot, so good that it has been claimed for Dunbar. The number of these contemporary makars and the metrical excellence of the poems ascribed to them show that Dunbar was not an isolated genius but the highest peak in a range of considerable general elevation.

The season for allegory was later in Scotland than in England. At a time when English allegory had fallen into the fumbling hands of Hawes, Dunbar and Douglas in Scotland were writing allegories that can still be read with some

E

pleasure.   Gavin Douglas (c. 1474–1522) was an earl's son
and a bishop.   His two allegories were youthful work.   In
The Pallice of Honour allegory seems to be largely an excuse for
decoration; fancy and learning are used, with touches of humour
and naturalism, to adorn the thesis that God alone is the
fountain of true honour.   The allegory in *King Hart* is firmer
and more consistent.   King Hart is Everyman, and the poem
tells once more the life-story of *Humanum Genus* as it passes
from youth to age: the picture of Age knocking at the gate
thrills the imagination.   These two poems are in the Chaucer-
Lydgate tradition, aureate in diction and elaborate, too
elaborate, in metre.   Douglas's chief work, his translation of
the *Aeneid*, is in a different style: it is written in plain heroic
couplets, and the language is much homelier, more purely
vernacular.   Douglas renders Virgil's surface meaning faithfully enough; he cannot render Virgil's overtones.   A Scot
reading the translation side by side with the original is painfully
aware of the rudeness of Douglas's medium.   Douglas was
aware of it himself, and grudgingly eked out his deliberately
archaic Scots with "bastard Latin, French, and English".   The
most original things in Douglas are found in the prologues
which he prefixed to the several books, above all in the prologue to Book VII, which describes the rigours of a Scottish
winter, a piece of landscape-painting showing Nature in her
sterner aspects such as we have not found before except in
Gawain and the Green Knight, and shall not find again till we
come to Thomson's *Winter*:

> Reveris ran reid on spait with watteir broune,
> And burnis hurlis all their bankis downe . . .
> The wind made wave the reid weid on the dyke.

The prologues to Books XII and XIII, describing May and
June, are fine too, but more conventional.

Douglas's *Aeneid* was finished in 1513, the year of Flodden.
The most important of the poets who survived in the enfeebled
and distracted kingdom was Sir David Lindsay (1490–1555).
In Lindsay the Chaucerian influence is waning; it is barely
discernible, except in verbal echoes, in his most characteristic
work.   Lindsay was not really a born poet; but he had wit and
wisdom, and a formidable gift of satire, which he put to better
use than Dunbar had done, flying at higher game than tailors
and souters and feigned friars.   His ambitious *Dreme* and

Monarchie are quite dead, in spite of, or because of, the history and geography they are crammed with. We can still find some amusement in *Squire Meldrum*, a lively biography of a neighbouring Fife laird. But the work by which Lindsay lives is his *Satire of the Three Estates*. It is a Morality Play in form, and was acted as such on several occasions; but though Lindsay makes his bow to morals and religion, his real object is political; his real hero is not *Rex Humanitas* but John the Commonweal, the poor misgoverned people of Scotland. The fearlessness, frankness, and (we must add) the scurrility of Lindsay's attacks on corruption in high places endeared him to the commons of Scotland for centuries, so that Scott could say in 1808,

> Still is his name in high account,
> And still his verse has charms;

and long after 1808, as we see from *Johnny Gibb*, "a blaud o' Davie Lindsay" still appealed to a popular Scottish audience.

By the time Lindsay died the drum ecclesiastic had begun to drown the voice of poetry. The ballad still flourished, and the drum ecclesiastic itself tapped out certain *Gude and Godly Ballates* in anti-Papist parody of popular songs, but literate poetry, as we see it in anonymous lyrics like "Quhen Flora has ourfret the firth" or "O lusty May, with Flora Queene", and in the known work of Alexander Scott (*c.* 1525–1584), Alexander Montgomerie (1556–*c.* 1610), and Alexander Hume (1560–1609), was gracefully dying. The spring of the Italian Renaissance came so slowly up that way that the Reformation overtook it before it had fairly begun to bloom. Still it had some effect, for till Queen Mary was deposed the Scottish court was in close contact with France: Montgomerie translated several of Ronsard's sonnets, and William Fowler (1560–1612) the whole of Petrarch's *Trionfi*. The new English poetry had some influence too; Scott's best-known poem, "Lo! quhat it is to lufe", is a Scotticised version of a lyric of Wyatt's. Scott was essentially a love-lyrist. His would-be robustious *Justing and Debait* is tame after *Christis Kirk*, which was his model; but his slender, elegant erotics, veering from courteous love to misogyny and worse, have, some of them at least, the accent of the new English poetry, and might have gained him a place in *Tottel's Miscellany* if he had been an Englishman. In Scotland they found no such favour as Montgomerie's *The Cherry and the Slae*, the last of Scottish allegories, which was reprinted even in the seventeenth century and became very popular in the eighteenth when Watson and Ramsay revived it. The allegory proper is confused and tedious, but the prelude is full of fresh, vivid natural description:

> The air was sobir, saft and sweit,
> Nae misty vapours, wind nor weit,
>   Bot quyit, calm and cleir,
> To foster Floras fragrant flouris,
> Quhairon Apollos paramouris
>   Had trinklit mony a teir;
> The quhilk like silvir schaikers shynd,
>   Embroydering Bewties bed,
> Quhairwith their heavy heids declynd,
>   In Mayis collouris cled;
>   Sum knoping, sum doping,
>   Of balmy liquour sweit,
>   Excelling and smelling
>   Throw Phebus hailsum heit.

The stanza too, the 'quatorzain', though over-alliterated, is very taking; it certainly 'took' Burns, who used it with brilliant effect in *The Jolly Beggars*. Montgomerie also wrote Spenserian sonnets, with five rhymes instead of the Shakespearian seven. He may have got that form from France; but if he invented the 'quatorzain', as he seems to have done, he was a considerable metrist. The "auld sang" came to a quiet close in the serene sunset beauty of Hume's *Day Estivall*:

> The time sa tranquil is and still,
>   That na where sall ye find,
> Save on ane high and barren hill,
>   An air of peeping wind.

With the removal of the court to London in 1603 Scottish courtly poetry died a natural death. But ballad and popular song lived on.

The diction of early Scottish poetry is grounded on Northern English, seen at its purest in popular poems like *The Wife of Auchtermuchty*. In the chronicles and the romances it is laced with Norman French; the "auld alliance" added some words from Central French; and the Chaucerians of course borrowed from their English models. Not content with this, the Chaucerians, especially Dunbar, often patched their Doric with

purple Latinisms, producing a barbarous grandiloquence
which they took for the Grand Style:

> Haile sterne superne! Haile in eterne!
>   In Godis sicht to schyne!
> Lucerne in derne for to discerne,
>   Be glory and grace devyne,
> Hodiern, modern, sempitern,
>   Angelicall regyne!

Similarly in metre they often erred by excess of technique,
throwing off fireworks of alliteration and inner rhyme to show
their virtuosity. Thus at the end of *The Pallice of Honour*
Douglas works up his inner rhymes till he gets one to every
foot:

> Hail rois maist chois till clois thy fois grete micht—

and so on throughout the whole stanza. But, after all, these
faults are only perversions of the instinct for style which they
share with Burns, and Carlyle, and Stevenson, as they share the
Scottish gift of visual imagination, which "leaves a picture on
the mind's eye for ever".

Chapter Six

THE TUDOR RENAISSANCE

THOUGH the fifteenth century was so barren in England, great things were being done elsewhere—the invention of printing, the invention of gunpowder, the discovery of America, and (what concerns us more immediately) the rediscovery of Ancient Greece. Petrarch was the first of the moderns to discern in Classical Antiquity the outlines of a real living civilisation. He himself discerned these things dimly, not having Greek enough to read the original texts. But from about 1400 Greek teachers began to be invited to Italy from Constantinople, and Greek studies made great progress in the peninsula, progress which was accelerated when the fall of Constantinople in 1453 drove many Greek scholars to seek refuge in Italy, bringing their manuscripts with them. A passion for Greek, and with it a new interest in classical as opposed to monkish Latin, fired the rival academies of Naples, Rome, and Florence, and led to that literary and artistic revival which we call the Italian Renaissance. The early Humanists were good Catholics, who saw in Classical Antiquity a preparation for, not a rival to, Christianity; later they became less orthodox.

England, as usual, lagged behind the Continent, but by 1500 Greek was being taught at Oxford. Later Erasmus taught it at Cambridge, where it was fostered by Smith and Cheke, the Sir John Cheke who, as Milton reminds us,

taught Cambridge and King Edward Greek.

Still the study remained academic; it scarcely influenced vernacular literature directly till the days of Spenser and Sidney. But long before that a breath of the Renaissance spring had begun to blow northward from Italy and to thaw the ice of scholasticism, asceticism, pessimism, and formalised emotion which encrusted the dying Middle Ages. We shall call this the First, or Tudor, Renaissance.

Henry VII was too busy establishing his dynasty to do much for letters, but under Henry VIII, eager to shine in the eyes of Europe and a bit of a poet himself, the English court became once more a centre of culture. In 1527 Sir Thomas Wyatt came back from a diplomatic mission to Rome with an enthusiasm for Petrarch and three measures new to English [1]—terza rima, ottava rima, and sonnet. He tried them all himself, but only the sonnet caught on in that generation. As a sonneteer Petrarch had invested the old troubadour theme of courtly love with a new subtlety of passion and a matchless perfection of form. Wyatt's sonnets are on the Petrarchan model except for their final couplets; but he himself was not exactly a model of the courtly lover. He did not "profess chastity", he admits; he was an ardent but not an abject lover; if his lady persisted in her cruelty he could remind her that beauty fades, and himself that there are other ladies and other things than love for a man in a world of men. Wyatt did good service to English poetry by introducing the sonnet, but intrinsically his sonnets are far inferior to the lyrics in which he recaptured the grace of the pre-Chaucerian lyric, wedding courtly sentiment to the melodious strains that had survived in popular song:

> My lute, awake! perform the last
> Labour that thou and I shall waste,
>   And end that I have now begun;
> For when this song is sung and past,
>   My lute, be still, for I have done.

Wyatt's versification is puzzling: many of his songs, written presumably to existing airs, are as smooth as the best Elizabethan, whereas in not a few of his sonnets metrical ictus clashes harshly against natural accent, producing such cacophonies as

> And there campéth, displaying his bannér.

It has been suggested that these sonnets are either prenticework, done while accent was still unsettled, or mere rough drafts to be polished afterwards: there is no evidence for either view. Wyatt died prematurely in 1542.

Henry Howard, by courtesy Earl of Surrey, was not so manly a man as Wyatt—a proud, impetuous boy rather—but might have proved as good a poet if he had not been judicially murdered in 1547, when he was barely thirty. We owe Surrey two things: he discarded the Petrarchan type of sonnet for the freer form which we call Shakespearian; and in his translation of Books II and IV of the *Aeneid* (for which he made some use of Gavin Douglas's version) he introduced blank

[1] Chaucer had used terza rima once.

verse.   But our debt to him is not merely formal: Surrey, like
Wyatt, was a poet in his own right.   His love poems lack
Wyatt's virile, personal note; they read rather like literary
exercises; but when he obeyed the Muse's command, "Look
in thy heart and write", he produced the charming account of
the boyhood he had spent in Windsor with the Duke of Rich-
mond, and the noble sonnet on his squire Clere who had saved
his life at the cost of his own.   Surrey was best inspired not
by the love of woman but by the love of comrades.

   Wyatt and Surrey printed nothing, content to have their
poems circulated in manuscript among their friends; but twelve
years after Surrey's death R. Tottel published a number of
them, with others by other (unnamed) members of the same
courtly set.   Tottel's *Miscellany of Songs and Sonnets* gives us a
fair sample at least of the poetic output of what we have called
the First, or Tudor, Renaissance.   One song, attributed to
Lord Vaux, has been immortalised, in a quaintly garbled form,
by the First Gravedigger in *Hamlet*.   Nicholas Grimald helped
to compile the *Miscellany* and contributed several poems of his
own.

   In the reigns of Edward VI and Mary Tudor English poetry
made no advance.   The lovely phrases and cadences of the
Book of Common Prayer, which appeared in Edward VI's reign,
cannot have fallen on ears that listened to them every Sunday
without producing effects that would one day be propitious for
poetry.   But the day was not yet.   At the time, England was
too sorely distracted by religious controversy to pay much
attention to poetry.   It is harder to understand why the first
twenty years of Elizabeth's reign should have remained so
barren.   She had settled the religious difficulty in a fashion;
the language too was fairly settled in accidence if not yet in
vocabulary; and the New Learning was beginning to pour in
fresh ideas and models for poetry.   Only a dearth of good
poets can really explain the phenomenon; but there were con-
tributory causes.   The purely accentual prosody on which
Skelton had fallen back when syllabic verse broke down lapsed
easily into 'doggerel', which went naturally with a commonplace style.   At the same time the new models were suggesting
a more regular verse and a style of more dignity.   The result
was twofold.   On the one hand we find a verse that is still
accentual in an emphatic, doggerel fashion, though rather more
regular in number of syllables, cast generally into alexandrines,

or fourteeners, or the mixture of these called "poulter's measure":

> The bird that dreads no guile is soonest caught in snare;
> Eche gentle herte devoide of craft is soonest brought to care.

On the other hand, if syllabic regularity is achieved, the effect is usually wooden. What is true of metre is true of style. Trying to escape from the slovenly speech of everyday, the poets over-emphasised such decorative elements as alliteration and antithesis:

> A captive clapped in chains of care, lapped in the laws of lethal love;

or again:

> The sturdy rock for all his strength
> By raging seas is rent in twain:
> The marble stone is pierced at length
> With little drops of drizzling rain.

There was no lack of poets, or at least of rhymesters, whose poems were issued in the anthologies that succeeded Tottel's, such as *A Hundreth Sundrie Flowres* (1573), *The Paradise of Dainty Devices* (1576, the most popular of all), *A Gorgeous Gallery of Gallant Inventions* (1578), *A Handful of Pleasant Delytes* (1584, but perhaps a first issue earlier). The poems in the first of these were taken over by, or for, George Gascoigne in his *Posies of George Gascoigne* (1575–1576), but examination has shown that they were by several hands, including probably Sir Christopher Hatton and possibly the Earl of Oxford. Poems of Oxford's are certainly found in *The Paradise of Dainty Devices* and later Elizabethan anthologies. He was highly esteemed by the Elizabethan critics, Webbe and Puttenham; and more recently Mr. Looney has claimed for him the dramas vulgarly ascribed to the yokel of Stratford. Such poems as are known for Oxford's do not bear out this estimate. The most typical, and by no means the worst, poet of this era of trial and error was George Gascoigne (1542[1]–1577). He broke new ground in prosody, general satire, prose comedy, and other fields. True, his *Notes of Instruction* are rudimentary; his *Steel Glass* is dim—blank verse is not the medium for satire; and his *Supposes* is only a translation from Ariosto. Gascoigne was too unstable to excel in anything, but let him have the praise of a pioneer. The rest, with their

---

[1] Confusion with a namesake, an M.P., has put his birth at 1525.

clownish diction and lolloping or lumbering metres, are dismissed in the notes to *The Shepheardes Calender* as "a rakehelly rout of rascally rhymers".

The one poem which helps to redeem these barren years is Sackville's *Induction* to the *Mirror for Magistrates*. The *Mirror* is a huge collection of 'tragedies' (in the Chaucerian sense), a sequel to Lydgate's *Falls of Princes*. It is a dull compilation; even the 'tragedy' which Sackville contributed, *The Complaint of Buckingham*, though it has some fine lines, is dull on the whole. Not so his *Induction*. It is modelled on Book VI of the *Aeneid*, which describes Aeneas's descent into Hell. But Sackville's genius is more Dantesque than Virgilian. The figures of Malady, Famine, and Old Age, expanded in detail from the personifications briefly indicated by Virgil, are etched with an iron pen: Virgil's *tristis senectus* becomes

> Crookebackt he was, toothshaken and blere eyed,
> Went on three feete, and sometime crept on fower,
> With olde lame bones, that rattled by his syde,
> His skalpe all pilde, and he with elde forlore:
> His withered fist still knocking at deathes dore:
> Fumbling and driveling as he drawes his breth:
> For briefe: the shape and messenger of death.

A true poet, possibly a great poet, was lost when Thomas Sackville took to politics, to become Earl of Dorset and later to sit in judgement on Mary Queen of Scots. Yet he can scarcely be counted among the promoters of English poetry; his face was turned to the past; he is rather the last of the mediaevals than the first of the moderns.

Barren as it was of original poetry, this age produced some useful translations, sowing seed that flowered in the next generation. Most of it flowered in drama and will be touched on later; but non-dramatic poetry too was to profit by such things as Arthur Golding's translation of Ovid's *Metamorphoses*. Meanwhile Raleigh, Spenser, Sidney and Lyly were growing up, to usher in the second, or Elizabethan, phase of the English Renaissance.

Chapter Seven

SPENSER, SIDNEY, AND THEIR CIRCLE

THE second phase of the English Renaissance was not like the first: the Reformation came between. Our earliest humanists had remained good Catholics, who hoped like Erasmus to reform the Church from within. Even Henry VIII's breach with Rome did not at first involve any fundamental change in creed or liturgy. But under Edward VI England went definitely Protestant, and after the Marian reaction Elizabeth established the English Church on that middle way on which it has stood ever since. Elizabeth herself was no zealot in religion, though circumstances at last forced on her the rôle of Protestant champion. The policy which kept England out of war, husbanding its strength, for nearly thirty years, bred a proud sense of nationality and independence, and made the Queen its idol. Confident in their strength and unity at home, Englishmen began to cast covetous eyes on the New World, which hitherto they had left Spain to loot. Protestantism, nationalism, imperialism—these notes occur again and again in Spenser's poetry.

Other more purely literary influences differentiated the second phase of our Renaissance poetry from the first. Wyatt and Surrey knew no Greek; Spenser and Sidney knew a good deal, if not a great deal. Again, in Tudor days the influence of Italy was paramount; but though the Renaissance began there it presently spread beyond the Alps, and by the middle of the sixteenth century the star of Italy was on the wane and primacy in literature had passed to France, where the Pléiade, brilliantly led by Ronsard, addressed itself to the reformation of French poetry in all its branches. Spenser's debt to Italian poetry is immense in *The Faerie Queene*, but the chief influence in his earlier poems comes from France not Italy. Finally, when Wyatt was in Rome Petrarchism for the moment was all the fashion, and it was Petrarch whom Wyatt took for his model. The influence of Petrarch persisted to the end of the century; it is frequently felt in Spenser, especially, of course, in the *Amoretti*; but by 1580 England had made the acquaintance of the new romantic epic which is the peculiar glory of the Italian

Cinquecento: it was Ariosto, not Petrarch, whom Spenser set himself to 'overgo' in *The Faerie Queene*.

Edmund Spenser was born in London in 1552. His father, it is thought, was a journeyman clothmaker, but well-connected. At Merchant Taylors' School, under the great Mulcaster, Spenser learned to "worship the English", and made his first essays in verse with some translations from Marot and du Bellay. From 1569 to 1576 he was at Pembroke Hall, Cambridge, absorbing the New Learning. The split between Anglican and Puritan had already begun; Spenser took the Puritan side: in politics he attached himself to the party of militant Protestantism, of which Leicester was the head. What he did on leaving Cambridge we do not know: the story that he stayed with relatives in Lancashire and there fell in love with the Rosalind of his *Shepheardes Calender* is a myth. In 1577 we get a glimpse of him at Limerick, but again we do not know what took him there. In 1578 he was at Rochester as secretary to the new bishop, who had been Master of Pembroke when Spenser was there. In the summer of 1579 we find him domiciled in Leicester House and on terms of some intimacy with Leicester's nephew, Philip Sidney, and his friend Edward Dyer. In October of that year he married—not his Rosalind, and in December *The Shepheardes Calender* was published with a flourish of trumpets. But he did not follow up its success, though up to April, 1580, he clearly meant to do so. The Duc d'Alençon, the French King's brother, was in England as a suitor for the Queen's hand; the prospect of such a match alarmed the Puritans; Sidney remonstrated and was banished from the court; and then, it would seem, Spenser took a hand with the satirical fable of *Mother Hubberd's Tale*, was disowned by Leicester, was packed off to Ireland as secretary to the new Lord Deputy, and published not another line for ten years. He accompanied his new chief, Lord Arthur Grey, in the Ravaging of Munster, where he saw such misery, he tells us, "as that any stony heart would rue the same". But the sight did not shake his loyalty to Grey, whom he afterwards immortalised as Arthegal. He lost his secretaryship on Grey's recall in 1582, but stayed on in Ireland, holding various minor offices, and about 1587 was granted a perpetual lease of the lands of Kilcolman in County Cork. Here Raleigh visited him in 1589, saw the first three books of *The Faerie Queene*, and carried him off to London to lay them at Elizabeth's feet. They were published in 1590. The visit is charmingly commemorated in *Colin Clout's Come Home Again*; but it did not yield Spenser the substantial prefer- ment he had hoped for, and in 1591 he returned to Ireland a disappointed man. After he had gone his publisher brought out some of his minor poems under the title of *Complaints*. Spenser's first wife had died before he settled at Kilcolman, and in 1594 he married again, celebrating his wooing in the *Amoretti* and his wedding in the *Epithalamion*. 1596 saw him back in London with three more books of *The Faerie Queene*. While there, he published his *Prothalamion* and *Four Hymns*, and wrote, but did not publish, his prose *Vue of the Present State of Ireland*. In September, 1598, he was nominated for the Sheriffdom of Cork, as a man "not unskilful or without experience in the wars". But preferment had come too late. Tyrone's rebellion had already broken out in Ulster; in October the Munster Irish rose and burned Kilcolman; Spenser fled to Cork, and thence to London, where he died, a broken man, in January, 1599. He was buried in Westminster Abbey. All his brother poets attended, with elegies which they threw into his grave, as a tribute to one whom all England acclaimed as the prince of poets in his time.

Spenser is the second father of English poetry. His *Shepheardes Calender* is a watershed in its history comparable only to the *Lyrical Ballads*. He had long meditated a heroic poem which should 'overgo' Ariosto and rival Virgil. But first he had to forge his instrument. So with the example of the Pléiade before him, and their precepts too as laid down by du Bellay, he set himself to do for English verse what they had done for French, to rescue it from the "rascally rhymers" into whose hands it had fallen, and to reform it in its 'kinds', metres, and diction. And remembering that Virgil wrote his *Eclogues* before attempting the *Aeneid*, he resolved to make his first essay in the humble form of the Pastoral.

There are six different kinds of poem in the *Calender*—love- lament, *débat*, roundelay, fable, paean, and dirge—the last two new to English; and thirteen different measures, three of them also new.

Most of the eclogues are in smooth iambi; but three of them, somewhat ruder in language than the rest, are in what look like rough accentual tetrameters. We pass with some surprise from the first eclogue—

> A Shepeheards boye (no better doe him call)
> When Winters wastful spight was almost spent,
> All in a sunneshine day, as did befall,
> Led forth his flock, that had been long ypent—

to the second—

> Ah for pittie, wil rancke Winters rage,
> These bitter blasts neuer ginne tasswage?
> The kene cold blowes through my beaten hyde,
> All as I were through the body gryde.

The explanation is that in these "rustic eclogues" Spenser believed himself to be imitating Chaucer's versification. But men had long forgotten how Chaucer spoke; they did not understand his pronunciation of final -e and -es, his rules for elision, or his accentuation of French words; they read

> Whan thát Aprílle wíth his shóurës sótë

as if it were

> When that Áprill wíth his shoúres sóte.

So Spenser, meaning to be faithful to Chaucer, represented his smooth pentameters by these rough tetrameters.

As for diction, Spenser enriched his vocabulary with loan words, dialect words, coinages, and archaisms; but he was careful always to graft his new shoots on an English stock, and in fact his main enrichment consisted of fine old English words retrieved from Chaucer and Langland. But diction covers more than vocabulary; a good writer thinks not only of his words but of the order of his words and the juncture of his sentences. It was here that Spenser scored his greatest, and least remarked, success. He is neither involved nor crabbed, but gives his syntax a movement, too copious perhaps, but admirably lucid, in fluent, well-knit sentences. Syntactically Spenser is one of the easiest of English poets.

These reforms would have been of little avail had not the reformer been himself a poet richly gifted in eye and ear; there is much melody and fancy in the laments and the lively fables, while the paean and (still more) the dirge hold promise of the stately harmonies of the *Epithalamion*.

Spenser's object in the *Calender* was not purely aesthetic. Like Mantuan, he would use the Pastoral for religious propaganda. Though the Elizabethan settlement was barely twenty years old, that rift in the Church of England had already begun to show which sixty years later widened into civil war. Already there were two parties in the Church, one leaning towards Rome, the other towards Geneva. Spenser belonged to the latter, and under cover of the pastoral convention he struck some shrewd blows for the Puritan cause, unmasking those grim wolves the seminary priests who were stealing English souls for Rome, satirising idle pastors who "for their bellies' sake" had crept into the Anglican fold, boldly attacking that proud prelate Bishop Aylmer, and extolling Archbishop Grindal who had been suspended for his Puritan sympathies.

Finally, in the October eclogue he strikes a more personal note and in a higher strain, a note that recurs in *The Tears of the Muses*, complaining of the neglect of poetry, the lack of patrons with whose encouragement he might have been writing epics and tragedies instead of humble pastorals.

> Thou kenst not Percie how the rime should rage,
> O if my temples were distaind with wine,
> And girt in Girlonds of wilde Iuie twine,
> How I could reare the Muse on stately stage,
> And teach her tread aloft in buskin fine,
> With quaint Bellona in her equipage.

Not all the poems in the *Complaints* volume are literarily complaints. Such as are are mostly prentice-work, translations from, or imitations of, du Bellay, notable chiefly as showing Spenser's fondness for the 'emblem', which appealed to his pictorial imagination; his devotion to du Bellay, though it was Ronsard, not du Bellay, who was the bright particular star of the Pléiade; and his obsession with the idea of change and decay, an idea that haunted him all his life; like Donne, he believed that the world was running down, a thesis which Milton contests in his early Latin poem: *Naturam non pati senium*. Two poems stand out from these jeremiads— *Muiopotmos*, a graceful, enigmatic story of a spider and a fly; and *Mother Hubberd's Tale*, which shows Spenser in a new light. "Sweet Spenser", "mild Spenser", Wordsworth calls him, but here is Chaucerian humour and satire as pungent as Pope's. The brilliant passage on the misery of a suitor's state was added in 1590 in resentment of his treatment by the court.

Of Spenser's other minor poems, *Daphnaida* is an epicede modelled, not very successfully, on Chaucer's *Boke of the Duchesse*; *Astrophel* a pastoral elegy on Sidney, so frigid as to make us wonder whether the two had ever been really intimate and whether Sidney's love for Stella was only an *amour courtois* after all. *Colin Clout's Come Home Again* is a masterpiece in a key not often struck with success in English verse, though Shelley retouched it in *Julian and Maddalo* and some later poems, the key of well-bred conversation.   Its rippling quatrains show how well a great metrist could write narrative in a measure commonly regarded as purely elegiac.   Its conception of love, not courtly or Platonic, but what we might call Lucretian, of love as the lord of generation and the author of harmony, is more fully developed in *The Faerie Queene* (III. 6) in the Garden of Adonis.   Spenser's sonnets, for all their linked sweetness, are not great, except the second Easter sonnet; but the *Epithalamion* is the greatest of all wedding-songs. Here for once Spenser's whole nature found expression, soul and sense reconciled in the sacrament of Christian marriage. The stanza, modelled on the Italian *canzone*, is unsurpassed in English poetry. The *Prothalamion*, a spousal verse for two of the Earl of Worcester's daughters, is equally perfect in its slighter kind.   Spenser never writes more delightfully than when he gives his imagination or fancy a perfectly free rein, unburdened by moral purpose or weight of thought.   The *Four Hymns* are important for the understanding of Spenser's philosophy, and we shall recur to them in that connection; in point of form the first two are among his most polished works, though he wrote them, he says, in the greener times of his youth.

But of course it is to *The Faerie Queene*, on which, torso as it is, he worked for nineteen years, that Spenser owes his place among the great poets.   To Spenser as to Sidney the true end of poetry was "delightful teaching".   He meant *The Faerie Queene* to be a text-book of morals and manners for noble and gentle persons, couched in the delightful form of a chivalric romance.   More than that—for he meant to rival Virgil as well as to 'overgo' Ariosto—he hoped, by drawing his characters, or some of them, from the life, to raise his romance into an epic to the glory of England and her Queen.   He thought his threefold object attainable because, just as for the author of *The Song of Roland* the eternal war of good and evil meant the war of Christian and Paynim, just as for us it means the struggle of Britain against "those evil men over there", so for Spenser it was embodied in the struggle of Protestant England against Catholic Spain.   "The eternal war of good and evil" —that is the real theme of *The Faerie Queene*.   It is not primarily an Allegory of Love.   No doubt love plays a great part in it as it does in life, and of love Spenser ever writes *con amore*; in this aspect the central figures of the poem are Britomart and Amoret, and its purpose is the exaltation of true love leading to fruitful marriage over the barrenness of courtly love, which leads only to adultery.   But love is not the whole of life, and it is with the whole of life that Spenser is concerned, the whole of man's moral and spiritual life, seen as a war against the sins that beset him.

In the first book he partially achieved his threefold object. We can read that book as a chivalresque romance, like the *Morte d'Arthur*; or as an allegory of the Christian life, like the *Pilgrim's Progress*; or we can see in it, dimly and by flashes, an outline of the history of the English Reformation in the sixteenth century, with Philip of Spain as Orgoglio and Mary Tudor as Duessa.   These identifications are obvious, and other figures in the poem have been identified more or less plausibly with other historical personages.   But even in Book I the historical parallel is far from complete, and in Books II, III, and IV we can discern no continuous historical allegory at all.   We may recognise Raleigh in Timias and Northumberland in the "hotspurre youth Paridel", but *continuous* historical allegory there is none till we reach Book V with its bleak allegorisings of recent events—the campaigns of Grey, Leicester, and Essex, and the trial of Mary Queen of Scots. In Book VI history disappears again, for Ben Jonson's assertion that the Blatant Beast means the Puritan party was evidently made in drink.   Its obvious meaning is slander as Spenser saw that at court (*Colin Clout*), and slanders in religious controversy. No doubt Spenser's contemporaries could identify many characters besides those we have named; but for us this aspect of the poem is a *roman à clef* to much of which we have lost the key.   Drawing from the life may have given some of the figures a firmer outline; otherwise the historical allegory adds nothing to the value of *The Faerie Queene* as poetry.

We must not dismiss the moral allegory so lightly, as Hazlitt did when he recommended *The Faerie Queene* to readers with the assurance that the allegory would not bite them.   The moral allegory is the backbone of the poem, without which it would fall into a heap of disjointed episodes.   What value it has for the imagination is another question, the answer to which depends on the depth to which it is rooted in Spenser's

F

own experience.   Few things could be more puerile than the House of Alma, with its detailed comparison of the human body to a castle; or more impressive than the figures of Despair, and Mammon, and Mutability.   And why?   Because Spenser himself had known despair, and the lure of riches, and world-weariness.   He is no mere decorative artist.   It is when his rich pictorial imagination is informed not so much by a moral purpose as by a moral experience that he rises to his greatest heights.   And this he does by means of allegory.

In Book I the spiritual allegory is well maintained.   The Redcross Knight is an elect Christian.   When he is parted from Gospel Truth by Hypocrisy, he falls under the spell of False Religion, succumbs to the arch-sin of Pride, and is rescued only by the Grace of God, but left so weak from his captivity to sin that he must undergo a long course of penance and instruction before he is fit to do battle with that old serpent which is the Devil.   Book I owes much to the Bible, still more to Protestant polemic, but nothing to Aristotle.   Temperance, on the other hand, is an Aristotelian virtue, and to deal with it in Book II Spenser dipped into the *Ethics*, not deep enough, however, to observe that his Temperance is Aristotle's Continence; that the arch-foe of Temperance is Acolasia, not Acrasia; and that virtue is a mean opposed to two extremes, excess and defect, not to excess only.   Book III, of Chastity, has three heroines.   Belphoebe, the virgin huntress, is a compliment to Queen Elizabeth.   But Spenser's ideal of chastity is not virginity, but true love culminating in marriage and motherhood, embodied in Britomart and Amoret.   The victory of true love over courtly love is symbolised when Britomart strikes Busirane down, and his gorgeous House forthwith becomes an empty shell.   Book IV, of Friendship, has two heroes, but they fade out after the second canto, and the rest of the book is a series of romantic episodes.   Book V consists of a slab of allegory dealing with distributive justice, a slab of romance, and one of recent history, the three slabs very imperfectly cemented.   In the opening cantos of Book VI Calidore gives some pretty examples of Courtesy; then he strays into Arcady, and forgets his quest.   From this pastoral valley we rise again to heights of allegory in the Mutability cantos which are all that remain of Book VII.   It will be seen that the moral allegory is much more persistent and consistent in the first half of the poem than in the second, though even in the first half mere romance keeps breaking in.

Apart from allegory, historical or moral, the mere romance delights us, not so much by the stories it tells as by the richness of its decoration and its music.   Spenser's experience in the Irish wars yielded some fine descriptive touches and one or two striking scenes of nightly bodrags, hues and cries; but story and decoration both owe less to actual experience than to literature and art.   Spenser ransacked poetry and romance, ancient and modern, for incidents and situations.   His debt to Ariosto is immense.   He stole some gems from Tasso, but Tasso came into his hands too late to colour his fable as Ariosto did.   He owes less to Malory than we should have expected, but a good deal to folk-romances like *Guy of Warwick* and folk-plays like *St. George and the Dragon*.   Then he had fed his imagination on pictures, tapestries, masques, and pageants.   To read things like the Masque of Cupid or the Pageant of the Seasons and the Months is like watching a colour film move slowly across the screen to the sound of music.   Half the charm of the poem comes from the music of the stanza that Spenser invented for it.   The invention looks simple enough: he took a stanza that Chaucer had used in *The Monk's Tale* and he himself in *The Shepheardes Calender*, a stanza of eight pentameter lines rhymed *ababbcbc*, and added a ninth line rhyming with the sixth and eighth.   But—and this was the stroke of genius—the line that he added was not a pentameter: it was a hexameter.   So Browning says of the musician that he takes three sounds and of them makes "not a fourth sound but a star".   Many later poets have used the Spenserian stanza, but none of them has got so much variety and melody out of it as its inventor.   He gets variety by shifting stresses and pauses, melody by lavish use of alliteration and assonance and consonants that the voice can dwell on.   It is not a perfect measure for narrative: no stanzaic measure is, certainly not one so heavily weighted at its close; but for description and meditation it is hard to surpass. The effect is cumulative: the verse of *The Faerie Queene* has been compared to a sea that rolls in, wave after wave, "each ninth wave breaking higher than the rest".

And what of the teaching which was to have been the true end of the poem?   There are many noble sentences in *The Faerie Queene*, but he who looks in it for a coherent system of moral philosophy will look in vain.   The reason is not so much that Spenser was a poet, who thought in images not in syllogisms, as that, being the child at once of the Renaissance and the Reformation, he had two strains in his nature which he never managed to reconcile.   His philosophy, to call it so, was a mixture of Calvinistic Christianity, popular Aristotelianism, and Florentine Platonism, all on a ground which was neither Christian nor Greek, but simply the chivalric cult of knightly honour; and the ingredients did not blend.   In the greener times of his youth Spenser thought to reconcile the love of woman with the love of God by the aid of the Platonic doctrine of Love and Beauty which he had learned from Ficino, according to which the love of earthly beauty is the lowest step of a ladder whereon the soul mounts to the vision of the Eternal Idea laid up in the heavenly places.   Such is the theme of his first two *Hymns*.   But when we pass on to the third *Hymn* what do we find?   Not the next step on the Platonic ladder, but simply the Puritan scheme of salvation through the atoning sacrifice of Christ.   Spenser's Platonism split on the rock of the Atonement.   We come nearest perhaps to his inmost thought in the very last stanzas of *The Faerie Queene*, the fragment which alone remains of the eighth canto of Book VII, where he turns away in loathing from the vain things of this unstable life, and yearns for that Eternal Sabbath "when no more change shall be".   In more senses than one, that is Spenser's last word.

The so-called "School of Spenser" faded out in the generation after his death; but in a wider sense all later poets have been his scholars.   Leigh Hunt was well inspired when he called Spenser the poets' poet.

At Leicester House Spenser found a gallant ally in Philip Sidney, a poet and militant Protestant like himself.   To unite the Protestant Powers against Rome and Spain was the cause for which Sidney lived and died; but his Protestantism did not inform his poetry as it informed Spenser's.   Sidney was a man of action; poetry was his passion but not his business.   Nevertheless no one except Spenser himself did more in that day for English poetry.   No doubt the gifts and graces which made him the paragon of his age, who joined the virtues of the knight to the accomplishments of the courtier, added weight to his eloquent *Defence of Poesy*, and helped to make his *Astrophel and Stella* the model for younger sonneteers.

The question that teases us in all Elizabethan love-sonnets, "How much of this is mere convention?", becomes acute in

Astrophel and Stella. Such sonnets must be read in the cross-lights of the known facts, if such there are, and of the Petrarchan convention to which they conform. In Sidney's case we do know that Stella was Penelope Devereux, daughter of the Earl of Essex; that when she was thirteen there was talk of marrying her some day to Philip Sidney; that, her father dying, the project fell through; that in 1581, at the age of eighteen, she married Lord Rich; and in 1583 Sidney married Frances Walsingham. Knowing these things we cannot but feel in *Astrophel and Stella*, full as it is of conceits and imitations, a pulse of real passion, chivalrous indeed, but not quite sublimed away like Petrarch's love for Laura. And we feel this not only in the sonnets but still more strongly in the much simpler songs with which they are interspersed, songs like the fourth with its refrain,

> "Take me to thee, and thee to me."
> "No, no, no, no, my dear, let be";

or the lovely eighth song, "In a grove most rich of shade"; songs fuller of youth and warm desire than any of the sonnets; surely these (we say) must come from the heart. But they are songs, and so one remove farther from reality than the sonnets. Honour was saved: Spenser's *Astrophel*, with its praise of Stella, was sponsored by Sidney's sister and dedicated to his widow. (The two famous sonnets at the end, bidding good-bye to Desire and the love "which reaches but to dust", were not part of the original series.)

Among Elizabethan sonnets Sidney's, as a whole, rank next to Shakespeare's. They are not so mellifluous as Spenser's, nor even as those of some lesser poets; but there is more fundamental brainwork in them, more realism too, "full, material, and substantiated", as Lamb put it, and couched in racy English idiom, with here and there a felicity of phrase, a condensed metaphor, that is quite Shakespearian. There are some good songs, too, among the verses scattered through Sidney's prose romance of *Arcadia*, "My true love hath my heart and I have his" being perhaps the best of them all.

Sidney had other poet-friends besides Spenser: there was Edward Dyer, who wrote "My mind to me a kingdom is", and Fulke Greville, who made poetry of statecraft and thought "Friend of Philip Sidney" epitaph enough. With these and others Sidney made what Spenser playfully called an Areopagus, to reform English verse on classical lines.   He tried to lure Spenser down that blind alley, but happily did not succeed for long; nor did he stray very far in that direction himself: his classical experiments are mere curiosities.

Sidney, Greville, and Dyer were not professional poets, but men of affairs.   So, still more conspicuously, was another friend of Spenser's, Sir Walter Raleigh.   Little of Raleigh's verse has been positively identified, but that little contains four masterpieces—*The Lie*, the sonnet prefixed to *The Faerie Queene*, *The Pilgrimage*, and the lines written on the eve of his execution—highly individual poems in that "lofty, insolent and passionate vein" so aptly characterised by Puttenham.

Sidney and Raleigh were Spenser's friends, but not his disciples.   It was among younger men that Spenser's influence was felt.

Chapter Eight

ELIZABETHAN POETRY

WHEN Spenser returned to England in 1589 he found the state of poetry more full of promise than when he wrote his *Tears of the Muses*,

> mourning for the death
> Of learning late deceas'd in beggary,

though indeed it is the lack of generous patrons which Spenser chiefly deplores. The nation was aglow with the triumph of the Armada, and a chorus of new poets was tuning up, several of whom Spenser enumerates under Latin names in *Colin Clout's Come Home Again*. In poetry other than dramatic the closing years of the century were years of experiment in one direction or another, as suggested by the poetry of Italy and France and, of course, Greek and Latin. There was much writing both of, and on, poetry,—the theory of poetry including its justification, the kinds of poetry, the diction and metre proper to poetry. Sidney's *Defence of Poesy*, printed in 1595, had been composed earlier. Puttenham's *Arte of English Poesie* appeared in 1589. Meres's *Palladis Tamia*, a comparative estimate of English poets and those of Greece and Rome, followed in 1598.

In one of the ambitions of which *The Faerie Queene* was the outcome, the reinspiration of the romantic epic, Spenser found no follower. The *Orlando Furioso* of Ariosto found a translator in Sir John Harington, and the *Gerusalemme Liberata* of Tasso was rendered in somewhat too Spenserian a style in the *Godfrey of Bulloigne* of Edward Fairfax (1600). But no poet tried to revive the old themes of Arthur and the Grail. Later narrative poems such as Chamberlayne's *Pharonnida* (1659) and others found their inspiration in the tedious Greek prose romances. It was the pastoral and allegorical Spenser, and the diffuse and musical poet, who appealed to his successors. They tried their hand at many kinds—legends after the manner of the *Mirror for Magistrates* but composed in a less didactic, more refined and 'passionating' style; overwrought Ovidian idylls; historical poems (a kind which Italian criticism distinguished from the epic proper); satire after Horace, Juvenal, and Persius; pastoral in a variety of forms; philosophical poems and epistles reflecting fashionable moods of feeling—sceptical, stoical, epicurean.   The whole trend was away from chivalrous romance.   The next great narrative poem was to be strictly classical in form, an epic after the model of Virgil.   Marlowe's splendid but unfinished *Hero and Leander*, probably known to many before its publication with Chapman's very different conclusion in 1598, probably set the fashion of mythological stories in verse after the manner of Ovid.   Marlowe's fragment professes to be a paraphrase of Musaeus; but its glowing speed and defiant sensuality are his own.   Lodge's *Glaucus and Scylla* (1592) was followed the next year by Shakespeare's brilliantly sensuous and 'conceited' *Venus and Adonis*, dedicated to his young patron the Earl of Southampton; to whom also was dedicated a year later the equally 'conceited' *Rape of Lucrece*, which one may, if one please, call a palinode—chaste Lucrece offsetting wanton Venus.   The latter poem has fine reflective passages, and the agitated conflict in Tarquin's mind suggests the later similar conflict in the mind of Macbeth, and the great sonnet:

The expense of spirit in a waste of shame.

It has not the sustained brilliance of *Venus and Adonis*, nor any such vivid piece of natural description as the horse or the hunted hare.   Drayton's *Endimion and Phoebe* (1594) belongs to the same *genre*, but with a difference.   Phoebe is the planet as well as the Goddess, and the Goddess of Chastity, on which much stress is laid, so that, while the poem has similar wealth of description, the metaphysical strain enters.   The poem was never completed.   Marston's *Metamorphosis of Pygmalion's Image* (1598) was regarded as passing the limit in frankness; and the poet had to plead for it a satirical purpose as a travesty. The fashion faded, though we have such later examples as Beaumont's *Salmacis and Hermaphroditus* (1602) and *Britains Ida* (1627), perhaps the work of the otherwise pious poet Phineas Fletcher.   Ovid is the model for these neo-pagan poems, but compared even with Ovid the Elizabethan poet sows his conceits with the sack.

In 1591, the same year as Spenser's *Daphnaida* and the *Complaints*, appeared Sidney's *Astrophel and Stella* and set the fashion of the sonnet sequence.   The *Hecatompathia* of

Thomas Watson had appeared some ten years earlier, frigid literary exercises often translated, as the poet acknowledges, from foreign models. But it was Sidney's passionate, gallant, insolent poems which established the vogue. Along with them were printed some twenty-seven sonnets of the more 'wailful' *Delia* of Samuel Daniel, which, completed and by itself, appeared in the following year, and in the same year came the *Diana* of Henry Constable. Watson's *Tears of Fancy*, still of the same year, show an advance on his earlier attempt. Drayton's *Ideas Mirror* (1594) was added to and improved in successive issues. He caught, one might say, in turn the manner of Watson, Daniel, Sidney, and perhaps at the end, of Shakespeare. Lodge's *Phyllis honoured with Pastoral Sonnets* (1593) consists largely of translations from the minor French follower of the Pléiade, Desportes. Spenser's *Amoretti* (1595) show his usual interest in rhyming experiment. These sonnets as published all belong to the sixteenth century. Shakespeare's were probably composed within the same years but were not made public till issued piratically in 1609. The Elizabethans wrote too many sonnets—those we have mentioned are by no means all the sequences—but there are gems in many of the collections. Spenser's Easter sonnet is one:

> Most glorious Lord of life, that on this day
> didst make thy triumph over death and sin:
> and having harrow'd Hell, didst bring away
> captivitie thence captive, us to win;

but the *Amoretti* are not his best work. Daniel's

> Care-charmer Sleep, son of the sable night

is a beautiful variation on a theme which goes back to the Latin poet Statius, and on which Sidney had already written:

> Come Sleep, O Sleep! the certain knot of peace!
> The Baiting place of wit, the balm of woe,
> The poor man's wealth, the prisoner's release;
> The indifferent judge between the high and low—

lines which Shakespeare recalled in *Macbeth*.

One might add for Daniel the four sonnets on death and the power of poetry to give enduring life (a favourite theme) beginning

> Look Delia, how we esteem the half-blown rose.

The latest and best of Drayton's sonnets, the now familiar

> Since there's no help, come let us kiss and part,

has the penetrating power of Shakespeare at his best, if not the close texture of thought.   But most of the sonneteers chanted the woes of "poor Petrarch" with a conventionality that drove Donne mad, and made Jonson curse Petrarch for pinning poetry down on the Procrustean bed of fourteen lines.   It will be interesting to note how Donne rehandles the often charming lines which open a sonnet in his more realistic way: for

> An evil spirit, your beauty, haunts me still

we get

> For God's sake hold your tongue and let me love.

Of Shakespeare's sonnets a word will be said later.

But some space must be given to two of those whom we have mentioned among the sonneteers.   In his *Colin Clout's Come Home Again* Spenser makes special mention by name of Daniel:

> And there is a new shepheard late upsprong,
> The which doth all afore him far surpasse:
> Appearing well in that well tuned song,
> Which late he sung unto a scornfull lass.
>
>   .   .   .   .   .
>
> Then rouze thy feathers quickly *Daniell*
> And to what course thou please thyself advance:
> But most meseemes thy accent will excell,
> In Tragick plaints and passionate mischance.

Of another he writes:

> And there though last not least is *Aetion*,
> A gentler shepherd may no where be found:
> Whose *Muse* full of high thoughts inuention
> Doth like himselfe Heroically sound—

that is Michael Drayton, author of the not yet published *England's Heroicall Epistles*, which Spenser doubtless had seen. These are the best, after Spenser, of all the non-dramatic poets, certainly the most copious and varied.

"Well languaged Daniel", as Browne calls him; "a good honest man but no poet", according to Jonson; a poet, "more historiographer than poet", whose "manner better fitted prose" (Drayton), followed up his wailful *Delia* with a 'passionating' legend, the *Complaint of Rosamond* (1592). His tragedies in the Senecan manner, but influenced by the French dramatist of the same school, Robert Garnier, were, if intended for the stage, a day too late. But in his choice of the *Civil Wars* for the subject of an heroic poem he was moving with the same favourable breeze as Shakespeare in his historical plays. His model was Lucan's *Pharsalia*. Daniel's style, as described above by Drayton, is not exciting, but Shakespeare could find what he might use in his description of poor Richard's humiliation:

> Behind him all aloof came pensive on
> The unregarded King, that drooping went
> Alone, and but for spite scarce looked upon:
> Judge if he did more envy or lament.

Hence Shakespeare's more vivid and moving "As in a theatre the eyes of men", etc. Daniel is most himself neither in drama nor in epic but in moralising epistles, which appealed to Wordsworth, poems such as *Musophilus or a General Defence of Learning: A Letter from Octavia to Marcus Antonius* (1599), and epistles to the Countess of Cumberland and Sir Thomas Egerton. That to the Countess is probably the best:

> Knowing the heart of man is set to be
> The centre of this world, about the which
> Those revolutions of disturbances
> Still roll; where all th' aspects of misery
> Predominate, whose strong effects are such
> As he must bear, being powerless to redress;
> And that unless above himself he can
> Erect himself, how poor a thing is man! [1]

In the reign of James Daniel composed two Masques, for misbehaviour at the performance of one of which Jonson and his friend the soldier and poet Sir John Roe were turned out of the hall. Poetically Daniel's highest level was reached in *Hymen's Triumph*, a pastoral play "full from first to last of beautiful thoughts and beautiful writing" (Beeching).

Drayton was an even more copious poet than Daniel, and more versatile, ranging from paraphrase of Scripture to pastoral, song, sonnet, epic, drama, and satire. His first real hit was with *England's Heroicall Epistles* (1597), verse letters in the manner of Ovid's *Heroides* between various historical lovers—

---

[1] Wordsworth quotes the whole stanza in *The Excursion*.

Henry and Rosamund, King John and Matilda, and many others, for Drayton always a little overdid whatever was the fashion.   But in these poems he cultivated a vein of eloquence in closed decasyllabic couplets which anticipate the Popean verse:

> Who would not rise to ring the morning's knell
> When thy sweet lips might be the sacring bell?
> Or what is he not willingly might fast
> That on those lips might feast his lips at last?
> On worldly pleasure who would ever looke
> That had thy curls his beads, thy brows his booke?

It was the same vein of eloquence rather than pure song which he carried over into another happy experiment, *Odes with Other Lyrick Poesies* (1619), odes composed in a variety of stanzas and rhythms all handled in the same spirited, exalted tone as the first *To Himselfe and the Harpe*:

> And why not I as hee
> That's greatest, if as free,
>   (In sundry strains that strive
>   Since there so many bee)
>   Th' old *Lyrick* kind revive?
>
> I will, yea, and I may;
> Who shall oppose my way?
>   For what is he alone,
>   That of himselfe can say,
>   Hee's Heire of *Helicon*?

The best are probably *To the New Year*, *To the Virginian Voyage*, and *To the Cambro-Britains and Their Harpe*, his *Ballad of Agincourt*. This last—"Fair stood the wind for France"—is the best known of Drayton's lyrics.   Nor are these the only fresh ventures of his later years.   In 1627, at the age of sixty-four, he produced *Nymphidia*, a delicious mock-romance in a metre resembling that of Chaucer's *Sir Thopas*. This is how Pigwiggin rides out to encounter Oberon:

> Himself he on an earwig set,
> But scarce upon his back could get,
> So oft and high he did curvet
>   Ere he himself could settle.
> He made him prance, to leap and bound,
> To gallop and to trot the round.
> He scarce could stand on any ground,
>   He was so full of mettle!

We are back in the world of *A Midsummer Night's Dream*. The sixth *Nymphal* of his *Muses Elizium* (1630) opens with one of the loveliest of decorative landscapes.

Drayton was the most conscious successor to Spenser, not only as a pastoral poet but because his *magnum opus, Poly-Olbion*, was inspired by the same motive as *The Faerie Queene*—love of England and loyalty to the Tudor-Stuart monarchy which had united Briton and Saxon and renewed the glories of Brut and Arthur. It is a huge gazetteer in verse of England, descriptions of county after county, the rivers taken as framework, all interspersed with history and legend. "Too much topographer in verse", a critic might have retorted on his gibe at Daniel. There are many long dull stretches. But there are nooks of beauty such as the passage about the English birds in the Thirteenth Song:

> When *Phoebus* lifts his head out of the Winters wave,
> No sooner doth the Earth her flowerie bosome brave
> At such time as the Yeere brings on the pleasant Spring
> But Hunts-up to the Morne the feath'red *Sylvans* sing,

and he proceeds to enumerate them. The alexandrines jingle along bravely through the thirty songs. But the failure of the first part to attract disappointed Drayton, and he ends in Northumberland before he could fulfil his intention of passing to Scotland. Drayton actually visited Scotland, and among his friends were Drummond and Alexander.

The songs of Elizabeth's reign have kept their freshness better than the sonnets. They owe their incomparable tunefulness to the fact that they were all composed to or for music, either madrigal or air. The madrigal was a continuous composition for several voices, the air a recurrent tune sung by a soloist to his lute. Most Englishmen could touch a lute in those days when England was the most musical country in Europe. The madrigal was an exotic from Italy, never completely naturalised; the air was akin to our native folk-song, and had a salutary effect on the lyric, formalising it a little perhaps, but curbing the exuberance to which the Elizabethans were prone.

The treasures of Elizabethan song have been gathered partly from the song-books of such composers as Byrd, Dowling, Morley, and Campion; partly from five Elizabethan anthologies: *The Phoenix Nest* (1595), *The Passionate Pilgrim* (1599),

England's Helicon (1600), *England's Parnassus* (1600), and *The Poetical Rhapsody* of the brothers Davison (1602); and partly from romances and dramas. Thus "My true love hath my heart and I have his" comes from Sidney's *Arcadia*, "Weep not my wanton" from Greene's *Menaphon*, and "Love in my bosom like a bee" is from Lodge's *Rosalind*, the romance whence Shakespeare drew *As You Like It*. As for drama, we expect songs in masques and court-plays, but the common stages also contributed their share. In fact, from Marlowe's smooth song, "Come live with me and be my love", down to Shirley's "The glories of our blood and state", there were few playwrights, Elizabethan, Jacobean, or Caroline, but had some lyric gift. Many of the songs in song-books and anthologies are anonymous, including some of the loveliest, even "There is a lady sweet and kind". Of known authors few, except Breton and Barnefield, are known only or even mainly for their songs.

Most of these songs are songs of love, sometimes plaintive, oftener gay—songs of happy love and youth and spring-time. Edwards leads off with "In youth is pleasure, in youth is pleasure"; Nash follows with "Spring, the sweet Spring, is the year's pleasant King"; and so on to "It was a lover and his lass" and "O mistress mine, where are you roaming?" Others strike a graver or a loftier note—patriotic in Drayton's *Agincourt* referred to above; heroic in his *Virginian Voyage* and Daniel's *Ulysses and the Sirens*; passionate in Shakespeare's "Take, oh take those lips away"; and grave in his "Fear no more the heat of the sun" (which the late Lord Oxford accounted the greatest of English lyrics); philosophic in Campion's "The man of life upright" and Wotton's "How happy is he born and taught"; religious in "Hierusalem my happy home" by an unknown author, and the rapturous *Burning Babe* of the Jesuit martyr, Robert Southwell.

Two traditions mingled in the Elizabethan pastoral—the Sicilian, coming down from Theocritus through Virgil and his imitators in Latin, French, and Italian; and the Arcadian, coming from the late Greek novelist Longus through the *Diana* of the Portuguese Montemayor. Spenser exemplifies both, the former in *The Shepheardes Calender*, the latter in the legend of Pastorella in *The Faerie Queene*, Book VI. Sicilian pastoral, natural and delightful in Theocritus, was conventionalised and made allegoric by Virgil, who introduced his friends and him-

self as shepherds.   This artificial pastoral proved a convenient
vehicle for personalia—elegiac, eulogistic, satirical, and especially (since "pastor" may mean a spiritual pastor) religious.   In
this direction the way had been led by the Italian Latinist
Baptista Mantuanus ("Ah! good old Mantuan!"), and Spenser
followed this as other pastoral fashions.   The pastoral elegy or
lament was to have an illustrious progeny in *Lycidas, Adonais,*
and *Thyrsis.*   In this period its most notable emergence was
in the number of laments for Sidney.   Matthew Roydon's is
by far the best; the rest, even Spenser's, are frigid.   But the
November eclogue in *The Shepheardes Calender,* a lament for
some lady, is not to be despised and was in Milton's memory:

> Dido is gone afore (whose turne shall be the next?)
> There lives shee with the blessed Gods in blisse:
> There drinks she *Nectar* with *Ambrosia* mixt,
> And joyes enjoyes, that mortall men doe misse.
> The honor now of highest gods she is,
>   That whilome was poore shepheards pride,
>   While here on earth she did abyde.
>   O happy herse
> Ceasse now my song, my woe now wasted is,
>   O joyfull verse.

Arcadian pastoral took another line.   "A prince in disguise
woos a shepherdess, who turns out to be of noble birth"—
such is the favourite formula, as we see it in *The Winter's Tale,*
the plot of which Shakespeare got from Greene's romance of
Dorastus and Fawnia.   Elizabethan romance is, in fact, a cross
between Arcadian pastoral and the romance of chivalry.   But
our immediate concern is with the effect, the curiously happy
effect, of this pastoralism on Elizabethan song.   Here the
convention wore very thin, "shepherd" and "shepherdess"
meaning simply lad and lass; and yet somehow it gives a song
a kind of classic grace, lifts it into a clearer air, to hear the lad
called Corydon, the lass Phyllis.   There is little realism in the
Elizabethan Arcadia; it is the country of a townsman's dream,
where eternal summer dwells and lovers are always a-Maying.
Of course all this could easily, and afterwards did, become a
trick; but in these songs it still enchants us, and the call,
"Nymphs and shepherds, come away", is still an invitation to
Eden.   All the great Elizabethans tuned the shepherd's reed
now and then, but none of them piped more sweetly than
Nicholas Breton who seldom attempted anything beyond that

humble instrument.   Sir Edmund Chambers has found place
for some twelve of his pieces.   There is none we would wish
away.

> Shall we go dance the hay, the hay?
> Never pipe could ever play
> Better shepherd's roundelay.
>
> Shall we go sing the song, the song?
> Never love did ever wrong.
> Fair maids hold hands all along.
>
> Shall we go learn to kiss, to kiss?
> Never heart could ever miss
> Comfort where true meaning is.
>
> Thus at base they run, they run,
> When the sport was scarce begun.
> But I waked, and all was done.

Elizabeth's last years were not all patriotism, song, and
pastoral.   Between 1597 and 1599 reaction found a voice in
the satires of Joseph Hall and John Marston, blusterers in the
manner of Juvenal and Persius rather than quite serious
reformers of manners.   The contemporary satires of Donne
were not published till much later.   Hall was a very young,
very superior person, but he could touch off a character
epigrammatically.   The authorities were suspicious of satire,
probably because of the Martin Marprelate tracts; and satires
were burned by the hangman.

Satire took another form in epigrams.   Along with Marlowe's translations of Ovid's *Amores* printed at Middelburg
came a number of Epigrams by J. D.   This was the later Sir
John Davies who, after some early troubles, gained the goodwill of Elizabeth by his fine poem *Nosce Teipsum* (1599).   He
had issued in 1596 a number of *Hymns to Astraea*, *i.e.* the
Queen, and a delightful and unusual poem *Orchestra*, *or a Poem
on Dancing*:

> This sudden, rash half-capreole of my wit.

The suitor Antinous inviting Penelope to dance, and rebuked
by her, goes on to show that the whole Universe is a dance,
from the first dance of the heavenly atoms to the heavenly
bodies and the social order of men—all is a dance taught by
Love:

Only the earth does stand forever still:
Her rocks remove not, nor her mountains meet:
(Although some wits enricht with learning's skill
Say Heaven stands firme, and that the earth doth fleet
    And swiftly turneth underneath their feet.)
Yet though the earth is ever stedfast seene,
On her broad breast hath Dauncing ever been.

The whole ends, so far as it does end, in a compliment to the
Queen. But it was the more serious *Nosce Teipsum*, in which
he brings together all the proofs of the independence and
immortality of the soul, that won her favour.

G

Chapter Nine

THE JACOBEANS

WHEN James I came to the throne Shakespeare and Jonson were at or near the zenith of their powers. Yet already we are aware of a change of atmosphere as if (despite the sense of relief with which the accession was received) England had passed her first climacteric and left some of the ardours of youth behind. The surprising outburst of satire that we noted in 1597–1599 looked like a premonitory symptom of a change of sentiment. Political and social causes help to account for the change. The glow of the Armada years had waned and with it the Queen's popularity. In her last years, after the death of Essex, she ceased to be the idol of the nation; and Englishmen found little to idolise in the pedantic, ungainly Scot who succeeded her. Nor was his policy of appeasement calculated to stir the blood of men who had crusaded against Spain, nor his anxiety to secure a Spanish wife for his son attractive to Protestant sentiment. Fissures began to show more clearly in the unity of the nation. Puritanism grew daily stronger, and court and City drifted apart.

But the relation between political history and literature is a complex one. Great happenings do not necessarily call forth great poets. That depends on factors over which we have no control. Great poets have made their appearance at times when their country was in a far from happy condition, as the case of Dante shows. Patriotism has its source, or one of its sources, in the desire of every man to have something of which he can feel proud. For most of us personal distinction is hardly attainable, and we seek distinction then, it may be, in our profession, our social status, our Church, and, often, in the country to which we belong, the England of Elizabeth, the France of the *roi soleil*, the England of Chatham:

> Time was when it was praise and boast enough
> In every clime, and travel where we might,
> That we were born her children. [Cowper.]

This is the note of Elizabethan literature, the motive of Spenser's *Faerie Queene*, England the champion of Protestant-

ism—"To Hell with the Pope"—of Shakespeare's historical
plays, of Drayton's *Poly-Olbion*; and it is this which grows fainter
as religious passions and the struggle for power between king
and parliament grew more intense.   But one must not exaggerate the effect of this change of tone on our literature.   The
opening years of the century are the greatest in the history of
our drama, the years of Shakespeare's great tragedies and the
more serious plays of Jonson, Webster, and Chapman.

More important than political changes are changes in the
common background to men's minds.   Despite Copernicus,
the world view of Elizabethans such as Sidney, Raleigh,
Hooker, Shakespeare, and Jonson was still much what it had
been to Chaucer.   Nor had the Reformation profoundly
altered the picture they inherited of the Christian faith and life.
Despite his hatred of the Pope, the discipline to which Spenser
subjects the Redcross Knight is just Christian, in detail more
Catholic than Protestant.   Shakespeare's world is, as Carlyle
divined, that of the Catholic Middle Ages.   It is with Donne
that the new philosophy begins to call all in doubt:

> The Sun is lost, and th' earth, and no man's wit
> Can well direct him where to looke for it.

In his religious poetry also we see the conflict in which a
sensitive soul might be involved as the first enthusiasm of the
Reformation spirit died down and the Counter-Reformation
was in full force.   The religious poetry of the new century will
reflect the various shades of feeling and individual reactions of
poets—Herbert, Milton, Traherne—more consciously and
vividly.

Some poets carried on the simpler, more singing note of
the Spenserians, the so-called "School of Spenser".   George
Wither (1588–1667), unlike most pastoral poets, was country-
bred, a native of Bentworth in Hampshire.   After a short
time at Magdalen College, Oxford, he became a member of
Lincoln's Inn.   His first printed book, *Abuses Stript and
Whipt*, was suppressed, and its reissue in 1613 brought the
author to the Marshalsea prison.   There he wrote his *Shepherds Hunting* (*c.* 1615), a pastoral dialogue between himself as
Philarete (lover of virtue) and William Browne as Willy.
Wither's style is easy, homely, and diffuse, comparatively little
tormented with conceits, and, when warmed with enthusiasm
for love and friendship, Nature and song and virtue, is capable

of a soaring flight. His feeling for Nature foreshadows a
later century. He had not Wordsworth's vision, but he shared
his delight in little things: the sight of a shady tree, or a daisy
closing at sunset, or the

> Murmur of a spring,
> Or a least bough's rustling

enraptured him, and the memory of them was his "bliss in
solitude". He loved the country-folk and their junketings
with the kindly gusto of Burns. Withal he was a man of fine
moral sensibility. Virtue is his mistress, a frank, self-confident,
self-pleasing Virtue. In *Fidelia*, a long Heroical Epistle, he
pleads, anticipating the author of *Clarissa*, with all his usual
ardour against the claim of parents to sunder lovers:

> For I do think it is not only meant
> Children should ask, but parents should consent:
> And that they err, their duty so much breaking
> For not consenting, as we for not speaking.

As he grew older and times sterner the Puritan in Wither
overshadowed the poet. When the Royalists took him prisoner
in the Civil War, Waller begged him off on the plea that, as
long as Wither lived, he himself would not be the worst poet
in England; and "Withers", as Pope called him, became a
synonym for a bad poet. But the Roundhead's verses must
not be judged by the Royalist's jest. Except for his pastoralism and diffuseness there is not much of the Spenserian
in Wither, nothing at all in his plain diction and tripping
trochaics.

William Browne of Tavistock (1591–1643) was also country-
bred. His *Shepherd's Pipe* (1613, 1625) imitated Spenser's
rustic eclogues, except for a silly tale which he introduced
from Occleve. To this volume Wither and others contributed.
He also composed a masque, as well as sonnets, jocular verses,
epigrams, and epitaphs—the best known of the last being the
famous epitaph often attributed to Jonson:

> Underneath this sable hearse.

His longest poem, *Brittanias Pastorals* (1613, 1616), was meant
for a pastoral romance, but the plot is a mere trickle, losing
itself in endless digressions and backwaters that lead nowhither.
One of the most pleasing of these digressions is that in which
he sings the praise of Spenser and other poets dead and living.

The poem is saved from silliness by occasional neat epigrams such as that on a fawning citizen:

> And lives a knave to leave his son a knight.

Best of all are his Homeric similes, little pictures of horse-shoeing, pike-fishing, squirrel-hunting, and suchlike country doings, clear vignettes drawn from the life, as good as the coursing in *Venus and Adonis*. Browne's heroic couplets, flowing but seldom overflowing, were Keats's early models.

The brothers Phineas and Giles Fletcher followed Spenser more closely, that is Spenser the pastoral poet and the allegorical and religious poet. The romantic disciple of Ariosto and Tasso found no successor. Phineas Fletcher (1582–1650) imitated the *Shepheardes Calender* in his *Piscatory Eclogues*, with fishermen for shepherds—a variety introduced by the Italian poet Sannazaro. *The Purple Island* was modelled on the House of Alma in *The Faerie Queene*. The island is the human body, and the first five books of the poem are allegorised physiology—an intolerable combination. The pastoral openings, however, to the different cantos are not without charm. The poem improves when it goes on to describe the sins assaulting the Church of England as Electa, in imitation of Maleger's assault on the House of Alma. King James at the end blows his trumpet and summons Christ to the rescue of the hard-pressed Church. Giles was happier in his choice of subject: in *Christ's Victory and Triumph, in Heaven and Earth, over and after Death* (1610) he describes Christ's heavenly intercession, earthly mission, resurrection, and ascension with a strength of religious feeling which rises at times to sublimity, not least in the closing description of the joys of the saints in Heaven:

> Full yet without satietie of that
> Which whets, and quiets greedy appetite,
> Whear never Sunne did rise, nor ever set,
> But one eternal day and endless light
> Gives time to those whose time is infinite,
> > Speaking with thought, obtaining without fee,
> > Beholding him whom never eye could see,
> And magnifying him that cannot greater be.

His account of the Temptation, Spenserian in its rather too decorative style, gave Milton suggestions for *Paradise Regained*. The Fletchers, both clergymen of the Church of England,

testify to the recovery of religious fervour with which the
Church met the challenge of Puritanism.   Both are Spenserian
in diction.   Their stanzas are variants of the Spenserian, Giles
omitting the seventh line, Phineas both the fifth and seventh,
unhappy variants both, since they bring three rhymes together
at the close and spoil the balance of the stanza.

William Drummond (1584–1649), a Scottish poet who
wrote in southern English, was a Spenserian less by discipleship than by natural affinity and choice of the same Italian
masters.   He had some of Spenser's pictorial imagination and
metrical skill, and was steeped like him in the poetry of Italy
and France, if to these he added Spanish and if his favourite
Italian was the decadent Marino.   Pity that so accomplished
an artist had so little to say.   At his mansion at Hawthornden,
near Edinburgh, he went on writing sonnets and madrigals
when the fashion was long over in London.   A third of them
are simply translations; many others are imitations in the
Renaissance sense of the word, which did not preclude originality of thought or sincerity of feeling.   There is sincere
feeling in his sonnets to his dead mistress, imitative as they are;
and if Drummond was not an original or consistent thinker,
the Christian and Platonic elements in his thought never quite
reconciled, yet the religious feeling of his *Flowers of Sion* is
sincere, the expression felicitous, and at moments, as in the
sonnet on John the Baptist, rememberable:

> Who listened to his voice, obey'd his cry?
> Only the echoes, which he made relent,
> Rung from their marble caves: "Repent! Repent!"

His other poems are either official eulogies on Royal persons
or literary exercises that helped, like his mechanical inventions,
to shield a sensitive Royalist from the cold airs of fanatical
Presbyterianism.   To his ear, attuned to Spenser and Sidney,
the innovations of Donne, his harshness and wit, were as
distasteful as some aspects of modern poetry are to a taste
nurtured on Tennyson.   Donne, he thought, should have
been the first of epigrammatists.

And this brings us to the anti-Spenserians, the reaction
against the poetry inspired by Italy and the French Pléiade.
Ben Jonson's non-dramatic poems are numerous.   They com-
prise many forms of verse—epigram, lyric, epistle, elegy,
epitaph, and epithalamium; but there are no Italianate sonnets

or madrigals among them. Jonson was all for the classics, and for the Latin poets more than the Greek. Horace was his model for lyric and Martial for epigram; but in his poem to the memory of Sir Lucius Carey and Sir H. Morison he essayed the Pindaric ode with its triple division—turn, counter-turn, and stand—hoping perhaps that it might supersede the Italian canzone which had been the model for elaborate lyrics by Spenser and Drummond. The whole poem is unknown to many who are familiar with the one stanza which Palgrave selected for the *Golden Treasury*, which exemplifies well the Horatian rather than Pindaric character of each stanza taken by itself:

> It is not growing like a tree
> In bulk, doth make man better be;
> Or standing long an oak, three hundred year,
> To fall a log at last, dry, bald, and sere:
> A lily of a day
> Is fairer far in May,
> Although it fall and die that night;
> It was the plant and flower of light.
> In small proportions we just beauties see;
> And in short measures life may perfect be.

Here as in his epistles and other poems Jonson excels in eulogy: his temper may have been censorious, but his heart was warm. His noble eulogy on Shakespeare:

> He was not of an age, but for all time,

on Shakespeare's genius and Shakespeare's art, shows him at his best. For other poets too, such as Drayton, Donne, and Fletcher, he had cordial praise; and mingled with the praise of the poet goes generally appreciation of the friend. Compared with Donne's his eulogies are more concrete, less abstract and far-fetched. His songs are gems, not flowers; the famous "Drink to me only with thine eyes" is a mosaic of fragments from the Greek, exquisitely fitted. Two of the finest, "Slow, slow, fresh fount", and "Queen and huntress chaste and fair", adorn the heaviest of his dramas, *Cynthia's Revels*. If such lyrics lack the freshness and spontaneity of the best Elizabethan song, they are free from its occasional extravagances; clean-cut and shapely. They, or their Latin exemplars, set the fashion for some of the Carolines: others followed the more dangerous and passionate lead of Donne. In translation Jonson clung to the close following of the original which Dryden was to reject for a freer rendering.

Some knowledge of Donne's life will help us to understand a poet who ranges from sensual elegies to holy sonnets. John Donne (1572–1631) was bred a Catholic. On his mother's side he came of a family of distinguished service to the Faith, for she was the granddaughter of a sister of Sir Thomas More. He went to Oxford at the age of eleven and thence to Cambridge when fourteen, but did not graduate, as that would have involved taking certain oaths which his religious upbringing made impossible. In his twentieth year he was entered at Lincoln's Inn. His father had died, and on coming of age in 1593 he entered on a patrimony of £3000 in money. It was probably in 1595–1596 that he went abroad, visiting Italy and Spain. Later he joined the expeditions of Essex to Cadiz in 1596, to the Azores in 1597, the occasion of two poems, *The Storm* and *The Calm*. For the rest we must think of him as a young man about town and haunting the court, the theme of one of his early satires, dividing his time between gallantries and the study of controversial divinity. As a result of this study he had by 1598 renounced Rome, for in that year he became secretary to the Lord Keeper, Sir Thomas Egerton, and threw himself enthusiastically into his duties, as the last of his five satires shows. But in 1601 he ruined his worldly prospects by a clandestine marriage with Ann More, Lady Egerton's niece. At the instance of his father-in-law he was dismissed and was for a short time in prison; and thereafter for fourteen years ate the bitter bread of dependence. In 1615, under strong pressure from the King, he took orders and, as Reader at Lincoln's Inn and later (1621) as Dean of St. Paul's, earned a fresh reputation as an eloquent preacher. But in 1617 his wife died, and Donne became "crucified to the world", an ascetic and a devotee. Donne's *Satires* are early work dealing topically with the commonplaces of Roman satire; but the third, which warns the reader to "doubt wisely" yet to

> strive so, that before age, death's twilight,
> Thy soul rest, for none can work in that night,

reveals the detachment rather than scepticism of the ex-Catholic. The *Songs and Sonets* and the *Elegies* contain Donne's strange testament of love. When first he came to town Petrarchan sonneteering was in full spate. Later in life when he paid court to noble ladies he could Petrarchise in his own way with the best, though none of his love-poems is in the sonnet form. Young Jack Donne was in revolt against the whole convention, not only the sugared sonnets in which it flowed (for which he substituted a more realistic use of language "such as men do use", and a more dramatic and passionate lyrical verse), but against the whole creed of chivalry and woman-worship. To Donne woman was no goddess but a creature, desirable indeed, but not adorable, though no poet has at times used the language of adoration more daringly to express the feeling of the moment. For there are several strands in Donne's songs and elegies. Some of the love-poems are frankly, even arrogantly, sensual: in others the tears of passion are brined with shame and scorn. Others again are directly and splendidly passionate: "For God's sake hold your tongue and let me love"; "If yet I have not all thy love"; "Twice or thrice had I loved thee"; "All kings and all their favourites"; "Take heed of loving me"; "Whoever comes to shroud me do not harm, Nor question much The subtle wreath of hair which crowns my arm. . . ." But there are still others in which Donne rises to a purer conception of love, neither Petrarchan nor Platonic, but something more concrete than either, compounded of passion and tenderness, mutual trust and entire affection. In *The Ecstasy* he develops a philosophy of love consonant with his later religious thought— the interdependence of soul and body. Knowing what we do of Donne's life, we cannot doubt that it was the love of Ann More that turned the wild gallant and lover of audacious paradoxes into the devoted husband who could attune his paradoxes to the utterance of simple affection:

> When thou sigh'st, thou sigh'st not wind,
>   But sigh'st my soul away.
> When thou weep'st, unkindly kind,
>   My life blood doth decay:
>   It cannot be
> That thou lov'st me, as thou say'st,
> If in thine my life thou waste,
>   That art the best of me.
>
> Let not thy divining heart
>   Forethink me any ill,
> Destiny may take thy part,
>   And may thy fears fulfill;

But think that we
Are but turn'd aside to sleep;
They who one another keep
Alive, ne'er parted be.

Was it possibly her death, or the thought of her death, that inspired the unfathomable desolation of the sublime *Nocturnal upon St. Lucies Day?* We know at least that when she died all Donne's love for her turned back to God from whom she came. He had written religious poems before, notably the *Corona* sequence of sonnets. But the *Holy Sonnets*, which for depth of passionate feeling have been compared by one critic with the sonnets of Michael Angelo, by another with the religious feeling in the work of Dostoievsky, were of these years; and with them the final hymns. The love of God which throbs through the sonnets so desperately was never, or never till the last, the perfect love that casts out fear—fear that at the last he should find that there is a way to Hell even from the gates of Heaven; but the hymns strike a note of peace and confidence.

Donne was the father of what Johnson, following Dryden, called the metaphysical school of poets. Whatever Johnson meant, much of Donne's poetry may be called metaphysical in the ordinary sense of the word, if philosophy be what Plato called it, "a practising for death". Donne brooded much on death and on the relation of soul and body. In his middle years his subtle, self-tormenting mind was in a flux, his early faith corroded by the scepticism and neo-paganism of the Renaissance, and the scheme of things which he had learned from the Schoolmen shattered by the discoveries of Copernicus and Galileo, so that in the *Second Anniversary* he concluded that the world, physical and moral, was dissolving in corruptions which human reason could not cure, and took refuge in the ark of the Church.

But what Johnson had in mind was not so much the substance of Donne's thought as the extravagant conceits in which he clothed it. Conceits, surprising collocations of ideas, are common enough in Elizabethan and Jacobean poetry; but no poet ever sprang so many and such strange surprises on his readers as Donne. Others had written of parted lovers, but who before Donne, at least in Western poetry, ever thought of comparing them to the legs of a pair of compasses? Donne's wit followed no fashion: it was the natural working of a mind abnormally quick to apprehend likeness in things divergent: from his multifarious learning analogies came into his head thick and fast, and were flung upon the paper. But conceits are not poetry unless they stir emotions deeper than mere surprise; and this Donne's often fail to do. Yet, not so infrequently as was for a time declared, in the best of his love-poems and his divine poems, wit and passion fuse in some electrifying phrase, and we are ready to declare with Ben Jonson that Donne is the first poet in the world "for some things". After a period in which he

> ruled as he thought fit
> The universal monarchy of wit,

Donne's poetry passed through a long eclipse, which began to lighten with De Quincey and Coleridge, and was impressively brightened by the admiration of Robert Browning, of all love-poets the most akin "for some things" to the great Jacobean. Of late he has regained a more discriminating but hardly less enthusiastic appreciation than he enjoyed in his own century.

Jonson also declared that for not keeping accent Donne deserved hanging; but another poet has said of the poet and his critic: "Donne is rugged: Jonson is stiff: And if ruggedness of verse is a damaging blemish, stiffness of verse is a destructive infirmity. Ruggedness is curable; witness Donne's *Anniversaries*: stiffness is incurable; witness Jonson's *Underwoods*" (Swinburne). The fact is that we must distinguish. The harshness of Donne's *Satires* is a deliberate imitation of Persius; the frequent harshnesses in his longer poems come from an attempt to force speech-rhythms on the verse-pattern; many of his songs are melodious enough, and perhaps more might be found melodious if we had the tunes they were set to. But even the lyrics suggest a spoken rather than a sung poetry, spoken with a varying speed and emphasis. In some of the effects he achieved Donne was more in line with the dramatists than with the poets his contemporaries.

Donne's influence was powerful for good and for ill. He smashed the Petrarchan convention with its sugared diction, and brought love-poetry some way back to Nature. If his conceits are extravagant, his vocabulary is simple. But for writers who had none of his passion and imagination no model could be worse, witness much of the poetry from Cleveland to Cowley.

Chapter Ten

SHAKESPEARE'S PREDECESSORS

THIS book is a study of English poetry, and of drama in so far as it is poetic.   English drama in the form of Miracle Play, Morality, and Interlude was a verse drama from the outset: a poetic drama one can scarcely call it; its style was almost always homely, not to say banal, its verse, in couplets or stanzas, rough accentual 'doggerel'.   Nor, with one exception, was it otherwise for many years with the plays which, under classical influence, struggled to take shape as regular comedies or tragedies.   Not till near the end of the sixteenth century did drama take to itself a fitting vesture of verse and prose, verse for the serious and romantic parts, prose for more comic or realistic effects.   By that time, happily, the diction of English poetry had acquired new beauty and dignity in the hands of Spenser and Sidney.   Then, but not till then, the abundant poetic genius of the age began to pour itself freely into dramatic channels, and produced the crowning glory of Elizabethan literature in a poetic drama comparable at its best with the great poetic drama of the Greeks.   We have now to trace the steps by which this result was reached.

Elizabethan drama had two roots.   In the Interlude our native drama came within a step of regular comedy, but the step was not taken without foreign aid.   A tentative advance was made in *Calisto and Meliboea* (c. 1520).   It called itself not inaptly "a comedy in English in manner of an Interlude", and was in fact a kind of tragi-comedy cut down from a long Spanish play; but it stands alone, and is too slight and moralistic to rob *Ralph Roister Doister* (c. 1553) of the glory it has long enjoyed of being our first regular comedy.   The author, Nicholas Udall, was Headmaster of Eton, where Latin plays were often performed.   One year, instead of Plautus, the boys presented an English play modelled on his *Miles Gloriosus*, a regular comedy in five acts, complete with plot and individual characters. Ralph, the braggart soldier, and his parasite Matthew Merrygreek are stock Plautine types, but the filling-in is good English stuff.   About the same time *Gammer Gurton's Needle* was performed at Cambridge.   No Plautine types here, but frank English fun, all turning on the Gammer's loss of her needle, which, after much farcical pother, turns up at last in the seat of Hodge's breeches.

It needed even more help from Latin to make a start in Tragedy, which could not take off from Interlude as Comedy did. It was 1562 before Sackville and Norton produced in *Gorboduc* the first English tragedy. Unhappily they modelled it on the so-called Seneca, whose declamatory Latin had debased the great Greek exemplars to horrible melodramas of revenge. *Gorboduc* has all Seneca's faults without his brilliant rhetoric. An old king abdicates in favour of his two sons; the younger murders the elder, and is murdered in revenge by their mother, who in turn is murdered by the incensed populace— a timely warning against the perils of a disputed succession. These bloody deeds are not acted but reported. Dull as *Gorboduc* is with its long tirades, messengers' speeches, and choruses, it is doubly important: it is a tragedy, and it is in blank verse—more 'blank' than 'verse', as Swinburne says, but still blank verse. Twenty-five years had to pass before Marlowe breathed into it the breath of life.

Meanwhile English tragedy floundered in search of a proper method, metre, and diction. Here as in France two ways were open, the classic and the romantic. In France the former soon prevailed; in England the latter, in spite of, or because of, the example of *Gorboduc*, carried all before it. It was in vain that Sidney in his *Defence of Poesy* scoffed at its lack of decorum in mingling tragedy with comic stuff, and its neglect of the unities of time and place; in vain that his sister and her protégé Daniel afterwards tried to turn back the clock. The English public wanted something more exciting than declamations and messengers' reports; Jonson himself could not bully them into applauding his frigid *Catiline*. But that was later. To return to the era of trial and error: Preston's *Cambyses* (*c.* 1569) is a fair example of the kind of tragedy that Sidney scoffed at. It presents the whole reign of that mad Persian monarch, and ranges from Persia to Egypt, interlarding its horrors with irrelevant buffoonery. The diction of its comic scenes is merely clownish; the serious use that kind of fustian which Pistol adored and Falstaff parodied when he spoke "in King Cambyses' vein". For metres the playwrights of this era use alexandrines, or fourteeners, or the ugly combination of these called "poulter's measure"; sometimes heroic couplets, or doggerel; not prose; rarely blank verse. The craving for drama was met partly by native talent like Preston's, partly by translations from French, Italian, or Spanish. Other translators meanwhile were laying in material for the drama of the future, the most important being William Painter, whose *Palace of Pleasure* (1566–1567) is full of *novelle* from Boccaccio, Bandello, and Cinthio, and Sir Thomas North, who translated Plutarch's *Lives*. Shakespeare got some plots for comedy and tragedy from Painter, and all the material for his Roman plays from North. Nor must we forget chronicles like Raphael Holinshed's (1577), which supplied the material for Shakespeare's plays of English and Scottish History. These were years of incubation, poor in performance, but rich in promise for the future.

A new era dawned for Comedy when Lyly's *Campaspe* appeared in 1579, the year of Spenser's *Shepheardes Calender*. Tragedy had to wait eight years longer for the advent of Marlowe. Then Elizabethan drama, in all kinds, burst into an astonishing efflorescence.

Elizabethan drama was of two kinds. First, there was the academic play as practised at the Universities, the Inns of Court, and the Royal Court, presented to select audiences by amateurs or singing-men and choir-boys. Its importance diminished as the court came more and more to rely for entertainment on plays composed for the "common stages" and the companies were summoned to the court for occasional performances. The antecedents of the common stages were humble enough. Before regular theatres were built troupes of strollers played in any available place, pits for bear-baiting and the like, but most often in inn yards. Imagine an old two-storeyed inn, like the one where Sam Weller was boots, built round a square courtyard with a balcony running round it on the first floor level. Against one wall of this yard the strollers set up a platform on trestles for a stage. The rooms behind it served as tiring-rooms, and the balcony above it became an extension of the stage enabling action on two levels to be shown. The gentles sat in the other balconies or the rooms behind them; common spectators, the 'groundlings', sat or stood in the yard. When the first regular theatre was built in 1576 it was on this model. The square became a hexagon, the two storeys three; the wall behind the stage was replaced by a curtain which when drawn disclosed a shallow alcove or back-stage, accessible from both wings.   Two doors set aslant before the curtain gave direct access to the main or platform stage.   Through these doors the actors entered.   The yard or pit was open to the sky, and performances were given by daylight, usually in the afternoon.   There being no scenery to shift, a play could be run through in a couple of hours or so.   On such a stage there could be little attempt at scenic illusion, but the actor was *en rapport* with the audience, which surrounded the stage on three sides at close quarters, ready to catch every gesture and intonation.   Admission cost from sixpence to half a crown.   Female parts were played by boys.

The Elizabethan theatre was popular in a sense unknown since the Restoration: it appealed to the whole people except the Puritan cits.   The closest resemblance to-day is to the lookers-on at a horse-race.   The playwright must therefore cater for all tastes, and the tastes of the groundlings accustomed to bear-baitings, witch-burnings, and public executions, demanded strong meat both tragic and comic.   Moreover the Elizabethans looked to the theatre for entertainment that we find in the novel and the music-hall.   They wanted a story first of all, and preferably a new story.   Long runs were unknown: the nine-days run of Middleton's *Game at Chess* was a nine-days wonder, and was due to political feeling.   The demand for new plays led to hasty production and collaboration: many plays are by two or three hands.   Heywood boasted that he had a hand, "or at least a main finger", in two hundred and twenty plays.   To the demand for music we owe many lovely songs.   Shakespeare's songs are dramatically appropriate, but inferior artists often made their characters break into songs quite irrelevant to the situation.

Ben Jonson put his finger on the three of Shakespeare's predecessors who matter most when he told, or declined to tell,

> How far thou didst our Lily outshine,
> Or sporting Kyd, or Marlowe's mighty line.

Of these and the other precursors of Shakespeare John Lyly (1554?–1606) alone devoted himself entirely to court drama. In his *Campaspe* he brought to prose comedy that gift of, and passion for, style which made his *Euphues* of the year before a landmark in English prose.   Lyly was not strong in plot or character, but *Campaspe* and the plays that followed it—

Sappho and Phao, *Galatea*, *Endymion*, and *Midas*—though encumbered with mythological machinery and political allegory, taught English comedy to speak the language of polite society. These scenes of polite, witty comedy are interspersed, as by Shakespeare later, with scenes between pages, yokels, and such like. Indeed Shakespeare did not hesitate to borrow from Lyly as well as to make fun of him. To us his stylised prose seems affected and fantastic, "playing with words and idle similes", and his wit too much of a see-saw between "that" and "this": but thus the Elizabethan smart set would have talked if they could, and in this school Rosaline and Beatrice learned their good wit. There are some charming lyrics in Lyly's comedies, but whether his own or supplied is disputed.

Lyly, as has been said, wrote exclusively for the court stage. The young Titan of the common stages was Christopher Marlowe (1564–1593). At twenty-three, fresh from Cambridge, he burst on the town with *Tamburlaine*, blazed in the theatrical firmament for six years, and then perished mysteriously, stabbed to death in a long-shore tavern. His genius and early death enhaloed Marlowe's image in the memories of his brother poets. "His raptures were all air and fire", says Drayton; and Shakespeare, so chary as a rule of personal allusion, refers regretfully to the "dead shepherd" who had written *Hero and Leander*. These impressions must be set against the charges of atheism and vice which hung over him when he died. Marlowe was in truth a rebel, not alone against the conventions of his day, but against the common limitation of our creaturely nature. In him alone among English poets the spirit of the Italian Renaissance was incarnated, its boundless aspiration after knowledge, and power, and beauty—beauty in every form except the beauty of holiness. Tamburlaine craves for infinite power, Faustus for infinite knowledge and the power which knowledge and magic gave; there is a touch of the infinite even in Barabbas's lust for gold. Only in *Edward II* Marlowe came down to earth and made a tragedy of human weakness.

Marlowe's dramaturgy is still rudimentary. *Tamburlaine* has no construction: the daemonic Tartar marches through seas of blood from conquest to conquest till he succumbs to the conqueror Death. *Doctor Faustus* opens magnificently with Faustus selling his soul to the devil for twenty-four years of magical power, and the final scene, where he awaits the stroke of midnight that is to sound his eternal damnation, is sublime beyond anything that any English poet had ever conceived; but the intermediate acts are ruined by scenes of clownish horseplay which we would fain believe to be interpolated. *The Jew of Malta* also begins greatly, only to break down half-way in an orgy of blood and horror.   *Edward II* comes nearer to the tragic model—here is situation, crisis, and catastrophe; but the original *nisus* of the tragedy is not strong enough to carry it forward to the end without a series of fresh impulses, and the pity and terror of the catastrophe are weakened by a too great insistence on mere physical suffering.

Nevertheless our debt to Marlowe is immense.   He gave English tragedy its true metre and diction, splendidly fulfilling his arrogant promise in the Prologue to *Tamburlaine*:

> From jigging veins of rhyming mother-wits,
> And such conceits as clownage keeps in pay,
> We'll lead you to the stately tent of war.

He took the stilted rhetoric of *Gorboduc* and filled it with the breath of passion.   In his hands its wooden blank verse became a trumpet, blaring out poetry and eloquence "in high astounding terms".   These were indeed great services; but Marlowe did more: he perceived, and he was the first English playwright to perceive, that tragic action must issue from, and be reflected in, character.   A string of carnal, bloody, and unnatural acts, such as abound in *Gorboduc* or *Cambyses*, may be enough for melodrama; it is not enough for tragedy.   The spring of the tragedy in *Tamburlaine*, and the centre of interest, is Tamburlaine himself; it is *his* tragedy.   So with Faustus, and Barabbas, and Edward II.   In each case the tragedy be-gins in the hero and ends with him.   Marlowe's characterisa-tion is simple; nevertheless his heroes are individuals; they all arouse sympathy in some degree, Faustus and Edward II in a high degree; and in their own natures are the seeds of their fates.   This was Marlowe's greatest contribution to English tragedy, greater even than his revivification of its diction and metre.   He was the morning star of Elizabethan drama, and when he perished suddenly in the pride of his youth men felt that Lucifer had fallen from heaven.

Thomas Kyd (1557?–1595?) had neither Lyly's wit nor Marlowe's poetry, but he had the *don du théâtre*, he could translate an exciting story into a tense series of striking situa-tions effectively linked by suspense and surprise.   In his

H

Spanish Tragedy Kyd employs the whole Senecan apparatus of horror—ghost, hanging, stabbing, madness, pistolling, and suicide—and employs them all with a skill which prepares his hearers and yet surprises them. The execution of Pedringano is a fair example of Kyd's technique. Pedringano mounts the scaffold jauntily, chaffing the hangman, for at the gallows' foot he sees, as he had hoped, a boy with a box in his hand. At every jest that Pedringano vents the boy points knowingly to the box. The audience knows that the box is empty, and so does the hangman; but Pedringano believes that it contains his pardon, thrusts his neck into the noose with a leer—and is launched into eternity, too astonished for terror. Devices like these made *The Spanish Tragedy* the most popular of all Elizabethan plays: with additions by Jonson it held the stage well into the seventeenth century. Shakespeare laughed and learned. How much he learned we could guess better if we had the *Ur-Hamlet*, as the Germans call it, and knew for certain who wrote it. All we do know is that in 1589 a play existed with a ghost in it which cried like an oyster-wife, "Hamlet, revenge!" There is no external evidence for attributing it to Kyd except a jest of Nash's; but the debt of Shakespeare's *Hamlet* to *The Spanish Tragedy* is so obvious as to make us suspect that there may once have been a bridge between them, *i.e.* a play by Kyd on the *Hamlet* theme.

Of the other members of the group sometimes known as the "University Wits", Robert Greene (1558–1592) made a hit with *Friar Bacon and Friar Bungay*—good English magicians to set against the foreign Dr. Faustus. Their harmless magic made a frame for a love-idyll, which gave scope to Greene's jovial English humour, his admiration for English womanhood, and his liking for the English countryside. The keeper's daughter, with an earl and a prince at her feet, is a charming creation. So are Ida and Dorothea, who partly redeem the skimble-skamble stuff of *King James Fourth*. But Greene's abundant talent was rather lyrical than dramatic. In tragedy he merely aped Marlowe, and did it so badly that his *Alphonsus* and *Orlando Furioso* read almost like parodies. George Peele (1558–1597?) is of more importance as a dramatist. Like Lyly, he was in the field before Marlowe; and if his blank verse has not the strength of Marlowe's, it is the sweetest and smoothest of the earlier writers. His *Arraignment of Paris*, a courtly play performed at Oxford before

Queen Elizabeth, is a charming blend of mythology and pastoral, ending in an extravagant compliment to Elizabeth, to whom Paris assigns the prize of beauty. For the common stage he reverted to the earlier tradition of chronicle plays in *Edward I*. *Edward I* is a genuine chronicle play, just one thing after another; and the Biblical *David and Bethsaba* is not much better. *Sir Clyomon and Sir Clamydes*, an example, like *Common Conditions*, of the dramatised long romance, which went completely out of fashion, is now regarded as being not by Peele but probably by Preston. We remember Peele chiefly because his *Old Wives' Tale* furnished the plot for *Comus*; but it has a lyrical strain of its own.

Lodge and Nash were men-of-all-letters who dabbled occasionally in popular drama.

Chapter Eleven

SHAKESPEARE

WILLIAM SHAKESPEARE'S father was a Stratford glover; beyond that we know nothing of his early life except four dates—his baptism in April, 1564; his marriage in November, 1582; the baptism of his daughter Susanna in May, 1583; and of the twins Hamnet and Judith in February, 1585. When next we hear of him in 1592 he is in London, acting and writing with such success as to excite Greene's envy. His next two years have been touched on in Chapter VIII. When the theatres reopened in May, 1594, he joined the Lord Chamberlain's company for good, and thereafter enjoyed unbroken, if modest, prosperity. He became part-proprietor of the rebuilt Globe, invested his savings prudently, bought the best house in Stratford, retired to it about 1610, and died in it in 1616.

The current of his inner life did not flow so smoothly. The death of his only son in 1596 ended his hope of founding a family. Some time in the 1590's, if we can trust the Sonnets, he conceived an adoring affection for a fair youth of higher rank than his own, and became infatuated with a dark married woman who played him false with his adored friend. The Sonnets reveal moods of dejection, self-disgust, and self-mistrust, and this in a season of worldly prosperity. The change that came over him after 1600 will be discussed when we come to that date.

Nature was prodigal to Shakespeare. He was a handsome, well-shaped man, of a very ready and pleasant smooth wit; very good company, but no debauchee; honest and of an open and free nature. So much we learn from Aubrey and Jonson. His plays and poems show that he had a keen eye for the beautiful and the characteristic in form and movement, a fine ear for tone and rhythm, and a sense of smell almost painfully acute. This capacity for sense-experience was invaluable to the poet; the dramatist had gifts still more precious—an unequalled capacity for moral experience, self-knowledge, and imaginative sympathy. Shakespeare knew what was in man, because he knew what was in himself.

Before we can discuss Shakespeare's writings we must make

up our minds as to what he *did* write. The disintegrators maintain that he had collaborators in all his plays. We believe, on the contrary, that, except for some gags and tags added by the actors, another hand is to be seen only in *Titus, 1 Henry VI, The Taming of the Shrew, Macbeth, Pericles,* and *Henry VIII.* A tradition as early as 1687 avers that *Titus* was by "a private hand", and that Shakespeare only gave it some touches and his name. Let us hope so! *1 Henry VI* was cobbled up to exploit the success of *2* and *3 Henry VI*; Shakespeare contributed little but the garden scene. *The Taming of the Shrew* recast an older *Taming of a Shrew*; only the Induction and the Petruchio-Katherina scenes are Shakespeare's. *Pericles* is not in the First Folio, which means that its editors did not regard *Pericles* as Shakespeare's; the latter part of it, however, is his, though why he added it we do not know. He gave Fletcher a hand with *Henry VIII*; perhaps he had come up from Stratford for the Princess Elizabeth's wedding in 1613. The case of *Macbeth* is different: apparently it was originally written for a court performance, and was afterwards padded out for the common stages with the Hecate scenes and some of the witches' songs; but that is not really 'collaboration'. Shakespeare *had* collaborators in *all* his plays; but they were not his fellow-dramatists; they were his fellow-actors with whom he rehearsed them.

Chronologically, Shakespeare's plays fall into six groups: (1) a Prentice Group, comprising *Titus Andronicus, The Comedy of Errors, Henry VI, Richard III, Love's Labour's Lost, The Two Gentlemen of Verona,* and *The Taming of the Shrew*; (2) a Lyric Group, comprising *Richard II, Romeo and Juliet,* and *A Midsummer Night's Dream*; (3) what Polonius would call a Historical-Comical Group, comprising *King John, The Merchant of Venice, Henry IV, The Merry Wives of Windsor, Henry V, Julius Caesar, Much Ado about Nothing, As You Like It,* and *Twelfth Night*; (4) four Problem Plays—*Hamlet, Troilus and Cressida, All's Well that End's Well,* and *Measure for Measure*; (5) six Tragedies of Passion—*Othello, King Lear, Macbeth, Antony and Cleopatra, Coriolanus,* and *Timon*; and (6) four Romances—*Pericles, Cymbeline, The Winter's Tale,* and *The Tempest.* (*Henry VIII* stands alone at the end.)

If we could believe the tradition that Shakespeare was once a schoolmaster in the country, we might imagine him coming to London with *Titus* in one pocket and *The Comedy of*

Errors in the other, for *Titus* apes Seneca's hideous *Thyestes*, and *The C. of E.*[1] is modelled on Plautus's *Menaechmi*. Actually the first play we have a written record of is *H. VI*. There are striking situations in the second part of *H. VI*, but the trilogy as a whole is a straggling chronicle with no proper dramatic construction. *R. III*, on the other hand, is a well-made play, with a very effective Marlovian hero-villain, wading through slaughter to a throne. All four plays show the influence of Marlowe. *Titus*, if it is Shakespeare's, is his only plunge into the Senecan horrors of Kyd, but some of the *motifs* of *The Spanish Tragedy* are transfigured, sublimated in *Richard III* and *Hamlet*. The comedies, other than *T. of S.*, are all experiments. *The C. of E.* is a comedy, or farce, of situation, cleverly, and even, by comparison with Plautus, delicately managed. Shakespeare's most interesting innovation is the serious background. In Plautus the parents of the Menaechmi have long been dead; in Shakespeare the father is a prisoner in Ephesus awaiting execution, and the mother, supposed dead, has been a nun in Ephesus for twenty years. *L. L. L.* is a comedy of dialogue, with patches of fine, youthful poetry. The snip-snap of the dialogue recalls, and sometimes parodies, Lyly. Again the most interesting thing is the serious close. Into the midst of the revels and flirtations of Navarre falls the news that the French King is dead; the ladies hasten back to sad and serious duties, and the gentlemen are put off for a year, which the mocker Biron is ordered to spend in visiting hospitals, straining his wit "to teach the pained impotent to smile". *The T. G. of V.* is Shakespeare's first experiment in romantic comedy, comedy that depends not on situation and dialogue but on plot and sentiment, the sentiment of course being love. It is a hasty piece of work, but contains some sketches that Shakespeare worked up afterwards, *e.g.* the trick of dressing a girl in boy's clothes. The fact that female parts were played by boys no doubt recommended the idea to him.

When Shakespeare returned to the stage after writing *Venus* and *Lucrece*, the poetic impulse was still strong in him. The plays of the Lyric Group are all bursting with poetry. Richard II is a fanciful poet whom Fate unhappily has made a king. *R. and J.* is not one of the greatest tragedies, but surely it is the greatest love-poem in the world. Out of the

---

[1] Having given all the plays their full names, we shall allow ourselves hereafter to refer to them by abbreviations when convenient.

black cloud of family hate the love of Romeo and Juliet flashes in a moment of intense, white light, and then "the jaws of darkness do devour it up". *M. N. D.* is not a full-blooded, human comedy like *T. N.*, but in its airy, symbolic way it is a gem, a gem, be it noted, in a firm setting supplied by the solid characters of Theseus and Hippolyta.

"The sweet, witty soul of Ovid lives in mellifluous and honey-tongued Shakespeare." Had Shakespeare died at thirty-one, these words of Meres might have served for his epitaph. But now the poetic impulse began to be dominated by, or transmuted into, a dramatic impulse: he began to create characters in the round. The first of Shakespeare's major characters who is fully individualised is the Bastard in *King John*; the next is Shylock; the next Falstaff. Bottom and Juliet's nurse are individuals, no doubt; but they play minor parts. Not so the Bastard. The moment he appears he takes the action on his back and walks away with it. This is the hall-mark of creative genius, that its creatures come to life on its hands and walk whither they will, which is not always whither their creator had intended or expected. The results are sometimes awkward for a dramatist tied to historical fact or comic convention. No modern reader is quite happy about the fate of Shylock or the rejection of Falstaff. Shakespeare's genius exposed him to another danger—or perhaps it is the same danger in another form. Except in *L. L. L., M. N. D.,* and *The Tempest,* Shakespeare always borrowed his plots; and sometimes the searchlight of his imagination brought out flaws that were not, or not glaringly, obvious in his material. Thus his handling of the serious plot of *Much Ado* brings out the essential ugliness of the story, and shows Claudio for the cad he is. In *A. Y. L.* and *T. N.* he was so happy as to find stories with no such flaw: the result is purely delightful. *T. N.* is the better-made play, but *A. Y. L.* is even more charming, for it contains Rosalind. These two plays are the pearls of our Romantic Comedy.

The winter of 1600–1601 was a watershed in Shakespeare's literary, and perhaps in his private, life. Before we go on let us look back over the ground we have traversed. Apart from *Titus* and the Yorkist Histories at the far end of the vista, it is in the main a sunny world, dancing to the old tune, "In youth is pleasure, in youth is pleasure". Its one tragedy is youthful; even there cheerfulness keeps breaking in, so that Shakespeare cannot keep it tragic without killing off Mercutio. When complications arise, as they must to make drama, they arise mostly from mere mistake, wilfulness, or self-conceit; if there is real malignity, as in Don John and Shylock, it is frustrated by the stupidity of its agents or the superior cleverness of the good. Furthermore, it is a world of gentlefolk. Shakespeare never touched bourgeois comedy except in *M. W. W.*, which he wrote by the Queen's orders to show Falstaff in love. His other plays all deal with the governing classes: the Histories show them in their business of war or politics, the comedies show them at leisure, love-making or merry-making. The politics of the Yorkist plays simply reflect the traditional view of the Wars of the Roses as a series of crimes avenged by crimes, till the heat of civil strife breeds a monster whom all the healthy elements in England combine to cast out. The politics of the Lancaster plays may be summed up in the sentence, "The King's government must be carried on",—but carried on for the good of the nation, not the pleasure of the King. What Shakespeare most fears is anarchy; and against anarchy there is no defence but subordination. He hates rebellion and despises democracy. Individually the people may be good fellows; collectively they are a mob; and the crowd in *Julius Caesar*, always trotting after the last speaker like sheep, shows what he thought of mob-psychology.

"In youth is pleasure, in youth is pleasure"—ah, yes, but youth's a stuff will not endure. The thought of the transience of youth and beauty, only hinted at in the Comedies, is the burden of the Sonnets. Apart from personal references they are a descant on Time and Death. How can beauty hold a plea with Death's rage? What can make defence against Time's scythe? 'Breed' is Shakespeare's first answer—but his fair friend will not marry. Then he will give him poetic immortality—but a rival poet appears, and Shakespeare consoles himself for a moment with the thought (which failed to console Spenser) that change itself is transient; in the Great Year the stars return to their places. Then at least true love is immortal. In the end he turns to the last place of refuge, his own soul:

> So shalt thou feed on Death, that feeds on men,
> And, Death once dead, there's no more dying then.

The remarkable change that comes over Shakespeare's work

after 1600 must surely reflect some change in himself. He
had left his youth behind; perhaps he was run down and sleepless from overwork; perhaps in his weak state the wounds that
the "dark lady" had dealt him began to ache again. One
thing may be said without any 'perhaps': he like others was
afflicted by the execution of Essex, whose henchman his patron
Southampton had been. Be these things as they may, it is
strange to pass from *A. Y. L.* and *T. N.* to the Problem Plays.
In the first place we find a singular change in Shakespeare's
attitude to sex. Hitherto he had thought love a natural, even an
ennobling thing; now he begins to be obsessed by its baser side.
This obsession appears first in *Hamlet*; it deepens to savagery in
Troilus, and taints the whole atmosphere of *Measure for Measure*.

Troilus is a strange, savage play; as if Shakespeare, surfeited
with Chaucer and Chapman, had said to himself, "I'll show
them what brutes these heroes of romance really were". The
free, open nature of Troilus makes him the dupe of a wanton;
Hector's chivalry exposes him to be butchered by the Myr-
midons; in this world of bullies, pimps, and harlots nothing
thrives but cold policy and brute force. There is no poetry
in the play, except in the speeches of Troilus, but it is knotty
with hard political wisdom expressed in a contorted style stiff
with uncouth Latinisms.

All's Well may be a recast of the *Love labours wonne* which
Meres attributed to Shakespeare. But whether written or
only rewritten in 1601, it was written against the grain. The
theme of the pursuing woman intrigued Shakespeare, but it
did not inspire him as it inspired Mr. Shaw. Bertram, forced
by the King to marry Helen, casts her off at the church door,
and swears never to acknowledge her till she show him a ring
off his finger and a child of his begetting. She fulfils these
conditions by means which no modern reader can stand; but
such a trick is a "set theme" (to use Mr. Lawrence's phrase)
which Shakespeare took over from the original story and his
audience accepted just as they accepted the theme of the caskets
in *The Merchant of Venice*. Comedy is provided by the un-
casing of a braggart; but he who can get a laugh out of Parolles,
his lungs must be tickle o' the sere.

Shakespeare had temporarily lost form when he wrote
All's Well, but he recovered it in *Measure for Measure*. Here
is the loveliest of all his songs, "Take, oh take those lips away";
here are some speeches as good as any in *Hamlet*; and here is

that priceless desperado, Barnardine. But here too is the *All's Well* trick of the substituted bedfellow; the place reeks with the sexual corruption that "bubbles in the stews"; and the forced happy ending so affronts us that we turn with positive relief to the Tragedies of Passion. With these we shall take *Hamlet*, though it was written some years earlier and is not strictly a Tragedy of Passion.

The world of the four great tragedies—*Hamlet*, *Othello*, *Lear*, *Macbeth*—is not youthful like that of the comedies. Shakespeare conceived Hamlet at first as a youth of nineteen, but he changed his mind as he went on; the Hamlet of the last act is thirty; Othello and Macbeth are middle-aged; Lear is "fourscore and upwards". Love plays little part in this world; in *Macbeth* it plays none at all. It is still, however, the world of the governing classes: Shakespeare inherited the mediaeval tradition that 'tragedies' meant "Falls of Princes". But he added certain elements which restored the Greek conception. His tragic heroes are not merely great personages; they are great men, great in intellect, or imagination, or passion, or power. But though great they are not perfect: each has some weakness that may endanger him. And the weakness of each is allied to his peculiar greatness—Othello's credulity is the weak side of his free and open nature, Lear's self-will of that authority which makes him "every inch a king". And each encounters the danger to which his weakness makes him peculiarly vulnerable. Finally, to the mediaeval mind a fall from prosperity was in itself tragic. Shakespeare's conception was more inward: his heroes fall and perish, but they also suffer—they suffer terribly: Hamlet is on the verge of suicide, Othello falls in a fit, Lear goes mad, Macbeth is on the rack.

What drags these heroes down to suffering and death? Not blind fate, nor the jealousy of the gods, nor some ancestral curse or hereditary taint—these ideas are foreign to Shakespeare—but simply human wickedness, the human will to evil, the corruption of man's heart. The evil which makes tragedy springs not from the lusts of the flesh but from the lust of power. It is lust of power that makes Claudius a fratricide, makes Iago "plume up his will" by torturing Othello, and turns Goneril and Regan into monsters. The callous cruelty that the lust of power begets not only horrifies Shakespeare, it amazes him. "What cause is there in Nature," Lear cries, "that makes these hard hearts? Let them anatomise Regan, see what breeds about her heart." In *Macbeth* Shakespeare attempted this anatomy, the anatomy of the evil will; but he could not probe the mystery. The evil in Macbeth is stirred into active life by the witches. There are powers in Nature, it seems, powers not ourselves, that make for wickedness.

But if the origin of evil is dark, its end is manifest. It is death. Claudius perishes, Iago perishes, Edmund, Goneril, Regan, Macbeth—all perish. The avalanche they have started overwhelms them.

The powers that resist evil take different guises according as they operate in the mediaeval Catholic world of *Hamlet*, or the purely secular world of *Othello*, or the pre-Christian world of *Lear*, where the gods are remote and inscrutable, or the primitive Christian world of *Macbeth*, where the supernatural reappears though only Hell's agents are visible. In all these plays, however, one or more of three forces are at work to resist evil and destroy it. First there is what we call accident. It plays a great part in *Hamlet*, where it works altogether for good, so that Hamlet sees in it the hand of God. In *Othello* and *Lear* it is much less important, and works (as we say) both ways—for evil when Desdemona loses her handkerchief or Edmund forgets to countermand Cordelia's execution; for good in Roderigo's momentary revival or the discovery of Goneril's plot. It plays no part in *Macbeth*. Next there is human goodness, the healthy instincts and impulses of the heart—the last flicker of motherly love in Gertrude and of manly honour in Laertes, the humanity that makes the serving-man draw his sword on Cornwall and give him his death-blow. In *Lear* and in the outward tragedy of *Macbeth* these impulses are embodied in the characters, at once virtuous and strong, of Kent, Albany, Edgar, Malcolm, and Macduff. But the most moving instance is in *Othello*. Iago is destroyed by a power on which he had never reckoned, the power of love. It is Emilia's love for her mistress, stronger than death, not to be silenced, that tears his plot to tatters. Finally, the self-destructiveness of evil appears overtly in *Lear*, where Goneril poisons Regan, inwardly, as we shall see, in *Macbeth*.

The evil, then, perish and are lost. What of the good who perish with them? The peace of Heaven awaits Hamlet. Othello has no such hope, but he knows now that Desdemona was true and dies upon a kiss. In *Lear* a new idea appears: suffering makes Lear a better man, humbled and pitiful; and

Gloucester draws the same lesson from *his* sufferings. But Desdemona, stunned by an incomprehensible calamity, does *she* learn from suffering? Is Cordelia made better? Does she need to be better? That way no consolation lies. But as we listen to Desdemona's dying whisper,

> Commend me to my kind lord. Oh, farewell,

and watch Cordelia going almost gaily to all but certain death, we feel that earthly happiness and misery, life and death themselves, are nothing beside such love and devotion. To pursue this thought would carry us into a region where tragedy, if it existed, could exist only in an inward form. This is the direction in which Shakespeare is moving in *Macbeth*.

In its outward aspect *Macbeth* is a story of crime and punishment, like *Richard III*. But what most interests Shakespeare is the inner tragedy, the conquest of a soul by evil and the effect of crime on the criminal. Macbeth's evil thoughts are in solution till the witches' prophecy precipitates them into a murderous purpose. The deed once done, remorse, which he mistakes for fear, drives him on from crime to crime; his human attributes drop from him; he reels back into the beast, and dies at last like a wild beast at bay; but his soul is dead already. The dissolution of the soul in Lady Macbeth is even more appalling; she has not the man's strong animal force; her guilt strikes in, and she loses even the will to live. As we look at these great, lost souls, we can only whisper with the Doctor, "God, God, forgive us all".

What remains when the tragic avalanche has swept by? The world remains. Tragedy is an episode; it passes, and the general life resumes its course. But since the tragic hero is a man of high degree, whose fate affects the common weal, provision must be made for carrying on his work. So in all these plays we find characters whose main or sole function it is to provide that the King's government shall be carried on. Fortinbras has no part in the domestic tragedy of *Hamlet*; yet we are told of him in the very first scene, and again before the crisis; in Act IV he crosses the stage, and at the very end he enters to assume the Danish crown. Albany and Malcolm have similar functions in *Lear* and *Macbeth*. The faintness of the political background in *Othello* is one of the things that make it so painful: we are too deeply absorbed in the private tragedy to think of the public issues involved.

Public issues bulk so large in the Roman plays that they divide our interest with the private tragedy.   These plays, in fact, are not true tragedies: there are no villains in them; the hero's fall is due to himself, and his end does not move pity and fear.   In *Antony and Cleopatra* Shakespeare, still following Plutarch, takes up the story near where he left it off in *Julius Caesar*.   The triumvirs have divided the world between them; the elimination of Lepidus leaves Antony and Octavian face to face and makes war inevitable.   Cleopatra cajoles Antony into giving battle at sea; then panic seizes her and she flies with the whole Egyptian fleet; Antony follows her, and all is lost.   In Act IV he kills himself on a false report of her death; in Act V she kills herself to escape being led through Rome in triumph. Antony's death saddens us, but it does not awe us like Macbeth's; he has lost the world, but not his soul.   And we acquiesce; for, little as we love Octavian, we recognise that he, not Antony, is the destined Emperor.   Cleopatra's death does not even sadden us; we exult to see her befool the cold-blooded Caesar and die as befits a princess "descended of so many royal kings".   Though the emotional tension of the great tragedies has relaxed, the sweep of Shakespeare's imagination is as superb as ever.   In the sunset splendour of the last two acts unsurpassable touches of verbal music are achieved by the simplest means.   "The bright day is done, And we are for the dark"— who but Shakespeare could have worked such a miracle with Saxon monosyllables?

The plot of *Coriolanus* also comes from Plutarch.   Coriolanus is a mighty warrior whose victory over the Volsci has been rewarded by the consulship, though his aristocratic pride can hardly stoop to solicit the votes of the plebs.   Their tribunes sting him into expressions for which he is indicted and banished as a traitor to the people.   He returns at the head of a Volscian army to burn Rome.   The city is at his feet; but his mother's prayers prevail; he withdraws his forces, and is killed by his Volscian rival.   We grieve to see so grand a creature fall; but we feel that his fall is due in the main to his own monstrous pride.   (Perhaps we sympathise more with the plebs than Shakespeare did.)   Shakespeare's powers have begun to flag; he is not in full imaginative sympathy with his subject; the verbal magic of *Antony* is gone; the style is harsh and contorted in places, as if Shakespeare were lashing himself into a passion to keep up the tragic strain.

Timon is obviously unfinished. Shakespeare may have abandoned it in disgust; but it is possible, nay, if we think of the cerebral excitement he had undergone in composing the great tragedies, we shall find it even probable, that while he was at work on *Timon* he had a nervous break-down which left him an altered man.   Certainly the gulf between the Tragedies and the Romances is as great as that which we noted between the Comedies and the Problem Plays.

There are common features in the plots of the Romances; in all of them families and friends, parted by accident or jealousy or treachery, are reunited at the end.   They have a common atmosphere too; a country air breathes through them all; they are fuller of country sights and sounds than anything Shakespeare had written since *L. L. L.*   It is as if Shakespeare, having retired to Stratford, had turned his back on London and tragedy.   These plays are neither tragedies nor comedies.   There are tragic possibilities in them all, but they are not driven to tragic issues.   And their happy endings are not forced like those which make the Problem Plays distasteful.   There is evil and suffering; but the evil, as a rule, is not heinous, and the suffering, as a rule, is atoned for, if not in one generation then in the next.   The idea of race, submerged since the Sonnets, reappears; and with it the ideas of repentance, forgiveness, and reconciliation.   "The greater action lies in virtue than in vengeance"; we must seek to overcome evil with good.   But Shakespeare will not deceive himself.   He had no theory of evolution to lull him with the dream that evil is only good in the making.   He believed that evil was evil, and might so overmaster a man that he could not repent.   Iachimo in *Cymbeline* repents and is forgiven; but the wicked Queen dies by her own hand, "shameless desperate".

There is a famous passage in *The Tempest* which the instinct of all readers has fastened on as Shakespeare's most personal utterance.   Prospero is gracing the betrothal of the lovers with a masque; suddenly he starts and speaks in agitation; the masque vanishes, and he turns to Ferdinand:

> Our revels now are ended; these our actors,
> As I foretold you, were all spirits, and
> Are melted into air, into thin air;
> And, like the baseless fabric of this vision,
> The cloud-capt towers, the gorgeous palaces,
> The solemn temples, the great globe itself,

> Yea, all which it inherit, shall dissolve,
> And, like this unsubstantial pageant faded,
> Leave not a rack behind.

What strange passion has moved him to this utterance?   It is
the sudden recollection of the foul conspiracy of the beast
Caliban,

> A devil, a born devil, on whose nature
> Nurture will never stick.

A world in which such irreclaimable evil exists cannot, he
declares, be real; and we feel that he speaks with Shakespeare's
voice.   In his normal moods Shakespeare very likely felt about
the last things much as his father had done before him; if his
father was a Catholic, as some hold, the local tradition may be
true that he himself "died a Papist".   But when his old brain
is troubled by the memory of irreclaimable evil, he falls back
into this mystical thought that the world of sense is illusion,
that we are all phantasms in the Red King's dream.   Meanwhile in this world of sense, which is the world of all of us,
there is happiness in friendship and family affection; for the
young there is love, and for the old the sight of their children's
happiness, and duty, and the meditation of death.   Prospero
will resume his dukedom, but every third thought shall be his
grave.

Such were the conclusions that Shakespeare came to at the
end of his long study of life.   He did not reach them by
abstract reasoning and then clothe them in drama; he was a
poet, not a metaphysician; but he was a poet with an unequalled
capacity for experience, and these were the conclusions to
which his experience led him.

So far we have dwelt mainly on Shakespeare's changing
attitude to life; it remains to say something of his art as
dramatist and poet.   Shakespeare wrote dramas for the stage,
not the study; to earn his living, not to air his views.   To
succeed, he had to bear two things in mind—the demands of
his audience and the resources of his theatre, such as we
described it in the preceding chapter.

Many effects possible in a modern theatre were impossible
in a playhouse that had no drop-scene, limelight, or painted
scenery, and few mechanical appliances.   Shakespeare recognised these limitations, apologised for them in *Henry V*, and
begged his audience to piece out his imperfections with their

thoughts, help him to unfold to their imaginations what he could not display to their eyes. For painted scenery he gave them word-pictures—the bank where the wild thyme blows, the floor of heaven "thick inlaid with patines of bright gold", the pleachéd bower in *Much Ado*, the two oaks in *As You Like It*, Macbeth's castle with its temple-haunting martlets; he abounds especially in pictures of dawn, none so glorious as Romeo's

> Night's candles are burnt out, and jocund day
> Stands tiptoe on the misty mountain-tops.

Nothing indeed shows his confidence in his audience more strikingly than the boldness with which he puts night scenes on a stage open to the afternoon sky.

The bare platform stage, projecting into the pit, gave little scope for scenic illusion; but it brought the audience nearer the actors, enabling them to catch every intonation, and reducing the artificiality of those favourite Elizabethan conventions, the soliloquy and the aside. Soliloquies and asides sound less unnatural when overheard at short range than when shouted across the footlights. Shakespeare's soliloquies improved as he went on. Richard III's opening soliloquy is a piece of declamation obviously addressed to the audience; but Hamlet's murmured "To be, or not to be" is overheard, not heard; in "Is this a dagger?" Macbeth seems to burst into uncontrollable speech. Another convention on which Shakespeare improved was the ghost. The ghosts in *Richard III* are simply dreams made audible and visible; the ghost in Hamlet is a substantial figure, kept ghostly by the fact that he is never both seen and heard at once except by Hamlet; while Banquo's ghost, heard by none and seen only by Macbeth, is so ghostly that many readers take him to be a hallucination like the air-drawn dagger.

There was a trap-door in the stage, and a 'machine' for letting celestial beings down from above; Shakespeare used the first only in *Macbeth* and the second only in *Cymbeline*. He used the balcony in some half-dozen plays to represent a balcony or upper room, but also the ramparts of a castle or walled town. The alcove was employed specifically for an alcove, bedroom, cell, or study; but also for a more general purpose: with the curtain before it closed, properties could be set out in the alcove while a scene proceeded on the platform; that scene over, and the curtain opened, the alcove became part of a full-stage scene, to which its properties gave a definite location, so that the two hours' traffic of the stage was not much held up by *entr'actes*.

After 1594 Shakespeare became a 'sharer' in the Lord Chamberlain's company, for which thenceforth he wrote exclusively. When he planned a new play he had to think of his 'fellows', and say to himself, not only "That part will do for A", but also "I must find a part for B—or make one". Unfortunately we do not know enough about A and B to say how these considerations affected his art. Burbage, his leading man, was probably too versatile to need to have parts written specially for him. Shakespeare himself was too busy producing and rehearsing to take major parts in his own plays; tradition says that he played Adam in *As You Like It* and the ghost in *Hamlet*. About the rest of the company we know little that helps us; but it is clear that for some five years after 1594 it contained two clowns who played opposite each other as Launce and Speed, the two Gobbos, Dogberry and Verges; also two boys, one taller and fairer than the other, who played Helena and Hermia, Portia and Nerissa, Rosalind and Celia. Kemp was the principal clown; after he deserted the company there are no more pairs of clowns; instead we find a single professional jester, who does Touchstone and Feste. If Kemp played Falstaff, his desertion early in 1599 may explain why Shakespeare did not bring on Falstaff in *Henry V*, as he had promised to do in the epilogue to *2 Henry IV*. After *Twelfth Night* the two boys also disappear, having shot up into men; even when he acted Rosalind in 1600 the fair boy was already grown "more than common tall". Possibly it was the need to find a part for him in *Much Ado*, and one for the jester in *As You Like It*, that suggested Beatrice and Touchstone: there are no such characters in the novels on which these plays are founded.

Most of Shakespeare's plays were written for the common stages with their mixed audiences. Gentles and groundlings might have different tastes in wit and humour, but what they all demanded was a story. Now Shakespeare, with all his gifts, was apparently no great 'plotter'; at all events he habitually borrowed his plots. He looked about for a likely story; if one story did not promise matter enough for the traditional five acts, he might 'contaminate' it with another. Then he would ask himself, "What kind of character would behave like this in these circumstances?" Having formed a conception, at first perhaps a somewhat vague conception, of his characters, he

I

set them to tell the whole story in action. The *whole* story: except in the English Histories, and not always there, he could not assume any knowledge of the story on the part of his audience, such as Sophocles could assume. His first care therefore was to make clear the situation out of which the story arose, and to do so dramatically. He was not always very good at this. Richard III's opening speech, as we have noted, is a thinly veiled prologue; even a mature play like *As You Like It* opens clumsily—"As I remember, Adam, it was upon this fashion . . ."; but the opening of *Hamlet* is a masterpiece: in fifteen natural, dramatic lines he contrives not only to tell us the names and relations of all the persons on the stage, the scene of the action, the time of day, and the state of the weather, but to convey a sense of excitement and foreboding, the reason for which will soon appear. Since he had to tell the whole story, Shakespeare could not start close on the crisis, as Sophocles could. The weakness in Shakespeare's mode of construction lies at the point where the crisis is past and the counter-stroke not yet ready. In *Hamlet*, *Lear*, and *Macbeth* he masks the weak point by changing the key from tragedy to pathos. The construction of *Othello* is different: there the whole of the long first act is really 'situation', needed to show us Othello in himself and in relation to his fellows; once the scene has shifted to Cyprus the action rushes down like an avalanche, and in thirty-six hours all is over, though there are suggestions of a longer lapse of time. Shakespeare has not written with his eye on the clock.

Shakespeare followed the Romantic tradition not only in telling the whole story but in mixing comic matter with tragic and ignoring the unities of place and time. But here we must distinguish. He did not interlard his tragedies with such lumps of irrelevant buffoonery and ribaldry as deface so many Elizabethan tragedies; he toned the comedy into keeping with the play to which it belonged. Moreover, as he advanced towards the tragedies of passion, he grew more chary of introducing comedy at all: wit and humour abound in *Romeo and Juliet*; in the long, discursive tragedy of *Hamlet* there is abundance of wit, but very little humour except in the grave-diggers' scene; in *Macbeth* there is only the porter's soliloquy; while in *Othello* the comic element is so faint that it costs us an effort to remember that the play contains a clown. Why did Shakespeare introduce such scenes at all? Not, we believe, to tickle the ears of the groundlings, but to remind us that beyond these palace-tragedies there is a world of common folk going its way as usual: "the murderer, leaving the house of his victim, meets the milkman with the milk".

His treatment of the unities is equally interesting.   When he took a plot (say) from Holinshed or Plutarch, he could not help himself: he had to follow his authority over land and sea, through months or years.   But there are three plays—*Love's Labour's Lost*, *A Midsummer Night's Dream*, and *The Tempest* —the plots of which Shakespeare invented himself; and these three plays have three interesting features in common: they seem all to have been written for private performance; in all of them Shakespeare is not dramatising a given plot but developing an abstract idea—that Love is irresistible, that Love is unaccountable, that forgiveness is better than vengeance; and finally in all of them he keeps very close to the unities.   There is only one scene in *L. L. L.*, and the action takes only two days; in *M. N. D.* there are only two places, and the action occupies two days and the night between them; after the first scene, the action of *The Tempest* is all confined to one small island, and occupies exactly six hours, as Shakespeare pointedly informs us.   From all which we infer that Shakespeare, Romantic as he was by tradition, was not blind to the advantages of the classical method, and experimented in it when he was free to do so.

But Shakespeare was also a poet, more conscious perhaps in his early work of himself as poet than as dramatist, a virtuoso interested in effects which, he must have known, only a section of his audience could fully appreciate.   Like other artists he felt his way under the guidance of others who had achieved success, and whose art appealed to his own not fully developed taste.   In the *Henry VI* plays his model in style and verse is Marlowe, yet there are interesting differences.   To Shakespeare these heroes of civil war are savage monsters, the whole pack of them—Suffolk, the Queen, Clifford, York—to the final culmination of this ruthless personal ambition in Richard, Duke of Gloucester.   In keeping with this feeling are the images drawn from wild animals:

> O tiger's heart wrapp'd in a woman's hide;

> She-wolf of France, but worse than wolves of France,
> Whose tongue more poisons than the adder's tooth;

> But you are more inhuman, more inexorable,
> Oh ten times more than tigers of Hyrcania.

The greater fertility of Shakespeare's imagination is obvious even in these vituperative speeches. Marlowe is apt to say one or two striking things and then to repeat or to weaken: Shakespeare's vituperation pours forth in a torrent of conceit, image, phrase all aflame with the savage temper of the speaker:

> What! will the aspiring blood of Lancaster
> Sink in the ground? I thought it would have mounted!
> See how my sword weeps for the poor King's death:
> O may such purple tears be always shed
> For those that wish the downfall of our house!
> If any spark of life be yet remaining,
> Down, down to Hell, and say I sent thee thither,
> I that have neither pity, love nor fear.

In comedy there was no such dominant influence as Marlowe, but Lyly affected Shakespeare's work as he did that of others. But here Shakespeare was freer to indulge his natural vein of poetry, to play upon words, conceits, rhymes, and stanzas. The puns and the quibbling wit are out of date, but the poetry is often delightful; and there is humour as well as quibbling in the scenes with Speed and Launce and Bottom and all the rest of them.

The style of these early comedies, moreover, was carried over into a couple of the histories whose style is not that of the Marlowesque *Henries*, viz. *King John* and *Richard II*. (The former certainly, for the original is extant, the latter probably, as Professor Dover Wilson has shown, is based on older work, in both cases possibly by the same author, someone more interested in accurate history and more Protestant in feeling than Shakespeare.) Compared with the earlier histories the characters, even the 'politicians', are more human, less rigidly fierce and ruthless. Bolingbroke is a type we can still recognise, an Essex of Shakespeare's day, cap in hand to all that meet him till his end is secured. The Bastard is a first sketch of John Bull. But the predominant interest for the poet in Shakespeare is the opportunity for poetic argument and eloquence,—Constance pleading for her child, Richard the eloquent exponent of his own wrongs and self-pity. Compared with Marlowe's Edward the difference again is in the greater fertility of the younger poet's brain. Edward is more

passionate and exalted in his first speech, which echoes the cry
of Faustus awaiting damnation:

> Continue ever, thou celestial sun;
> Let never silent night possess the heavens;
> Stand still, you watches of the elements;
> All times and seasons rest you at a stay,
> That Edward may be still fair England's King.

Richard's moods are more varied, the play of his wit and fancy
more surprising:

> Now is the golden crown like a deep well
> That owes two buckets filling one another,
> The emptier ever dancing in the air,
> The other down, unseen and full of water;
> That bucket down and full of tears am I,
> Drinking my grief while you mount up on high.

Eloquent self-pity is the note throughout. In his own eyes
Richard is a betrayed and martyred Christ:

> Though some of you with Pilate wash your hands,
> Showing an outward pity; yet you Pilates
> Have here delivered me to my sour cross,
> And water cannot wash away your sin.

In what, as regards verse and style, may be called the middle
period of his dramatic activity, the plays in the third and
fourth groups enumerated above, the dramatist and the poet
are better balanced. That equipoise is in part secured by the
combination of verse and prose, prose for the purely comic
scenes, verse for those in which the sentiment takes a higher
flight. But even the poetry is less fanciful, the language and
imagery more natural and appropriate. Compared with the
passionate flights of Constance, the rich fancies of the despairing Richard, Mark Antony's speech is a masterpiece of effective
eloquence, fulfilling the conditions of successful persuasion
indicated in the *Rhetoric* of Aristotle—the superficial arguments:

> He hath brought many captives home to Rome,
> Whose ransoms did the general coffers fill:
> Did this in Caesar seem ambitious?

and so on; the subtle appeal to his own character:

> I am no orator as Brutus is;
> But as you know me all, a plain, blunt man
> That love my friend;

the whole culminating in the direct assault upon the emotions of the mob which have been gradually worked up:

> I only speak right on;
> I tell you that which you yourselves do know;
> Show you sweet Caesar's wounds, poor, poor dumb mouths,
> And bid them speak for me; but were I Brutus
> And Brutus Antony, there were an Antony
> Would ruffle up your spirits, and put tongues
> In every wound of Caesar, that should move
> The stones of Rome to rise and mutiny.

It is from these plays that many of the best-known Shakespearian commonplaces, passages the thought and form of which have made them memorable, are derived: "The quality of mercy is not strained"; "Sweet are the uses of adversity"; "All the world's a stage", etc.; to say nothing of "To be or not to be" and other passages which have made *Hamlet* strike one at times as a play made up of quotations. Finally there is much less of rhyme and stanza in these plays, and the blank verse has not the rigid march of the earlier plays, but curves and overflows, with medial as well as terminal pauses just as may suit the message conveyed.

It was in the tragedies of passion that Shakespeare's style underwent its last and most striking change. It is in part the same change that we noted in passing from the Elizabethan Petrarchists to the *Songs and Sonets* of Donne, a closer approximation, even in poetry that is not satirical, to the language that men do use under the influence of strong feeling, natural in diction and syntax including the order of words, this last made easier by the quickening of the overflow through weak and light endings, the pause medial more often than final. The imagery is realistic and dramatic rather than picturesque and fanciful:

> I offered to awaken his regard
> For's private friends: his answer to me was,
> He could not stay to pick them in a pile
> Of noisome, musty chaff; he said 'twas folly
> For one poor grain or two to leave unburnt,
> And still to nose the offence.

When the passion grows more intense the image may become even ugly:

> Nay, but to live
> In the rank sweat of an enseamed bed,
> Stew'd in corruption, honeying and making love
> Over the nasty sty.

Image hurtles after image so hurriedly as to leave the impression of confusion and mixed metaphor:

> Besides, this Duncan
> Hath borne his faculties so meek, hath been
> So clear in his great office, that his virtues
> Will plead like angels trumpet-tongued against
> The deep damnation of his taking off:
> And pity like a naked, new-born babe
> Striding the blast, or heaven's cherubins horsed
> Upon the sightless couriers of the air,
> Shall blow the horrid deed in every eye,
> That tears shall drown the wind.

But if an image may be realistic to the limit of ugliness, another will soar as far in the direction of the sublime:

> Like to the Pontic sea,
> Whose icy current and compulsive course
> Ne'er feels retiring ebb, but keeps due on
> To the Propontic and the Hellespont,
> Even so my bloody thoughts with violent pace
> Shall ne'er look back, ne'er ebb to humble love,
> Till that a capable and wide revenge
> Swallow them up.

We have said that the change is of the same kind as that which distinguishes Donne and Jonson and the satirists from the Spenserians; but there is more in it than that. Shakespeare has our language more at large than Donne or any other poet of the period. To the end he is a virtuoso delighting in experiment in language. There is not a play of these years in which there is not some strange word, used perhaps only here, or some fresh application of a familiar word: "our terrene moon", "exsufflicate and blown surmise", "a bookish jealousy", "the guiled shore", "the ribaudred nag", and countless others which have lured commentators into endless conjectures. Even in an impassioned speech images will emerge which only a poet could have conceived, and which are not quite such as would spring naturally to the lips of the character as presented:

> One whose subdued eyes,
> Albeit unused to the melting mood,
> Drop tears as fast as the Arabian trees
> Their medicinal gum.

The English language comes alive under Shakespeare's creative hand. Indeed at times his delight in language has led him to endeavour apparently to evoke an atmosphere by rare words, harsh constructions, bold metaphors, that it is a little difficult for us to apprehend the guiding motive of, in *Troilus and Cressida* for example. But in that play these difficult speeches are made the vehicle for shrewd wisdom, brutal truths, transcendent passion:

> Within my soul there doth conduce a fight
> Of this strange nature, that a thing inseparate
> Divides more wider than the sky and earth;
> And yet the spacious breadth of this division
> Admits no orifex for a point as subtle
> As Ariachne's broken woof to enter.
> Instance, O instance! strong as Pluto's gates!
> Cressid is mine, tied with the bonds of heaven;
> The bonds of heaven are slipp'd, dissolv'd and loos'd;
> And with another knot, five-finger tied,
> The fractions of her faith, orts of her love,
> The fragments, scraps, the bits and greasy relics
> Of her o'er-eaten faith are bound to Diomed.

In the plays of the last group, the romances, Shakespeare returns to the poetry of the early comedies, but with a difference:

> Where are the songs of Spring, aye where are they?
> Think not of them, thou hast thy music too.

The interval is well illustrated by a comparison of *A Midsummer Night's Dream* with *The Tempest*. In the former all is gaiety and light-winged poetry, the troubles but the shifting imagery of a dream. In *The Tempest* evil has accumulated upon evil, plot on plot; yet all turns to joy, a tempered joy, sin to repentance, revenge to forgiveness, the sorrows of one generation redeemed by the happiness of those who succeed. The style is generally simpler than in the tragedies, though there are ever and anon the same daring felicities. The verse has the same freer movement, the blank verse at times a lyrical grace and lightness. Compare with the "I know a bank" lines in *A Midsummer Night's Dream* the lines from *The Winter's Tale*:

> What you do
> Still betters what is done.   When you speak, sweet,
> I'ld have you do it ever: when you sing
> I'ld have you buy and sell so, so give alms,
> Pray so; and for the ordering your affairs
> To sing them too: when you do dance I wish you
> A wave o' the sea, that you might ever do
> Nothing but that ; move still, still so,
> And own no other function : each your doing,
> So singular in each particular,
> Crowns what you are doing in the present deed,
> That all your acts are queens.

Finally contrast both with the lines on the opposite page and realise the range of Shakespeare's dramatic poetry.

Chapter Twelve

SHAKESPEARE'S CONTEMPORARIES AND SUCCESSORS IN DRAMA

SHAKESPEARE was at the height of his comic power when Ben Jonson (1573?–1637) threw down the gauntlet, not so much to him as to the whole idea of Romantic Comedy. Jonson was a born leader of revolt—honest, opinionative, and pugnacious—he killed two men in single combat. He revolted against Romantic Comedy as being Italianate, improbable, sentimental, loose in construction, high-flown, and purposeless; whereas comedy should be realistic, using

> language such as men do use,
> And persons such as comedy would choose;

and it should have a social purpose beyond mere entertainment. Jonson's conception of the purpose of comedy is bound up with the doctrine of the 'humours'. Human folly is due to the excess of this or that 'humour', which so colours a man's whole conduct as to make him, so to speak, that humour incarnate: the confirmed braggart brags on all occasions, and the jealous man is jealous of his shadow. It is the function of comedy to reduce such excesses by showing folly her own image exaggerated, as it were in a distorting mirror. Jonsonian comedy looks back to the Morality and forward to the Comedy of Manners. Its danger is that it walks a razor's edge between homily and caricature. In *Every Man in His Humour* Jonson kept his balance well enough, and Bobadil, though he is not a new type and is pasteboard compared to Falstaff, does excellently for the braggart soldier. But in *Every Man out of his Humour* Jonson toppled over into caricature, and even, it would seem, into caricature of living persons. Satire became lampoon in *Cynthia's Revels* and *The Poetaster*, where he fell foul of Dekker and Marston. They gave him as good as they got, and Jonson broke off the engagement to show Shakespeare how to write a Roman play; and try "if tragedy have a more kind aspect". *Sejanus* (1603) is carefully constructed and scrupulously documented, but it is dead, though not so dead as *Catiline* (1611) with its long speeches and choruses. By

1604 Jonson had made it up with Marston, and joined him and Chapman in *Eastward Ho!*   The spirit of satire betrayed them into poking fun at the King and his "thirty pound knights", and Chapman and Marston were thrown into prison, Jonson voluntarily accompanying them.   Luckily he escaped by pleading his clergy, and afterwards became a favourite with the scholarly King, who employed him frequently to write masques.

Between 1605 and 1613 Jonson wrote his four masterpieces, of which *Volpone* was the first.   Volpone is an old sensualist who pretends that he is dying; his friends, who are as hateful as himself, load him with presents, and are ready to give up wives and children to his lust in hope of inheriting his wealth. From this savage satire Jonson swung round to the farcical comedy of *The Silent Woman*.   Morose is an old monomaniac whose 'humour' is a horror of noise.   His nephew, whom he has threatened to disinherit, tricks him into marrying (as he believes) a dumb woman, who at once recovers her tongue and fills his house with a clattering mob that drives him to frenzy, till the nephew, having gained his object, reveals that the silent woman is a boy in disguise.   *The Silent Woman* is a well-made play, but *The Alchemist* is better, with a simple, straightforward plot that keeps strictly to the unities.   Subtle, a pretended alchemist, obtains occupation of a house in the owner's absence, where, with the help of the caretaker, he fleeces a succession of dupes; then the owner unexpectedly returns, and Subtle is bilked by his accomplice.   The play, though full of rogues and gulls, is not savage like *Volpone*.   Among the dupes, Sir Epicure Mammon is almost Marlovian in his boundless concupiscence.   "We of the separation" are the kind of pious frauds whom Jonson, like Dickens, detested.   *Bartholomew Fair* is not nearly so well constructed; the motley crowd of characters is far more than the plot can hold together; but several of the characters are very diverting: there is the pig-wife; and Zeal-in-the-Land Busy, the Puritan who gets drunk; and Arthur Bradley who demands both ale and beer, "Ale for Arthur and beer for Bradley"—in short, if you are not too squeamish, there is all the fun of the fair.   There is more real fun in *Bartholomew Fair* than in all Jonson's other plays together.

After *The Devil is an Ass* (1616) Jonson turned from comedy to masque.   After King James's death in 1625 he fell out of favour at court, and came back to the stage; but his hand had lost its cunning. It would be unkind to dwell on what Dryden called his 'dotages', with their "jests so nominal". After 1632 he left "the loathed stage". But, like Drayton, he had a second spring; the unfinished *Sad Shepherd* is a pastoral play of Robin Hood, revealing a feeling for Nature and a vein of tender sentiment that we should scarcely have expected in this angry satirist with his mountain belly and his rocky face.

Jonson's reputation has suffered from Drummond, who took down in malice what Jonson said in drink. The man who wrote the noble lines "To the Memory of my Beloved the Author Master William Shakespeare", who was himself beloved by Beaumont, and round whom so many young wits gathered, proud to be called "sons of Ben", cannot have been simply the drunken praiser of himself and disprizer of others that Drummond depicts. No doubt he was arrogant, and his arrogance betrays that lack of imaginative sympathy which debars him from the highest ranks of drama. He has created no living character. Moreover, his censorious temper gives a rough tang to most of his writing: after Shakespeare's genial and gracious creations his world seems to be peopled wholly by fools and knaves. Compared with Molière (a fairer comparison) he seems heavy-handed, bludgeoning his victims instead of pinking them. For all that, he towers above all his contemporaries except Shakespeare, not for his book-learning but because he was a tireless observer of men and manners and had a literary conscience. He put more brain-work into his plays than any of his fellows except Shakespeare. Some of them surpass him in single scenes, but they never keep it up; Jonson's good plays are good as wholes.

No other of Shakespeare's contemporaries is known to ordinary readers now for more than one or two plays, and these are all that we shall have room to mention. George Chapman (1559–1634) stands a little apart, a grave senior who took to drama rather late in life and wrote mostly for the private theatres. *The Gentleman Usher* is the best of his few comedies; *The Widow's Tears* dramatises the most cynical story in Petronius. His most characteristic work is in his tragedies of recent French history—*Bussy d'Ambois*, *The Revenge of Bussy d'Ambois*, *Biron's Conspiracy*, and *The Tragedy of Biron*. They are all very ill-constructed, and of the two heroes Bussy is a bravo and Biron a braggart. Where Chapman shines is not in plot or character, but in what Aristotle calls διάνοια, thought.   His full and heightened style, often full to bombast and heightened beyond comprehension, impedes his utterance; but when he gets his throat clear he can speak out loud and bold, venting through the mouths of his characters strong antinomian and pantheistic views on suicide, marriage, kingship, and man's relation to the All.   Chapman was not a good playwright either made or born; but he was a great humanist, and he lives by his translation of Homer.

The work of the other minor playwrights may be roughly divided into tragedies, often of Italian or (later) of Spanish origin, and comedies, generally English and unborrowed; but most of them tried both kinds, or a mixed kind, frequently in collaboration.   Thomas Heywood (1575?–1641) and Thomas Dekker (1570?–1641) are at their best on English soil, where good-nature and good-humour are native.   Of the 220 plays that Heywood had a finger in, only seventeen remain—sixteen too many, some would say; but all agree that in *A Woman Killed with Kindness* he found a subject exactly suited to his genius—the story of a woman taken in adultery, forgiven, and dying under the weight of forgiveness—and produced a domestic tragedy full of delicate feeling and unforced pathos. Thirty years later he used a similar *motif*, not without success, in *The English Traveller*.   Heywood's low comedy is trash, but he had a pleasant lyric gift.

Dekker lacked Heywood's command of pathos, but he had humour and poetry: his songs rank next to Shakespeare's. Much must be pardoned to playwrights like Heywood and Dekker, wage-slaves of the managers, often in debt and sometimes in debtors' prisons, scribbling for their lives.   Dekker's gallant Cockney spirit bore him up; gaiety bubbles through *The Shoemaker's Holiday*: the hero, Sim Eyre, is company for a king, as in fact he becomes when made Lord Mayor.   Dekker's brave temper, clean, bright prose, and gift of song make him the most attractive of all these minors.   There are evidences in his plays of dramatic power and of pathos which happier conditions might have developed.   Of the scenes in *The Honest Whore* which depict Bellafonte, her father Orlando Friscobaldo, and her betrayed and spendthrift husband Hazlitt has written: "It is as if there were some fine art to chisel thought and to embody the inmost movements of the mind in everyday actions and familiar speech".

John Marston (1575?–1634) had considerable satiric and some comic force. His *Dutch Courtesan* is a pretty good comedy, and *Eastward Ho!*, in which he had a hand, is capital; but a dirty mind and a turgid style are not a sufficient outfit for tragedy: the first part of his *Antonio and Mellida* was the worst tragedy in English till the second part appeared. Young Marston strikes us as a shifty, hectoring fellow: we are glad to think that Jonson beat him and took his pistol from him. Yet he cannot have been black-blooded, for he bore Jonson no malice. In early middle life he quitted the stage, in charity (he says) with all men, took orders, and retired to a country cure and the study of Epictetus.

Thomas Middleton (1570?–1627) was unequal even for an Elizabethan. He first made his name in realistic comedy of all sorts, from the clever intrigue of *A Trick to Catch the Old One* with its Charles Surface hero to the gross farce-medley of *A Chaste Maid in Cheapside*. Then he turned to tragedy or tragi-comedy, generally in collaboration with William Rowley, writing the serious verse himself while Rowley threw in comic relief in rough-and-ready prose often quite irrelevant to the main plot. In *A Fair Quarrel* we actually find two plots of nearly equal length and interest, with no connection whatever between them except that a character in the one has a sister in the other. The two halves of *The Spanish Gipsy* do not cohere much better. Yet the serious plots of both plays have great merit: the struggle in Ager between honour and conscience and Roderigo's revulsion from his act of violence are very effective. But Middleton's masterpiece is De Flores in *The Changeling*, an ugly ruffian whose black heart is consumed by a passion for Beatrice-Joanna. She employs him to murder her betrothed, that she may enjoy the man she loves. Her incredulous horror when he demands her virginity as the price of his crime—

> Why, 'tis impossible thou canst be so wicked,
> Or shelter such a cunning cruelty,
> To make his death the murderer of my honour!

is truly Shakespearian; and so is the subtle change in her feeling for him when she has yielded. Middleton's rough strength might have done great things had his literary conscience been less lax. (His *Witch* is interesting chiefly because it contains a Hecate like the Hecate in *Macbeth*, and has in full the songs of which *Macbeth* gives the first lines.)

John Webster (1580?–1625?) for his *White Devil* and *Duchess of Malfi* is counted second to Shakespeare in tragedy. He had studied Shakespeare to good purpose, and believed with him that the wages of sin is death.   But his plots are so clumsy that Lamb himself could not have made *Tales from Webster*; and his construction is so defective that Vittoria, the White Devil herself, almost fades out of the play after the third act.   He has created no really sympathetic character; even the Duchess of Malfi has a sensual strain in her which qualifies our sympathy with her nobler traits.   The piled-up horrors with which her brothers try to drive her mad—the dead man's hand, the dance of madmen, the effigies of her murdered children— wring our nerves but not our hearts.   And the gloom is seldom lightened by those touches of common humanity and glimpses of wider horizons which Shakespeare is so careful to indicate. Yet Webster's dark, laborious spirit can move pity if not terror; he has pages of lucid beauty, eloquence, and pathos; haunting dirges, and strokes like "I am Duchess of Malfi still", which compel admiration.   We do not surrender freely to Webster, but he carries our feelings by storm.   Cyril Tourneur (1575?– 1626) does not, though he tries hard.   The Senecan tradition culminates in *The Revenger's Tragedy*, when Vendice forces the wicked Duke to kiss a skull smeared with corrosive poison. His only other play, *The Atheist's Tragedy*, is inferior.   Tourneur's carrion imaginings move little but horror; yet he too has his great moments, as when Castiza cries to the mother who is tempting her to sin, "Mother, come from that poisonous woman there!" Tourneur's scenes are laid in Italy, sixteenth-century Italy as Englishmen conceived it: they might with more propriety be laid in Hell.

Besides other playwrights too numerous even to name, many anonymous dramas survive from that age, some of them so good that they have been attributed, quite unwarrantably, to Shakespeare.   *Arden of Feversham* and *The Yorkshire Tragedy* are bourgeois tragedies of a kind that Shakespeare never handled, founded on actual murders recently committed.   We would rather, if the evidence allowed, see Shakespeare's hand in *The Merry Devil of Edmonton*, one of the pleasantest things the Elizabethans have left us.

By the time Shakespeare retired a younger generation of playwrights was coming to the front, headed by Francis

Beaumont (1584–1616) and John Fletcher (1579–1625). The social changes which their plays reflect have been touched on in Chapter Nine. The change that most affected drama was the widening gulf between the City and the court. Heywood, Dekker, and Middleton were all connected with the City and wrote for City audiences; Beaumont and Fletcher were gentlemen born and wrote with an eye on the court. Dryden thought that they understood and imitated the conversation of gentlemen better than Shakespeare; which means that the gentlemen of James I's day talked much like those of Charles II's. They had shed the Euphuisms, conceits, and verbal wit in which the Elizabethans delighted. They had shed other things too. When we turn from Shakespeare and Jonson to Beaumont and Fletcher we are conscious of a relaxation of tension: tragedy gives way tò tragi-comedy, pity and terror to pathos and sentiment, serious satire to comedy of manners, bold bawdry to veiled indecency.

Of the fifty-odd plays that go by the name of Beaumont and Fletcher only six are certainly their joint production, viz. *The Scornful Lady, The Coxcomb, Philaster, The Maid's Tragedy, A King and no King,* and *Cupid's Revenge.* We can distinguish their shares not by any marked difference in style or spirit but by a marked difference in versification: Beaumont modelled his verse on Shakespeare's middle style, with run-on lines and varied pauses; Fletcher affected end-stopped lines with feminine endings. By this test we can pick out the scenes which each actually *penned*; beyond that we can scarcely go, so intimate was their collaboration. It is pretty clear, however, that Beaumont, though the younger in years, was the senior partner; the plays he had a hand in are fuller and firmer than the rest.

Each of them had written a play or two before their partnership was cemented. Beaumont's *Knight of the Burning Pestle* is a skit (suggested by *Don Quixote*) on the City craze for chivalric romance, to which Heywood had pandered in his *Four Prentices of London.* A citizen and his wife in the audience, suspicious of the play they are witnessing, insist that their prentice shall play the hero, to the glory of grocers. The two plots are dexterously sandwiched, and the result is simply the best burlesque in English. Fletcher's *Faithful Shepherdess* might hold the same place among pastoral plays but for its sensual taint; it is beautifully written, and so mellifluous that Milton deigned to steal from it.

Their joint work is seen at its best in *The Maid's Tragedy* and the tragi-comedy of *Philaster*. In the former, the King makes Amintor discard the maid Aspasia and marry Evadne. On their wedding night she tells him that she is the King's mistress and will be his wife only in name. Amintor, a fanatical loyalist, acquiesces. But Evadne's brother wrings the secret from her, and forces her at the dagger's point to repent and seal her repentance by murdering the King. Then she proffers Amintor her love, is repulsed, and stabs herself; while Aspasia, in man's clothes, gets herself killed by Amintor. Here are strong situations in plenty! But the whole thing does not bear reflection. Evadne is unconvincing, Amintor feckless, Aspasia a mere wraith. Character is sacrificed to situation. We feel this less in the more poetic *Philaster*. The hero is wooed and won by his suzerain's daughter. They use his page as a go-between. Hence mistakes and jealousies, as in *Twelfth Night*, till they find that the page is Euphrasia, a young girl, who has followed Philaster "in the lovely garnish of a boy". Sentimental as it is, the play has many beauties: Euphrasia's words, when she thinks herself dying, are at once pathetic and felicitous in the wonderful Elizabethan manner:

> 'Tis not a life,
> 'Tis but a piece of childhood thrown away.

After Beaumont's death Fletcher found other associates, notably Massinger, and with their help poured out plays at the rate of four a year, often taking his plots from Spanish sources, where he found the sharp contrasts and piquant situations that he loved. Mass-production has left its mark on these later plays: read in the lump they weary us with repetition, taken one at a time they do very well; at least they all "go to a good tune", as Scott put it. Fletcher's faults are obvious—his readiness at all times to sacrifice truth to effect, his flippancy, his indecency. He is not brutal, nor cynical, nor even (by Jacobean standards) obscene; he simply does not know what modesty means. *Per contra*, his wit and invention never flag, he knows all the tricks of his trade, and, best of all, he has a fine, copious lyric vein. Fletcher is the chief link between Elizabethan and Restoration drama.

None of these later dramatists has worn better than Philip Massinger (1583–1640). Massinger had few of the gifts that made Fletcher popular. He had not much humour, or wit,

K

or poetry; and he seems to have had no lyric gift at all. But he had the one thing needed for a dramatist; he had the gift of the theatre—his plots hold us to the last line. Within seventy lines of the end of *The Maid of Honour* the Duchess says,

> For my part,
> I cannot guess the issue;

and the candid reader says, "No more can I". Sometimes, it must be owned, Massinger cuts the knot by a sudden conversion; but as a rule his denouements, though surprising, do not offend our sense of probability and poetic justice. His attempts to gratify the groundlings with scurrility are pitiful; his natural instincts were serious and noble. *The Virgin Martyr* is unique among the plays of that age in having a distinctively Christian subject, and in other plays Massinger expresses truly Christian and liberal views on duelling, suicide, the divine right of kings, and the position of women and slaves. His most successful plays were *A New Way to Pay Old Debts* and *The City Madam*: the former was still on the boards in Lamb's day. These are satirical comedies—more satire than comedy—in Jonson's sternest manner. The usurer Overreach in *A New Way* and the hypocrite Luke in *The City Madam* recall the pen that drew Volpone, and anticipate that which created Ralph Nickleby. Massinger's own favourite among his plays was *The Roman Actor*, a tragedy modelled on *Sejanus*. The title rôle is certainly what actors call a fat part; but modern readers will prefer *The Maid of Honour*, an admirable tragi-comedy, nobly planned, and marred only by the slight part of the fribble Sylli, who is supposed to supply comic relief.

John Ford (1583–1640?) is an enigmatic figure. He sits in the shadows with his hat drawn over his eyes, as a contemporary 'drollery' depicts him:

> Deep in a dump John Ford was alone got,
> With folded arms and melancholy hat.

We know little of him except that he came of a good Devonshire family and was entered at the Middle Temple in 1602. Though he collaborated with professional playwrights like Dekker and Rowley—with the former in *The Sun's Darling* and with both in *The Witch of Edmonton*—Ford was not himself a professional playwright, but a lawyer with literary ambitions. Among his unassisted dramas *Perkin Warbeck* is a sound chronicle play, the last of that species; but there he had Bacon's broad shoulder to lean on.   He stands or falls, as Saintsbury says, by *'Tis Pity She's a Whore* and *The Broken Heart*.   Of the former we find it hard to write.   Its morbid psychology has a horrifying fascination.   The man who makes a tragedy of incest, whether Ford, Scott, or Shelley, runs the risk of awakening a broad resentment fatal to the pleasure proper to tragedy, confesses that he cannot arouse tragic emotion by lawful means: the scene in which Giovanni rushes in with his sister's heart transfixed on his dagger exceeds what is legitimately probable or tolerable in drama.   More subtly repulsive than physical horror is the sympathy that Ford implicitly demands for the victims of passion, as if passion excused everything.   *The Broken Heart* aims at a different effect, a still tragedy of inward suffering.   The scene is laid in Sparta, the traditional home of fortitude.   There is little violent action: to stab a helpless man and then open your own veins—Shakespeare would not have boggled at that.   The tragedy is in the wringing of heart-strings.   There are two broken hearts in the play.   Penthea, the unhappy wife, wails her woes, goes mad, and starves herself to death.   Calantha, the Spartan princess, breaks her heart in silence.   The famous scene in which she leads the revels and dances on and on to the end, while tale after tale of death—of father, friend, lover— is poured into her ears, moved Lamb to declare that Ford was of the first order of poets.   But to agonise thus for a point not of honour but of etiquette, is that the way of high tragedy? We ask the question, but we ourselves are not agreed on the answer; and greater critics than we have agreed no better: Lamb can be cited on the one side and Hazlitt on the other. Of Ford as a poet something more will be said.

James Shirley (1596–1666) owed more to books than Nature in tragedy: his *Cardinal* is Webster-and-water.   Most of his comedies, however, are still readable; *Hyde Park* deserves praise less faint; Mistress Carol in that play is a distant cousin of Beatrice and Millamant.   His morals, compared with Fletcher's, reflect the improved tone of the court under Charles I.   Shirley wrote one noble poem, *Death the Leveller*; otherwise his poetry, like his wit, is rather thin.   The wine of English drama was on the lees by the time Parliament closed the theatres in 1642.

Elizabethan drama is no longer rated so high as it was in

the nineteenth century, when criticism was still bewitched by
Charles Lamb. Affection transferred to Lamb's judgement
of drama the respect rightly paid to his exquisite taste in poetry.
But the things Lamb loved—recondite beauty, high-wrought
sentiment, and sudden glimpses into the secret places of the
heart—do not of themselves make drama, though they may
enrich it provided they subserve its main purpose of showing
human nature in action. So when we pass on from Lamb's
Specimens to the complete plays we too often find the bulk not
answering to the sample. Lamb was not the only Romantic
to eulogise the Elizabethans. Hazlitt admired them too; and
so, quite independently, did Scott; and their praises were
repeated by poets and critics till near the end of the century.
Rossetti indeed protested angrily that the ordinary Elizabethan
vintage was "rank as turpentine", swallowed only because it
came from the same cellar as Shakespeare. Swinburne, on
the other hand, was the loudest eulogist of all. In the second
series of *Poems and Ballads* he addressed a passionate invocation
to Marlowe:

> For thou, if ever godlike foot there trod
> These fields of ours, wert surely like a god.
> Who knows what splendour of strange dreams was shed,
> With sacred shadow and glimmer of gold and red
> From hallowed windows, over stone and sod,
> On thine unbowed bright unsubmissive head?

And to *Tristram of Lyonesse* he appended a series of sonnets to
the Elizabethan dramatists, including even *Anonymous Plays*
and *The Many*. But that this enthusiasm was confined to
critics and poets is proved by the complete failure to give a
continued life on the stage to any of the lesser dramatists.
Lamb could still see plays by Jonson and Massinger on the
stage, and actors make a name in the parts of Abel Drugger or
Overreach. Those days are long past. Occasional revivals
by amateurs of Jonson or Webster or others have now and then
gained a *succès d'estime*: that is the most that can be said. By
the end of the nineteenth century the critics too had gone cold:
critics whose ideal was the realistic prose drama of Ibsen found
little to their taste in the rich, crude stuff of the Elizabethans.

The truth is that, except Shakespeare generally and Jonson
in his prime, there is not one of these dramatists who can be
trusted to produce a play that shall be good as a whole, not
marred by some structural flaw, violation of probability in

incident or character, or gross intrusion of buffoonery, bawdry, or ranting melodrama. But equally there is scarcely one of them but may at any moment surprise us by a fine excess, a flash of sheer beauty, a snatch of song, a line, a speech, even a whole scene that makes us exclaim 'Shakespearian'! It will help us to understand this anomaly if we recall what was said in Chapter Ten of the composition of an Elizabethan audience, the multifarious demands which the playwrights tried to satisfy, and the hand-to-mouth conditions under which they often worked. Courthope describes these "men of great skill and much learning", as he calls them, as "dramatists by profession, poets only in a subordinate sense". We should prefer to put it, "dramatists by profession and necessity, poets by inspiration and the grace of heaven". It remains a problem how audiences who loved crude melodrama and broad comedy enjoyed, or tolerated, the poetry in which the dramatist delights to indulge on every opportunity.

Of Shakespeare and Marlowe we need not say more. But take the two chief tragedians after them, Webster and Ford. Whatever one may think of *The White Devil* and *The Duchess of Malfi* as dramatic constructions, or of the probability of the characters, their moods and changes, it is impossible to deny the poetic beauty of Webster's treatment of certain dramatic moments. The death scene of the Duchess may include not a few extravagances, but at least there is poetry in the scene of repentance which follows:

> *Bos.* Fix your eye here.
> *Fer.* Constantly.
> *Bos.* Do you not weep?
>   Other sins only speak; murder shrieks out.
>   The element of water moistens the earth,
>   But blood flies upwards and bedews the heavens.
> *Fer.* Cover her face : mine eyes dazzle: she died young.
> *Bos.* I think not so: her infelicity
>   Seemed to have years too many.

Webster's poetical passages do not always have so close a bearing as this on the immediate action: they are sometimes there for their own beauty, like Antonio's speech on ancient ruins. And what is true of Webster is equally true of Ford. How much the poet predominates in Ford is shown by the rather absurd introduction into a serious, if romantic, drama of the contention of the nightingale and the musician which he, like Crashaw, has translated from the Latin of Strada. The Spartan scene which closes *The Broken Heart* may tax our credulity, but the poetry of the whole is sustained to the last speech:

> Oh, my lords,
> I but deceived your eyes with antick gesture,
> When one news straight came huddling on another,
> Of death, and death, and death: still I danced forward;
> But it struck home, and here, and in an instant.
> Be such mere women, who with shrieks and outcries
> Can vow a present end to all their sorrows,
> Yet live to court new pleasures, and outlive them:
> They are the silent griefs which cut the heart-strings:
> Let me die smiling. . . .
> One kiss on these cold lips, my last!

The effect of these scenes in Webster and Ford is romantic or melodramatic rather than tragic in the sense in which Shakespeare is tragic, for they have not been led up to so convincingly and with such overwhelming power as the great scenes in *Lear* or *Othello*.

The romantic is still the dominant note in Beaumont and Fletcher, Dekker, and Massinger. One of the finest of Swinburne's sonnets on the dramatists describes what is best in Massinger:

> Grave and great-hearted Massinger, thy face
> High melancholy lights with loftier grace
> Than gilds the brows of revel: sad and wise
> The spirit of thought that moved thy deeper song.
> Sorrow serene in soft calm scorn of wrong
> Speaks patience from thy majestic eyes.

In justification of this judgement we cite one example from *The Bondman*:

> Wilt thou then confirm
> That love and jealousy, though of different natures,
> Must of necessity be twins, the younger
> Created only to defeat the elder,
> And spoil him of his birthright? 'Tis not well.
> Nor will one syllable or tear express
> How deeply I am wounded with the arrows
> Of your distrust: but when that you shall hear,
> At your return, how I have borne myself,
> And what an austere penance I take on me
> To satisfy your doubts; when like a vestal
> I show you to your shame the fire still burning,

Committed to my charge by true affection;
When by the glorious splendour of my sufferings
The prying eyes of jealousy are struck blind,
The monster too that feeds on fears e'en starved
For want of seeming matter to accuse me,
A sharp reproof expect, Leosthenes,
From my just anger.

Dekker was one of the most careless of playwrights, but also
one of the most natural and lyrical of poets: witness these lines
from *Old Fortunatus*, absurd enough as a drama:

To-morrow? aye to-morrow thou shalt buy.
To-morrow tell the Princess I will love her;
To-morrow tell the King I'll banquet him.
To-morrow, Shadow, will I give thee gold.
To-morrow Pride goes bare and Lust a-cold.
To-morrow will the rich man feed the poor,
And vice to-morrow virtue will adore.
To-morrow beggars will be crowned kings.
This no-time, morrow-time no sweetness brings.

The note of romantic pathos in Beaumont and Fletcher is
much more self-conscious and studied. One may, or may not,
be moved by the purple passages of pathos and eloquence in
The Maid's Tragedy, and *Philaster*, and *Bonduca*, happy figures
like

Strive to make me look
Like sorrow's monument; and the trees about me
Let them be dry and leafless; let the rocks
Groan with continual surges; and behind me
Make all a desolation.

There is purer poetry in the lyrical descriptive parts of *The
Faithful Shepherdess*:

Do not fear to put thy feet
Naked in the river sweet:
Think not leech, or newt, or toad
Will bite thy foot when thou hast trod;
Nor let the water rising high
As thou wad'st in make thee cry
And sob, but ever live with me,
And not a wave shall trouble thee.

Equally poetical are the songs scattered through their plays.
Almost all these dramatists had the gift of song. Fletcher has
the most copious vein, if Dekker comes closest to Shakespeare

in his fine careless raptures, and Webster's "Hark, now everything is still" recalls Desdemona's willow-song. But here again it is the appropriateness with which Shakespeare introduces his songs that gives them their peculiar charm.

Weight and dignity of thought and expression are the qualities that distinguish Jonson and Chapman. These qualities are not wanting in Shakespeare, but he does not give the impression of being out to philosophise. What he has to say of life and death and kindred themes is strictly dramatic: it is Macbeth, not Shakespeare, who calls life "a poor player". Jonson and Chapman wish to teach. Jonson will give his tragedy "gravity and height of eloquence, fulness and frequency of sentence". In the two great comedies, *The Alchemist* and *Volpone*, there are passages of weighty thought on human nature and its weaknesses. Recent research has lessened Chapman's claim to be an original thinker; but, whencesoever suggested, his great passages have weight, and a soaring spirit that recalls Marlowe rather than Jonson:

> Give me a spirit that on life's rough sea
> Loves to have his sails fill'd with a lusty wind,
> Even till his sailyards tremble, his masts crack,
> And his rapt ship run on her side so low
> That she drinks water, and her keel ploughs air.
> There is no danger to a man that knows
> What life and death is; there's not any law
> Exceeds his knowledge; neither is it lawful
> That he should stoop to any other law.
> He goes before them, and commands them all,
> That to himself is a law rational.

It is interesting to compare the poetry of the dramatists with that of their non-dramatic contemporaries. There are plenty of conceits in Shakespeare, but not the learned, intellectual conceits of Donne and his followers: they could scarcely have been got across. The dominant feature in the diction of the dramatists is the wealth of sensuous and emotional imagery, the range of which in Shakespeare's plays was illustrated in Chapter Eleven. "Pestered with metaphor" is Dryden's complaint; and in fact this feature of Shakespeare's style made it a dangerous model for later dramatists. But with this lavishness of imagery the dramatists combined a natural use of the spoken language that links them with the poetry of the Jacobean period. This combination of the poetic and the colloquial is found not in Shakespeare alone; such a dramatist

as Ford, for example, can use it with fine tragic effect, as in the
last scene between Giovanni and Annabella:

Gio.   Why, I hold fate
        Claspt in my fist, and could command the course
        Of time's eternal motion, hadst thou been
        One thought more steady than the ebbing sea.
        And what? you'll now be honest, that's resolved?
Anna. Brother, dear brother, know what I have been,
        And know that now there's but a dining-time
        'Twixt us and our confusion: let's not waste
        These precious hours in vain and useless speech.

The other characteristic which these dramatists have in common is just their wealth of thought, *dianoia*, large generalisa-
tions more or less dramatic in their relevancy.   There has
never been anything again quite like the Elizabethan drama in
its combination of obvious faults of structure and dramatic
convincingness with pregnant thought and great poetry.

Chapter Thirteen

THE CAROLINES

IN the latter half of the period 1625–1660 the voice of poetry was almost drowned in the clash of arms, though it was during these years that many plays and poems which had circulated in manuscript found their way into print.   But before the storm broke the Royalist poets went on singing of or to their real or fancied mistresses, while Milton let grow his wings at Horton peaceably enough, with but one ominous note in *Lycidas*. Otherwise the poets were as unaware of the storm which was brewing as the Georgian and later poets of our own day were of the approaching war:

> What though the German drum
> Bellow for freedom and revenge, the noise
> Concerns not us, nor should divert our joys;
> Nor ought the thunder of their carabines
> Drown the sweet air of our tuned violins.
> Believe me, friend, if their prevailing powers
> Gain them a calm security like ours,
> They'll hang their arms upon the olive bough,
> And dance and revel then, as we do now:

so Carew sang in 1632–1633.   Except Milton the age produced no great poet, and its most ambitious attempts— Chamberlayne's *Pharonnida* (1659), Davenant's *Gondibert* (1651), and Cowley's *Davideis* (1656)—were still-born.   On the other hand no generation, till perhaps our own, produced more good poets of all but the first rank or more short poems and songs of high excellence.   Spenser was forgotten, except by Milton and by Cowley in his youth.   In lyrical and love poetry the master influences were Jonson and Donne, the classical and the metaphysical.   It was Jonson who gave to the lyric the carefully builded form which superseded the "woodnotes wild", the folk-song note which is still that of the songs scattered through the plays of Shakespeare, Fletcher, and others.
    Jonson's chief disciple and the best of the Royalist poets was Robert Herrick (1591–1674), the son of a London goldsmith,

fit parent for the carver of such jewels of song.   After graduating at Cambridge Herrick spent some years in London,
where he was sworn of the Sons of Ben:

> Ah Ben!
> Say how or when
> Shall we thy guests
> Meet at those lyric feasts,
> Made at the Sun,
> The Dog, the Triple Tunne?
> Where we such clusters had,
> As made us nobly wild, not mad:
> And yet each verse of thine
> Outdid the meat, outdid the frolic wine.

In 1629 the King presented him to a living in Devon—whence
the name of his volume later, *Hesperides*—of which the Parliament deprived him in 1647.   Poems of Herrick's circulated
in manuscript, and a few found their way into print, but it was
not till 1648 that he published *Hesperides: or the Works both
Humane and Divine of Robert Herrick Esq.*, the latter entitled
Noble Numbers.   Of the divine poems the best are the *Litany*
and the quaint *Thanksgiving*; the rest are more witty than
devout.   Indeed wit peeps out even in the *Litany*:

> When the artless doctor sees
> No one hope but of his fees,
> And his skill runs on the lees;
>   Sweet Spirit comfort me!
>
> When his potion and his pill,
> Has, or none, or little skill,
> Meet for nothing, but to kill;
>   Sweet Spirit comfort me!

Of the varied themes of the poems he gives a delightful roll in
the opening lines:

> I sing of brooks, of blossoms, birds and bowers . . .

and similarly of the Latin poets who, with Ben, were his models,
in the lines *To Live Merrily and Trust to Good Verses*.   Though
he never was quite reconciled to his "salvage" parishioners, he
came to enjoy their merry-makings, seeing them too through
the spectacles of Latin poetry; for despite *Noble Numbers*, he is
the most pagan of English poets, beseeching his Perilla:

> Dead when I am, first cast in salt, and bring
> Part of the cream from that religious spring;

With which (Perilla) wash my hands and feet;
That done, then wind me in that very sheet
Which wrapt thy smooth limbs (when thou didst implore
The gods protection but the night before).
Follow me weeping to my turf, and there
Let fall a primrose and with it a tear;
Then lastly, let some weekly strewings be
Devoted to the memory of me:
Then shall my ghost not walk about, but keep
Still in the cool and silent shades of sleep.

The Hock Cart, Twelfth Night, and *Corinna's Going a-Maying,* are among his happiest verses. The beauty of Nature did not move Herrick to ecstasy as it did Wither. It filled him rather with pensive melancholy to see the meadows bare of flowers, and the daffodils decay:

Fair daffadils, we weep to see
You haste away so soon:
As yet the early-rising sun
Has not attained his noon.
Stay, stay,
Until the hasting day
Has run
But to the evensong;
And, having prayed together, we
Will go with you along—

a poem in which, as in *To Primroses fill'd with Morning Dew* and others, he shows his skill in weaving original and charming stanza-patterns. Being a poet he claimed the licence to sing of youth and love and "cleanly wantoness", if his epigrams cannot all claim the last epithet. But the many mistresses whom he celebrates—Julia, Anthea, Corinna, Perilla, Dianeme— probably lent him nothing but their pretty names; nor is his note passionate. Yet in two poems, *Night-piece to Julia* and *To Anthea, who may command him anything,* he catches the directness and movement of intenser feeling:

Bid me to live, and I will live
Thy Protestant to be:
Or bid me love, and I will give
A loving heart to thee.

.   .   .   .

Thou art my life, my love, my heart,
The very eyes of me:
And hast command of every part,
To live and die for thee.

Herrick attempted nothing great but, if allowance be made for the different levels on which they moved, he may claim with Milton and Gray the merit, which Pattison would allow to no other English poet, of being a poet and a careful artist, sweeter and fresher than his master Jonson and no less clear and terse.

"Jocund his muse was, but his life was chaste"—so Herrick says of himself. It is certainly more than Thomas Carew could have said; but if a libertine he was a conscientious artist. Moreover his Masque *Coelum Britannicum* shows he was not unread—it was based on Bruno's *Spaccio della Bestia*—and the *Elegy on Dr. Donne* that he could criticise and distinguish. It is the best of the bundle. His lines also *To my worthy Friend, Master George Sandys on his Translation of the Psalms* (1638) make explicable the sentence pronounced on him by Clarendon: "His glory was that after fifty years spent with less severity and exactness than it ought to have been he died with the greatest remorse for that license and with the greatest manifestations of Christianity that his best friends could desire". Carew's lyrics have not the range of Herrick's, but in the narrow field of amorous compliment and disdain he laboured for perfection. Moreover some of them catch a tone of passionate eloquence which is not Herrick's:

> Ask me no more where Jove bestows,
> When June is past, the fading rose:
> For in your beauty's orient deep,
> These flowers as in their causes sleep.

If that suggests anything it is such lyrics as Byron's "She walks in Beauty like the night", or "There be none of Beauty's daughters"; and there is the same note of oratory in "When thou poor excommunicate", and in

> Now you have freely given me leave to love
>   What will you do?
> Shall I your mirth or passion move
>   When I begin to woo?
> Will you torment or scorn or love me too?

Compared with Carew the poems of Sir John Suckling (1609–1642) read like improvisations. Suckling was the Cavalier of tradition and fiction,—gay, gallant, loyal, and careless of fortune as of life. His *Ballad on a Wedding*, "Why so pale and wan fond lover?", "Out upon it I have loved Three whole days together", have a sparkling insouciance, a natural grace, to which Carew's laboured perfection is as still wine to champagne. Suckling could write reverently of true love too.

Richard Lovelace (1618–1658) and the Marquis of Montrose (1612–1650), the noblest and most hapless of the Cavaliers, are remembered each for two poems, Lovelace (though he wrote much more) for *To Lucasta, Going to the Wars*:

> Tell me not Sweet, I am unkind
>   That from the nunnery
> Of thy chaste breast and quiet mind
>   To war and arms I fly;

and *To Althaea, from Prison* with the famous closing verse:

> Stone Walls do not a Prison make,
>   Nor iron bars a cage;
> Minds innocent and quiet take
>   That for an hermitage;
> If I have freedom in my Love
>   And in my soul am free;
> Angels alone that soar above
>   Enjoy such liberty;

Montrose by

> My dear and only Love, I pray
>   This noble world of thee,
> Be govern'd by no other sway
>   But purest Monarchy;

and the lines that he wrote on the eve of his execution:

> Let them bestow on every airth a limb.

The Cavaliers followed Jonson in the main; Donne's influence is strong in the divines,—Herbert, Crashaw, Vaughan, and others. One trait both groups have in common, the absence of a distinctively "poetic diction". Donne's avoidance of words felt at once to be "poetic" is almost without parallel in English poets, as a glance at the recently published *Concordance* of his English poems will show. Such words as Professor Wyld cites as making their first appearance with Spenser will be sought for in vain: "the *daedal* earth", "to be *eternised*", "the *verdant* fields", "the golden altars *fumed*", "night's *humid* curtain", and many others, to say nothing of Spenser's archaisms or of Latinisms which did not live on, such as "pulcrytude", "facundyous", etc. Jonson is not quite so sparing, being fond of using a Latin word like 'numbers', or 'religion' in its original or an admitted sense:

> I should believe the soul of Tacitus
> In thee, most weighty Savile, liv'd to us:
> So hast thou rendred him in all his bounds,
> And all his *numbers*, both of sense and sounds;

and again "that unto me doth such *religion* use"; and one could find in Jonson words recognisable as "poetic",—"his *lucent* seat", "*to apt* their places", but they are rare; and the same is true of these poets, both the love-poets and the more "metaphysical" divines. Theirs is what Coleridge called the "neutral" style, equally adapted to poetry and prose.

In none of these devout poets is the influence of Donne so strong as in George Herbert, son of the Lady Magdalen Herbert to whom Donne addressed his *Holy Sonnets*. Wit and scholar, nobly born and in favour with King James, Herbert seemed marked out for high office in the State, nor was he without ambition, witness *Affliction* or *The Collar*. But the death of James and other influential friends dashed these hopes; and in 1630, under the influence of Laud, he took orders, accepted a country living, Bemerton in Wiltshire, and wore out the rest of his life in the work of a parish priest, borne up on the wave of religious zeal which the Puritan challenge had raised in the Church of England. The Church's middle way seemed good to Herbert:

> Beautie in thee takes up her place,
> And dates her letters from thy face,
> When she doth write;

for what other churches miss,

> The mean, thy praise and glory is.

Its care for order, decency, and beauty appealed to one who was neither a mystic nor a fanatic, and had been a courtier. His *Church-Floor* is paved with patience and humility, cemented by love and charity. It had cost Herbert much to turn his back on the world, but when once he has taken Jesus for his master, he dares to expostulate with God knowing that his heart's desire is wholly bent on Him. This loving, reasonable temper sweetens all the verses of *The Temple*, making us excuse, even find pleasure in, his metrical flourishes—a three-lined stanza for the Trinity, seven for the Sunday, poems shaped like wings and altars—and his innumerable conceits. Herbert's conceits are sometimes penetrating by their homely quaintness, never electrifying like those of Donne; they are the products of Fancy not of Passion and Imagination, "emblems" in the manner of Quarles. His most deeply felt poems, as *Discipline* and *Love*, have none of them. Unsubtle wit in the service of piety made the *Divine Emblems* of Quarles exceedingly popular; doubtless the woodcuts helped. The polite sneered at a homeliness that often sank into bathos. It is a curious comment on the sneers that his fine poem, "Why dost thou hide thy lovely face?", was for long attributed to Rochester, who "improved" it into a rather blasphemous poem *To His Mistress*.

Richard Crashaw (1612–1649) called his first book *Steps to the Temple* in honour of Herbert. But "the Mean" which Herbert loved did not for long satisfy Crashaw. Deprived of his Cambridge fellowship for refusing the Covenant, he retreated to the Queen at Oxford, thence to Paris, where his *Carmen Deo Nostro*, *Te Decet Hymnus*, *Sacred Poems* was printed, not without errors, in 1652, and ultimately died a Canon of Loretto. Study of the flamboyant Neapolitan Marino merely encouraged Crashaw's natural bent to extravagance, "happy fireworks"; but the Spanish mystics fanned his zeal to a flame in which his very extravagances are transfigured till they seem the natural language of adoration. When the glow fades they reveal themselves as ludicrous conceits. Donne's humour and Herbert's good sense would have saved him from the "brisk cherub" who supped the Magdalene's tears, "the cream upon the Milky Way", so that his song

> Tastes of his breakfast all day long.

Conversion to an authoritative Church relieved Crashaw of the pain of thought. Faith transcends all conflict:

> Faith can believe
> As fast as Love new laws can give.
> Faith is my force; Faith strength affords
> To keep pace with those powerful words,
> And words more sure, more sweet than they,
> Love could not think, Truth could not say.

To colder natures there seems to be something febrile in a piety that clothes itself in erotic imagery. But when all is said there is nothing in English to match the rapturous eloquence of

Crashaw's *Hymn to St. Teresa* or the adoring tenderness of his *Shepherds' Hymn*. Among his secular pieces the *Wishes to his (Supposed) Mistress* shows that he could have held his own with the courtly poets.

Henry Vaughan (1622–1695) was a disciple of Herbert in a more intimate sense. It was Herbert's holy life and work that, he tells us, converted his Muse from secular to sacred poetry, though his "profane" poems are of a very mild and innocuous character. His *Silex Scintillans* (1650–1656) abounds in echoes of *The Temple*. But he was not a priest like Herbert and Crashaw; he found God not only in the Bible and the Church but in Nature, animate and inanimate:

> I would (said I) my God would give
> The staidness of those things to man! for these
> To his divine appointments ever cleave,
>   And no new business breaks their peace;
> The birds not sow, nor reap, yet sup and dine,
>   The flowers without clothes live,
> Yet Solomon was never drest so fine;

and these too expect the revelation of the sons of God:

> And do they so? Have they a sense
>   Of ought but influence?
> Can they their heads lift and expect
>   And grone too? Why the Elect
> Can do no more: my volumes said
>   They were all dull and dead,
> They judged them senseless, and their state
>   Wholly inanimate.
>   Go, go; seal up thy looks,
>   And burn thy books.

His mysticism like Wordsworth's is grounded in his recollections of childhood. But sin has dimmed the eye of the soul; life is now a cloudy vale between two bright eternities into which he can only peep in angel-visited dreams or transcendent moments of waking life, as when in *Night* he sees his Lord's head wet with the dew, or in the hush of dawn each leaf has its morning hymn, or when at sunset he meditates with sadness but confidence on departed friends:

> They are all gone into the world of light!
>   And I alone sit lingering here;
> Their very memory is fair and bright,
>   And my sad thoughts doth clear.

L

And as with the individual so with the race: the world's grey fathers had lost Eden but

> still Paradise lay
> In some green shade or fountain.

In his tent Abraham might converse with angels.   As a more modern poet has stated the same thought:

> What bard,
> At the height of his vision can deem
> Of God, of the world, of the soul
> With a plainness as near
> As flashing as Moses felt
> When he lay in the night by his flock
> On the starlit Arabian waste?

It is such glimpses into Eternity—

> I saw eternity the other night
> Like a great ring of pure and endless light—

that make Vaughan's charm, but they are rare, and there are long flat intervening passages.   Vaughan was Welsh—Silurist he calls himself after the ancient Silures of South Wales—and his English sometimes suggests that Welsh was his native tongue.

The poems of Thomas Traherne (1637?–1674) lay unknown for more than two centuries.   Their discovery in 1903 revealed a poet worthy to be named with Herbert, Crashaw, and Vaughan.   His mysticism is more absolute than Vaughan's. It was only in rare and transcendent moments that Vaughan recovered his childhood's vision.   Traherne recaptured it by "high reason", and possessed it thenceforth as a thing of every-day.   Heaven lies about us here and now, if we will but look with the eyes which God has made on purpose that through them He may behold the beauty of His creation and rejoice. Our beatific vision is His:

> Our blessedness to see
> Is even to the Deity
> A beatific vision!   He attains
> His ends while we enjoy.   He in us reigns.

Traherne was not a master of verse; he proclaimed his gospel less clearly in his *Poems of Felicity* than in the lovely, translucent prose of his *Centuries of Meditations*.

Andrew Marvell (1621–1678) was the only Puritan among these Metaphysicals; no sour precisian, however, but a humanist, a wit, and a high-minded patriot who could praise Cromwell without defaming Charles:

> He nothing common did or mean
> Upon that memorable scene:
>> But with his keener eye
>> The axe's edge did try:
> Nor called the Gods with vulgar spite
> To vindicate his helpless right,
>> But bow'd his comely head,
>> Down as upon a bed.

As M.P. for Hull after the Restoration he maintained a manly independence. His Satires were written then, his poetry mostly between 1650 and 1653, when he was tutor to Lady Mary Fairfax at Appleton House. His verses smell of its small meadows and gardens. Marvell's feeling for Nature, though not mystical, rises in *The Garden* to a kind of ecstasy. In *Appleton House* we find Wordsworthian touches of minute observation:

> And through the hazel boughs espy
> The hatching throstle's shining eye,

touches that please even more than his graceful little pastorals. His love-poems were mostly tissues of conceits, but in *The Definition of Love* the wit is daringly metaphysical:

> My love is of a birth as rare
>> As 'tis for object strange and high:
> It was begotten by despair
>> Upon impossibility;

and in *To his Coy Mistress* wit is shot through with passion. In these poems Marvell is the supreme metaphysical poet. Generally, though not always, his fondness for conceit is controlled by the masculine taste that makes his *Horatian Ode to Cromwell* truly and nobly classical. In his most characteristic poems, as the *Song of the Emigrants in Bermuda* and *The Nymph Complaining for the Death of her Fawn*, we think not of influences, metaphysical or classical, only of the "witty delicacy", as Lamb called it, the clean, terse style, the simple, firmly handled metre. His central thought was simple too, clearly uttered in *A Dialogue between the Resolved Soul and Created Pleasure*:

> Earth cannot show so brave a sight
> As when a single soul doth fence
> The batteries of alluring sense;
> And heaven views it with delight.

To the second edition of *Paradise Lost* Marvell prefixed some lines which anticipate Dryden's treatment of that poem:

> Well mightst thou scorn thy readers to allure
> With tinkling rhyme, of thy own sense secure;
> While the Town-Bays writes all the while and spells,
> And like a pack-horse tires with all his bells:
> Their fancies like our bushy-points appear,
> The poets tag them, we for fashion wear.
> I too transported by the mode offend,
> And while I meant to praise thee, must commend.
> Thy verse created like thy theme sublime
> In number, weight and measure needs not rime.

The difference between Marvell's style and Milton's is instructive in view of the changes that were coming.

Abraham Cowley (1618–1667) was the most popular poet of the day, to Langbaine, even in 1692, the first of English poets. Two generations later Pope could ask, "Who now reads Cowley?" Both facts are significant. *The Faerie Queene* made Cowley a poet at the age of twelve and his *Poetical Blossoms* were published when he was fourteen, by which time he had gone over to the Metaphysicals. He had another vein, the playful, in which he praised wine in his *Anacreontics* and catalogued his (supposed) mistresses in *The Chronical*; but what his contemporaries admired was his pointed wit. It was wit without passion. Cowley was capable of affection as his moving elegy on his friend Hervey shows, but not of passion. (Imagine Donne content with "a mistress moderately fair"!) His wit found an unresisting medium in the so-called *Pindarique Ode*. Horace unable to scan Pindar had called his numbers "lawless": in lawless numbers and structureless arabesques of verse Cowley coruscated to the admiration of his contemporaries. But when conceits went out of fashion, and wit came to mean not what was never thought of before, but what oft was thought but ne'er so well expressed, Cowley could not stand. The most significant thing about him is his interest in science: he praised Bacon and Hobbes, and helped to found the Royal Society. The new science fascinated his bright, dry intellect. He did not perceive that its spirit was alien to a poetry rooted in the fantasies of the old philosophy. So he fell between two stools. In Pope's day he was remembered chiefly for his pleasant prose essays with occasional verses interspersed: "I prefer", Lamb said later, "the graceful rambling of his essays to the courtly elegance and ease of Addison—abstracting from the latter's exquisite humour".

These are the chief poets, Milton excepted, of the Caroline age. Some others, mostly Sons of Ben, are remembered for one or two poems. The oldest of them, Bishop Richard Corbet (1580–1636), is rather Jacobean than Caroline by date, but the light grace of his famous "Farewell, rewards and fairies" allies him with Herrick and Suckling. Another Bishop, Henry King (1592–1669), a friend of Donne's, was the author of many complimentary verses: the exquisite "Tell me no more how fair she is" is worthy to stand beside Carew's "Ask me no more where Jove bestows"; but he is still better remembered for his moving *Exequy* on his wife. Sir Richard Fanshawe (1608–1666) deserves to be remembered for his graceful translations from Horace's Odes, and for his own Ode, in Horace's manner, on the Royal proclamation of 1630 commanding the gentry to reside on their estates. Then there is Charles Cotton (1630–1687), author of the second part of *The Compleat Angler* and translator of Montaigne, who wrote many poems of which both the language and the wit are natural and pleasing if not inspired. Moreover, the Commonwealth witnessed the issue not only of countless collections of sermons, but of numerous miscellanies of verse which by no means bear the stamp of the Puritan temper of the age: *The Academy of Compliments* (1650); *The Marrow of Compliments* (1655); *Wits Interpreter* (1655); *Parnassus Biceps* (1656); *Choyce Drollery* (1656)—these are only a few of such miscellanies, the titles of which suggest that England was still Merry England at heart even under the rule of the saints.

Chapter Fourteen

MILTON

JOHN MILTON (1608–1674) towers over all his contemporaries "like Teneriffe or Atlas unremoved". His father, a prosperous London scrivener, discerned his genius early, had him carefully schooled and tutored, gave him seven years at Cambridge, and six more of studious leisure in his country house at Horton, and finally supplied him with funds for a tour in Italy. Moreover, being himself a skilled musician, he had him taught the viol and the organ. At thirty Milton was perhaps the most accomplished young man in England, so far as music and books could make him; of some other things more important for the conduct of life he was and remained invincibly ignorant.

In 1639 he came back to England to bear his part in her struggle for liberty. On the way home he learned of the death of his bosom friend, Charles Diodati. It was an irreparable loss: in later years Milton had many admirers but no intimates. He settled in London, teaching his two nephews while he meditated the great poem that was to be his contribution to the national effort and justify his long apprenticeship to the Muse. The meeting of the Long Parliament in 1640 filled him with exalted hopes. Surely God was about to reveal Himself anew to men, and first, as His wont was, to His Englishmen: Parliament would make God's will prevail in Church and State, and pave the way for Christ's second coming. In 1641 he threw himself into the pamphlet war against Prelacy.

About Whitsuntide 1642 he suddenly went down into Oxfordshire, and returned with a wife, a girl of sixteen, the daughter of a thriftless Cavalier squire. Six weeks later she left him for a visit to her parents, and refused to return. Her desertion dealt him a wound that never healed. Milton was of a nature at once chaste and ardent; he had staked his hopes of happiness on "a contented marriage", and now he was indissolubly yoked to "a dull and spiritless mate" who refused to live with him. In the next two years he issued four tracts demanding the legalisation of divorce for incompatibility. (Some of these were unlicensed, which led to his famous plea

for unlicensed printing in the *Areopagitica*.)   After Naseby his
wife returned and threw herself at his feet; he took her back,
and next year, when Oxford fell, received her refugee family
under his roof.   He might now have resumed poetry—he had
allowed his early poems to be printed in 1645—but pupils and
in-laws made his house a Babel.

In 1648 he returned to politics, and became, first as a
volunteer later as a salaried official, the literary champion of the
regicides.   The Council of State rewarded his *Tenure of Kings
and Magistrates* by making him their Secretary for Foreign
Tongues, in which capacity he wrote his two *Defensiones pro
Populo Anglicano* in reply to shocked champions of Royalty on
the Continent.   In 1652 he became totally blind, his eyes
"over-plied in liberty's defence".   Thereafter his official duties
were gradually lightened, so that in 1655 he began to meditate,
and in 1658 to write, his long-deferred epic.

After the Restoration Milton lay in hiding till the Act of
Oblivion in August 1660 made it safe for him to reappear.
Thenceforth, politics being forbidden, he devoted himself
(except for one sally against Popery in 1673) to poetry and to
the composition of his *De Doctrina Christiana*, which came to
light in 1823.

From the time he left Cambridge, circumstances drove
Milton more and more to the Left both in religion and in
politics.   Prelatical tyranny made him join the Presbyterians,
till their reception of his tracts on divorce convinced him that
Presbyters were as tyrannous as Prelates, and drove him into
the Independent camp.   But as time went on he grew too
independent for any church that had other members than John
Milton: his *De Doctrina* is inscribed in Latin "John Milton,
Englishman, to all the Churches".   If he sympathised with
any sect at last, it was with the Quakers.   Similarly in politics
he moved from Constitutional Monarchy to Parliamentary
Republicanism, and then to something not unlike Dictatorship.
Liberty was his lodestar always.   But he was no democrat; he
thought that liberty was possible only to the wise and good.
His ideal, in fact, was aristocracy in the true sense, government
by the best.   He thought to find it first in the Long Parliament, then in the Council of State, then in Cromwell.   But
even Cromwell disappointed him, and the Restoration found
him "crying to the earth and stones", an unteachable, indomit-
able idealist.

Almost from boyhood Milton took poetry for his vocation, and laboured by study and self-discipline to fit himself to write something that the world would not willingly let die.   He was himself from the first.   "He confessed to me", Dryden says, "that Spenser was his original"; but though his lines *On the Death of a Fair Infant* show Spenser's influence clearly enough, even these lines, written at seventeen, have something Miltonic in them, some promise of the *os magna soniturum*, not in the thought, which is a mere boyish conceit, but in the choice diction and the stateliness which he has imparted to the rhyme royal by prolonging the final line.

This promise was more than fulfilled in the *Nativity Ode*, which he wrote at twenty-one.   Some conceits still cling to the opening and the close, and there is some ostentation of learning; but how nobly the poem evolves in long crescendo and diminuendo, as the great stanza peals on like a carillon proclaiming "*hodie Christus natus est*".   There are some notable differences between the *Ode* and *Paradise Lost*.   The heathen gods are not identified with the rebel angels, as they are in *Paradise Lost*. Christ's birth drives Satan from more than half of his usurped sway: not so, as we shall see, in *Paradise Lost*.   The difference in temper is still more striking: there is a note of tender adoration in the *Ode* such as we never hear in the epic:

> Oh, run! prevent them with thy humble ode,
> And lay it lowly at his blessed feet.

'Humble', 'lowly'—not thus does the poet of *Paradise Lost* speak of his "adventurous song".

> My hasting days fly on with full career,
> But my late spring no bud nor blossom showeth—

so Milton wrote of himself on his twenty-third birthday.   He made nothing of having written the *Nativity Ode*, the brilliant epitaph on Shakespeare (for which he was inclined later to apologise), and the stately verses *On Time* and *At a Solemn Music*, not to speak of *Arcades* and the *Epitaph on the Marchioness of Winchester*, which, formal as they are, contain such magical phrases as

> branching elm star-proof,

and such cadences as

> Here be tears of perfect moan,
> Weept for thee in Helicon.

All that was prentice work.   Even in the Horton poems, which
seem to us so perfect, he was only pluming his wings for a
loftier flight.   *L'Allegro* and *Il Penseroso* are studies, *Comus*
and *Lycidas* occasional pieces.   *Comus* was written in 1634 to
grace the installation of the Earl of Bridgewater as Viceroy of
Wales in Ludlow Castle, in the hall of which its action ends.
The plot is slight and the issue foreseen; but we must not judge
Comus as we judge a regular play.   *Comus* was the libretto of a
masque which depended for its effect not on speech only but
on song, dance, and spectacle.   The blank verse is like early
Shakespeare with touches of Fletcher, so smooth that at one
point it glides easily into rhymed couplets.   Sir Henry Wotton
praised the "Doric delicacy" of the songs; indeed the whole
play is Doric in its purity of line; Doric but romantic too, full
of classical reminiscences but also of echoes or overtones of
notes struck by Spenser and Shakespeare and Fletcher.   The
moral is neither classic nor romantic; it is Puritan:

> Love Virtue; she alone is free.
> She can teach you how to climb
> Higher than the sphery chime.

A shining creed; but it casts a dark shadow:

> But evil on itself shall back recoil,
> And mix no more with goodness, when at last,
> Gathered like scum, and settled to itself,
> It shall be in eternal restless change
> Self-fed and self-consumed.

The Hell of *Paradise Lost* is prefigured in these lines.

L'Allegro and *Il Penseroso* describe specimen days and nights
(not, as is often said, a single day and night) in the poet's life
at Horton.   In cheerful mood he wakes at the song of the lark,
and goes out to watch the rustics at work, or climbs the
Chilterns to see their sports, or runs up to town for a masque,
wedding, or play.   So too in *Il Penseroso* the song of the
nightingale, the sight of the moon, the seat by the fire, the
reading of philosophy or poetry "in some high lonely tower"—
these are alternative delights.   And always he ends with music.
The style is less Shakespearian than in *Comus*, more Jonsonian,
but with a fineness beyond Jonson.   The iambic tetrameters
are enlivened with trochees, twice as freely in *L'Allegro* as in
the sober *Penseroso*.   The *legato* close of *L'Allegro* has a linked

sweetness matched only by the close of *Comus*.

Lycidas is a pastoral elegy on Edward King, who had been at college with Milton and was drowned in 1637. Criticisms of *Lycidas* are at bottom criticisms of the pastoral convention. "Easy, vulgar, and therefore disgusting", Johnson called it; but a convention to which we owe *Lycidas*, *Adonais*, and *Thyrsis* needs no defence. It does not matter whether King and Milton had been close friends like Clough and Arnold, or barely acquainted like Keats and Shelley. *Lycidas* is not a cry of personal grief. The thought of this young poet "dead ere his prime" makes Milton ask what study and self-discipline avail if one should die before they bear fruit. The thought of this young priest's death makes him turn wrathfully on the corrupt clergy whom death has spared—but Judgement will not spare. From such thoughts he turns for a little to "dally with false surmise", then lifts his eyes to Heaven, where he will find his reward, as Lycidas has found his. These thoughts, not in themselves remarkable, are invested with a splendour of words and music that made Tennyson call *Lycidas* the touch-stone of poetic taste. It moves in successive waves of rising emotion, from each of which, as it breaks, the poet retires to his pastoral ground. These undulations are communicated to, and by, the verse, which runs not into stanzas but *laisses* of varied length, variously rhymed, with unrhymed verses and trimeters here and there, plastic to every change in the poet's mood. For Milton's biography the most significant thing in *Lycidas* is the outburst against the Laudian clergy. Spenser too had discharged some arrows at idle shepherds from under the shield of the pastoral; but Milton is far angrier and more threatening: the gulf between Anglican and Puritan had widened perilously since 1579.

After *Lycidas* Milton wrote no English verse for twenty years except a fragment of tragedy (to which we shall recur) and a handful of sonnets. Milton's sonnets are not love-poems, nor are they in sequence. They are occasional pieces, ranging from scoldings at the detractors of his divorce pamphlets to invitations to dinner, compliments to pious ladies, and exhortations to great generals. Two stand out above the rest—the noble sonnet *On his Blindness* and the trumpet-blast of *On the Late Massacres in Piedmont*. Few as they are, Milton's sonnets are important in the history of English poetry. The form had quite gone out of fashion in England. When

Milton took it up he went behind Shakespeare and Spenser back to the pyramidal Petrarchan model. One liberty he allowed himself; as often as not he runs the sense on from the octave to the sestet; but only once does he end with a couplet. When the Romantics revived the form they took Milton for their model rather than Shakespeare; it was Dorothy's reading of Milton's sonnets that made Wordsworth a sonneteer.

Milton knew he was a great man. Great men are those who do great deeds, or counsel their doing, or celebrate them when done. His task was to write a great poem which should be "doctrinal and exemplary for a nation". At first he thought of an Arthuriad; but study convinced him that the Arthurian story was a mass of fables; and a national epic must be true. About 1641 he made notes of ninety-eight possible subjects for tragedy, sixty Biblical, thirty-eight British. The one that attracted him most was the Fall; he drafted four scenarios for a play on that theme, and even wrote the opening lines of the speech, "Oh thou, that with surpassing glory crowned", which he used afterwards in *Paradise Lost*. Then, for reasons already mentioned, he put all that aside. In 1655, when he had been blind for three years, his official duties were so far lightened that he could begin to think of poetry again. But now it seemed to him that the national epic which he so long contemplated had in a sense been written. Was not *this* the heroic age of England? And had not he celebrated its deeds and its heroes in his two *Defensiones*? So he turned to the other theme which had once attracted him, and resolved to make an epic of that. He meditated it for three years, and in 1658, being now on the pension list, sat down at last to write. He finished the poem in 1663 or 1664. These dates are important. In 1658 the good old cause was not yet lost; in 1660 "the Philistines triumphed, and the ark of God was taken"; the shadow of that crowning disaster darkens the last books of *Paradise Lost*.

For two centuries after it appeared *Paradise Lost* imposed itself on the Protestant imagination with an authority almost Scriptural. Even the few who did not take it literally saw in the Fall a symbol of some primeval catastrophe which had defeated God's purpose in creation. When Darwin made Milton's cosmogony incredible, our fathers, while surrendering his theodicy, still counted *Paradise Lost* the greatest of English poems. To-day a determined attempt is being made to dethrone Milton even as a poet. We are told that he corrupted the English language; that he began that "dissociation of sensibility" which has vitiated our poetry ever since; that his eye was poor, and his ear so despotic that the evolution of his periods is guided not by sense but sound. There is something in these charges, but not much.

Addison put the first of them more elegantly when he said of Milton that the language "sunk under him". Milton did invent a new diction for *Paradise Lost*, as Spenser did for *The Faerie Queene*, and for much the same reason: he felt that the language of serious poetry had been vulgarised by popular writers like Quarles; that he must raise it to the height of his great argument; and, since he had been writing Latin for years, to Latin he naturally turned. But he did not so much coin new words from Latin as re-mint words already current in English but debased by vulgar handling, restoring their character and evocative power by so using them as to recall their original sense. It is less easy to defend the occasional lapses into Latin idiom and syntax into which his love of conciseness led him. But on balance he enriched poetic diction more than he corrupted it. The sins of his imitators should not be visited on Milton.

If "dissociation of sensibility" means that thought and passion are not fused in Milton as they are (say) in the best of Donne, the charge holds as against the theological parts of *Paradise Lost*, notably those speeches in which "God the Father turns a school divine". But of the really great things in the poem it is simply not true. Blake put it better: "Milton wrote in fetters when he wrote of Angels and God, and at liberty when of Devils and Hell". It is the chief structural flaw in *Paradise Lost* that the interest declines after the first two books, in which Milton wrote "of Devils and Hell", his imagination impassioned and free to create unfettered by the Bible story.

If, however, the critics mean that there is no such fusion of sense-impressions in Milton as there is (say) in Shakespeare, the charge invites to a comparison of the two poets in respect of their sense-endowment, a comparison which will help us to deal with the last charge also. Certainly Milton had not Shakespeare's quick eye for movement. Nor was he observant of near and little things; he seems always to gaze into the distance. This sense of distance, of space, was strangely

MILTON

3222222

2222222

heightened by his blindness. His prayer to the Celestial Light—

> Shine inward, and the mind through all her powers
> Irradiate—

was answered: creation widened on his view: his inward vision surveyed the depths of interstellar space,

> From Libra to the fleecy star that bears
> Andromeda far off Atlantic seas.

Milton is the supreme master of the material sublime. Even Dante's universe, compared to his, is no bigger than "a star of smallest magnitude close by the moon".

Milton's ear may have been no finer than Shakespeare's by nature, but it was much more highly cultivated. His father was a composer of distinction; his home was full of music; music was his lifelong solace, and no poet has written so movingly of its power to exalt and soothe:

> . . . such as raised
> To highth of noblest temper heroes old . . .
> Nor wanting power to mitigate and suage
> With solemn touches troubled thoughts, and chase
> Anguish and doubt and fear and sorrow and pain
> From mortal or immortal minds.

His eye dwelling habitually on the distant, and his ear delighting most in orchestral harmonies, his verse assumed a corresponding amplitude. As in rhyme he found stanza too strait for *Lycidas*, so in blank verse his units are periods often of many lines:

> As when far off at sea a fleet descried
> Hangs in the clouds, by equinoctial winds
> Close sailing from Bengala or the isles
> Of Ternate or Tidore, whence merchants bring
> Their spicy drugs, they on the trading flood
> Through the wide Ethiopian to the Cape
> Ply, stemming nightly toward the pole: so seemed
> Far off the flying fiend.

Rejecting the trivial embellishment of rhyme, he exhausted the resources of the language for other embellishments that should give the pleasure we expect from verse—beauty, variety, and flow of rhythm. But "the true beauty of verse", as he calls it, depends not only on rhythm but on what is rhythmed, the actual sounds of vowels and consonants chiming in alliteration and assonance. Milton uses consonantal alliteration more artfully, if less lavishly, than Spenser: in the passage we have quoted it serves to link the end of the period to its beginning. Now and then we find a lovely vowel alliteration:

> The angel ended, and in Adam's ear.

Assonance of long vowels makes

> To save the Athenian walls from ruin bare,

perhaps the most beautiful line in the language. Considerations of sound, then, constantly dictated Milton's choice of words; but they did not deflect the current of his argument.

Nor is it true that he never fuses sense-impressions. Impressions of sight and smell are fused in the passage we have quoted, and in the similar passage where

> out at sea north-east winds blow
> Sabaean odours from the spicy shore
> Of Araby the blest.

Fusion of sound and smell, rare in all poets, is exemplified in *Comus*, where the Lady's song

> Rose like a steam of rich distilled perfumes.

Fusion of sight and sound yields some of Milton's happiest effects, none happier than the description of the banyan grove,

> a pillared shade,
> High over-arched, and echoing walks between.

Where Milton was hopelessly inferior to Shakespeare was not in sense-endowment but in imaginative sympathy. He could not take a hundred shapes like Shakespeare. He was a humourless idealist, better read in books than in human nature. Pride, heroism, constancy—qualities importing strength of will —these he understood from himself, and has portrayed sympathetically in Satan and Samson and Abdiel; but what other qualities has he sympathetically portrayed?

The freedom of the will is the keystone of Milton's creed. His theodicy amounts to this: God made Adam free; he abused his freedom and fell; God is blameless. That is how he justifies God's ways *to man*. But man's fall is the sequel to another and more stupendous tragedy, the fall of the angels. By lifting his argument to that plane Milton raises the problem of evil in a more intractable form, the nature of which, veiled by poetry in *Paradise Lost*, is clear enough in the *De Doctrina*.   Milton held that God created all things, not out of *prima materia* (as Dante held), but out of Himself.   Out of Himself He made matter and spirit (which is but a finer kind of matter); He made evil also.   There was evil in Heaven before Satan rebelled: Pride, Lust, Ire, and Avarice were there.   At the exaltation of the Son these forces erupted and were cast forth.   But God suffered them to escape from Hell and infect the Earth.   And then the tragedy was re-enacted, but with a difference—"Man shall find grace".   But he must lay hold of it by an act of free-will.   The elect do this effortlessly, but for the ordinary man salvation means an act of choice constantly renewed. When Milton began the poem, his exalted hopes for mankind, though damped by repeated disappointments, were not all quenched.   God's speeches in Book III hold out good hope of salvation for the ordinary man: He will exclude none from His mercy but such as neglect His grace.   But in Book XII Michael prophesies that after the Apostolic Age religion will again grow corrupt; some few elect there will always be, but the rest, "far greater part", will sink into superstition; and so the world will go on,

> To good malignant, to bad men benign,

till the day of Judgement, when the wicked shall be turned into Hell, and its gates shut down on them for ever.

Paradise Lost will always be admired for its style, its verse, and its command of the material sublime; but it will not hold a place among the world's greatest poems unless men continue to find in its substance something of enduring and universal value.   They will not find that in a theology which reveals no sense of the mystery of evil, and makes God's command an arbitrary ukase and man's redemption a legal transaction. They will find it, if at all, in the heroic temper of the poem, its unconquerable faith in reason and the power of the will.

When Milton's Quaker friend Elwood handed him back the manuscript of *Paradise Lost*, he observed, "Thou hast said much here of Paradise lost, but what hast thou to say of Paradise found?"   The question showed Milton that, though he had said something of the Redemption, he had not said enough for the Friends whom he respected.   *Paradise Regained* is a sequel to *Paradise Lost*, but not a continuation of it.   The two poems differ widely in scope and treatment.   In his tract *The Reason of Church Government urged against Prelaty* Milton had distinguished two kinds of epic, 'diffuse' like the *Iliad*, and 'brief' like the Book of Job. *Paradise Regained* belongs to the latter kind. It resembles its prototype not only in being brief but in containing more argument than action; Job's patience too foreshadows Christ's.

If Milton's theme was the Redemption, why did he choose an episode so briefly related in the Gospels? The answer is clear; Paradise was lost when Adam yielded to the Tempter, regained when Jesus withstood him:

> Winning by conquest what the first man lost
> By fallacy surpris'd.

In whatever sense Milton held the doctrine of the Atonement, he nowhere dwells on the miraculous efficacy of Christ's sacrifice in washing away sin; for him redemption means the victory of reason over passion; and of this the Temptation is the supreme example.

The Restoration shattered Milton's hopes of civil and religious freedom; but he still possessed that inner freedom which comes of willing submission to God's will, and can raise itself an Eden in the waste wilderness. It was in this spirit of resignation that he wrote *Paradise Regained*. In the order of the temptations he follows St. Luke. He treats the first temptation lightly as a preliminary test of Jesus' claim to Sonship; the third he regards as merely a parting insult flung out by the baffled Tempter. It is on the second that he expatiates —"the kingdoms of the world and the glory of them", to which he adds an item not warranted by Scripture—the temptation of learning. Power and glory are disposed of by arguments familiar to Stoic and Christian alike; but the disparagement of Greek poetry and philosophy is strange. Can Milton have gone so far beyond Arianism as to represent Jesus as possessed by Jewish prejudice? No; he is speaking his own mind. There is one thing needful, and it is not learning. The warrior-saints of the Commonwealth were not learned. The true believer needs only the Word of God, and the Inner Light to read it by. The Humanist in Milton has succumbed to the Puritan.

The virtues that the poem exalts are the restrictive, Puritan virtues; not love and mercy, but patience, fortitude, temperance, self-control. In truth the Jesus of *Paradise Regained*, who stoops to sophistry and calls the people "an indiscriminate rabble", is more like Milton himself, the controversialist, the aristocrat, than the Jesus of the Gospels.   The Adversary has lost his original brightness, the ruined archangel shrunk into a grey dissembler.   Yet his two great speeches—

> 'Tis true.   I am that spirit unfortunate,

and

> Let that come when it comes.   All hope is lost—

are strangely moving; nay more, though Jesus denounces them as lies, they do not strike us as wholly false.   Milton has put so much of himself into Satan that we cannot deny him all sympathy.   Had Milton himself known despair in 1660? Was it that knowledge which has made Satan's words so poignant?

The style of *Paradise Regained* is in marked contrast to that of *Paradise Lost*.   The opening books of that poem are starred with splendid similes; there is not a single simile in the first three books of *Paradise Regained*.   Milton has allowed himself two purple patches, as if to show that he had not lost his skill: the description of the Table in the Wilderness is full of that magic which always touches Milton's style when he thinks of mediaeval romance:

> Of Fairy Damsels met in forest wide
> By Knights of *Logres*, or of *Lyones*,
> *Lancelot* or *Pelleas*, or *Pellenore*;

the magnificent eulogy on Athens is the Humanist's adieu to the glory that was Greece.   Elsewhere, and markedly in the narrative, the style is deliberately quiet and plain, so plain that many readers (but not the poets!) find it bald.   It is Milton's speaking voice.   The vocabulary is less heavily Latinised than in *Paradise Lost*, the syntax less periodic.   The verse matches the style—not sonorous, but moving quietly on with constant subtle variations of pause and cadence, and here and there a beauty of chiming vowels that defies analysis:

> Food to *Elijah* bringing even and morn.

Paradise Regained and *Samson Agonistes* were published together in 1674, but their composition was separated by some years, during which Milton's mood changed from resignation to rebellion, a mood no doubt more painful, but for that very

M

reason a symptom of returning strength, like the growth of Samson's hair. And as strength returned the hope revived that God would avenge His own elect even in this life. To speak politically, he began to hope that the Stuart tyranny would not last for ever; perhaps he saw signs of the rise of the Whig opposition which presently overthrew it. Charles's policy of indulgence, Baxter tells us, "made every Protestant heart to tremble"; which encouraged Milton to issue in 1673 his tract *Of True Religion*, a product of the same period and the same mood as produced *Samson*.

As far back as 1641 Milton had noted Samson as a possible subject for tragedy. What drew him to it now was the resemblance that he saw between Samson and himself. His dedicated and abstemious youth, his marriage with a daughter of the enemy, his triumphs in liberty's defence, the ruin of his cause, his blindness, even his gout—for all these he found parallels in Samson. But at one point the resemblance ends: Samson had sinned, as Milton had not done; he had sinned and been justly punished. This is what links Samson to *Paradise Lost* and *Paradise Regained*, and makes it the third article in Milton's confession of faith. Adam yielded to temptation and fell; Jesus resisted it and stood; Samson yielded, repented, and was received again into God's grace.

Johnson complained that *Samson* had a beginning and an end but no middle, not seeing that the intervening episodes mark the stages by which Samson moves from self-reproach and self-pity through despair to resolve and action, the crisis being the entrance of Dalilah. The chorus have dropped gall into his wounds; Manoah's hopefulness has plunged him in despair; then Dalilah enters. Her pleas and blandishments rouse Samson to a flaming wrath which burns up despair, so that he drives Harapha from the stage with insults and threats, and defies the Philistines' command. Then comes another change. His manhood and faith reasserted, he hears God's voice once more; an inner impulsion prompts him to rise and follow the returned messenger to triumph and death. Death, not suicide; Milton is careful to acquit Samson of that.

Samson is strictly modelled on Greek tragedy, except that the stasima are not strophic. In particular it recalls the *Oedipus Coloneus*: in both, the heroes are blind, remain seated against a leafy background, and leave the stage to meet their end. Its purpose, too, is Greek. Tragedy, says Milton after

Aristotle, "has power, by raising pity and fear or terror, to purge the mind of these and such-like passions".   Whatever it does for the reader, this tragedy purged Milton's own bosom of some perilous stuff that had festered there since his wife's desertion, and allowed him in a parable to defy the Philistines and reassert Eternal Providence.   *Samson* is the most personal of Milton's poems, and the most passionate.   The agonised cry of

> Oh, dark, dark, dark, amid the blaze of noon,

and the despairing moan of

> All otherwise to me my thoughts portend,

are the most moving things he ever wrote.

Many who admire Milton's poetry are repelled by his theology, his misogyny, and his hard, unforgiving nature. Hereafter perhaps a sterner age will do more justice to his faith and matchless fortitude.

Chapter Fifteen

COWLEY TO DRYDEN

THE change which was coming over the spirit of poetry, even while Milton was composing the great poem on which his mind had dwelt for so long, is clearly reflected in the work of Dryden's immediate predecessors. In Butler's *Hudibras* (1662, '63, '78) one can recapture the feeling of anger and relief which Pepys has described so vividly as breaking out when Monk declared for a free Parliament, inaugurating the end of the rule of saints and major-generals: "Indeed it was past imagination both the greatness and the suddenness of it. . . . All along burning and roasting of rumps. Bowbells and all the bells in all the churches were ringing." Anyone who was in New York when, with the advent of two-per-cent beer, the passing of prohibition was heralded, had something of the same experience, the general sense of relief, for just so will the human spirit react from any too prolonged endeavour to hold it above its capacity for restraint and well-doing by compulsion. *Hudibras* is a strange poem, a burlesque satire on the fanaticism and knavery of Presbyterian and Independent, interwoven with satire on other frauds and follies of the period, and with disquisitions on themes of more general import such as marriage. Dryden was critical of Butler's choice of the octosyllabic metre, but for Butler's purpose, the degradation and ridicule of the godly, it was entirely suitable. Butler had no thought of drawing any of the Commonwealth worthies, not even Cromwell, as Dryden would later draw Shaftesbury, doing justice to his nobler qualities, as a "great, bad man". Sir Hudibras, the Presbyterian knight, and his

> Squire whose name was Ralph
> That in the adventure went his half,
> Though writers, for more stately tone,
> Do call him Ralpho, 'tis all one:
> And when we can with metre safe,
> We'll call him so ; if not plain Ralph;
> For rhyme the rudder is of verses
> With which like ships they steer their courses,

are a pair at once of arrant knaves and canting zealots, each

ready at any moment and at any length to argue for their
respective principles, the Scriptural authority for Presbyterian
order, "provincial, classic, national", or the infallibility of the
inner light.   The exploits which they undertake, in ludicrous
fashion and with disastrous effects for themselves, are in tune
with the spirit of the time, the suppression of all popular
pastimes such as bear-baiting, etc.:

> A vile assembly 'tis, that can
> No more be prov'd by scripture than
> Provincial, classic, national,
> Mere human-creature cobwebs all.
> Thirdly it is idolatrous;
> For when men run awhoring thus
> With their intentions, whatsoe'er
> The thing be, whether dog or bear,
> It is idolatrous and pagan
> No less than worshipping of Dagon.

With which compare what Baxter has to say of all that made
England merry.   Equally characteristic is the resort of Sir
Hudibras to the astrologer, for then, as now in time of war, the
future was scanned by the help of the stars if not yet of the
pyramids.   But while the contemptuous and witty satire of
the godly is the main theme, Butler touches on other themes
relevant to the period.   The long and rather tedious wooing
of the widow by Hudibras is, we take it, a satire not only on
hypocrisy but on the contrast between the treatment in the
romances of which Dorothy Osborne was so interested a reader
and the actual financial basis of marriage.   In parts too, as in
the long disquisition on marriage, Butler lets his mind range
freely, as he was already doing in other poems which did not
appear till after his death, in the genuine *Remains* (1759).   Here
he satirised the doings of the Royal Society as Swift was to do
later, in *The Elephant in the Moon*, which proves to be a mouse
in the telescope; and the to-and-fro arguments of the Heroical
Plays, *Repartees between Cat and Puss*; and he dilates on the
Weakness and Misery of Man in a vein more sombre than satirical,
for Charles and his crew were almost justifying the forebodings
of the Saints and Fanatics.   They

> Make jests of greater dangers far
> Than those they trembled at in war;
> Till unawares they've laid a train

> To blow the public up again;
> Dally with horror, and in sport
> Rebellion and destruction court,
> And make Fanatics, in despight
> Of all their madness, reason right
> And vouch to all they have foreshown,
> As other monsters oft have done,
> Although from truth and sense as far
> As all their other maggots are:
> For things said false, and never meant,
> Do oft prove true by accident.

In satirising Charles and the court, *Satire upon the Licentious Age of Charles*, the disappointed and neglected Butler was moving with the tide of disillusion to which Pepys bears witness. Satire, direct, undisguised, political satire of a peculiarly savage kind, was becoming the vogue. Not the least truculent, but the most sincere in his disgust and indignation, was that sweet singer of the previous age, Andrew Marvell. Not all the satires ascribed to him are certainly his, but the best, the *Last Instruction to a Painter* (1678), one of a series suggested by an adulatory poem of Waller's, is certainly Marvell's. It is coarse enough on the loves and ladies of the court, and fierce enough on the humiliations of the Dutch invasion of the Medway. But Marvell can rise to poetry which is not much in evidence in these satires generally:

> Paint last the King, and a dead shade of night,
> Only dispers'd by a weak taper's light;
> And those bright gleams that dart along and glare
> From his clear eyes, yet these too dark with care.
>
> .   .   .   .
>
> Shake then the room, and all his curtains tear,
> And with blue streaks infect the taper clear:
> While the pale ghosts his eye doth fixt admire
> Of grandsire Henry and of Charles his sire.
> Harry sits down, and in his open side
> The grizly wound reveals of which he died,
> And ghastly Charles, turning his collar low,
> The purple thread about his neck doth show:
> Then whispering to his son in words unheard,
> Through the lock'd door both of them disappear'd.

The wider sweep that satire in such an age of disillusionment was bound to take is seen, as in Butler's poem quoted above, in the dissolute Rochester's *A Satyr against Mankind*:

> Which is the basest creature, man or beast?
> Birds feed on birds, beasts on each other prey;
> But savage man alone, does man betray.
> Press'd by necessity, they kill for food;
> Man undoes man, to do himself no good.

John Oldham's *Satyres upon the Jesuits* (1681) appeared in the same year as Dryden first took the field on the court side. But the best of his satires is that *Address'd to a Friend that is about to leave the University and come abroad in the World*, with the parable of the wolf whose ambition to become a well-fed dog is checked by the sight of the marks of the collar on the dog's neck.

When one turns from satire to the poems of a higher ambition, the work of Dryden's predecessors, what one finds is: in Cowley the last extravagance of wit; in others a more natural vein of thought and feeling that, however, seldom rises above the commonplace, occasional elegance, occasional dignity. Davenant's *Gondibert* even with Hobbes's introduction sleeps on the shelves. But he could write some charming eulogy, as in *To the Queen entertain'd at Night by the Countess of Anglesea*, and *For the Lady Porter*. He is also the author of two lovely songs: "The lark now leaves his watery nest", and *To a Mistress Dying*, with its taking if daring hyperboles:

> From this vext world when we shall both retire,
>   Where all are lovers, and where all rejoice;
> I need not seek thee in the Heavenly Quire;
>   For I shall know Olivia by her voice;

and there is dignity in *The Christian's Reply to the Phylosopher*:

> O harmless death! whom still the valiant brave,
>   The wise expect, the sorrowful invite,
> And all the good embrace, who know the grave
>   A short dark passage to eternal life.

To Sir John Denham, Dryden assigns "strength", to Waller "sweetness". The former lives in text-books and some anthologies by his *Cooper's Hill*, an example of what Johnson called local poetry. Four lines that were added later *are* good poetry and exemplify well what Pope meant by correctness, the coherence of the rhetorical with the metrical accents, and the closed couplet structure:

> O could I flow like thee, and make thy stream
> My great example, as it is my theme!

> Though deep yet clear; though gentle yet not dull;
> Strong without rage, without o'erflowing full.

But it is in Waller, who took Cowley's place in Dryden's early eulogistic verses, that one sees the direction in which poetry was moving as "wit" fell out of fashion and "form" became the chief preoccupation. Waller's style has not yet acquired the "poetic diction" which was later to supply and disguise triviality of content, for trivial the thought is. Yet his lines run smoothly and catch at times a singing note which Dryden was to reproduce in his early complimentary addresses to Charles and others:

> While in the park I sing, the listening deer
> Attend my passion, and forget to fear.
> When to the beeches I report my flame,
> They bow their heads as if they felt the same.
> To gods appealing, when I reach their bowers
> With loud complaints, they answer me in showers.
> To thee a wild and cruel soul is given,
> More deaf than trees, and prouder than the heaven!

Of his shorter lyrics Johnson gave the preference, not unjustly, to that *To Amoret*:

> Fair, that you may truly know
> What you unto Thyrsis owe,
> I will tell you how I do
> Sacharissa love and you,

and to that beginning

> Anger in hasty words and blows,

describing the vanity of resisting love:

> So the tall stag, upon the brink
> Of some smooth stream about to drink,
> Surveying there his armed head,
> With shame remembers that he fled
> The scorned dogs, resolves to try
> The combat next: but if their cry
> Invade again his trembling ear
> He straight resumes his wonted fear,
> Leaves the untasted spring behind,
> And, winged with fear, outflies the wind.

Modern anthologists have preferred "Go lovely rose" and *On a Girdle*. Once at any rate Waller rose to a higher level, in *A Panegyric to my Lord Protector*, whose only fault, says Johnson, is its choice of a hero. To this one may add *Of the Last Verses in the Book*:

> The seas are quiet when the winds give o'er;
> So calm are we when passions are no more!
> For then we know, how vain it was to boast
> Of fleeting things, so certain to be lost.
> Clouds of affection from our younger eyes
> Conceal that emptiness which age descries.
> The soul's dark cottage, battered and decayed,
> Lets in new light through chinks which time has made;
> Stronger by weakness, wiser men become,
> As they draw near to their eternal home.
> Leaving the old, both worlds at once they view,
> That stand upon the threshold of the new.

John Dryden occupies much the same position relative to the poetry didactic, satirical, oratorical, conversational of the end of the seventeenth and greater part of the eighteenth century as Spenser did to Elizabethan poetry. In each period there had been precursors,—Wyatt and Surrey, Gascoigne, Sackville in the sixteenth century, Cowley, Denham, Davenant, Waller in the seventeenth, precursors whose tentatives were taken up, completed, and combined in the work of the greater successor. Each has been called a "poets' poet", so definite and continuous has been their influence not only on their immediate successors but recurringly in the history of our poetry. One may not subscribe to Johnson's dictum that "What was said of Rome adorned by Augustus may be applied to English poetry embellished by Dryden, *lateritiam invenit, marmoream reliquit*, he found it brick and he left it marble"; but Scott claimed for him without hesitation the third place among English poets, as Gray had done in the *Progress of Poetry*. Keats learned from Dryden to tighten up and strengthen his rhyming couplets in *Lamia*; and a recent critic, the late Professor Verrall, doubted whether the work of such nineteenth-century poets as Wordsworth and Tennyson would prove more permanent than that of Dryden. If some of us feel that with all its excellence Dryden's poetry lacks something, an element of pure beauty, a want which places it in a different class from the poetry of the very greatest poets, as Spenser and Shakespeare, and to us Wordsworth and Shelley and Keats, it is the more necessary to do full justice to what Dryden did achieve.

To do so is to trace the history of his development as a poet, the changes his style underwent as he turned from one theme to another in quest of an audience and a livelihood, for Dryden is the first English poet who lived mainly or wholly by his pen. No Elizabethan poet did so unless he was also a dramatist. There was only one choice for a Spenser, a Daniel, a Drayton, a Peele—either to find a patron of wealth or to write for the players, those "upstart crows beautified with our feathers"; and Dryden too had to live mainly by plays,—comedies, heroic dramas, tragedies, no one of which can honestly be said to be fully alive to-day. But Dryden was also the first English poet to discover and prove that a poet might play a part in the political life of the country, that if he was to secure the patronage of its chief dispenser, the court, it was not to be by the fair eyes of his Muse alone, but by taking an active part in the warfare which the court of Charles and James was waging against formidable odds—and in doing so there was always the risk, as Dryden was to find, of backing the wrong horse. But if in the end he was left to depend on his own resources, on the booksellers and the theatre, Dryden inaugurated a brief period in the history of our literature in which men of letters enjoyed a recognition and substantial patronage such as they had never enjoyed before, and have never enjoyed since. "There was perhaps never a time", writes Macaulay in his essay on Addison, "at which the rewards of literary merit were so splendid, at which men who could write well found such easy admittance into the most distinguished society, and to the highest honours of the state. The chiefs of both the great parties . . . patronised literature with emulous munificence." He goes on to illustrate from the fortunes of Congreve, Rowe, Hughes, Ambrose Philips, Gay, Prior, Swift, and Addison. Pope was excluded from political patronage by his Catholicism. The period ended with the accession of George I, who had no taste for "boetry or bainting", and the more sordid and economical corruption by which Sir Robert Walpole kept himself in power.

But if authors have a definite and responsive audience they must supply what that audience can appreciate. Poetry and prose alike had to deal with the subjects, social and political, which absorbed the interest of the town, and in a style which reflected the taste for brilliant conversation or dignified and sonorous oratory. The changes in Dryden's style mark his advance towards such a command of argumentative conversation or debate. From the outset his choice of theme is determined by his recognition of what will pay—the eulogy of possible patrons, and of fellow-poets who will respond in kind, dramas adapted to the changing taste which followed the advent of Charles, satire and didactic poetry defending what seemed to him for the moment the policy in favour at court.

It was as a "metaphysical" that Dryden began. He had evidently read Donne with care and appreciation; from no poet does he borrow with less acknowledgement. He appreciated the condensation and pregnancy of "metaphysical" poetry, and one might say that his achievement as a poet was to combine this pregnancy with some of the sweetness which Waller was bringing back by rejection of that "rich and pregnant fancy" which Carew admired in Donne, to retain the pregnancy while making the thought more natural, more commonplace, if the deeper, more imaginative, passionate strokes which give power and sincerity to Donne's conceits have disappeared. Cowley's more superficial, clever wit is Dryden's model in his first extant verses, contributed when he was eighteen to a volume of elegiac poems, *Lachrymae Musarum*, on the death of the young Lord Hastings, just such a volume as that in which *Lycidas* had appeared twelve years previously. The young man had died of smallpox and Dryden asks:

> Was there no milder way but the small pox
> The very filthiness of Pandora's box?
> So many spots like naeves on Venus soil?
> One jewel set off with so many a foil.

That is the metaphysical style at its worst, as in the verses of Bishop Corbet, Cleveland, and even Cowley, for which Dryden was to substitute in time, not the more moving, imaginative touches of Donne at his best, such as

> her pure and eloquent blood
> Spoke in her cheeks, and so distinctly wrought
> That one might almost say her body thought,

but the felicities of an effective oratorical appeal. Metaphysical still, but growing in weight and dignity, are the lines with which Dryden some nine years later commemorated the greatness of the departed Cromwell (1659). His immediate model is Waller, who had written (1655) on the same theme in what is almost his best poem:

> Still as you rise, the State exalted too
> Finds no distemper, while 'tis changed by you.
> Changed like the world's great scene, when without noise
> The rising sun night's vulgar lights destroys.

Dryden has no stanza quite so fine as that, but it is in the same vein that he writes

> Swift and resistless through the land he passed,
>   Like that bold Greek who did the East subdue,
> And made to battle such heroic haste,
>   As if on wings of victory he flew.

Having composed *Heroic Stanzas* upon the death of Cromwell did not prevent Dryden, any more than it did Waller, from hailing the return of Charles, *Astraea Redux* (1660), in exultant strains in which the sweetness of Waller blends with his own more vigorous and pregnant style:

> How shall I speak of that triumphant day
> When you renew'd the expiring pomp of May!
> (A month that owns an interest in your name:
> You and the flowers are its peculiar claim.)
> That star, that at your birth shone out so bright,
> It stain'd the duller sun's meridian light,
> Did once again its potent fires renew,
> Guiding our eyes to find and worship you.
> And now time's whiter series is begun,
> Which in soft centuries shall smoothly run;
> Those clouds that overcast your morn shall fly,
> Dispell'd to farthest corners of the sky.

To His Sacred Majesty, A Panegyric on his Coronation (1661), followed in the same exalted strain:

> Music herself is lost; in vain she brings
> Her choicest notes to praise the best of kings:
> Her melting strains in you a tomb have found,
> And lie like bees in their own sweetness drown'd.
> He that brought peace, and discord could atone,
> His name is music of itself alone.

The Chancellor, Lord Clarendon, was complimented too in a more complicated series of conceits.

No patron forthcoming, Dryden turned to the stage, the revived theatre, with comedies in which Fletcher, and Fletcher's model, the Spanish comedy of intrigue, showed the way, and with heroic plays of love and adventure. Of Dryden's

comedies none can be said to be effectively alive, and he himself recognised that it was not his forte, and fully acknowledged
the superiority of Congreve later.   The heroic plays are mainly
interesting as the field in which Dryden cultivated his peculiar
gift for forcible reasoning in verse.   Commenting on a scene
in the *Rival Ladies* (1663) the late Professor Saintsbury
remarks in a note: "Here begins the first of the scenes of
amatory battledore and shuttlecock on which Dryden was to
waste his talents, and which are known to most readers from
the *Rehearsal* [1671: a parody of the kind by the Duke of
Buckingham] and Butler's *Cat-and-Puss Dialogue*", to which
one might add Fielding's *Tom Thumb* (1730–1731).   What
has outlived the dramas themselves are the critical dedications
and introductions (suggested by, and occasionally borrowing
from, the *Discours* and *Examens* of Corneille) in which Dryden
shows his vital, if not always consistent, interest in the technical questions of criticism: diction, verse, the dramatic
unities, etc.   The best known of these critical asides, *An
Essay of Dramatic Poesy*, a delightful dialogue, was published
in 1667–1668.   It is in intention a defence of drama as the
highest type of poetry, and of "rhyming and heroic tragedies
as the most legitimate offspring of the drama" (Scott).   But
more interesting than the main thesis (and Dryden deserted
later both rhyme and the heroic drama) are the discussions of
Greek, French, and English plays, the unities and their practical difficulties, which include a brilliant series of appreciations
of Beaumont and Fletcher, Jonson, and Shakespeare, "the man
who of all modern and perhaps ancient poets had the largest
and most comprehensive soul".

In the same year as the *Essay*, the theatres being closed,
Dryden wrote and issued his first poem of any length, the
Annus Mirabilis.   It is a strange poem to have appeared in the
same year as *Paradise Lost*.   To read them together, not of
course for purpose of comparison in merit, which would be
grossly unfair to Dryden, but as kinds, is to understand what
Arnold meant by distinguishing between poetry begotten in
the imagination and poetry begotten in the wits.   Dryden's
poem is not, he is careful to point out, an epic but an historical
poem, being a detailed and accurate account of the two great
naval battles of the year and the Fire of London, a detailed,
in parts prosaic, account made poetic as Dryden conceives, by
the "sonorous" verse (taken over from *Gondibert*) and by the

deliberate heightening of the descriptions by an image borrowed generally from the classics or a conceit often felicitous,
always surprising:

> To nearest ports their shattered ships repair,
>   Where by our dreadful cannon they lay awed;
> So reverently men quit the open air
>   When thunder speaks the angry gods abroad.
>
> .   .   .   .   .
>
> Amid whole heaps of spices lights a ball,
>   And now their odours arm'd against them fly,
> Some preciously by shatter'd porcelain fall,
>   And some by aromatic splinters die.

The most sustained attempt at imaginative, vivid description
is of the Great Fire, yet even here the deliberate personification
of the flames produces an odd effect:

> The daring flames peeped in and saw from far
>   The awful beauties of the sacred quire;
> But since it was profaned by civil war
>   Heaven thought it fit to have it purged by fire.

The poem abounds in compliments to possible patrons, from
the King to the City of London.   It is an extraordinary *tour de
force* if hardly a great poem.

Continuing his work for the stage Dryden produced in 1672
the crown and flower of the Heroic Drama, the *Conquest of
Granada*.   Scott in his *Life of Dryden* has described well the
features of the type, the sublimated ideal of love derived from
the French "long-winded romances", a love "neither to be
chilled by absence, nor wasted by time, nor quenched by
infidelity"; the ingenious dialogue in which "the lover hopes
everything from his ingenuity and trusts nothing to his
passion"; the "solemn feasts and processions, battles by sea
and land . . . sudden and violent changes of fortune".   "Fortune has been compared to the sea, but in an heroic poem her
course resembled an absolute Bay of Biscay or Race of Port-
land, disturbed by an hundred contending currents and eddies
and never continuing in one steady flow".

That plays of such exalted absurdity should provoke satiric
comment was inevitable.   The second part of the *Conquest of
Granada* was anticipated or was followed by *The Rehearsal*,
Bayes the hero being so dressed and spoken of as to make his
identification with Dryden unmistakable.   But Dryden was

quite as well aware as his critics of the absurdities of the fashionable kind, despite his critical defence. No poet more deliberately cultivated the taste of his audience, and if the public taste was changing he was ready to try some other course. He had given close study to Shakespeare and Milton, and he turned to both as possible models. What led him to attempt a dramatisation of *Paradise Lost* was, we venture to think, the opportunity it offered for just such spectacular effects as contributed to the popularity of the Heroic Drama. But the *State of Innocence* was never produced on the stage. Characteristically, Dryden does not accept Milton's dogmatic and simple acceptance of the compatibility of Divine omnipotence with human free-will. The most distinctive scene is that in which Adam, already a metaphysician, argues the point with Raphael.

The direction in which Dryden's mind was moving is traceable in *Aurungzebe* (1675), the last of the Heroic plays, and like the rest a tissue of absurdities. Everyone falls in love at first sight—the men with Indamore, the women with Aurungzebe. But he is experimenting in character-drawing. The heroine is induced by fear to falter in her fidelity to love; and the verse abounds in dramatic half-lines. Then with *All for Love* (1678) Dryden abandoned rhyme, and concentrated on character-drawing—a passionate but also sentimental Antony, torn between love and fame, but also between Octavia and Cleopatra, dominated always in the last resort by passion. It was the first play, Dryden declared, that he wrote for himself, *i.e.* to please his own judgement, not to capture the applause of the audience.

Three years later Dryden found an occasion for the use of his now fully developed power of reasoning in verse, and his easy command of the whole range of the English language, not in the battledore and shuttlecock of amorous nonsense, but in a political satire on the burning question of the day, a satire, but conceived and planned on the scale of an epic poem. Dryden had spoken in the dedication of *Aurungzebe* of his wish to make the world "amends for many ill plays by an heroic poem". *Absalom and Achitophel* (1682) is not that poem, but in it Dryden has made a more effective use of *Paradise Lost* than in the *State of Innocence*. For here is a threatened rebellion, not in Heaven but in England; and the *dramatis personae* on either side, not angels but politicians, are presented with a dignity, and in the greater figures a roundedness, which only makes more telling the easy certainty with which the poet exposes the vanities, vices, and follies alike of individuals and the mob. Pope's satires are more witty, more crammed with malice. No satire in English is at once so weighty, and gives such an impression of the satirist's superiority to his victims, as this poem and its sequels, *The Medal* (1682) and *Mac Flecknoe*, which furnished a model for Pope's more laboured *Dunciad*. The subject is the Whig poet Shadwell, who is declared by the dullest of preceding poets to be his legitimate heir to the throne of dulness:

> Shadwell alone my perfect image bears,
> Mature in dulness from his tender years;
> Shadwell alone of all my sons is he
> Who stands confirm'd in full stupidity.
> The rest to some faint meaning make pretence,
> But Shadwell never deviates into sense.

There are in these satires occasional Drydenian witticisms, more clever than in good taste, not quite appropriate to the sentiment which the subject spoken of is fitted and intended to evoke. The poet who in the *State of Innocence* talks of "all the sad variety of Hell' and of cherubs who "dissolved in Hallelujahs lie" is capable of describing Nadab (Lord Howard of Escrick) as one

> Who made new porridge for the paschal Lamb.

But it is with Milton's style, and even to some extent his verse, that *Absalom and Achitophel* will bear comparison if one keep in mind that the subject is mundane and the purpose satirical.

In these satires and the closely connected didactic, argumentative *Religio Laici* (1682) and *The Hind and the Panther* (1687) Dryden found for a time subjects of more solid interest and wider appeal than the Heroic Drama. He had to fight, and he was a good fighter; to reason, and he was a vigorous reasoner. How far his own convictions and deeper feelings were enlisted is another question. The greatest want in Dryden's poetry is that quality which Tolstoi places first, the impression of sincerity, that the poet is writing first for himself and secondly for those like-minded with himself. He is not a showman setting off to advantage the wares he knows his readers demand, expressing *their* feelings, not his own. Well, in all these poems Dryden is confessedly fighting the cause of his employers, those to whom he looked for patronage, if Charles's pleasures were too expensive, his favourites too greedy (as Scott says), to make it easy for him to notice or reward genuine merit.   Yet there is no doubt that Dryden had a sincere contempt for the mob, and for politicians who disguised self-seeking under the specious cover of constitutional and religious liberty—a sincere hatred also for anarchy, and a conviction that order is the indispensable condition of a life that is worth living.   More interesting is the impression conveyed by the two religious poems.   The *Religio Laici*, composed while Dryden was still a Protestant, is a little masterpiece of reasoning in verse, in a style that, aiming at none of the higher effects of poetry, yet justifies the use of verse.   *The Hind and the Panther*, in which he writes as one who is now a Catholic and follows obediently the course of poor James's policy, is in part a more beautiful if also a more unequal poem.   Johnson was doubtless right in describing the *Religio Laici* as a "voluntary effusion", a poem written to satisfy Dryden himself and the friend he addresses, rather than a contribution to the public controversy.   It expresses as nearly as may be what was Dryden's everyday religious conviction or mood of mind—scepticism tempered by a sense of Everyman's need of, or desire for, forgiveness and security.   In the Catholic poem Dryden rises, in the personal passages, to a higher level of feeling—a more passionate sense of sin, a more ardent devotion to the Church whose promises of forgiveness and security are given with so much greater a consciousness of authority and infallibility.   But the general tone of the poem is argumentative and satirical.   One might not unfairly say that the two poems are rather poems about religion than religious poems.   More purely devotional and ecstatic is the poem *Britannia Rediviva*, in which Dryden hailed what Catholics deemed a miracle, Protestants a fraud,—the birth of the Prince who was later to be known as the elder Pretender, by Jacobites as James III. "Dryden," says Scott, "who knew how to assume every style which fitted the occasion, writes here in the character of a devout and grateful Catholic, with much of the unction which pervades the hymns of the Roman Church", of which hymns Dryden was the translator of the *Veni Creator Spiritus*, the *Te Deum*, and the hymn for the *Nativity of John the Baptist*.   On the *Britannia Rediviva* Johnson notes "the exorbitant adulation, and that insensibility of the precipice on which the King

N

was then standing, which the laureate apparently shared with the rest of the courtiers. A few months cured him of controversy, dismissed him from court, and made him again a playwright and a translator."

The plays of Dryden's last years include one, *Don Sebastian* (1690), which, with *All for Love*, is reckoned the best of his numerous but mainly forgotten dramas. As a translator he dealt in his free, vigorous, eminently readable manner with Juvenal and Persius, prefixing to his versions an essay on satire which included a more interesting series of reflections on the heroic or epic poem; with Ovid; with Lucretius, with whom of all the Latin poets his genius had the most in common; with Theocritus, and with Homer, whose two epics he tells us he would have preferred to Virgil if he had been free to choose which he would translate.

But the two chief works of these years were a complete translation of the poems of Virgil,—*Eclogues, Georgics*, and *Aeneid*; and the volume of imitations or re-renderings of poems and tales from Boccaccio and Chaucer entitled the *Fables* (1700). To these should be added some of the best of his numerous addresses and epistles, notably that to Congreve on his comedy *The Double Dealer* (1694), and that *To My Honoured Kinsman John Driden of Chesterton in the County of Huntingdon* (1700):

> How blessed is he who leads a country life,
> Unvexed with anxious cares and void of strife!

In 1697, his work on Virgil concluded, Dryden wrote a poem by which he is probably known to more readers than by anything else; *Alexander's Feast; or, the Power of Music, An Ode in Honour of St. Cecilia's Day*. When congratulated by a young man on having written the finest and noblest ode that had ever been written in any language, Dryden is said to have replied: "You are right, young man, a nobler ode never was produced nor ever will." On the strength of the same ode Scott declares that "in lyrical poetry Dryden must be allowed to have no equal". In the light of earlier and later odes one may, or may *not*, allow the truth of this estimate, while acknowledging to the full the brilliance of Dryden's achievement in his particular manner.

Of his method as a translator Dryden has spoken at considerable length, elsewhere and in his *Dedication of the Aeneis*:

"On the whole matter I thought fit to steer between the two extremes of paraphrase and literal translation; to keep as near my author as I could, without losing all his graces. . . . I have endeavoured to make Virgil speak such English as he would himself have spoken if he had been born in England, and in the present age." The last words are important, for they point to the truth that there can be no final translation. What seemed to Dryden and Pope the manner in which Virgil or Homer would have spoken and versified had they been Englishmen does not necessarily seem so to us to-day, to whom Wordsworth, Tennyson, and others have taught a different style and other cadences. Dryden's *Virgil* is probably not much read to-day, but it is still readable, allowing for the changes we have indicated. His rendering of the *Georgics* is both faithful and animated.

But the best of this last work is the *Fables*, his retelling of Chaucer's *Palamon and Arcite*, of *The Cock and the Fox*, of the Chaucerian *Flower and the Leaf*, of Boccaccio's *Sigismunda and Guiscardo* and other tales. No work of Dryden remained so long popular. "To this day", writes Macaulay, "*Palamon and Arcite, Cymon and Iphigenia, Theodore and Honoria* are the delight of both critics and schoolboys." Macaulay's school-boys were always rather an ideal lot. We doubt if many schoolboys to-day would stand an examination on the *Fables*; or if many critics would echo without qualification the statement of Scott that "there is not in our language a strain of more beautiful and melodious poetry than that so often quoted in which Dryden describes the sleeping nymph and the effect of her beauty upon the clownish Cymon". Fashions change; yet, read with some historical and literary interest in a past manner, one will find much to admire. The oratorical couplet grows a little wearisome in a long narrative poem, and tempts the poet to a rhetorical heightening of the original. The best of the pieces is probably the *Palamon and Arcite* just because the imaginative and emotional range of the poem is not outside Dryden's scope. But the gentler, more insinuating manner, the more sinuously moving verse of Chaucer, are gone; and in the humorous pieces one misses the archness, the delicate sly-ness of Chaucer's satire. The stories from Boccaccio are well told, but here again Dryden excels in passages of passionate, masculine eloquence. He lacks delicacy of feeling, moving pathos, variety of mood.

Dryden dominated the age in which he worked to a degree that no single one of the distinguished writers of the reign of Anne quite attained to. To-day his prose is perhaps for us even more interesting than his poetry. His prose has not, to use the words of Johnson, "the formality of a settled style in which the first half of the sentence betrays the other. The clauses are never balanced, nor the periods modelled; every word seems to drop by chance, though it falls in its proper place. Nothing is cold or languid; the whole is airy, animated, vigorous: what is little is gay; what is great is splendid." Indeed if easy strength is a quality of prose Dryden can hardly be surpassed. Swift's more incisive style requires behind it the force of Swift's malice. Dryden gives always, in spirit and form, the impression of a finer magnanimity. Whether he is eulogising a patron, with entire disregard of truth but with a complete understanding of what will please, or driving an enemy to the ropes with one easily delivered, but well directed, blow after another, Dryden's combination of mastery with ease is unrivalled. The father of English criticism, Johnson calls him, and if his opinions are often inconsistent with one another, they are the judgements of one who writes from a wide experience and a respect, without idolatry, for tradition. Dryden is one of the commanding figures in our literature, as Ben Jonson had been earlier, and Dr. Johnson was to be later.

In satire and polemic Dryden "ruled as he saw fit The universal monarchy of wit", so much so that most of his rivals survive only as flies preserved in the amber of his verse. But in the provinces of drama and lyric his sovereignty was by no means undisputed. In comedy, as we saw, he frankly yielded the laurel to Congreve; in tragedy he had a formidable rival in Thomas Otway (1652–1685), whose *Orphan* and *Venice Preserved* held the stage far longer than any play of Dryden's. Otway has been loudly praised by some good judges: Gosse calls *Venice Preserved* the greatest tragedy between Shakespeare and Shelley; Scott declares that in scenes of passionate affection Otway rivals and sometimes excels Shakespeare; "more tears", he says, "have been shed, probably, for the sorrows of Belvidera and Monimia"—the heroines of *Venice Preserved* and *The Orphan*—"than for those of Juliet and Desdemona". It is true that Otway's plays, barring the execrable comic scenes, are well constructed and pathetic: he understood stagecraft, having been an actor; and his short,

unhappy life had known heart-break; but his passion is of the
stage stagey, and pathos like his is not very hard to achieve
if, in Johnson's phrase, you abandon your mind to it.   Other
tragedians of that age, such as Nathaniel· Lee (1653–1692)
and Thomas Southerne (1660–1746), are mere names to-day:
that Lee's *Alexander* and Southerne's *Oroonoko* continued to
be performed now and then for a hundred and fifty years shows
how low English tragedy had sunk.   Nicholas Rowe (1674–
1718), though his *Jane Shore* was a favourite in the eighteenth
century, is remembered now not as a dramatist but as the first
editor and biographer of Shakespeare.   The genius of that
unheroic age was in truth apter for comedy than tragedy; and
comedy had gone over entirely to prose.

In lyric, too, Dryden had equals if not superiors.   He himself thought *Alexander's Feast* the noblest of odes; to other ears
its music sounds like that of a brass band.   In the mob of
gentlemen who wrote with ease at Charles II's court there were
some voices more tuneful than Dryden's.   The *musa proterva* of
the Restoration is not always fit for chaste ears; but Sir Charles
Sedley (1639–1701) and the· Earl of Dorset (1638–1706) could
be graceful and witty without immodesty.   Sedley's

> Not, Celia, that I juster am
> Or better than the rest,

and Dorset's

> To all you ladies now at land
> We men at sea indite,

are in the true Cavalier tradition: other wits sometimes affected
the Metaphysicals.   The Earl of Rochester (1647–1680) was
the greatest rake of them all, and the best poet.   There is
nothing in Restoration verse so sincere and touching as his cry
of penitence:

> When wearied with a world of woe
> To thy safe bosom I retire,
> Where love and peace and truth does flow,
> May I contented there expire.
> Lest once more wand'ring from that Heaven,
> I fall on some base heart unblest;
> Faithless to thee, false, unforgiven,
> And lose my everlasting rest.

In another and (we fear) a more habitual mood he declared,

> Cupid and Bacchus my saints are,
> May drink and love still reign.

The Restoration Cupid is an arch, Anacreontic god; but in her astonishing

> Love in fantastic triumph sate

Aphra Behn (1640–1689) "set him up a deity" with something of the terrible in his aspect. Outside Society there were still poets who worshipped other gods than Cupid and Bacchus. Bishop Ken's two famous hymns,

> Awake, my soul, and with the sun,

and

> All praise to Thee, my God, this night,

belong to this age; so do Bunyan's few verses, which at their best have the tonic quality of his prose. The pastoral still had charms for some; John Norris of Bemerton (1637–1711) put into smooth verse the philosophy he had learned from the Cambridge Platonists; Thomas Flatman is remembered not for his Pindarics or his Anacreontics but for one sombre and strangely modern poem, "O the sad day", which sounds like a passing bell.

Besides poems by known authors the age of Dryden has left many *adespota* in such collections as Playford's *Select Ayres*, *Wits Interpreter*, and various *Drolleries*, etc. Formally it added little or nothing to the range of English verse: satire and criticism went into heroic couplets as a matter of course, if Dryden's couplets united smoothness and strength as no earlier poet had done; the lyrists as a rule were content with the measures they had inherited from the Carolines; but the pleasant anapaests of Walter Pope's *Old Man's Wish* seem to anticipate Matt Prior.

Chapter Sixteen

THE AGE OF POPE AND OTHER AUGUSTANS

IN his moving epistle to Congreve Dryden declares that he alone is his true successor:

> O that your Brows my Lawrel had sustain'd,
> Well had I been depos'd if you had reign'd!
> The Father had descended for the Son,
> For only You are lineal to the Throne.
> Thus, when the State one *Edward* did depose,
> A greater *Edward* in his Room arose;
> But now, not I but Poetry is curst,
> For *Tom* the Second reigns like *Tom* the First.

But Congreve, who had abandoned poetry and the drama for the last twenty and more years of his life, was not to be Dryden's successor as a poet, to say nothing of the laureate-ship. That was reserved for a little, deformed poet, a Catholic as Dryden had become, who was born a few months before the Revolution which ended Dryden's hopes. In a "Memorial List of Departed Relations and Friends" written by Pope in an Elzevir Virgil the opening note runs: "Anno 1700, Maij primo, obiit semper venerandus, poetarum princeps, Joannes Dryden aet. 70". Pope's early translations from Statius, Ovid, and Chaucer were modelled on the *Fables* of Dryden. "It was in perusing the works of Dryden", says Johnson, "that he discovered the most perfect fabric of English verse"; and indeed Pope's so-called 'correctness' is found mainly in the heightened finish he gave to the rhetorical couplet. And as with Dryden so with Pope, most of the subject-matter of his poems was supplied from without, if the *Moral Essays* and *Imitations* included his own satirical and somewhat spiteful observation of men and women. But Dryden had the educa-tion of a scholar, a pupil of Westminster School and Cam-bridge. Pope was educated by priests at home, in Catholic seminaries, and by his own reading; and in his reading his aim was to learn how to write. "He was very industrious", writes Mark Pattison, "and had read a vast number of books, yet he was very ignorant, that is, of everything but the one thing which he laboured with all his might to acquire, the art of happy expression. He read books to find ready-made images and to feel for the best collocations of words. His memory was a magazine of epithets and synonyms, and pretty turns of language."

However, Pope did learn some Latin, and his earliest experiments, apart from the *Ode to Solitude*, are translations in Dryden's manner from Statius, the first book of the *Thebaid*, Ovid's *Sappho to Phao*, and a version of Chaucer's *The Wife of Bath's Prologue*. These Pope dates as early as 1703, but his statements are never to be quite trusted. The first of his poems to be published were the *Pastorals*, issued in 1709 in a *Miscellany* which began with pastorals by Ambrose Philips and closed with those of Pope. In 1709 Pope was twenty-one, but the poems had been written, he declares, "at the age of sixteen and passed through the hands of Mr. Walsh, Mr. Wycherley and others, all of whom gave our author the greatest encouragement, and particularly Mr. Walsh, whom Mr. Dryden . . . calls the best critic of his age". It was Walsh, a minor poet, author of two good songs, *The Despairing Lover* and "Caelia, too late you would repent", who gave Pope the advice which more or less determined the direction of his ambition: "Though we had several good poets, we never had any one great poet that was correct; and he desired me to make that my study and care". Walsh had written an introduction on Pastoral Poetry in Dryden's Virgil, so gave his full approval to Pope's efforts. What Walsh meant by 'correctness' was at once a closer approach to the 'Ancients', and just the qualities which Pope's poetry was to illustrate, a sustained felicity of style and sweetness of versification seen to perfection in the well-balanced couplet, with none of the lapses in which the poetry of Dryden, Pope's great model, abounds. You must not approach Pope's *Pastorals* with Wordsworth in your mind. His shepherds and scenery are taken from his classical models. "It is surely sufficient", says Johnson, "for an author of sixteen not only to be able to copy the poems of antiquity with judicious selection, but to have obtained sufficient power of language, and skill of metre, to exhibit a series of language and versification which had in English poetry no precedent, nor have since had an imitation." We may prefer the music of *Lycidas* and the *Epithalamion*, to go no farther, to Pope's sweet

but limited, somewhat monotonous rhythms, and his uninter-
rupted succession of couplets.   Yet there is a music in Pope's
couplets which one may still enjoy:

> O deign to visit our forsaken seats,
> The mossy fountains and the green retreats!
> Where'er you walk, cool gales shall fan the glade;
> Trees where you sit shall crowd into a shade;
> Where'er you tread, the blushing flowers shall rise,
> And all things flourish where you turn your eyes.

The exact chronological order of Pope's poems is hard to
settle.   We propose therefore to consider the poems of the
two main groups, which do correspond to some extent to
earlier and later poems.   Dates given will be those of publication.   The first is the group of poems which, like the pastorals,
call to be considered just as poetry,—poems of feeling, imagination, and harmony.   The second is that in which the predominant element is intellectual—witty poetry, satirical and
didactic.   In an interesting detailed study of Pope's poetry
issued by Joseph Warton in 1756, completed in 1782, it is in
the latter class that Pope is, he claims, pre-eminent.   He is a
great wit, not a great poet.   But Warton recognises that Pope
had produced poems which claim respect as works of imagination.   These are: *Windsor Forest* (1713), *The Rape of the Lock*
(1711, 1714), the translation of Homer's *Iliad* (1715–1720)
(the *Odyssey* is only partially his own work), *Eloisa to Abelard*
(1717), *Elegy to the Memory of an Unfortunate Lady* (1717); to
which one might add *The Temple of Fame* (1715) from Ovid,
and the *Ode for St. Cecilia's Day* (1713).   When the reaction
against Pope and eighteenth-century poetry set in, the tendency
was to disregard these, to set them aside as examples of Pope's
rhetoric applied to themes which demand another kind of treatment.   But they are well worth study and will bear comparison
with poems of the same kind by later poets,—*The Rape of the
Lock* with, *e.g.*, *The Princess*; *Eloisa to Abelard* with Tennyson's
Oenone or his *Lucretius*, or some of Browning's *Dramatis
Personae*, or Swinburne's *Anactoria*; *To the Memory of an Unfortunate Lady* with (say) Donne's *Second Anniversarie* or even
Lycidas.   It will be found that which one may prefer depends
a little on the poetic manner to which one has grown accustomed.   One may call them rhetorical, or more justly oratorical,
eloquent, but despite Verlaine's command, "Take rhetoric and

wring its neck", which applies to lyrical poetry and that of a special kind, there is an oratorical element in a great deal of good poetry,—Homer, the Greek Tragedians, Virgil, Shakespeare, Marlowe, Milton. It is for your own individual judgement to decide whether the eloquence is or is not in place. One may take exception to certain conventions,—periphrases of a pompous kind like "the fleecy flock", "the thundering tube", etc. Nevertheless *Windsor Forest* is a readable descriptive poem, though not in Wordsworth's spirit or manner:

> The patient fisher takes his silent stand,
> Intent, his angle trembling in his hand:
> With looks unmov'd, he hopes the scaly breed,
> And eyes the dancing cork, and bending reed.
> Our plenteous streams a various race supply,
> The bright-ey'd perch with fins of Tyrian dye,
> The silver eel, in shining volumes roll'd,
> The yellow carp, in scales bedropp'd with gold,
> Swift trouts, diversified with crimson stains,
> And pikes, the tyrants of the wat'ry plains.

If the closing lines of the *Unfortunate Lady* are not poetry it is hard to say what is. But the best of these poems are *Eloisa to Abelard* and *The Rape of the Lock*. The first is based on the English version of a corrupt French version of the Latin letters, whose genuineness we need not here discuss. It is Pope's art which lends the poem poetic and dramatic value, his eloquent rendering of the ebb and flow of passion, the conflict between human love and religious devotion. It is the last and the best of the English poems suggested by Ovid's *Heroides*. "Here", says Johnson not unjustly, "is particularly observable the *curiosa felicitas*, a fruitful soil and careful cultivation. Here is no rudeness of sense or asperity of language."

But the gem of Pope's work as an imaginative, inventive poet is *The Rape of the Lock*, a little mock-heroic poem which is also a vivid little satiric picture of Society, a more pointed expression of that attitude towards "the fair sex" which inspired all that Addison wrote on the subject in the *Spectator*. Between the older chivalrous feeling of which Pope and Addison knew nothing and such a later revival of respect for women as is evident in the novels of Richardson, the only intermediary was poor Dick Steele, for whom to know her whom he loved was a liberal education. Even in its final form, when Pope introduced the machinery of the sylphs, gnomes, nymphs, etc., the mock-heroic element, if by that one means a constant reminder of and contrast with the serious epic of Homer, Virgil, Milton, is not the predominant interest of the poem, but rather the brilliant picture of fashionable life,—the lady's toilet, the voyage up the river, the coffee at Hampton Court, the game of ombre, etc. The effect of the machinery is to heighten the irony, the satiric treatment of the fair sex such as one finds for example in Addison's essay on "A Lady's Library". Like Addison, but with the heightened effect of his pointed style and finished versification, Pope treats with airy contempt all the trivialities of fashionable life and the vagaries of the feminine mind. The satire is so obvious throughout that it is little wonder that the lady, the loss of whose lock was the occasion for the poem, was only displeased and offended.

"I think one may venture to remark", wrote Warton, "that the reputation of Pope as a Poet among posterity will be principally owing" to the poems we have mentioned. But that, as we have said, was not the trend of later criticism. In a selection from Pope's poems Mark Pattison would include only *The Satires* and *Epistles* with Prologue, the *Moral Essays*, *The Essay on Man*, *Essay on Criticism*, the *Dunciad*, and *The Rape of the Lock* which links the two groups.

But to enjoy Pope's Satires you must to some extent be able to share Saintsbury's conviction that in poetry the form is everything, for even he has to admit a number of qualifications to the enjoyment if, like most of us, one is interested in the matter as well as the form. Pope's satire is inspired by no large view of human nature, its vices and weaknesses; no such dark misanthropy as at once arrests and horrifies us in Swift, and occasionally quickens in Byron; no such moral sincerity as we find in Juvenal, though Pope will on occasion pose as

To virtue only and her friends a friend.

His satires do not blend anger and pure fun as do Burns's *Death and Dr. Hornbook* or the more outrageous *Holy Willie's Prayer*. Personal animosity is the feather with which Pope's satiric arrows are fledged; and accordingly to do full justice to the *Dunciad* (1728) and the *Moral Essays* (1732–1735) and *Imitations of Horace* (1733–1737) one must be familiar with the social history of the time or be ready to plough through endless notes. The *Dunciad* is a monument of misapplied power. Of all the poets, dramatists, and critics assailed only two are familiar to most readers—Daniel Defoe and Richard Bentley.

The *Dunciad* was an outcome of the work which occupied the middle period of Pope's life, the translation of the *Iliad* and in part of the *Odyssey*. As early as 1708 Pope had been urged by a friend, to whom he had sent a version of the Sarpedon episode, to make a complete translation. His own circumstances and his exclusion, as a Catholic, from political patronage induced him in 1713 to issue proposals and invite subscriptions. The proposal was taken up with enthusiasm by his friends, especially Swift, and in 1715 the first volume appeared. But in the same year was issued a version of the first book of the *Iliad* by Tickell, a friend of Addison, which many suspected, and Pope was convinced, was the work of Addison himself, whom, for several reasons, Pope regarded as "a timorous foe, and a suspicious friend". Moreover the financial success of the *Iliad*, of which the version was completed in 1720, and of the *Odyssey*, in which he had collaborators, in 1725–1726, had raised up a number of jealous critics, such as Kipling and Barrie have suffered from in our own time. And to these attacks Pope laid himself open by undertaking an edition of Shakespeare for which he had not the necessary knowledge of Elizabethan drama and vocabulary, but to which he prefixed a brilliant appreciation. The errors in Pope's work were pointed out by Theobald in *Shakespeare Restored* (1726), who later, as Johnson puts it, "in a formal edition detected his deficiencies with all the insolence of victory; and as he [*i.e.* Pope] was now high enough to be feared and hated Theobald had from others all the help that could be supplied by the desire of humbling a haughty character". To all this Pope prepared to reply as his work on Homer drew to a close. With Swift and Arbuthnot to aid he issued in 1727–1732 a Miscellany of verse and prose including *The Art of Sinking in Poetry*, illustrated from various writers of the day. To the anger provoked by this Pope replied with the *Dunciad*, in which Theobald figures as the Laureate of dulness. In a later edition he was displaced by Colley Cibber.

Pope's *Homer* was for long familiar to more readers than his satires or didactic poems. Whatever its faults as a translation it is a brilliant piece of work, at its best in passages of eloquent declamation. If it is less known to-day, that is largely because all translations must for success be in the manner of the day, and Pope's is not that of the age of Tennyson and Browning or the poets of to-day, if there be a recognised manner of to-day. Every age will wish to have its own rendering; but it is doubtful if any will enjoy the popularity that Pope's did for well over a century.

The third period of Pope's activity began with the completion of his Homer, and was devoted mainly to satire, but included his philosophical poem, the *Essay on Man*. A close study of the *Dunciad*, the earliest of these, will reward a curious appreciator of Pope's marvellous cleverness in the use of word and phrase and pointed verse. Otherwise it is rather a weariness, and a sampler might well follow Johnson's selection and read the publishers' pursuit of a poet (II, 35-50, 109-120), the young fop's tour abroad (IV, 293-336), and "the crowded thoughts and stately numbers which dignify the concluding paragraphs". The last passage also indicates well what was the pose assumed by Pope and Swift throughout these years. They are the last survivors under the Hanoverian and Walpolian reign of corruption and dulness, the last survivors of an age of wit, culture, and politeness.

Before coming to his later satires a word on the great philosophical poem the *Essay on Man* (1730). Pope had already written a didactic poem of interest, the *Essay on Criticism* (1711). There is nothing original in Pope's doctrines. They are those of the Neo-Classical School, but expressed with rememberable point and felicity. Here are the two main dogmas of the school, honoured often more in the breach than the observance: follow Nature and imitate the classics:

> First follow Nature, and your judgment frame
> By her just standard, which is still the same;

and our guides in thus following Nature are the classics. To them we owe the rules,

> Those rules of old discover'd, not devis'd,
> Are Nature still, but Nature methodiz'd.

The youthful Virgil, according to Pope, had thought at first that he might steer by the light of Nature and his own genius, but a closer examination convinced him:

> Nature and Homer were, he found, the same.
> Convinc'd, amaz'd, he checks the bold design:

> And rules as strict his labour'd work confine
> As if the Stagirite [Aristotle] o'erlook'd each line.
> Learn hence for ancient rules a just esteem:
> To copy nature is to copy them.

This is, of course, all nonsense.   Neither Homer nor Aristotle
laid down rules for epic poetry.   The former supplied Virgil
with good models for his descriptions of the voyages and the
battles of Aeneas.   The so-called "rules" concerned the drama,
on which Pope has nothing to say.

But what does Pope mean by Nature?   Certainly not what
Wordsworth meant.   One might reply in one word "sense",
"good sense", the opposite of the "wit" of the Metaphysicals.
One should read with the *Essay on Criticism* Addison's essays in
the *Spectator* on "False Wit" and "Mixed Wit".   Sense is the
constantly recurring word in Pope's poem:

> True wit is nature to advantage dress'd,
> What oft was thought, but ne'er so well express'd;
> Something whose truth convinc'd at sight we find,
> That gives us back the image of our mind.
>
> Yet let not each gay turn thy rapture move,
> For fools admire but men of sense approve.
>
> Be niggard of advice on no pretence,
> For the worst avarice is that of sense.
>
> Horace still charms with graceful negligence,
> And without method talks us unto sense.

The last reference is to Horace's *Ars Poetica* which, with
Aristotle's *Poetics*, was one of the chief authorities on the laws
of art.

Had the *Essay on Man* been all that Pope and his mentor
Bolingbroke intended it would have been his *Paradise Lost*, his
most serious work, a poem devised

> To vindicate the ways of God to Man.

Here again Pope had nothing new to say.   He took over from
his friend Bolingbroke the philosophy, so far as either of them
understood it, of Leibnitz, on which Voltaire was to pour scorn
in *Candide* (1757) and which Johnson rejected in a more serious
spirit in *Rasselas* (1759), the doctrine that all is well in this the
best of all possible worlds:

> All are but parts of one stupendous whole,
> Whose body Nature is, and God the soul;

As full, as perfect in vile man that mourns,
As the rapt seraph that adores and burns;
To him no high, no low, no great, no small;
He fills, he bounds, connects, and equals all.

According to this philosophy everything as it is is necessary and good. It is our shortsightedness which makes us complain when we suffer from toothache or poverty or any other apparent ill; which is no consolation to the sufferer who cannot see the whole. Moreover, and here Pope got himself, as a Christian, into trouble, among these necessary things are bad men:

Respecting man whatever wrong we call,
May, must be right, as relative to all.

.   .   .   .   .

But errs not nature from this gracious end,
From burning suns when livid deaths descend,
When earthquakes swallow, or when tempests sweep
Towns to one grave, whole nations to the deep?
"No," 'tis replied, "the first Almighty cause
Acts not by partial but by general laws:
The exceptions few; some change since all began,
And what created perfect?" Why then man?
If the great end be human happiness,
Then nature deviates, and can man do less?

.   .   .   .   .

If plagues or earthquakes break not heaven's design,
Why then a Borgia or a Catiline?
Who knows but he whose hand the lightning forms,
Who heaves old ocean and who wings the storms,
Pours fierce ambition in a Caesar's mind,
Or turns young Ammon loose to scourge mankind?

But the Christian view is that this is not a perfect but a fallen world, and that men are free agents and responsible for their actions. When the unorthodoxy of the poem was pointed out by a Swiss divine, Crousaz, Pope was greatly alarmed, and was much relieved when a divine of the day, William Warburton, afterwards Bishop of Gloucester, came to his defence in a series of letters. Warburton became his chief friend and after his death the first editor of his works. Apart from the main doctrine which Pope took over without realising its full implications, the Essay is a series of either commonplace or very disputable propositions. "He tells us much that every man knows and much that he does not know himself." But here as in the *Essay on Criticism* Pope's wording is so felicitous, his eloquence so flowing, that commonplaces acquire a new attractiveness. From no poet except Shakespeare have so many phrases passed into use by people who do not know from whence they came. "Never were penury of knowledge and vulgarity of sentiment so happily disguised."

Yet it is in the satires of this last period that Pope's style is at its best. Satire was his element. Indeed the *Essay on Criticism*, *The Rape of the Lock*, and the *Essay on Man* all alike bear witness to the predominance of the satirical vein in the mind of Pope—the follies of poets and critics, the follies and foibles of women, the follies of mankind, are his central themes in the three. In his later work Horace became his chief model, though the temper of Horace as a satirist is very remote from that of Pope. Two of what became the *Moral Essays* had appeared before the *Essay on Man—Of False Taste* (1731) and *Use of Riches* (1732). To these were added later *Characters of Men* (1733) and *Characters of Women* (1734), and an attempt was made to represent them as part of the larger philosophical poem. But the philosophy is merely an excuse for satirical pictures of individuals. In the *Characters of Men* he dilates on a topic he had already developed in the *Essay on Man*, the ruling passion, in order to draw a telling picture of

> Wharton, the scorn and wonder of our days,
> Whose ruling passion was the lust of praise.

The Duchess of Marlborough is made the shining example of the doctrine that "Most women have no characters at all". She is the perfect embodiment of fickleness in passionate loves and hates:

> Scarce once herself, by turns all womankind!
> Who with herself, or others, from her birth
> Finds all her life one warfare upon earth;
> Shines in exposing knaves and painting fools,
> Yet is whate'er she hates and ridicules.
> . . . . .
> Full sixty years the world has been her trade,
> The wisest fool much time has ever made.

In the *Use of Riches* Pope illustrates its abuse by the corruption of political life under Walpole, its use by the picture of the Man of Ross and his benevolence on the large income of £500 a year; as in the last poem the picture of the Duchess as Atossa is balanced by that of Pope's friend Martha Blount. Pope is never so delightful, said Lamb, as when he is complimenting his friends. The example of the sublimity of false taste is taken by Pope from the gorgeous seat of the Duke of Chandos, but as the Duke had shown him considerable kindness he denied the identification.

The *Imitations of Horace*, the last of Pope's satires, were suggested by Bolingbroke. The most amusing are the first (Horace, *Satires*, II, 1) and that *To Augustus* (Horace, *Epistles*, II, 1). Nothing could illustrate better the difference between Horace's genial and often good-humoured satire and Pope's condensed malice. For every stab of Horace's Pope gets in three or four, and even Horace's compliments to Augustus are converted into satire of Hanoverian George. But more delightful than the imitations are the so-called *Prologue to the Satires*, composed as an *Epistle to Arbuthnot*, and the two dialogues, issued as *One Thousand Seven Hundred and Thirty Eight*, which became the *Epilogue* to the Satires. In these Pope undertakes his own cause as a satirist devoted only to the defence of truth and virtue. He has always been, he declares, the defender, not the attacker. The *Dunciad* was evoked by endless insults and insinuations. This is far from being the whole truth. The other plea he develops is that he and his friends are the last survivors of an age of honest politics, of true not pedantic learning, and of good poetry, in an age when Hanoverian kings and Whig statesmen have corrupted the country by South Sea bubbles and the bribery of politicians and the Press. "In the letters of Swift and Pope", writes Dr. Johnson, "there appears such narrowness of mind as makes them insensible of any excellence that has not some affinity with their own, and confines their esteem and approbation to so small a number, that whoever should form his opinion of the age from their representation would suppose them to have lived amidst ignorance and barbarity, unable to find among their contemporaries either virtue or intelligence, and persecuted by those that could not understand them."

Be that as it may, the most charming lines in Pope's poetry are those in which in the *Epilogue* he enumerates his political friends:

> But does the Court a worthy man remove?
> That instant, I declare, he has my love:
> I shun his zenith, court his mild decline;
> Thus Somers once, and Halifax were mine.

o

Oft in the clear, still mirror of retreat,
I studied Shrewsbury, the wise and great:
Carleton's calm sense, and Stanhope's noble flame,
Compar'd, and knew their generous end the same;
How pleasing Atterbury's softer hour!
How shin'd the soul unconquer'd in the Tower!
How can I Pulteney, Chesterfield forget,
While Roman spirit charms and Attic wit?
Argyll, the state's whole thunder born to wield,
And shake alike the senate and the field?
Or Wyndham, just to freedom and the throne,
The master of our passions and his own?
Names which I long have lov'd, nor lov'd in vain,
Rank'd with their friends, not number'd with their train;
And if yet higher the proud list should end,
Still let me say: no follower but a friend.

Pope was the high priest of a rationalistic and social age. It is difficult to speak too highly of the brilliance of his talents and the completeness with which he achieved his special task. To the wisdom of common sense, to the generous feelings of the social man, to the wit and satire of a keen observer of the foibles of men and women in society he has given finished expression in language natural, condensed, and felicitous, and in verse smooth and resonant which heightens by its balanced rhythm the luminousness of an aphorism, the poignancy of an epigram, and the sonority of an impassioned declamation.   His defect is moral rather than artistic, for one has a right to judge the soundness and sincerity of a poet who sets up as a teacher and judge.   Pope's wisdom is too limited and worldly; his satire too occasional and personal and prejudiced.   Had his insight into life been deeper, and his sympathies more generous and just, the shining beauty of his style would have given to his work not only the admiration of those who appreciate literary workmanship but enduring worth and influence.

If Pope was the high priest of our witty poetry in a very special period of the history of English poetry and English political life, he was not the only poet.   Most of the wits wrote verse as well as prose, the chief exception being Steele.   Of them all Matthew Prior (1664–1721), statesman and poet (he took an active part in the negotiations which led up to the Peace of Utrecht (1713) and thereby became obnoxious to the Whigs who came into power in 1714), is the most charming in virtue of his blend of wit and sentiment and his command, so much admired by Cowper, of "the familiar style . . . of all styles the most difficult to succeed in, to make verse speak the language of prose without being prosaic". His long serious poem, *Solomon, or the Vanity of the World* (1718), in decasyllabic couplets and three books, had no success. The lighter *Alma, or the Progress of the Mind* (1718) and on the same underlying theme, *que scais-je*, is pleasanter reading:

> For Plato's fancies what care I?
> I hope you would not have me die,
> Like simple Cato in the play,
> For anything that he can say?
> E'en let him of ideas speak
> To heathens in his native Greek.
> If to be sad is to be wise,
> I do most heartily despise
> Whatever Socrates has said
> Or Tully writ or Wanley read.
> Dear D——, to set the matter right
> Remove these papers from my sight;
> Burn Mat's Descartes and Aristotle;
> Here! Jonathan, your master's bottle.

But Prior lives by the best of his lighter lyrics: "While blooming youth and gay delight";

> Celia and I the other day
> Walk'd o'er the sandhills to the sea;

> The merchant to secure his treasure
>   Conveys it in a borrow'd name;
> Euphelia serves to grace my measure,
>   But Chloe is my real flame;

and others in the same vein and verse with a few in delightful anapaestics, as the *Better Answer*, *i.e.* to Chloe Jealous, with its charming if ungrammatical closing verse:

> Then finish, dear Chloe, this pastoral war,
>   And let us like Horace and Lydia agree;
> For thou art a girl as much fairer than her
>   As he is a poet sublimer than me.

To these add the *Lines Written in the Beginning of Mezeray's History of France*, which Scott cited to Lockhart on one of their last walks together: be life as it may, we all cling to it:

> The man in graver tragic known,
> Though his best part long since was done,

> Still on the stage desires to tarry:
> And he who play'd the harlequin,
> After the jest still loads the scene,
> Unwilling to retire though weary.

One of his cleverest hits was a verse-by-verse reply to Boileau's Ode on the taking of Namur by Louis when that town was retaken by William.

Swift too could use the language of prose effectively in verse. He began indeed in what Johnson calls, when speaking of Watts, "the Pindaric folly", but warned off by Dryden who told him, "Cousin Swift, you will never be a poet" (whence Swift's vicious attacks on Dryden in the *Battle of the Books*), he abandoned the higher levels of poetry, but showed in occasional poems that what could be said in prose could be equally well said in verse:

> And let me in these shades compose
> Something in verse as true as prose.

Indeed one element in Swift's wit, for surprise is an invariable element of wit, is just the surprise of finding a quite prosaic content—realistic, coarse, sensible, satirical—appropriately expressed in verse. If Prior uses the language of prose yet it is to some extent winged; Swift can write what is just good straightforward prose in effective verse:

> Swift had the sin of wit, no venial crime.
> Nay 'tis affirmed he sometimes dealt in rhyme.
> Humour and mirth had place in all he writ;
> He reconciled divinity with wit;
> He mov'd and bow'd and talk'd with too much grace,
> Nor show'd the parson in his gait or face:
> Despis'd luxurious wines and costly meat,
> Yet still was at the tables of the great.

So he describes himself, and he is equally truthful when his theme is Stella. There is no flattery, no profession of anything stronger in his feelings than friendship, but also no disguise of that sincere friendship and admiration undiminished by the enumeration of her faults:

> Thou, Stella, wert no longer young
> When first for thee my harp was strung,
> Without one word of Cupid's darts,
> Or killing eyes, or bleeding hearts:
> With friendship and esteem possest
> I ne'er admitted love a guest.

Her great attraction is a combination:

> Say, Stella, was Prometheus blind,
> And forming you, mistook your kind?
> No; 'Twas for you alone he stole
> The fire that forms a manly soul;
> Then, to complete it every way,
> He moulded it with female clay:
> To that you owe the nobler fame,
> To this the beauty of your frame.

And she has her faults:

> Resolv'd to mortify your pride
> I'll here expose your weaker side.
>   Your spirits kindle to a flame
>   Mov'd with the lightest touch of blame.

In the same matter-of-fact style in *Cadenus and Vanessa* he relates the history of his second Platonic flirtation. He can describe with minute detail a shower in town, or the rising of the sun, or all that can disgust him in a lady's bedroom. His favourite metre is the Hudibrastic couplet; but he wrote ballads, and also one or two poems in the colloquial style of uneducated servants and in doggerel verse: *Mrs. Harris' Petition*, that the chaplain may be made to marry her, "or instead of him a better", and *Mary the Cookmaid's Letter to Dr. Sheridan*. A tragic strain flows as an undercurrent through all Swift's verse and prose, coming to the surface in the lines *On the Death of Dr. Swift* and in the witty blasphemy of *The Day of Judgment*:

> While each pale sinner hung his head,
> Jove nodding shook the heavens and said:
> "Offending race of human-kind,
> By nature, reason, *learning*, blind;
> You who, through frailty, stepp'd aside;
> And you who never fell, *through pride*;
> You who in different sects were shamm'd,
> And come to see each other damn'd—
> (So some folk told you, but they knew
> No more of Jove's designs than you:)
> —The world's mad business now is o'er,
> And I resent these pranks no more.
> —I to such blockheads set my wit!
> I damn such fools!   Go, go, you're bit."

The pet, one might almost say, of the Pope, Swift, Arbuthnot group, the antagonists of Walpole and the Whigs, was Gay, if Parnell was also a protégé. Congreve and Prior were more loosely attached. Gay was the somewhat helpless sort of person who invariably finds friends and patrons when in a scrape. As a poet, a female friend of Johnson pronounced him "of a lower order. He had not in any great degree the *mens divinior*, the dignity of genius." His work shows the influence of his stronger friends. *The Shepherd's Week* (1714) was a contribution to Pope's quarrel with Philips and Steele over pastoral poetry. It is an amusing application of pastoral and Virgilian themes and clichés to the actualities of English rustic loves and life. The chief recurrent themes are there: the quarrel and competition, the forsaken maiden's complaint:

> Ah, Colin! canst thou leave thy sweetheart true?
> What I have done for thee will Cic'ly do?
>
> .   .   .   .   .
>
> I lagg'd the last with Colin on the green;
> And when at eve returning with thy car
> Awaiting heard the jingling bells from far;
> Straight on the fire the sooty pot I plac'd,
> To warm thy broth I burnt my hands for haste;
> When hungry thou stood'st staring like an oaf,
> I slic'd the luncheon from the barley loaf,
> With crumbled bread I thicken'd well the mess.
> Ah, love me more or love thy pottage less.

There is a Dirge and a Spell, and even the lofty strain of Silenus is echoed in the drunken songs of Bowzebeus. The best song again in Gay's mock-tragedy, *What d'ye call it* (1715),

> 'Twas when the seas were roaring—

is declared by Cowper on good authority to be a joint production with Swift, Arbuthnot, and Pope. Two lines from it were quoted by Scott on a tragic evening in his life:

> No eyes the rocks discover
> That lurk below the deep.

Trivia (1716) describes the streets of London with the minute detail, the realistic effect, of Swift's *A City Shower*, while giving to the whole a suggestion of the mock-heroic by the recurring interjection of epic similes; which was to be Arnold's device for such Homeric effects in *Sohrab and Rustum*. *The Beggar's Opera* (1728) sprang from a suggestion by Swift of a Newgate Pastoral, that is that Gay should do for thieves and rogues what he had done for English rustics. Fortunately Gay chose to parody Italian Opera which Addison had made fun of in the *Spectator*. It was his greatest stroke of invention. "We owe", says Johnson, "to Gay the Ballad Opera: a mode of comedy which at first was supposed to delight only by its novelty, but has now, by the experience of half a century been found so well accommodated to the disposition of a popular audience that it is likely to keep long possession of the stage." The century that followed on Johnson's prophecy in 1781 has seen it confirmed, most conspicuously by Gilbert and Sullivan. In the kind of ballad too that was coming into vogue, which Cowper admired and Johnson despised, the ballad in which simplicity, not yet romance, was the effect aimed at, Gay excelled, not alone in those supplied to the two operas, for *Polly* was the sequel to his first attempt but was censored. *Sweet William's Farewell to Black-eyed Susan* is a good example of the combination of simplicity and elegance which was admired. On the other hand Gay's *Fables*, of which he wrote so many, are frankly tedious reading. They catch nothing of the peculiar character of the animals introduced to point the somewhat cynical philosophy which Gay took over from his friends.

Thomas Parnell, Dean of Clogher in Ireland, was another poet whom Pope took up and made a Tory of. He has been praised as more essentially a poet than many of his contemporaries mainly on the strength of two meditative poems, the *Night Piece on Death* and the *Hymn to Contentment*, and the tale in verse *The Hermit*. The two first have been described as intermediaries between Milton and Wordsworth. Well, the verse is that of Milton's two poems and the subject is Nature, which is Wordsworth's. There is not much more in the comparison. They are tolerable poems in the manner which the Wartons were to cultivate later. *The Hermit* is an adequately told tale in decasyllabic couplets on a theme which has a long literary history, and has been rehandled in an interesting way in the *Bridge of San Luis Rey*, the providential purpose which we might discover underlying the apparently most arbitrary happenings, a belief which must lurk in every religious mind.

In what might be called Addison's or the Whig camp the poets were not many or important,—Addison himself, Ambrose Philips, Thomas Tickell. Complimentary poems to political patrons actual or prospective, translations from or imitations of the classical poets, odes and elegies were common products of all the poets of the period. Addison's poems, including *The Campaign* on the battle of Blenheim, so highly extolled by Macaulay, do not rise above the level of good prize-poems. Philips's Pastorals, overpraised and perhaps over-censured, are forgotten. He lives, if at all, by the name Namby-Pamby which he acquired by the verses in short lines "by which he paid his court to all ages and characters from Walpole, the 'steerer of the realm' to Miss Pulteney in the nursery". Tickell's *To the Earl of Warwick on the Death of Mr. Addison* has been extolled by both Johnson and Macaulay, and the opening is impressive by its truthful record of a moving scene:

> Can I forget the dismal light that gave
> My soul's best part forever to the grave!
> How silent did his old companions tread
> By midnight lamps the mansions of the dead,
> Through breathing statues, then unheeded things,
> Through rows of warriors, and through walks of kings!
> What awe did the slow solemn knell inspire;
> The pealing organ, and the pausing choir;
> The duties by the lawn-rob'd prelate pay'd;
> And the last words, that dust to dust convey'd!

It was this truth to the facts that Johnson preferred to the more indirect approach of a classical elegy such as *Lycidas*.

What has survived of these and other poets of the time are things to which they attached little importance, at least regarded as *parerga*: the *Colin and Lucy* of Tickell; the *Admiral Hosier's Ghost* of Glover, who was guilty of a once much admired epic *Leonidas* (1737); the *Margaret's Ghost* of Thomson's friend, David Mallet, who was also the author of *Edwin and Emma*, and anticipated Wordsworth in the title of a poem, *The Excursion*. The great Addison himself is known as a poet to many who have never read and probably never will read *The Campaign* by two or three hymns:

> The spacious firmament on high,
> With all the blue ethereal sky,
> And spangled heavens, a shining frame,
> Their great Original proclaim.

Better known are

> When all thy mercies, O my God!
> My rising soul surveys,

and "How are Thy servants blest, O Lord", two lines of which made a powerful appeal to the young imagination of Burns:

> For though in dreadful whirls we hung
> High on the broken wave,

and perhaps

> When rising from the bed of death
> O'erwhelmed with guilt and fear,
> I see my Maker face to face,
> O how shall I appear.

The fact is that the ballad and the hymn constitute an interesting thread through the poetry of the century. Of the ballad we shall speak later when, with Percy's *Reliques*, the charm of simplicity is reinforced by that of romance. Of the hymn we may say a word here. Both ballad and hymn satisfied one of the requirements of the classical doctrine as set forth in Pope's *Essay*: truth to nature, to what unsophisticated people do actually feel, if to Johnson they both seemed to lack the other requirement of "nature to advantage dressed", nature made interesting to a mind that can think and calls for some elaboration and dignity of expression. Johnson deals as sweepingly with Watts's hymns as with Warton's ballads.

The Calvinist Reformation in this country did not produce a crop of hymns as the Lutheran Church did in Germany. Some of the German hymns of the seventeenth century are among the greatest hymns after the Latin hymns of an earlier age. The English devotional poets of the same century, Donne, Herbert, Vaughan, etc., are not hymn-writers. They express not the communal experience and feelings of Christians as such but their own individual experiences and reactions, as Newman did at a later period. The reason for this blank in our literature is the Puritan dogma that nothing is to enter into the service of God in Church which is of merely "human composition". The only poems which may be sung there are the directly inspired Psalms of David. These might be and were reduced to metre. It was as late as 1695 that Bishop Ken printed two hymns that are well known to us to-day: "Awake, my soul, and with the sun" and "All praise to thee, my God, this night". It was in the eighteenth century that the hymn found its way into religious devotion, and the first prolific author of hymns was Isaac Watts (1674–1748). The titles which

210 A CRITICAL HISTORY OF ENGLISH POETRY

he gave to his volumes show how well aware he was of his innovation: *Hymns and Spiritual Songs in Imitation of the Psalms* (1707); *Psalms of David Imitated in the Language of the New Testament* (1719). In the Preface to this last volume he defends his practice. The language of the Psalms is not always suited for Christian use. "Where the Psalmist has described Religion by Fear of God, I have joined Faith and Love to it." The greatest of all the many hymns Watts wrote is often sung as a supplement to, and might well take the place of, a national anthem:

> Our God, our help in ages past,
> Our hope for years to come,
> Our shelter from the stormy blast
> And our Eternal Home.

To this one might add:

> Jesus shall reign where'er the sun
> Doth his successive journeys run.

The Divine and Moral Songs for Children (1720) are often of a rather alarming character, suitable for children brought up on the lines laid down in the *Fairchild Family*. But they had their influence on the very different *Songs of Innocence* of William Blake. Watts's chief successor was Charles Wesley, that sweet singer of Israel, author of "Jesus, lover of my soul", "Hark, through all the welkin rings", "Love divine, all love excelling", "Lo, he comes with clouds descending", "Christ the Lord is risen to-day", and others. John Wesley was responsible for some of the translations from the German, and collaborated with his brother. Philip Doddridge (1702–1751) is the author of "Hark the glad sound, the Saviour comes". John Wesley's Calvinist opponent, Augustus Toplady, closed a passionate defence of salvation only by grace by bursting into the now famous hymn, "Rock of Ages, cleft for me". Of Cowper and Newman we shall hear again.

The fate of many hymns illustrates well what must have happened to many ballads, though the record is not preserved. Both ballad and hymn are written for a community whose feelings the writer is trying to express. But such an audience knows what it wants, and, if it is absurd to speak of communal authorship as meaning something composed jointly by a singing throng, what it does mean is that the audience can react on the ballad or hymn—selecting, rejecting, altering as feeling dictates. Hardly one of the hymns referred to has preserved its original text throughout. Stanzas have been dropped, others modified as the community felt its sentiments were or were not expressed as they desired.

One poem of this age stands alone, the *Song to David*, of the otherwise undistinguished Christopher Smart (1722–1771). It is not a hymn in the sense which we have defined; it is a paean of adoration rising to a rapturous close: Rossetti called it the most accomplished poem of its century. Like Clare's best poem, it was written in an asylum; but any incoherence in its evolution is outweighed by the ecstasy of the poet's reaction to the poetry of the Psalms.

Chapter Seventeen

THOMSON TO COWPER

WITH the death of Queen Anne and the advent of the Hanoverians and the dominance of the Whig party under Walpole, who came into power with the collapse of the South Sea Bubble, ended the period of the dignified patronage of letters, and with it gradually came the end of the witty literature addressed to the town. Walpole's economical mind found the expense too great for the return. He preferred simpler and surer methods of corrupting politicians and the Press. The result for our literature is interesting to consider. It meant the loss of a definitely conceived, if limited, audience such as Steele and Addison, Swift and Pope wrote for. Men of letters were thrown back on the booksellers to take the place of patrons. It was to Cave that Johnson made his first appeal, to Cave's *Gentleman's Magazine* that he made his first contributions. Griffiths and the *Monthly Review* were Goldsmith's first haven. Hackwork such as translation became a necessary portion of a struggling author's labours. Johnson's great achievement was a Dictionary of the English Language; Goldsmith compiled grammars and histories, biographies and anthologies; and even wrote on Natural History. What, leaving such tasks aside, would determine an author's choice of a subject and the manner of treating it? Necessarily he would be in some measure guided by what had been, and still was, in vogue. The *Tatler* and the *Spectator* had made the periodical essay-paper a fashion which prevailed till almost the end of the century: Johnson's *Rambler* and *Idler*, Goldsmith's *Citizen of the World*, the *Adventurer* of Hawkesworth, to which Johnson contributed, are only a few. But the important thing to note is the change of tone. Johnson does not write for the town, the fashionable world. He conceives of his audience as mainly people like himself. The wit and sparkle of the earlier essayists, a reflection of the tone and manners of the circle in which the writers lived, is gone, its place taken by the weightier moral tone of the teacher or preacher. It was for the same kind of audience that Richardson's novels were composed, if Fielding had a wider outlook and a tone of better society in the narrow sense of the word. Even poetry acquired some of the same moralising, didactic, one might even say utilitarian tone, for with Walpole began quite definitely the utilitarian epoch in British history:

> For idle ages, starting, heard at last
> The Lusitanian Prince, who heaven-inspired
> To love of *useful* glory roused mankind,
> And in unbounded commerce mixed the world.

(So Thomson, whose claim for Britain is that she joins industry with liberty.) The *Essay on Criticism* and the *Essay on Man* were sparkling, witty poems, and dealt with themes of immediate general interest for intellectual circles. There are few or no poems so dreary as the didactic blank verse poems of the mid-eighteenth century: *Liberty, Field Sports, Night Thoughts, Pleasures of the Imagination* (Addison's essays recast in blank verse), *The Fleece, The Sugar Cane, The Art of Preserving Health,* etc.

But there was gain as well as loss. Liberated from the consciousness of an audience which welcomed, but to some extent controlled, his choice of theme and form, the poet was freer to look into his own soul, to say what he himself felt and thought, to appeal to a wider if more indefinite audience. Johnson's *Vanity of Human Wishes* is not so brilliant a poem as the *Essay on Man*. It is a far more sincere and ethically a much finer poem. There is a steady deepening of the personal note throughout the century—Collins, Gray, Johnson, Goldsmith, Cowper, Crabbe—insomuch that finally the blank verse didactic became in the *Excursion* and the *Prelude* a poem confessional rather than didactic, if still didactic in intention.

Moreover, as preoccupation with the town decreased, the range of interest widened to include interest in external nature, the world of earth and sea and sky. In the Nature-poetry of the century scientific and poetic interest are blended in a somewhat complex way, the experimental science of Bacon and Newton, which had enlarged the conception of the rule of law in the universe, and the imaginative delight in the life and beauty of Nature inherent in the British people, which becomes always fully self-conscious as Nature is mastered and primitive fears dispelled.

Nature was, of course, no new interest in English poetry. Even the Augustans had composed pastorals and locally descriptive poems of the type of *Cooper's Hill* by Denham and *Windsor Forest* by Pope. What was new in this landscape poetry was a fresh accuracy of description of the details of a scene, partly scientific in origin, but also due to the growing recognition of the imaginative appeal of a vivid even if objective description. It was something new to find in poetry such details as Lady Winchelsea notes in her *Nocturnal Reverie* (1714), which Wordsworth singled out just on this score:

> In such a night when passing clouds give place,
> Or thinly veil the heavens' mysterious face,
>
> .   .   .   .   .
>
> When the loos'd horse now, as his pasture leads,
> Comes slowly grazing through the adjoining meads,
> Whose stealing pace and lengthening shade we fear
> Till torn up forage in her teeth we hear.

The effect of such detail may be prosaic; it may be, as the pre-Raphaelite poets were to discover, poignantly emotional:

> From perfect grief there need not be
> Wisdom or even memory:
> One thing then learnt remains to me,—
> The woodspurge has a cup of three.

The poet in whose poetry the new objective, scientific interest, scientific but also imaginative, is made the main theme is the young Scotsman, James Thomson (1700–1748), who in 1725, deserting his theological studies in Edinburgh, came to London and found a publisher in 1726 for a blank verse poem *Winter*—a thin folio of sixteen pages sold for one shilling. *Winter* was much altered and added to in later years, and out of it grew successively *Summer* (1727), *Spring* (1728), and ultimately in 1730 *The Seasons*, including *Autumn* and the closing hymn,

> These as they change, Almighty Father! these
> Are but the varied God.   The rolling year
> Is full of thee.

The poems were composed in patches, but in the final form of each a certain method is observed,—the succession, most obvious in *Winter*, of the different phases of the season, between which are interspersed reflective passages and occasional descriptions of the season in other regions as the poet has learned of them from books of travel, of which, like Cowper,

Crabbe, and Wordsworth, he was a great reader. In *Summer* a somewhat different plan is followed, the progress of a single day from when

> yonder comes the powerful king of day
> Rejoicing in the east

to when

> Low walks the sun, and broadens by degrees
> Just o'er the verge of day. The shifting clouds
> Assembled gay, a richly gorgeous train,
> In all their pomp attend his setting throne.

It is the descriptive passages of Scottish and South of England scenery that alone are of interest to-day. Thomson was a close and accurate observer:

> The yellow wall-flower, stained with iron-brown.

> The pale descending year, yet pleasing still,
> A gentler mood inspires; for now the leaf
> Incessant rustles from the mournful grove,
> Oft startling such as studious walk below,
> And slowly circles through the waving air.

> The cherished fields
> Put on their winter-robe of purest white.
> 'Tis brightness all,—save where the new snow melts
> Along the mazy current. Low the woods
> Bow their hoar heads; and ere the languid sun
> Faint from the west emits his evening ray,
> Earth's universal face deep hid and chill
> Is one wide dazzling waste that buries wide
> The works of man.

And if it is on the selection and vivid rendering of the objective details that he relies for his main effects, Thomson when moved can give the transfiguring epithet which betrays the reactions of the poet's imagination:

> the *mournful* grove,
> And the sky *saddens* with the gathering storm,

and the lines in which the feelings of the hunted deer are so vividly reflected:

> He sweeps the forest oft and sobbing sees
> The glades mild opening to the golden day,
> Where in kind contest with his butting friends
> He wont to struggle, or his loves enjoy.

Three main strands are blended in Thomson's *Seasons*: his own observation and love of scenery, the scientific interest inspired by Newton, Locke, and the English philosophy of observation and experiment which Voltaire loved to contrast with the high-flying a-priorism of Continental philosophy dominated by Descartes and Leibnitz, and lastly a religious mood which justifies to the poet's mind the Miltonic character of the diction and verse. Thomson's religion is not Milton's stern reading of Christian doctrine. It is the Deism to which Newton's revelation of the wide sweep of the reign of law had given a genuinely religious support, and which had pervaded the scientific teaching Thomson received at Edinburgh University. Thomson's theme, writes a contemporary, "is Nature and its explorer (*i.e.* Newton) and its author (*i.e.* God). What indeed could without prophaneness be added to the praises of the Great Creator but His works and Newton? He speaks his sublime wisdom and goodness to us in them, and Newton is his interpreter." It will be interesting to note how this religion of God as seen in Nature will show itself in later poets such as Cowper and Wordsworth, and the shock given to this feeling by the Darwinian doctrine of evolution.

After a reference to Shakespeare and Milton among the British "Sons of Glory", Thomson continues:

> Nor shall my verse that elder bard forget,
> The gentle Spenser, fancy's pleasing son,
> Who like a copious river poured his song
> O'er all the mazes of enchanted ground.

Spenser was his model in the other poem by which Thomson lives, for neither the declamatory blank verse of *Liberty* (1735–1736) nor his poetic dramas, of which the best is probably *Tancred and Sigismunda* (1745), have anything but an historic interest. But the *Castle of Indolence* (1748), a little allegory in two cantos, has some delightful descriptions. Following Spenser's narrative of the Bower of Bliss and its destruction in the second book of *The Faerie Queene*, Thomson describes with an undertouch of humour the Castle and its inhabitants, including the poet:

> A bard here dwelt more fat than bard beseems.

In the second canto we hear of the Knight of Industry, his achievements and his destruction of the Castle and liberation of those fit to be set free.   Though the poem is a *jeu d'esprit*, Thomson dilates on his favourite philosophical and political themes—the ascending scale of being, and Britain as the great inheritor and home of Liberty and Industry.   It was for a masque composed in conjunction with his Scottish friend Mallet that he wrote what is the most widely known of his verses:

> Rule Britannia, rule the waves,
> Britons never will be slaves—

as the refrain originally ran.

In the same year as Thomson's *Winter* appeared what might be called a landscape poem, *Grongar Hill*, by John Dyer (1700–1758).   In four-foot trochaics the poet describes the impression of scenery as it opens to the eye of the climber:

> Now I gain the mountain's brow,
> What a landscape lies below!
> No clouds, no vapours intervene,
> But the gay, the open scene
> Does the face of Nature show
> In all the hues of Heaven's bow.

In characteristic fashion the landscape suggests a moral:

> As yon summits soft and fair
> Clad in colours of the air,
> Which to those who travel near
> Barren, brown and rough appear,
> Still we tread the same coarse way,
> The present's still a cloudy day.

Dyer's more ambitious poem, *The Ruins of Rome* (1740), is in the too declamatory style of so many poems of the day.   "The title", says Johnson, "raises greater expectation than the performance gratifies."   It is otherwise with *The Fleece* (1757). "The woolcomber and the poet appear to me such discordant natures that an attempt to bring them together is to couple the serpent with the fowl."   Yet in the opening part which deals with the sheep there are some very English landscapes which pleased Wordsworth:

> See, the sun gleams; the living pastures rise
> After the nurture of the fallen shower.
> How beautiful! how blue the ethereal vault,
> How verdurous the lawns, how clear the brooks!
> . . . such spacious flocks of sheep
> Like flakes of gold illuminate the green.

P

What Johnson says of *The Fleece* is true of Somerville's *The Chase* (1735), in which the influence of Thomson is obvious. Lively pictures of a hare hunt, a fox hunt, and a stag hunt, with a digression to describe a hunt of wild animals under Aurungzebe, hardly compensate for tedious didactic accounts of the best method of worming dogs, etc.

But in fact to follow in detail the course of the more ambitious poetry of the mid-century—Browne's *Pipe of Tobacco*, Glover's *Leonidas*, an epic, Green's *The Spleen*, Somerville's *Field Sports*, Young's *Night Thoughts*, Blair's *The Grave*, Akenside's *Pleasures of the Imagination*, Armstrong's *Art of Preserving Health*, all between 1736 and 1750—is not a very repaying task. Some are more tedious than others. Young's *Night Thoughts* (1742), at once gloomy and booming, enjoyed wide popularity in France as well as in England. For them and for Blair's *Grave* (1743) Blake was to do designs. Only two short extracts from *Night Thoughts* have found their way into the *Oxford Book of Eighteenth Century Verse* (1926). One understands Johnson's dislike and distrust of blank verse, because it seemed to be thought that one wrote poetry if one discussed any subject in this measure. Wordsworth did not entirely abandon the habit. But if one cannot read with much pleasure or profit the blank verse poems of the century one must not fail to do justice to the songs. They are not lyrical poems such as are the songs of the Elizabethans or the later romantics. They have not much of the lyric cry. But there are many charming songs in a lower key: after Gay one has Carey's "Of all the girls that are so smart", the anonymous "In good King Charles's golden days", James Miller's *The Life of a Beau*, Byrom's "Christians awake, salute the happy morn", Dyer's "Ye poor little sheep, oh well may ye stray", Fielding's spirited Hunting Song:

> The dusky night rides down the sky,
> And ushers in the morn;
> The hounds all join in glorious cry,
> The Huntsman winds his horn!
> *And a-hunting we will go—*

and many others in the same vein.

But we must confine ourselves to tracing the main currents, dwelling shortly on poems which are still alive with a view to understanding the changes which came about as the century drew to an end. What one may call the orthodox poetry is didactic and satiric. The subject should be one capable of poetic treatment, but even so it must have something to teach. "I do not see that *The Bard* promotes any truth moral or political", says Dr. Johnson, who defines poetry as the art of bringing imagination to the help of truth. And Johnson's two poems, and those of his great friend and disciple Goldsmith, show what can be done in poetry weighted with an impressive theme. *London* appeared in the same year as Pope's *One Thousand Seven Hundred and Thirty-Eight,* afterwards the *Epilogue to the Satires.* Johnson imitates Juvenal as Pope had imitated Horace. It is from London, not Rome, that the speaker is flying, and for the "graeculus esuriens", the greedy and parasitic Greek, Johnson substitutes the French:

> Studious to please and ready to submit,
> The subtle Gaul was born a parasite.

But Johnson was not really in sympathy with Juvenal's theme. He loved the town and hated the country. "People live in the country who are fit to live there." But one note he did strike with conviction and dignity—the woes of poverty:

> This mournful truth is everywhere confess'd,
> Slow rises worth by poverty depress'd.

Eleven years later appeared the *Vanity of Human Wishes,* based on Juvenal's tenth satire. Here Johnson had a theme entirely to his mind: "Man is not born for happiness", a theme he was to reinforce later in his prose novel, if it can be so called, *Rasselas* (1759). Johnson's rendering of Juvenal's theme with modern for ancient examples is weighted with sombre conviction. But at the close he departs from both Juvenal and his earlier translator Dryden. In the religious reference of both the latter there is a satiric tone:

> Ut tamen et poscas, etc.

"Still, that you may also prefer some prayer and offer at the shrines vitals and consecrated sausages from a tiny white pig contrived" (Owen). So Juvenal, and Dryden substitutes rather than translates:

> Yet not to rob the priests of pious gain,
> That altars be not wholly built in vain.

Johnson breathes into the closing paragraph his sincere, passionate spirit of religious resignation:

> Enquirer cease, petitions yet remain
> Which heaven may hear, nor deem religion vain.
> Still raise for good the supplicating voice,
> But leave to heaven the measure and the choice.
>
> .   .   .   .   .
>
> Yet when the sense of sacred presence fires,
> And strong devotion to the skies aspires,
> Pour forth thy fervours for a healthful mind,
> Obedient passions and a will resign'd;
> For love, which scarce collective man can fill;
> For patience, sovereign o'er transmuted ill;
> For faith, that panting for a happier seat,
> Counts death kind nature's signal of retreat.
> These goods for man the laws of heaven ordain,
> These goods he grants, who grants the power to gain;
> With them celestial wisdom calms the mind,
> And makes the happiness she does not find.

Johnson's prologues and his occasional and lighter poems are often excellent. The most moving and rememberable are the lines on the death of the poor physician who found, with others, a home under Johnson's roof:

> His virtues walked their narrow round,
>   Nor made a pause, nor left a void,
> And sure the Eternal Master found
>   The single talent well employ'd.

Something of Johnson's sombre philosophy found expression in the gentler, more charming poetry of his friend Oliver Goldsmith. *The Traveller* (1764), the record of Goldsmith's wanderings as a casual medical student, a street fiddler, an academic disputant, has for its moral Johnson's conviction that the sum of human happiness is much the same in all countries and under all sorts of governments:

> How small of all that human hearts endure
> That part which laws or kings can cause or cure.

Each people, Goldsmith contends, has its peculiar source of happiness, which pursued to excess "begets peculiar pain". But Goldsmith had a clearer perception than his master of what was the evil of his own day and country, the sacrifice of the poor to the increasing wealth of the few:

> Each wanton judge new penal statutes draws,
> Laws grind the poor, and rich men rule the laws.

That became even more definitely the burden of his *Deserted*

Village (1770), the sweetest poem which the eighteenth century has left us. The picture of the village is doubtless coloured by the tender idealism of memory, and the poem was attacked from two sides. On the one hand it was affirmed, as Goldsmith admits in the dedication to Sir Joshua Reynolds, that the "depopulation is no where to be seen, and the disorders it laments are only to be found in the poet's lamentation". Johnson was one of the critics; and later Macaulay would comment on the fallacies in Goldsmith's political economy. Recent research, like that of the Hammonds, *The Village Labourer* (1900), suggests that Goldsmith was the truer observer. On the other hand Crabbe was to include Goldsmith among the pastoral idealists who pictured a scene which had never existed, and to be scornful over the parson "passing rich with forty pounds a year", which, if we may believe the dedication of the *Traveller*, was the salary of the poet's brother Henry: "A man who despising fame and fortune has retired to happiness and obscurity with an income of forty pounds a year". In no poems of the century so fully as in the *Vanity of Human Wishes* and the *Deserted Village* is the personal feeling of the poet expressed with such power as in the first of these, with such winning sweetness as in Goldsmith's:

> In all my wanderings round this world of care,
> In all my griefs—and God has given my share—
> I still had hopes my latest hours to crown,
> Amidst these humble bowers to lay me down;
> To husband out life's taper at the close,
> And keep the flame from wasting by repose;
> I still had hopes, for pride attends us still,
> Amidst the swains to show my book-learn'd skill,
> Around my fire an evening group to draw,
> And tell of all I felt and all I saw;
> And as a hare whom hounds and horns pursue
> Pants to the place from whence at first he flew,
> I still had hopes, my long vexations past,
> Here to return—and die at home at last.

Goldsmith's lighter verses, *The Haunch of Venison*, *Retaliation*, *The Death of a Mad Dog*, *Mrs Mary Blaize*, are delicately and charmingly humorous. Indeed Johnson's epitaph is one of the truest of his sweeping judgements: *nullum fere genus scribendi non tetigit: nullum quod tetigit non ornavit*. Goldsmith's *Deserted Village*, his *Vicar of Wakefield*, and his comedies are among the most living things bequeathed us by the century.

Johnson and Goldsmith were both in theory and practice upholders of the orthodox poetry of the century: didactic, satiric, pastoral, occasional. But orthodoxy is most aware of itself when heresy is in the air; and it is clear from their words that there were fashions in poetry which they did not approve. "What criticisms have we not heard of late", writes Goldsmith, "in favour of blank verse, and Pindaric Odes, choruses, anapaests and iambics, alliterative care and happy negligence. Every absurdity has now a champion to defend it: and as he is generally much in the wrong, so he has always much to say, for error is ever talkative." "I take up books to be told something new; but here as it is now managed the reader is told nothing. A parcel of gaudy images pass on before his imagination like the figures in a dream; but curiosity, inductive reason, and the whole train of affections, are fast asleep" (*Citizen of the World*, xcvii). These words were written between 1760 and 1762, and we fear that Gray's odes were the poems in view, or among them, those "Wonderful Wonder of Wonders", as Johnson calls them, "the two Sister Odes, by which, though at first either vulgar ignorance or common sense universally rejected them, many have since been persuaded to think themselves delighted". But one must go a little further back than 1757, when these odes were published, to trace the source and nature of the heresy. Some ten years earlier, two small collections of odes were issued, the one by William Collins, the other by Joseph Warton. The preface to the latter contains the revolutionary challenge: "The public has been so much accustomed of late to didactic poetry alone, and essays on moral subjects, that any work where the imagination is much indulged, will perhaps not be relished or regarded. . . . But he [the author] is convinced that the fashion of moralising in verse has been carried too far, and as he looks upon invention and imagination to be the chief faculties of the poet, so he will be happy if the following odes may be looked upon as an attempt to bring poetry into its right channel." This was to be the text of Joseph's later *Essay on Pope* (1756–1782). "I revere the memory of Pope, I respect and honour his abilities, but I do not think him at the head of his profession. In other words, in the species of poetry wherein Pope excelled he is superior to all mankind; and I only say that this species of poetry is not the most excellent one of the art." This is the kind of statement to which Johnson could only answer: "If Pope be not a poet, where is poetry to be found?"

Joseph (1722–1800) and Thomas (1728–1799) Warton were the sons of an older Thomas (1688–1745), himself a poet and professor of poetry, some of whose poems were published by his son in 1747 as *Poems on Several Occasions*. Both the sons were poets, but also, and more important, ardent lovers and students of our older poets. The purpose of Joseph's *Essay on the Genius and Writings of Pope* was to distinguish between Pope and "our only three sublime and pathetic poets, Spenser, Shakespeare and Milton". He edited later the shorter poems of Milton with the commentary of a student and a lover of poetry. Thomas issued in 1753 a volume of *Observations on the Faerie Queene*.

This then was the new direction which was to be given to poetry—feeling and imagination, not instruction or satire. Of our older poets the most inspiring were Spenser and the Milton of *L'Allegro* and *Il Penseroso*, which with the other shorter poems had been overlooked in the general admiration of *Paradise Lost*. *The Enthusiast, or the Lover of Nature*, a blank verse poem by Joseph, breathes the spirit of Milton's poems throughout:

> But let me never fail in cloudless nights,
> When silent Cynthia in her silver car
> Through the blue concave slides, when shine the hills,
> Twinkle the streams, and woods look tipp'd with gold,
> To seek some level mead and there invoke
> Old Midnight's sister, Contemplation sage.

The *Ode to Fancy* and the shorter *Ode to Solitude* are composed in the metre of Milton's poems. Thomas in his *Pleasures of Melancholy* is equally enthusiastic about Nature and "Mother of Musings, Contemplation sage", and his poem *On the Approach of Summer* is quite in the manner of *L'Allegro*:

> Hence iron-sceptred Winter, haste
> To bleak Siberian waste. . . .

But Thomas could be humorous and write a panegyric in Miltonic style and verse *On Oxford Ale*.

More interesting is the poet who appeared along with Joseph in 1746, William Collins, Joseph's friend and first poetic collaborator at both Winchester and Oxford. His earliest volume was a collection of pastorals strangely entitled

Persian Eclogues (he spoke of them later as Irish eclogues), but his reputation rests upon the little volume of *Odes* referred to above. They were twelve in number, described as *On Several Descriptive and Allegoric Subjects*, which title, if one omit that on the *Death of Colonel Charles Ross*, covers the remainder,—*Pity, Fear, Simplicity, The Poetical Character, Mercy, Liberty*, "How sleep the brave", *Peace, The Manners, The Passions*, leaving *To Evening* as the descriptive ode. The logic of Collins's odes is uncertain, and even the grammar can go astray. What opens well may tail off to vagueness or flatness. Speaking of his later decline Johnson says: "His disorder was no alienation of mind, but general laxity and feebleness, a deficiency rather of his vital than intellectual power". The same is true of his odes. In a long ode like that to *Liberty* the poet seems to grow out of breath before the end, which tails off to what Swinburne described as "the prostration of collapse". Only three of the odes have found their way regularly into anthologies,—the short and quite perfect "How sleep the brave", the *Ode to Evening*, and *The Passions, An Ode for Music*. Yet there is some peculiar quality that appeals, if fitfully, in all the odes. It is not passion. Collins is not a singer, despite Swinburne's claim in an extravagant essay inspired partly by the desire to differ from Arnold. Nor are "the whole train of the affections", of which Goldsmith speaks, very obviously quickened even in the two delightful poems composed later than the *Odes—On the Death of Thomson* and the *Dirge in Cymbeline*. What attracts us in Collins is a delicate sense of beauty which is always present if it only occasionally finds quite adequate expression. Collins's personifications are, like Shelley's, not mere abstract nouns with an opening capital letter. They are real if faintly outlined figures by the help of which he is able to express a delicate mood of feeling without too disturbing detail—"Spring with dewy fingers cold", "Honour a pilgrim gray", "Freedom a weeping hermit". What Mrs. Barbauld and Mr. Garrod complain of in the poem on Thomson, that there is no direct expression of sorrow or characterisation of Thomson, is just what gives its peculiar charm to the poem. Pity and Ease and Health and Love and Fancy and Joy suggest without making too concrete those who are touched by these moods. The sorrow is transmuted into a mood of passion recollected in tranquillity. The one long poem which Collins wrote after the *Odes*, the *Ode on the Popular Superstitions of the Highlands* (1749–1750), was not published till many years after the poet's death and has come to us in an unfinished state. Like his other poems it is unequal, but like these also reveals how fully he was a poet of imagination, how he responded to the influences which were quickening the spirit of the coming revival of romance. Of all the early, and some of them minor, precursors he is most entirely free of the didactic spirit with which Warton had declared war. Even Gray has his closing moral. Collins is the precursor of those of the later poets in whose work the predominant shaping influence is the spirit of beauty.

In the year before that in which Warton and Collins made their joint appearance another poet had published a volume of *Odes on Several Subjects* (1745), and these were followed in 1747 by Gray's *Ode on a Distant Prospect of Eton College*. "Akenside", Johnson declared once in a rather petulant mood, "was a superior poet to Gray and Mason." And later another excellent, but also prejudiced, critic, Hazlitt, pronounced Akenside's odes superior to those of Wordsworth; and the late Sir William Watson was an admirer of the careful finish of Akenside's work. But Johnson's praise of Akenside did not extend to the odes. "When he lays his ill-fated hand upon his harp the former powers seem to desert him . . . his thoughts are cold and his words inelegant." Perhaps "tame" would be an even juster word than "cold", for Akenside's disquisitions in various forms of the ode. There is no strong personal note, nothing that through the abstractions and arguments tells of the poet's own feelings.

It is otherwise with the odes of Thomas Gray, the most learned of English poets after Milton; and Gray's learning was wider, his knowledge of Greek more accurate, than Milton's. There is personal feeling in all Gray's odes except it be *The Bard*. He is strong too where Collins is weak. There is no failure in the logic, the poetic logic, of an ode, whereas Collins is apt to falter half-way through as if not quite sure what the drift of the whole poem was to be. Gray has always something quite definite to say. His personifications are clearly conceived and presented:

> Wisdom in sable garb arrayed,
>   Immersed in rapturous thought profound,
> And Melancholy, silent maid,
>   With leaden eyes that love the ground,

> Still on thy solemn steps attend
>   Warm Charity, the general friend,
> With Justice to herself severe,
> And Pity dropping soft the sadly pleasing tear.

This is from the *Ode to Adversity* which, with the *Ode to Spring* and the *Ode on a Distant Prospect of Eton College*, was composed in 1742. The ode *On the Death of a Favourite Cat* in 1747 was followed in 1750 by the *Elegy Written in a Country Church-yard*, which with Goldsmith's *Deserted Village* is probably the most widely known poem of the century. But the most elaborate of Gray's finished and sustained odes are the two Pindarics of which Johnson spoke so contemptuously. So far from not having "spoken out", as Arnold declares, Gray has, one feels, said with great completeness all he had to say, but that is not very profound. The progress of poetry, hand in hand with freedom, is a rhetorical topic not very remote from "When Britain first at heaven's command". The prophecies of *The Bard* are too neatly historical to produce the impression of such prophetic poetry as the Hebrew, or even the closing lyrical portions of *Prometheus Unbound*. Gray's poetry is more solid, more convincing, when the core of it is his own personal feelings as in the Eton ode, or the *Hymn to Adversity*, and the *Elegy*. The *Elegy* deserves its fame. The thought of Death the Leveller is a commonplace, no doubt; but it is one of those commonplaces that never grow old. A tender heart beats under the stiff brocade of the style. The stately argument moves steadily on from the lovely hushed opening to the wistful close:

> On some fond breast the parting soul relies.

"The close", we call it, for here the real elegy ends: the lines that follow about the poet's own imagined fate are fanciful by comparison.

The Ode then, with its personified abstractions, was one form taken by the revolt, a somewhat timid revolt, against the dominance of the didactic and satiric. Its effect on lyrical poetry is traceable into the Romantic Age, witness the early poems of Coleridge and even of Byron.

But if the ode offended Johnson and Goldsmith by its want of any definite teaching (for Johnson excepts Gray's *Adversity* as "at once poetical and rational"), and by the "cumbrous splendour", the classical mythology, and use of "a language deemed to be more poetical as it is more remote from common use", there was another heresy showing its head which offended by its over-simplicity and its harking back to less enlightened ages. The impulse came from the quickening of interest in other older literatures besides the classical. Old Scandinavian poetry, which as represented by *The Death-Song of Ragnar*, had attracted the interest of Sir William Temple, found translators in Bishop Percy, *Five Pieces of Runic Poetry* (1763), and Gray whose two Norse Odes, the *Fatal Sisters* and the *Descent of Odin*, were included in the 1768 edition of his poems. But the exciting discovery was not Scandinavian but Celtic, Caledonian poetry, as that was revealed to the world in the Ossian poems by James Macpherson. Here was the poetry of a primitive people with all the nobility and sensibility which the century was determined to ascribe to barbaric nations whether in America or in Scotland, a people who had warred with and defeated the degenerate Romans. And Macpherson's poetic prose had real merits of imagination and rhythm not least in the descriptions of Scottish scenery—moor and rock and mist and desolation. But the most enduring and genuine influence in the revival of an imaginative poetry was our own older poetry, and especially the ballads of England and Scotland.

The manner in which the ballad became an influence in poetry shows interestingly that what has been cited to justify one effect may help to quicken something very different. In his conflict, a conflict continued after the foe was really dead, with the conceits of metaphysical poetry, Gothic as he called it, Addison undertook in the *Spectator* to show how much of the "truth to nature" which criticism found in classical poetry, in the Ancients, was discoverable in an obviously simple and popular poem such as *Chevy Chase* or *The Babes in the Wood*. "I know nothing which more shows the essential and inherent perfection of simplicity of thought above that which I call the Gothic manner in writing than this, that the first pleases all kinds of palates, and the latter only such as have formed to themselves a wrong artificial taste upon little, fanciful authors and writers of epigrams. Homer, Virgil, Milton, so far as the language of their poems is understood, will please a reader of plain common sense who would neither relish nor comprehend an epigram of Martial or a poem of Cowley; so on the contrary an ordinary song or ballad that is the delight of the common people, cannot fail to please all such readers as are not unqualified for the entertainment by their affectations or ignorance;

and the reason is plain, because the same *paintings of nature* which recommend it to the most ordinary reader will appear beautiful to the most refined" (*Spectator*, No. 70). Accordingly Addison goes on to show that "the old song of Chevy Chase obeys the rules of the critics and is full of the same beautiful strokes" of feeling as the *Aeneid*. Like that, it has a lesson to teach, "an important precept of morality"—to deter barons from civil conflict. As to touches of feeling, when Douglas is dying and

> Earl Percy took
> The dead man by the hand,
> And said, Earl Douglas for thy life
> Would I had lost my land,

"the beautiful line . . . will put the reader in mind of Aeneas' behaviour toward Lausus", whom he had slain as he came to the rescue of his father:

> At vero ut voltum vidit, etc.—

in Dryden's version:

> The pious prince beheld young Lausus dead:
> He grieved, he wept, then grasped his hand and said.

Truth to Nature carried to this degree of simplicity did not appeal to Johnson: "People talk of nature. But mere obvious nature may be exhibited with very little power of mind." "Chevy Chase pleased the vulgar but did not satisfy the learned; it did not fill a mind capable of thinking." But there was more in the ballads than simplicity, as became apparent when better ballads than the particular version of *Chevy Chase* known to Addison became available. *A Collection of Old Ballads, etc.* appeared in 1722, the most of them the kind of ballad which Scott calls "stall-ballads", ballads which had already been printed in broadsides or in small miscellanies known as "Garlands", generally flat and insipid ballads of the kind which Dr. Johnson disliked and Wordsworth too much admired. The great, the revealing collection of ballads was that issued by Bishop Percy in 1765 as *Reliques of Ancient English Poetry consisting of Old Heroic Ballads, Songs, and other Pieces of our earlier Poets, Together with some few of later Date*. As the title and the preface indicate ballads, English and Scottish, were not the sole contents. With them "to atone for the rudeness of the more obsolete poems" there were to be "a few modern attempts in the same kind of writing", "little elegant pieces of the lyric kind", and some "specimens of the composition of contemporary poets of a higher class". But the pith and marrow of the volumes is the ballads which Percy discovered in an old MS. volume half of which had been used up to light fires. To these were added ballads supplied to him by friends, especially Sir David Dalrymple and other Scottish enthusiasts. Moreover the whole work had been planned in connection with the poet William Shenstone (1714–1763), the author of at least two charming poems, *The Schoolmistress* (1741), a delightful humorous poem in the Spenserian stanza, and the *Pastoral Ballad* in the anapaestic verse which Prior had used before and Cowper was to use later:

> When forced the fair nymph to forego,
>   What anguish I felt in my heart!
> Yet I thought—but it might not be so—
>   'Twas with pain that she saw me depart.
>
> She gazed as I slowly withdrew;
>   My path I could hardly discern;
> So sweetly she bade me adieu,
>   I thought that she bade me return.

Shenstone was responsible, Percy states, for the selection and arrangement of most of the modern pieces, and probably for a good deal of the dressing to advantage which enraged the antiquary Ritson, but, as Scott insists, made the ballads more acceptable to general readers.

A glance through the *Reliques*, of which the best is the fourth edition prepared by the Bishop's nephew Thomas Percy, a fellow of St. John's College, Oxford, is sufficient to show what there was to appeal to the reawakening interest in the poetry of feeling and imagination: *Chevy Chase* in an older version, *Otterbourne, The Jew's Daughter, Edward, Edward, Sir Patrick Spens, Edom o' Gordon*—all in the first volume. Others are *The Notbrowne Mayden, The Lord of Linne, Glasgerion, Child Waters, Fair Margaret and Sweet William, Barbara Allan's Ghost*. The names themselves suggest the new ferment which was to bring back to poetry romance—chivalrous, thrilling, mysterious. In the best of the ballads one gets the quintessence of the romantic which often suffers in longer poems, such as Scott's lays, from the alloy of more detailed description of scenery and character and action. If asked to define "romantic" one might adopt Arnold's suggestion for the testing of poetry generally and cite single verses:

> Half ower, half ower to Aberdour
> 'Tis fifty fadom deep,
> And ther lies guid Sir Patrick Spens
> Wi' the Scots lords at his feet.

As has been said, the *Reliques* included some poems from later authors, as well as such imitations of the old ballads as *Hardyknute*, Hamilton's *Braes of Yarrow*:

> Busk ye, busk ye, my bonny, bonny bride,

and *Admiral Hosier's Ghost*, also poems from Elizabethan and seventeenth-century poets, with one or two from Middle English. But how little of Middle English poetry was familiar is evident from the singular story of the *Rowley Poems* of poor Thomas Chatterton (1752–1770). Under the spell of the beautiful church of St. Mary Redcliffe in Bristol, this untaught boy discovered for himself the charm of the Middle Ages, whose unrivalled churches and cathedrals were despised by the virtuosi of his day, with whom 'Gothic' was a synonym for 'barbarous'. In a mass of old MSS. released from the muniment room of St. Mary's he professed to have found the poems of one Thomas Rowley, a fifteenth-century priest; they were in fact his own. Chatterton knew little of Middle English beyond what he had gathered from the glossary to Speght's *Chaucer*, and equally little of Chaucer's prosody. His decasyllables run almost as smoothly as Pope's, though in one or two poems he catches the accentual rhythm which Coleridge later claimed to have invented. Spenser, Shakespeare, and Dryden were his masters; fifteenth-century Bristol was the world of his imagination. The mystification of the Rowley poems has long been cleared up; but the poetry remains. They *are* poems; two of them, the *Balade of Charitie* and the lyric "O, sing untoe my roundelaie", deserve a place in any anthology. From Chatterton Keats caught the Pre-Raphaelite note, which, through *The Eve of St. Mark*, he transmitted to Rossetti and Morris, both of whom expressed their admiration for the marvellous boy who "perished in his pride" before he was eighteen.

Chapter Eighteen

COWPER

"OH, mamma," says Marianne Dashwood in Jane Austen's *Sense and Sensibility*, "how spiritless, how tame was Edward's manner in reading to us last night! . . . To hear those beautiful lines, which have frequently almost driven me wild, pronounced with such imperturbable calm, such dreadful indifference!"

"He would certainly have done better justice to simple and elegant prose. I thought so at the time; but you *would* give him Cowper."

"Nay, mamma, if he is not to be animated by Cowper! . . ."

We hardly think to-day of Cowper, if we read him at all, as a passionate, animating poet. The romantics who followed were to provide us with so much more stimulating, not to say intoxicating, beverages that Cowper appeals, if he appeals at all, by way of contrast, as a poet of pious sermons or more frequently, *e.g.* to Sainte-Beuve, as the poet of quiet rural and domestic life, a life of quiet, controlled, pious epicureanism, a type of life which has apparently passed away for ever. Yet historically considered, to his own and the next generation it was the combination of sensibility with naturalness, the truth of feeling which the poets of "Feeling" often lacked that constituted the appeal of Cowper's blend of sermon and self-revelation. Indeed one might say that Cowper the man, revealed in his poems and letters supplemented by the facts of his life, is of greater interest to-day than his poems themselves, witness the recent *Stricken Deer* of Lord David Cecil.

For a History of Literature, a detached study of that poetry, it is necessary to distinguish the different strata in Cowper's, if not complex yet divided, personality. There is first the Cowper of the days before his nervous collapse in 1763 and confinement in a private asylum at St. Albans till 1765. Injury had doubtless been done to a not strong nervous system by his early experience of school in Bedfordshire.

But the years he spent at Westminster School, and in law-chambers later, are always recalled by him as, in the main, days of happiness and of innocent levity,—laughing over the *Arabian Nights' Tales* with his cousin Harriet Cowper, "giggling and making giggle" with Thurlow in law-chambers, "cutting capers for victories obtained under Chatham's auspices", making love to his other cousin Theodora, Harriet's sister, and writing verses amorous or humorous,—verses inspired by his huge admiration for the charming ease of Prior's poems: "Every man conversant with verse-writing knows, and knows by painful experience, that the familiar style is of all styles the most difficult to succeed in. To make verses speak the language of prose without being prosaic . . . to marshal the words of it in such an order as they might naturally take in falling from the lips of an extemporary speaker, yet without meanness, harmoniously, elegantly, and without seeming to displace a syllable for the sake of rhyme, is one of the most arduous tasks a poet can undertake." That is the Cowper of early days, a Cowper who, despite the storms which descended upon him, remained till almost the end of his life the composer of light, occasional poems in ballad, fable, or other form as well as the writer of matchlessly charming and humorous letters. His favourite metres are Prior's octosyllabics, and the same writer's anapaests, as:

> Dear Chloe, how blubber'd is that pretty face,

which is the metre of Cowper's:

> The rose had been washed, just washed in a shower.

There was, even in the young man of these years, an undercurrent of religious melancholy which found a certain satisfaction in the poems of George Herbert, a master also of the natural style.

The second Cowper is the man who emerged from the sanatorium at St. Albans in 1765, a sane but also a converted man—saved by the blood of Christ, the Everlasting Mercy, aware that his own righteousness was as filthy rags but that he is clothed in the eyes of God in the imputed righteousness of the Saviour. His chief correspondent during these years, 1765–1773, was a Mrs. Cowper, sister of the Reverend Martin Madan whose son afterwards afflicted Cowper sorely by his prescription of polygamy as the punishment and cure for adultery. The most direct expression of the mood of these years is to be found in the *Olney Hymns,*

> Jesus whose blood so freely flow'd
>   To satisfy the law's demand;
> By thee from guilt and wrath redeem'd
>   Before the Father's face I stand,

and

> This heart a fountain of vile thoughts,
>   How does it overflow!
> While self upon the surface floats
>   Still bubbling from below.

The best known of Cowper's hymns—for a large number of the Olney Hymns were by Dr. Newton—are probably "There is a fountain fill'd with blood" and "Hark, my Soul, it is the Lord". These were the years, Lord David Cecil believes, in which alone Cowper was really happy. Had the mood lasted we should have had only hymns, pious letters, and the more didactic portions of the longer poems, if these at all. Cowper can think of nothing but his great experience. Nature, gardening, hares, humorous letters were all out of his reckoning as yet. When his brother, a clergyman, visits him, Cowper complains that he gives the conversation a turn "that we have not been used to, so much said about nothing, so little about Jesus is very painful to us". But ecstasy is a dangerous form of happiness, especially for one who felt so acutely as Cowper, whose nerves were so delicately strung: "So long as I am pleased with an employment I am capable of unwearied application. I never received a *little* pleasure from anything in my life; if I am delighted it is in the extreme" (May 8, 1780). "The meshes of that fine network, the brain, are composed of such mere spinner's threads in me that when a long thought finds its way into them, it buzzes about at such a rate as seems to threaten the whole contexture." The reaction which ecstasy provokes came to Cowper at first in the not unusual form of a complete dryness of soul; but it deepened into a suicidal mania, and in the end left him deprived for life of the joy, the conviction, the hope in which he had lived during these years. Henceforth he was, even when sane in other respects and physically well, to remain convinced that his was a lost soul, singled out by God's inscrutable will for damnation.

The direct expression of this fixed mood, occasional in his letters, is still rarer in his poetry. There are the lines in *The Garden* from which Lord David Cecil has taken the title of his Life of Cowper:

Q

> I was a stricken deer that left the herd
> Long since; with many an arrow deep infixt
> My panting soul was charg'd;

and even that does not strike the final note of despair. He closes on the memory of the earlier experience of relief:

> soliciting the darts
> He drew them forth, and heal'd and bade me live.

Besides this is the short poem to Newton on his return from Ramsgate, and last, most poignant of all, written in his final mood of hopeless suffering, *The Castaway*.

These are the chief strata of Cowper's temperament as man and poet, and these some of the poems in which the one or the other finds direct expression. In the main body of his work they are combined in various ways. The early poems, gay and amorous, were never included by himself in any of the volumes issued from 1782 onwards. They were preserved by Theodora Cowper and published, with the permission of her sister Harriet, Lady Hesketh, as late as 1825. One poem written during the first onset of insanity was issued with his autobiography in 1816:

> Hatred and vengeance, my eternal portion,
> Scarce can endure delay of execution,
> Wait with impatient readiness to seize my
> Soul in a moment.

The use of the Sapphic stanza was probably suggested by Isaac Watts's ode on the Day of Judgement. Cowper confesses his admiration of Watts's poetry in commenting on Dr. Johnson's criticism of that and of all devotional poetry, "It is sufficient for Watts to have done better than others what no man has done well", a generalisation on religious poetry to which Cowper takes exception.

With his recovery in 1775 Cowper resumed the habit of writing occasional verses, a few religious, but in the main on subjects of public or personal interest, including some of the best of his fables in octosyllabics, *The Bee and the Pineapple*, *The Nightingale and Glowworm*, the moral of which is not so convincing as charming:

> Did you admire my lamp, quoth he,
> As much as I your minstrelsy,
> You would abhor to do me wrong
> As much as I to spoil your song;

For 'twas the selfsame power divine
Taught you to sing and me to shine;
That you with music, I with light,
Might beautify and cheer the night;

to which the nightingale might have only too truthfully replied that the selfsame power had decreed that "I should eat you. Neither of us exists to beautify the night for poets."

Like others, Cowper found in employment the best distraction, the only counteractive to melancholy; and it was when carpentering, gardening, keeping such pets as hares and dogs, had all lost their first charm that he began, when settled at Olney with Mrs. Unwin, his regular and strenuous work as a poet with a mission.

Satire was still the vogue, and during the years of Cowper's illness a school friend of his, remembered by him always with affection and admiration despite the wide divergence of their lives, Charles Churchill, had given a new animus and edge to satire in both octosyllabic and decasyllabic verse. Satire was to be Cowper's first serious venture (though he does not call his poems satires), and they are satires very different in temper and motive from Churchill's, if like Churchill's the style and verse recalled Dryden rather than Pope. *The Progress of Error*, a subject suggested by Mrs. Unwin, opened the series, written in December, 1780. In January, 1781, came *Truth*, followed in March by *Expostulation*, in May-June by *Hope*, then June-July *Charity*, July-August *Conversation*, August-October *Retirement*. The last written, *Table Talk*, was composed as an introduction to the series.

Cowper's attitude as a satirist and didactic poet in these first attempts, and in the later *The Task*, is both representative and personal, if it is the predominance of the personal element which has made the later series the more interesting. Representatively Cowper is the first, perhaps the only, satirist whose point of view is definitely of the Calvinist and Evangelical school of thought. Whatever he felt as to his own unhappy lot, Cowper in the poems adheres unwaveringly to the truth which in 1765 had brought him for a time deliverance from hopeless melancholy to a supreme ecstasy; the all-atoning sacrifice of Christ, the worthlessness of all human virtue. Neither Whitefield nor Watts is so thorough going a Calvinist as Cowper, the pupil of "the little Doctor" Cotton and the great Dr. Newton. This is the theme throughout of *Truth*

236 A CRITICAL HISTORY OF ENGLISH POETRY

which followed *The Progress of Error*:

> And is the soul indeed so lost? [Pride] cries;
> Fall'n from her glory, and too weak to rise?
> Torpid and dull, beneath a frozen zone,
> Has she *no* spark that may be deem'd her own?
> Grant her indebted to what zealots call
> Grace undeserved—yet surely not for *all*!
> Some beams of rectitude she yet displays,
> Some love of virtue and some power to praise.
>
> .   .   .   .
>
> Perish the virtue, as it ought, abhorr'd,
> And the fool with it who insults his Lord.
> Th' atonement a Redeemer's love has wrought
> Is not for you—the righteous need it not.
> See'st thou yon harlot, wooing all she meets,
> The worn out nuisance of the public streets;
> Herself from morn to night, from night to morn,
> Her own abhorrence, and as much your scorn!
> The gracious show'r, unlimited and free,
> Shall fall on her when heaven denies it thee.
> Of all that wisdom dictates, this the drift—
> That man is dead in sin, and life a gift.

That is the Evangelical text on which Cowper preaches in *Truth*, and indeed throughout these poems. There is little of satire as we think of satire in Juvenal, Pope, Swift—no angry attacks on individuals. Lord Chesterfield (Petronius) is handled somewhat severely; Charles Wesley (Occiduus) is reproved for his love of music; and Voltaire is contrasted with the village matron who knows her Bible and only that. Cowper's affinity as a satirist is with Horace, the Horace of the more hortatory satires and of such epistles as those to Maecenas and Lollius and Numicius where Horace dilates on the best life, or estimates the comparative value of what men esteem as good. Indeed if one takes *The Task* along with these early poems one sees Cowper as a kind of Evangelical Horace. If he does not share Horace's enthusiasm for wine and women he has his own peculiar pleasure in tea and sympathetic ladies; and all, perhaps more than all, Horace's love of retirement and the country. Moreover Cowper is not only an Evangelical preacher of doctrine and morals but, like Horace, he is a patriot, a Whig of the glorious age of Chatham, who has lived into the disastrous years of the American war and its consequences in Europe:

Poor England!   Thou art a devoted deer,
Beset with every ill but that of fear.
The nations hunt, all mark thee for a prey,
They swarm around thee, and thou stand'st at bay.
Undaunted still, though weary and perplex'd,
Once Chatham saved thee; but who saves thee next?

So Cowper writes in the opening *Table Talk*, a patriot and a
Whig—a Whig, suspicious of kings, the champion of liberty
as the birthright of Englishmen, he is also the champion of
order, distrustful of self-called "patriots".   Lastly, like Horace,
Cowper dilates at times on literature, on the progress of poetry
and its connection with morals and religion, on satire in the
hands of Addison, and Pope and Swift and Arbuthnot and
Charles Churchill.   Cowper has no small measure of Horace's
lightness of touch, especially in the dialogue passages where
doubtless Horace is his model; and Evangelical as he was,
Cowper had been in his early days, and within measure, a man
of the world, and he was always a gentleman.

But first and foremost Cowper is an Evangelical preacher.
If England is in trouble it is that God is punishing her sins—
so in *Table Talk* and at greater length in *Expostulation* where the
history of the Jews is held up as a lesson and a warning.   And
what are the sins of England?   Vice and corruption certainly,
but also those recurrent themes of Puritan and Evangelical
reprobation—cards, hunting, dancing, music if indulged to
excess, by the clergy, and on Sundays:

If apostolic gravity be free
To play the fool on Sunday, why not we?
If he the tinkling harpsichord regards
As inoffensive, what offence in cards?
Strike up the fiddle, let us all be gay!
Laymen have leave to dance if parsons play.

Cowper and Newton were profoundly shocked by the Handel
Commemoration of 1784.   The beginnings of Biblical criticism and the evils of the Press are the main themes of *The
Progress of Error*.   To *Charity* a special interest is given by
Cowper's passionate feeling—which he shared with Johnson
—regarding the cruelty which attended the conquest of the
uncivilised world, and the institution of slavery.   In *Retirement*, which closed the series, there is more of the poetry which
was to relieve the similar preachments of *The Task*, for in it
Cowper reveals his own sincere love of Nature:

> The deep recess of dusky groves,
> Or forests where the deer securely roves,
> The fall of waters, and the song of birds,
> The hills that echo to the distant herds.
>
> .   .   .   .   .
>
> Oh Nature! whose Elysian scenes disclose
> His bright perfections at whose word they rose,
> Next to the power who formed thee and sustains
> Be thou the great inspirer of my strains.

His own melancholy too and the joy of his first recovery are described with vivid touches—the loss of the sense of beauty and of joy, the bliss of their recovery:

> Then heav'n eclips'd so long, and this dull earth,
> Shall seem to start into a second birth;
> Nature, assuming a more lovely face,
> Borrowing a beauty from the works of grace,
> Shall be despis'd and overlook'd no more,
> Shall fill thee with delights unfelt before,
> Impart to things inanimate a voice,
> And bid her mountains and her hills rejoice;
> The sound shall run along the winding vales,
> And thou enjoy an Eden ere it fails.

The first group of poems had been undertaken at the instance of his constant companion, Mrs. Unwin, aware that occupation was the poet's best or only antidote to the melancholy which beset him. The suggestion for *The Task* came from Lady Austin, that brilliant butterfly who, in 1781, fluttered into the quiet life of Cowper and Mrs. Unwin with an effect stimulating to begin with, if in the end disturbing. When she urged him to write in blank verse he asked for a theme, and she replied "Oh, you can never be in want of a subject: you can write upon any: write upon this sofa!" Hence the general title and that of the first poem, to be followed by *The Time-Piece, The Garden, The Winter Evening, The Winter Morning Walk,* and *The Winter Walk at Noon*.

In purpose and general theme *The Task* does not differ essentially from the earlier poems. This too is a series of sermons—sermons on the religious life and the vanities of the world. Cowper is still the champion of Divine Grace as the sole security of man whose own efforts have no merit:

> Grace makes the slave a free man, 'tis a change
> That turns to ridicule the turgid speech
> And stately tone of moralists.

He is still the patriot, the *laudator temporis acti*, the glorious
days of Chatham:

> Time was when it was praise and boast enough
> In every clime, and travel where we might,
> That we were born her children.   Praise enough
> To fill the ambition of a private man,
> That Chatham's language was his mother tongue,
> And Wolfe's great name compatriot with his own.
> Farewell these honours, and farewell with them
> The hope of such hereafter!

England has fallen—the colonies lost, France and Spain united
in arms against her, etc., and in it all Cowper of course traces
the hand of God.   When a season of fogs sets in he is inclined
to suspect the approaching end of the world, which alas! (for
Cowper's humour is never quite in abeyance) has not all the
effect it ought to have on the poorer inhabitants of Olney:
"This very Sunday morning the pitchers of all have been
carried into Silver End [*i.e.* to the Cock Inn] as usual, the
inhabitants perhaps judging that they have more than ordinary
need of that cordial at such a juncture" (June 29, 1783).

But neither Cowper's piety nor his patriotism interests us
to-day.   It is the humanism of his poems—his love of Nature,
the country, animals, and domestic retirement.   In *The Sofa*,
a half-humorous opening leads up to a description of the
scenery around Olney in which Cowper's power reveals itself,
his gift of being able to convey his feelings, not so much for
Nature generally nor for the sensuous and sublime in Nature,
but for scenes made familiar by their constant presence and
woven into the poet's own emotional life:

> Here Ouse, slow winding through a level plain
> Of spacious meads with cattle sprinkled o'er,
> Conducts the eye along its sinuous course
> Delighted.   There, fast rooted in their bank
> Stand, never overlooked, our favourite elms,
> That screen the herdman's solitary hut;
> While far beyond, and overthwart the stream
> That as with molten glass inlays the vale,
> The sloping land recedes into the clouds,
> Displaying on its varied side the grace
> Of hedgerow beauties numberless, square tower,
> Tall spire, from which the sound of cheerful bells
> Just undulates upon the listening ear,
> Groves, heaths, and smoking villages, remote.

> Scenes must be beautiful which daily viewed
> Please daily, and whose novelty survives
> Long knowledge and the scrutiny of years.

There follow the lines on sounds in Nature for which Cowper, like Crabbe and Wordsworth, had a delicate ear.

It is in the Winter poems that are to be found some of Cowper's finest descriptions of scenery, for to the poet whose love of Nature is rather emotional than sensuous winter is often the most appealing of the seasons. We do not ourselves think that Cowper is superior to Thomson as a poet of Nature. Thomson's range is wider, his descriptions as faithful as Cowper's. It would be difficult to choose between the snow-storm in the *Winter* (ll. 223-240) of Thomson and that of Cowper in *The Winter Evening* (ll. 311-322). There are some touches of imaginative transfiguration in the Scottish poet's work that Cowper has not surpassed, if equalled:

> The whole loosen'd Spring,

and

> Or where the northern ocean in vast whirls
> Boils round the naked melancholy isles
> Of farthest Thule, and the Atlantic surge
> Pours in among the stormy Hebrides;

or again the lines in the description of the hunted stag:

> He sweeps the forest oft and sobbing sees
> The glades mild opening to the golden day.

It is the greater intimacy of Cowper's descriptions, the simplicity of his style, the less sonorous blank verse that attract. To Wordsworth's more mystically transfiguring suggestion of a spirit in Nature Cowper's closest approach is in the lines in *A Winter Walk at Noon*:

> The night was winter in his roughest mood;
> The morning sharp and clear,

leading up to the lovely lines,

> No noise is here, or none that hinders thought.
> The redbreast warbles still, but is content
> With slender notes and more than half suppress'd:
> Pleas'd with the solitude and flitting light
> From spray to spray, where'er he rests he shakes
> From many a twig the pendent drops of ice
> That tinkle in the wither'd leaves below.

Stillness accompanied with sounds so soft,
Charms more than silence.   Meditation here
May think down hours to moments.   Here the heart
May give an useful lesson to the head,
And learning wiser grow without his books.
Knowledge and wisdom, far from being one,
Have ofttimes no connection.   Knowledge dwells
In heads replete with thoughts of other men,
Wisdom in minds attentive to their own.

 . . . . .

Knowledge is proud that he has learn'd so much,
Wisdom is humble that he knows no more.

The drift of the whole is that of Wordsworth's well-known
poem:

Books! 'tis a dull and endless strife;
Come hear the woodland linnet;
How sweet his music, on my life,
There's more of wisdom in it.

But Cowper does not mean all that Wordsworth meant, or
thought he meant.   To Cowper Nature and Solitude may pre-
dispose the mind to receive religious truth, but that Truth can
come from one source only and in one way.

In *The Garden* Cowper dilates on what was his second chief
source of happiness:

Domestic happiness, thou only bliss
Of Paradise that has survived the Fall!

This is the theme on which Sainte-Beuve found Cowper a
unique poet, a poet such as Port Royal might or should have
produced: "It has caused me at times surprise and regret that
there has not been found at Port Royal, or among those who
followed, a poet like William Cowper.   Like Pascal, Cowper
was struck with terror at the idea of the vengeance of God.
He knew the fears which inspired Saint-Cyran, and yet how
tenderly he sang."   Retirement in the country, the beauty of
Nature, the joy of the fireside, the garden, the greenhouse, the
pets—these are the things in which Cowper's wounded spirit
found consolation.   For a time it had seemed to himself that
he had found more than an escape—joy, ecstasy, a duty to
perform, the duty of the converted, that is to convert others by
preaching.   His own hope had departed, but he would still
preach in his poems and he could still delight in Nature and

domestic life, the affections. *The Garden* is largely an account of his own life, his first conversion:

> I was a stricken deer, that left the herd
> Long since; with many an arrow deep infixt
> My panting side was charg'd, when I withdrew
> To seek a tranquil death in distant shades;

his daily life beside Mrs. Unwin, the morning tea:

> the fragrant lymph
> Which neatly she prepares;

his light labours in the garden and the greenhouse. Of others who do not share his tastes he has no understanding, and therefore little sympathy to spare them. They are the victims of the world, or are led astray by pride of intellect to believe that they can correct what God has communicated to Moses:

> Some drill and bore
> The solid earth, and from the strata there
> Extract a register, by which we learn
> That He who made it and reveal'd its date
> To Moses, was mistaken in its age.

The Winter Evening opens with the famous description of the joys of home:

> Now stir the fire, and close the shutters fast,
> Let fall the curtains, wheel the sofa round,
> And while the bubbling and loud-hissing urn
> Throws up a steamy column, and the cups
> That cheer but not inebriate wait on each,
> So let us welcome peaceful evening in.
> Not such his evening who with shining face
> Sweats in the crowded theatre.

For Cowper can never sing of what he loves without these pointed contrasts. He combines the egotism of the invalid with that of the pious. The things *he* likes are those which all men ought to like.

On the *Tirocinium* which followed *The Task*, and the translation in blank verse of Homer, we need not dwell. The former was an indictment of the cruelty for a sensitive boy of boarding-schools. More interesting is the incomplete *Yardley Oak*, in which Cowper combined a Miltonic dignity of verse with a characteristic strain of reflection found in many of his letters—reflection on the inevitable flight of time and on change, "the diet on which all subsist".

But of Cowper's shorter poems, ballads, and lyrics a word must be said, for they have a charm which may appeal to readers who cannot bring themselves to take much interest in the didactic and descriptive poems of the "maniacal and Calvinist and coddled poet", as Byron calls him. His love-poems addressed to his cousin Theodora Cowper were not printed till twenty-five years after his death. They are not passionate poems, but have some quite unmistakable qualities—sincerity, a pretty wit (it was not for nothing that Cowper counted Donne among his ancestors and admired the poetry of Cowley and Waller and Prior), and the perfect naturalness of the language in diction and order of words. Each turns on a simple, natural conceit:

THE SYMPTOMS OF LOVE

Would my Delia know if I love, let her take
My last thoughts at night and the first when I wake;
With my prayers and best wishes preferr'd for her sake.

Let her guess what I muse on when rambling alone
I stride o'er the stubble each day with my gun,
Never ready to shoot till the covey is flown.

Let her think what odd whimsies I have in my brain
When I read one page over and over again,
And discover at last that I read it in vain.

Let her say why so fix'd and so steady my look,
Without ever regarding the person who spoke
Still affecting to laugh without hearing the joke—

and so on. In later years the shorter poems are mainly occasional verses in which Cowper combines the lightness of Prior with an undertone of more serious and delicate feeling. Among the best of these are such fables as *The Nightingale and the Glow-worm* and others, *The Poplar Field*, the delightful *Dog and the Water-Lily*, *The Rose*, *Epitaph on a Hare*. Of the ballads the best known, and best, is *John Gilpin*, if its attraction for us is rather a puzzle for Frenchmen. Of odes the best is that on the *Loss of the Royal George*, though *Boadicea* deserves a reading. The pathos, if not the full tragedy of Cowper's life is beautifully adumbrated in the *Lines on the Receipt of my Mother's Picture*. The fuller tragedy speaks in two lyrics, more explicitly than in the lines in *The Garden* cited above, for there the poet ends in an escape which Cowper came to believe was for him an illusion. The one is the short lines on Newton's return from Ramsgate:

> That ocean you of late surveyed,
>   Those rocks I too have seen,
> But I afflicted and dismay'd,
>   You tranquil and serene.
>
> You from the flood-controlling steep
>   Saw, stretch'd before your view,
> With conscious joy the threatening deep,
>   No longer such to you.
>
> To me the waves, that ceaseless broke
>   Upon the dangerous coast,
> Hoarsely and ominously spoke
>   Of all my treasure lost.
>
> Your sea of troubles you have past,
>   And found the peaceful shore;
> I tempest-toss'd, and wreck'd at last,
>   Come home to port no more.

But Cowper's supreme lyric is *The Castaway*, a unique combination of the reserve and formality of the best eighteenth-century lyric with passionate feeling, of Cowper's courtesy with Cowper's despair:

> No poet wept him: but the page
>   Of narrative sincere,
> That tells his name, his worth, his age,
>   Is wet with Anson's tear.
> And tears by bards and heroes shed
> Alike immortalise the dead.
>
> I therefore purpose not, or dream
>   Descanting on his fate,
> To give the melancholy theme
>   A more enduring date:
> But misery still delights to trace
> Its semblance in another's case.
>
> No voice divine the storm allay'd,
>   No light propitious shone;
> When, snatch'd from all effectual aid,
>   We perish'd each alone:
> But I beneath a rougher sea,
> And whelm'd in deeper gulfs than he.[1]

---

[1] The incident occurred during the terrible voyage of Anson's ship, the *Centurion*, in rounding Cape Horn in the winter month of April, the description

of which by the Chaplain, Richard Walter, who compiled the Voyage, in its matter-of-fact description of place and incident and the reactions of his feelings to these is worth a lot of deliberate picturesque writing: "As our ship kept the wind better than any of the rest, we were obliged, in the afternoon, to wear ship, in order to join the squadron to the leeward. . . . And as we dared not venture any sail abroad, we were obliged to make use of an expedient which answered our purpose; this was putting the helm a-weather and manning the fore-shrouds" (*i.e.* using the crew as sails). "But though this method proved successful for the end intended, yet in the execution of it one of our ablest seamen was canted overboard; and notwithstanding the prodigious agitation of the waves, we perceived that he swam very strong, and it was with the utmost concern that we found ourselves incapable of assisting him; and we were the more grieved at his unhappy fate since we lost sight of him struggling with the waves, and conceived from the manner in which he swam that he might continue sensible for a considerable time longer of the horror attending his irretrievable fate." The details of the throwing overboard of cask and coop and floated cord to help the swimmer are supplied by Cowper's imagination and sympathy. Where the accident occurred such help could have availed nothing except perhaps to prolong the suffering. It was, we do not doubt, "the horror attending his irretrievable fate" that moved Cowper to the comparison.

Chapter Nineteen

CRABBE

COWPER'S satires, as we have called them, were published
in 1782. Next year appeared *The Village*, by George Crabbe
(1754–1832). Each poet had already written much and published a little—Cowper the *Olney Hymns* in 1779, and *Anti-
Thelyphthora* (a satirical poem on his cousin Madan's defence
of polygamy as a punishment, and cure, for adultery) in 1781;
Crabbe *The Candidate* (1780), *The Library* (1781). But it was
the volumes of 1782 and 1783 which marked the definite début
of the two as individual, remarkable poets.

Crabbe, like Cowper, had passed through troubled waters
before emerging as an author, but troubles of a very different
kind. Cowper's afflictions came entirely from within. Given
a sound nervous system, Cowper's life would have passed
smoothly enough, as it glided from one sinecure to another.
Poor Crabbe's troubles were of a more solid character,—
poverty, an uncompleted scanty education, degrading employment, and finally some weeks of agitation and despair in Grub
Street, hoping against hope for the patronage of statesmen,
relieved at last through the generosity of Burke, and floated
into the haven of the Anglican Ministry and such various
provision as patrons could supply,—curacies, chaplainries,
parishes.

The differences in the experiences are vividly reflected in the
work of the two poets,—Cowper's sermons, his withdrawal
from and narrow condemnation of all that he personally shrank
from, his epicurean delight in the country and the quiet fireside; Crabbe's vivid, detailed, sombre pictures of human life,
of human nature's bitter struggles with adverse circumstances
without, with passions and frailties within: the poet

> Loves the mind in all its modes to trace,
> And all the manners of the changing race.
>
> . . . . .
>
> He finds what shapes the Proteus-passions take,
> And what strange waste of life and joy they make.

His father was a George Crabbe in Aldeborough, Suffolk,

who combined a collectorship of salt duties with an interest in fishing, a man of great mental and physical energy, a lover of mathematics but also of the poetry of Milton and of Young, passionate, and in his later years addicted to drink. The poet was born on Christmas Eve, 1754. His mother, a Mary Lodwick, "was a woman of the most amiable disposition, mild, patient, affectionate and deeply religious". To school Crabbe went, when very young, in Bungay, where he suffered from a savage discipline, and when twelve years old, in Stowmarket, where he was the victim of a bully. He shared his father's interest in mathematics, and he learned a little Latin, but the best of Crabbe's education came from his own reading and his own observation. "I read every book which I could procure." The distinctive feature of Crabbe's poetry is, however, its debt not so much to books as to his minute, eager observation of scenes, objects, events, manners, and characters. In the account of his own life given by Richard, the younger brother in the *Tales of the Hall*, Crabbe has described his own youth, his interest in everything around him, his power of sympathetic listening which won him the heart especially of women, often of women much older than himself, as, later in life, of women much younger:

> Where crowds assembled I was sure to run,
> Hear what was said, and mused on what was done;
> Attentive listening in the moving scene,
> And often wondering what the men could mean.
>
> .   .   .   .   .
>
> Whatever business in the port was done,
> I, without call, was with the busy one,
> Not daring question but with open ear
> And greedy spirit ever bent to hear.
> To me the wives of seamen loved to tell
> What storms endangered men esteem'd so well;
> What wondrous things in foreign parts they saw,
> Lands without bounds, and people without law.
>
> .   .   .   .   .
>
> The open shops of craftsmen caught my eye
> And there my questions met the kind reply:
> Men when alone will teach, but in a crowd
> The child is silent, or the man is proud.
>
> .   .   .   .   .
>
> I made me interest at the Inn's fireside,
> Amid the scenes to bolder boys denied;

> For I had patrons there, and I was one,
> They judged, who noticed nothing that was done.
> "A quiet lad," would my protector say,
> "To him now this is better than his play:
> Boys are as men; some active, shrewd and keen,
> They look about if aught is to be seen;
> And some, like Richard here, have not a mind
> That takes a notice—but the lad is kind."

Shepherds, smugglers, vagrants were other friends; and these brief extracts will suggest what the whole piece explains, the quiet eagerness, the sympathy, the intelligence and shrewdness with which Crabbe stored his mind and prepared himself to write poems which, whatever the limitation of their music, are unique in our literature. A more imaginative chord was touched by Nature:

> I loved to walk where none had walked before
> About the rocks that ran along the shore;
> Or far beyond the sight of men to stray,
> And take my pleasure when I lost my way.
> For then was mine to trace the hilly heath,
> And all the mossy moor that lies beneath;
> Here had I favourite stations, where I stood
> And heard the murmurs of the ocean-flood,
> With not a sound beside, except when flew
> Aloft the lapwing or the gay curlew,
> Who with wild notes my fancy's power defied,
> And mocked the dreams of solitary pride.

For if a reader and an observer Crabbe was also a dreamer:

> Thus with my favourite views for many an hour
> Have I indulged the dreams of princely power.

But in later days Crabbe's mature interest was not so much in the dreams themselves, their content as wish-fulfilments, as in the psychology of dreams, their vividness and withal their unaccountable mutability.

Leaving school at the age of thirteen, Crabbe was apprenticed to a surgeon or apothecary who was also a farmer, and Crabbe took his share in both activities. This was at Wickham Brook, and from it Crabbe passed to a similar appointment at Woodbridge, where his duties consisted mainly in compounding drugs. While at Woodbridge he accompanied a friend to the village of Parham where he formed the acquaintance of, and a strong attachment to, the Sarah Elmy who was

the Mira of his early poems and ultimately became his wife.
Returning to Aldeborough when twenty-one he received an
appointment as parish doctor, such as that was; but going to
London to improve his medical knowledge he lost the post.
After some years of casual work, medical and other, he finally
in 1780 resolved, almost in despair, to put his fortune to the
touch, go to London with such poems as he had in MS., and
seek the patronage of Lord North, Lord Thurlow, and others.
His disappointments and sufferings in London, where he was
an eye-witness of the Gordon riots, the reports of which
agitated Cowper, who saw in them both the manifest hand of
God and the hidden hand of the French, are recorded in Crabbe's
journal. At last, in the spring of 1781, a moving letter to
Edmund Burke evoked a response; and, after revision and the
obtaining of subscriptions, *The Library* was issued in June of
that year.

The *magnum opus* of eighteenth-century poets was not, as in
the seventeenth, an epic but a didactic poem on some larger or
smaller general subject,—*Essay on Criticism, Essay on Man,
The Seasons, Art of Preserving Health, Pleasures of the Imagination, Liberty, The Fleece, Vanity of Human Wishes, Enthusiasm,
The Sugar Cane*, etc. Crabbe had already printed at Ipswich
a poem on such a general edifying topic, *Inebriety*, a poem in
three parts. Echoes and parodies of Pope are obvious in this
early work, but his own bent of mind is seen in the choice and
treatment of the subject. *The Library* is a less colourful piece,
a series of reflections on books in general and books on various
themes, as medicine, law, etc. It was not till after he had taken
orders and become chaplain to the Duke of Rutland at Belvoir
Castle that Crabbe found himself as a poet, that he was enabled
to bring the whole weight of his own bitter experiences into his
poetry,—his intimate knowledge of the English peasantry in
the condition to which the enclosure of commons, and the high
tariffs that benefited farmers and landlords, had reduced them.

As has been indicated in a previous chapter, the pastoral
tradition of a Golden Age and a life where, as Johnson puts it,
"we are to meet with nothing but joy and plenty and contentment, where every gale whispers pleasure and every shade
promises repose", had given way steadily to the growing
interest in Nature as Nature actually is, Nature and country
life. Even Goldsmith's idealism is the idealism of memory,
not of convention. Crabbe had no such memories. In the

R

country and the life of the peasantry he found neither peace nor leisure nor innocence—no Elysian region of joy and plenty and contentment: quite the reverse; and he would tell the truth:

> No; cast by Fortune on a frowning coast
> Which neither groves nor happy valleys boast;
> Where other cares than those the Muse relates,
> And other shepherds dwell with other mates;
> By such examples taught, I paint the cot
> As truth will paint it and as bards will not.

The Italian poet Sannazaro had written Piscatorial eclogues (to which Johnson took exception inasmuch as few people associate any idea of pleasure with the sea), and Crabbe's pastoral is piscatorial in so far as it deals with fishermen as well as shepherds and peasants; but they are wreckers as well as fishers. As for the peasants, however, even if the country which Crabbe knew had been richer, their portion of it would be small:

> . Where Plenty smiles—alas! she smiles for few.

The peasant's actual life is one of never-ending and excessive labour, ill-health and insufficient food, a neglected old age, and finally the poorhouse, where he is fed by a grudging hand, visited by a careless doctor, and left unvisited by a more careless, fox-hunting, self-indulgent parson:

> And does not he, the pious man, appear,
> He, "passing rich with forty pounds a year"?
> Ah! no, a shepherd of a different stock,
> And far unlike him, feeds this little flock.

He will not attend even to read the funeral service.

Crabbe had found his *métier* as a poet; but he was singularly slow in following up his first success. He did not publish another poem till twenty-two years had elapsed, for *The Newspaper* (1785) was an earlier work in the conventional, Popean manner of *The Library*. The outward events of Crabbe's life during these years are the difficulties and migrations of his clerical career. The chaplainry to the Duke of Rutland at Belvoir Castle brought unpleasantness and trouble, clearly suggested in a later poem, *The Patron*. A curacy at Stathern near Belvoir Castle was followed by the gift of two small livings, Muston in Leicestershire, and Allington in Lincoln-

shire. In 1783 he married Sarah Elmy. From Muston
Crabbe, on coming into some money through his wife's relatives, transferred himself to Parham, much to the discontent
of his Muston parishioners. He wrote abundantly, among
other things two prose novels, but destroyed most or all of
what he wrote. An illness traceable to some disturbance of
his digestion, and inducing fits of giddiness, led to his taking
opium; and it was probably under the influence of the drug
that he wrote two remarkable poems in stanzas, on dreams,—
Sir Eustace Gray and *The World of Dreams*. To Muston and
his grumbling parishioners Crabbe returned in 1805, and there
completed *The Parish Register*, which, with his previously
printed poems, was issued in 1807. *The World of Dreams*,
though probably written at this time, was not printed till after
his death, but *Sir Eustace Gray*, *The Birth of Flattery*, *Reflections*,
and *The Hall of Justice* were included in the *Poems* of this year.

The *Birth of Flattery* is a slight but characteristic little
allegory. Flattery, the child of Poverty and Cunning, is
assured by the evil fairy Envy that

> The good shall hate thy name, the wise shall fear;
> Wit shall deride, and no protecting friend
> Thy shame shall cover or thy name defend.
> The gentle sex who, more than ours, should spare
> A humble foe, will greater scorn declare;
> The base alone thy advocates shall be
> Or boast alliance with a wretch like thee.

But the unhappy parents are reassured by another fairy. The
name of Flattery will be condemned, but the reality will always
be welcomed under some other name:

> Envy himself shall to thy accents bend,
> Force a faint smile and sullenly attend
> When thou shall call him Virtue's jealous friend,
> Whose bosom glows with generous rage to find
> How fools and knaves are flattered by mankind.

Reflections is a not less characteristic poem. When at last
men have acquired wisdom and have mastered their passions,
our time is drawing to its close: "Chilling Age comes creeping
on". We can make no use of the wisdom we have acquired:

> What is possessed we may retain,
> But for new conquests strive in vain.

Only in another life can we hope to reap the fruits of what we have gained.

Sir Eustace Gray and *The Hall of Justice* are more moving poems. The latter, in ballad stanzas, is a story of crime and incest for whose setting Crabbe has drawn on his early acquaintance with gipsies and vagrants, a tale of murder and incest passionately related by the victim, not, as in Crabbe's usual method, by some outsider, whether another character or the poet himself.

As late as 1813, Crabbe in writing to Sir Walter Scott asks him if he knows "the ancient mariner or Poet's reverie written by a friend" [of Wordsworth] "Mr. Lambe", and describes it as an interesting attempt which "does not describe Madness by its effects but by Imitation, as if a painter to give a picture of Lunacy should make his Canvas crazy and fill it with wild unconnected Limbs and Distortion of features . . . yet, one or two of the limbs are pretty". It is a strange comment on *The Ancient Mariner* by the author of *Sir Eustace Gray*, a strange comment, for both are dream-poems, the dreams of madness, and in each poem these dreams are presented with a vividness that owes something to the poet's acquaintance with opium. Sir Eustace's madness is a punishment, not for shooting an albatross, but for his neglect of God in the days of his prosperity when he was a generous host at Grayling Hall, and the happy husband of a beautiful and virtuous wife:

> But my vile heart had sinful spot,
>   And Heaven beheld its deep'ning stain;
> Eternal Justice I forgot,
>   And Mercy sought not to obtain.

His wife is seduced by a friend, his children die, and he becomes insane. Like Cowper, who heard a voice saying "*Actum est de te, periisti*", Sir Eustace too believes himself to be the victim of supernatural powers:

> . . . cast from out my state
> Two fiends of darkness led my way.

These are the "ill-favoured" ones of Bunyan's dream. What follows recounts Sir Eustace's dreams, which have some of the vividness of Coleridge's and the horror of De Quincey's:

> They placed me where those streamers play,
>   Those nimble beams of brilliant light;

> It would the stoutest heart dismay,
>   To see, to feel that dreadful sight;
>   So swift, so pure, so cold, so bright,
> They pierced my frame with icy wound,
>   And all that half-year's polar night
> Those dancing streamers wrapp'd me round.

In the end Sir Eustace seems to escape, if not from madness altogether, yet from his worst sufferings, by a conversion of the same kind as Cowper experienced:

> This slave of sin, whom fiends could seize,
>   Felt or believed their power had end;
> "'Tis faith," he cried, "my bosom frees,
>   And now my Saviour is my friend."

What then is the difference which Crabbe felt between his own poem and Coleridge's?   It is, presumably, that we are aware, we learn from the physician who has brought the visitor to see him, that Sir Eustace is mad.   We know that we are listening to a madman's account of his imagined experiences.   We are not asked to believe in the objectivity of the experience described.   In Coleridge's poem, on the other hand, and this puzzled Crabbe, it is never made clear whether what is described was an objective experience or the vivid dream of one at least temporarily crazed.   The wedding guest and we remain inside the Mariner's mind from first to last.

The stanza which Crabbe used for his poem is, like Shelley's in *Lines written in Dejection at Naples*, the Spenserian adapted to the more lyrical manner in which the story is told; but Crabbe does not, as Shelley does, preserve the closing alexandrine.   Crabbe, realist as he was, loved Spenser's poetry. Two Spenserian stanzas introduce *The Birth of Flattery*, because Crabbe feels that he is venturing into Spenser's fairy land of allegory.

In *The Parish Register*, the *pièce de résistance* of the 1807 volume, Crabbe resumes the tone and form of *The Village*.   He is now himself a parson and he will, turning over the pages of his register of births, marriages, and deaths, tell us something of the various people recalled to his memory.   Once more he contrasts the village of the poet's imagination with actuality:

> Since vice the world subdued and waters drown'd
> Auburn and Eden can no more be found.

The cottage of a thriving peasant is then described, the picture
on the wall, the books he reads, the Bible

> . . . with choicest notes by many a famous head,
> Such as to doubt have rustic readers led;
> Have made them stop to reason *why?* and *how?*
> And where they once agreed to cavil now.

From the fairer scenes of village life Crabbe passes to those of
vice and misery, and thence to the details of the register and
all the incidents of disappointment, suffering, disillusionment
which, despite some interludes of happiness and humour, made
up the story of the greater number—base-born children, ruined
beauty in the story of Phoebe Dawson, solid worth in Isaac
Ashford, saved in the end from the disgrace of the poorhouse
only by death, the love of power in conflict with the hopes of
Heaven:

> Heaven in her eye and in her hand her keys,

the vagabond at heart and all the vicissitudes of his life, etc.

The Parish Register was succeeded in 1812 by *The Borough*,
a long poem on which Crabbe had been engaged since 1801.
Here again, but on a larger canvas, he describes the village,
Aldeborough in the main but with additions drawn from his
clerical experience.   We get first a series of clerical figures, the
vicar and his starved curate whose growing family has defeated
the hopes which learning had awakened.   Then come the
religious sects:

> . . . who all the Church maintains approve
> But yet the Church herself they will not love.

There are the few survivors of Roman days; Baptists whose
early fervour has declined:

> This I perceive, that when a sect grows old
> Converts are few, and the converted cold.

There are Swedenborgians, Jews:

> Amazing race!   Depriv'd of land and laws,
> A general language and a public cause;
> With a religion none can now obey,
> With a reproach that none can take away:
> A people still whose common ties are gone;
> Who, mixed with every race, are lost in none.

There are Independents, whom he treats with some respect in

The Frank Courtship.   Crabbe's pet aversion is the Methodists. For their doctrines of sudden conversions, all-prevailing grace, and imputed righteousness, Crabbe had none of Cowper's affection, as some of his later tales will show clearly.   Lawyers and their tricks, doctors and quacks follow; and a survey of trades, clubs and social meetings, inns, actors, the alms-house and its trustees and inhabitants, the hospital and its governors, the poor of the borough (at great length), prisons and schools complete the survey, all illustrated by characters and incidents. The most impressive scene, and the finest poetically, even metrically, is that of the two occupants, a woman and a man, of the condemned cell.   In the dream of his last night the man who is to die next morning is carried back to the days of innocence and youth and early love as he wanders in imagination across the heath and beside the sea:

> . . . There behold the bay!
> The ocean smiling to the fervid sun—
> The waves that faintly fall and slowly run—
> The ships at distance and the boats at hand;
> And now they walk upon the seaside sand,
> Counting the number and what kind they be,
> Ships softly sinking in the sleepy sea.

They search for crimson weeds and bright red pebbles, jelly-fish, pearl shells, and star-fish.   But in his dream the prisoner suddenly thinks that the girl whom he loves is caught by a wave:

> . . . Oh! Horrible! A wave
> Roars as it rises—"Save me, Edward, save"
> She cries: Alas! The watchman on his way
> Calls and lets in—truth, terror and the day.

It has been said that Crabbe's tone in this and *Tales* and *Tales of the Hall* is less pessimistic than in *The Village*.   That is so far true that in *The Village* he is correcting a false picture of the life of the poor, and thus naturally emphasizes the points of contrast with pastoral poetry, including Goldsmith's *Deserted Village*.   In *The Parish Register* and in *The Borough* we find accordingly other aspects presented of the life of the poor,— "My friend the weaver" and his delight in moths, butterflies, and flowers; and more than once Crabbe stresses the happiness which may come from poverty and content in contrast with the loss of affection which the ruthless pursuit of wealth brings in its train, *e.g.* Walter and William in *Trades* in *The Borough*.

Nevertheless the main effect of the broadening of Crabbe's view to include other classes than the poor alone is rather a deepening of his sombre picture of life. All are unhappy. To Crabbe as to Johnson scenes of gaiety only disguise the unhappiness that lurks in each individual bosom. The rustic who in *Amusements* gazes with envy at a party of holiday visitors enjoying themselves in a boat is warned:

> Ah! Go in peace, good fellow, to thine home,
> Nor fancy these escape the general doom;
> Gay as they seem, be sure with them are hearts
> With sorrow tried; there's sadness in their parts:
> If thou couldst see them when they think alone,
> Mirth, music, friends, and these amusements gone;
> Couldst thou discover every secret ill
> That pains their spirit, or resists their will;
> Couldst thou behold forsaken Love's distress,
> Or Envy's pang at glory and success,
> Or Beauty, conscious of the spoils of Time,
> Or Guilt alarmed when Memory shows the crime;
> All that gives sorrow, terror, grief and gloom;
> Content would cheer thee trudging to thine home.

No; as Crabbe's view goes up the social scale the melancholy truth is but reinforced—happiness is the exception. For most men life is a progressive disillusionment.

In his descriptions of environment and professions and characters Crabbe had sketched shortly the history of this or that individual,—the scholarly curate, a predecessor of Anthony Trollope's Mr. Crawley in *The Last Chronicle of Barset*; Swallow the dishonest attorney; the adventure on the tidal island in Letter IX, *Amusements*; Blaney the wealthy heir who closes his life in the alms-house; Clelia in the same retreat; and Benbow; the clerk Jachin and how his honesty was seduced; Ellen Orford; Abel Keene. Indeed, the stories of the last three characters occupy each a whole Letter. Crabbe had also experimented, but without success, in the prose novel. With *Tales*, published in 1812, he became, one might fairly say, Chaucer's chief successor in the short story in verse.

Crabbe had not Chaucer's subtle humour, his lightness of touch, his dramatic power in presenting characters and incidents. He does not enter into his characters with such detached sympathy and humour; nor finally has his verse the easy varied charm of Chaucer's. Crabbe is more of the onlooker and preacher, enforcing the moral of his tale. The Popean or Johnsonian couplet with its limited compass and monotonous rhythm is not well fitted for a progressive narrative. On the other hand Crabbe covers a far wider range; and in his narrative poems his style gained, perhaps under the influence of Wordsworth, in simplicity, and his verse in variety of movement. Few prose novelists even have described a greater variety of characters or laid bare more convincingly the surprising turns of which human feeling is capable, the different modes in which human beings are capable of defeating their own happiness. There are in *Tales* some humorous and even gay stories— *Jessie and Colin, The Frank Courtship, Arabella*; but, as M. Huchon in his admirable study says, the common element of most of the stories is "the pathos of disenchantment". There are in all twenty-one stories, of which the most poignant are probably *Procrastination,* which tells how in consequence of too prolonged delay a lover gradually yields place in a woman's heart to the love of possessions; *The Mother,* a very modern story of the possessive and destructive partiality of a parent; *Edward Shore*; *The Brothers*; and *The Parting Hour.* The last of these is in part the source of, and in its sheer truthfulness and absence of all sentimentality an admirable contrast to, Tennyson's decorative *Enoch Arden.* The lovers are parted because he must seek his fortune abroad. Captured by the Spaniards, he settles in a South American colony and lives happily there with his Spanish wife and their children. Threatened with persecution on religious grounds but in fact, as so often, because he has money, he is compelled to flee. On arriving in England he is at once pressed into the Navy. After further years he reaches his native town to find that most of those he had known are dead, their names hardly remembered. But one has survived, a widow in a village near. It is Judith, his early love, and she becomes his nurse. Yet in his feverish attacks it is not of her and their early love that he dreams, but of his wife and children. Few novelists have surpassed Crabbe in the knowledge of how human feelings do act in contrast with the way in which we think they will or ought to act; and it is on such fluctuations of feeling that his tragic issues depend, not, as too often with Thomas Hardy, on coincidences, mere accidents.

The *Tales* were followed by *Tales of the Hall* in 1819, stories told to one another by two half-brothers who have been separated throughout their lives but are united at the close. The elder brother has become the proprietor of the Hall in his native village which had been the cynosure of his eyes in youth. The younger, Richard, in the description of whose early life Crabbe, as we have indicated, drew upon his own experiences, had gone to sea and after numerous vicissitudes returned a poor man but happily married, while his elder brother's experience as a lover has had a tragic conclusion.

Crabbe, as the account of Richard shows, had from his early days been readily loved by women. He had loved intensely and tenaciously the Sarah Elmy who helped him during the critical month in London, and in 1783 had married her. In her later days, after the loss of a child, she sank into a state of dejection and ill-health and died in 1813. In the following year a much younger woman indicated her readiness to marry him; and on a wave of feeling Crabbe became engaged on September 22. The excitement, however, the feeling of a break with his past life, was too much for him, and on December 12, as his journal notes, "Charlotte's picture was returned". These facts remembered make it easier to understand why love and marriage bulk so largely in *Tales of the Hall*. This is the rock on which so many lives are wrecked. For the whole collection of stories Crabbe might have used the motto he prefixed to *The Widow's Tale* in the 1812 collection:

> Ah me! For aught that ever I could read,
> Could ever hear by tale or history,
> The course of true love never did run smooth.

The disillusionment is sometimes brought about in almost too brutal a manner. George the elder brother has worshipped for years a lady whom he had seen only once. He meets her in later life—the painted, sluttish mistress of a merchant from whom he has to collect the payment of a debt. The younger brother relates as a story told to him by one of the old dames of his youth one of Crabbe's most poignant and, in the closing lines, most poetical tales, the story of Ruth robbed by the press-gang of the man whom she had loved and who was to have married her before the birth of her child, pursued later by a seemingly pious, sensual preacher, escaping only by suicide:

> And she was gone! The waters wide and deep
> Roll'd o'er her body as she lay asleep.

She heard no more the threatening of mankind;
Wrapped in dark weeds, the refuse of the storm,
To the hard rock was borne her comely form.

> .   .   .

She had, pray heaven!—she had that world in sight,
Where frailty mercy finds, and wrong has right;
But sure, in this her portion such has been,
Well had it still remained a world unseen.

A very characteristic story is *The Natural Death of Love*, which describes in an amusing yet moving dialogue the discovery by a husband that with their marriage love has taken wings and departed.   Not less characteristic in its truth to life is *The Preceptor Husband*, the story of a young man who has married one who, he hopes, will share his intellectual interests, only to find, when it is too late, that her reading had been only of sentimental novels and

> . . . all the works that ladies ever read,
> Shakespeare and all the rest.

Writing in 1825, Hazlitt could describe Crabbe as "one of the most popular and admired of all living authors".   Saintsbury, writing some sixty or more years later (1889), contrasts the popularity which Hazlitt records, a popularity that included such names among his admirers as Scott, Lockhart, Byron, Jeffrey, Wilson, with the fact of "the almost total forgetfulness of his works"; and Canon Ainger in 1903 endorses Saintsbury's pronouncement: "As Crabbe is practically unknown to the readers of the present day, *Sir Eustace Gray* will be hardly even a name to them".

It has, however, been the fate of more than one poet, as of some musicians, to suffer a long period of neglect after greater or less contemporary recognition.   What was known of Donne's poetry between Dryden and Coleridge?   The appeal that a poet makes will depend largely on the temper of the time, and there are not wanting signs that Crabbe has still readers and that in an increasing number.   It would be strange indeed if the present reaction from the romantics and taste for realism both in poetry and fiction should not revive an interest in Crabbe's poetry.   It is more important to define as clearly as possible the character of Crabbe's realism, his attitude towards his own stories.

Where Hazlitt is unjust to Crabbe is in declaring that there are in the poet's survey of life no flowers of hope or love or joy. Not so great a poet as the author of *Ecclesiastes*, his philosophy is much the same, supplemented by an at least intellectual acceptance of a Christian doctrine of immortality. There is none of Hardy's incessant arraignments of Providence, nothing like "the President of the Immortals had finished his sport with Tess". Crabbe was not like Cowper a Calvinist, a believer in the doctrines of predestination, election, conversion, salvation by the grace of God and that alone, which is the theme of the poem *Truth* in Cowper's first volume. What Crabbe thought of these doctrines in the abstract is not clear. He leaned for his own faith on the historical rather than the theological. What he did dislike was the manner in which the doctrine of conversion and grace seemed to him to work in practice, as he shows in the story of Abel Keene in *The Borough*. For Cowper the sinner,

> The worn-out nuisance of the public streets,

was in a happier condition for grace to work upon than the moral man, and this is what the "good man" tells Abel:

> "Once thou wert simply honest, just and pure,
> Whole as thou thoughtst, and never wished a cure:
> Now thou hast plung'd in folly, shame, disgrace;
> Now thou'rt an object meet for healing grace;
> No merit thine, no virtue, hope, belief,
> Nothing hast thou but misery, sin and grief,
> The best, the only titles of relief."

> "What must I do," I said, "my soul to free?"
> "Do nothing, man; it will be done for thee."
> "But must I not, my reverend guide, believe?"
> "If thou art call'd, thou wilt the faith receive."

The result of such waiting was for Abel—as for Cowper incidentally—despair. In belief as in other things, Crabbe thinks men must use their will, doing the best they can. Unbelief is most often the consequence of shallow vanity, and he gives some examples, as of the Gentleman Farmer. The nearest Crabbe comes to any comment on the course of events is in the closing lines in the story of Ruth:

> Well had it still remain'd a world unseen.

In the last resort, however, it is not a poet's choice of subject, his being a realist or a romantic, that makes him a poet, but

the manner in which he treats his subject, the charm which he
lends to it by depth of feeling, beauty of language, music of
verse.   The most serious charges which have been brought
against Crabbe are that his treatment is didactic rather than
poetic, and that his verse is wanting in music.

But to say that Crabbe is didactic is simply to say that he
was an eighteenth-century poet, for every poet of that century
thought it his duty to be didactic.   Yet the effect of a tale by
Crabbe is not in the end didactic.   It is not the lesson, the
warning, that one remembers, but the inevitability of what has
been related.   Such is human nature; so man will act and so in
consequence he will suffer; or such are men's hopes, and so are
they too often disappointed.   Virtue itself is no guarantee of
happiness.   "Consider the work of God, for who can make that
straight which he has made crooked? . . . there is a righteous
man that perishes in his righteousness, and there is a wicked
man that prolongeth his life in evil-doing."   That is the
burden of the *Book of Job*, of Johnson's *Rasselas* and *Vanity of
Human Wishes*, and it is the burden of Crabbe's stories, told
dramatically in his dry yet for that reason effective manner,
the story left to speak for itself.   But for Crabbe, as for the
author of *Ecclesiastes*, there are good things in life—love,
affection, kindness, pity, the beauty of Nature, wisdom.   Nor
have all his tales a didactic intention.   What lesson is taught
by *The Parting Hour*?   Pity is the dominant mood in all
Crabbe's most serious pictures of life from *The Village* onwards.
"What made Crabbe a new force in English poetry", Canon
Ainger justly wrote, "was that in his verse Pity appears, after
a long oblivion, as the true antidote to sentimentalism . . . if
Crabbe is our first great realist he uses his realism in the cause
of a true humanity, *facit indignatio versus*."

By the complaint that Crabbe does not envisage his subject
poetically, Saintsbury had doubtless in view, as well as the
didactic tone, the matter-of-fact style in which he describes his
scenes, characters, and incidents, and the occasional flatness
of his diction and verse.   Wordsworth's criticism, when he
invites comparison with Crabbe, of his own tales of peasant's
life and suffering in *The Excursion* is Saintsbury's but with a
difference.   Crabbe does not invest, as Wordsworth endeavours
to do, his story with an atmosphere which suggests that there
is more than pathos in the tale, that there is something that
helps us to transcend or sublimate the sadness, to discover:

Sorrow that is not sorrow but delight,
And miserable love that is not pain
To hear of, for the glory that redounds
Therefrom to human kind and what we are.

But the sheer truthfulness of Crabbe's tales has a power which any attempt to interpret or adorn might easily mar. Is there nothing of the miserable love that is not pain to hear of in *The Parting Hour* or *Ruth*? Crabbe had passed through the bitter experiences of life as Wordsworth had not. For his purpose the matter-of-fact style,—"poetry without an atmosphere", as he himself calls it—even the occasional descents—and he had not so far to descend as Milton and Wordsworth—are better suited than a more decorative style, a more swelling verse. But it is the verse on which Saintsbury based his final summing-up against Crabbe, the want of variety in his music; and this is not to be altogether denied. Yet his style and verse are the fitting garb of his feeling and themes, nor is his style always flat, his verse always monotonous. When deeply moved, as in the account of the condemned man's last night or the story of Ruth, there is both moving description and adequate rhythm. Where he is least successful is in the satirical, half-humorous tales, where he wants the art of Chaucer, the more sinuous movement of his verse.

Chapter Twenty

THE REVIVAL OF SCOTTISH POETRY

WHILE these things were happening in England, Scottish poetry was following, in the main, an independent course. We observed in Chapter Five that with the removal of the court to London in 1603 Scottish courtly poetry died a natural death. Several Scotsmen—Drummond of Hawthornden, the Earl of Stirling, the Marquis of Montrose, Sir Robert Ayton —wrote courtly poetry after 1603, but they wrote it in English; popular songs and ballads continued to be made in Scots and transmitted orally; but of written Scots verse there is no trace until, about the middle of the century, we come on Robert Sempill's *Life and Death of the Piper of Kilbarchan*, otherwise *The Epitaph of Habbie Simson*, a poem which became the model for those humorous elegies in which Ramsay and Fergusson and Burns delighted—"Standart *Habby*", Ramsay calls it. It is in that strain which we now call the Burns stanza; actually it is much older than either Burns or Sempill. Francis Sempill, Robert's son, wrote *The Banishment of Poverty*, a dull poem in rime couée, and has been credited with the much livelier *Blythsome Wedding*. William Hamilton of Gilbertfield followed with *The Last Dying Words of Bonnie Heck, a Famous Greyhound*, which suggested Burns's *Poor Mailie's Elegy*. Lady Wardlaw's *Hardyknute* imitated the old ballad well enough to deceive Percy at first and delight the childhood of Scott. But the best of all these seventeenth-century poets was Lady Grizel Baillie. Alas! she survives only in one short, tender poem, *Werena My Heart Licht*, and one idyllic fragment, *The Ewebuchting's Bonnie*. Though these poets all chose homely subjects, or, in Lady Wardlaw's case, the homely form of the ballad, they all belonged to the class of the nobility or the gentry; the upper classes still spoke Scots familiarly, though they were ceasing to write in it on serious subjects.

The publication of Watson's *Choice Collection of Comic and Serious Scots Poems*, in 1706, 1709, and 1711, made something of an epoch in the Scottish Revival. The loss of her Parliament, impending in 1706, accomplished by 1709, made Scotland cling jealously to such symbols of nationhood as were left—her language among them—while at the same time she was dazzled by the brilliance of English letters, then in their Augustan zenith. When Hamilton of Gilbertfield modernised the fiercely anti-English *Wallace* of Blind Harry, in 1722, he did so by turning it into English in the style of Pope's *Homer*! So, while Watson's is a collection of Scots poems in the sense that all the poems were written by Scots, only thirteen of the seventy-three are written in Scots: only four of the thirteen are older than 1600; but these include *Christis Kirk on the Green* and *The Cherry and the Slae*, which, with "Standart *Habby*", provided Ramsay and Burns with their favourite measures, the sixain, the quatorzain, and the octave with refrain.

The same combination of Scottish nationalism with deference to English taste is seen in Allan Ramsay (1686–1758), the chief promoter of the Scottish Revival. Scottish Jacobitism being more a nationalist than a dynastic sentiment, Ramsay's Jacobitism proved him a patriotic Scot; but it did not prevent him from keeping one eye on London, where his pretty songs, Scotch but not too Scotch, were vastly popular at Ranelagh and Vauxhall. Besides songs and a political allegory (*The Vision*), Ramsay wrote humorous elegies, familiar epistles, satires, and fables. He used three languages—English, Scots, and Anglo-Scots, the last chiefly in his songs. The Scots of his elegies is broader; so is the humour; and both sometimes smack of the gutter. There is a touch of vulgarity in the relish with which this canny epicurean describes the thrifty guzzlings and tipplings of Old Edinburgh. As a rule he is genial; but *Lucky Spence's Last Advice* to her houris shows that on occasion he can rival Dunbar in grossness, as he often does in vivacity and metrical skill. Ramsay's imitations of Horace are among his happiest efforts. The urbanity of his model keeps his worst faults in check, and his Scots, like Charles Murray's in our own day, catches surprisingly often the curious felicity of the Latin.

> Then fling on coals, and ripe the ribs,
> And beek the house baith butt and ben,
> That mutchken stoup it hads but dribs,
> Then let's get in the tappit hen,

is good value, in its homelier way, for

> Dissolve frigus, ligna super foco
> Large reponens, atque benignius
> Deprome quadrimum Sabina,
> O Thaliarche, merum diota.

In his masterpiece, *The Gentle Shepherd* (1725), Ramsay emulated the pastoral strains of the English Augustans, and easily surpassed them all. *The Gentle Shepherd* is a pastoral comedy of rustic life and courtship among the Pentland Hills. It follows the Arcadian convention in that hero and heroine turn out to be 'gentle'; but it is full of fresh, shrewd touches of Nature, and, in fine, comes nearer to the natural pastoral of Theocritus than anything else in any form of English.

Ramsay contributed even more to the Scottish Revival as an editor than he did as an original poet. In 1724 the Bannatyne manuscript came into his hands, and he published great part of it in *The Evergreen*, a collection, as he described it, of Scots poems "wrote by the Ingenious before 1600". The seventeenth century had neglected all the old makars except Blind Harry and Davie Lindsay; Watson had printed only four pieces "wrote before 1600"; *The Evergreen* added some old ballads, some of the *Gude and Godly Ballates*, some of Henryson, a good deal of Alexander Scott and other minors, and a great deal of Dunbar. Ramsay treated his texts cavalierly, modernising, vulgarising, and improving as he saw fit; but he rendered an inestimable service to Scottish poetry by revealing the wealth of its inheritance. *The Tea-Table Miscellany* (1724, 1725, 1729, 1732) did for the songs of Scotland what *The Evergreen* did for her literate poetry. It is a mixed bag of songs old and new, Scots and English; the old songs are treated as cavalierly as the poems in *The Evergreen*; but it gave a powerful stimulus to the reviving interest in popular song; and much may be forgiven to the editor who first printed *O Waly, Waly*, *The Bonnie Earl o' Murray*, *Willie's Drowned in Yarrow*, *Barbara Allen*, *The Gaberlunzie Man*, and *Toddlen Ben*. Ramsay served Scotland well not only in poetry but in drama and the fine arts; for many years his bookshop was the centre of Edinburgh's literary and artistic life.

The Scottish Renascence did not come to full bearing till Burns appeared, but between Ramsay and Burns it yielded a remarkable crop of minor poets. With the exception of Fergusson they are known only for one or two songs apiece, but these are of singularly high and uniform quality. Finest of all is Jane Elliot's *Flowers of the Forest*, which gives perfect utterance to the unforgotten pain which even in Scott's day made old men in Ettrick Forest burst into tears at the mention of Flodden. Mrs. Cockburn's song of the same name laments,

s

in more conventional English, the financial ruin of certain Ettrick gentlemen. To the Borders also belong two poems that Burns had in mind when he wrote

> Yarrow an' Tweed, to monie a tune,
>   Owre Scotland rings,

namely, Robert Crawford's *Leader Haughs and Yarrow* and William Hamilton of Bangour's *Busk Ye, Busk Ye, My Bonnie, Bonnie Bride*, a song which Wordsworth also admired. In Alexander Geddes's *O, Send Lewie Gordon Hame* Jacobitism is still a living sentiment, not the literary pose that it afterwards became. Lady Anne Barnard's *Auld Robin Gray* and the anonymous *Logie o' Buchan* are tragedies of humble life, the wail of a heart-broken woman whose lover comes back too late, the plaint of a girl whose lad has been pressed for the wars. The latter theme appears again in John Mayne's sweet pastoral *Logan Braes*. Scottish song is sweetest when saddest, but it has other notes than pathos. Alexander Ross's pastoral romance of *Helenore* had only a local reputation, being in Northern Scots; but all Scotland lilted his gay *Wooed and Married and A'*, *The Bridal O't*, and *The Rock and the Wee Pickle Tow*. Humour still more rollicking gives life and mettle to John Skinner's *Tullochgorum*, which Burns declared the best Scots song Scotland ever saw. That charming domestic piece, *There's Nae Luck Aboot the Hoose*, is claimed for W. J. Mickle. Tradition assigns the idyllic *Ca' the Yowes to the Knowes* to the ale-wife Tibbie Pagan. It will be seen that pathos and humour, not passionate love, are the dominant notes in these mid-century songs; and that gentlefolk are still prominent among the singers.

Robert Fergusson (1750–1774) wrote no songs in Scots, but in other forms of poetry he has left a body of work remarkable in one who died so young. His father's death forced him to leave college to earn his bread as a copying-clerk. He sought relief from drudgery in the tavern; but he was too frail for such a life, and died in a mad-house at twenty-four. In poetry other than song Fergusson is the chief link between Ramsay and Burns. He was not so versatile a metrist as Ramsay, but he was a sounder and more original poet. He broke new ground in *The Farmer's Ingle* and in the dialogues of *Plainstanes and Causey* and *The Ghaists*. He was the laureate of Auld Reekie, whose jollifications he celebrated with cleanly glee in *The Daft-Days*, and *Hallow-Fair*, and *Leith Races*. In *The Farmer's Ingle* he went afield for his subject: his odes to the caged goldfinch and the butterfly seen in the street bring Nature into the city, and show the same sympathy for the lower creation as charms us in Cowper and Burns. He had not Burns's gift of phrase, nor his virility—his impetuous blood; but he blazed the trail for him in several directions: his *Leith Races*, *Plainstanes and Causey*, and *Farmer's Ingle* were the models which Burns 'emulated' in *The Holy Fair*, *The Twa Brigs*, and *The Cotter's Saturday Night*—rough diamonds, no doubt, beside Burns's polished gems, but diamonds for all that.

This is how *Leith Races* opens:

> In July month, ae bonny morn,
>   Whan Nature's rokelay green
> Was spread o'er ilka rigg o' corn
>   To charm our roving een;
> Glouring about I saw a quean,
>   The fairest 'neath the lift;
> Her EEN ware o' the siller sheen,
>   Her SKIN like snawy drift,
>   Sae white that day.

And here is the opening of *The Holy Fair*:

> Upon a simmer Sunday morn,
>   When Nature's face is fair,
> I walk-ed forth to view the corn,
>   An' snuff the caller air.
> The rising sun, owre Galston Muirs,
>   Wi' glorious light was glintin';
> The hares were hirplin' down the furs,
>   The lav'rocks they were chantin
>   Fu' sweet that day.

We see at once how much Burns owes to Fergusson and how quickly his "emulating vigour" carries him beyond his original.

Chapter Twenty-One

BURNS

THE poetry of Robert Burns (1759–1796) presents a crowning example of the complex relation between Scots and English which has existed ever since the fifteenth century. The Scottish tongue is a distinct variety of English, with a history of its own, and, as such, continued to be spoken by people of all classes till into the first quarter of the nineteenth century. "Scotch was a language which we have heard spoken by the learned and the wise and witty and the accomplished, and which had not a trace of vulgarity in it but, on the contrary, sounded rather graceful and genteel . . . it was different from English as the Venetian is from the Tuscan dialect of Italy, but it never occur'd to anyone that the Scottish, any more than the Venetian, was more vulgar than those who spoke the purer and more classical.—But that is all gone." So Scott writes in 1822, and ten or more years later Cockburn gives evidence of the use of Scottish on the Bench and at the Bar, but also of its gradual disappearance in the mouths of cultivated and professional people, its gradual supersession by what might be called "lingua inglese in bocca scozzese".

Moreover in this Scottish tongue literary work of a distinguished and distinct character had been produced by the great makars of the fifteenth and sixteenth centuries. Even in this poetry the influence of Chaucer and his southern forms is traceable, but nevertheless the genius of their language is Scottish throughout. It was the Reformation and the change in the stratification of Scottish thought and feeling which followed from the close of the "auld alliance", and the suppression of the old Faith, from the dependence of the Reformers on English support, and finally from the accession of a Scottish king to the throne of England, which determined what was to be the interrelation of the tongues. From the sixteenth century onwards an educated Scot is aware that he has two tongues to choose from according to his purpose, that if he will (say) preach and print sermons it will be in the vernacular; if he writes a thesis on a controversial point in theology or ecclesiastical practice, if he does not use Latin—and in every country

the Reformation and Counter-Reformation, with their appeal
to a more popular audience, were encouraging the use of the
vernacular—then the same Scot will write in English as best
he can.   The consequence is that when Scottish poetry reawoke
in the eighteenth century, it is in varying degree in individual
poets, varying degrees in individual poems by the same author,
an Anglo-Scottish poetry, Scottish in spirit and choice of subject and in the main Scottish in language and form, but
traversed ever and again by veins of feeling that come from the
English literature of the day, and allowing a poet ever and
again to pass from a Scottish to an English diction, and even
in the Scottish parts permitting an occasional convenient use
of an English rather than a Scottish form.   And further, the
ever-growing prestige of Southern English as the politer
tongue, the tongue proper for a literature addressed to cultured
and polite circles, hangs over the heads of all these poets.
One and all of them will attempt to write in the more polite
tongue, not least Robert Burns.   He spoke in English, Dugald
Stewart tells us, not only with fluency, precision, and originality
but with a careful purity in his turn of expression, avoiding
"more successfully than most Scotchmen the peculiarities of
Scottish phraseology", *i.e.* Scotticisms.   Indeed such education as Burns received from tutor or school was directed to
making him a master of English.   "Though it cost the schoolmaster some thrashings, I made an excellent English scholar,
and by the time I was ten or eleven years of age I was a critic
in substantives, verbs, and particles."   So Robert, and Gilbert
confirms.   And the books Burns read and took as his models
for conversation and for letters were English—Addison: "The
earliest composition that I recollect taking pleasure in was
The Vision of Mirza and a hymn of Addison's beginning *How
are thy Servants blest, O Lord!*   I particularly remember one
half-stanza which was music to my boyish ear—

> For though on dreadful whirls we hung
> High on the broken wave.

I met with these in *Mason's English Collection*, one of my school-
books."   Again, "I had met with a collection of Letters by
the wits of Queen Anne's reign, and I pored over them most
devoutly.   I kept copies of any of my own letters that pleased
me, and a comparison between them and the composition of
most of my correspondents flattered my vanity."   He read

Pope and Shakespeare, and his own mind responded readily to the doctrine of "Truth to Nature" as handed on from Pope to Johnson and from Johnson to Cowper and Crabbe, for he was no romantic; but his heart responded more warmly to the note of sensibility audible in such well-loved writers as Thomson, Shenstone, Sterne, and Mackenzie, the doctrine of the kind heart as an atonement for all weaknesses and vices. His conversation in Edinburgh was equally remarkable for its strongly satirical turn and its capacity, when his mood was that of feeling, to sweep an audience, especially a female audience, off their feet; and to such audiences he doubtless spoke in the politer tongue.

All this is true and must not be forgotten in trying to make an estimate of his poetry. That one might write more or less well, more or less purely, in the Scottish tongue entered the head of none of his teachers or his Edinburgh patrons and admirers. They were all more or less Anglicisers, bent on eschewing Scotticisms. The Scottish tongue, so far as serious study was concerned,

> Lay like some unkenn'd of isle
>   Beside New Holland,
> Or whare wild-meeting oceans boil
>   Besouth Magellan.

The language of the Highlands, the presupposition of Macpherson's *Ossian*, was already a subject of greater interest to *virtuosi* than this "English of the Northern Parts", which to the polite was just English debased by passing through the mouth of the vulgar. Yet it was not in the English which he studied and practised so assiduously that Burns was to write anything of enduring merit, but in the homely Scots which he learned by daily use in his family and among his associates, from his study of old Scottish songs and ballads, and from the practice of the Edinburgh poets, his predecessors, Ramsay and especially Fergusson. Speaking of his twenty-third year, and his stay in Irvine, he says, "Rhyme, except some religious pieces that are in print, I had given up; but meeting with Fergusson's Scottish Poems I strung anew my wildly-sounding lyre with emulating vigour". In the course of three years that followed he composed *The Death and Dying Words of Poor Mailie*, the first herald of this Fergussonian, dramatic, rural poetry; but it was in the closing months of his twenty-sixth

year (1784) and throughout the year which followed that he
got into his full stride and proceeded to pour forth the poems
which were to be issued in the Kilmarnock volume of 1786
and, with additions, in the Edinburgh volume which followed
in 1787.   It is not a pure Scots, less pure than that of Fergusson.   It contains an infusion of "hamely westlin" Ayrshire
dialect, possibly even a touch of his father's Mearns dialect;
but in the main it is the Scots of the Edinburgh poets with a
varying intermixture of English stanzas, lines, or words.   The
religious poems are generally in English throughout.

What then is the peculiar character, the worth, of these
poems that has won for them among readers who can judge a
far wider than local and patriotic interest?   Of many of the
charms of the romantic poetry which was to come, Burns,
though he is frequently classed with the romantics, had little
or none—the subtle and bold imaginative quality steeped
in religious feeling of William Blake, the deeply blended,
sensuous, and spiritual quality of Wordsworth's Nature poetry,
the intimate personal quality of the best poems of another
peasant poet, poor John Clare.   He was not at any period of
his life the dreamer, loving solitude and the building of castles
in the air, that Scott had been in youth according to his own
description and that, to one who has eyes to see, he remained,
amid all his social and financial activities, till disaster overtook
him.   Burns's description of himself indicates very clearly
certain aspects of his poetry: "a strong appetite for sociability,
as well from native hilarity as from pride of observation and
remark; a constitutional melancholy or hypochondriasm that
made me flee solitude.   Add to these incentives to social life
my reputation for bookish knowledge, a certain wild logical
talent, and a strength of thought something like the rudiments
of good sense, and it will not seem surprising that I was
generally a welcome guest where I visited, or any great wonder
that always when two or three met together there was I among
them.   But far beyond all other impulses of my heart was
un penchant à l'adorable moitié du genre humain."   A sociable
being himself, Burns's poetry is a social poetry as entirely as
the satires and epistles and didactic poems of Horace or Pope
or Johnson, or the essays of the *Spectator*—a poetry written to
amuse and interest as definitely conceived an audience as
Horace's or Pope's, though a very different audience.   But
anything that can justly be called a poetry of the people has this

definitely social quality—ballads, songs, tales, flytings, satire, elegy, epistles. Sociability is the note of the Scottish poetry revived in Edinburgh by Ramsay and Fergusson, their verse-epistles and satires and festive poems on *Leith Races* or *The Daft-Days*. If Clare is a poet, as Mr. Symons says, because of qualities that unfitted him to be a peasant, one of the qualities that distinguishes his poems from those of Burns is just the inwardness of an essentially solitary soul. When Burns attempts to retreat into himself in religious melancholy his language becomes English, his poetry negligible. He took over the themes, the forms, the spirit of his Scottish predecessors, but gave to that spirit a new intensity. Speaking of the dissipations of even cultured circles in the Edinburgh of 1787 Currie says, "Burns entered into several parties of this description with *the usual vehemency of his character*". If that vehemency of character was to prove his own undoing as a man, it is to that same vehemency we owe all that is best in his poetry,—pictures of life and revelry that will hold their own in comparison with some of the great Falstaff scenes in Shakespeare; an ardour of generous sentiment which raises the humanitarian sensibility of the later eighteenth century to a white heat; satire in which scorn and fun are blended as perhaps in no poet since Aristophanes; love songs, or fragments of love songs, which, if written in Greek and dug up in the sands of Egypt, would add to the reputation of Sappho.

The Kilmarnock volume of 1786 contained some twenty-eight poems, three songs, and a few epitaphs. Of the poems seven, written in English and in a vein of hypochondriacal melancholy, are entirely negligible. A poet-laureate of the day could have written better, and of the epitaphs that on himself alone deserves any attention. This leaves—omitting songs for the moment—twenty-one poems in the Scots which was Burns's natural language. To these he added in the Edinburgh edition of 1787—they had been composed earlier —some ten more poems in the same vein. *The Jolly Beggars*, a work probably of the same Mossgiel period, was not printed till much later. *Tam o' Shanter* was the only poem of the same kind composed after the critical visit to Edinburgh. It is on these poems and the songs, of which later, that Burns's reputation rests, and we propose to consider their various themes and treatment.

The forms which Burns used were those he inherited from

his Edinburgh models, themselves derived from much older mediaeval Scottish and French poets—the famous sixain which bears his name; the nine-line bob-wheel stanza of *Christ's Kirk on the Green*, which he uses (*e.g.*) in *The Holy Fair* and *Halloween*; and the 'quatorzain' of *The Cherry and the Slae*, which he uses with brilliant effect in *The Jolly Beggars* and the *Epistle to Davie*.

In addition to these Scottish measures Burns uses the familiar English and Scottish octosyllabics and decasyllabics; and like many of his favourite English poets of the century he tries his hand at the Spenserian stanza in (*e.g.*) *The Cotter's Saturday Night*. For themes as well as verse forms Burns was largely indebted to his predecessors, to Fergusson especially. His most ambitious bucolic poems of Scottish life and revelry have their exemplars in Fergusson's "Scots Poems". Fergusson was to Burns a little of what Marlowe was to Shakespeare. Indeed one feels at times that Fergusson's was rather the more original mind, if he cannot give to what he describes or feels the same warm vivid glow, or the same artistic finish. After all Burns owes something to his English reading. It taught him the classic virtues of clearness, conciseness, and point—precisely the stylistic qualities in which his Scots verse surpasses Fergusson's.

To say that Burns's poetry is not individual, personal, introvert in the same way as John Clare's or Shelley's or the religious poetry of Herbert, Vaughan, and Traherne, is not of course to say that Burns does not put himself into his poems, far from it; the themes of which he sings are just the main interests of his life. There are the poems which deal with incidents of his own life as a farmer: *The Death and Dying Words of Poor Mailie*, *The Auld Farmer's New Year Morning Salutation to his Auld Mare, Maggie*, the addresses *To a Mouse* and *To a Mountain Daisy*. Another group deals with the social gaieties, pious and bacchic, which relieved the life of the peasant and farmer struggling with an ungrateful soil unrelieved by any rotation of crops,—"the cheerless gloom of a hermit with the unceasing moil of a galley-slave", so Burns describes his own early days. But Saturday came—if Sunday loomed ahead with its woeful exercises and sermons and the possibility of having to appear on the cutty-stool and be reproved—and Burns went down the road to Tarbolton, his eyes shining with joyous expectation of hours to be spent in song and talk, himself generally the leader, with boon-companions among the

Free Masons or others, or more moving and dangerous hours with the lasses, dancing and daffing. And it is the reflection of his own ardent temperament which shines in his descriptions of the innocent amusements of *Halloween*, his satirical enjoyment of the blended piety, jollification, and sensuality of *The Holy Fair*; the more reckless debauchery of *The Jolly Beggars* or *Tam o' Shanter*:

> Kings may be blest, but Tam was glorious,
> O'er a' the ills o' life victorious.

And there are the Epistles—to James Smith, to Davie, to J. Lapraik, to William Simpson, in which he gives vent to his joys and ambitions as poet and patriot, and airs his philosophy of life. There remain the poems which could only have been written by a Scot—the satires on the religious creeds and discipline and clergy of the Kirk of Scotland as Burns knew it. Andrew Lang regretted they had ever been written. To Swinburne they seemed the greatest things Burns composed:

> Above the storm of praise and blame
> That blur with mist his lustrous name
> His thunderous laughter went and came
>   And lives and flies;
> The roar that follows on the flame
>   When lightning dies.

Any regrets should include the doctrines, practices, and penalties which evoked them. Our concern with them is only as poems, and we doubt whether there exists in English literature a greater humorous satire than *Holy Willie's Prayer*.

Originality of theme or form or sentiments is not characteristic of Burns as a poet or letter-writer. His gift to Scottish poetry and poetry generally was his amazing temperament, a temperament which when it finds adequate expression suggests nothing so much as that which we divine through the fragments of Sappho. But these fragments have only one motive—love, and, as we shall see, it is only in a few of his songs—perhaps, to be quite just, in one or two stanzas—that Burns achieves anything like the perfect and burning felicity of the Greek fragments. Byron thought of himself, and was accepted by his generation, as the poet of passion, but except when anger becomes the predominant motive, as in the unjust stanzas on Castlereagh, his passionate poetry is rhetorical and unconvincing. . What we want to indicate in dealing with these

early poems is that the passionate strain in Burns's genius
diffused itself through poems whose theme is not love, in a
joie de vivre unequalled in English poetry except it be in some
of the great scenes in Shakespeare's comedies—and these are
generally in prose.

That Burns cared for natural scenery for its own sake, as Sir
Walter Scott did, we do not believe.   But what Burns had was
something more vital, a passionate response to the life of Nature
as it flowed round and through him from day to day:

> O, sweet are Coila's haughs an' woods,
> When lintwhites chant amang the buds,
> And jinkin' hares, in amorous whids,
>   Their loves enjoy,
> While thro' the braes the cushat croods,
>   With wailfu' cry:
>
> Ev'n winter bleak has charms to me
> When winds rave thro' the naked tree;
> Or frosts on hills of Ochiltree
>   Are hoary gray:
> Or blinding drifts wild-furious flee,
>   Dark'ning the day!

But for Burns, as for Dr. Johnson, and for the same reasons—
sociability of temperament and gifts, a hypochondriacal
shrinking from solitude—the tide of human life at its full was
more attractive than scenery.   "Many others", wrote Mrs.
Dunlop after the poet's death, "may have ascended to prouder
heights in the region of Parnassus, but none certainly ever outshone Burns in the charms—the sorcery I would almost call it,
of fascinating conversation, the spontaneous eloquence of social
argument, or the unstudied poignancy of brilliant repartee;
nor was any man, I believe, ever gifted with a larger portion
of the *vivida vis animi.*"   "The rapid lightenings of his eye
were always the harbingers of some flash of genius whether
they darted the fiery glances of insulted and indignant
superiority, or burned with the impassioned sentiment of
fervent and impetuous affection. His voice alone could
improve upon the magic of his eye."   Comparatively little of
that *vivida vis*, which shone in his eye and echoed in his voice,
found its way into his too carefully composed letters.   But it
is present in all its force in the poems descriptive of peasant
life and revelry.   *Halloween* is in a slightly quieter key of

gaiety; but in *The Holy Fair*, *The Jolly Beggars*, and *Tam o' Shanter* it overflows in a torrent,—a torrent of vivid description and rollicking humour:

> Here, farmers gash, in ridin' graith,
>   Gaed hoddin' by their cotters;
> There, swankies young, in braw braid-claith,
>   Are springin' owre the gutters.
> The lasses, skelpin' barefit, thrang,
>   In silks an' scarlets glitter;
> Wi' sweet-milk cheese, in monie a whang,
>   An' farls, bak'd wi' butter,
>   Fu' crump that day.
>
> Here, some are thinkin' on their sins,
>   An' some upon their claes;
> Ane curses feet that fyl'd his shins,
>   Anither sighs an' prays:
> On this hand sits a chosen swatch
>   Wi' screw'd-up, grace-proud faces;
> On that, a set o' chaps at watch,
>   Thrang winkin' on the lasses
>   To chairs that day.
>
> Now butt an' ben, the change-house fills,
>   Wi' yill-caup commentators;
> Here's crying out for bakes an' gills,
>   An' there the pint stowp clatters;
> While thick an' thrang, an' loud an' lang,
>   Wi' logic, an' wi' Scripture,
> They raise a din, that, in the end,
>   Is like to breed a rupture
>   O' wrath that day.

But the highest pitch in this strain of *joie de vivre* is reached in *Tam o' Shanter* and *The Jolly Beggars*, between the merits of which critics have been seriously divided. In our view *Tam o' Shanter* has the more equal and sustained flow of narration, vivid description, and dramatic humour, all lit up with the glow of the hero's mind. Dramatic touches abound as—

> And at his elbow Souter Johnie,
> His ancient, trusty, drouthy crony:
> Tam lo'ed him like a very brither—
> *They had been fou for weeks thegither.*

Perhaps the subtlest is that which describes the gathering of

superstitious impressions in Tam's mind as he rides, preparing
him for the spectacle of Kirk-Alloway and all that was there
transacting:

> By this time he was cross the ford,
> Whare in the snaw the chapman smoor'd;
> And past the birks and meikle stane,
> Whare drunken Charlie brak's neck-bane;
> And thro' the whins, and by the cairn,
> Whare hunters fand the murder'd bairn;
> And near the thorn, aboon the well,
> Whare Mungo's mither hang'd hersel'.

There is in *The Jolly Beggars* a strain which is not purely
Scottish, an echo of *The Beggar's Opera*, especially in the songs,
but the thunder of reckless laughter and defiance in the closing
song speaks the spirit of the abandonment that recalls the
poetry of Villon.   Here at any rate Burns seems to justify his
deviation into English.   Nevertheless there is a purer strain,
less earthly and spirituous, of the same *joie de vivre* in the verse-
epistles where he gives the same glow and animation to the
expression of his joy in poetry, in the beauties of his own
countryside, the passionate patriotism with which he surveys
the history of his country, the long struggle for independence
which made early Scottish poetry, as Professor Brie has recently
emphasised, the first distinctively patriotic poetry:

> Ramsay an' famous Ferguson
> Gied Forth an' Tay a lift aboon;
> Yarrow an' Tweed, to monie a tune
>   Owre Scotland rings,
> While Irwin, Lugar, Ayr, an' Doon,
>   Naebody sings.
>
> Th' Ilissus, Tiber, Thames, an' Seine,
> Glide sweet in monie a tunefu' line:
> But, Willie, set your fit to mine,
>   An' cock your crest,
> We'll gar our streams and burnies shine
>   Up wi' the best.
>
> We'll sing auld Coila's plains an' fells,
> Her moors red-brown wi' heather bells,
> Her banks an' braes, her dens an' dells,
>   Where glorious Wallace
> Aft bure the gree, as story tells,
>   Frae southron billies.

At Wallace' name, what Scottish blood
But boils up in a spring-tide flood!
Oft have our fearless fathers strode
    By Wallace' side,
Still pressing onward, red-wat-shod,
    Or glorious dy'd.

The same *joie de vivre* is the note of Burns's satires, not anger, as Swinburne's lines suggest, but Aristophanic laughter. The earliest example is the piece of local satire *Death and Dr. Hornbook* with its delightful description of the somewhat unsteady poet making his way home:

The rising moon began to glower
The distant Cumnock hills out-owre:
To count her horns, wi' a' my power,
    I set mysel';
But whether she had three or four,
    I could na tell.

But the finest stroke of the poem is the drunkard's reaction to Dr. Hornbook's victory over Death:

"Wae's me for Johnny Ged's Hole now,"
Quo' I, "if that thae news be true!
His braw calf-ward whare gowans grew,
    Sae white an' bonnie,
Nae doubt they'll rive it wi' the plew;
    They'll ruin Johnnie!"

The greatest of all Burns's satires, to our minds the most perfect bit of satire in English poetry, is *Holy Willie's Prayer*, and it too is steeped in laughter, Aristophanic, inspired not so much by anger as by delight in contemplating the turns and returns of the hero's mind seeking to achieve the peace of repentance with forgiveness but without consequences, while leaving, by doctrinal aid, the door open for fresh relapses:

O Lord! yestreen, thou kens, wi' Meg,—[1]
Thy pardon I sincerely beg,—
O! May't ne'er be a livin' plague
    To my dishonour,
And I'll ne'er lift a lawless leg
    Again upon her.

[1] A line which recalls in its effective pauses so different a parallel as
"Eyeless, in Gaza, at the Mill, with slaves."

Maybe thou lets this fleshly thorn
Beset thy servant e'en and morn,
Lest he owre high and proud should turn,
          'Cause he's sae gifted;
If sae, thy han' maun e'en be borne,
          Until thou lift it.

It is in the poems and songs conceived in this spirit of reckless *joie de vivre* and overflowing humour that Burns has no
rival.   It is not, of course, the quality which constitutes the
chief tie between himself and the Scottish people.   That is to
be found rather in the pieces touched with pathos—*To a Mouse*,
on turning up her nest with the plough, *To a Mountain Daisy*,
on turning one down with the plough, *The Cotter's Saturday
Night*, and others, poems certainly not without charm and
appeal, but in which Burns has both rivals and superiors.
The Deserted Village is worth them all put together,—to say
nothing of *Michael*, *Margaret*, or, despite the prim stiffness of
its versification, Crabbe's *The Parting Hour*.

Nor will it ultimately be found very different when one
turns from the poems to the songs.   It was in these that Burns
found new life as a poet after the disastrous visit to Edinburgh which, but for *Tam o' Shanter*, one might say killed
the poet of rural life and satire and humour, the great inheritor
of the tradition of Ramsay and Fergusson.   The Edinburgh
gentlemen made of the poor poet a hard drinker and an
author of worthless English poems and bombastic, worthless
English letters.   But James Johnson, the Edinburgh
engraver and publisher, saved the Scottish poet by enlisting
him in the work of collecting and editing and writing songs
for his *The Scots Musical Museum* (6 vols., 1787–1803).   To
the first volume of 1787 he contributed two songs—"Green
grow the rashes" and the more decorative, Anglified "Young
Peggy blooms"; but in the second volume came "A rose-bud
by my early walk", "Blyth, blyth and merry was she", "The
Birks of Aberfeldy", the pompous and English "Clarinda,
mistress of my soul", the fiery "McPherson's Farewell", "How
pleasant the banks of the clear, winding Devon", "The Young
Highland Rover", "Hey Tutti, Taiti":

              Landlady, count the lawin'.
              The day is near the dawin';
              Ye're a' blind drunk, boys,
              And I'm but jolly fou.

Hey tutti, taiti,
How tutti, taiti,
Hey, tutti, taiti,
Wha's fou now?

To the same volume belong "Musing on the roaring ocean", "O whistle, and I'll come to you, my lad", "Raving winds around her blowing", "Stay my charmer, can you leave me", "No cruel fate shall bid us part", "Thickest night, surround my dwelling", "Tibbie, I hae seen the day", "When braving angry winter storms", "When Guilford good our pilot stood". Thereafter Burns became not only the chief collector and contributor but, one might say, the controlling editor. The result has been well described by Professor Hecht. Whereas the work had opened in the tradition of Allan Ramsay and "the elegant poets of the seventeenth and eighteenth centuries", with Burns "the philandering with English 'correct poetry' ceased, and, supported by the whole treasury of Scottish melodies, carefully supplemented by new collections, by the most suitable songs of contemporary native poets, and by the still existent texts and fragments of old traditional lyrics, which found in Burns a congenial restorer and adapter animated by a very real understanding of the people, there rose up the imposing structure of a comprehensive collection of Scottish song". This is in the main true and important, yet one must not forget that here again there is a complex, mixed tradition. Scottish and English do not stand apart sheer and distinguishable. As Mr. Henderson well sums up, "from the time of Ramsay *down to and including Burns* the stream of Scottish popular song—whether as regards words or music—ceased to be of purely Scottish origin, and in many ways—ways that are as yet but imperfectly and confusedly disclosed—is intermingled with the stream of broadside and claptrap literature which reached its highest watermark in the eighteenth century".

Leaving the elucidation of these interrelations to the work of slow, and probably never to be completed, research, it is enough here to define as far as can be done what Burns did in the work for Johnson, and later—less happily, more tempered by the editor's regard for elegance and propriety and his own declining powers—for George Thomson's *Select Collection of Original Scotch Airs for the Voice*. In the first place he collected assiduously old airs and, if they existed, the words to which they were the accompaniment. He touched up such songs, supplying better lines for what were imperfect, or had too much of the hilarious indecency characteristic of the songs and fragments in (say) David Herd's [1] collection, or in Burns's own *The Merry Muses*. He wrote fresh songs to old airs, very often starting from an existent chorus, as in "Duncan Gray" from a chorus in Herd's MS. It is still difficult to say of many of Burns's songs, this is entirely Burns's work.

Taking it then as it stands, what is the peculiar quality, the special excellence of Burns's songs? For Burns an old song was somewhat as an old play to Shakespeare, but with a difference. In the recast by Shakespeare the old play—say *The Troublesome Reign of King John*—practically disappears. All that is dramatic and poetic is due to Shakespeare. It is not quite so with Burns's songs. The old note of folk-song is audible through the new song, is indeed a quality—its simplicity for example, humour, pathos—which the poet is fain to preserve. He does not always succeed, for Burns too at times succumbs to the taste of the day for elegance and decoration. Burns's *Wandering Willie* has not the perfect, the poignant simplicity of the original as preserved by Herd. Let us cite the original, as it will serve a double purpose:

> Here awa, there awa, here awa Willie,
>   Here awa, there awa, haud awa hame;
> Lang have I sought thee, dear have I bought thee,
>   Now I have gotten my Willie again.
>
> Thro' the lang muir I have followed my Willie,
>   Thro' the lang muir I have followed him hame,
> Whate'er betide us, nought shall divide us;
>   Love now rewards all my sorrow and pain.
>
> Here awa, there awa, here awa Willie,
>   Here awa, there awa, haud awa hame:
> Come Love, believe me, nothing can grieve me,
>   Ilka thing pleases while Willie's at hame.

There is the essential simplicity of the folk-song whether its theme be sentiment or bawdry. The poet goes straight to the heart of the matter with no embroidery, metaphysical or decorative. Burns adds a little of both:

> Come to my bosom, my ain only dearie,
>   And tell me thou bringst me my Willie the same.

[1] "The most indefatigable and the most conscientious of the old Scottish collectors" (Henley and Henderson, *The Poetry of Burns*, vol. iii, p. 296).

T

So run the closing lines of the first stanza, Burns adding a plea which the older poet has never dreamed of. In his poem the love is taken for granted. And then Burns becomes the eighteenth-century decorator with classical tags:

> Rest, ye wild storms, in the cave o' your slumbers.
> How your wild howling a lover alarms. . . .

What village maiden ever troubled her head about Aeolus and his cave, or indulged in such refinements as

> Wauken ye breezes, row gently ye billows,
> And waft my dear laddie ance mair to my arms?

But there is another aspect of Burns's best lyrics which must be borne in mind when he is commended as the great restorer of Scottish folk-song, *"ultimus Scotorum*, the best expression of the old Scots world" (Henley). He is something more. He is a great lyrical poet, using one might almost say by chance rather than by choice, the Scottish or Anglo-Scottish vernacular in which the greater number of the songs which he knew and loved were composed; but into the best of his songs he puts a great deal that one will not find in the pure folk-song, so far as one can identify such a song in the very mixed tradition from which Johnson and Burns drew. For one can exaggerate the merits of folk-song. Its range is very limited. The song we have cited above is a good example, and there are abundance of such among the songs which Burns supplied to Johnson. Such songs have, and the same is true of many of the mediaeval lyrics amorous or religious in almost every language of Western Europe, a simplicity and charm that is irrecoverable. But the human mind will not rest for ever content with simplicity, witness the sophistication which love-poetry underwent as it became the interest of more cultivated circles Provençal or Italian. *"Chevy Chase"*, Dr. Johnson said, "pleased the vulgar but did not satisfy the learned; it did not fill a mind capable of thinking strongly." *Chevy Chase* has in fact pleased the learned, as have many other things in which simplicity came as a relief to an outworn or conventional complexity of thought and feeling. But what Johnson is driving at is clear and just. The cultivated and thinking mind cannot be satisfied with a great deal that charms it in an earlier or a simpler, more popular literature. But that was in its way the relation of Burns to these songs. If he is not content to leave to some of

them the entire simplicity of feeling, thought, and diction which
is their charm, into his best songs he pours an intensity, a
variety of sentiment, passionate, pathetic, or humorous, which
goes far beyond the range of the average folk-song. Consider
an early song such as *Mary Morison*, "O Mary, at thy window
be". What simple folk-song would give you so dramatic, so
thrilling a verse as

> Yestreen, when to the trembling string
>   The dance gaed thro' the lighted ha',
> To thee my fancy took its wing,
>   I sat, but neither heard nor saw?

But the same seems to us to be true of all the best of Burns's
lyrics. The mould may be that of traditional, popular song,
but into it Burns pours more both of passion and intellect than
the traditional song-writer would either have been capable of
or have deemed appropriate.

But the poet is not always equally successful in his endeavour
to give to his songs a greater depth of feeling and variety of
adequate analysis and elaboration. After all he was not a
cultivated, sophisticated poet, and the poetry of his century
English and Scottish could teach him little, indeed more easily
mislead. He had not Shakespeare's sonnets before him as
a model of how variously the feelings of longing, devotion,
reproach, and all the sad train which gather in the heart and
brain of the lover may adorn and subtilise themselves. And
so it is only in fragments, in single lines or stanzas, that Burns's
more tragic love-songs have some of the passionate Sapphic
quality we spoke of earlier,—poems such as "Thou lingering
star", "Highland Mary", and verses such as

> The wan moon is settin' behind the white wave,
>   And Time is settin' wi' me o,

or

> Had we never loved sae kindly,
> Had we never loved sae blindly,
> Never met—or never parted—
> We had ne'er been broken-hearted.[1]

No single passionate love-song that Burns wrote is comparable
to Rochester's

> Absent from thee I languish still,

---

[1] Which, as Scott says, "contains the essence of a thousand love-tales". The
rest of the song is comparatively mere verbiage.

or Emily Brontë's

> Cold in the earth and the deep snow piled above thee,
> Far, far removed, cold in the dreary grave,
> Have I forgot, my only love, to love thee,
> Severed at last by Time's all-severing wave?

In one lyric and one only, it seems to us, has Burns achieved and preserved throughout the note of moving pathos:

> It was a' for our rightfu' king
> We left fair Scotland's strand;

and that is so unlike the usual lyric by Burns that Scott, imagining it on Hogg's authority to be an old song, borrowed its closing cadences for a song of his own in *Rokeby*.

But there is another kind of love-song in which Burns has no rival, the song not of tragic alienation or parting but of mutual contented love, sometimes exquisitely blended with humour. Songs like "Of a' the airts the wind can blaw", "Go, fetch to me a pint o' wine", "O my luve's like a red, red rose", "When o'er the hill the eastern star", seem to us as supreme in their own kind as Shelley's "I arise from dreams of thee", or "Life of life! thy lips enkindle", and, as Matthew Arnold would insist, saner, more true to natural human feeling.

No poet again has succeeded quite so finely as Burns in uniting humour with a strain of genuine feeling as in *Tam Glen* (another favourite of Arnold's), *Duncan Gray*, "Last May a braw wooer", and one of the most attractive of the songs, though comparatively little quoted, *The Country Lass*, with its dramatic contrast between the "old struggler" to whom experience has taught caution and the frank, generous-hearted young girl:

> It's ye ha'e wooers mony ane,
>   And, lassie, ye're but young, ye ken;
> Then wait a wee, and cannie wale
>   A routhie but, a routhie ben:
> There's Johnnie o' the Buskie-glen,
>   Fu' is his barn, fu' is his byre;
> Tak' this frae me, my bonnie hen,
>   It's plenty beets the lover's fire.
>
> O gear will buy me rigs o' land,
>   And gear will buy me sheep and kye,
> But the tender heart o' leesome love
>   The gowd and siller canna buy:

We may be poor—Robie and I,
   Light is the burden love lays on;
Content and love brings peace and joy,—
   What mair ha'e queens upon a throne?

It is only in a very wide sense of the word that songs such as these can be called folk-songs.   If in "Here awa', there awa'" Burns diverges from folk-song in the wrong direction, that of elegant, conventional sentiment and phrasing, the manner of Percy in his retouching of the old ballads, in these song he diverges from folk-song by making it the vehicle of a more passionate content and by a fuller elaboration.   The difference will be felt at once by a comparison of such songs with the great majority of those which Burns contributed to the *Museum*. Of most of them it is just to say that they must not be judged apart from the music to which they are set.   This is not true of songs such as "When o'er the hill", or *Mary Morison*, or "It was a' for our rightfu' king".   These have a music of their own to the reader, which to some of us (not musical people doubtless) can be lost when the melody predominates.   Of them in a measure is true what Madame Goldschmidt pointed out to J. A. Symonds—referring to Shelley's songs—"How the verbal melody was intended to be self-sufficient.   How full of complicated thoughts and changeful images the verse is . . . how the tone of emotion alters and how no melody-phrase could be found to fit the daedal woof of the poetic emotion."

It is then upon a somewhat narrower base than that of its appeal to his own countrymen that Burns's reputation as a poet in the field of English Literature in its full extent must rest— some incomparable poems of country life, revel, and satire, some lyrics poured into the mould of traditional folk-song but charged with a higher power.   But this is to confine oneself to consideration of Burns as an artist.   He owes his reputation also to the contribution his whole temper and spirit made to the development of the democratic spirit.   Burns and Napoleon were in their different ways the living evidence of the ultimate meaning of democracy—the fundamental equality of men in the sense not that all men are equal intellectually, morally or physically, but that no stratification of society will ever corre- spond to the realities of individual ability and character, "La carrière ouverte aux talents".

Chapter Twenty-Two

THE REVOLUTIONARY AGE

THE movement in English literature which we call variously the Romantic Revival, or the Return to Nature, or the Renascence of Wonder, according as we think chiefly of Scott or Wordsworth or Coleridge, was an eddy in a far wider movement which affected the whole of Western Europe. We have reached a stretch in the stream of Time which is broken by the cataract of the French Revolution. Everything within that stretch seems to be either sweeping towards the cataract or issuing from it. We cannot understand the work of Blake, Wordsworth, and Coleridge, or later of Byron and Shelley, till we know something of the ideas which led up to the French Revolution or arose from its effects.

When we look back over the eighteenth century we see many signs of impending change. All these years Orthodoxy was fighting a drawn battle with Deism; many English Presbyterians had gone over to Unitarianism, which the orthodox considered little better than Deism; and beyond the left flank of the Deists lay adversaries still more dangerous, sceptics and infidels like Hume and Gibbon in England, Voltaire and Diderot in France. The climate of opinion thus created in the upper classes of society, though it suited satire and didacticism well enough, was very unfavourable to the poetry of the imagination and the higher emotions. It is a strange, and perhaps a significant, fact that of the English poets who are looked on as the precursors of the Romantic Revival, Cowper, Collins, and Smart were all at times mad, Blake can scarcely be regarded as at all times sane, and Gray, though in no sense insane, was deeply melancholic.

And yet this so-called Age of Reason was also the great age of English hymnology. Beneath its cold, rationalistic surface a warmer current flowed, something that its dispraisers called 'enthusiasm'. The essence of 'enthusiasm' was simply personal religion, resting on the belief that man could know God. Its great practical manifestation was the Methodist Revival, the most important event, Leslie Stephen declares, in the history of England during the eighteenth century. When

Methodism became Dissent, 'enthusiasm' within the Church embodied itself in the Evangelical party, which in time secured the abolition of the slave trade.   Methodism contributed directly to English poetry in the hymns of Charles Wesley. Allied somehow to 'enthusiasm', in so far at least as it appealed from the head to the heart, was the singular movement called Sentimentalism.   Audible in the essays of Steele and the *Seasons* of Thomson, its classics are Rousseau's *Nouvelle Héloïse*, Goethe's *Sorrows of Werther*, Sterne's *Sentimental Journey*, and Henry Mackenzie's *Man of Feeling*, which Burns carried in his pocket.   As a literary fashion it was short-lived, but what was healthy in it produced some effect on the brutal manners of the century, made people more humane to man and beast.   It was at this time and under this influence that the love of animals first became a subject for poetry, as we see in Cowper, Fergusson, and Burns.

We have already mentioned another and a more purely literary movement in this age, exemplified in the revived interest in Spenser, and in Gray's poems on Norse and Welsh subjects, Collins's *Ode on the Superstitions of the Highlands*, Percy's *Reliques*, Walpole's pseudo-Gothic *Castle of Otranto*, and the fakes of Macpherson and Chatterton.   In all of them we note a new interest in literatures and legends other than those of Greece and Rome.   It was in effect a revolt of the English imagination against the neo-classicism which prevailed from the days of Pope to those of Johnson.   The Romantic Revival had in fact begun.

The business of the sceptics was to clear the ground of the débris of mediaevalism and superstition.   The architect of the future was Jean-Jacques Rousseau.   In 1761 he published two books that electrified Europe—*Du Contrat Social* and *Émile*.   Their ideas were not all new: some of them can be found in the sober pages of Locke; but passed through Rousseau's glowing mind they acquired a voltage which, as we said, electrified Europe.   "Man is born free, and everywhere he is in chains": so the *Contrat Social* begins.   "God made all things good; man meddles with them and they become evil": that is the first sentence of *Émile*.   These two sentences sum up Rousseau's gospel.

The *Contrat Social* is the most brilliant exposition of the theory that the state is not a Divine institution but a human contrivance, a voluntary association of men for their mutual benefit. The Divine Right of Kings is a fable. The people alone is sovereign: the King is merely its Chief Executive Officer. In forming themselves into civil societies men surrender their natural freedom, and obtain security and civil liberty instead, on this condition always, that each man shall submit his will to the general will, which means in practice that under civil government the will of the majority shall prevail.

Liberty is not safe without equality. Rousseau does not demand absolute equality in wealth; but thus much there must be, that no man shall be rich enough to buy another or so poor as to be forced to sell himself.

Liberty, Equality, and the Sovereignty of the People are the leading ideas of the *Contrat Social*; they became the watchwords of the Revolution.

The *Contrat Social* was not meant for a historical account of the origin of civil government; it was an analysis of the grounds of civil obligation. Rousseau was not telling us how men became citizens, but why they should be citizens. But that was not how most people understood him. They believed that once upon a time all men had been free and equal; that they had then combined and chosen governors to protect them; and that these governors had abused their trust and reduced their fellow-citizens to slaves. It was this misconception that, in Hegel's phrase, gave the idea of the Social Contract hands and feet, and made it terrible as an army with banners.

Rousseau knew that his own generation was not fit to remodel institutions in which it had itself grown up. We must look to the children for that. Therefore in *Émile* he set forth a scheme of education which might in time produce citizens fit to build the New Jerusalem and worthy to dwell there.

"God made all things good; man meddles with them and they become evil." Leave man's meddlings, then, and get back to things as they came from God's hand: return to Nature. What did Rousseau mean by Nature? In the first place he meant the country as opposed to the town. A child's education should begin with the education of his senses: Émile's senses should be trained not in the smoke and din of Paris but among the pure sights and sounds of the country: "God made the country, and man made the town". In the second place Rousseau meant what we call the simple life. Parisian society is corrupt; but virtue still exists among the herdsmen of the Alps. Both these ideas are familiar to us from Wordsworth, though Wordsworth invested the first of them with a mystical significance that was all his own. Nature had yet a third meaning for Rousseau. If Émile is to be educated according to Nature, he must be educated according to his own nature. A child is not a little man: childhood is a definite stage in human life, with laws of its own, which the educator must discover and obey. With this simple maxim Rousseau revolutionised European education. But for students of literature the most important thing in *Émile* is that first clause, "God made all things good"; for in these five words Rousseau repudiated the doctrine of Original Sin.

These ideas of Rousseau's, and others like them, imperfectly apprehended, mingling in the mass of misery and wrong that had accumulated in France for centuries, produced an explosive mixture which blew the old régime to pieces. They inspired an implacable resentment against the present, and a vague, immense hope for the future. If Divine Right and Original Sin were fables, if human nature was not corrupt at the source, if God meant man to be happy, if such was Nature's holy plan, what might not men achieve if they broke their chains and claimed the birthright that kings and priests had filched from them? This revolutionary hope had all the fervour of a new religion. There had been nothing like it in Europe since the sun of Christianity rose on the weary Roman world:

> Bliss was it in that dawn to be alive,
> But to be young was very Heaven!

The news of the French Revolution was at first received in Britain with considerable favour. The Radicals exulted; Fox declared that the fall of the Bastille was the best thing that had ever happened; most of the Whigs agreed with him; and the Tories, though apprehensive, were not at first openly hostile. Then, in October, 1790, Burke published his *Reflections on the French Revolution*. The most authoritative voice in Britain was raised in passionate denunciation of the Revolution, pouring scorn on its feverish legislation and its frenzied finance, prophesying mob-rule and military dictatorship, and declaring, in fine, that France had no good cause for revolution at all, since she had a constitution that had worn well for centuries and could easily have been mended to wear for centuries more; instead of which she had torn it up, and was rushing down a steep place into a sea of anarchy.

The permanent value of Burke's *Reflections* lies not in these denunciations but in the sublime passage in which he outlines his own conception of the true nature of the Social Contract as a spiritual partnership between the living, the dead, and the unborn, adumbrating in prophetic fashion that organic conception of the state which is the first principle of all wise Conservatism. But these lofty thoughts bore no fruit at that time.

Burke's *Reflections* provoked many replies, but none so effective as Tom Paine's *Rights of Man*. Paine knew what he was talking about: he had been in France during the Revolution, and demonstrated conclusively that by 1789 France was so enmeshed in oppression and misery that nothing short of revolution could set her free. Then he proceeded to declare the Rights of Man and preach Liberty, Equality, and the Sovereignty of the People.

Paine's pamphlet went like wild-fire. The Government took fright, suspended Habeas Corpus, and got five reformers tried for sedition at Edinburgh and sent to Botany Bay. Emboldened by this success, they indicted twelve London reformers for high treason. But William Godwin, in a masterly *exposé*, showed that in English law high treason meant attempting the King's life or levying war on him, crimes of which none of the accused could conceivably be deemed guilty. The prosecution collapsed.

This William Godwin was the most uncompromising of our Revolutionary thinkers. For a little while his *Political Justice* was the Bible of Reform. He was a philosophical anarchist, who held that government was at best a necessary evil, which would practically disappear in a perfect society. In morals he was a thorough-going rationalist. Actions must be judged solely by their consequences. The Moral Law is the Calculus of consequences: the moral man is he who, disregarding convention, instinct, and private affection, chooses always the course best calculated to promote the general good. "The *general* good"—for man is naturally benevolent and rational; all social evils are due to "positive institution"; abolish that, and the millennium will dawn. For man is not only benevolent and rational by nature; he is perfectible; the power of the mind over the body is far greater than people imagine; the free exercise of reason may in time enable men to overcome desire, and old age, perhaps death itself. Then indeed the millennium will have come, in communities of ageless, deathless, sexless, childless citizens, satisfying their simple wants by one hour's work a day, and spending their ample leisure in endless discussion.

Godwin modified some of his opinions afterwards; but that is the cream of the pure milk of the word as poured out in the first edition of *Political Justice* in 1793.   It sounds absurd when thus summarised; yet there is something sublime in Godwin's perfect faith in the power of reason and virtue.   What gave his ideas "hands and feet" was the widespread, rankling sense of social injustice which he voiced with such apparently rigorous logic.   His book had a great, if transient, success; for a year or two he had some of the ablest young men in England, Wordsworth among them, sitting at his feet.   It is for his influence on Wordsworth, and later on Shelley, that Godwin must be noticed in any account of English poetry.

The French Revolution had little influence on any of the older poets except Blake.   Crabbe might never have heard of it, for all his poems show; Cowper was attracted at first, then shrank back in terror; Burns sang of human equality in "A man's a man for a' that", and composed "Scots wha hae" on hearing of the sentence on the first of the Edinburgh reformers, but nothing else of value in his verse was inspired by the Revolution.   It was otherwise with Blake and the younger generation represented by Wordsworth, Coleridge, and Southey.

Chapter Twenty-Three

BLAKE

IT would be difficult to conceive a greater and more illuminating contrast than that between the poetry of Robert Burns and the poetry of William Blake (1757–1827). If Burns is to be reckoned a contributor to the romantic revival it must be done by giving to that phrase a wider and vaguer significance than hitherto attaches to it, for Burns's poetry, as has been said, is essentially unromantic, if we think of romantic in terms of what is most significant in the poetry of Wordsworth, Coleridge, Scott, Shelley, and Keats. Addison did not go altogether astray when he chose to compare a simple popular ballad, *Chevy Chase*, with the *Aeneid* in order to illustrate his ideal, and that of the neo-classical school generally, of a poetry based on good sense, truth to Nature, understanding by Nature what seemed to them most remote from the "wit" of the so-called "metaphysical poets" from Donne to Cowley. Romantic poetry was no revival of this witty, fantastic poetry, though it made gradually possible a juster view of what there was in that poetry over and above wit and overstrained fancy. But romantic poetry was a poetry into which the impassioned imagination entered as a transfiguring, a modifying, in its greatest products a creative factor, giving us Nature as interpreted by Wordsworth, or a past that in great measure never had been a present, whether the Middle Ages or the "glory that was Greece", or the future as dreamed of by Shelley.

Of all this there is no vestige in Burns, whereas William Blake might be reckoned the extreme representative of the effort to discover and interpret the truth of things not by the understanding, by Addison's "good sense", but through and by the imagination, the vehicle, as Blake claimed, of poetic and prophetic inspiration: "All art is inspiration. When Michael Angelo or Raphael or Mr. Flaxman does any of his fine things, he does them in the spirit"—in which there is much truth, if it was Blake's error to believe that the fact of inspiration made unnecessary a slow and careful training in the technique by which the content of the artist's inspiration is to be communicated to less sensitive and gifted minds.

An uneducated, at least a self-educated, man—his most thorough training was as an engraver under Basire—Blake belongs with those exemplars, Boehme, Tauler, George Fox, of a native, untrained inspiration to whom Coleridge in the *Biographia Literaria* acknowledges a debt in his progress from Hartley and empiricism to a more transcendentalist, creative conception of the part played by reason and imagination in the knowledge which the unphilosophic mind too readily accepts as something simply given to it from without. "It takes deeper feeling and a stronger imagination than belong to most of those to whom reasoning and fluent expression have been as a trade learned in boyhood, to conceive with what might, with what inward strivings and commotion, the perception of a new and vital truth takes possession of an uneducated man of genius. His meditations are almost inevitably employed on the eternal or the everlasting, for the world is not his friend, nor the world's law!" No words could better describe Blake and the inspiring motive of his work, whether as artist or poet.

If the chief sources of Blake's thought were, to begin with, Swedenborg, Jacob Boehme, and, above all, the Bible read and interpreted in his own fashion, his early artistic and literary models were the Gothic tombs in Westminster Abbey which he was commissioned to draw by Basire, Elizabethan poetry, the ballad, Chatterton (whose poems he accepted as genuinely Gothic), Collins, Gray, the Bible again, and, unfortunately, the Celtic poetry of Ossian as that is discoverable in the tumid prose of Macpherson.

The *Poetical Sketches* of 1783, printed by the help of friends, consist mainly of quite early experiments after various models— dramatic blank verse of an irregular kind in *Edward II*, blank verse lyrics, a little after the manner of Collins, in the Addresses to the Seasons, ballads, and a passionate *War Song to Englishmen*, on what occasion composed or for what purpose, perhaps a drama that was never written, it is impossible to discover; *Blind Man's Buff*, an anticipation to some extent of *Songs of Innocence* in which the influence of Shakespeare and of Milton (*L'Allegro*) are both obvious. The gems among these early poems are the lyrics: "How sweet I roamed from field to field", "My silks and fine array", "Love and harmony combine", "I love the jocund dance", "Memory, hither come", and *The Mad Song*. In these, especially the two last, Blake shows himself already, as in the best of those which were to follow, an even more quintessential lyric poet than Shelley. In the poem *To the Muses* Blake indicates his personal dislike of contemporary lyric poetry, but in general the lyrics are, so far, not personal but dramatic. Blake had not yet become absorbed in the problem of happiness and suffering, of innocence and the inexplicable sense of guilt, which were both to quicken and ultimately to disintegrate his metrical poetry. If Blake achieves the light-winged music of the Elizabethan songs, he pours into them, by way of suggestion rather than by definable content, a passionate imaginative quality which is all his own. Indeed, if anyone both as artist and poet is the ancestor of modern developments which aim at the direct communication of the artist's or poet's mind with a bold disregard for truth of representation in the design or definable content in the poem, it is William Blake.

The *Poetical Sketches* (1783) were published, as has been said, by the help of friends to whom Blake had been introduced by Flaxman but among whom he found no really congenial and understanding spirits. It was Blake's great misfortune that he knew no brother-poets. Five years later he engraved, in his own peculiar fashion, and coloured, the first poems in which the prophetic note is heard, the note of a poet who believes that he has something of his own to say. What led him to compose the *Songs of Innocence*, whether he had already any clear foresight of a further development, is not certain. Two things may have contributed to the composition of poems so full of passionate sympathy and joy—his own childless marriage, and Dr. Watts's *Divine and Moral Songs for Children*. If indeed the inscription on an early engraving, Joseph of Arimathea among the Rocks of Albion (1773), was not appended later, then already Blake's mind was moving in a direction which ran counter to the spirit of the age of reason and yet was not to run entirely parallel to the Romantic movement as that shows itself in the poetry of Wordsworth, Coleridge, Shelley, and Keats. "This", runs the inscription, "is one of the Gothic artists who built the Cathedrals in what we call the Dark Ages, wandering about in sheep-skins and goat-skins, of whom the world was not worthy. Such were the Christians in all ages." Blake was in his, to our eyes, erratic course to touch on every aspect of the Romantic movement,—the Gothic or Mediaeval (including what remained to Sir Walter Scott a sealed book, the religious spirit of the

Middle Ages), the delight in Nature and in what is most akin
in natural things to the mind of man, the revolutionary spirit
and passion for liberty—but to one and all Blake makes his
own individual, often contradictory approach, at once bewildering, and yet in its own way enlightening.

Wordsworth could not take a purer and intenser joy in the
life of natural things—

> And 'tis my faith that every flower
> Enjoys the air it breathes—

than Blake does in the life of children as he observes and inter-
prets their moods, for if Blake's songs were suggested by those
of Watts, he was no preacher, no moralist playing on the fears
of childhood. The inspiration of his songs is sympathy and
encouragement. The spirit of the whole is Christian, but
only on the one side, that of love and hope and a deepening of
joy and confidence. Whatever one may think of Blake's interpretation of childhood—as of Wordsworth's of the life of
Nature and of natural things on which Blake himself was later
to pass condemnation—the *Songs of Innocence* combine an
impression of pure childishness with the same suggestion of
something profound and mysterious in this life of joy and
innocence as Wordsworth found in the life of birds and
flowers:

> The birds around me hopped and played,
> Their thoughts I cannot measure:—
> But the least motion which they made
> It seemed a thrill of pleasure.

Just so Blake:

> O what a multitude they seem'd, these flowers of London town!
> Seated in companies they sit with radiance all their own.
> The hum of multitudes was there, but multitudes of lambs,
> Thousands of little boys and girls raising their innocent hands.

But Blake's is the more passionate voice. In the best of these
songs, *Introduction, The Echoing Green, Laughing Song, Holy
Thursday*, he is the purer lyrical poet, the diction and the verse
combining to suggest more than is communicable by the
thought considered apart.

And just because Blake's convictions were more passionately
held, with the passion of the self-educated mind of which
Coleridge speaks in the words cited above, he was to make a

more daring attempt to interpret the significance of these early experiences when brought into contact and contrast with the harsh facts of life as these revealed themselves even in the fate of children (as chimney-sweepers in Blake's day), than Wordsworth was to attempt or achieve in *The Prelude* or *The Excursion*. Blake's was the more daring attempt, for Wordsworth's inspiration gradually dried up, if on the other hand Blake's prophetic books were to prove too turbid and fitful, too apocalyptic to permit of any clear and convincing interpretation of the whole.

The Book of Thel (except the last section, which is of later date and written in an entirely different spirit) was engraved in the same year as the *Songs of Innocence*, and conceived in the same spirit of love and of confidence in God and Immortality. It was in the *Marriage of Heaven and Hell* (1790) that the storm broke, and Blake began his furious quest of such a reading of Life and Death, of Heaven and Hell, as should harmonise the painful antinomies of life. In this amazing piece of vivid, if unintelligible, visions and incisive paradoxes Blake makes quite clear his moral anarchism, his rebellion against all that seems to him to put restraint upon the free play of passionate energy and creative imagination. The *Proverbs of Hell* form a series of paradoxes in perhaps every one of which there is a germ of truth: "What is now proved, was once only imagined"; "The bird a nest, the spider a web, man friendship"; "Damn braces, Bless relaxes". Not a few of Blake's paradoxes are indeed among the bricks of which Nietzsche's philosophy was to be builded: "The weak in courage are the strong in cunning"; "The apple tree never asks the beech how he shall grow, nor the lion the horse how he shall take his prey".

From the nervous prose and relative clarity of the *Marriage of Heaven and Hell* Blake returned to the loose fourteeners of the *Book of Thel*, and began the composition of what we may call his Revolutionary Prophecies, to distinguish them from the later Prophetic Lays and the still later Prophetic Epics. Of these Revolutionary Prophecies *The Daughters of Albion* (1793) is an impassioned symbolisation of the wrongs of women; *America* (1793) and *Europe* (1794) were inspired by the success of the American and the hopes of the French Revolution. With these we may include the earlier *French Revolution*, which is not a prophecy, merely a visionary description of the Convocation of Notables before the summoning of

the States General.   All four poems were apparently products
of Blake's closer intimacy with such champions of the Revolution as Paine, Godwin, Holcroft, Mary Wollstonecraft, and
others who met at Johnson the printer's, for Johnson actually
printed the first book of *The French Revolution* in 1791.   To
Blake's mind, more excited and visionary than those of the
dreamers of Pantisocracy on the banks of the Susquehanna, or
of the young Wordsworth for whom

> Bliss was it in that dawn to be alive,
> But to be young was very Heaven,

both the American and the French Revolutions were incidents
in the emancipation of men's minds not from political chains
alone but from all conventional and moral inhibitions.   Blake's
prophetic books are an extreme example of the products of
such a period of fermentation as in their different ways are
Milton's pamphlets on episcopacy, divorce, and regicide,
Godwin's *Political Justice*, and Shelley's poems, to say nothing
of Continental revolutionary literature from Rousseau onward.
We are living through a similar period and know how difficult
it is to forecast what element of any real social and human
progress may emerge and survive when all the tumult is over.

More interesting than these Revolutionary Prophecies is the
volume of poems in which Blake set out the dual aspect of life
from which emerged his passionate, confused quest of a solution, viz. the *Songs of Experience* (1794), engraved and coloured
by his hand as their predecessor had been.   Combined in one
volume, Blake described the whole as *Songs of Innocence and
Experience, Showing the Two Contrary States of the Human Soul.*

The effect of the deeper passion with which Blake's soul
was shaken is evident in both the form and the content of what
is best in these songs, if gradually the effect of the new wine
poured into old bottles is also evident.   The best of these later
lyrics have a tone and timbre which moves a reader even when
their full significance remains hard to divine.   Nothing could
well be sweeter than the *Introduction* to *Songs of Innocence*:

> Piping down the valleys wild . . .

Into the *Introduction* to the *Songs of Experience*, in the appeal of
the Bard to the Earth to shake herself free from the fetters of
convention and moral laws and religious taboos, there has come
a new reverberant intensity:

U

Hear the voice of the Bard!
Who Present, Past, and Future sees;
Whose ears have heard
The Holy Word
That walk'd among the ancient trees,

Calling the lapsèd Soul,
And weeping in the evening dew;
That might control
The starry pole,
And fallen, fallen light renew!

"O Earth, O Earth, return!
Arise from out the dewy grass;
Night is worn,
And the morn
Rises from the slumberous mass.

"Turn away no more;
Why wilt thou turn away?
The starry floor,
The wat'ry shore,
Is giv'n thee till the break of day."

It requires of course some study of the main aspects of Blake's revolutionary thought to apprehend aright the drift of this passionate invocation and the reply of the Earth, but no one with any ear can miss the more sonorous and vibrant music of the poem.

In the songs which constitute the body of the volume Blake shows in one after another the counterpart, the corrective of what has been the burden of the earlier songs, or he weaves point and counterpoint together in the same short lyric. In *The Clod and the Pebble* the altruism and the egoism of love are proclaimed with equal condensation and force:

"Love seeketh not Itself to please,
Nor for itself hath any care,
But for another gives its ease,
And builds a Heaven in Hell's despair."

So sung a little Clod of Clay
Trodden with the cattle's feet,
But a Pebble of the brook
Warbled out these metres meet:

"Love seeketh only Self to please,
To bind another to Its delight,
Joys in another's loss of ease,
And builds a Hell in Heaven's despite."

In *The Tyger* again Blake gives sublimely imaginative expression to what is the theme of the whole, the insoluble contrasts presented in the world of natural things (as in the life of man), the overwhelming beauty of aspects of Nature which to us are terrible, aspects which Wordsworth's poetry tended to ignore:

> When the stars threw down their spears,
> And water'd heaven with their tears,
> Did he smile his work to see?
> Did He who made the Lamb make thee?

That is probably the greatest lyric in the collection, if the loveliest is the simple yet also enigmatic:

> Ah, Sun-flower! weary of time,
> Who countest the steps of the Sun;
> Seeking after that sweet golden clime,
> Where the traveller's journey is done;
>
> Where the Youth pined away with desire,
> And the pale Virgin shrouded in snow,
> Arise from their graves, and aspire
> Where my Sun-flower wishes to go.

But the stress and storm in Blake's mind was too great to allow him ever again, except in brief intervals, to achieve any sustained beauty of form. The lyrics which he wrote after *Songs of Experience* were all occasional. One or two of them he engraved but most of them have been published posthumously from the so-called Rossetti and Pickering manuscripts. Of these miscellaneous poems, many are crude, hasty, unfinished polemics including epigrams occasionally effective but often enough merely wilful and angry. What seems the most ambitious endeavour after a poem of some length is represented by a series of fragments composed about 1810, *The Everlasting Gospel*, in which the poet appears to have tried again and again to elaborate his passionately heretical reading of the Gospel. Christ came, he says, to replace the Mosaic law by the law of love, whose sole commandment is the forgiveness of sins, and to establish on Earth the Kingdom of Heaven, which is the Human Imagination.

"Was Jesus humble?" he asks, and makes God answer:

> If thou humblest thyself, thou humblest Me;
> Thou also dwell'st in Eternity.
> Thou art a Man, God is no more,
> Thy own humanity learn to adore.

Again,

> Humility is only doubt,
> And does the Sun and Moon blot out.

These short, pithy lines remind one of the *Marriage of Heaven and Hell*. Among the lyrics are other symbolic reiterations of Blake's conflict with conventional morality, such as *The Smile*, *The Golden Net*, *The Crystal Cabinet*, and *The Grey Monk* with its one famous stanza:

> For a tear is an intellectual thing,
> And a sigh is the sword of an angel king,
> And the bitter groan of the Martyr's woe
> Is an arrow from the Almighty's bow.

But among them is also such a pure and lovely lyric, unburdened with angry doctrine, as *The Birds*, in the Rossetti manuscript.

The *Songs of Experience* were followed by what we have called the Prophetic Lays—*The First Book of Urizen* and *The Book of Ahania* in 1794, *The Book of Los* and *The Song of Los* in 1795. These lays are written in short lines of three or four feet, strongly stressed. Their general drift, so far as we understand it, may be set forth most simply by analysing the central figure of Urizen. Like some of the figures in Dante, he has four aspects, which yet are one. Politically he represents the *ancien régime*, opposed by Orc, the spirit of Revolution, the fiery heart (*cor*) of man. Theologically he is the Jehovah of the Old Testament, as Blake conceived him, a jealous God, enmeshing man in nets of religion and priestcraft. Morally he is the spirit of servile obedience to law, convention, and "positive institution"; in this aspect his opponent is Luvah, passion. Psychologically he represents the cold, logical understanding which builds on the evidence of the senses, embodied for Blake in Bacon, Newton, and Locke; over against him is Los, the imagination, incarnate in creative artists like Blake himself.

In 1800 Blake was engaged by Hayley to engrave the illustrations to the *Life of Cowper*, and he stayed for some years at Felpham in Sussex. They were an ill-matched couple, the mild but not unexacting Hayley and the intransigent Blake. Moreover, while at Felpham, Blake involved himself in a quarrel with a soldier who wandered into his garden, and found himself in consequence on trial for the use of seditious language.

He was acquitted, for the soldier was an obvious liar, and
Hayley and others rallied to the support of his character and
innocence. One result was that Schofield, the soldier in the
case, appears as one of the symbolic figures in the great Prophetic Epics begun at Felpham and engraved by Blake after
his final breach with Hayley and return to London in 1803.
These include *The Four Zoas*, an attempt to rewrite an earlier
Vala in the light of the change of spirit which he felt had come
over him at Felpham. "Though I have been very unhappy,
I am so no longer. I have again emerged into the light of
day. I still and shall to Eternity embrace Christianity, and
adore Him who is the express image of God." The mythology of the earlier Prophetic Lays is non-Christian. Man,
apparently, can himself overthrow Urizen, and by his own
efforts sweep away kings and priests, repressive morality, and
"positive institution". But by the time he came to write these
later Prophetic Epics Blake has returned to Christianity as he
interpreted it. Urizen has become merely one of the Four
Zoas; his central place is taken by Satan, who for his selfhood
falls from Heaven into the abyss of nonentity. Adam also
falls; but his fall is stayed; the Divine Mercy creates for him
a world of Space and Time, that Mankind may have a place
for repentance, and may reascend to Heaven through the power
of Jesus teaching the forgiveness of sins.

The two works in which he elaborated, or strove to elaborate,
his new position, the "illumination" to which he had attained,
are *Milton* and *Jerusalem* (engraved in 1804 and some following
years). In the introduction to *Milton* he engraved one of the
best-known of his later lyrics:

> And did those feet in ancient time
>   Walk upon England's mountains green?
> And was the holy Lamb of God
>   On England's pleasant pastures seen?
>
> And did the Countenance Divine
>   Shine forth upon our clouded hills?
> And was Jerusalem builded here
>   Among these dark Satanic Mills?
>
> Bring me my Bow of burning gold!
>   Bring me my Arrows of desire!
> Bring me my Spear! O clouds, unfold!
>   Bring me my Chariot of fire!

I will not cease from Mental Fight,
  Nor shall my Sword sleep in my hand
Till we have built Jerusalem
  In England's green and pleasant Land.

It is in *Milton* and *Jerusalem* that Blake's most careful expositors, Messrs S. Foster Damon, Sloss and Wallis, and more recently Mr. Milton O. Percival, have found or sought to find the most complete exposition of Blake's philosophy. Much remains obscure, but there is also much in Blake that even the ordinary man may understand. He has emphasised certain truths, whether or not we understand or accept the deductions which he draws from them. The enigma of life, the fundamental contradiction in which life is involved, set forth in the *Songs of Innocence* and the *Songs of Experience*, consists in the fact that the spirit of man is profoundly divided against itself. It is this division which to Blake is the result of the Fall. Man is not what he has been and yet may be, when he has passed through the door of death:

The Door of Death is made of gold,
That mortal eyes cannot behold;
But when the mortal eyes are closed,
And cold and pale the limbs reposed,
The Soul awakes; and wondering sees
In her mild hand the golden Keys:
The Grave is Heaven's golden Gate.

Christ has come into this vegetative world, the world of Nature, in which we live, or dream that we live, perfect God because perfect Man, to restore that unity of our being which was lost when Urizen, Reason, or perhaps more justly the Understanding of Kant's philosophy, broke away from the imagination which is the inspiration of the artist, the prophet, and the poet, and made himself, Urizen, master of that world to which men are confined by the limitation of the senses: "Man has no Body distinct from his Soul, for that called Body is a portion of Soul discerned by the five Senses, the chief inlets of Soul in this age". The Fall of man at whatever time it took place, if there be such a thing as time, has its source in this tyranny of reason, the calculating faculty which has given us modern, materialistic science. Bacon, Locke, Newton, all who follow the guidance of the understanding and the senses, are for Blake atheists, for their faith is not in inspiration and imagination which alone are the sources of truth. As against all such Blake

is heart and soul a Christian, as he affirms in the passage we
have quoted, refusing even to allow that there is such a thing
as superstition if the so-called superstition finds its justification
in the heart and the imagination.   Superstitions may be tares
springing from a fruitful soil, but they are not easily to be
rooted up (as indeed Protestantism has discovered) without
doing injury to the grain that grows with them.   From the
same work of abstract reason flow all attempts at establishing
a so-called natural religion.   There is no such thing, Blake
affirms dogmatically; and Hume reached the same conclusion,
if in a guarded manner, in the *Dialogues on Natural Religion*.
But it is from this same source that proceed many things with
which the priests, Blake contends, have corrupted Christian
truth—jealous moral codes and formulated creeds crying
"anathema":

> I went to the Garden of Love,
> And saw what I never had seen:
> A Chapel was built in the midst,
> Where I used to play on the green.
>
> And the gates of the Chapel were shut,
> And "Thou shalt not" writ over the door;
> So I turn'd to the Garden of Love
> That so many sweet flowers bore;
>
> And I saw it was filled with graves,
> And tombstones where flowers should be;
> And Priests in black gowns were walking their rounds,
> And binding with briars my joys and desires.

So Blake had written in the *Songs of Experience* and the same
thought recurs and ever recurs.   In *Milton* it is Satan through
the person of Rintrah who

> created Seven deadly Sins, drawing out his infernal scroll
> Of moral laws and cruel punishments upon the clouds of Jehovah,
> To pervert the divine voice in its entrance to the earth
> With thunders of war and trumpet's sound, with armies of disease;
> Punishments and deaths mustered and numbered; saying, I am God
>   alone,
> There is no other; let all obey my principles of moral individuality.
> I have brought them from the uppermost, innermost recesses
> Of my Eternal Mind; transgressors I will rend off for ever,
> As now I rend this accursed Family from my covering.

For Blake, in short, the source of our unhappiness is to be found (as Shelley was beginning to divine in *Adonais*) in our separate, self-centred individualities, each intent on its own satisfaction and so at war with one another on the battle-field, in the law courts, in church councils and formulated creeds. When he wrote the *Marriage of Heaven and Hell* Blake had seen in Milton's Satan the embodiment of that energy and freedom which alone is true life, but in the same Miltonic Satan he now sees also the other side. Satan has become the abstract limit of opaque individuality turning for ever on himself. To Adam, the earthly man, has been granted a limit to this self-centredness, in the imagination which can transcend self, and does so most manifestly in the artist and in the genuinely religious spirit: "God sent his two servants, Whitefield and Wesley: were they prophets? Or were they idiots and madmen? 'Show us miracles.' Can you have greater miracles than these? men who devote their life's whole comfort to entire scorn, injury and death?" If Blake's religion is ultimately pantheism, it is (so far as one can divine) a pantheism in which individuality is not lost or absorbed, but rather transcended by love and the mutual forgiveness of injuries. Even in the ever-recurrent defence of free love, to which we have referred, his condemnation of jealous inhibitions or clerical taboos, it is love that Blake is thinking of, not lust, for lust is one of the consequences of our disintegrated personality: "What is the joy of heaven but improvement of the things of the spirit? What are the pains of hell but ignorance, bodily lust, idleness and devastation of the things of the spirit?" Lust and cruelty become impossible the more one has the imagination to transcend the limits of one's own personality. Virtue is knowledge, Socrates had taught; but Socrates, Plato, and Greek and Latin authors generally were anathema to Blake as the chief of the rationalists who had corrupted the world. Yet for Blake, too, virtue is knowledge, if that knowledge is revealed through the imagination: "The Eternal Body of Man is the Imagination. That is God Himself, the Divine Body, Jesus. We are his members." Los, the imagination as it lives and moves in poets, artists, and prophets, is ever building the City of Golgonooza, which is the never-perfected counterpart of that New Jerusalem which lies behind the veil of illusion, the city of the Perfect Man in whom the warfare is over, reason and passion and sense have surrendered their abstract claims, absorbed into the full life of the spirit, restored

to the innocent joy of childhood.   Urizen, repentant, acknowledges his error in that he has been

> Through chaos seeking for delight and in spaces remote
> Seeking the eternal which is always present to the wise,
> Seeking for pleasure which unsought falls around the infant's path,
> And on the fleeces of milky flocks who neither care nor labour.

But to reconcile the inconsistencies in Blake's occasional
angry and excited affirmations about ethics and religion or to
interpret adequately the greater Prophetic Books is beyond our
power.   His interpreters seem to us generally as obscure as
the original.   Nevertheless these books retain an interest
which is not to be measured in full by the degree to which they
can be made clear to the understanding.   They represent in
an extreme form what was the very pulse of the Romantic
movement, a movement not confined to literature, the reaction
namely of the heart and the imagination against the spirit and
the limitations of the Age of Reason, the *Aufklärung*.   Moreover, through their wild divagations and what seem wilful
obscurities they yet convey an exciting sense of some elements
of profound truth in their indictment of scientific, ethical, or
religious conclusions which leave the heart and the imagination
unsatisfied.   To live most men must have a credible, sustaining
myth.   The Christian myth seemed to be disintegrating under
the scrutiny of abstract reason.   Blake in his own wild way
was striving to reconstruct, to revaluate that myth; and for
Blake as for Milton the Bible, not Greek philosophy, is the
only and final source of religious and spiritual truth—the Bible
read with the imagination.   Lastly, for readers who may
remain indifferent to all this ado about Heaven there remains
the lyrical beauty of many passages of description and of
passionate thought.

The last of Blake's prophetic poems was evoked by Byron's
drama of *Cain*, and in it again Blake preaches his central
doctrine of sin and the forgiveness of sin, of Christianity as he
understood it.   The punishment of Cain carries within it the
germ of the Crucifixion on Calvary.

Chapter Twenty-Four

WORDSWORTH AND COLERIDGE: EARLY POEMS AND LYRICAL BALLADS[1]

THE British Public took a long time to make up its mind whether the imposing appearance called Wordsworth was a mountain or a cloud: it was convinced at last that he was a mountain, the most massive in that lofty range which we call the Romantic Revival. William Wordsworth (1770–1850) was born at Cockermouth, where his father was an attorney. He was educated at the little old public school of Hawkshead in the heart of the Lake District. The boys boarded in the village, and after school-hours were as free as air. These years at Hawkshead were the first great formative period in his life; the second was the year he spent in France. In his boyhood the remoter Dales were still "an almost visionary republic" of peasant proprietors, and a sense of human equality still survived between masters and men. At Cambridge he found another kind of republic, where all were equal as scholars and gentlemen. Thus his mind was ready soil for the ideas of the French Revolution. It was not the French Revolution, however, that first inspired his Muse, but the "dear native regions" to which he vowed lifelong fealty in schoolboy verse.

As a schoolboy Wordsworth was much like his hardy, north-country classmates, except for one peculiarity, which he probably kept to himself: he was prone at times to strange trances, in which the external world seemed to melt, as it were, into his soul, become "a dream and prospect of the mind", so that he had to grasp some solid object to assure himself that anything existed outside him. At the time he read no special meaning into these trances, of which, in fact, he was at first afraid.

In his boyhood, strictly so called, Nature was simply his playground; if she stirred any deeper emotion in him, it was only in moments of panic or nervous excitement. But in adolescence he came to love her for her own sake, with a passion "that had no need of a remoter charm", but with no

[1] Some expressions in Chapters Twenty-Four and Twenty-Five are taken from Dr. Smith's *Study of Wordsworth*, by permission of Messrs. Oliver & Boyd.

clear sense as yet of the Divine in her.   With this passion for
Nature he discovered that he possessed rare gifts of observation, and was struck by the multitude of natural appearances
that the poets had ignored.   To remedy this neglect was the
prime motive of his first considerable poem, *An Evening Walk*,
and fresh, exact description of "natural appearances" is its most
obvious, though not its only, merit: Coleridge justly praised its
"fine balance of truth in observing with the imaginative faculty
of modifying the objects observed".   But there is something
more than that in *An Evening Walk*.   The most striking
passage in the poem—more striking in the original edition of
1793 than in the later version—is the poignant description of
the starving widow and orphans of the soldier who lies

> Asleep on Bunker's charnel hill afar.

During his first Long Vacation, which he spent at Hawkshead,
Wordsworth met a discharged soldier: the meeting is impressively described in *The Prelude*.   Other men in like case, now
that the American War was over, were straggling back to the
Dales; from what he heard of or from them Wordsworth conceived a profound horror of war, with all the misery it inflicts
on poor women.   The soldier's widow in *An Evening Walk*,
the female vagrant in *Guilt and Sorrow*, and Margaret in *The
Ruined Cottage*, are all victims of war.

Descriptive Sketches commemorates a walking tour in the
Alps in the summer of 1790.   The descriptions are more
grandiose than those of *An Evening Walk*, but less clear-cut,
the scenes not having been engraved on the poet's memory by
long association like the Lakeland scenes of the earlier poem.
The most wonderful of Wordsworth's experiences in the Alps,
the revelation of the Divine in Nature that came to him in the
Simplon Pass, is not recorded in *Descriptive Sketches*.   The
Rousseau-like denunciation of tyranny near the end of the
poem belongs to 1793, when it was published, not to 1790.

Both these poems are in Popean couplets, in the late-
Augustan poetic diction which Wordsworth afterwards derided.
Descriptive Sketches is the worse of the two in this respect:
when the chamois-hunter opens a vein in his foot,

> He opens of his feet the sanguine tides.

When he passed through France on his way to Switzerland,
Wordsworth found the whole nation wild with joy of their
new-won liberty—

France standing on the top of happy hours,
And human nature seeming born again.

The memory of their joy drew him back to France in November, 1791. At Orleans he met Annette Vallon and fell vehemently in love with her; she bore him a daughter in December, 1792. At Blois he met Michel Beaupuy, an officer in garrison there, a fervent republican. Beaupuy's eloquence and the misery he saw with his own eyes converted him; his heart was all given to the people, and his love was theirs. Before the end of 1792 he was dragged back to England by mere want of funds. No doubt on obtaining them he meant to go back to Annette and her child, but the outbreak of war in February, 1793, cut off his return. In October, however, he contrived to slip across the Channel, reached Paris, found the Terror raging, and fled for his life. These were wretched years for Wordsworth, afflicted with public and private cares and ghastly nightmares of the Terror. His state of mind at this time is reflected in that remarkable poem, *Guilt and Sorrow*. Two victims of social injustice meet in darkness and cold on Salisbury Plain; one a sailor, a pressed man, who, defrauded of his prize-money, has robbed and murdered a traveller; the other a female vagrant whose soldier-husband and children have all died in the West Indies. The poem is in the Spenserian stanza, the style much plainer than that of the two earlier poems, strangely impressive, but flat with the flatness of despair.

In 1795 the cloud began to lift. A small legacy enabled Wordsworth to set up house with his sister Dorothy at Racedown in Dorset. There he began once more to smell the dew and rain and relish versing. The first thing he 'versed' was *The Borderers*. As a tragedy it is quite unactable, almost unreadable; but biographically it is of great interest. When the Terror chilled his Revolutionary ardour, Wordsworth sought intellectual support for his views in the philosophy of Godwin. In *The Borderers* we see him casting off that spell. The hero is a simple-minded idealist who, on a Godwinian "calculation of consequences", leaves a blind old man to perish on the moor, and is then overwhelmed with unavailing remorse. By the time he wrote that, Wordsworth had done with Godwinism; but for the moment he saw no alternative and, abandoning moral questions in despair, turned to a humble tragedy of real life. *The Ruined Cottage* he called it at first; some years later he wrapped it up in a longer poem to be called *The Pedlar*, in which form it was afterwards incorporated in *The Excursion*. Divested of these wrappings, it is sheer tragedy, the story of poor Margaret, whose husband has been forced to enlist, and who waits for him year after year, while her cottage goes to ruin, and dies in it,

> Last human tenant of these ruined walls.

Sheer tragedy; yet the effect is not flat despair; the torturing hope that endears her cottage to Margaret "shares the nature of infinity". The style is simple, though not with the aggressive simplicity of the *Lyrical Ballads*, austere but not homely, forecasting the style that Wordsworth made his own in *Michael*, and heightened to statelier effects in *Tintern Abbey*.

Thus much Wordsworth had written by 1797, but only *An Evening Walk* and *Descriptive Sketches* had been published. These early poems have one quality in common: they are *solid*, the product of direct observation of Nature and human life.

It was a fateful day for English poetry when, in June, 1797, Coleridge jumped the fence at Racedown and ran across the field to greet the Wordsworths. William he had met before. Both men were poets and democrats, but their temperaments were as unlike as their experience had been. The one had passed through fires which the other had never come near. Wordsworth was naturally vehement and passionate, active in habit, a lover of the mountains and the moors; Coleridge was passive, a dreamer and a bookworm from his childhood. Samuel Taylor Coleridge (1772–1834) was the son of a Devonshire parson; he was educated at Christ's Hospital in the heart of London, seeing nothing of Nature but the sky and the stars, and taking no such delight as Lamb took in the city crowds. He dreamed, and read, and talked, expounding Plotinus to the wonder of the passers-by. At Cambridge he was fired by the news from France, and trumpeted his hatred of tyranny in blank verse, ode, and sonnet. Later he collaborated with Southey in a fustian tragedy on *The Fall of Robespierre*, planned with him and his friend Lovell a pantisocratic colony on the Susquehanna, and became engaged to one of the three Fricker sisters, Southey and Lovell being engaged to the others. Pantisocracy came to nothing, but the engagement held; by the time he visited Racedown he was married, and happy enough. "Happy enough"—Coleridge was never passionately in love with his wife, or with any woman. At school he had argued himself into love with Mary Evans, but her refusal did not break his heart. In truth Coleridge, the most affectionate of men, was incapable of real passion, incapable of facing reality in any form. The sense of his weakness drove him at times to opium to allay his mental and physical pain; and so he was gradually sucked into a maelstrom that drowned his shaping spirit of imagination, made him incapable of the labour of creation, by the time he was thirty.

Coleridge's early poems belong mostly to the class that Wordsworth called "Poems of Sentiment and Reflection" and Coleridge himself calls "Effusions". Metaphysics, politics, and love supply their themes. The metaphysics is a kind of vaporous neo-Platonism, condensed into poetry only in the lines on *The Eolian Harp*—even Coleridge could not make poetry of the Plotinian monads. Politics obtrudes on metaphysics in *Religious Musings* and *The Destiny of Nations*, and inspires the Jacobinical *Fire, Famine, and Slaughter* and the *Ode on the Departing Year* (1796); in the much finer ode on *France* (1797) he recants his Jacobinism, shocked by the French invasion of Switzerland, and finds true liberty in his own free soul communing with Nature. The love-poems are tepid; those addressed to Sara Fricker are little better than album verses; even the elaborate *Love*, of somewhat later date, which tells us how he won his Genevieve by singing an old and moving story, leaves us asking, "Was ever woman in this manner won?"

The diction of the odes reminds us that Coleridge, like Wordsworth, was a child of the eighteenth century, though his models were not Pope and Darwin but Collins and Gray. The *Monody on the Death of Chatterton*, the *Ode on the Departing Year*, and the ode on *France*, read in that order, show his growing mastery of the most difficult of lyric forms. The sonnets are in a simpler style, learned from Bowles. He once said in his enthusiastic way that Bowles made him a poet. It did not need the mild influence of Bowles to make a poet of Coleridge; but Bowles certainly revived the sonnet, wholly neglected since Milton's day, and showed that poetry could speak a simpler language than Gray and Collins had used.

These early poems, unequal as they are, show plenty of promise; even their 'ebullience' (to use Coleridge's own word) is a promising sign in a youthful poet. But the strange thing

is that the promise they show is not the promise that was fulfilled in the poems that made Coleridge immortal.   There are
hints in *Lewti* of that delicate perception of atmospheric effects
which we find in the poems of his Golden Year, but never a
hint of the narrative power, the vivid, abundant imagery, the
mystery, and the magic of phrase and cadence that enchant
us in *Kubla Khan*, and *The Ancient Mariner*, and *Christabel*.
What wrought that transformation we have now to inquire.

After Coleridge's visit the Wordsworths moved to Alfoxden
in Somerset, three miles from Coleridge's cottage at Nether
Stowey.   For eleven months, from July, 1797, to Midsummer,
1798, the two poets were much together, Dorothy often
making a third or walking alone with Coleridge.   It was a
fruitful partnership—"three bodies with one soul", as Coleridge
put it.   In that air his genius bloomed as it had never bloomed
before and was never, alas, to bloom again.   He sat at Wordsworth's feet.   He had long admired his published poems; at
Racedown he had heard, or read, *Guilt and Sorrow*, *The
Borderers*, and *The Ruined Cottage*, and been thrilled by their
union of imagination with veracity and simplicity of language.
His discipleship to Wordsworth is patent in the blank verse
poems which he wrote at this time, *Frost at Midnight* and *Fears
in Solitude*.   Thoroughly Wordsworthian they are in their
attitude to Nature, Wordsworthian too in the expression of it,
yet with descriptive touches here and there of a delicacy beyond
the compass of Wordsworth's narrower, if more intense,
sensibility, such as the description of the icicles

> Quietly shining to the quiet moon,

or of the unripe flax,

> When through its half-transparent stalks at eve
> The level sunshine glimmers with green light.

Dorothy perhaps did something to sharpen Coleridge's perception of such nuances of atmospheric effect: several of the
most famous descriptive touches in *Christabel*—the one red
leaf, the thin grey cloud, the slow-coming spring, the moon
that looks both small and dull—have their prose counterparts
in Dorothy's Alfoxden Journal, though it is hard to say who
borrowed from whom.

Yet this sharpening of his sense-perceptions, and his newly-
discovered delight in concreteness and simplicity, do not go

very far to explain the magic of *Christabel*, still less of *The Ancient Mariner*, least of all of *Kubla Khan*. There was another agency at work: Coleridge had already begun to take opium, though as yet in small doses, and opium, which ended by benumbing his imaginative powers, began by stimulating them. *Kubla Khan* is an opium dream. It was composed in a sleep induced by "an anodyne", theme and rhythm suggested by a sonorous sentence of Purchas, which Coleridge was reading when he fell asleep. It has all the marks of a dream—vividness, free association, and inconsequence. Short as it is, it runs off the rails before the end: the "Abyssinian maid" has nothing to do with the subject.

The *Ancient Mariner* also is a kind of dream, not a dream of sleep like *Kubla Khan*, but a waking dream, a 'reverie' as Wordsworth insisted on calling it to Lamb's annoyance. It was begun as a joint composition, but Wordsworth soon dropped out; not, however, before he had contributed two of the points of support between which Coleridge was to spin his glittering gossamer web—the killing of the albatross and the navigation of the ship by dead men. These, with a dream of his friend Cruickshank, were all the data that Coleridge had to work on. But once his imagination began to flow free, a thousand ideas and images welled up from his subconscious mind. Coleridge had read enormously, and retained, consciously or subconsciously, great masses of what he had read; and now memory after memory floated up, one following another by force of literary association, as Professor Lowes has brilliantly demonstrated in *The Road to Xanadu*. But the material which his subconscious memory, his dreaming mind, supplied, was controlled by his waking intelligence, his active imagination, and by it shaped into a work of art. How firmly the artist controlled the dreamer is strikingly shown by the rigour with which Coleridge revised the poem for the second edition of *Lyrical Ballads*, dipping his web in the vat afresh, expunging all the "ballad slang", all that was bizarre or gruesome in the first version, and embroidering on it a prose rubric worthy of the verse—a feat only less remarkable than the original act of creation and of the same imaginative order. As for the form of the poem, Coleridge set out to imitate the rude traditional ballad; but soon we find him extending its simple quatrain to stanzas of five, six, even nine lines, enriched with inner rhyme, alliteration, and assonance. The result is all magic and music, magic that unsealed springs of wonder which had not flowed since Shakespeare wrote *The Tempest*, music such as had not been heard since Milton wrote *Comus*. Up to the lifting of the curse the poem is perfect; after that it moves less surely, for now Coleridge has to bring us back from the enchanted sea to common earth, and for that purpose to use homely touches which sometimes verge on the grotesque. The conclusion of the poem may seem too trite for machinery so tremendous; but when Coleridge said it had too much moral, he was only retorting on Mrs. Barbauld, who said it had none. In truth the moral is embedded in the poem, and gives articulation to what without it would be a phantasmagoria.

Seemingly *Christabel* should have told of the struggle for the heroine's soul between her good and evil angels, the spirit of her dead mother and the witch Geraldine; but how Coleridge would have worked it out we cannot divine, nor perhaps could he, for of the six parts which he projected only two were ever written, and only the first part belongs to his Golden Year. A marvellous fragment it is, giving promise of a magic even finer and more subtle than that of *The Ancient Mariner*, and of a music no less delicate. There are no such 'miracles' in it as Lamb disliked in *The Ancient Mariner*, no phantom ships and dead men working the ropes; all is inward. The marvellous wins on us not by direct description but by suggestion, suggestion so potent that Shelley fainted when first he heard the line

> A sight to dream of, not to tell.

This subtle, inward magic is reflected in the imagery of the poem, not strong and vivid like that of *The Ancient Mariner*—"blue, glossy green, and velvet black"—but all delicate and misted over as if lit by a wan moon shining through thin clouds. Metre and diction have the same delicacy. The principle of counting beats, not syllables, was not really new, as Coleridge believed, but no poet ever used syncopation and resolution with more delicate skill.

When Wordsworth withdrew from *The Ancient Mariner*, he left to Coleridge the task of making the supernatural seem natural by the dramatic truth of the emotions depicted, and applied himself to the other half of their joint enterprise, that namely of making the common seem new and strange by imaginative interpretation. Apart from some pieces of earlier date, including a long extract from *Guilt and Sorrow*, Words-

x

worth's contribution to the volume consisted chiefly of lyrical ballads properly so called, written for the purpose we have just defined; but to these he added four delightful, spontaneous lyrics—"It is the first mild day of March", "I heard a thousand blended notes", *Expostulation and Reply*, and *The Tables Turned* —which give voice to his recovered sense of the life and joy of Nature, and a long poem written, to use Coleridge's words, "in his own character, in the impassioned, lofty and sustained diction which is characteristic of his genius", namely the *Lines Written above Tintern Abbey*, the medium of which is neither ballad nor lyric, but an elevated blank verse. It is only in these lines that we perceive the influence of Coleridge, or rather, as we shall see, the effect of his advice.

Wordsworth put forth the lyrical ballads, properly so called, as an experiment designed to ascertain "how far the language of conversation in the middle and lower classes is adapted to the purpose of poetic pleasure". That is the literary, or aesthetic, way of putting it; in a deeper sense these ballads were a democratic manifesto. The invasion of Switzerland had shocked Wordsworth out of his Republicanism, but he was still a democrat at heart, his goal still "joy in widest commonalty spread". If he cannot change society by political revolution, he will try what poetry can do to change people's hearts and enlarge their sympathy for men as men. He will not write heroics for the amusement of a corrupt Society; he will write of simple folk in simple language. With his Republicanism Wordsworth had shed his rationalism; he had come to recognise that there are powers in human nature, primary instincts and emotions, more august and authoritative than the logical reason. Now it is the mark of democracy that it lays stress on the things men have in common, not on those in which they differ. And these primary instincts and emotions are precisely what men have in common, and so are the proper themes for a democratic poet. Therefore Wordsworth seeks his subjects not among Godwinian intellectuals but among forsaken women, old men in distress, children, and crazy persons, in whom these instincts and emotions show themselves in their simplest and most recognisable forms. He chose the medium of the ballad as being the natural vehicle of popular poetry. Unfortunately the grand old ballads of romance and gramarye were not suited to his purpose, as they were to Coleridge's, and he fell back on banal broadside ballads of the type of *The Babes in*

the Wood. The occasional baldness and flatness of Wordsworth's lyrical ballads are due in part to his unlucky choice of
models. Nevertheless, even in the original edition of the
Lyrical Ballads, he succeeded in showing what depths of feeling
may lie in simple natures when their primary instincts are
violated or their primary emotions stirred. As he thus
explored the penetralia of human nature, he discovered powers
that filled him with awe: the strength of the maternal instinct
which madness cannot quench in Martha Ray and the Mad
Mother, the devotion of Betty Foy to her idiot son, the idiot's
night-long rapture before the waterfall—these things seemed
to him to exalt our common nature towards that infinitude
which is its heart and home. *Goody Blake,* on the other hand,
is a study of the uncanny effect of a curse upon a coarse but
superstitious mind. For when he withdrew from *The Ancient
Mariner* Wordsworth did not lose all interest in the supernatural. Only his interest lay not in spinning vivid webs of
dream-phantasy but in exploring the causes which beget in
simple minds a sense of the 'numinous', the supernatural.
Peter Bell is a palmary instance. *Peter Bell* was composed in
1798, the year of the *Lyrical Ballads,* though in deference to
Lamb's judgement it was withheld from publication till 1819.
Had it been included among the *Lyrical Ballads,* as Wordsworth possibly meant it to be, it would have counterbalanced
The Ancient Mariner, and shown the world how that poem
should have been written, or at least how Wordsworth would
have written it. Wordsworth objected to the Old Navigator,
as Coleridge loved to call him, that he had no definite character,
personal or professional. Certainly no such objection lies
against Peter Bell. He is a potter to trade, an itinerant hawker
of earthenware, a hardened ruffian with a dozen wedded wives,
whose crust of insensibility is broken down by a succession of
blows which we know to be natural happenings but which his
superstitious mind believes to be dealt by the hand of God. In
short, *Peter Bell,* like Mr. Masefield's *The Everlasting Mercy,*
is a study in the psychology of conversion. As such it is very
interesting; but it is not sufficiently informed with feeling to
be good poetry. Wordsworth was so bent on teaching, on
tracing, as he put it, "the manner in which we associate ideas
in a state of excitement", that he sometimes forgot in practice
the maxim which he acknowledged in theory, that Poesy only
instructs as it delights. *Peter Bell* does not delight.

These lyrical ballads owed nothing to Coleridge beyond encouragement; no more did the four lyrics which voiced Wordsworth's joy in convalescence. That is not quite true of the *Lines Written above Tintern Abbey*. Wordsworth's French experience had left him so perturbed with political passions and private cares that for a time he lost his ecstatic love of Nature, and the visionary power which that love had evoked. In the poems of these years Nature, which to him had been all in all, became only a bleak background to tales of human guilt and sorrow. At Racedown, in the sunshine of Dorothy's love, he gradually regained his mental tone, his sense of the life and joy of Nature, and even at moments his visionary power, the sense sublime

> Of something far more deeply interfused

than human guilt and sorrow. He owed his recovery in the main to Dorothy; but it was Coleridge's more metaphysical mind, we believe, which suggested to him that in the ecstatic experiences which he had enjoyed in the high beatitude of youth lay the key to the riddle of this painful earth. Further we believe that it was on Coleridge's instigation that he resolved to compose a great philosophical poem, embodying the reflections of a poet-recluse

> On Man, on Nature, and on human life,

reflections of which the *Lines Written above Tintern Abbey* give us a foretaste. But when he essayed this *magnum opus* he found that he must first render an account of the steps by which he had attained his mount of vision. This was the origin of *The Recluse* and *The Prelude*. How he accomplished, or failed to accomplish, these tasks will be discussed in the next chapter. Here it is enough to note the service which Coleridge rendered to Wordsworth by directing him to what was to be the haunt and the main region of his song, or at least of all that is most characteristic in it. Wordsworth acknowledged the debt; *The Prelude* in its original form was addressed to Coleridge.

Chapter Twenty-Five

WORDSWORTH AND COLERIDGE: LATER POEMS

IN September, 1798, Coleridge and the Wordsworths sailed for Germany. At Hamburg they parted, Coleridge to study philosophy at Ratzburg and Göttingen, the Wordsworths to hibernate in the little Saxon town of Goslar. It was a fateful winter for both poets. It turned Coleridge from poetry to metaphysics. The translations that he made next year from Schiller's *Piccolomini* and *Wallenstein's Death* contain some fine things that are not in the German—"The fair humanities of old religion" is pure Coleridge—but of original poetry henceforth he wrote very little. In October, 1800, he came to Grasmere and delighted the Wordsworths with the second part of *Christabel*. The second part of *Christabel* is a fine poem in its way: it contains one wonderful stroke of psychology in the lines which tell how Christabel was so fascinated by the serpent eyes of Geraldine that her own features

> passively did imitate
> That look of dull and treacherous hate;

but from the rest of it the magic has somehow faded; the poet seems to be marking time; and when the herald is ordered out with

> Bard Bracy! Bard Bracy! your horses are fleet,

we seem to have left the world of Coleridge for the world of Scott.

In April, 1802, Wordsworth visited Coleridge at Keswick and read to him the first four stanzas of his *Immortality* ode: Coleridge replied with the ode on *Dejection*. Structurally the ode on *Dejection* is a magnificent performance in a very difficult kind, finer even than the ode to *France*. But it marks a parting of the ways. In the Nether Stowey days Coleridge had accepted Wordsworth's view of Nature as living and Divine; since then he had learned from Kant that Nature furnishes only the raw material of sensation on which the mind imposes its own forms of thought:

O William! we receive but what we give,
And in our life alone does Nature live.

He tells Wordsworth that the celestial light in which he had
once seen the earth apparelled came from the eyes of the
beholder:

Joy, William! is the spirit and the power,
Which wedding Nature to us gives in dower
A new Earth and new Heaven.

Such joy had once been his also, but now it is gone—drowned,
though he does not say so, in opium; and with it has gone his
shaping spirit of imagination.   It has been truly said that the
ode on *Dejection* is the swan-song of Coleridge the poet.   The
few poems that he wrote thereafter are often beautiful and
touching: the lines which he addressed to Wordsworth on
hearing him read *The Prelude* are poignant in their self-abase-
ment; but they are all, like his early verses, "poems of Sentiment and Reflection", pensive, elegiac pieces mostly, gentle
laments for vanished hopes:

Verse, a breeze mid blossoms straying,
Where Hope clung feeding like a bee—
Both were mine!   Life went a-maying
With Nature, Hope, and Poesy,
When I was young!

For Wordsworth too the winter in Germany was crucial.
That melancholy dream, as he calls it, taught him that his
passion for Annette and for France was dead.   He yearned for
England and his first love: the Lucy poems were born of that
yearning.   In December, 1799, he returned to the Lakes; in
1802 he married his first love, Mary Hutchinson, and settled
down to a quiet routine, frequently varied by lengthy tours in
Scotland and elsewhere, most of which yielded crops of
'Memorials' of diminishing poetic value.   Three external
events must be mentioned as powerfully affecting the current
of his thoughts—his visit to Calais in 1802, the death of his
brother John in 1805, and the invasion of Portugal in 1807.

In January, 1801, he brought out an enlarged edition of the
Lyrical Ballads.   Among the additions were four of the Lucy
poems, along with *The Fountain, Poor Susan, Ruth,* and *Lucy
Gray,* lyrics of a sweet and grave simplicity unmatched in
English.   To these he added two long 'pastorals', *Michael* and
The Brothers, in plain, dignified blank verse.

In 1802, during the Peace of Amiens, he spent a month at Calais with Annette and their daughter, and no doubt made some settlement on them in view of his approaching marriage. That visit completed his disillusionment with France. He saw that the liberator had turned aggressor, and that war was inevitable. He had already begun to practise the sonnet; now in his hands as in Milton's it became a trumpet, to rouse England and nerve her for the coming struggle. The best of his sonnets on *National Independence and Liberty* are among the glories of English poetry, equalled in their kind only by Milton, and by Milton only at his best.

In 1803 a tour in Scotland yielded the first crop of *Memorials*, among them the perfect *Solitary Reaper*. But Wordsworth's main occupation in these years was *The Prelude*. In 1800 he had attacked that "great philosophical poem *The Recluse*", which was to be his *magnum opus*; but after describing his return to Grasmere and proclaiming his purpose in tones so lofty that Blake thought them blasphemous, he found that he could not go on till he had rendered that account of his own life which we know as *The Prelude*. *The Prelude* is not Wordsworth's *Confessions*; it is what it professes to be, a record of the growth of a poet's mind. It was not published till after his death, and then in a revised version, but the original version, which fortunately has survived, was completed in May, 1805.

Three months before that Wordsworth's sailor brother John, to whom he was passionately attached, went down with his ship. It was the first great personal calamity that had befallen Wordsworth since his boyhood, and it shook him to the depths of his soul. Solitary communion with Nature had sufficed him hitherto; but now a deep distress has humanised his soul, he yearns for Christian fellowship, and cries

> Farewell, farewell, the heart that lives alone,
> Housed in a dream, at distance from the kind.

Echoes of that deep distress may be heard in *The White Doe of Rylstone*, finished, but not published, in 1808, the story of a soul so purified by suffering that it becomes an inhabitant of Eternity while yet in the world of Time, companioned in its desolation by the innocence of Nature symbolised in the mystical form of the white doe—a strange, difficult poem, perhaps the most finely conceived of all Wordsworth's longer poems.

These were Wordsworth's great years. The two volumes published in 1807 contain, besides the sonnets on *National Independence and Liberty*, and the *Memorials of a Tour in Scotland*, such masterpieces as *Resolution and Independence*, *The Affliction of Margaret*, the *Ode to Duty*, the *Elegiac Stanzas suggested by a Picture of Peele Castle*, *The Happy Warrior*, the *Immortality* ode, and the *Song at the Feast of Brougham Castle*, poems on loftier themes and in a more elevated style than the simple lyrics and plain pastorals of 1801. The change of style may have been due in part to the study of Sidney and Daniel, whose acquaintance Wordsworth made at this time: certainly Daniel's "middle style" was congenial to him; but the sonnets are wholly Miltonic in style as in spirit.

In 1808 the Convention of Cintra roused Wordsworth to passionate indignation. In a great prose tract, Miltonic in its wrath and high-piled eloquence, he thundered against the generals who had sacrificed the interests and the honour of our allies. In the same mood he wrote a second series of sonnets on *National Independence and Liberty*. But for some years after 1808 he was occupied mainly on *The Excursion*. In 1804, with the end of *The Prelude* in sight, he had bethought him of the neglected *Recluse*, and appealed to Coleridge for ideas. They never reached him, and without Coleridge's aid he could not go on. Now he thought of another plan: he decided to take up *The Pedlar*, which had lain by him since 1802, and to carry it on, adding two more characters, the Solitary and the Pastor, and using them, with the Pedlar, to voice ideas which he held, or had held, at different times in his life. His poetic powers were beginning to decline. *The Excursion* is inferior to *The Prelude* and the second series of sonnets on Liberty to the first. The psycho-analysts tell us that this decline was the nemesis of repressed passion. We doubt it. Wordsworth's passion for Annette troubled the surface of his mind for some years, but not its depths. The nightmares that afflicted him continually for years after his return from France came not from repressed passion but from remembered terrors. The proximate cause of the withering of his genius, we believe, was over-work. The labour of composition bore very hard on Wordsworth. Again and again in her Grasmere Journal Dorothy records that William has made himself ill with writing, that he is tired to death, worn to death, nervous and sleepless. By 1809 he had been working at this high pressure for a dozen years. Moreover, we must not exaggerate. *The Excursion* has many beauties; the second series of sonnets on Liberty contains noble tributes to the Tyrolese and the Spaniards; and quite at the end of 1814 Wordsworth wrote two remarkable poems in a new style, a classic style suggested by his re-reading of Virgil. If we read *Laodamia* or *Dion* without knowing the author, we should say at once, "That's great", but not at once, "That's Wordsworth". The stern conclusion of *Laodamia* was an after-thought: it distressed sentimental readers, but it expresses his true mind of the Divine Justice, which no weak pity moves. The end of *Dion* is still more striking: when Dion has expiated his one crime by death, we seem to be lifted into a region where individuality is transcended.

After 1814 the decline in Wordsworth's powers is undeniable. He still wrote verse—a third of his poems are of later date than 1814—but he attempted no sustained flights. Instead we have 'Memorials' of his various tours, and sonnet-sequences—three long series of *Ecclesiastical Sonnets*, a series on the River Duddon, another on the punishment of death. He had grown very facile in the sonnet, and found it an apt receptacle for his observations and reflections. His power of observation was unimpaired, though what his eyes saw seldom fired his imagination. He had still much of value, though not always of poetic value, to say, and he chose to say it in verse. He had always regarded verse as an 'accomplishment', something 'superadded' to the matter of poetry; and as he possessed the accomplishment he would not deny his readers the superadded pleasure. It is less easy to account for the ladylike style which he adopted for the narrative poems of 1830— *The Armenian Lady's Love*, *The Russian Fugitive*, and *The Egyptian Maid*—as if he had picked up the tinkling lyre of Mrs. Hemans. Again, we must not exaggerate. Wordsworth's fire was never quite extinguished till long after 1814. When he was deeply moved he could write as well as ever. There is nothing in English more poignant than the sonnet "Surprised by joy, impatient as the wind", inspired by the sudden recollection of his dead child Catherine. What moved him most often to high poetry in these later years was the thought of man's mortality, whether brought home to him by the deaths of old friends like Coleridge and Lamb and Scott, or suggested by some contrasted aspect of Nature, by her unending life in the noble conclusion to the Duddon series:

I thought of thee, my partner and my guide,

by her old felicities in the beautiful sonnet on the Trossachs:

There's not a nook within this solemn pass.

The great voice is heard for the last time in the *Effusion on the Death of James Hogg*:

Like clouds that rake the mountain summits,
Or waves that own no curbing hand,
How fast has brother followed brother
From sunshine to the sunless land.

We think of Wordsworth first as a poet of Nature, and rightly; for, though the Concordance shows that Nature was less often his theme than Man, it is by his poetry of Nature that he is unique, and it was the love of Nature, he tells us, that led him to the love of Man.   Indeed what he loved and revered in men were the things most akin to great natural forces, their primitive unreasoned instincts.   Wordsworth's unique apprehension of Nature was determined by his peculiar sense-endowment.   His eye, though not exceptionally quick, was at once far-seeing and penetrating; he looked through the visible scene to what he calls its "ideal truth", poring over objects till he fastened their images on his brain, and brooding on these in memory till they acquired the liveliness of dreams; dwelling especially on the larger features of the scene, the mountain and the deep and gloomy wood, the clouds, the sky; enraptured above all by sunrise and sunset—it was in the sweetness of a summer dawn that he first knew himself a dedicated spirit, and his last glimpse of the celestial light that had once apparelled the earth came to him on an evening of extraordinary splendour and beauty.   He had a keen ear too for all *natural* sounds, the calls of beasts and birds, and the sounds of winds and waters: the 'soughing' of boughs in a high wind set his mind working, and he composed thousands of lines wandering by the side of a stream.   On the other hand he had no ear for music, at least for instrumental music; he had practically no sense of smell at all; and compared with a poet like Keats he was poorly endowed in the less intellectual senses of touch, taste, and temperature.   'Fragrant', 'smooth', 'luscious', 'warm'—these are no epithets for Wordsworth's world.   It is an austere world; it is almost bleak—

The bare trees and mountains bare.

Thus, among the senses, it was only in sight and hearing that Wordsworth was exceptionally gifted, and even in these, so far as we have seen, he differed from his fellows only in degree.   For infant sensibility is the common birthright of all men.   But in the poet this birthright is augmented and sustained.   And this it is that determines his function in society. The true poet, like all true men, seeks to make his fellows happier; but he does so, as poet, not by adding to their material conveniences but by enlarging the sphere of their sensibility. The infant sensibility, which in him has been augmented and sustained, has in most of us been dimmed by a film of familiarity; it is the poet's office to remove this film, to restore the innocence of the eye, and so reveal endless sources of happiness in common things that lie around us.   This was the aspect of Wordsworth's poetry that appealed to those whose opinion of it was formed before *The Prelude* appeared; this is what Arnold had in mind when he said of Wordsworth—

> He laid us as we lay at birth
> On the cool flowery lap of earth.

That is true and beautifully said; but it is not the whole truth, nor perhaps the deepest truth, about a poet who said of himself,

> The outward shows of sky and earth,
> Of hill and valley, he has viewed;
> And impulses of deeper birth
> Have come to him in solitude.

We have now to ask what these deeper impulses were, and how they came to him "in solitude".

And first we note that Wordsworth possessed above all poets the ear for silence, silence

> That is not quiet, is not ease,
> But something deeper far than these,

a silence beyond silence—

> Of silent hills, and more than silent sky;

next, that he could hear, or believed he could hear,

> The ghostly language of the ancient earth;

and finally that he had a sense of space so remarkable that he seems almost to have *felt* the earth as a solid globe and *sensed* its diurnal rotation: he sees Lucy in death,

Rolled round in earth's diurnal course,
With rocks, and stones, and trees.

Such perceptions made up, or contributed to, that sense of the material sublime in which Wordsworth comes near to Milton.

Still, it may be said, these are sense-perceptions, implying no more than an abnormal, or supernormal, acuity of hearing and sight; but Wordsworth believed himself to possess a higher faculty, a mode of perception that was beyond sense. He calls it vision, thereby allying it less to sense-perception than to dream and reverie, activities of the subconscious or semi-conscious mind. He was a great dreamer: "Dreams, books, are each a world", he says; and his own dream-world appears to have been singularly vivid, bright, happy, glorious, and fresh. At times he indulged in prolonged day-dreams or reveries, peopling the forest-glades of the Loire with the creatures of Ariosto's fancy, or the downs of Salisbury Plain with memories of the Ancient Britons. But dreams and reveries are purely subjective; they tell us nothing of anything outside ourselves. Vision is veridical: the visionary sees into the life of things, as if sense and the objects of sense were for a moment in abeyance and the soul had direct perception of reality. At its highest this is the distinctively mystical experience called Ecstasy, the "serene and blessed mood" of *Tintern Abbey*, the "high hour of visitation from the living God" of *The Excursion*. Other poems record experiences which, though lower than Ecstasy, have yet something of the same visionary quality, suggesting a world beyond the world of sense. This is true in particular of the class of poems which he calls "Poems of the Imagination". All imagination, in Wordsworth's sense, is vision in some degree.

These visionary experiences usually came to Wordsworth only when communing with Nature in solitude, though even in the heart of London he could make an island of solitude for himself. In boyhood, it would seem, they were rare, and were strongly coloured with fear, even with terror. There is nothing in Wordsworth's psychology more remarkable than the stress he lays on "the impressive discipline of fear". In the high beatitude of adolescence his blissful communion with Nature was apparently untroubled by fear, but it was also devoid of any clear religious significance. It was in the awe-inspiring sublimity of the Simplon Pass that the Divine in Nature was first clearly revealed to him, that he first beheld all the elements of the visible scene as workings of one mind,

> Characters of the great Apocalypse,
> The types and symbols of Eternity,
> Of first, and last, and midst, and without end.

The immediate effect was trance; but looking back on that experience afterwards he perceived its tremendous significance for himself:

> But to my conscious soul I now can say—
> "I recognize thy glory"—

the glory, that is, of his own soul: the soul that perceives the Divine in Nature must itself be Divine:

> Our destiny, our nature, and our home,
> Is with infinitude, and only there.

Thenceforth the light of that revelation illuminated for him the riddle of human life and human suffering—until God put forth his hand and touched his bone and his flesh.

Though most of Wordsworth's poems deal with human life, we should scarcely call him, as we might call Shelley, the Poet of Humanity. It is true that in the first ardour of his conversion by Beaupuy he avowed himself a patriot of the world; but Humanity was too abstract a conception to move Wordsworth to poetry. It was not till from a patriot of the world he became a patriot of England that his passion for Humanity condensed upon a definite object and inspired the great sonnets *On National Liberty and Independence.* His winter in Germany had taught him what love he bore to England. Now he saw her threatened with destruction. As the peril deepened—

> Another year, another deadly blow—

his courage rose to meet it—

> Oh dastard, whom such prospect does not cheer!

At the worst moment his song never shrank from hope,

> the paramount *duty* that Heaven lays,
> For its own honour, on man's suffering heart.

Wordsworth's patriotism was not jingoistic, nor even imperialistic. He held that Britain, having kept herself free, should help other nations to freedom. Foreign conquest was a violation of a nation's personality, and to Wordsworth the personality of every nation was sacred. Thus he was the

prophet of Nationalism, the first man to discern and comprehend the force that has moulded the destinies of Europe from
that day to this.   But his Nationalism, like his patriotism, was
unaggressive, generous, and sane.

So much, in brief, for what Wordsworth has to say of men
as citizens.   Of men and women as individuals he has also
much to say, within a certain range.   The city proletariat lay
beyond his ken; it was not for him to sing

> the fierce confederate storm
> Of sorrow barricaded evermore
> Within the walls of cities;

but rather

> To hear humanity in woods and groves
> Pipe solitary anguish.

The primary instincts and affections which are common to all
mankind, these were his chosen subjects, and he looked for
them in humble, rural life, where they

> Exist more simple in their elements.
> And speak a plainer language—

plainer, but more dignified from association with the grandeur
of Nature.   Of these primary instincts and affections, love is
the greatest.   Wordsworth is not a love-poet in the usual
sense.   He was not incapable of passion, but except in
Vaudracour and Julia he eschewed it as a theme for poetry.
The Lucy poems breathe a deep and tender affection, but they
are not passionate.   The love which moved Wordsworth to
poetry was not sexual passion but love of country, family, and
friends.   In Wordsworth family affection was a passion, even
a tragic passion; in Dorothy's words, he had "a violence of
affection": his brother's death almost overwhelmed him; the
death of his second boy aged him by ten years; Dora's death
broke his heart.   It was his violence of affection that enabled
him to enter into, and render with unequalled power, the love
of father for son, of brother for brother, of mother for child,
in *Michael*, *The Brothers*, and *The Affliction of Margaret*.

Such love has in it something of the infinite, revealed when
it is perfected by suffering.   It is not true that Wordsworth
'averts his ken from half of human fate".   He did avert his
ken from the dark side of Nature, in a Rousseau-like faith
which we now find hard to share; but with human suffering,

if not with human guilt, he dealt unflinchingly, not only in the poems we have named but in many of the *Lyrical Ballads* and the tales that fill Books VI and VII of *The Excursion*. But, after *Guilt and Sorrow*, if he tells a lamentable tale, he tells it not to arouse our indignation or even our pity, but for the light it sheds on the hiding-places of man's power, and for

> the glory that redounds
> Therefrom to human kind and what we are.

When Coleridge first met Wordsworth in 1795, he found him "at least a semi-atheist". He was still in the gall of bitterness, his visionary power impaired. When he recovered it, and began with Coleridge's aid to realise all that it meant, he enjoyed for some years, and at rare moments, those visionary experiences which he has tried to describe in *Tintern Abbey*, *The Simplon Pass*, and *The Pedlar*, and, more boldly, in an unpublished fragment which Mr. de Selincourt has retrieved, in which he speaks of that one interior life to which sensation, intellect, and will are mere accidents, an inner life

> In which all beings live with God, themselves
> Are God, existing in the mighty whole,
> As indistinguishable as the cloudless east
> At noon is from the cloudless west, when all
> The hemisphere is one cerulean blue.

Whether we call this pantheism or panentheism, we cannot call it orthodox Christianity. It is in Nature, and in Nature only, that the visionary communes with God; she is the soul of *all* his moral being.

Wordsworth's private illumination had faded when he set himself to philosophise upon it in the ode on *Intimations of Immortality*, finding in the doctrine of pre-existence a notion that unified his mystical experiences with his memories of his childhood. We come from God, and our true life is a striving towards Him. As the auroral light which lay about our infancy fades, and we can no longer live by impulse, relying on the genial sense of youth, we must learn to walk by the light of duty; but the memory of that other light remains, nay, in seasons of calm weather we still have glimpses of it, to remind us of "our destiny, our nature, and our home".

Before Wordsworth had finished the great Ode, the death of his brother changed the current of his thoughts, and turned them to seek the consolations of revealed religion, with its promise of personal immortality. How else could he escape the intolerable thought that mortal man is more loving than his Maker? The story of his reconversion is to be read in *The Excursion.* The Solitary represents the eclipse of faith through which he had passed in the 1790's; the Wanderer the mystical religion of Nature described in *Tintern Abbey*; the Pastor the orthodoxy to which he was returning. The Pastor has the last word, but there is no conflict between him and the Wanderer; the religion of Nature is not abjured, but melts into the fuller light of revelation.

This change in Wordsworth's religious attitude coincided with a change in his political attitude which reinforced but did not cause it. Hatred of Napoleon had driven Wordsworth into the camp of the Tories, who alone were whole-hearted in the prosecution of the war. Then fear of revolution at home made him identify himself more and more closely with the landed interest and the Established Church, in which he saw the only bulwarks of the old England that he loved. He ensconced himself deeper and deeper in English institutions, and studied their history, especially the history of the Church of England, which he versified in his *Ecclesiastical Sonnets.* Otherwise these later developments, though biographically and even historically important, are of little interest to the student of his poetry. But the timidities and prejudices of Wordsworth's old age must not blind us to the fact that if to love the people and to value the things which men have in common above those in which they differ be the essence of democracy, he was still a democrat at heart. "Joy in widest commonalty spread" was still his aim, though he had changed his mind as to the means for attaining it. And even as to the means, he was not, at the last, "completely Toryfied": near the end of his days he declared, "As far as the people are capable of governing themselves, I am a democrat". In all this, strange as it may seem, his closest link is with Sir Walter Scott. Scott's feudal sympathies never gave an authentically aristocratic tone and temper to his novels: it was in the fundamentally human qualities of men and women, whatever their rank, that he and Wordsworth alike found the essential subject of their work.

In this way, and in others, by his theory as well as his practice, Wordsworth effected a revolution in English poetry. He demolished the eighteenth-century convention of poetic diction; but this service, great as it was, was only incidental to his main purpose, which was to proclaim the true nature, end, and best themes of poetry, and the true function of the poet in society. By his exaltation of the poet's office, and the noble consistency with which he himself exercised it, he established in England a tradition of serious poetry which remained unchallenged until twenty years ago.

Chapter Twenty-Six

SCOTT

WE have noted that the movement which we are discussing in these chapters has been variously called the Return to Nature, the Renascence of Wonder, the Romantic Revival. The first of these names makes us think of Wordsworth, the second of Coleridge, the third of Sir Walter Scott (1771–1832). Historically, Scott's poetry is very important: it effected a revolution in taste, a "shift of sensibility" which made Wordsworth and Coleridge acceptable and paved the way for Byron, Shelley, and Keats: in a word, it popularised romance. Intrinsically too its value is far from negligible: if Scott's long poems have sunk in the estimation of critics, his songs have risen, till so good a judge as Professor Elton can maintain that he is the best lyric poet between Burns and Shelley.

Like many other poets, Scott began as an imitator. He had a natural gift for mimicry: his *Poacher* is pure Crabbe; the lines in *Old Mortality* beginning "Thy hue, dear pledge, is pure and bright", are very Byronic; the song,

> Oh, say not, my love, with that mortified air,
> That your spring-time of pleasure is flown,

might be Tom Moore's; mimicry is too base a word for so noble a poem as *Glencoe*, but its form obviously came from Campbell's *Hohenlinden*. These, however, were casual imitations, and had no sequels: the line Scott followed up was the line he began on—translation and imitation of German romance. German romance was in part a revolt against French classicism: Bürger carried it to extremes in wild folk-tales of crude supernaturalism. The taste for the supernatural may have come from England, from Horace Walpole's mock-solemn *Castle of Otranto*; it was re-imported, in full solemnity, by Mrs. Radcliffe and 'Monk' Lewis. A craze for German had been started in Edinburgh by Henry Mackenzie, the Man of Feeling; Scott caught it, and learned German enough to translate Bürger's *Lenore* and *Der Wilde Jäger*, and Goethe's *Götz*. Happily he escaped from this High Dutch miasma into the pure native air of romance when he took to collecting Scottish

ballads. He had loved ballads from his cradle. As a child
at Sandyknowe he learned *Hardyknute*, and bawled it at visitors
"like a cannon". At twelve he discovered Percy's *Reliques*.
From the 'raids' that he made into Liddesdale in his youth he
brought back ballads as well as "auld nick-nackets". Then
he set himself to do for the Borders what Percy had done for
the country at large. What attracted Scott was not the simplicity of the broadside ballad that had appealed to Wordsworth but the thrilling elements of chivalry, romance, and
gramarye in which the old Scottish ballads excel. Hogg and
Leyden helped him, and Hogg's mother gave him some of his
best versions, though she deplored their publication.

Scott's treatment of the ballads was influenced by his view of
their origin and history. He believed that ballads were made
by minstrels, who, in the decline of romance,

> tuned to please a peasant's ear
> The harp a king had loved to hear.

That was probably not how the ballad-form originally arose; [1]
but it may well be true of the full-grown ballads that Scott
collected. Ballads, once made, were transmitted orally, and
garbled and mutilated in the process. It was Scott's aim to
present them as the old minstrels first made them, "cured and
perfect in their limbs", or as near that as he could come. He
did not treat the ballads as Burns had treated the folk-songs of
Scotland, as material from which to fashion something new;
his object was to recover something old. When he found two
or three versions of a ballad, he took the best bits from each
and pieced them together, sometimes mending the metre a
little, or adding a picturesque touch like

> The blows fell thick *as bickering hail*—

in short, giving it a cocked hat and feather, as he phrased it.
If there was "a hole in the ballant", he might patch it from the
whole cloth of his own invention. But beyond such titivating
and patching he did not go, except in *Kinmont Willie*, and there
he owned up, pleading that he had only rags and tatters to
work on. *Otterburn* supplies a good example of his methods.
Hogg got that ballad, he says, from "a crazy old man and a
woman deranged in her mind". At one point they could only
give him a prose version, with an odd line or two of verse.

[1] See Chapter Four.

This material Hogg 'harmonised'—and Scott, we guess, reharmonised.   The result is the finest passage in the poem:

> "My nephew good," the Douglas said,
>   "What recks the death o' ane?
> Last nicht I dreamed a dreary dream,
>   And I ken the day's thy ain.
>
> My wound is deep, I fain wad sleep;
>   Take thou the vanguard o' the three,
> And bury me by the bracken bush,
>   That grows on yonder lily lee.
>
> O bury me by the bracken bush,
>   Beneath the blooming brier.
> Let never living mortal ken
>   That ere a kindly Scot lies here."

We suspect that these lines owe more to Scott and Hogg than to the crazy old man and the woman deranged in her mind!

The Minstrelsy of the Scottish Border appeared in 1802 and 1803.   Scott was now thirty-one.   He had made a name as editor and collector, but his claim to be counted an original poet rested on little beyond some mediocre imitations of the ballad style—*The Eve of St. John, Glenfinlas, Cadzow Castle*—which he had appended to the *Minstrelsy*.   He was now to essay a bolder flight.   Lady Dalkeith told him a story about a Goblin Page, and suggested that he should make a ballad of it. Scott decided to try something bigger, something on the scale of those Middle English lays on which he had been working with George Ellis.   Such was the genesis of *The Lay of the Last Minstrel*.   But he did not mean to write a purely romantic, fairy-like story, such as these old lays mostly are.   Writing later about *The Lady of the Lake*, he said, "There is a want of truth in all the verses or rather epics"—he had Southey's in mind—"which we have in modern days.   They present us heroes when we would rather have a lively display of real men and manners."   What Scott had in view was what he carried out more fully in novels like *Ivanhoe*, an imaginary story, but laid in a definite historical period and with a definite local setting.   In his best poems, as in his novels, he trusted less to imagination than to memory, to his unsurpassed knowledge of Scottish history, legend, and topography.   A Border raid, a Highland foray, Flodden, Bannockburn—these supply the historical background; and the action is laid among scenery he

knew and loved—the Borders, the Trossachs, the environs of
Edinburgh, the Western Isles. In *Rokeby*, the least successful
of his poems in these respects, we see him moving towards the
novel of character.

For the metre of the *Lay* Scott found what he wanted in
Christabel, the first part of which he had heard recited.

> The feast was over in Branksome tower,
> And the Ladye had gone to her secret bower—

we scarcely need the "Jesu Maria, shield us well" which follows
to tell us where *that* opening came from. Much of the *Lay*
is in this *Christabel* metre, though Scott could not manage its
syncopations and resolutions with the delicate art of Coleridge.
There are also many regular tetrameter couplets, and a good
deal of rime couée, simple or extended. Unfortunately, as he
went on, Scott fell back more and more on the regular tetrameter couplet, in which he grew dangerously facile. Except
for the inset songs, most of *The Lady of the Lake* and all of
Rokeby is in this metre—an excellent metre for a poem of the
length of *Tam o' Shanter*, not so good for a poem as long as
Rokeby.

The *Lay* appeared in 1805, and was immediately successful.
Marmion (1808) was even more successful. *The Lady of the
Lake* (1810) was the most successful of all. After that Scott's
popularity declined. We may pass over *The Vision of Don
Roderick*, which was written to raise funds for the relief of
distress in Portugal. But in *Rokeby* (1813) Scott made a
serious attempt, visiting Greta Bridge to get local colour on
the spot. But the scene was English, the period the English
Civil War; his foot was no longer on his native heath; and
though the poem sold well enough at first, Scott himself felt
that he had fallen off. Perhaps for that reason his next long
poem, *The Bridal of Triermain*, was published anonymously.
It would not do. A new star had appeared on the horizon,
and for his hour (in Burke's phrase) was lord of the ascendant.
The first two cantos of *Childe Harold* had come out in 1812;
next year came *The Giaour* and in 1814 *The Corsair*. Byron
gave the public a racier and more novel article than Scott could
provide. Byron 'bet' him, as he put it afterwards, and he
turned philosophically to prose fiction. But before abandoning verse altogether, he determined to try his luck once more.
Surely Bruce and Bannockburn would appeal more, to Scots

at least, than these outlandish Giaours and Corsairs. So in December, 1814, five months after *Waverley* had appeared anonymously, he issued *The Lord of the Isles* in his own name. It came too late: the Giaours and Corsairs held the field; and Scott went on to *Guy Mannering*.

Scott's narrative poems have faults that are perhaps more obvious to us than they were to his contemporaries. In the first place, he was unhappy in his imaginary plots. He felt bound, apparently, to provide a love-interest, though he had no real interest in love as a literary motif. The Clare-Wilton business in *Marmion* wearies us; the tearful Maid of Lorn in *The Lord of the Isles* is an afflicting, almost a comic figure. If Scott had cut the love-affairs out of *Marmion*, and told the story of the whole campaign as he has told the story of the final battle, he might have produced something worthy to be called an epic.

His execution, too, is often faulty. When he is at a loss for a rhyme, he helps himself out with feeble expletives and irritating inversions. Even in a show piece like the death of De Bohun he can write:

> And at King Edward's signal soon
> Dashed from the ranks Sir Henry Bohun. . . .
>
> He spurred his steed, he couched his lance,
> And darted on the Bruce at once.

That "soon"! That "at once"! They would have wrung a cry of pain from Matthew Arnold.

These verbal laxities are symptomatic; the root of the trouble lay deeper: it lay in the fact that Scott did not take poetry seriously enough. His ideal was the man of action, not the poet. And if he did not take any poetry very seriously, least of all did he take his own. In all this he was poles apart from Wordsworth, Wordsworth with his lofty conception of the function of poetry, and of himself as a *sacer vates*. Wordsworth had a message. "I wish," he said, "to be regarded as a teacher or as nothing." Scott had no such wish: innocent pleasure was all he sought to give. His hatred of Revolutionary ideas put him out of sympathy with the progressive thought of his time. Indeed he had not much interest in ideas at all; none of that craving for the infinite which possessed Wordsworth and Shelley, and even, in his own fashion, Byron;

little of that sense of mystery which was Wordsworth's peculiar gift. This last deficiency spoils his treatment of the supernatural. When he could show it through the medium of a temperament, and play on it with his humour, he produced a masterpiece in *Wandering Willie's Tale*; but he could only do that in prose.

Against these faults we must set Scott's merits. First, his objectivity—surely a cardinal virtue in a story-teller. Wordsworth's own mind was the haunt and the main region of his song; Scott was not interested in his own mental processes: he wanted to tell a story. Now for a good story two things are needful—an interesting background, and an exciting action set out upon it. Scott's backgrounds are admirable, both the historical and the natural. In *Marmion* and *The Lord of the Isles* the historical background is everything, the imaginary plot is naught. His natural backgrounds are equally excellent. He may not have seen into the life of Nature as Wordsworth did, but her picturesque surface he did see with a painter's eye, and rendered with a vividness that delighted Ruskin. Think of the opening of *Marmion*:

> Day set on Norham's castled steep,
> And Tweed's fair river, broad and deep,
> And Cheviot's mountains lone;

of the opening of *The Lady of the Lake*:

> The stag at eve had drunk his fill,
> Where danced the moon on Monan's rill;

of the scene in Melrose Abbey when Deloraine breaks open the wizard's tomb:

> Full in the midst his Cross of Red
> Triumphant Michael brandished. . . .
> The moon-beam kissed the holy pane,
> And threw on the pavement a bloody stain.

On these backgrounds an exciting action is energetically set forth. Scott is at his best in describing rapid movement, especially the movement of large bodies of men and horse. His masterpiece in this kind is the last canto of *Marmion*, where he describes the battle of Flodden, not directly but as seen through the eyes of spectators, English spectators. But as the battle draws to its close, the *personae* are forgotten, and Scott is with his countrymen locked in the struggle:

> But as they left the darkening heath,
> More desperate grew the strife of death.
> The English shafts in volleys hailed,
> In headlong charge their horse assailed:
> Front, flank, and rear, the squadrons sweep,
> To break the Scottish circle deep,
>   That fought around their king.
> But yet, though thick the shafts as snow,
> Though charging knights like whirlwinds go,
> Though bill-men ply the ghastly blow,
>   Unbroken was the ring;
> The stubborn spearmen still made good
> Their dark, impenetrable wood,
> Each stepping where his comrade stood,
>   The instant that he fell.
> No thought was there of dastard flight,
> Linked in the serried phalanx tight,
> Groom fought like noble, squire like knight,
>   As fearlessly and well.

Here, at least, Scott rose to epic heights.

In the *Lay*, *Marmion*, and *The Lady of the Lake* Scott prefixed an introduction to each canto.   In the *Lay* these refer to the minstrel himself; the interludes in *The Lady of the Lake* are short reflective pieces, Spenserian in manner and metre; those in *Marmion* are much longer and more personal.   They are in the form of letters to various friends, dealing with things that filled Scott's mind at the time after his visit to London—home politics, the war with Napoleon, the deaths of Nelson, Pitt, and Fox, his own return to Ashestiel and his memories of the Borders; for though he made no great success of the personal lyric, Scott liked to talk about himself in season.   These epistles were much criticised at the time; to us some of them seem better than all but the best of the narrative.   In particular the lines on Nelson, Pitt, and Fox, in their firm, epigrammatic style, illustrate the variety of Scott's poetic gifts, and remind us that the great Romantic was a child of the eighteenth century.

There was yet another side to Scott's nature, best illustrated in his songs, but seen occasionally even in the narrative poems. These are in the main poems of action; but here and there we come on passages of sentiment and reflection, which reveal the strain of melancholy that underlay Scott's love of action, and made Ruskin declare, "Of all poetry that I know, none is so sorrowful as Scott's".   Like Tennyson, he was haunted by

the sense of the past, the past that has vanished, the memories
that remain:

> Sweet Teviot! on thy silver tide
>   The glaring bale-fires blaze no more;
> No longer steel-clad warriors ride
>   Along thy wild and willowed shore;
> Where'er thou wind'st by dale or hill,
> All, all is peaceful, all is still. . . .
>
> Unlike the tide of human time,
>   Which, though it change in ceaseless flow,
> Retains each grief, retains each crime,
>   Its earliest course was doomed to know,
> And, darker as it downward bears,
>   Is stained with past and present tears.

The tide of time did indeed grow darker with Scott as it bore
downward: near the end of his days he declared that no man
could bear to live if he saw life as it really is.

When Scott retired from the contest with Byron, he had by
no means done with verse: some of his best poetry was still
to be written in those snatches of song which occur in his
novels. Scott's lyric range was limited by the fact that he was
not a love-poet. There are some dramatic love-songs in the
novels, tepid things like "Ah, County Guy, the hour is nigh"
and "Leonard tarries long"; but his own love-story has left no
trace in his poetry except *The Violet* and *The Response*, and two
other pieces, equally mediocre, first printed in *Blackwood's* in
1937. Several of Scott's songs, including *Bonnie Dundee,
Jock o' Hazeldean, The Maid of Neidpath, The Massacre of
Glencoe*, and "Waken, lords and ladies gay", appeared separately in periodicals or anthologies; the rest are found as insets
in the long poems and the novels. The *Lay* gives us *Rosabelle*,
a dirge as decorative as the chapel of Roslin which it refers to.
In *Marmion* there are two strangely contrasted songs in *Young
Lochinvar* and "Where shall the lover rest?" *The Lady of the
Lake* is exceptionally rich in songs; besides the ballad of *Alice
Brand* there are the Coronach, the Boat Song, "Soldier, rest,
thy warfare o'er", that mysterious fragment, "The toils they
are pitched, and the stakes are set", and others. *Rokeby* is
lighted up with *Brignal Banks* and "A weary lot is thine, fair
maid".

The songs in Scott's novels are comparable with the songs
in Shakespeare's plays, far more so than those songs of Burns

which Carlyle selected for comparison. They are dramatic lyrics, but not quite in Browning's sense; not expressions of the minds of particular individuals in particular moods and situations, but objective and universal; proper indeed to the singer and the occasion, but that occasion one which, like death, is part of the common lot of man.   In *Waverley*, to name only the best, we have Davie Gellatley's song, "Hie away, hie away"; in *Guy Mannering* Meg Merrilies's mystical spells for birth—

> Twist ye, twine ye!   Even so
> Mingle shades of joy and woe;

and for death—

> Wasted, weary, wherefore stay,
> Wrestling thus with earth and clay?

In *The Antiquary* there is the wonderful ballad of *Harlaw*, sung by old Elspeth—surely Scott's masterpiece in balladry; and there are the impressive lines on Time:

> Why sit'st thou by that ruined wall,
> Thou aged carle, so stern and grey?

The scene of Madge Wildfire's death in *The Heart of Mid-lothian* is the most Shakespearian thing Scott ever wrote. Madge's dying songs, like Ophelia's, are the flotsam of a wrecked mind.   First there floats up a jolly song of harvest-home:

> Our work is over—over now,
> The goodman wipes his weary brow,
> The last long wain wends slow away,
> And we are free to sport and play.

Then comes what sounds like a Methodist hymn:

> When the fight of grace is fought,—
> When the marriage vest is wrought . . .
> Doff thy robes of sin and clay;
> Christian, rise, and come away.

Then a snatch of what might be an old ballad:

> Cauld is my bed, Lord Archibald,
>   And sad my sleep of sorrow;
> But thine sall be as sad and cauld,
>   My fause true-love, tomorrow.

And then, last of all, the incomparable "Proud Maisie".
As if to show the range of his lyric powers, there followed, in

The Bride of Lammermoor, Lucy Ashton's song, "Look not thou on beauty's charming", and, in *Ivanhoe*, Rebecca's noble hymn:

> When Israel, of the Lord beloved,
>   Out of the land of bondage came,
> Her fathers' God before her moved,
>   An awful guide, in smoke and flame.

There are many lyrics of sorts in *The Pirate*, but the one that haunts us is Claud Halcro's

> And you shall deal the funeral dole;
>   Ay, deal it, mother mine,
> To weary body, and to heavy soul,
>   The white bread and the wine.

The later novels contain fewer songs; but even so late a novel as *Woodstock* yields "One hour with thee".

Scott's songs may be distinguished according as they deal with life or with death. Those of the former class are songs of action; they have the merits of the long narrative poems, without their occasional *longueurs* and false diction. They are real songs, made to the tunes that rang in Scott's head from the days when he compiled the *Minstrelsy*. Of the songs of the latter class, Lord Tweedsmuir has written in words which we cannot better:

> But there is a second type of lyric or lyrical ballad, mostly to be found in the novels, which mounts still higher, which at its best, indeed, is beyond analysis, producing that sense of something inexplicable and overwhelming which is the token of genius. Its subjects are the mysteries of life, not its gallant bustle, and the supreme mystery of death. It deals with enchantments and the things which "tease us out of thought", with the pale light of another world, with the crooked shadows from the outer darkness which steal over the brightness of youth and love.

These lyrics, he continues, "are Scott's final credentials as a poet, even as a great poet, for they have the *desiderium* of great poetry".

Chapter Twenty-Seven

BYRON

WHEN we pass from the first generation of Romantics to the second we are in a new world. Wordsworth and Coleridge were young in the dawn of the French Revolution, when to be young was very Heaven; when Byron and Shelley began to write the Napoleonic War was ending, and when it ended the tide of reaction set in. By that time Wordsworth was middle-aged, soothed and tamed into acceptance of the *status quo* in politics if not in economics, and returning step by step to the Anglican fold; Byron and Shelley were young, high-spirited aristocrats, rebels against convention, the one a sceptic, the other a professed atheist.

The force that overthrew Napoleon was nationality. Unfortunately it marched to victory under the banners of three absolute monarchs, the rulers of Russia, Austria, and Prussia. These now formed a Holy Alliance, to maintain law and order in Europe on true Christian principles. The Holy Three, as Byron called them, were well-meaning men, who believed firmly in the Divine Right of Kings; the right of subjects, whether of individual subjects to personal liberty or of subject peoples to national independence, they rigorously suppressed. Castlereagh kept Britain out of the Holy Alliance; but he could not help subject peoples in land-locked countries like Hungary and Poland. Later, it is true, Canning brought British sea-power to bear, prevented Spain from crushing Portugal, and when her South American colonies revolted, held out a hand to the United States in support of the Monroe Doctrine and "called in a new world to redress the balance of the old". But on the continent of Europe the Holy Three were all-powerful. Their first rebuff came in 1830, when the second French Revolution sent the Bourbons packing and helped Belgium to independence.

In Britain the cause of Parliamentary Reform had made no progress during the war, and when it was won the oligarchy that had won it had no mind to relinquish power; but the rapid growth of the unenfranchised industrial towns in population and wealth was too much for them. In 1832 the

Reform Bill became law, and political power began to pass into the hands of the middle classes. The Victorian Age was approaching.

The economic condition was worse than the political. In the "dear years" that followed Waterloo the workers of Britain touched depths of misery such as they had not known since the Peasants' Revolt. One-fourth of the rural labourers in England were paupers: in Scotland the Highland clearances drove thousands of crofters out of their blazing cottages to emigrate or starve. Old people told us in our boyhood that in those days oatmeal was as great a luxury in Scotland as wheaten bread was in normal times. It was still worse in the new manufacturing towns, rushed up in the fever of the Industrial Revolution without regard to comfort, health, or even decency. What women and children suffered in the mills and the pits can be read in Mr. and Mrs. Hammond's *Town Labourer*. We shall mention only two facts, but they tell a grim tale: the average wage of British workers was £11 a year; the average age of cotton-spinners was forty. The Government did nothing to help the oppressed. On the contrary *Habeas Corpus* was suspended; all combinations of workers were declared illegal; and every attempt they made to improve their lot was treated as sedition, which the military might be called out to suppress. At Peterloo in 1819 a squadron of yeomanry charged an unoffending crowd of workers and sabred them by the score. The economists offered the poor no comfort: even the Benthamites, who were Liberals in politics, accepted the orthodox economic doctrine of *laissez-faire*—the greatest happiness of the greatest number would be best promoted by leaving things to the unescapable laws of supply and demand: Governmental interference would throw a spanner into the works—a doctrine highly agreeable to the hard-faced mill-owners who were coining child-slavery into guineas. Not that there were no protests. These years saw the birth of British Socialism. Owen's communal experiments failed, but they set an example which was not forgotten. After the ten "dear years" things began to mend a little even in the social field; and it is worth noting that while political reform was the work of the Whigs, the beginnings of social reform owed more to the Tories.

Such was the world in which Byron (1788–1824) and Shelley (1792–1822) found themselves.

The poetry of Byron broke upon the public of England, and of Europe, with a startling effect which it is difficult for us quite to comprehend, either in its character or its range. Of the Romantic poets none except Byron attracted much attention abroad, for it was to the novels that Scott owed his wide reputation. The French showed none of the interest in Wordsworth and Coleridge, or later in Shelley and Keats, that they had shown in Pope and Swift and Thomson and Young, to say nothing of writers whose interest was not mainly literary —Locke, Newton, Shaftesbury, Hume, Adam Smith. The quickening influence of Byron's poetry was felt from one end of the Continent to the other. Of Scott Goethe could say in 1823, "Byron alone will I let stand by myself; Walter Scott is nothing beside him".

The reactions in this country were more conflicting. Something like it had been evoked, one can divine, but necessarily over a much narrower range, by Marlowe's *Tamburlaine*, *Faustus*, and *Jew of Malta*, which had presented something of the same challenge to accepted conventions religious, ethical, and social. Whatever we may think of the purely literary merits of the tales which Byron poured forth in the years following his return from the first visit to the Mediterranean, from *The Giaour* to *Parisina*, they brought a new note, the note of passion, passion its own justification, into our poetry, such as had not been heard since at least Pope's *Eloisa to Abelard* (itself somewhat of a *tour de force*), and some of the Elizabethan dramatists—Marlowe, Webster, and Ford. As before, and as again when *Poems and Ballads* appeared in 1866, it was at once an attractive and a repelling force, ultimately a releasing one. And the repulsion was felt not alone by readers whose traditions were still those of the older didactic poetry, but by some who were themselves rebels against traditions literary and social—Wordsworth, Coleridge, Lamb, even Hazlitt, and others; for they too were moralists and, whatever their theoretic tenets, Christian in sentiment. This was not, they felt, the direction in which they wished to move. Here was a poet who in *Childe Harold* flaunted his own vices, and in his tales in verse found the heroic in men for whom love was a law to itself, careless alike of prudence and conventional morality. But others, in widely separated classes, found something at once stimulating and releasing in the absorbing, self-forgetting passion of such a song as that of Medora in *The Corsair*:

Deep in my soul that tender secret dwells,
  Lonely and lost to light for evermore,
Save when to thine my heart responsive swells,
  Then trembles into silence as before.

There, in its centre, a sepulchral lamp
  Burns the slow flame, eternal—but unseen;
Which not the darkness of despair can damp,
  Though vain its ray as it had never been.

What, compared with such intensity of feeling, reappearing again in *The Giaour*, *The Corsair*, *The Bride of Abydos*, *Parisina*, were the mild bleatings of Bowles's sonnets, or the poems inspired by them in the volumes of joint work by Coleridge, Lamb, and Lloyd? or *The Pet Lamb* and *The Idiot Boy*? Even in 1812 the finer poetry of Coleridge and Wordsworth was the possession only of the few. Nor is the moral balance so entirely on the side of Wordsworth as Lamb claims: "Why, a line of Wordsworth is a lever to lift the immortal spirit! Byron can only move the spleen", for as another critic justly says: "We do not understand how moral it is to yield unreservedly to enthusiasm. . . . It is rare to meet now even with young people who will abandon themselves to heroic emotion, or who if they really feel it do not try to belittle its expression. Byron's poetry above most tempts and almost compels surrender to that which is beyond the common self", the prudent self. Reckless courage is perhaps better than moral timidity.

A Byron and a Gordon, the young poet, who began life in lodgings in Aberdeen, inherited difficult impulses from both sides, obvious in his dissolute father and unruly, passionate mother. Nor was life made easier for a sensitive, proud soul by being suddenly converted into a peer of the realm without the means to support the position or friends to assist; nor by the gift of personal beauty marred by a club-foot. "Byron's countenance is a thing to dream of", said Scott, who met him for the last time in September, 1815. At Harrow and Cambridge too Byron came under the influence of the aristocratic tradition of life and manners which the late Sir George Trevelyan has described so vividly in his *Early Life of Charles James Fox*. On the other hand, the attention drawn to his poetry owed something to his rank and to his early friendship with the influential Rogers. His first venture, *Hours of Idleness* (1807), showed little evidence of what was to come from this complex and stormy temperament. Brougham's sarcastic review in the *Edinburgh* evoked, however, a spirited, if boyish, assault on both the new poets and the reviewers who still stood in the main for the old Popean tradition, to which Byron himself was later to proclaim his attachment.

But it was when he returned from a three-years visit to the Peninsula and the Mediterranean, and published, after some hesitation, the first two cantos of *Childe Harold*, that he sprang into fame. The poem itself owed its attraction partly to adventitious circumstances, first to the determination of readers to identify the character of the hero, a somewhat Mrs. Radcliffian type, with that of the poet and young peer; and secondly to the picturesque and romantic scenes described, Spain where our armies were fighting, the classic lands of Greece and the East. But if *Childe Harold* attracted lovers of poetry, it was the tales in verse which followed, suggested doubtless by those of Scott, that won him his wider popularity. It was in these, *The Giaour* (1813), *The Bride of Abydos* (1813), *The Corsair* (1814), *Lara* (1814), *The Siege of Corinth* (1816), that a new gale of passion blew through English poetry, startling and arresting. And the passion, love and hatred, gave to Byron's verse a weight and speed which distinguishes it from Scott's flowing and at times facile verse. On the whole the tales in octosyllabics—*The Giaour*, *The Bride*, *Parisina*—are the best, the language most natural, the flow most rapid. In the decasyllabic lines of *The Corsair* and *Lara*, especially the former, Byron's style retains some of the more radical faults of the eighteenth-century tradition, the use of a language that is not "such as men do use", and yet gains no really poetic effect from the departure, and the recurrent fault of inverting for the sake of the rhyme and thereby throwing a quite undue emphasis on some unimportant word:

> This casket India's glowing gems unlocks (Pope);
>
> Here too the sick their final doom receive (Crabbe);
>
> For the wild bird the busy springes set,
> Or spread beneath the sun the dripping net (Byron).

If inversion in the first line, why not in the second? In the much later *The Island* (1825) Byron showed an easier command of a naturally moving verse.

The note of passion, a romantic setting, these gave to Byron's slight and melodramatic poems a charm they have hardly retained; but they contain passages that were once favourites in every anthology, if one seldom meets them now:

> He who hath bent him o'er the dead
> Ere the first day of death hath fled,
> The first dark day of nothingness,
> The last of danger and distress—

with its continuing appeal to the spirit of Greece, for whose cause Byron was to lay down his life; or again:

> Know ye the land where the cypress and myrtle
> Are emblems of deeds that are done in their clime?

and

> Slow sinks, more slowly ere his race be run,
> Along Morea's hills the setting sun.

These are good examples of poetic rhetoric; but if all rhetoric were taken out of poetry much extant poetry would disappear. In the same years too Byron wrote several of his best lyrics:

> I enter thy garden of roses,
> Beloved and fair Haidée;

and

> And thou art dead, as young and fair
> As aught of mortal birth;

and

> She walks in beauty, like the night
> Of cloudless climes and starry skies.

To which we may add: "Oh! snatched away in beauty's bloom"; "When coldness wraps this suffering clay"; "There's not a joy the world can give like that it takes away"; and of the Hebrew melodies at least "The Assyrian came down like the wolf on the fold". If Byron's lyrics have not the lyric lightness of the best of Scott's, or the lyric cry of Shelley's, they have a weight and impetus of their own.

But the best of his poems were written in the years of exile in Italy, when he was to himself the centre of a storm of conflicting passions—the consciousness of his own delinquencies, indignation at the outcry raised against him, and finally boredom absolute at the severance from his countrymen and equals. The second part of *Childe Harold* struck Scott, to whom it was sent for review in the *Quarterly*, as nothing Byron had hitherto published: "It is wilder and less sweet, I think,

z

than the first part, but contains even darker and more powerful pourings-forth of the spirit which boils within him. . . . We gaze on the powerful and ruined mind which he presents as on a shattered castle within whose walls, once intended for noble guests, sorcerers and wild demons are supposed to hold their Sabbath. There is something dreadful in reflecting that one gifted so much above his fellow-creatures should thus labour under some strange mental malady that destroys his peace of mind and happiness although it cannot quench the fire of his genius."

Byron and all his troubles and inner conflicts face to face with Nature and with human history and great men are the themes of the third canto, composed in Geneva, and of the fourth, written when, after settling in Venice, he made a tour to Rome. The first predominates in the third canto, and in the Faustish drama *Manfred*, and in *The Prisoner of Chillon*. In Switzerland he met Shelley, and through him acquired a better understanding of Wordsworth, which is reflected in his treatment of Nature in the Swiss scenes. But here are also Waterloo and Napoleon and Rousseau and Gibbon. In the fourth canto it is Italy, her great cities and men—Venice and Florence and Rome; Dante and Petrarch and Boccaccio and Michael Angelo and Alfieri and Galileo and Machiavelli. But Nature is here too, sunset over Venice, and finally the sea. The descriptions of men and scenery are interrupted ever and again to give voice to his own wrongs and the conflict in his own soul, the consciousness of his own wrongdoing and the passionate conviction of being more sinned against than sinning.

The imperfections and inequalities of Byron's style in these poems are well described in Scott's review: "The harmony of verse and the power of numbers, nay, the selection and arrangement of expressions, are all so subordinated to the thought and sentiment as to become comparatively light in the scale. His poetry is like the oratory which hurries the hearers along without permitting them to pause on its solecisms and singularities. Its general structure is bold, severe, and as it were Doric, admitting few ornaments but those immediately suggested by the glowing imagination of the poet—rising and sinking with the tones of his enthusiasm, roughening into argument or softening into the melody of feeling and sentiment, as if the language for either were at the command of the poet, and the numbers not only came uncalled, but arranged themselves with little care on his part into the varied modulation which the subject requires." It was a little hard, indeed, on the stanza to which Spenser had given such sweetness and melody, to treat it in this cavalier manner; and fortunately, when *Childe Harold* was hardly finished, Byron found another model in the mock-heroic poetry of the Italians which was admirably suited to this constant variation of mood—the ottava rima which, as Swinburne justly says, Byron made his own. His first experiment was the little, almost Chaucerian, picture of Venetian manners and morals, with satirical digressions, *Beppo* (1818); and from that he passed to his second great epic, a satirical epic of modern life in the upper classes of Europe, *Don Juan*, which occupied him off and on from 1819 to 1824. It is an extraordinary medley of the grave and the gay, narrative and description, philosophy and satire. The first cantos, including the letter of Donna Inez, and the story of the shipwreck and of the love of Juan and Haidée on the Greek island, contains the most beautiful poetry that Byron was to write. But Juan's adventures carry him from Greece to Turkey, and thence to Russia and Catherine (Voltaire's great heroine), and then by way of Germany to England, where, just as a fresh intrigue is beginning, the poem breaks off. The whole flows with the ease and naturalness of Byron's conversation as described by Colonel Stanhope: "a stream sometimes smooth, sometimes rapid, and sometimes rushing down in cataracts—a mixture of philosophy and slang—of everything". Of the verse Swinburne has written with perhaps a touch of exaggeration: "Across the stanzas of *Don Juan* we swim forward as over the broad backs of the sea. They break and glitter, hiss and laugh, murmur and move like waves that sound or that subside. There is in them a delicious resistance, an elastic motion which salt water has and fresh has not. There is about them a wide wholesome air full of vivid light and constant wind which is only felt at sea." Perhaps Swinburne, like Homer, has a little forgotten his subject in the pleasure of his simile.

Of the verse dramas on which Byron expended so much labour between 1821 and 1824 there never was much to be said—*Marino Faliero* (1821), *The Two Foscari* (1821), *Sardanapalus* (1821), *Cain* (1821), *Werner* (1822), *Heaven and Earth* (1822), *The Deformed Transformed* (1824). The three first are historical dramas; *Cain* and *Heaven and Earth* are from the

Bible, whose Old Testament stories had taken hold of Byron's imagination in his early Aberdeen days. *Werner* and *The Deformed* are based on prose fictions. "In passing from description to drama", Professor Herford has well said, "Byron instantly betrayed the rhetorical quality of his imagination. In passing from rhyme to blank verse he betrayed still more the limits of his sense of melody, for no poet of comparable rank ever wrote verse so unutterably blank." But one or two of the dramas have a personal interest, *The Deformed Transformed* obviously:

> *Bertha.* Out, Hunchback!
> *Arnold.* I was born so, Mother.

In *Sardanapalus* and *Cain,* as in *Manfred,* one can hear again the conflict that raged in Byron's mind between the consciousness of wrongdoing and rebellion against the doctrine of the individual's entire responsibility irrespective of Nature and Fortune, Heredity and Environment—

> That which I am, I am; I did not seek
> My life, nor did I make myself.

The reactions of Byron and Shelley respectively to their being cast out by society deserve more consideration than they have received. They were both social beings, conscious of their human ties, of the social instinct in which the moral conscience has its root. To Shelley, aware of his own entire goodwill to his fellow-men, his sympathy with their lot, the sense of being an outcast because of his separation from Harriet and marriage to Mary was one of dazed incomprehension. He believed that his own motives had been good. To Byron, aware of his own sins, accepting, as Shelley did not, the standards by which he was judged, the conflict was to escape from the full sense of guilt in an inescapable fatalism. One may too, like Sardanapalus, have been a voluptuary, and yet be capable of heroic action and death.

In 1822 Byron wrote two poems of real excellence which have had a very different degree of recognition—*The Vision of Judgement* and *The Island.* The latter is a well-told tale in decasyllabic couplets. The former is, with *Absalom and Achitophel,* the greatest political satire in our language. The main attack is on Southey, the Tory Poet Laureate, who had celebrated the arrival of George III in Heaven. Byron does the same in his very different way.   In *The Age of Bronze* he turned his satire on the Holy Alliance and the greed of land-lords and farmers determined to keep up the high prices of war at the expense of the poor.

Byron's fame as a poet reached its nadir in the closing years of the last century, assailed by Swinburne and forsaken by others who had once spoken more appreciatively.   The war brought back to some young readers a sense of something in Byron's picture of life that Wordsworth, the Romantic who made a good end, as Mr. Lewis calls him, had overlooked.   At any rate, after the vicissitudes that one has witnessed in the popularity of such poets as Pope, Donne, Crabbe, it would be rash to believe that Byron's poetry is dead.   There are some things that cannot die.   Rhetorical his poetry has been called. A fairer word would be 'oratorical', for the word 'rhetoric' has come to suggest an element of insincerity and elaboration of diction, neither of which is chargeable to the poetry of one who spoke the truth as he saw it.

Chapter Twenty-Eight

SHELLEY

NO poet suffered severer reprobation in his life and none perhaps has evoked more ardent sympathy and admiration in later years than this strange offshoot from an otherwise undistinguished aristocratic family who was born in 1792 and drowned in the Gulf of Spezzia in 1822. "I am regarded by all who know or hear of me, except, I think, on the whole, five individuals, as a rare prodigy of crime and pollution" (to Peacock, April 6, 1819). However they may vary in their treatment from time to time of Wordsworth, Coleridge, Byron, the early reviews of the century are at one in regarding Shelley as something outside the pale. The condemnation was in part the consequence of his early marriage and the tragic fate of poor Harriet Westbrook, for which indeed no excuse can be made except that of Mrs. Campbell in her *Shelley and the Antiromantics* of youth and an hysterical vein in the young poet's constitution. But the general attitude towards Shelley was even more due to the outspoken attack on Christianity in his first poems, especially *Queen Mab*, which put him in the same category as the author of *The Age of Reason*. Even to less prejudiced critics like Lamb and Hazlitt Shelley's poetry seemed "thin sown with profit and delight", too full of wild theories and nostrums.

A reaction set in after his death, due at once to the recognition of the sheer beauty and music of the poetry of his maturer years, and also the conviction that, despite the errors of his early life and work, that work was inspired by an unwavering idealism, that Shelley was one of the rare beings for whom the thought of the suffering of his fellow-men was intolerable. If Keats was to Tennyson potentially the first of the poets of the age just passed away, Browning's earliest poems were inspired by love of Shelley:

> Sun-treader, light and life be thine for ever!
> Thou art gone from us; years go by and spring
> Gladdens, and the young earth is beautiful,
> Yet thy songs come not, other bards arise,
> But none like thee;

and Shelley's central faith in the perfectibility of man was Browning's also, with a difference.   But the reaction has itself done Shelley some harm by evoking a spirit of idolatry which has not served him well.   Shelley, like Burns, has had to pay for the ardent apologies of his admirers.

For Shelley, as for Wordsworth, a determining experience in his life was the school.   At home with his sisters he seems to have been happy enough; but when ten years old he was sent to a school bearing the ominous name of Sion House to board with "the sons of London shopkeepers of rude habits and coarse manners".   Thence, when only thirteen, he passed to Eton, where "are our young barbarians all at play", and thence to Oxford, where dons of settled habits disliked the challenge of youth full of enthusiasm in the quest for truth.   Shelley's *The Necessity of Atheism*, a challenging pamphlet based on his reading of Hume and sent to various persons, was even more obnoxious to the fellows of University College than the excessive zeal of Charles Wesley and his friends had been to those of Christ Church earlier, and was more easy to punish.   Shelley was expelled and the young man launched on life, for his father refused him permission to come home, with nothing to guide him but his own passion for humanity, a passion which had become aware of itself while he was still at Eton:

> Thoughts of great deeds were mine, dear Friend, when first
> The clouds which wrap this world from youth did pass.
> I do remember well the hour which burst
> My spirit's sleep: a fresh May-dawn it was
> When I walked forth upon the glittering grass,
> And wept, I knew not why; until there rose
> From the near schoolroom voices that, alas!
> Were but one echo from a world of woes—
> The harsh and grating strife of tyrants and of foes.
>
> And then I clasped my hands and looked around—
> But none was near to mock my streaming eyes,
> Which poured their warm drops on the sunny ground—
> So without shame I spake:—"I will be wise,
> And just, and free, and mild, if in me lies
> Such power, for I grow weary to behold
> The selfish and the strong still tyrannize
> Without reproach or check." I then controlled
> My tears, my heart grew calm, and I was meek and bold.

It is more easy to will to be wise than to become so, as

Shelley's life and poems were both to show; nor is love in which, as Blake has well emphasised, the egoistic and altruistic impulses are so complexly mingled, the surest guide to wise conduct: "good", he was to write towards the end of his life, "far more than evil impulses, love far more than hatred, has been to me . . . the source of all sorts of mischief". But whoever has imagination and sympathy enough to enter into the feeling of the lines quoted above, and appreciate the experiences that lay behind them, will understand the essential spirit of Shelley's poetry—a poetry of rebellion and of escape; rebellion against everything that seemed to him, rightly or wrongly, to be the creation of "the selfish and the strong", whether the Christian doctrine of eternal punishment, the rule of kings and tyrants, or a too rigid law of monogamy; but a poetry also of escape, escape from human life with all its jars and inhibitions into the joyous, because free and irresponsible, life of Nature, of clouds and birds and streams, or into pure dreams as in the *Witch of Atlas*, or lastly, into that dream which Christianity had inherited from the Hebrew prophets, of a New Age, a Second Coming, when "the wolf shall dwell with the lamb, and the leopard shall lie down with the kid; and the calf and the fatling together; and a little child shall lead them", and when man's will,

> A spirit ill to guide, but mighty to obey,
> Is as a tempest-winged ship, whose helm
> Love rules, through waves which dare not overwhelm,
> Forcing Life's wildest shore to own its sovereign sway.

And it is here that Shelley suggests comparison with Milton. It may be true as Clutton-Brock declared that "Milton's whole imagination was political, that he could not keep politics out of *Lycidas* or *Paradise Lost*. His devils debate like statesmen. His Supreme Being makes speeches from the throne. But Shelley even where he means to be political combines poetry with politics only with manifest difficulty, and on any pretext escapes into another world where there is no need for any statesmanship." But that is not the whole truth. If Milton flung aside poetry for politics for some twenty years it was not because *his* genius had a practical, political bent. It was because he too was fired, on the meeting of the Long Parliament, with the vision of a new, a regenerate world, a Second Coming. In a word, both Milton and Shelley (and the same is true of the early Wordsworth) were not political but religious poets, expecting something from political movements which they can never give us—a new Earth, the Kingdom of Heaven. But Milton had, as Wordsworth and Shelley with their natural pantheism had not, a definite creed to work with and on; and when he came to his chief poems a traditional symbolism to give a fresh life to. Moreover, Milton was a stronger and sterner man, as well as a greater artist, than either Wordsworth or Shelley. If he had hoped for a new era to dawn with the meeting of the Long Parliament, a preparation at least for a Second Coming, he knew in the end where to put the blame, on the weakness of men, the triviality of their lives; and he accepted, with variations of his own, the stern orthodox Christian doctrine that this world will never be other than a mixture of good and evil, a place where—not the Elect in the full Calvinistic sense of the word—yet the few, the heroic, the strong of will alone are prepared for a better world elsewhere. There are some indications that on Shelley also was dawning the stern truth of the invincibility of human folly and weakness. On the other hand he retained to the end what Milton too early lost, a feeling of love and pity for his fellow-men:

> Me—who am as a nerve o'er which do creep
> The else unfelt oppressions of this earth—

which has made him, despite all his faults on which the criticism of to-day dwells so severely, an influence which kept alive in the hearts of many, especially the young, a passion for justice and human-kindness that even in these dark days is not altogether extinct. Moreover, in some of the sweetest of Shelley's lyrics there is neither rebellion nor prophecy. Like the nightingale of tradition he leans his breast against the thorn of his own despair and pours forth an eloquent lament.

In his quest of an explanation of human ills and a way of escape Shelley had, of course, various guides. Godwin early, and to Godwin's central doctrine, the perfectibility of man, he remained loyal to the end; Plato later. But he took them in his own way. There is no consistent philosophy, Godwinian or Platonic, to be sought for in his poetry; and so finally we may turn to that poetry just as poetry and consider its essential merits, its, to some minds, serious or fatal defects. One fact presents itself at once as distinguishing the development of Shelley's genius as compared with that of Milton or Keats—the absence of great poetry or poetry of any note at all as an early shaping factor.   Milton trained himself in the composing of Latin *Elegies*, but shows also in his earlier verses evidence of his reading of Sylvester's *Du Bartas* and Spenser.   Keats, after some aberrations in the manner of Moore and Miss Tighe, finds his way through Leigh Hunt to the shaping influences of Spenser and Milton and Shakespeare.   Of all this there is little or nothing in the early records of Shelley.   His excitable, and in these earlier years one must add unbalanced, mind— exposed almost indecently in the letters to Elizabeth Hitchener —was attracted first by the sensational Ann Radcliffe, 'Monk' Lewis type of fiction; then by the magical potentialities of chemistry and the physical sciences; and finally by philo- sophical and political speculation; and his interest in the two latter is of the same kind, not purely scientific or speculative, but inspired by a hope to find in both means to promote the coming of the millennium.   Knowledge for the sake of know- ledge, poetry for the sake of poetry, were never Shelley's con- scious aim.   When not merely relieving his own feelings he is seeking to regenerate mankind.   Even in *The Cenci* good and evil are set over against one another with the sharp distinction beloved of the preacher and moralist.

But it is perhaps from this very fact that his poetry has for the poet an end beyond itself, "to awaken public hope and to enlighten and improve mankind", that one of its most striking qualities flows.   Shelley, far more than Wordsworth despite theory and prefaces, is content to use only the language of the day.   No poetry of the period—except Byron's, and Byron's poems are more rhetorical than poetic—is so free of "poetic diction" in the sense in which Wordsworth uses that word in his famous preface, whether the conventional epithets and personifications of the school of Gray and Collins, from which the early work neither of Wordsworth nor Coleridge is exempt, or the newer poetic diction, more sensuous, eclectic, and imaginative, of which Keats was to be master.   Shelley's style abounds in personification and metaphor and other of those natural figures which we all use, as best we may, to describe vividly what we see and feel, or to express what passionately moves us.

Now Shelley's mind was at once abstract and imaginative, so that he sometimes wondered if he were fitter for metaphysics or for poetry.   His natural mode of thinking was to abstract, to isolate, some element in Nature, or man, and then, being a poet, to body it forth in imagery. This is the process which yields the familiar figure of Personification. Only, as he once explained to Godwin, the elements which Shelley loved to isolate and then personify were "minute and remote distinctions of feeling", which could only be bodied forth in remote and impalpable shapes. But when analysed, the strangest and most remote of these figures will be found elaborated in words current, not either traditionally poetic or coined for the occasion, though like every poet and every vivid writer Shelley will use current words in a new and striking manner and will form new compounds, an always fresh shoot in every living language.

It was the same taste which drew Shelley to Mrs. Radcliffe and 'Monk' Lewis, and which produced in his early years *Zastrozzi* and *The Rosicrucian*, that made Southey for him the most interesting, to begin with, of the Romantic poets—the strange journeyings and happenings of *The Curse of Kehama* and *Thalaba the Destroyer*. But though Southey too is an emphatic moralist, there is a mighty difference between his mythological stories and Shelley's *Queen Mab* (1813), the poem which followed his expulsion from Oxford in 1810 and his hasty marriage. Southey's irregular metre is adopted, mingled with passages in regular blank verse, but the Queen Mab of fairy tales and of Shakespeare never underwent a stranger sea-change than when she became the guide of Ianthe through scenes of cruelty and suffering, and the expounder of Godwinian doctrines concerning the evils of tyranny and superstition, necessitarianism, vegetarianism, and the perfectibility of mankind. It is in *Alastor* (1816), the poem which followed, that we get the first glimpse of the Shelley who was to appeal to lovers of poetry and not merely such addicts of revolution as were responsible for the frequent reprinting of *Queen Mab*. It is a strange poem, a confused yet eloquent record of a confused state of feeling through which a young poet, who never quite understood either himself or other men, was passing. Neither the preface nor the motto from St. Augustine (which was added in later editions) has much to do with the content and spirit of the poem. The second title, "The Spirit of Solitude", comes nearer, for the poem is a record of Shelley's intense consciousness of his own loneliness in life and a passionate contemplation of the mystery of death, for Shelley believed himself to be a victim of consumption. What it is he wants the wandering poet does not know himself. In dreams he enjoys at once spiritual and physical union with a woman who shared his aspirations:

> Knowledge and truth and virtue were her theme,
> And lofty hopes of divine liberty.

But she vanishes with the dream. Nature gives him no sympathy, and here Shelley suggests, as Wordsworth never does, Nature's refusal "to partake of our moods". She stands aloof and alien:

> The cold white light of morning, the blue moon
> Low in the west, the clear and garish hills,
> The distinct valley and the vacant woods,
> Spread round him where he stood.

But the dominant thought of the poem is the mystery of death. The inspiration of Shelley's poem is a profound self-pity:

> Art and eloquence,
> And all the shows o' the world are frail and vain
> To weep a loss that turns their lights to shade.
> It is a woe too 'deep for tears', when all
> Is reft at once, when some surpassing Spirit,
> Whose light adorned the world around it, leaves
> Those who remain behind, not sobs or groans,
> The passionate tumult of a clinging hope;
> But pale despair and cold tranquillity,
> Nature's vast frame, the web of human things,
> Birth and the grave, that are not as they were.

From such eloquent if indistinct lament over his own inability to adapt himself to a hard world, and morbid if eloquent contemplation of death, Shelley turned back to his mission of converting this stubborn world to his own ideals of liberty and love in *The Revolt of Islam* (1818), entitled first *Laon and Cythna*, the hero and heroine to be brother and sister as well as lovers. No knocks however bewildering could persuade Shelley to compromise in his warfare with whatever seemed to him cruel and irrational conventions. It was too much for the publisher, however, and the relationship as well as the title of the poem was altered. For the Wordsworthian, but more sustainedly musical, blank verse of *Alastor* was substituted the Spenserian stanza which Shelley again masters at once, if in his own more lyrical fashion. The music of the

verse, indeed, and the poetic imagery are the chief, perhaps the
sole, interest of the poem:

> the visions of a dream
> Which hid in one deep gulf the troubled stream
> Of mind . . .
>
> And every bosom thus is rapt and shook,
> Like autumn's myriad leaves in one swoln mountain-brook;
>
> And cast the vote of love in hope's abandoned urn . . .
>
> With hue like that when some great painter dips
> His pencil in the gloom of earthquake and eclipse.

The story itself is the wildest absurdity, combining Shelley's
two invariable motives, a passionate philanthropy and an equally
passionate eroticism. His three favourite characters are there
—the generous young man devoted to the cause of freedom
and justice, of love as the ruling principle of human society;
the generous and ardent young woman his associate; the wise
old man whom age and experience have freed from all selfish
motives. The liberation of man is to be achieved by eloquent
persuasion. In the end defeated and perishing together at the
stake, the hero and heroine are borne in the spirit to some
Valhalla of peace and love beyond the bonds of human
experience:

> Motionless resting on the lake awhile,
>   I saw its marge of snow-bright mountains rear
> Their peaks aloft, I saw each radiant isle,
>   And in the midst, afar, even like a sphere
>   Hung in one hollow sky, did there appear
> The temple of the Spirit; on the sound
>   Which issued thence, drawn nearer and more near,
> Like the swift moon this glorious earth around,
> The charmed boat approached, and there its haven found.

So Shelley escapes, and will escape always, from his insoluble
political problems, men being what they are.

Rosalind and Helen which followed is less readable, a reflection, more morbid and less imaginative and elevated, of his
confused feelings in the years before his final exile,—the same
blend of self-pity, eroticism, anticipation of death, and protest
against what seems to him the needless cruelties of society and
convention,—all in the metre of Scott, Coleridge, and Byron's
tales.

But all the early longer, and some of the shorter, poems are the work of a sick man. With the transition to Italy in 1818 came a complete recovery in Shelley's health—he had probably imagined himself more ill than he really was, his complaint being nervous, not organic,—and with it a strengthening and clarification of his style.

But it was not alone the change of climate and the recovery of health which gave a new strength and clarity to Shelley's poetry. Before leaving England he had, Mrs. Shelley tells us, resolving on poetry rather than metaphysics as his life-work, "educated himself for it . . . and engaged himself in the study of the poets of Greece, Italy and England, Greek poetry pre-eminently". It was in his first year in Italy that he translated the Homeric *Hymn to Mercury* with some of the shorter hymns and a fragment of that to Aphrodite. The *Cyclops* of Euripides was the work of the following year.

The effect of translating such poems on his own style was beneficial. It encouraged him to moderate the over-ecstatic strain in his earlier poems, stimulated, as that was, by his dreams of human perfectibility, taught him to cultivate an easy, natural tone, the tone of conversation, conversation with even a touch of humour in it, and so doing drew him nearer to the mood of less exalted minds. This is the chief effect, whatever influence Greek poetry had or might have had on the thought and substance of his poems. For there is no radical change in the tenor of the two chief poems composed in 1818: *Julian and Maddalo* and the *Lines written among the Euganean Hills*. The latter opens in the same morbid contemplation of death, and closes in the familiar dream of an escape to a land where music and moonlight and feeling are one. But the descriptive parts have the peculiar Shelleyan quality in dealing with effects of light and cloud and atmosphere in which he has, it seems to us, no rivals. The, in general catalectic, trochaic lines are written with the lyrical music Shelley could contribute to any measure he essayed. The political references to Venice and Padua have little value except as giving to the melancholy a less egoistic tone, being a reminder that Shelley's sorrow, like Milton's anger, is not purely personal but reflects his passionate response to the thought of cruelty and injustice.

Julian and Maddalo (1818) shows the influence of Byron, the Byron of *Beppo* and *Don Juan*, which the then much more famous poet must have read to him, and suggests, with the later *Letter to Maria Gisborne*, how well Shelley could write when, as in the translations, he curbed his genius and wrote as one who can talk as well as sing. The first part of the poem, describing the day with Byron, is admirable in diction, natural (yet unmistakably the conversation of a gentleman in the full sense of the word), admirable also in the management of the couplet with overflow and varying pause. The episode of the visit to the mad-house is somewhat of a puzzle and makes for Byron's pessimism rather than for Shelley's confidence in human nature, but the significance of the episode is left obscure. Perhaps again there was an intention to suggest too close a kinship. The best of the poem is conversational and descriptive. The maniac is another Alastor, revealing again Shelley's want of any clear grasp of his own feelings about life.

Julian and Maddalo was the outcome of his visit to Venice from the Baths of Lucca to which he and his wife had proceeded from Milan and Leghorn. *The Cenci* was composed at Rome in 1819, when Shelley came on a very incomplete and untrustworthy version of the story. It is a product of Shelley's reading of Shakespeare and the Elizabethan dramatists, and his own intense and hysterical reaction to a story of cruelty. For if horrors are piled on horrors in the manner of the lesser Elizabethan tragedians, it is not with their eye to a popular dramatic effect, but as the expression of Shelley's own, single-minded reaction to the horrors of cruelty and of a Church that could condone crime for money. It has been overpraised as a tragedy, if in diction and verse it is far superior to any verse-play of the day. There are reflections of Shakespeare, and Shelley is not Shakespeare, yet his language has always a distinction of its own. On the other hand it has been unduly depreciated of late, represented as just one more example of Shelley's self-pity—"there is nothing grasped at the core of the piece. Instead there is Beatrice-Shelley, in whose martyrdom the Count acts Jove." But to be just to Shelley's self-pity as to Milton's self-confidence, one must recognise that his own self is identified with the cause of suffering wherever he finds it. He would have laid down his life as readily as Byron did later for the cause of justice and humanity, however wild his confidence in pacifist principles and the power of reasonable persuasion. But *The Cenci* fails to be a great tragedy, first because of the poet's inability to paint otherwise than in black and white, and secondly because in the one character whom he does make a serious effort to present dramatically, Beatrice, he failed to get through to any clear, defensible, or at least arguable principle. It was a bold stroke to make her at once the instigator to the murder of her father and the boldest in maintaining her innocence later. But he does not develop, he had not thought out clearly, what might be her defence, defence suggested by her own cry:

> Mother,
> What is done wisely, is done well. Be bold
> As thou art just.

His single-tracked mind saw only the infinite pathos of the sufferers' fate, the limitless cruelty of their oppressors, and the cowardice of their defenders.

Prometheus Unbound, begun at Este in 1818, the second and third acts completed at Rome in 1819 ("The bright blue sky of Rome, and the effect of the vigorous awakening spring in that divinest climate, and the new life with which it drenches the spirits even to intoxication, were the inspiration of this drama"), the fourth act an afterthought added at Florence at the close of the same year, is the most ambitious and central attempt of the poet to render his reading of life, the mystery of good and evil, and to give adequate embodiment to his own ambition as poet and reformer: "I have what a Scotch philosopher characteristically terms 'a passion for reforming the world'". For the drama is a symbolic rendering of the same sequence of ideas as was given the form of an imaginary piece of history in *The Revolt of Islam*. The relation of Shelley's drama to the *Prometheus Bound* of Aeschylus is very simple. Prometheus, the champion of humanity, will not surrender to Jupiter as, in some way left unknown, was to take place in the Greek trilogy. Shelley's treatment is entirely his own.

The note of spring which he strikes in the introduction as quoted above is dominant throughout, for to understand the symbolism (if some of the details are purely fanciful, and some quite unintelligible, as the Zoroastrian apparitions in the first act) one must realise from the outset that the deliverance of mankind is not brought about by the *action* of Prometheus and Asia, though they are to give it the guidance of wisdom and love, without which the revolution may end in such a disaster of anarchy and mutual slaughter as has disfigured the history of Christianity and wrecked the promise of the French Revolution. The agent of the revolution which is to give to

men the rule of wisdom and love, Prometheus and Asia, is
Necessity, embodied in Demogorgon, that inscrutable power
which, as had been described in the opening canto of *The
Revolt of Islam*, has brought the world alternations of tyranny
and liberty:

> Two Powers o'er mortal things dominion hold,
> Ruling the world with a divided lot,
>   Immortal, all-pervading, manifold,
> Twin Genii, equal Gods—when life and thought
> Sprang forth, they burst the womb of inessential Nought.

The ultimate source is an impenetrable mystery, but in the
drama Shelley has apparently a thought that goes beyond the
Revolt:

>   If the abysm
> Could vomit forth its secrets . . . But a voice
> Is wanting, the deep truth is imageless;
> For what would it avail to bid thee gaze
> On the revolving world?   What to bid speak
> Fate, Time, Occasion, Chance, and Change?   To these
> All things are subject *but eternal love,*

the love which endures when all is dark; for the service which
Prometheus and Asia have, in different degrees and ways,
rendered to the coming change is *passive*.   They have loved,
and hoped, and endured, and now Necessity is bringing round
the hour of fulfilment.   And Prometheus is just Shelley and
Hunt and all who have refused to be carried away by the tide
of reaction which overwhelmed Southey and Coleridge and
Wordsworth.   For Shelley believed that the worst of the
reaction which followed Waterloo was beginning to pass, the
rule of the Triple Alliance abroad and of Castlereagh at home.
So Prometheus passes through the last hour of suffering, the
darkest vision in which is the evil that good intentions have
wrought when their fulfilment passed into the hands of men
wanting wisdom and love:—the Christian revelation:

> Hark that outcry of despair!
> 'Tis his mild and gentle ghost
> Wailing for the faith he kindled;

or the French Revolution:

> See a disenchanted nation
> Springs like day from desolation;

AA

> To Truth its state is dedicate
> And Freedom leads it forth, her mate;
> A legioned band of linked brothers
> Whom Love calls children—
>   'Tis another's.
> See how kindred murder kin!
> 'Tis the vintage time for Death and Sin.

The burden of the comforters' songs is the evidence which they have found of the goodness, the spirit of self-sacrifice, which are also in that complex thing, the mind of man. But Spring has come. The dreams of Panthea, the vision of Asia, the winds that blow and the voices which call "Follow, follow" (which got on Mrs. Campbell's nerves), are yet all part of the evidence that the time has come, not by any action of Prometheus but in the order of fate. Jupiter, whether as a tyrannous and revengeful God created in and by man's own mind and now outgrown, or the tyranny which has taken the place of the freedom hoped for at the time of the American and French revolutions, is cast down. And in Prometheus who is Wisdom that has learned the final lesson of forgiveness, and Asia who is Love, the world has a guarantee that the hopes will not be quenched by another night of anarchy leading to a fresh tyranny. The final act is a lyrical rhapsody, more satisfying than the long declamatory speeches in which Shelley attempts to give some concrete picture of the unimaginable results of the great delivery. Nor is Shelley's rhapsody so void of thought as some critics have been tempted to say, if it is as vague as are the prophecies of the genuine Hebrew prophets. It is always the fraudulent prophets who are definite. He seems to us to transcend some, or most, of the dreamers of a golden age. Neither man's free will with its inherent capacity for evil as well as good, nor yet human pain and suffering, are to disappear, but they will be transcended and transmuted by the power of mutual love:

> Familiar acts are beautiful through love;
> Labour and pain and grief in life's green grove
> Sport like tame beasts, none knew how gentle they could be!

It is all a dream, a wish-fulfilment, and if in these evil days it seems a difficult one, yet it does indicate the one direction in which human nature has struggled forward, if often relapsing,

—the conquest of the will to injure or avenge, the heroic alleviation of pain and suffering.[1]

To the same years as *Prometheus Unbound* belong some poems strangely different at first sight, but inspired by the same active interest in the course of political events: the polemical *Mask of Anarchy*, and two shorter poems in the same vein: *Lines Written during the Castlereagh Administration*, and the *Song of the Men of England*:

> Men of England, wherefore plough
> For the Lords who lay ye low?

They were evoked by Shelley's horror at the massacre of Peterloo. But all the thoughts of the *Prometheus* are repeated in the more direct and concrete poems: hope, love, forgiveness, and liberty. To these should be added the *Ode . . . before the Spaniards had recovered their Liberty*, perhaps the finest of all:

> Bind, bind every brow
> With crownals of violet, ivy and pine:
> Hide the bloodstains now
> With hues which sweet nature has made divine:
> Green strength, azure hope, and eternity:
> But let not the pansy among them be;
> Ye were injured and that means memory

The three chief poems which followed the *Prometheus* are

[1] We owe this reading of the myth to an interesting article by Kenneth Neil Cameron in PMLA, vol. lviii, No. 3. We have not detailed or discussed his identifications and proofs from the prose writings. But we accept the view that the *Prometheus Unbound* is not, like the *Prometheus Vinctus* of Aeschylus, primarily a philosophical and religious drama but had for Shelley an immediate political interest. Shelley's religion and philosophy were those which he had learned from Hume and Godwin, modified by a growing strain of Plato. The *Prometheus* is, like *The Revolt of Islam*, an appeal to the young and generous intellectuals not to yield to despair and cynicism: a change is coming. Their duty is to give to that when it comes the guidance of wisdom, love, and the spirit of forgiveness, failing which the French Revolution drove France into the arms of Napoleon, and thence back to the Old Anarch, Custom and Legitimacy. But any immediate didactic intention is sublimated in a wish-fulfilment expressed in image and music: "Didactic poetry is my abhorrence . . . my purpose has simply been to familiarise the highly refined imagination of the more select classes of poetical readers with beautiful idealisms of moral excellence; aware that until the mind can love, and admire, and trust, and hope, and endure, reasoned principles of moral conduct are seeds cast upon the highway of life which the unconscious passenger tramples into dust, although they would bear the harvest of happiness. Should I live to accomplish what I purpose . . . a systematic history of what appear to me to be the genuine elements of human society", he would take Plato rather than Aeschylus as his model.

certainly, whatever we think of them, poems which nobody but Shelley could have dreamed of or composed. He once wrote, Platonising to John Gisborne, "Some of us have, in a prior existence, been in love with an Antigone". All his life Shelley was seeking this lost Antigone, and thinking he had found her in a living, breathing woman—Harriet Grove, Mary Godwin, Emilia Viviani, perhaps Jane Williams. In the ecstatic *Epipsychidion* (inscribed to Emilia V——) he dreams that he has escaped with his Antigone to a lone and lovely isle in the Aegean. The gem of the poem is the description of this ideal island, into which are woven reminiscences of pastoral poetry and aspects of the Italian scenery with which Shelley had become familiar, all blended in the poet's liquid and undulating verse. But now he knows that the lady and the isle alike are dreams.

Adonais, written in June of the same year on the death of Keats in Rome, is a stronger poem because not so purely a poem of escape. Here Shelley has to face the inescapable facts of life and death, and there is clear evidence of advance in thought on the eloquent but confused *Alastor*. Shelley's models are of course Bion's *Lament for Adonis* and Moschus's *Lament for Bion*, "Adonais" being just a modification of "Adonis" intended to suggest that Keats was as dear to Urania, the goddess of heavenly love and the muse of high poetry, poetry that quickens in men's souls the love of liberty, as Adonis was to Aphrodite. From the Greek poems Shelley borrows phrases, elaborating them at times into mere conceits, at others (v. 18) illuminating them with a new splendour of passion and description and cadence. His mythology is in the main his own, a mythology of abstractions:

The quick Dreams,
The passion-wingèd Ministers of thought. . . .
. . . Desires and Adorations,
Wingèd Persuasions and veiled Destinies,
Splendours, and Glooms, and glimmering Incarnations
Of hopes and fears, and twilight Phantasies;
And Sorrow, with her family of Sighs.

The subject of the whole is of course less Keats than Shelley himself. Keats indeed had suffered martyrdom, but more because of the political sins and literary vulgarities of Leigh Hunt than his own. It is of himself as the poet of liberty and an outcast from society that Shelley is thinking both through-

out the poem and in the description of the shepherds who come
to mourn the dead poet:

> Midst others of less note, came one frail Form,
> A phantom among men . . .
>   . . . sad Urania scanned
> The Stranger's mien, and murmured: 'Who art thou?'
> He answered not, but with a sudden hand
> Made bare his branded and ensanguined brow,
> Which was like Cain's or Christ's—oh! that it should be so!

It is from the thirty-ninth stanza onwards, however, that the
poem gathers strength; and the theme is just that of *Alastor*, the
mystery of death.   But the poet's treatment is now boldly
pantheistic or transcendental.   Indeed Shelley seems to
glimpse at last the ultimate source of his own and mankind's
suffering.   It is not just kings and priests that are the source
of evil (one might add to-day capitalists and communists and
fascists).   It is individual existence with all which that involves
of inevitable conflict, the fierce competition for power: "Thou
shalt starve ere I starve".   Only in some mystical unity in
which individual existence is transcended can all the ills which
Prometheus was to have cured find their true end:

> The One remains, the many change and pass;
> Heaven's light forever shines, Earth's shadows fly;
> Life, like a dome of many-coloured glass,
> Stains the white radiance of Eternity,
> Until Death tramples it to fragments.—Die,
> If thou wouldst be with that which thou dost seek!

To escape into such a One as Keats has become part of is the
passionate desire with which the poem closes:

> I am borne darkly, fearfully, afar;
> Whilst, burning through the inmost veil of Heaven,
> The soul of Adonais, like a star,
> Beacons from the abode where the Eternal are.

The *Hellas* of 1822 is a shorter lyrical drama than the
Prometheus.   Its model is the *Persae* of Aeschylus—a drama of
waiting and the arrival of messengers with conflicting news
of the warfare, the whole interspersed with choral odes.   Some
of these are the best that Shelley ever wrote, notably that on
Christianity which he was beginning to see as a development,
if not (so his note emphasises) a final development of much

that was best in Hellenic thought. But more and more Shelley's line of escape was moving in the direction of transcendental idealism, little as he may have known of the German philosophers. Thought is the ultimate and only reality:

> Thought
> Alone, and its quick elements, Will, Passion,
> Reason, Imagination, cannot die;
> They are, what that which they regard appears,
> The stuff whence mutability can weave
> All that it has dominion o'er—worlds, worms,
> Empires, and superstitions. What has thought
> To do with time, or place, or circumstance?

And so Hellas, in virtue of the seminal thoughts which she bequeathed to the world, is not something which was and is gone; she is still alive and active:

> Greece and her foundations are
> Built below the tide of war,
> Based on the crystalline sea
> Of thought and its eternity.

The temporary defeat of the Greek cause turns Shelley's thought towards America, as the land of freedom; but the final song is in the spirit of Shelley's most eloquent lyrics of sorrow, a reminder once more that the sorrow is not purely personal, but is a lament for unfulfilled and apparently hopeless ideals:

> Oh, cease! must hate and death return?
> Cease! must men kill and die?
> Cease! drain not to its dregs the urn
> Of bitter prophecy.
> The world is weary of the past,
> Oh, might it die or rest at last!

That Shelley was himself beginning to feel there was something amiss in human life which no political revolution on Godwinian lines, no mere deliverance from kings and priests and foreign tyrants would heal, is obvious, as we have said, in the closing stanzas of *Adonais*, while it is the main theme of the strange fragment which he left unfinished, *The Triumph of Life*, with its significant close:

> "Then what is life?" I cried.

Shelley's experiment here in the terza rima, like that of other English poets, was not based on a sufficiently close study of

Dante's verse. Instead of each triplet closing more or less completely, he used the run-on movement of the poems in rhyming couplets or blank verse, with an effect which is somewhat giddying.

In satire, for which Shelley had not much natural aptitude, his closest approximation to success is the parody on Wordsworth's *Peter Bell*. The *Letter to Maria Gisborne* illustrates, like the earlier *Julian and Maddalo*, his ability to write in the manner of easy, natural, yet poetical conversation. In sharp contrast to these attempts at a more mundane style is *The Witch of Atlas*, the most elaborate and delightful poem of pure escape, of fancy weaving a myth of deliverance from all Shelley's imagined troubles, personal and human, composed in the ottava rima of Byron's latest and best poems. If less masculine than Byron's, Shelley's stanzas are not less natural and easy, and infinitely more delicately musical.

Whatever may be the fate of Shelley's longer poems, philosophic or would-be philosophic, it is impossible to believe that he will ever be otherwise regarded than as one of the greatest of English lyrical poets. Yet it was late before he found his special gift. The first unmistakably Shelleyan lyric, Shelleyan at once in its poignant note of self-pity and its mastery of metre and form, is the *Stanzas Written in 1814*:

> Away! the moor is dark beneath the moon,
> Rapid clouds have drank the last pale beam of even.

In 1815 came "We are as clouds that veil the midnight moon", the beautiful *A Summer Evening Churchyard, Lechlade, Gloucestershire*, and the equally characteristic *Hymn to Intellectual Beauty*, the earliest appearance of a Platonic note in Shelley's poetry:

> The awful shadow of some unseen Power
> Floats, though unseen, among us.

But the best of Shelley's songs, as of his longer poems, were composed in Italy, the *Invocation to Misery* and *Stanzas Written in Dejection near Naples*, both of the same year as *The Cenci* (1818). To 1819 belongs *The West Wind*, in which Shelley combined the Italian terza rima with the construction of the Shakespearian sonnet, for the poignancy of Shelley's lyrics is not more remarkable than the variety of his emotionally effective stanzas. To 1820 belong his chief nature lyrics,—*The Sensi-*

tive Plant, The Cloud, To a Skylark, Autumn: a Dirge, The Question, the stately *Hymn of Apollo,* and the more wonderful *Hymn of Pan.* Wordsworth had seen in Nature, or thought he saw, the happiness which flows from the untroubled acceptance of the law of one's being. To Shelley natural things, clouds and birds, seemed to enjoy the entire emancipation from all constraints of law and convention for which his own spirit craved; but he could also, as in *Autumn,* find in Nature the reflection of his own passing melancholy moods. In 1821 a slight change came over the tone of these shorter lyrics. The predominant note is that of a piercing, yet a more resigned and controlled, sorrow:—"Orphan hours, the year is dead", "Swiftly walk over the western wave", "Far, far away, oh, ye Halcyons of Memory", "Rarely, rarely comest thou, spirit of delight",

> O world! O life! O time!
> On whose last steps I climb,
> Trembling at that where I had stood before;
> When will return the glory of your prime?
> No more—Oh, never more!

In the love-songs the tone of a singer blends with that of one who talks in gentle winning accents:

> One word is too often profaned
> For me to profane it,
>
> Do you not hear the Aziola cry?
>
> The serpent is shut out from Paradise,
>
> When the lamp is shattered
> The light in the dust lies dead,

and *To Jane: The Recollection,* that delicate and vivid record of a day of "peace in Shelley's mind". Minute criticism, as of faulty rhymes or occasional vagueness of meaning, is of no avail when applied to poems of such unique beauty, spiritual and formal, and of such entire originality, lyrics unique not alone in English but one might almost say in European literature, which have, though their full recognition had to await the subsidence of the Byronic storm, exercised a penetrating influence on some of what is finest in the lyrical poetry of the Continent.

It may be that Shelley's poetry stands less high in recent English estimation than it did even before the war. To Saintsbury, who detested Shelley's politics, he was nevertheless the quintessential poet; to Herford, witness the chapter in the *Cambridge History of Literature*, as to A. C. Bradley and Gilbert Murray, he was still both poet and prophet. The poets of to-day are not lyrical. For them the long-enduring connection between poetry and song is broken. Insensible to the lyrical music of Shelley's poems, they have, not inexplicably, fastened their attention on his defects as a thinker. To deny thought to Shelley altogether is of course unjust, but he is a fitful thinker, unable either to work out a dominant idea to its full implication or to subject the impulses of his single-track mind to adequate criticism. Nevertheless it is not only the musical ecstasy of his lyrical poetry as poetry which gained for him so marked an influence at home and abroad. It is the spirit of that poetry, the fact that in it he has given rapt and musical expression to a profound longing of the human heart, obscured but not extinguished in the hardest, the most cynical of realists, the spirit which sent Byron to Greece, and which in manifold, if also on the face of them often absurd, forms carries on the unceasing warfare with cruelty and stupidity, which were never more predominant than at the present moment.

Chapter Twenty-Nine

KEATS

O latest born and loveliest vision far
Of all Olympus' faded hierarchy!

SO Keats hails Psyche, and so one feels inclined to hail Keats himself.   He was the last of the great Romantics to be born (in 1795, the same year as Thomas Carlyle) and the first to die. His early death was the greatest loss that English poetry ever sustained.   When he died, at twenty-five, he had written *Lamia, Isabella, The Eve of St. Agnes, The Eve of St. Mark,* and *Hyperion,* besides four of the finest sonnets, five of the greatest odes, and one of the finest ballads in the English language.   A marvellous performance! and more marvellous still when we look closer into the facts.   Keats was not exceptionally precocious.   He published nothing till he was nearly twenty-two; and for the last thirteen months of his life he was a dying man, sunk too deep in sickness and despair to write any poetry except one great sonnet, composed on the small, comfortless ship that carried him and Severn to Italy: "Bright star, would I were steadfast as thou art".   Except that sonnet, and one early sonnet on Chapman's *Homer,* all the master-pieces mentioned above were written in twenty months, between February 1818 and October 1819.   Well might Tennyson say, "Keats with his high spiritual vision would have been, if he had lived, the greatest of us all."   It is of course possible that the disease which carried him off, and the passion of love which simultaneously consumed him, may have quickened this astonishing efflorescence, and that his genius might have faded as speedily as it flowered.   But of the direction in which his work might have developed more will be said later.

In contradistinction to Shelley's early rather feverish taste for the terror novel of the day, the hidden mysteries of chemistry, and Utopian political theories, is John Keats's early and eager delight in poetry for the sake of poetry.   No poet has left on record in verse and in prose letters a fresher picture of the period when a young man discovers the charm of poetry. It was in the spirit of discovery that Keats revelled in *The*

Faerie Queene and phrases like "sea-shouldering whales" and described in a sonnet the joy with which he walked home while "keen fitful gusts are whispering here and there" and "the stars look very cold about the sky", but can feel nothing except the memory of hours spent in congenial company reading Milton's *Lycidas* and Petrarch's sonnets to Laura. "Whenever you write", he tells Reynolds in 1817, "say a word or two on some passage in Shakespeare that may have come rather new to you which must be continually happening . . . for instance the following from *The Tempest* never struck me so forcibly as at present: Urchins

> Shall for the vast of night that they may work
> All exercise on thee . . .

How can I help bringing to your mind the line

> In the dark backward and abysm of time?

I find I cannot exist without poetry—without eternal poetry—half the day will not do it—the whole of it—I begin with a little, but habit has made me a Leviathan." Again he writes: "One of the three books I have with me is Shakespeare's Poems; I never found so many beauties in the Sonnets—they seem to be full of fine things said unintentionally—in the intensity of working out conceits. Is this to be borne? Hark ye!—

> When lofty trees I see barren of leaves,
>   Which erst from heat did canopy the herd,
> And Summer's green all girded up in sheaves,
>   Borne on the bier with white and bristly beard.

He has left nothing to say about nothing or anything: for look at snails—you know where he talks about 'cockled snails'—well in one of these sonnets[1] he says:

> As the snail, whose tender horns being hit,
>   Shrinks back into his shelly cave with pain,
> And there all smothered up in shade doth sit,
>   Long after fearing to put forth again:
> So at his bloody view her eyes are fled
> Into the deep, dark Cabins of her head.

He overwhelms a genuine lover of poesy with all manner of abuse, talking about

> a poet's rage,
> And stretched metre of an antique song

[1] Keats corrects this to *Venus and Adonis*.

which, by the bye, will be a capital motto for my poem, won't it?—and 'April's first-born flowers'—and 'Death's eternal cold'." Keats was not, of course, the only person delighting in the rediscovery of the wealth of imagery in our older poetry, and the felicity of phrase. There were Lamb and Hazlitt, to say nothing of Coleridge and many lesser names. But Keats read as a poet conscious of his own creative impulse. "I had become all in a tremble from not having written anything of late—the Sonnet overleaf did me good. I slept the better last night for it—this morning, however, I am nearly as bad again. Just now I opened Spenser, and the first lines I saw were these:

> The noble heart that harbours virtuous thought
> And is with child of glorious intent
> Can never rest until it forth have brought
> The eternal brood of glory excellent."

To Shelley poetry was from the first a vehicle for his passionate polemic, his Utopian enthusiasm:

> Drive my dead thoughts over the Universe
> Like withered leaves to quicken a new birth.

To Keats poetry was an art to be mastered, an art in which his masters were the English poets of an age greater than that of Pope and his followers, and which was an end in itself, poetry for poetry's sake. In protest against the didactic, hortatory strain which he detects in Wordsworth he declares boldly for the detachment of the poet, his imaginative interest in every aspect of life,—an Iago as well as an Imogen. "We hate poetry that has a palpable design upon us . . . poetry should be great and unobtrusive, a thing which enters into one's soul and does not startle it or amaze it with itself—but with its subject." "I think poetry should surprise by a fine excess, and not by singularity. It should strike the reader as a wording of his own highest thoughts and appear almost as a remembrance. Its touches of beauty should never be half-way, thereby making the reader breathless instead of content. The rise, the progress, the setting of imagery should, like the sun, come natural to him, shine over him and set soberly although in magnificence, leaving him in the luxury of twilight." It would be hard to find a better description than those last two sentences of the effect achieved in the great odes of his last volume.

Approaching poetry in the spirit of a poet, more entirely

than any of his contemporaries, except it be Coleridge in the months in which he wrote his few perfect poems, Keats's earliest experiments are not the lyrics, so often a poet's first essays. He was never to be quite the pure singer, the Aeolian harp responding to the breath of the spirit, that Blake and Shelley were. Like Shakespeare's two poems, Keats's are narrative-descriptive poems, poems in which the narrative and dramatic elements are overburdened by a wealth of description and imagery. It is seldom, however, that a young poet derives from one of an earlier century the direct impulse to write. That comes generally from some contemporary who has already blazed a track: a Marlowe, or Spenser or Dryden, in John Keats's case Leigh Hunt. It was from *The Story of Rimini*, in its original version of 1816, that Keats caught the first notes of the style that, always growing richer and maturer, was to be his own. For Leigh Hunt in that poem did add a definite quality to the varied music and picture of the poetry inspired by the life and beauty of Nature. He is the earliest herald of the Pre-Raphaelite manner to which Keats was to contribute most distinctively in *The Eve of St. Mark*. The predominant feature of Hunt's descriptions is the poet's enthusiastic sensuous delight in small, easily overlooked details in the object described. What the later group of poets did was to make these details of a significance more emotional than sensuous. Wordsworth had indeed led the way in a quite conscious and declared endeavour to supply the deficiency of earlier poets in the noting of the infinite variety of natural appearances. But Wordsworth's detailed descriptions in the two early poems are some of them more prosaic and factual, others touch a deeper, more spiritual note. For Hunt, and still more for Keats, the predominant, perhaps the sole, interest is sensuous beauty.

As a dramatic telling of the story, presented with such dramatic and condensed power by Dante, Hunt's tale has the glaring faults of taste which earned for himself and Keats the title of the Cockney School of Poets, but the descriptive parts have freshness and charm, a joy in the sensuous, aesthetic aspects of a scene that is new in the landscape poetry of the tradition which runs from Thomson and Dyer to Cowper and the early Wordsworth:

> The sun is up, it is a morn in May
> Round old Ravenna's clear-shown towers and bay,

A morn the loveliest which the year has seen,
Last of the Spring yet fresh with all its green;
For a warm eve, and gentle rain at night
Had left a sparkling welcome for the light,
And there's a crystal clearness all about;
The leaves are sharp, the distant hills look out;
The smoke goes dancing from the cottage trees,
And when you listen you may hear a coil
Of bubbling springs about the grassy soil,
And all the scene in short—sky, earth and sea
Breathes like a face that laughs out openly.

And see the later description of the wood through which the returning betrothal troop have to pass:

It was a lovely evening, fit to close
A lovely day, and brilliant in repose,
Warm, but not dim, a glow was in the air,
The soften'd breeze came smoothing here and there;
And every tree in passing one by one
Gleamed out with twinkles of the golden sun, etc.

It was this sensuous, enthusiastic vein in Hunt's descriptions of Nature which delighted the young admirer of Spenser. All that is best in the volume of 1817 is inspired by Hunt, and the rapid progress which Keats's poems reveal was in the mastery of this, in Arnold's phrase, "natural magic". But from the outset Keats displayed the greater wealth of his sensuous endowment. His organic sensibility, that diffused consciousness of physical well-being which, with the tendency that Hume emphasises of the human mind "to spread itself on external objects", gives in an imaginative mind life and personality to the objects described, is less strong in Keats than in Wordsworth and Shelley. But he surpasses them both in the acuteness of his special senses. To illustrate from his maturer poems consider the verse from the *Ode to a Nightingale*:

I cannot see what flowers are at my feet,
    Nor what soft *incense* hangs upon the boughs;
But, in *embalmed* darkness, guess each *sweet*
    Wherewith the seasonable month endows
    The grass, the thicket, and the fruit-tree wild,
White hawthorn and the pastoral eglantine,
Fast fading violets covered up in leaves,
    And mid-May's eldest child,
The coming musk-rose, full of dewy *wine*,
    The *murmurous* haunt of flies on summer eves.

Scent, warmth, colour, taste, sound—all are woven in.   Or
again:

> O, for a draught of vintage! that hath been
> Cool'd a long age in the deep-delved earth;

or the description of the banquet set forth for the sleeping
Madeline in *The Eve of St. Agnes*, appealing by the smoothness
of the fruits to the sense of touch, as by their suggested sweetness to the taste:

> Of *candied* apple, quince, and plum, and gourd,
> With *jellies* soother than the *creamy curd*.

It is the acuteness of these less intellectual senses in Keats that
has laid him open to the charge of being merely a sensuous
poet.   But carry on the last two quotations a little farther:

> O, for a draught of vintage . . .
> Tasting of Flora and the country green,
> Dance, and Provençal song, and sunburnt mirth.
>
> Of candied apple. . . .
> Manna and dates, in argosy transferr'd
> From Fez; and spiced dainties, every one,
> From silken Samarcand to cedar'd Lebanon.

His senses, we perceive, are the servants, not the masters, of
his imagination.

It is this approach to poetry as an art rather than a vehicle
for prophecy that accounts for the marked distinction between
the diction of Keats and that of either Wordsworth or Shelley.
He escapes in fact more entirely than Wordsworth from that
periphrastic, "pseudo-poetic diction" which Wordsworth condemned but succumbed to not infrequently, "female" for
"woman", "itinerant vehicle", and the like.   But Keats quite
consciously uses language as Spenser and the Elizabethans and
Milton had used it, as one who is free of it, not confined to the
"language of the age", but at liberty to revive old words that
have taken one's fancy, to coin words, and not only, like all
poets, fresh compounds but epithets and verbs, to make verbs
of nouns and nouns of verbs, free of the order of words, the
epithet after the noun, etc. etc.   A glance at the glossary to
Professor de Selincourt's admirable edition will show to what
extent he robbed the older poets of their sweets—Chaucer,
Spenser, Shakespeare, Chapman, Browne, even Thomson.   He
is like these one of the shapers of our poetic diction.   But in

this quest for a diction to his taste he is guided by the colour, the atmosphere which he wishes to give to the poem as a whole, his narrative of mythical ages or past history. In the sonnets, where he is expressing his own feelings, the diction will be found simpler, more "such as men do use".

The Story of Rimini was issued early in 1816. Keats had read it before he composed the epistle *To Charles Cowden Clark* in September. In May of that year Hunt printed in the *Examiner* Keats's sonnet:

> O Solitude! if I must with thee dwell,

and in October his first really great sonnet:

> Much have I travell'd in the realms of gold,

inspired by the reading of Chapman's *Homer*. In that month the two poets met, and before the end of the year Keats had written the two poems of the 1817 volume most directly inspired by Hunt's exuberant enthusiasm for lovely things: "I stood tip-toe upon a little hill" and *Sleep and Poetry*. If the undated *Specimen of an Induction* and *Calidore* were not written in the same months, they express the same mood and abound in the same fine sensuous felicities:

> the sweet buds which with modest pride
> Pull droopingly in *slanting curve aside*
> Their scantly leav'd and finely tapering stems.

The poet who tells how

> I must tell a tale of chivalry
> For while I muse, *the lance points slantingly*
> *Athwart the morning air*; some lady sweet
> Who *cannot feel for cold her tender feet*
> From the worn top of some old battlement
> Hails it with tears,

is the same as will later with more finished art tell how Madeline

> Unclasps her *warmèd* jewels one by one.

In *Sleep and Poetry*, written in Hunt's house, Keats adumbrates his ambitions as a poet, his joy in the new poetry which has come back to England after the reign of Pope and the doctrines of Boileau:

> All hail delightful hopes!
> As she was wont, th' imagination

Into most lovely labyrinths will be gone,
And they shall be accounted poet kings
Who simply tell the most heart-easing things.

That is the ideal of Hunt, and of Keats in this early poetry. But the poet must move on to higher tasks:

Yes, I must pass them for a nobler life
Where I may find the agonies, the strife
Of human hearts.

This strain of thought was to run through all Keats's letters, the consciousness that he had not yet attained to the highest themes, that the sensuous felicity of his work in which the poems from 1817 to 1820 show a continuous advance, culminating in the perfection of the great odes, was not the final goal of a poet. But two different conceptions of what that higher achievement was to consist in, seem to have been to some extent confounded in his mind. The one is that exemplified in the development of Shakespeare's art, as dramatist and poet, when he passed from the early comedies with the sensuous charm of their poetic flights—"I know a bank where the wild thyme blows" or "How sweet the moonlight sleeps upon this bank", and endless other passages—to the tragedies with their homely but startling phrases and imagery:

And my poor fool is hang'd! No, no, no life!
Why should a dog, a horse, a rat, have life
And thou no breath at all?

The development is that of the poet *as* poet whose vision of life grows wider and deeper, bringing with it a corresponding change in the technique of style and verse. But the poet makes no claim to be a prophet or teacher. Any lesson or philosophy the poem may convey flows directly from the picture of life presented or adumbrated. And no one has described better than Keats what one feels was the character of such an imagination as that of Shakespeare. It is contained in the letter to his friend Woodhouse of October 27, 1818, a letter on the poetical character as "distinguished from the Wordsworthian or egotistical sublime". The poetical character, as he finds it in Shakespeare and himself, "is not itself—it has no self. It is everything and nothing—it has no character—it enjoys light and shade; it lives in gusto, be it foul or fair, high or low, rich or poor, mean or elevated. It has as much delight in conceiving an Iago as an Imogen. What shocks

BB

the virtuous philosopher delights the chameleon poet. It takes no harm from the relish of the dark side of things, any more than from its taste for the bright one, because they both end in speculation. A poet is the most unpoetical of any thing in existence, because he has no identity—he is continually in, for, and filling some other body." That is the Keats of *Isabella, or The Pot of Basil*, and *The Eve of St. Agnes* and *Lamia*—to say nothing of the Odes and *La Belle Dame sans Merci*. But into the conception of his two most ambitious poems, *Endymion* and the incomplete *Hyperion*, there enters another idea of the poet's development, his duty, his mission, an ideal which both attracted and repelled Keats. He could not help disliking it in Wordsworth, and it made him unable to do justice to the poetry of Shelley. It is the idea that the poet must be also the prophet, at least a teacher, his great work a poem "doctrinal to a nation". It was hard for Keats to escape from such a conception of the poet's goal in an age of active humanitarianism. Moreover the two poets who had excited Keats's early admiration, Spenser and Milton, had both written with such great didactic ends in view, if one may doubt whether this was the element in their poems which delighted the young poet. But the prophet as well as the poet must be born. The wish to be a teacher, pressed upon him by his admiring readers, was responsible for what has proved most open to later criticism in the poetry of Tennyson, especially in the poetry of his middle period. For the danger which besets the too deliberately, too self-consciously ethical or religious poet, is that he is tempted to express what he thinks he ought to feel as well as what he actually does feel.

That the *Endymion*, with which in 1818 Keats followed up his first volume, is an allegory is clear enough to every reader, an allegory Spenserian not in the use of abstractions but by the blend of diverse stories and the predominant sweetness and decoration of the style. What lesson the poet meant to inculcate is also fairly clear. It is that already hinted at in *Sleep and Poetry*: Endymion's quest of the ideal in love and beauty is not to be realised until into his conception has entered by sympathy an understanding of the human heart, the simpler affections. That is the end of the quest which has carried him over and under the earth and under the sea. But neither the lesson which is indicated rather than deeply felt, nor the chaotic story which on the dramatic, the emotional side has the

faults of the Cockney School, the too great readiness to swoon
in the ecstasies of love, is the real interest in the poem.   It is
the poetry.   There are poems which we approve, even admire,
yet are apt, in Dr. Johnson's phrase, to lay down and forget to
take up again.   *Endymion* is rather the poem in which every
critic can detect the faults but in which a young, genuine lover
of poetry will always find much to delight him.   Keats has
taken over from Hunt, not only the easy movement and even
too abundant overflow of the decasyllabic couplet but, as in the
first volume, a good deal of his descriptive manner strengthened
and enriched.   In the rejected passages which Mr. Garrod
prints in the notes one can see the younger poet substituting
for a too Huntian description a finer rendering of his own; and
it is these scattered passages that abide in the memory.   There
are the opening lines, and following them the whole scene of
the sacrifice in which Keats has interwoven the beauties of
natural scenery with the beauty of Greek life as he conceived
it in a manner which he was to bring to perfection in the *Ode
on a Grecian Urn*.   It was doubtless from the Elizabethans that
Keats derived some of his enthusiasm for the Greek myths and
the opportunity they offered to the poet for a rehandling of his
own.   But the picture of Greek life which shaped itself in his
imagination must, we think, have owed something from the
very outset to what he saw of Greek art as much as to anything
he read.   Then there is the *Hymn to Pan* which Wordsworth
characterised as a "pretty piece of Paganism", which it is and
is not.   There is more than one thread in the web.   But it is
surpassed by the Indian maiden's song and the description,
suggested by Titian's picture, of the Bacchic procession:

> And as I sat, over the light blue hills
> There came a noise of revellers: the rills
> Into the wide stream came of purple hue—
> > 'Twas Bacchus and his crew!
> The earnest trumpet spake, and silver thrills
> From kissing cymbals made a merry din—
> > 'Twas Bacchus and his kin!
> Like to a moving vintage down they came,
> Crown'd with green leaves, and faces all on flame;
> All madly dancing through the pleasant valley,
> > To scare thee, Melancholy!

And there are little spots of description the felicity of which
engraves them on the memory:

Hereat, she vanished from Endymion's gaze,
Who brooded o'er the water in amaze:
The dashing fount pour'd on, and where its pool
Lay, half asleep, in grass and rushes cool,
Quick waterflies and gnats were sporting still,
And fish were dimpling, as if good nor ill
Had fallen out that hour.

With all its faults, and they are abundant, there is more of the quintessence of poetry in *Endymion* than in the early poems of any of his contemporaries except it be Blake.

If *Endymion* is somewhat of a Spenserian allegory, a poem with a moral about which one does not much trouble oneself while enjoying the poetry, *Hyperion*, which he began after turning aside to compose *Isabella*, his first story pure and simple, was conceived and begun on Miltonic lines, an epic in blank verse on a war in Heaven, opening in the middle of the action and among the fallen in the combat—just so opens *Paradise Lost*. And the amazing advance in power of conception and in command of language and verse was at once to impress even his most sceptical readers and critics. But after he had got as far as the first apparition of Apollo, Keats seems to have realised that for the kind of conflict and development which he wished to adumbrate the most suitable medium was not the Homeric-Virgilian epic, of which the central theme is war. The effort to tread in Milton's steps had also, he felt, given his style too artificial a cast. In his reaction from Milton's Latinisms he was tempted to declare that Chatterton was the model of pure English: "The *Paradise Lost*, though so fine in itself, is a corruption of our language. It should be kept as it is—unique, a curiosity, a beautiful and grand curiosity, the most remarkable production of the world; a northern dialect accommodating itself to Greek and Latin inversions and intonations. The purest English, I think—or what ought to be the purest—is Chatterton's. . . . Chatterton's language is entirely northern. I prefer the native music of it to Milton's cut by feet. I have but lately stood on my guard against Milton. Life to him would be death to me. Miltonic verse cannot be written but as the verse of art. I wish to devote myself to another verse alone." Keats was no Middle English scholar, but by "northern" he did not mean a North English dialect but simply that English is a non-Mediterranean tongue. In verse he has in view the accent as the basis

of English verse, not a time-foot.   But Milton was not unaware
of the importance of accent despite his attempt to accommodate its use to the syllabic foot, witness his rules for slurring.
Chatterton Keats did not take as his model, but during or after
his tour in Scotland he read Cary's translation of the *Divine
Comedy*, and with that in mind and ear he began an introduction to the poem which was to make of it, not a Miltonic epic,
but a vision of life to which none might have access but those

> to whom the miseries of the world
> Are misery and will not let them rest.

But a word of that later; for with *Isabella, or The Pot of Basil*
Keats had entered on that other path of development, more
natural to his genius as a poet whose function was not to preach
but to communicate an ever fuller and deeper vision of the
tragic mystery and beauty of life, the path of Shakespeare, not
of Wordsworth or Milton, the path that had led, not to a
Paradise Lost or *Regained* or an *Excursion*, but to *King Lear*
and *The Tempest*.   This was Keats's first attempt to tell a tragic
story pure and simple, unburdened by any message.   Two
models were at least in the background of his mind, first, the
Elizabethans who as tellers of story in verse did not achieve
such a perfect accommodation of the style and verse to the
story as Chaucer had done, because all of them, including
Shakespeare, were disposed to overlay the dramatic interest by
a too elaborate garment of conceit and phrase; and secondly,
Chaucer in those of his tales, such as the tales of Constance and
Griseldis, in which the poet becomes himself a sympathetic
chorus commenting on the tragic significance of the incident:

> O queenes living in prosperitee,
> Duchesses and ye ladies everichone,
> Haveth some routh on *hir* adversitee;
> An emperoures dohter stant alone,
> She hath no wight to whom to make hir mone.
> O blood royal, that stondest in this drede,
> Far ben thy freendes at thy grete nede.

Just so Keats comments on the various turns of his story:

> O Melancholy, linger here awhile!
> O Music, Music, breathe despondingly! etc.

There is more of human sympathy and feeling in the poem
than in *Endymion* where the only effective suggestion of real

flesh and blood is to be found in the relation of Endymion and his sister Peona. Yet a story told just in this way, whether by Chaucer or Keats, achieves pathos rather than tragic force. The verse, the ottava rima, is managed with some inequality.

In *The Eve of St. Agnes*, to which he turned on laying aside the fragment of *Hyperion*, he chose a simpler theme, a more single central emotion. It is, with the Odes, the supremely successful example of his sensuously decorative manner because, for one thing, the central emotion is not of a kind to demand a more nakedly poignant treatment. The theme has two sources, a popular superstition regarding St. Agnes' Eve, and the theme, treated tragically by Shakespeare in *Romeo and Juliet*, gaily by Scott in *Young Lochinvar*, a passion which transcends the barriers of a family feud. Like Scott's, Keats's story ends happily, but the passion is interesting mainly for the warmth and colour which it lends to the descriptive, sensuous detail rich in all the devices of contrast and harmony —the cold of the night and "the poppied warmth of sleep", the noise of storm without and revelry within against the silence of the chamber:

> The boisterous, midnight, festive clarion,
> The kettle-drum and far-heard clarinet,
> Affray his ears, though but in dying tone:—
> The hall-door shuts again, and all the noise is gone.

The colours of the window which are shed on the kneeling maiden as she prays, the fruits piled for a feast which never takes place, all combine in a wealth of sensuous impression almost unique in English poetry, if there is more of passion in the *Hero and Leander* of Marlowe with which Swinburne compared and contrasted it.

The third and last of these verse tales was *Lamia* composed in the summer and autumn of 1819. The source of the story is Burton's *Anatomy of Melancholy*. For the form and handling of the rhyming decasyllabic couplet Keats turned from Hunt to the Dryden of the *Fables*, whence the more restrained overflow, the occasional weighting of the verse by an Alexandrine or a rhyming triplet. It is the best told of the tales, moving better from point to point, with less of decoration for its own sake and less of the eloquent sympathetic accompaniment of *Isabella*; but that the significance of the whole is deeper, more charged with the poet's personal sense of the tragedy of life and love, is not clear to us. The most distinctive note is perhaps the almost petulant complaint of the hopeless contrast between life as the heart and imagination would envisage it and the stern facts as science and philosophy reveal them. Like all the Romantics, Keats is a poet of escape; but the arts exist to provide an escape without which life would be even less tolerable than it is.

The year 1819 marked the culmination of Keats's productive work. In 1818 he had composed, and forwarded to his brother and sister in America, the most delightful of his lighter poems in octosyllabic verse: *Robin Hood*, *Lines on the Mermaid Tavern*, *Fancy*, and *Bards of Passion and of Mirth*; and had written the fragmentary *Ode to Maia*. But to 1819 belong the five great odes, to say nothing of that to *Indolence*. The Odes are the last and most perfect product of what might have come to be described as Keats's early manner, had life and his genius permitted such a transition as was Shakespeare's from the decorative imagery, natural and mythological of (say) *A Midsummer Night's Dream* or *The Merchant of Venice* to the more dramatic, realistic imagery of *Hamlet* and *Macbeth*.

The form given to the stanzas of the Odes was reached through experiments in the sonnet. And what of their comparative merits? It is difficult to say, each is so unique. *The Nightingale* is the most passionate strain of song. *Autumn* is surely the most perfect, or one of the most perfect, poems in the language, with its wonderful double evolution, the rising of the passionate movement in the second stanza marked by the transition from concrete description to transfiguring personification, and that followed in the final stanza by the return to the calmer rendering of objective details:

> Hedge-crickets sing; and now with treble soft
> The red-breast whistles from a garden croft,
>   And gathering swallows twitter in the skies.

But with this emotional rise and fall goes the passing of the season from autumn at the close of summer:

> And still more, later flowers for the bees,
> Until they think warm days will never cease,
>   For Summer has o'er-brimm'd their clammy cells,

to the time of reaping and gathering; and hence to autumn trembling on the verge of winter. The *Grecian Urn* is the

happiest stroke of invention, the sudden and surprising detachment of beauty from the flow of time and change. *Melancholy*
is a subtle Baudelairean expression of the mood in which
sensuous beauty is most deeply realised. *Psyche*, if artistically
less perfect than the others, is perhaps the most interesting,
the fullest expression of the profound charm exercised by the
Greek myths on Keats's imagination. No poet has felt so
deeply their radiant and suggestive beauty.

A lyrical poet pure and simple like Shelley and Blake,
Keats was not, but there is a charm of its own, not unlike
that of *L'Allegro* and *Il Penseroso*, in such meditative chants,
half songs, half chants in lyrical measures, as *Robin Hood* and
"In a drear-nighted December"; and his ballad *La Belle Dame
sans Merci* has in a fuller measure, because with more of passion
in it, the mysterious charm of Coleridge's *Christabel*.

What possible developments were in store for Keats had he
lived we shall never know, and it is vain to guess, but that there
was more in his mind than ever found expression in his verse
is clear from the letters, which, considering his age, his education, and environment, are of singular interest. With Lamb's
they seem to us the most interesting of any of the poets of
the period. They are not cluttered with wild theories like
Shelley's or pretentious metaphysics like Coleridge's, but they
are not less concerned with the problems of life. Of their
interest as revealing the purity and depth of his love for poetry
as poetry a word has already been said. They bear evidence
of his loyal and wise affection for his family, brothers and sister,
and his friends as Hunt and Haydon, and Reynolds and others.
He came to realise the faults which beset Hunt's work as
critic and adviser, but this is expressed, it must be remembered,
in letters not intended for the public eye, and his criticisms are
just. He could not, through his connection with Hunt and
the Liberal wing in politics, escape from the rather shallow
anti-Christian feeling and the Humanitarianism of the time.
The latter found expression, strangely enough, not only in
Endymion and the second *Hyperion* but in *Isabella*, strangely
because the feeling would have been incomprehensible to
Boccaccio, whose young men and women react to the plague in
Florence by retiring to a safe and beautiful retreat where they
may interchange charming, and not all very edifying, tales.
But Keats's central interest in life is religious, and certainly
not unchristian in feeling and hope; the misery of the world,

how is one to envisage it? "Were it in my choice I would reject a Petrarchal coronation on account of my dying day and because women have cancers." Like the rest of us he can but surmise, his guide the Imagination, which for him as for Wordsworth is the Reason in its highest workings. "I am certain of nothing but the holiness of the heart's affections and the truth of Imagination. What the Imagination seizes as beauty must be truth. . . . For I have the same idea of all our passions as of Love, they are all in their sublime creative of essential beauty." It is the Imagination alone which can adumbrate a solution of the problem of pain and death. "Well, I compare life to a Mansion of many apartments two of which I can only describe, the doors of the rest being as yet shut upon me. The first we step into we call the infant or thoughtless chamber, in which we remain so long as we do not think . . . but we are at length imperceptibly impelled by the awakening of the thinking principle within us—we no sooner get into the second chamber, which I will call the Chamber of Maiden Thought, than we become intoxicated with the light and the atmosphere, we see nothing but pleasant wonders, and think of delaying there for ever in delight: however, among the effects this breathing is father of is that tremendous one of sharpening one's vision into the heart and nature of Man—of convincing one's nerves that this world is full of Misery and Heartbreak, Pain, Sickness, and Oppression—whereby this Chamber of Maiden Thought becomes gradually darkened, and at the same time, on all sides of it, many doors are set open—all leading to dark passages— we see not the balance of good and evil—we are in a mist— we are now in that state—we feel the burden of the Mystery. To this point was Wordsworth come when he wrote *Tintern Abbey*." That is a singularly happy description of some of the phases and developments of a young man's experience who is capable of thinking. In Keats it led to no Godwinian or Shelleyan belief in human perfectibility: "But in truth I do not at all believe in this sort of perfectibility—the nature of the world will not admit of it—the inhabitants of the world will correspond to itself. . . . Look at the Poles and the Sands of Africa, whirlpools and volcanoes—let men exterminate them and I will say that they may arrive at earthly happiness. The point at which Man may arrive is as far as the parallel state in inanimate Nature, and no farther. . . . The common cognomen of this world among the misguided and superstitious is a vale of tears from which we are to be redeemed by a certain arbitrary interposition of God and taken to Heaven—what a little circumscribed notion! Call the world if you please the Vale of Soul-making. Then you will find out the use of the world (I am speaking now in the highest terms for human nature, admitting it to be immortal, which I will take for granted for the purpose of showing a thought which has struck me concerning it); I say *Soul-making*—Soul as distinguished from an Intelligence"—and so on he goes developing a thought which we venture to believe is closer to the best Christian thought of to-day than that which he sets aside. These are doubtless the thoughts of a young man letting his imagination play on the problem of life. How they might have been modified, or to what extent Keats would have found for them adequate expression in his poetry, it is impossible to say. The attempt to recast *Hyperion* shows that it was his wish to do so. Mr. Babbitt pronounces the attempt "a dismal failure". That is not the feeling of all Keats's readers.

Lastly there is another direction in which Keats's poetry shows some signs of development or at least of enlargement. Excepting in occasional sonnets his poetry was, almost as little as Shakespeare's, made the vehicle for his own passing experiences and the feelings they evoked. His poems are not, like Shelley's lyrics and even most of his longer poems, *Alastor*, the *Euganean Hills*, *The Witch of Atlas*, *Adonais*, the record of his own emotional reactions to this or that experience or mood of mind. Keats's poems are dominated by his great central passion for the abstract idea of beauty. "I never was in love," he writes to his friend Reynolds in September 1818, "yet the voice and shape of a woman has haunted me these two days. . . . This morning poetry has conquered—I have relapsed into those abstractions which are my only life—I feel escaped from a new, strange and threatening sorrow.—And I am thankful, for it is an awful warmth about my heart like a load of Immortality." "The roaring of the wind is my wife and the stars through the window-pane are my children. The mighty abstract idea I have of beauty in all things stifles the more divided and minute domestic happiness." It was but a few months later that a passionate love, and contemporaneously a final break in his health, came upon Keats, with the shattering effect reflected in his letters to Fanny Brawne, such pathetic lines as those *To Fanny*, and the last three of his sonnets. Given health and some good fortune, one can believe that a man of Keats's character, as shown in the letters we have cited, might have come through the personal experience back to an objective but a more comprehensive picture of human life and character.

Chapter Thirty

LANDOR TO TENNYSON

IN the same year as the *Lyrical Ballads* (1798) there was issued in Warwick, as a sixpenny pamphlet, a poem *Gebir*, which attracted little general attention, but caught the eye of Southey, himself then meditating epic poems on heroic and religious subjects. He reviewed the poem enthusiastically in the *Critical Review*. Through Southey Lamb got wind of it, and writes to Southey: "I have seen Gebor! Gebor aptly named from Geborish *quasi* Gibberish. But Gebor hath some lucid intervals. I remember darkly one beautiful simile veiled in uncouth phrases about the youngest daughter of the Ark." The simile thus cited is not the best of its kind:

> Never so eager when the world was waves
> Stood the less daughter of the Ark, and tried
> (Innocent this temptation) to recall
> With folded vest, and casting arm, the dove.

But the chief beauty of *Gebir*, as of most of what Landor was to write, is just these occasional moments, picturesque, sculpturesque, at their best dramatic. The poem as a whole is somewhat of a puzzle. Professedly an heroic poem, dealing with some shadowy invasion of Egypt, and including a not very impressive descent to Hell, its central themes are two love stories of a sentimental kind. The whole professes even to have a moral, "the folly, the injustice, the punishment of invasion", and combined with this an encouragement of the colonisation of empty lands. There are satirical sketches of kings, as George III, for whom Landor, like his later disciple Swinburne, had a Whiggish, aristocratic, somewhat empty scorn. But the interest of the poem is in the style and verse.

The author of *Gebir*, Walter Savage Landor (1775–1864), had already published, and withdrawn, a volume of Popean poems including an *Apology for Satire*, a *Moral Epistle*, and an *Abelard to Eloisa*, an imaginary reply to Pope's brilliant poem and in his style. In *Gebir* he swung over from the closed couplet to the varying cadence of a blank verse suggested by Milton and the classical poets, of whom he claimed Pindar as

his model: "If I could resemble Pindar in nothing else, I was
resolved to be as compendious and exclusive". The descriptive touches in *Gebir* show at times the close observation we
associate with Tennyson:

> Sweet airs of music ruled the rowing palms:
> Now rose they glistening and aslant reclined,
> Now they descended and with oné consent
> Plunging seem'd swift each other to pursue,
> And now to tremble wearied o'er the wave.

Just so Landor had seen the boats on the river at Oxford.
Others are more elaborately decorative:

> And the long moonbeams on the hard wet sand
> Lay like a jasper column half uprear'd;

and, perhaps the best known of all:

> But I have sinuous shells of pearly hue
> Within, and they that lustre have imbib'd
> In the sun's palace-porch, where when unyoked
> His chariot wheel stands midway in the wave:
> Shake one, and it awakens: then apply
> Its polish'd lips to your attentive ear,
> And it remembers its august abodes,
> And murmurs as the ocean murmurs there.

Speaking of his handwriting, Landor's biographer, John
Forster, comments on the identity of that in his earliest and his
latest letters. What is true of his handwriting is equally true
of his thought, feeling, and manner in style and verse. After
Gebir there is nothing that can be called development, no
expanding or deepening conception of Nature or beauty or
liberty or love as in the poetry of Wordsworth or Shelley or
Keats. He experimented in dramas, dramatic scenes, idylls,
and occasional lyrics, epigrams, and other short poems. Of
the dramas *Count Julian*, the most ambitious and best, is rather
a series of dramatic scenes than a dramatically developed story.
The subject is the story of the Spanish Count's revenge for
the violation of his daughter by the King, revenge taken by
bringing the Moors into Spain, as more recently German and
Italian mercenaries were brought into Spain to crush the freedom of that country. But the main action is over before
the play opens. He has conquered. Even such dramatic
moments as the discovery by the daughter's lover of what has
happened are not presented on the stage. What we have is a

successsion of scenes in which there is less of direct, passionate utterance than of imaginary conversations in the tone of passions recollected in tranquillity, interesting eddies and turns of thought, dramatic moments suggested by a statuesque pose, a felicitous image. Thought and style predominate over action:

>   too true! when love
> Scatters its brilliant foam, and passes on
> To some fresh object on its natural course,
> Widely and openly and wanderingly,
> 'Tis better; narrow it, and it pours its gloom
> In one fierce cataract that stuns the soul.

>   I touch the hand
> That chains down Fortune to the throne of Fate.

>   Ah, Sisabert,
> Wretched are those a woman has forgiven:
> With her forgiveness ne'er hath love return'd.

>   every germ
> Of virtue perishes, when love recedes
> From those hot shifting sands, a woman's heart.

Of the idylls which he composed throughout his lifetime, in Latin frequently to begin with, *Idyllia Heroica* (1814), *Hellenics* (1847), the best are *Iphigenia* and *The Death of Artemidora*; but there are many and they are generally readable in their peculiar way, which is the way described above—statuesque scenes of dramatic import. To almost the last moment Iphigenia can plead in a persuasive and pathetic rather than passionate strain. Then:

> A groan that shook him shook not his resolve.
> An aged man now entered, and without
> One word stept slowly on, and took the wrist
> Of the pale maiden. She looked up and saw
> The fillet of the priest and calm, cold eyes.
> Then turned she where her parent stood, and cried:
> "O father, grieve no more; the ships can sail."

Such a command of style made Landor a master of occasional verses,—lyric, epigrammatic, elegiac, laudatory, or satirical: *e.g.* the delightful *Corinna to Tanagra*:

> Sweetly where cavern'd Dirce flows
>   Do whitearm'd maidens chant my lay,
> Flapping the while with laurel-rose
>   The honey gathering tribe away;

And sweetly, sweetly, Attick tongues
Lisp your Corinna's early songs;
To her with feet more graceful come
The verses that have dwelt in kindred breasts at home.

Oh, let thy children lean aslant
    Against the tender mother's knee,
And gaze into her face, and want
    To know what magic there can be
In words that urge some eyes to dance,
While others as in holy trance
Look up to heaven; be such my praise!
Why linger?   I must haste, or lose the Delphick bays.

Few anthologies lack the lovely *Rose Aylmer*, or the epigram so true to Landor's image of himself, so untrue to the facts of his stormy life:

I strove with none, for none was worth my strife;
    Nature I lov'd and next to nature art:
I warm'd both hands before the fire of life;
    It sinks, and I am ready to depart.

In a *Gradus ad Parnassum* which Byron drew up for himself in the year 1813 Scott stands at the head.   Rogers, Moore, and Campbell come next, followed by Southey, Wordsworth, and Coleridge: thereafter the many.   Of these Rogers and Southey have definitely fallen out.   Each is represented in the *Oxford Book of English Verse* by one poem.   Southey's is the lines on *His Books*.   To that one might add the quaintly effective *Battle of Blenheim*:

"Great praise the Duke of Marlborough won,
    And our good Prince Eugene."
"Why, 'twas a very wicked thing!"
    Said little Wilhelmine.
"Nay, nay, my little girl," quoth he.
"It was a famous victory."

Coleridge and Wordsworth were not the only writers of ballads on the supernatural in the closing years of the century. Southey was composing *Lord William*, *The Old Woman of Berkeley*, *Mary the Maid of the Inn*, and the like.   If the *Ancient Mariner* and *The Thorn* and *Peter Bell* illustrate complementary ways of approaching the subject, Southey's are an incontestable example of how *not* to attempt the supernatural story. He has been commended by Saintsbury for his bold use of the trisyllabic foot, but it is a very wooden-legged hop, step, and jump. Southey's epics evoked the scorn of Byron:

> Next see tremendous Thalaba come on,
> Arabia's monstrous, wild and wondrous son,
> Domdaniel's dread destroyer, who o'erthrew
> More mad magicians than the world e'er knew;

and one may doubt if even *Roderick* or *Madoc* is ever read to-day. Against this it is fair to set their early influence on Shelley, and Newman's "Southey's beautiful poem of *Thalaba* for which I had an immense liking". Perhaps the youth of the reader counted for something in each case. Certainly Shelley did not benefit either by Southey's example or by his advice later.

Of Rogers's poems the *Oxford Book of English Verse* cites *A Wish*:

> Mine be a cot beside the hill,

which is not beyond the range of many a minor poet. *The Pleasures of Memory* (1792) and *Italy* (1822) are more interesting in Turner's illustrations than in the poems: nor can *Human Life* be called exhilarating poetry. It would not be just to dismiss Thomas Moore (1779–1852) quite so readily, though certainly Southey's good sense and sound if limited morality and excellent prose give him claims to respect that one might hesitate to extend to the more popular poet and greater social success. It was a little hard for the author of *Thalaba* (1801) and *The Curse of Kehama* (1810) to see *Lalla Rookh* (1816) sold for three thousand pounds, paid before publication,—the same sum as was paid for Scott's *Rokeby*. Southey had to console himself with the thought that he wrote for posterity. But, if more readable than either Scott's poem or Southey's, Moore's has gone, and with it his *Loves of the Angels* (1823) and other poems. Such reputation as his poetry retains depends on the *Irish Melodies* (1807) and *National Airs* (1815), which made him once the Irish national poet *par excellence*. The perfect adaptation of the words to the music is a measure at once of their success and their limitations. Down at least to the present writers' generation some of the songs were among their early experiences of poetry: "Go where glory waits thee", "O breathe not his name", "When he who adores thee has left but a name", "The harp that once through Tara's halls", "She is far from the land where her young hero sleeps", "At the mid hour of night when stars are weeping I fly", "'Tis the last rose of summer", "The minstrel boy to the war is gone", "When first I met thee warm and young", "Oft in the stilly night", and others linger, if always with the memory of a tune too. Stephen Gwynn has claimed, not unjustly, that Moore used the triple foot with a lightness and confidence which no other poet had quite attained to; and he points out that in fitting words to the old tunes he reproduced the rhythms of Irish folk-song; and "in three of his songs he achieved a metrical effect wholly new in English":

> At the mid hour of night when stars are weeping I fly;

and again in

> The dream of those days when first I sung thee is o'er.

"The peculiarity of these metres—the dragging, wavering cadence that half baulks the ear—is the distinctive Irish manner." When, however, Moore's songs are detached from the music, or the memory of the music, their thinness is clear. It is often said that Burns's lyrics must be sung to be appreciated. That is not strictly true. Some of the best of them lose a good deal of their passionate quality when trilled by singers. Moore's have not the same passionate quality. Again, to put a lyric by Moore beside one by Shelley is to realise the difference between poetry lightened, simplified, to let music have its chance, and one whose music is internal and its own. Thomas Campbell too (1777–1844) has left one or two lyrics which once heard are not easily forgotten, lyrics less suggestive of a tune, more oratorical in cast, especially two: "Ye mariners of England" and "Of Nelson and the North". The form of the latter poem was criticised on its appearance, but to-day it is the compact line (suggested possibly by Cowper's "Toll for the brave") which keeps the poem alive. To these one may add *Lord Ullin's Daughter* with its very imaginative stanza:

> By this the storm grew loud apace.
> The water wraith was shrieking,
> And in the scowl of heaven *each face*
> *Grew dark as they were speaking,*

and last, but not least:

CC

On Linden when the sun was low
All bloodless lay the untrodden snow,
And dark as winter was the flow
  Of Iser rolling rapidly.

But Linden show'd another sight
When the drums beat at dead of night,
Commanding fires of death to light
  The darkness of her scenery.

The sensitive, not to say timid, poet had seen the field of battle from the walls of a monastery at Ratisbon, and was at Altona when the Danish fleet was made captive.

Both these poets belong to what might be called the school of Scott.   They wrote, leaving aside such survivals of didactic poetry as Campbell's *Pleasures of Hope*, tales in verse such as Campbell's *Gertrude of Wyoming*, reflective poems, patriotic songs, and songs akin to folk-songs.   None of them quite penetrated to the higher precincts in which Wordsworth, Coleridge, Shelley, and Keats lived and moved.

Of Scottish poets in Sir Walter's day the best known is probably James Hogg (1770–1835), the so-called Ettrick Shepherd.   In his *Domestic Manners of Sir Walter Scott* Hogg declares that he said to Scott apropos of some ballads: "Dear Sir Walter, ye can never suppose that I belong to your school of chivalry.   Ye are the king o' that school, but I am the king of the faery school, which is the higher ane nor (than) yours." Well, Scott made no great thing of the fairy world in *The Monastery*; but the merits of *Kilmeny* have perhaps been exaggerated.   It opens beautifully and ends well, but the central part is strangely confused.   Hogg has to our mind confounded to some extent two kinds of escape from this world of sorrows, escape to a world where there is no sin and all passions are absorbed in the love of God:

But it seemed as the harp of the sky had rung,
And the airs of heaven play'd round her tongue
When she spake of the lovely forms she had seen
In a land where sin had never been;

but with this is blended the idea of a world where the escape is not from sin but from law, the world of Yeats's *Wanderings of Oisin* or Shelley's *Witch of Atlas*:

But we in a lonely land abide
Unchainable as the dim tide,

With hearts that know nor law nor rule
And hands that hold no wearisome tool,
Folded in love that fears no morrow,
Nor the gray wandering osprey Sorrow.

And with all this are further blended obscure references to Scottish history. Of Hogg's songs the Jacobite are like Moore's, good to sing but not much otherwise. His ballads are too long and the humour is merely grotesque. In fact the editor of *Ward's English Poets* was not far wrong in confining his selection to one lyric which, like Mrs. Browning's "What was he doing, the great God Pan", deserves to live if all the rest were forgotten:

Where the pools are bright and deep,
Where the grey trout lies asleep,
Up the river and over the lea,
That's the way for Billy and me.

Where the blackbird sings the latest,
Where the hawthorn blooms the sweetest.
Where the nestlings chirp and flee,
That's the way for Billy and me.

Where the mowers mow the cleanest,
Where the hay lies thick and greenest,
There to track the homeward bee,
That's the way for Billy and me.

.   .   .   .

Why the boys should drive away
Little sweet maidens from their play,
Or love to banter and fight so well,
That's the thing I never could tell:

But this I know, I love to play
Through the meadow, among the hay;
Up the water and over the lea,
That's the way for Billy and me.

Hogg's Jacobitism was a literary pose. There is more real feeling in the Jacobite songs of Lady Nairne (1766–1845), of which "Will ye no come back again?" is perhaps the most famous. She had humour too as well as pathos; witness the delightful *Laird o' Cockpen*.

In 1816 there appeared the first edition of Leigh Hunt's *Story of Rimini*, the effect of which on Keats's verse was discussed in the preceding chapter. As a poet, in truth, Leigh

Hunt is memorable chiefly for his influence on Keats; as a critic he deserves our gratitude for his warm championship of the Romantics. Another work which we mentioned as influencing Keats, Henry Cary's translation of the *Divina Commedia*, appeared complete in 1814. Cary's *Dante*, like Chapman's *Homer*, is an English poem in its own right. No better blank verse had been written since Milton, though by choosing that medium Cary sacrificed the movement of the terza rima, with all that that movement conveys. His diction, on the other hand, in its plain severity, owes more to Dante than to Milton. The influence both of Cary's style and of his metre can be felt in *Hyperion*.

In 1835 Hogg died, and in one of the few tolerable poems of his later years Wordsworth records the roll of those who had passed away in the last three years: Hogg, Scott, Coleridge, Lamb, Crabbe, and Mrs. Hemans. The best lines are those which record the friend and inspiration of his earlier days:

> Nor has the rolling year twice measured
> From sign to sign its steadfast course,
> Since every mortal power of Coleridge
> Was frozen at its marvellous source;
>
> The rapt one of the godlike forehead,
> The heaven-eyed creature sleeps in earth:
> And Lamb the frolic and the gentle
> Has vanished from his lonely hearth.

And what of the younger poets who should have now been securely settled in their place? They alas! had died ten years earlier,—Keats in 1821, Shelley in 1822, and Byron in 1824: "whom the gods love die young". It was on rather a blank scene that a real lover of poetry looked round in 1835, for if Wordsworth was still alive and to be so for fifteen more years, the "romantic who made a good end", the poet in him was dead. Before we venture on the greater poets to whom the torch was to pass we may say a word on some whose promise was not quite fulfilled: John Clare, whose *Poems descriptive of Rural Life* appeared in 1820; Thomas Lovell Beddoes, *Improvisatore, Bride's Tragedy*, 1822; George Darley, *Errors of Ecstasy*, 1822, *Nepenthe*, 1825; Charles Jeremiah Wells, *Stories after Nature*, 1822, *Joseph and his Brethren*, 1824; Thomas Wade, *Tasso*, 1825; *Mundi et Cordis Carmina*, 1835; Thomas Hood, *Whims and Oddities*, 1826–1827, *Plea of the Midsummer*

Fairies, 1827. In immediate popularity they were all probably outshone by L. E. L. (Letitia Elizabeth Landon), of whose verse modern anthologies are destitute.

Another poetess often bracketed in her own day with L. E. L. was Felicia Hemans, whose death in 1835 was mourned by Wordsworth in the poem from which we have quoted:

> Mourn rather for that holy Spirit,
> Sweet as the Spring, as ocean deep;
> For Her who, ere her summer faded,
> Has sunk into a breathless sleep.

Some of Mrs. Hemans's poems were familiar to, and loved by, the present writers in early years. Her longer poems were, and are, unknown to us, and are never likely to be revived. But one or two of her lyrics, lyrics of sentiment rather than sentimental, had that in them which touched the imagination. Such was this stanza from *The Graves of a Household*:

> One midst the forests of the West,
>   By a dark stream, is laid;
> The Indian knows his place of rest
>   Far in the cedar's shade;

and this from *The Landing of the Pilgrim Fathers*:

> The ocean eagle soared
>   From his nest by the white wave's foam:
> And the rocking pines of the forest roared,—
>   This was their welcome home!

The interest of Mrs. Hemans's poetry, and not of hers alone, is social rather than purely literary. No one can judge aright of middle-class feeling in the Victorian Age and ignore such poetry altogether.

Time has shown that Clare made a small, but definite and distinguished, contribution to poetry that lives. There is something of Shelley, the sensitive Shelley who lamented his loneliness, loving Nature yet longing for human sympathy. The *Address to Plenty* is a pathetic arraignment of the evils of poverty, in the verse and even in the mood of *Lines Written Among the Euganean Hills*:

> Oh, sad sons of poverty,
> Victims doomed to misery;
> Who can paint what pain prevails
> O'er that heart which want assails?

·   ·   ·   ·

Oh, how blest amid those charms
I should bask in Fortune's arms.
She defying every frown
Hugs me on her downy breast,
Bids my head lie easy down
And on winter's ruins rest.
So upon the troubled sea,
Emblematic simile,
Birds are known to sit secure
While the billows roar and rave,
Slumbering in their safety sure,
Rock'd to sleep upon the wave.

Clare wrote some simple but lovely lyrics such as *Song's Eternity*, but the most moving of all are the lines written on his own desolate condition when confined to an asylum:

I am: yet what I am who cares to know?
My friends forsake me like a memory lost.

. . . . .

I long for scenes where never man has trod:
A place where woman never slept or wept;
There to abide with my creator God.
And sleep as I in childhood sweetly slept:
Untroubling and untroubled where I lie;
The grass below, above the vaulted sky.

The antithesis to Clare's simple but at times piercing lyrics are the exotic poems of Beddoes, probably the most promising of the poets before the emergence of the Victorians proper. He was the author of two tragedies in the Elizabethan manner as regards both incident and style: *The Bride's Tragedy* and *Death's Jestbook: or the Fool's Tragedy* (1850). Of the dramas as such Swinburne has said the last word: "Beddoes, whose noble instinct for poetry could never carry him in practice beyond the production of a few lofty and massive fragments of half-formed verse which stand better by themselves when detached from the incoherent and disorderly context" (*George Chapman*). But Beddoes is the author of some fascinating exotic lyrics of a character a little difficult to define. They are not personal, though a perverse element in his own temperament doubtless lent colour to his moods. They are dramatic lyrics of an Elizabethan character, dramatic but with no definite suggestion of character or occasion such as Browning was to give to many of his songs. Beddoes's "If there were dreams to sell" and "If thou wilt ease thine heart" are the forerunners of such lyrics as Tennyson's "Where Claribel low lieth" and "Mariana in the South" and "A Spirit haunts the year's last hours", and Browning's "Heap cassia, sandal buds and stripes Of labdanum and aloe-balls". But Beddoes is at his best in single stanzas or lines. "If there were dreams to sell" has gained in Quiller Couch's selection by losing two stanzas. Of some of them it is the rhythm which clings to the memory, the run-on effect of:

> We have bathed where none have seen us,
>   In the lake and in the fountain,
> Underneath the charmed statue
>   Of the timid bending Venus,
> Where the water-nymphs were counting
>   In the waves the stars of night,
> And those maidens started at you,
> Your limbs shone through so soft and bright.
>   But no secret dare we tell,
>   For thy slaves unlace thee,
>   And he who shall embrace thee
> Waits to try thy beauties' spell.

Professor Saintsbury assigns a special importance in the history of prosody to Beddoes and to his immediate rival Darley.

George Darley, whom a painful stammer cut off from a profession and from easy social intercourse, was a trenchant critic of literature and a competent critic of painting. His first poem, *The Errors of Ecstasy*, in which "ecstasy" means the acute sensibility of the poet, is a strange dialogue between the 'ecstatic' and the moon. The theme of the whole is the wisdom of avoiding extremes, which, the author tells us, was also the purpose of the unfinished *Nepenthe*, the most rememberable thing in which is the description of the death of the Phoenix:

> O blest unfabled incense tree
> That burns in glorious Araby.

Of his shorter lyrics one found its way into the *Golden Treasury* from the editor's belief that it was a seventeenth-century poem:

> It is not beauty I demand,
> A coral brow, the moon's despair,

the theme of which is that of the longer poems, the conflict between imagination and good sense; and in none of them does it quite come off.

Thomas Hood made no such ecstatic flights as Darley. He knew what he was aiming at and generally achieved his purpose. He wrote poems of several kinds, in each leaving something to be remembered: philanthropic poems as *The Bridge of Sighs* and the *Song of the Shirt*; humorous poems abounding in puns as *Miss Kilmansegg and her Precious Leg*, which has also a philanthropic, satiric purpose. But Hood also wrote true poems of feeling and fancy. No poet need be altogether ashamed of his work who has left such verses as *Ruth*, *The Haunted House*, *Autumn* (not quite unworthy to be read after Keats's poem), "We watched her breathing through the night", "I remember, I remember", *The Last Man*, and the *Dream of Eugene Aram*.

Thomas Wade and Charles Wells have from time to time found readers eager to redress what seemed to them undue neglect, but with no great success. No poem of theirs has found its way into even so limited an anthology as the *Oxford Book of Regency Verse*. They both wrote verse-dramas, the best known by name being Wells's *Joseph and his Brethren*. Two of Wade's plays were acted, but his best poems, *The Contention of Death and Love* and *Helena* in *Mundi et Cordis Carmina*, are interesting chiefly as illustrating how the place of Wordsworth and Byron as influences with younger poets was being usurped by Shelley and Keats even before these poets had gained their whole due with the general reader and the regular reviews. "The disappearance of Shelley", wrote Beddoes in 1824, "seems to have been followed by instant darkness and owl-season; whether the vociferous Darley is to be the comet or tender-faced L. E. L. the milk and watery moon of our darkness are questions for the astrologers." In 1830 appeared *Poems chiefly Lyrical*, followed in 1832 by *Poems*; but to the critics of the day Tennyson was more akin to L. E. L. than to the greater poets his predecessors.

Chapter Thirty-One

THE EARLY VICTORIANS

(1) *Tennyson*

WE cannot fully understand Wordsworth or Byron or Shelley till we view them against their political background.   It is not quite so with Tennyson (1809–1892).   Except for a sonnet on Poland, the only foreign affairs that moved Tennyson to write were such as affected Britain, like the threat of French invasion in 1854 and the Crimean War.   Nor did domestic politics yield him much to make a song about.   He shared the watery Liberal faith in progress into which the millenary hopes of the Revolutionary Age had deliquesced, believing that the battle for the franchise had in principle been won, and now Freedom would slowly broaden down from precedent to precedent.   At first the prospect was clouded by the Chartist agitation; in the hungry forties he had visions of a starving people coming on,

as a lion creeping nigher,
Stares at one that nods and winks behind a slowly-dying fire.

Hunger was in fact the driving force in that agitation; it died out when the Repeal of the Corn Laws assured the people of cheap bread.   Then England entered on an era of peace and plenty, broken only by the Crimean War and the Indian Mutiny.   But there was another side to Tennyson; though he was a Liberal in politics, his temper was in many ways conservative.   He hated pacifism, and was always ready to sound the call to arms when Britain was threatened.   He was the first of Liberal Imperialists.   Love of valour and pride of race inspired some of his most stirring poems—the *Ode on the Death of the Duke of Wellington*, *The Charge of the Light Brigade*, *The Charge of the Heavy Brigade*, *The Defence of Lucknow*, and the superb *Revenge*.   Born and bred in a country rectory, he was deeply attached to English institutions and the English countryside; in his old age he came to fear that both were being endangered by the growth of democracy and the spread of industrialism in cities of slums; he voiced these fears in *Locksley Hall Sixty Years After*.

But all these poems put together make only a small fraction

of his output. As a poet he found his chief themes not in public issues but in private lives. The background that we need for Tennyson is therefore not so much political and economic as religious and scientific. He went up to Cambridge at a time when English society was undergoing a remarkable change. The middle classes were coming into their own not only in politics but in morals and manners. The tone of the Universities was set no longer by raffish aristocrats like Byron but by serious, high-minded scions of the upper-middle class, like Gladstone and Hallam. At Oxford there was a religious revival, Romish in tendency. At Cambridge the set to which Tennyson belonged inclined to the Broad Church view that Christianity was a growing faith which must be adjusted to the growth of knowledge. Adjustment became harder as knowledge of Nature grew from more to more. The modern conflict between science and religion had begun. It does not date from the appearance of *The Origin of Species* in 1859: Darwin did not invent the evolutionary hypothesis; what he did was to provide a carefully documented theory of the machinery of evolution by means of natural selection. Doubtless this embittered the conflict, for natural selection could not be squared with Genesis; but the general idea of evolution had long been in the air. If any one man invented it, it was Lamarck. In Britain it was most firmly entrenched in the science of Geology: see Chambers's *Vestiges of Creation* (1844). Tennyson was deeply perturbed by the repercussions of evolutionary doctrine on the belief in personal immortality which was the heart of his creed. What he feared was not only his own extinction, nor even the ultimate extinction of human life on earth; he feared that if men ceased to believe in the immortality of the soul all that he valued in this present life would perish, morality would crumble, and man reel back into the brute. These doubts and fears weighed heavy on him after the death of his beloved friend Arthur Hallam in 1833, but there is little trace of them in his early poems, though there is some; it was after brooding on them for sixteen years that he gave them full utterance in *In Memoriam*.

If ever a poet lisped in numbers it was Tennyson. From the age of eight he wrote reams of verse, imitating whatever poet he had read last. In 1827 he and his brother Charles produced *Poems of Two Brothers*. Two lines of Alfred's show his early interest in astronomy:

The rays of many a rolling central star,
Aye flashing earthward, have not reached us yet.

Most of these poems, however, are mere echoes of Scott, Moore, or Byron. Byron had been his idol; when the news of his death reached England, the boy Tennyson wrote in the sandstone, "Byron is dead", and felt that the world had come to an end.

In 1830 and 1833 he brought out two more volumes, but they were so mauled by some of the reviewers that he drew back into his shell and published no more for nine years. The reviewers had some excuse for their savagery; there was a good deal of triviality and missishness in these volumes; but any critic with an eye and an ear ought to have discovered that here was a coming poet. The two volumes of 1842 proved triumphantly that he had come. The poems of 1842 were partly new, partly redactions of earlier poems, marvellously recomposed, chastened, or enriched. They are not prophetic utterances; nor, except for "Break, break, break", are they lyrical cries of passion or pain; in the main they are studies in which the artist seeks by every refinement of diction and metre to paint a picture which shall perfectly communicate a mood. The subjects are drawn mostly from Greek legend, Arthurian romance, or English country life. Tennyson was the heir of the Romantic Revival; he had outgrown Byron, he found Shelley thin, but he had learned something from Coleridge and Keats, and tried to learn something from Wordsworth; and he had a solider backing of classical scholarship than any of them. The Arthurian poems in particular suggest Keats by their pictorial quality. But Tennyson was not so richly endowed as Keats in the less intellectual senses of smell, taste, touch, and temperature. One may read pages of Tennyson without lighting on an image drawn from any sense but sight or hearing. Hence his effects are more purely pictorial, less profuse and multiform than Keats's. "Colour like the dawn", said Emerson, "flows over the horizon from his pencil in waves so rich that we do not miss the central form." And the colours are pure and distinct, the whole picture set out in true perspective. In *The Lady of Shalott* there is the background of blue sky and yellowing barley, in the middle distance the willow-fringed river, in the foreground the island with its four grey walls and four grey towers. It is a landscape in water-colour. And the picture is shown to the music of flutes.

Tennyson did not invent many new metres, but he could use every melodic device of alliteration, assonance, and quantity. (He once said that he knew the quantity of every English word except 'scissors'!) His art is not always concealed, perhaps, but the result is always delightful. It was the rhymed poems above all that charmed FitzGerald with their "champagne flavour". Among the blank verse pieces *Oenone* and *Ulysses* are specially interesting as Tennyson's first essays in dramatic monologue, that typically Victorian form which Browning made his own. Tennyson's knowledge of human nature was not so wide, nor perhaps so deep, as Browning's; but simple types and single moods he could render with a firm pictorial touch. The English Idylls are not so successful. It is true that Wordsworth said of one of them, "Mr. Tennyson, I have been endeavouring all my life to write a pastoral like your *Dora*, and have not succeeded"; but Arnold pronounced the simplicity of *Dora* affected; certainly nothing could be less Wordsworthian than the opulent *Gardener's Daughter*; and the other two Idylls might as well have been written in prose. Tennyson's attempts at light verse were even less successful: "Alfred cannot trifle," said FitzGerald. Actually Alfred had a broad streak of rustic humour in him, as he showed afterwards in those capital dialect poems, the two *Northern Farmers* and *The Entail*, but his sombre temper did not fit him to shine in *vers de société*. Besides these 'studies' the 1842 volumes contained two or three poems in which Tennyson approached those ultimate problems of death and life and the purpose of life with which he was to grapple in *In Memoriam*. Such are *The Two Voices*, *The Vision of Sin*, and (in part) *The Palace of Art*. With these we may class *Locksley Hall*, in which he first essayed a theme to which he was to return in *Maud* and *Enoch Arden*— the theme of love and loss and renunciation. The moral note, though heard most distinctly in these poems, is seldom absent from Tennyson. The virtues he values most are the Puritan virtues, "self-reverence, self-knowledge, self-control".

Emerson's praise contained an ominous qualification: "colour . . . in waves so rich that we do not miss the central form". And he went on: "But he wants a subject, and climbs no mount of vision to bring its secrets to the people". If that sounds harsh, it is not half so harsh as what Tennyson once said about himself. "I don't think", he once said to Carlyle, "that since Shakespeare there has been such a master of the

English language as I." "To be sure," he added, "I've nothing to say." "He wants a subject"; "To be sure, I've nothing to say"—all his life Tennyson was in search of a subject on which he might write a great poem and find something to say worth bringing to the people. He never found it except in *In Memoriam*, and even *In Memoriam* is not so much a great poem as a great series of short poems, many of them exquisite, but not built up into a great whole.

Emerson's criticism was written after a visit that he paid to England in 1847. That same year Tennyson produced his first long poem, *The Princess*. Had he found his subject? We do not think so; he did not think so himself. The ostensible subject of *The Princess* is the higher education of women. If Tennyson succeeded in treating it poetically, it was by not treating it quite seriously. The setting is serio-comic; there are serio-comic touches in the body of the poem; the action is thrown back into a fantastic time, when ladies lecture on the nebular hypothesis in the classroom while knights tilt in the lists outside. And the conclusion, that "woman is not undeveloped man", what light does it throw on her higher education? No, *The Princess* is not a great poem; but it contains some jewelled phrases, and the third edition was enriched by half a dozen lovely songs: "Tears, idle tears" seems to well from the poet's heart; and in "The splendour falls" he used all his wonderful gifts of colour and melody to body forth one of those vague, high-charged moods in which poetry passes over into music, and in rendering which he rivals Shelley.

In Memoriam appeared in 1850, the year in which Tennyson became Laureate. Unlike *Lycidas* and *Adonais*, it is a cry of grief for a personal loss. But it is much more: it is a record of all the fluctuations of faith and doubt, hope and despair, that had filled Tennyson's mind for sixteen years. He could not take refuge with Newman on the rock which is Peter, nor with Gladstone on the impregnable rock of Holy Scripture, from the waves of doubt that swept over him, doubt as to the immortality of the soul, the final issue of the evolutionary process, and the purpose of the ultimate Power behind it, "the Power in darkness whom we guess". Nor had he the assurance which Wordsworth drew from his private illumination, the "sense sublime" which did not believe but saw. Tennyson too had mystical experiences; *In Memoriam* records one such, evoked as he read Hallam's old letters alone in a still summer night:

So word by word, and line by line,
  The dead man touched me from the past;
  And all at once it seem'd at last
The living soul was flash'd on mine;

And mine in this was wound, and whirl'd
  Above empyreal heights of thought,
  And came on that which is, and caught
The deep pulsations of the world,

Aeonian music measuring out
  The steps of Time—the shocks of Chance—
  The blows of death.   At length my trance
Was cancelled, stricken through with doubt.

"Stricken through with doubt": the ecstasy left no lasting assurance.   If faith conquers in the end, it is not by the aid of such rare and fitful illuminations, nor of dogmatic theology, but by the strength which it draws from the poet's own deathless love.   In the absence of such a theology as Dante inherited, the steps by which the poet rises to the *amor intellectualis Dei* are not traced with the assured firmness which gives unity to the *Divina Commedia*.   And in these days, when Heaven is falling, the consolations of *In Memoriam* mean less than they did to a generation that was still living on the victory of Waterloo.   But the vignettes that shine out as we turn its pages— "Calm is the morn without a sound", "The Danube to the Severn gave", "Dip down upon the northern shore", "By night we lingered on the lawn"—these lovely pictures of the dear English landscape have not faded and will not fade.   *In Memoriam* is the keystone in the arch of Tennyson's fame.   On none of his poems did he bestow such loving care; in none are his gifts of delicate observation and phrasing more manifest. The metre too fits his theme as the terza rima fitted Dante's: he was not the first to use it, as he thought, but he made it his own.

  Maud followed in 1855.   It is a series of soliloquies by one and the same speaker; Tennyson called it "a monodrama", and hoped that its variety of moods and metres would yield an effect not unlike that which drama secures by variety of characters.   *Maud* was Tennyson's favourite among his poems, the one he loved best to read aloud; he put a good deal of himself into the hero.   But the British public did not take to this morbid young man, who raved at cotton-spinning pacifists,

and plunged enthusiastically into a war in which they had
begun to fear that they had backed the wrong horse. Yet
Maud contains some of Tennyson's finest lyrics; there is the
dazzling dance-rhythm of "Come into the garden, Maud";
there are the tender lines out of which the whole poem grew:

> Oh that 'twere possible,
>   After long grief and pain,
> To find the arms of my true love
>   Round me once again—

lovely and tender lines, but not more lovely than the snatch of
sixteenth-century verse that suggested them:

> Oh western wind, when wilt thou blow,
>   That the small rain down can rain?
> Christ! that my love were in my arms,
>   And I in my bed again!

Even after *Maud* Tennyson was not widely read. What put
him on every parlour table was *The Idylls of the King*, the first
instalment of which appeared in 1859, and was followed by
others in 1869 and 1872. Had Tennyson found his subject
at last? He must have thought so, to give so many years to it.
He was deceived. Taken as a whole, *The Idylls of the King* do
not make a great poem. Indeed they cannot be "taken as a
whole", for they have no continued plot to give them unity.
Tennyson tried to unify them with a thread of allegory,
"shadowing sense at war with soul"; but the allegory is an
afterthought; where is the allegory in *Geraint and Enid* or
Lancelot and Elaine? They are novelettes in verse. Still each
Idyll might have been a gem in itself, if Tennyson had been
faithful to his originals, as he was in the 1842 *Morte d'Arthur*,
where he retold nobly, if too elaborately, the noble close of
Malory's romance. But in these later Idylls, dedicated to
Queen Victoria, and sacred to the memory of Prince Albert,
he tried to infuse Victorian morality into the legends of an age
whose ideas of love and marriage were far from Victorian. In
so doing he degraded the fateful, tragic love of Tristram and
Iseult to a vulgar intrigue. Lancelot and Guinevere fare little
better. So long as Arthur remains an abstraction, a personified conscience, our sympathies are with the lovers; but when
Tennyson tries to make him a real man, a true lover, and a
perfect husband, the loves of Lancelot and Guinevere become
plain adultery. For all that, there are many beauties in the

Idylls, not in the narrative—Tennyson was no great story-teller
—but the descriptions.   Tennyson was still a master of blank
verse, though now he sometimes made its surface so smooth
that the mind slips on it; and he had not lost his gift of phrase
and delicate observation.   He watched Nature,

As careful robins eye the delver's toil,

looking out for 'bits', of which he made thumb-nail sketches,
to be worked up at leisure; there are many such in *The Idylls
of the King*.

In 1864 he took a holiday from *The Idylls of the King* to
write *Idylls of the Hearth*, afterwards named *Enoch Arden*.   It
is a simple story of a fisherman who was given up for lost, came
back to find his wife remarried, and did not reveal himself.
In spite of its gorgeous description of a tropical island, the
poem displeases by the mannerism which calls fish in a creel
"ocean-spoil in ocean-smelling osier".

In the 1870's Tennyson tried drama.   He added nothing
to his reputation by doing so.   *Harold* and *Queen Mary* were
still-born; *Becket*, though Irving gave it a considerable run,
has long been dead also; *The Cup* and *The Falcon* had better
have been left as Plutarch and Boccaccio told them; and Tennyson himself recognised that *The Promise of May* was a failure.
We may therefore pass these things over, and turn to the last
and most remarkable phase of his long poetic life.

Between his seventieth and his eightieth year Tennyson produced a series of poems which, though they did not recapture,
or seek to recapture, the golden flow of his prime, were filled
with a deeper, more turbulent music, like the surge of the sea.
The Revenge, Rizpah, the second *Locksley Hall, In the Children's
Hospital, Vastness, Parnassus, To Virgil*, all belong to these
years.   A wonderful second spring!   There has been nothing
like it since Sophocles died.   Tennyson's faith in progress,
the march of mind, the steamship and the railway, had withered
as he saw democracy and industrialism threatening the glory
and the beauty of England, and heard in individual lives cries
of anguish more poignant than the echoes of battles long ago.
Hence the realism of *Locksley Hall Sixty Years After*, the terrible
Rizpah, and the painful *Children's Hospital*.   At first he had
thought, and had Darwin's assurance for thinking, that Dar-
winism was no foe to Christianity; but as time went on natural
science grew more materialistic every year, and physical science

more menacing.   His old fear assailed him again, fear that the drama of creation would end, not in some far-off divine event, but in a dead earth revolving round a dying sun:

> What is it all if we all of us end but in being our own corpse-coffins at last,
> Swallow'd in Vastness, lost in Silence, drown'd in the depth of a meaningless past?

The poet calls on the Muses to help him up Parnassus, that he may roll his voice from the summit, "sounding for ever and ever".   But look!—

> Who are these two shapes high over the sacred fountain,
> Taller than all the Muses, and huger than all the mountain?
> See, in their deep double shadow the crown'd ones all disappearing.
> Sing like a bird, and be happy, nor hope for a deathless hearing,
> "Sounding for ever and ever."   Pass on; the sight confuses.
> These are Astronomy and Geology, terrible Muses.

Yet again faith conquers in the end, and conquers as before by the strength of his own undying love for the friend of his youth:

> Peace, and let be; for I loved him, and love him; the dead are not dead but alive.

The revolt against Tennyson set in even before his death. In part it was mere youthful petulance; but in the main it was a healthy reaction against the idolatry which worshipped Tennyson for his very faults, a new return to Nature, led, this time, by Kipling and Yeats.   Later, Tennyson suffered in the general 'debunking' of Victorians which Lytton Strachey made fashionable for a time.   Now the debunkers have been debunked in their turn, and Tennyson is securely seated, not indeed on the summit of Parnassus, but high on its slopes. Few poets have been gifted with greater sensibility of eye and ear; none ever laboured more diligently at his art.   He was not a great original thinker, but through a long life he kept abreast of the thought of his time.   He remains the representative poet of the Victorian Age.

DD

Chapter Thirty-Two

THE EARLY VICTORIANS

(2) *Robert Browning*

THE second major prophet of the Victorians was Robert Browning (1812–1889). The Victorian prophets differed from those of Israel inasmuch as they came less to curse than to bless, to encourage rather than to warn, for they too shared, at least to begin with, the confident belief in progress as the solution for the ills which beset mankind, a faith in the "one far-off divine event to which the whole creation moves,"

> I know there shall dawn a day
> —Is it here in homely earth?
> Is it yonder worlds away,
>   Where the strange and new have birth?
> That Power comes full in play,

therefore let us "greet the unseen with a cheer". It is true that the first buoyant hopefulness was clouded in various ways as the century ran its course, and, as we have seen, the tone of Tennyson's poetry underwent a surprising and impressive change. No shadow completely darkened the courageous hopefulness of Browning, but the tone of his poetry did become more combative, more conscious of a defensive attitude.

If politics counted for little in Tennyson's poetry, it counts for less in Browning's. He lived for many years in Italy and loved her, but only in two or three places does he so much as touch on the *risorgimento*. He wrote a long poem on Napoleon III, but the interest is solely psychological. Love of England inspired *Home Thoughts from Abroad*; but two lines about the corn laws are all he has to say of home politics. The explanation lies in the dedication to *Sordello*: "The historical decoration was purposely of no more importance than a background requires; and my stress lay on the incidents in the development of a soul: little else is worth study". In a word, for both Tennyson and Browning the fundamental interest is religious not political, if in *Maud* Tennyson showed himself more aware than his 'equal' of the social problem which disturbed Carlyle and Ruskin, also (be it remembered) Victorian

prophets.   The temper and attitude of the two poets is characteristic of the cleft in English religious life.   Tennyson was an
undogmatic Christian of the English rectory and village church
type, rich in the charities and simpler pieties.   Browning's
parents were Dissenters, fairly well-to-do, cultured, and pious.
The poet was a pious lad himself except for a month or two
when Shelley's *Queen Mab* made him an atheist and a vege-
tarian.   But he had felt, and was never to forget, the fervour
of evangelical religion.   In *Christmas Eve and Easter Day*,
published in the same year as *In Memoriam*, the visionary has
been carried to Tübingen, the citadel of the Higher Criticism,
and to Rome with its tradition of ecclesiastical ceremony, but
returns in spirit to the dissenting chapel from which he had
set out, where religion spoke to the heart:

> I praise the heart and pity the head of him,
> And refer myself to THEE instead of him,
> Who head and heart alike discernest,
>   Looking below light speech we utter,
>   When frothy spume and frequent sputter
> Prove that the soul's depths boil in earnest.

But if different in feeling the religion of both the poets was
that Liberal Christianity, Broad Churchism, which we are told
now is not only out of fashion but entirely dead.   Neither of
them could accept with complacency Milton's stern creed that
the "regenerate are few" and the fate of the unregenerate such
as will not bear thinking of.   They both clung to what was
known as the "larger hope":

> That nothing walks with aimless feet;
>   That not one life shall be destroy'd,
>   Or cast as rubbish to the void,
> When God has made the pile complete.

To Tennyson that was a hope, to Browning a conviction rooted
in his sense of the significance of love, in man and in God as
revealed in Christ.

Browning's best work was done between 1840 and 1869, if
to the end he remained a lyrical poet of a spontaneity as
remarkable as is the subtlety of his moods.   Before 1840 he
was experimenting; after 1869 he allowed his poetic vein to be
too often smothered by casuistry, and 'jawed' instead of singing.
We may even make a finer distinction: Browning's greatest
love-poems—and they are his greatest poems—were all written

between 1845, when he first met his wife, and 1861, when she died; and the influence of her spirit can still be felt in the *Dramatis Personae* of 1864; the influence of her *spirit*, we say; no literary influence, her or another's, is perceptible in his mature work. He got over his Byronic measles at twelve and worked off his passion for Shelley in *Pauline* by the time he was twenty; after that he was himself, knowing no master. There is little evidence in anything that has come down to us of such tuning and mastering of his instrument as is represented by the changes in the poems of Tennyson as these appeared in successive editions. Browning plunged at once into the most ambitious themes, themes of so vague and transcendent a character as to make any concrete dramatic treatment very difficult. Inspired in part by Shelley's Godwinian dream of human perfectibility, in part by his own buoyant temperament and unshakeable faith in God, he chose as theme for three poems of considerable length, *Pauline* (1833), *Paracelsus* (1835), and *Sordello* (1840), the man inspired by vast ideals of human capacity, the desire to "be all, have, see, know, taste, feel all", but in some way baffled by an inherent weakness in himself and the limits set by God to human endeavour as such. *Pauline*, an early poem which he would fain have withdrawn, but which found an admirer in so important a person as Rossetti, has more both of Shelley and of the poet's own self than the older Browning cared to acknowledge. After that he would wear a dramatic mask, choosing as historical characters (treated with the utmost freedom) Paracelsus, the Renaissance alchemist and chief opponent of the Galenist tradition in medicine, and Sordello, the troubadour whom Dante met and embraced in Purgatory:

> "O Mantovano, io son Sordello
> Della tua terra." E l' uno l' altro abbracciava.

But Browning's heroes have little to do with their historical counterparts. Paracelsus is a man who would know everything and finds, like Goethe's Faust, that life has slipped away in a vain pursuit, and that meantime he has made no use for humanity of the knowledge he has acquired, sacrificed love to "this wolfish hunger after knowledge". But to tell the truth it is so difficult to form any definite conception of what it would be like to know everything or to love everything like the poet Aprile whom Paracelsus encounters at a turning point of his life, that one has the feeling that a great deal of eloquent talk is circling round an invisible centre. The beauties of the poem are to be sought in the descriptive touches, which are managed with dramatic fitness, as when after a night's despondent talk the hero sees

> morn at length. The heavy darkness seems
> Diluted; grey and clear without the stars:
> The shrubs bestir and rouse themselves, as if
> Some snake, that weighed them down all night, let go
> His hold; and from the East, fuller and fuller,
> Day, like a mighty river, flowing in:
> But clouded, wintry, desolate and cold.
> Yet see how that broad prickly star-shaped plant,
> Half down in the crevice, spreads its woolly leaves
> All thick and glistering with diamond dew.

The closing speech of the dying Paracelsus gives the completest statement of the faith which was, and was to be, Browning's, in God who through human imperfections is working out some end that transcends human conjecture.

Sordello too fails, fails both in song and in statecraft, because he has not the single eye. *Sordello* is notoriously difficult; to the intangibility of *Paracelsus* it added an obscurity of style such as, till twenty years ago, one would have thought no poet would allow himself. *Paracelsus* had been censured as diffuse; *Sordello* shall at all costs be succinct; but *"brevis esse laboro, obscurus fio"*, as Horace found. Tennyson complained that he only understood two lines of the poem—the first, "Who will may hear Sordello's story told"; and the last, "Who would has heard Sordello's story told"—and that they were both lies. Nevertheless, through the compressed, elliptical style shine ever and again, as through the imperfect medium of an early, spotty film, vivid touches of description—scenery and interiors, the landscape of northern Italy and her towns with the turbulent life of the streets in peace and war, as well as individual figures; for some of the lesser characters, Salinguerra and Palma, are dramatically drawn. Only the hero remains a shadowy figure, for a reason that becomes plain when we turn to Browning's experiments in drama for the stage. Whatever its faults as a poem, *Sordello* is of interest biographically in so far as it reflects the state of Browning's mind in the years when he had outgrown his mother's simple creed, and was seeking for something that would give him back faith and hope and love, provide an object for the superabundant energy which urged him on, like the hero of *Pauline*, to "be all, have, see, know, taste, feel all", and help him to turn from the self-centred strivings of adolescence to a nobler life of service, as Sordello turns from Palma to the beggar maid.

Before *Sordello* was published Browning had turned aside to try his hand at drama for the stage in *Strafford*, which Macready presented at Covent Garden (1837); and this was followed at intervals by others of the kind—*King Victor and King Charles* (1842); *The Return of the Druses* (1843); *A Blot in the Scutcheon* (1843), which proved too much for the audience; *Colombe's Birthday* (1844); and *Luria* (1846). But actable drama was not within Browning's compass any more than Tennyson's, if for a different reason. Drama demands a sustained plot, as was proved at an earlier date by the failure of the Senecan plays. Browning's stress lay on the development of souls; but he values souls not for what they are but for what they would, whereas the dramatist's business is to show character in action. That is where he fails. Djabal and Luria, the Francophil Arab and the Moor who loves Florence, are interesting studies, but they *do* nothing except kill themselves. But such lack of action is not fatal to dramatic lyric and monologue, and it was just here that Browning was at last to achieve success.

With *Pippa Passes* (1841) Browning got his feet on the ground. *Pippa* is a drama of a kind, but not for the stage. It consists of four successive episodes in each of which Pippa's song as she passes strikes into a fateful situation and precipitates the issue. They are strange songs for Pippa to have sung, but entirely Browningesque. One of them has been taken too readily as an expression of his philosophy, that ending

> God's in his heaven—
> All's right with the world,

which is just a poetical way of saying the day is fine and Pippa very happy. Close on the heels of *Pippa* came *Dramatic Lyrics* (1842),[1] and revealed, just as clearly as Tennyson's volume of the same year, that here was a poet of the first order; for here was God's plenty. They are, as the title indicates, lyrics in the main, but some are long lyrical monologues—as *Old Pictures in Florence*, *Saul*, *Any Wife to Any Husband*, *Popularity*, *Master Hugues of Saxe-Gotha*, *By the Fireside*. But

[1] See note at end of chapter.

even the lyrics pure and simple are dramatic, often with a definite setting picturesque and dramatic: *Cavalier Tunes*, which have a singing note in them such as Tennyson was incapable of; *Soliloquy in a Spanish Cloister*; *The Laboratory*; *The Confessional (Spain)*; *A Lovers' Quarrel*; the delightfully humorous and Italian *Up at a Villa, Down in the City*; *A Toccata of Galuppi's*; *De Gustibus*, and others. But the best are the love-songs, and of Browning's love-songs and the variety of moods they express more will be said later. Three years later came *Dramatic Romances* (1845).[1] Here are a few lyrics too, but the majority of the poems are narratives or monologues, including such well-known poems as *My Last Duchess*, *The Italian in England*, *The Englishman in Italy*, *In a Gondola*, *Waring*, *The Last Ride Together*, *The Pied Piper of Hamelin*, *A Grammarian's Funeral*, and perhaps the most powerful dramatic lyric that Browning ever wrote, *The Heretic's Tragedy*, the dreadful story of the end of the Templars:

> John of the Temple, whose fame so bragged,
>   Is burning alive in Paris square!
> How can he curse if his mouth is gagged?
>   Or wriggle his neck with a collar there?
> Or heave his chest while a band goes round?
>   Or threat with his fist, since his arms are spliced?
> Or kick with his feet, now his legs are bound?
>   —Thinks John, I will call upon Jesus Christ.

To these add the bizarre *Holy-Cross Day*, and *The Statue and the Bust*. In some of these poems one may trace what have been called the corollaries of Browning's central doctrines. But how unnecessary it is to seek for such morals is clear from *Childe Roland to the Dark Tower Came*, which is untroubled with any meaning.

Men and Women (1855),[1] which followed close on *Christmas Eve and Easter Day*, contains only dramatic monologues, mainly in blank verse. The best as poems are *Pictor Ignotus*, *Fra Lippo Lippi*, *The Bishop Orders His Tomb*, *Rudel to the Lady of Tripoli*, and the closing *One Word More* in which, dedicating his poems to E. B. B., he speaks for the first and last time in his own person:

> There they are my fifty men and women
> Naming me the fifty poems finished!
> Take them, love, the book and me together:
> Where the heart lies let the brain lie also.

[1] See note at end of chapter.

None of Browning's spoken poems is so simply musical and comprehensible. For those interested in his later apologetics *The Strange Medical Experience of Karshish*, on the raising of Lazarus, and *Bishop Blougram's Apology* are striking poems. The strangeness of the story of Lazarus is added to by the presence of an Arab physician some centuries before the advent of Arab learning and culture. The apologetic note is stronger in the *Dramatis Personae* which in 1864 closed the series of such monologues. Here are *Gold Hair: A Story of Pornic*, illustrating he thinks the doctrine of original sin, rather perhaps the variety of forms which lunacy may take, and the delightful *Caliban upon Setebos*, which is a picture of much more than savage religion alone, and *Mr. Sludge the Medium*; and, probably the most admired of the apologetic poems, *A Death in the Desert*. It is in the poems of these four volumes that one may study best the art of Browning and not a little of the best of his thought. There is the vividness of his occasional descriptions. Of Nature Browning writes occasionally, as in the closing part of *Paracelsus* and again in *Saul*, with some of Wordsworth's deep sense of the life of Nature, if never with his vision of her mystery. But he can also describe with some of the sensuous richness, at least the varied colour, of Keats:

> Most like the centre spike of gold
>   Which burns deep in the blue-bell's womb,
> What time, with ardours manifold,
>   The bee goes singing to her groom,
>   Drunken and overbold.

And there is the variety of the scenery appropriate to the theme and mood of the poem,—scenery English, French, Italian, Palestinian. To this add the variety of the lyrical rhythms, adapted as these are too to the particular poem. All contribute to the dramatic effect. For in each, whatever the method adopted, the aim is to get inside the soul of his subject and see him as he sees himself. No doubt Browning's probe often touches motives that have not risen above the threshold of consciousness. He sees more in his subject than that subject sees himself.

Music, painting, love, and religion are his favourite themes. There is Abt Vogler, the musician whom God whispers in the ear; there are Andrea del Sarto, the faultless painter who lacks the inspiration of a woman's love, and Fra Lippo Lippi, the

irrepressible realist whose religion it is to paint things as he
sees them for the God of things as they are; and Pictor Ignotus,
whose art is a dedication and who shrinks from the vulgar world
to which it is something to be priced and criticised:

> Wherefore I chose my portion.   If at whiles
>   My heart sinks, as monotonous I paint
> These endless cloisters and eternal aisles
>   With the same series, Virgin, Babe and Saint,
> With the same cold calm beautiful regard,—
>   At least no merchant traffics in my heart;
> The sanctuary's gloom at least shall ward
>   Vain tongues from where my pictures stand apart.

Love is a word of all work, as George Eliot said, and there
are forms of love—love of country, love of family, the manly
love of comrades—about which Browning says little or nothing.
The love he writes of is love between man and woman, and
that he knows in many phases, from the fierce animal passion
of Ottima in *Pippa Passes* to the romantic love ("Queen
Worship" he called it) so exquisitely rendered in *The Last
Ride Together* and *Rudel to the Lady of Tripoli*.   But he knew a
better way of love than that—the love whose object is not an
imagined goddess but a real woman, whom a man loves not
because she is his ideal but because she is herself, loves for the
way she has with her curls, her dented chin, her little tricks of
speech, all the causeless laughters, the little private jokes and
common memories that are the stuff of intimacy.   That is the
real thing, and in that kind of love-poetry Browning is a
master.   *Too Late, A Lovers' Quarrel, Love Among the Ruins,
By the Fireside*—such poems are among his best titles to
immortality.

The natural end of such love is marriage, and Browning,
like Donne in an earlier age, is the chosen poet of wedded love.
Yet he was less Victorian than Tennyson in his attitude to
what might be called free love.   Had we been sanctioned
lovers, says the speaker in *Respectability*,

> How much of precious life were spent
> With men whom every virtue decks,
> And women models of their sex,
> Society's true ornament,—
> Ere we dared wander, nights like this,
> Thro' wind and rain, and watch the Seine,
> And feel the Boulevart break again
> To warmth and light and bliss?

In the more passionate of these love-poems Browning has a certain affinity with Donne rather than with the poet of "Come into the garden, Maud". There is nothing in him of the deep, tormented, sensual strain that at once attracts and repels us in Donne; but there is the same activity of intellect, the same rush of thought through the impassioned mind, in such poems as *Too Late*, *The Last Ride Together*, *Cristina*, etc. In *Too Late* the lover has, like Dante, seen his love married to another; but he has always hoped that some day, some way, she may yet be his; now she is dead, and his mind races through a press of thoughts irrelevant and trifling:

> And alive I shall keep and long, you will see!
> I knew a man, was kicked like a dog
> From gutter to cesspool; what cared he
> So long as he picked from the filth his prog?
> He saw youth, beauty and genius die,
> And jollily lived to his hundredth year.
> But I will live otherwise: none of such life!
> At once I begin as I mean to end.
> Go on with the world, get gold in its strife,
> Give your spouse the slip and betray your friend!
> There are two who decline, a woman and I,
> And enjoy our death in the darkness here.

Browning's contemporaries, however, were less interested in his love-poems than in his poems of religion, which comforted many tender souls in that Victorian twilight of faith, though his arguments, being the arguments of a poet, are sometimes no more than extended metaphors. His creed was not really new in substance, however novel some of its applications might be. For him, as for Kant, the "Ideas of the Reason", God, Freewill, and Immortality—a God of love, for

> A loving worm within its clod
> Were diviner than a loveless God,

and personal immortality—were the postulates of the moral life.

Browning had a religious nature, but it was his wife's influence that turned the undogmatic theist of the earlier poems into the Christian apologist of *Cleon*, and *Karshish*, and *A Death in the Desert*, and the second part of *Saul*. Cleon, the weary, all-accomplished Greek, has heard of Paulus; heard too that his doctrine could be held by no sane man. Karshish, the Arab physician, has examined Lazarus, and reports to a brother doctor that Lazarus's 'death' must have been simply an epileptic trance; but even as he writes comes the blinding thought, "What if Lazarus's tale be true?"—

> The very God! think, Abib; dost thou think?
> So, the All-Great were the All-Loving too—
> So, through the thunder comes a human voice
> Saying, "O heart I made, a heart beats here!
> Face, my hands fashioned, see it in myself!"

In *A Death in the Desert* the dying apostle, author of the Fourth Gospel, foresees a day when not his testimony only but his very existence will be doubted, and proclaims that doubt is a necessary stage in the progress of souls, which else might perish of their over-assurance, like lamps flooded with oil.   In *Saul* the inspired shepherd-boy has a vision of the Christ that is to be.

When he finished *Dramatis Personae* in 1864, Browning addressed himself sedulously to "the Roman murder story" on which he had meditated at intervals for years.   In 1868–1869 it appeared as *The Ring and the Book*, and was hailed at once as his masterpiece.   *The Ring and the Book* tells the story of the murder of Pompilia by her husband, Guido Franceschini, a decayed nobleman, tells it from ten different angles.   Pompilia's own story as she told it on her deathbed is full of pathos; there are noble things in the version of Caponsacchi, the priest who rescued her; the Pope's summing-up rises at times to sublimity; and Guido's cry of terror when he sees his executioners approaching—

> Abate,—Cardinal,—Christ,—Maria,—God . . .
> Pompilia, will you let them murder me?—

is a thing to chill the blood.   But the views of the three parties in Rome are drawn out with a wilful prolixity that gave point to Calverley's parody—

> And might, God bless you, in judicious hands,
> Extend from here to Mesopotamy;

and the speeches of the two lawyers are mere *tours de force*, crammed with bad law and bad Latin.   In truth the whole poem is too like a gigantic *tour de force*.

The Ring and the Book left Browning's imagination exhausted, but not his intellect: his last twenty years produced fifteen more volumes.   Not all these later poems are original: *Balaustion's Adventure* and *Aristophanes' Apology* are 'transcripts' from Euripides, each set in a frame of monologue; he also wrote a translation of the *Agamemnon*, which one can make out with the help of the Greek.   Sometimes he took up contemporary topics: *The Inn Album* and *Red Cotton Nightcap Country* are reconstructions of an actual murder and an actual suicide recently committed in France; *Prince Hohenstiel-Schwangau* is Napoleon III's *apologia pro vita sua*.   *La Saisiaz* recalls *A Death in the Desert* when it argues that immortality is, and ought to be, a matter of faith, not of knowledge.   Much in these poems is mere psychologising, casuistical pirouettings that lead nowhere.   In *Pacchiarotto* and *Parleyings with Certain People* especially he flaunts all his eccentricities in the face of the British Public, "you who love me not".   Yet his poetic fire was never quite extinguished.   Some of the *Dramatic Idylls* show that he could still tell a brave story bravely; and the Prologue and Epilogue to *Fifine*, *Bifurcation*, *Prospice*, "Never the time and the place", and some of the songs in *Ferishtah's Fancies* are worthy of his prime.   So is the Epilogue to *Asolando*, which appeared on the day he died.

In his own day Browning was overrated as a thinker and underrated as a poet.   His philosophy, as we have seen, was not really new, though he applied it with amazing freshness to many novel situations.   But philosophy, pure or applied, is not poetry until it has been so transmuted as to appeal to the emotions through the senses and the imagination.   It is this aspect of Browning's genius that we have now to consider.

Like all true poets, this intellectual acrobat was a dreamer. *Childe Roland to the Dark Tower Came* is a pure dream; not a dream of sleep like *Kubla Khan*, but a waking dream like Wordsworth's on the banks of the Loire, a reverie induced by the rhythmical motion of the Channel steamer rolling in time to that strange snatch from *King Lear*.   *How They Brought the Good News*, *Through the Metidja*, and *The Last Ride Together* have the same dream-like quality.   In all four cases, be it noted, the dream-state is induced not by a sight or a sound but by a rhythmical movement, actual, remembered, or imagined.   And this brings us to a point of great importance; in Browning the dominant sense was not, as with most poets, the sense of sight nor, as with Milton, of hearing, but the muscular sense, the sense of pressure.   What strikes us first of all in Browning is his superabundant energy. Since the main haunt and region of his song was the soul, his energisings are chiefly mental; he does not brood and meditate, but darts on his prey in every direction, like a spider that "feels in each thread and lives along the line". It is the same with his descriptions of physical objects and actions; he loves bold, jagged outlines: it is the leaping from rock up to rock that yields David the wild joy of living. What he adores in Nature is not beauty or sublimity, but life, the pressure of life in plant, insect, bird, and beast, when spring returns and God renews His ancient rapture. Browning's mental jumps and jerks often bewilder us; he is sometimes harsh and grotesque when harshness and grotesquerie are out of place; he flings his immense, multifarious vocabulary about too recklessly; but all these faults are only so many symptoms of his superabundant energy.

Browning's visual endowment was peculiar; he had one telescopic and one microscopic eye, one that could distinguish objects on the horizon, and one that could read small print by twilight. His colour-sense was not delicate; he rejoiced in vivid primary colours, reds and blues that were really red and blue. Like Dickens, he had a quick eye for the characteristic rather than for the beautiful: a quaint German beer-jug delighted him as much as a sunset.

As for his ear, it seems strange at first that this accomplished musician should have no such care for verbal melody as Tennyson, who could not tell "God Save the Queen" from "Pop goes the Weasel"; but that only shows that melody means one thing in music and another in verse. Browning could be melodious when he cared enough; such a line as

All the face composed of flowers, we say

has a caressing, wistful sweetness that Shelley might envy. But generally it was in rhythm, not in melody, that he excelled. The variety of his metres is prodigious. He excelled above all, as we might expect, in the rendering of movement: compare the galloping amphibrachs of *How We Brought the Good News* with the cantering amphimacers of *Through the Metidja*; mark how the jog-trot iambi of *The Last Ride Together* break at intervals into swinging anapaests. Even the harshness we complained of may be put to good use: see how the discords are resolved in these lines from *Abt Vogler*:

Man, brute, reptile, fly,—alien of end and of aim,
  Adverse, each from the other heaven-high, hell-deep removed,—
Should rush into sight at once, as he named the ineffable Name,
  And pile him a palace straight, to pleasure the princess he loved!

Browning wrote too much. Most of his longer poems, whether early or late, and many of his dramas are already dead, and there is a danger that even the magnificent things in *The Ring and the Book* will be buried under its débris; but *Dramatic Lyrics*, *Dramatic Romances*, *Men and Women*, and *Dramatis Personae* will live as long as English is read.

NOTE TO PAGES 414 AND 415

In 1868 Browning redistributed most of the fifty poems published in 1855 as *Men and Women*. Of the poems named on pages 414 and 415, he transferred *Popularity, Master Hugues, By the Fireside, Up at a Villa, A Toccata of Galuppi's,* and *De Gustibus* to *Dramatic Lyrics*; and *The Last Ride Together, A Grammarian's Funeral, The Statue and the Bust,* and *Childe Roland* to *Dramatic Romances*. *Per contra,* he transferred *Rudel* from *Dramatic Lyrics* and *The Tomb at St. Praxed's* and *Pictor Ignotus* from *Dramatic Romances* to *Men and Women.*

Pages 414 and 415 should be read with this correction.

Chapter Thirty-Three

THE EARLY VICTORIANS

(3) *Mrs Browning and Others*

THE typically Victorian poets took themselves very seriously. Their poetry was not to be merely the expression of their own personal feelings, their delight in their art as such. They were bards with a message for their age and for humanity. Tennyson was worried all his later life by the consciousness that he was expected to write a great poem "doctrinal to a nation". But the impulse came too much from without, from the critics, not as with Milton from the inner impulse of his own soul. Browning, too, tells us the tale of *Sordello*, so far as we can follow it, and of *Paracelsus*, with an ethical purpose. It is as against this bent in their poetry that one must understand the insistence of the pre-Raphaelites, as Swinburne, on the doctrine of "art for art". It was in great measure a demand for sincerity, since the danger of setting out to convey a message is that the poet endeavours to express what he more or less consciously thinks he ought to feel rather than what he does feel; and if he is a great poet, the final effect of a *Paradise Lost* may be not quite that which the poet set out to produce.

Elizabeth Barrett (1806–1861), who became Elizabeth Barrett Browning, shared to the full this high ideal of the poet and his mission. Descended from a line of wealthy, slave-owning Jamaica traders in rum and tobacco, herself the daughter of one of these in whom the sense of power and will to command had hardened into a monomania, Elizabeth's early life had been one of acute sensibility which a series of shocks and bereavements deepened into illness partly real, partly hysterical, imaginary, cultivated as an art, a pattern of her life to herself. What she needed was not a darkened room, an overshadowing father, a doctor feeling her pulse and graduating thereby her doses of morphine but, what she got at last in Robert Browning, a healer who would say to her, "Take up your bed and walk".

It is a little difficult to understand what it was in Miss Barrett's published poems which so strongly attracted Browning before he made her personal acquaintance: "I love your verses with all my heart, dear Miss Barrett" (10/1/45). In a later letter he names four poems. *Bertha* is a somewhat sickly ballad of two sisters and a lover who has engaged himself to the wrong one, the discovery of the error, and the death of the disappointed bearer of the engagement ring:

> And, dear Bertha, let me keep
>   On my hands this little ring,
> Which at night, when others sleep,
>   I can still see glittering.
> Let me keep it out of sight,
>   In the grave, where it will light
> All the dark up, day and night;

all this and more to the poor sister who is to have the lover, so readily does the sentimentalist indulge his *ego* in the conscious-ness of self-sacrifice. *A Drama of Exile* is a bold but senti-mental attempt at a lyrical drama on the Fall and the Redemp-tion. The other two which the letter mentions are *The Rhyme of the Duchess May* and *The Romaunt of the Page*, ballads in various lyrical measures on faithful lady-loves and their tragic fate. It is difficult to understand Browning's high apprecia-tion of these poems unless one recognises that in the more robust poet there was also a vein of the same characteristically Victorian sentiment which had replaced the romantic passion for Nature, liberty, beauty of the previous age. For it is not by these nor the more ambitious *Aurora Leigh* (1857), a novel in blank verse with a strain of the humanitarian feeling which links it with such novels as *Alton Locke*, *Sybil*, and others, nor yet her later political poems on the Italian struggle for inde-pendence, *Casa Guidi Windows*, that Mrs. Browning lives for us so far as she does live, but by those poems in which she is content to record her own inner life and feelings. Her too slipshod art, and the spasmodic strain in her imagery, deprive these ambitious poems of the beauty of art which might com-pensate for their sentimentality. But in the *Sonnets from the Portuguese* there are a few perfect utterances of a woman's heart: "I thought once how Theocritus had sung",

> Go from me. Yet I feel that I shall stand
> Henceforward in thy shadow,

"Yet love, mere love is beautiful indeed", "If thou must love me, let it be for nought Except for love's sake only", "When our two souls stand up erect and strong", "My own beloved, who hast lifted me". Yet even in these, as in her poems on larger themes, Mrs. Browning stands a little on tiptoe, does not lose her self-consciousness in the single passion. She is always conscious of herself as a woman and a poet, a frail woman on whom has been laid the burden of a poet and a champion of her sex. This dual consciousness found expression in one immortal lyric, a jet of song that flows from first to last without a check, in a manner that recalls Shelley's great lyric the *Hymn of Pan*, and Mrs. Browning's concern is also with Pan:

> What was he doing, the great god Pan,
>   Down in the reeds by the river?
> Spreading ruin and scattering ban,
> Splashing and paddling with hoofs of a goat,
> And breaking the golden lilies afloat
>   With the dragon-fly on the river.
>
>   .   .   .   .   .
>
> Yet half a beast is the great god Pan,
>   To laugh as he sits by the river,
> Making a poet out of a man;
> The true gods sigh for the cost and pain,—
> For the reed which grows nevermore again
>   As a reed with the reeds in the river.

Her *Bianca Among the Nightingales* has some fine stanzas in which Italian scenery and passion are blended, but the poem is marred by faults of taste and form. Some of her simpler ballads too are not without charm, as *The Romance of the Swan*, *Wine of Cypress*, *The Deserted Garden*, and perhaps others, but all suffer from the carelessness of her rhyming.

Macaulay's ballads were inspired at once by his admiration for the poems of Scott, whose *Lay of the Last Minstrel* he early knew by heart, and by his scholarly interest in the theory of Perizonius and Niebuhr that the "romantic tales which fill the first three or four books of Livy came from the lost ballads of the early Romans. I amused myself in India with trying to restore some of these long-perished poems." The elder Arnold, to whom two of them were shown before they were printed, was delighted. The more critical Matthew described them as "pinchbeck", which perhaps they are if taken too seriously. Macaulay describes them himself as "trifles". All the same, Macaulay caught more of the chivalrous, genial spirit of Scott than Byron had, and few poems after Scott's *Marmion* gave some of us more pleasure in the first discovery of poetry.

EE

Macaulay's battle-pieces, moreover, have some of the intenser spirit of Byron in, *e.g.*, "The Assyrian came down like the wolf on the fold". In *The Battle of Naseby* and *Ivry, A Song of the Huguenots* he senses and renders the fierce spirit of combatant Protestantism as we, like him, can judge of it from history:

> Down, down, for ever down with the mitre and the crown,
>   With the Belial of the Court, and the Mammon of the Pope;
> There is woe in Oxford Halls: there is wail in Durham's stalls;
>   The Jesuit smites his bosom: the Bishop rends his cope.
> And she of the seven hills shall mourn her children's ills,
>   And tremble when she thinks of the edge of England's sword;
> And the kings of earth in fear shall shudder when they hear
>   What the hand of God hath wrought for the Houses and the
>   Word.

The malevolent emotions have been inspirers of much poetry since the days of Homer. It is more difficult to feel sure of rendering with conviction the inspiring motives of incidents in so remote a history as that of Rome. The best things in the Roman Lays are the descriptive touches in which Macaulay blends his learning with vivid imagination:

> From lordly Volaterrae
>   Where scowls the far-famed hold
> Piled by the hands of giants
>   For godlike kings of old;
> From sea-girt Populonia
>   Whose sentinels descry
> Sardinia's snowy mountain-tops
>   Fringing the southern sky;

and so on. But nothing of Macaulay's shows such sincerity of poetic feeling as *A Jacobite's Epitaph*, the epitaph of a Jacobite exile, who has sacrificed all for his King, and "pined by Arno for his lovelier Tees".

Readers have had to wait long before securing a quite adequate text of the poems of one who was a more intense, if less variously accomplished, poet than Mrs. Browning. Not till 1942 did we get Emily Brontë's poems distinguished from poems by her sister Charlotte, with a text correctly divined from her difficult and minute handwriting, and rid so far as may be of the corrections of her more timid and conventional sister. Her art is that of Mrs. Hemans and L. E. L. rather than of Mrs. Browning; but into the comparatively simple forms she has breathed an intenser passion than can be easily matched in English poetry since Marlowe, of whose reckless spirit the author of *Wuthering Heights* has not a little. The best of her lyrics—"Often rebuked, yet always back returning", "Cold in the earth, and the deep snow piled above thee", "Riches I hold in light esteem"—burn themselves into the memory; and in her great personal confession, "No coward soul is mine", she has written the most daring and exulting religious poem in the language. Many of her poems were meant for the lost Gondal Saga, that interminable romance with which she and her sister Anne amused themselves for years. The wonderful fragment which Charlotte printed as *The Prisoner* is now known to be part of a long Gondal poem; but it is none the less revealing for that: we cannot doubt that the mystical experience which it records had been Emily's own:

He comes with western winds, with evening's wandering airs,
With that clear dusk of heaven that brings the thickest stars.

  .   .   .   .   .

But first a hush of peace, a soundless calm descends;
The struggle of distress and fierce impatience ends;
Mute music soothes my breast—unuttered harmony
That I could never dream till earth was lost to me.

Then dawns the Invisible, the Unseen its truth reveals;
My outward sense is gone, my inward essence feels—
Its wings are almost free, its home, its harbour found;
Measuring the gulf it stoops and dares the final bound!

Oh, dreadful is the check—intense the agony
When the ear begins to hear and the eye begins to see;
When the pulse begins to throb, the brain to think again,
The soul to feel the flesh and the flesh to feel the chain!

The wave of enthusiasm for liberty, which the French Revolution had roused, and which, rising or falling, had swept through the poetry of the Romantics from Wordsworth and Coleridge to Shelley, spent itself with the passing of the Reform Bill. Its place was taken by a rather watery faith in progress, the best aspect of which was a growing practical interest in social reform quickened by the industrial problem of masses of workers—men, women, and children—living under shocking conditions of hardship and uncertainty. With this went a deepening interest, at least among the middle classes, in religion, an interest stimulated on the one hand by the rumours blowing in of the effects of the study of Biblical criticism in

Germany, and on the other by a revival of Catholic feeling in the Church of England, as it became more and more aware of the threat to its position following the increase of political power in dissenting circles. Of both these tendencies there are occasional echoes in poetry as well as in the novel.

The Chartist agitation and demand for the abolition of the Corn Laws found a poet in Ebenezer Elliot, *The Village Patriarch* (1829), *Cornlaw Rhymes* (1831). His political poems have gone the way of most occasional poetry, but one or two of his lyrics have value as poetry: "Child, is thy father dead?", "Day like our souls is fiercely dark"; and one has a wider reference:

> Dark deep and cold the current flows
> Unto the sea where no wind blows,
> Seeking the land which no one knows.
>
> O'er its sad gloom still comes and goes
> The mingled wail of friends and foes,
> Borne to the land which no one knows.
>
> . . . . .
>
> Though myriads go with him who goes,
> Alone he goes where no wind blows
> Unto the land which no one knows.
>
> . . . . .
>
> Alone with God, where no wind blows,
> And Death his shadow—doomed he goes:
> That God is there the shadow shows.
>
> O shoreless deep where no wind blows!
> And thou O land which no one knows!
> That God is all the shadow shows.

It was Carlyle's *Past and Present* (1843) which stated the industrial problem with an emphasis which could not be ignored. "I think the effect of Carlyle's *Past and Present* and of Disraeli's *Sybil*," said the Conservative, Stafford Northcote, "upon me has been to unsettle any opinions, if ever I had any on political subjects." The influence is seen in many novels, and in the poetry of Hood and Mrs. Browning and Kingsley, and even in such work of the Victorian Dioscuri as Browning's *Sordello* (from which it needs some fishing up) and Tennyson's *Maud*. It cannot be said that it produced any poetry comparable to the prose of Carlyle's work mentioned above.

In religious circles the Evangelical movement had spent itself as a freshening force by the first years of Victoria, which

is not to say that it was dead.   The first clear signal of the
reaction against Liberal influence in the Church is generally
taken to be the sermon preached by Keble in 1833 entitled
"National Apostasy".   He had already, in 1827, published
the *Christian Year*, a volume of religious, Anglican verse.   In
the Oxford Movement which followed, with the publication of
Tracts for the Times, the dominant figure that emerged was
John Henry Newman, a master of English prose but also a
poet of greater depth of feeling than Keble.   He appeared as
a poet in *Lyra Apostolica* along with four others.   Later he
published alone, now a Roman, *The Dream of Gerontius* (1865)
and *Verses on Various Occasions* (1868).   Keble followed up the
Christian Year with *Lyra Innocentium* (1846) and *Miscellany
Poems* (1869).   The Oxford Movement with its Catholic
tendencies provoked no little opposition which in poetry found
expression in the work of Kingsley, *Saint's Tragedy* (1848),
Andromeda and other Poems (1856).

Johnson's judgment on religious poetry, which Cowper
resented, that it is always "unsatisfactory", "The paucity of
its topics enforces perpetual repetition, and the sanctity of the
matter rejects the ornaments of figurative decoration", would
require fuller consideration than can be given it here.   There
are two categories under which such poetry may come, the
hymn, or what is of the nature of a hymn inasmuch as it undertakes to give voice to the sentiments of the Christian as such,
the congregation.   But there is also the poetry which records
the reactions of the individual to religious experiences or
dogmas.   Of the former few would deny poetic value to the
best of the great Latin hymns of the earlier Church.   When
Johnson tried to repeat the *Dies Irae* he could never pass the
stanza ending *Tantus labor non sit cassus* without bursting into a
flood of tears, so says Mrs. Piozzi.   Nor are we without some
hymns which have poetic value, including Watts's "O God,
our help in ages past" which might well take the place of any
national anthem.   Of the other kind of religious verse the best
examples before the date of Keble and Newman had been the
religious poetry of the seventeenth century: Donne, Herbert,
Vaughan, Traherne.   Even the poems which Donne calls
hymns, "In what torn ship soever I embark" and "Wilt thou
forgive that sin where I begun", are too personal for congrega-
tional use, though the latter was, Walton tells us, set to music
and "often sung to the organ by the choristers of St. Paul's",

to the great comfort of Donne in his last days. It is with this poetry that one must compare the poetry of Keble, Newman, and their fellows.

One may note a twofold purpose present consciously or not in such a personal religious poem,—the record of the individual's own reactions and a sermon preached to himself and others. The less intense the personal reaction the stronger the tendency to preach. There is more of it in Herbert than in Donne or Vaughan. The sermon naturally and obviously predominates in the poems which Keble writes appropriate in Anglican feeling to the particular day. Each poem, or most of them, starts from a text taken from the Gospel, Epistle, or one of the Lessons for the day. It was a belief of Keble that "the example of the Jews as a nation is there" (in the Old Testament) "held out in such a way as to regulate and correct the religious conduct of us Christians as individuals." Keble can thus use for edification incidents in the history of the conquest of Canaan from which our minds are prone to turn away, as when in a poem named by Saintsbury among the best he describes the Israelite contemplating with complacence the work of the man he has slain or despoiled which is now his own:

> It was a fearful joy, I ween,
> To trace the heathen's toil,
> The limpid wells, the orchards green
> Left ready for the spoil,
> The household stores untouched, the roses bright
> Wreathed o'er the cottage walls in garlands of delight.

Just so has the poetry of Greece, "dear land of glorious lays", become the inheritance of the Christian who finds in it a deeper significance (*Third Sunday in Lent*). Newman strikes a deeper, more personal note in the poem which, not quite justifiably, the Churches have adopted as a hymn, "Lead, kindly light", for there is a very individual note in

> I was not ever thus, nor prayed that thou
> Shouldst lead me on;
> I loved to choose and see my path; but now
> Lead thou me on.
> I loved the garish day, and, spite of fears,
> Pride ruled my will: remember not past years.

But one splendid hymn is at once Christian and Catholic, for

the emphasis laid in "Praise to the holiest" on transubstantiation has not excluded it from *Hymns Ancient and Modern*:

> And that a higher gift than grace
> Should flesh and blood refine,
> God's presence and his very self,
> And essence all-Divine.

In *The Dream of Gerontius* there is the same combination of
Catholic doctrine and deep personal feeling:

> Take me away, and in the lowest deep
> There let me be,
> And there in hope the lone night-watches keep
> Told out for me.
> There motionless and happy in my pain
> Lone, not forlorn,—
> There will I sing my sad perpetual strain
> Until the morn.
> There will I sing, and soothe my stricken breast,
> Which ne'er can cease
> To throb and pine, and languish, till possest
> Of its Sole Peace.
> There will I sing my absent Lord and Love—
> Take me away,
> That sooner I may arise, and go above,
> And see Him in the truth of everlasting day.

It is a unique poem in our literature that no one else could
have written.

Once or twice a translation has taken its place in our literature almost as an original poem, as indeed for many it has been.
Chaucer's two longest single poems *Troilus and Criseyde* and
Palamon and Arcite which became the *Knight's Tale* are in great
measure translations from the Italian of Boccaccio. Of the
sixth book of *The Faerie Queene* a considerable part is almost
to the same extent a translation from the *Gerusalemme Liberata*
of Tasso. But Pope's *Homer* is the most outstanding example
of a translation which for some hundred years was read as an
English poem by many to whom the rest of Pope's work was
comparatively little known. "The train of my disquisition",
writes Johnson in 1780, "has now conducted me to that poetical
wonder, the translation of the *Iliad*; a performance which no
age or nation can pretend to equal". "It is certainly the noblest
version of poetry which the world has ever seen; and its publication must be considered as one of the great events in the

annals of literature." Johnson's estimate may be exaggerated, but he could never have used such language had the popularity of the poem not been to all appearances finally established. No other translation has taken its place. Something of the same unique reputation has been acquired by the very free translation of the *Rubáiyát*—or a selection from them—of the Persian poet Omar Khayyám by Edward FitzGerald. The *Rubáiyát* in Persian are "independent stanzas, consisting each of four lines of equal, though varied, Prosody; sometimes all rhyming but oftener . . . the third line a blank". So says the translator and he has adopted the form with the third line blank:

> Awake! for Morning in the Bowl of Night
> Has flung the Stone that puts the stars to flight:
> And Lo! the Hunter of the East has caught
> The Sultan's Turret in a Noose of Light.

So the poem opens in the first edition of 1859, which attracted little or no attention till accidentally discovered on a book-stall by Swinburne. The author, Edward FitzGerald, friend of Thackeray and Tennyson, had already published translations from the Spanish of Calderon but withdrawn them, and had tried his hand at other Persian poets. But in Omar Fitz-Gerald found a great poet, and one the tone and tenor of whose poetry appealed in the strongest manner both to his own bent of thought and also to that of many more than himself. In Omar Khayyám is heard the note that was to be emphasised by Hardy, the voice of those who cannot accept the orthodox claim that all man's troubles are the result of his own erring will:

> Oh Thou who didst with Pitfall and with Gin
> Beset the Road I was to wander in,
>   Thou wilt not with Predestination round
> Enmesh me, and impute my Fall to Sin,

to which he added, the snake and the last line his own:

> Oh Thou who man of baser earth didst make,
> And even with Paradise devise the snake:
>   For all the Sin wherewith the Face of Man
> Is blacken'd—Man's forgiveness give—and take!

FitzGerald's "daring genius gave Omar Khayyám a place for ever among the greatest English poets" (Swinburne). Like Chaucer he was not content to be solely a translator. There is no equivalent of the last stanza quoted in the original. But it is not these audacities alone which gave the poem its attraction. It was also the poetry pure and simple.

Alfred was not the only one of the sons of the Rector of Somersby who wrote poetry. Both the elder Frederick and the younger Charles were real if not great poets. In each of them one finds a side of the greater poet isolated. For there are two Alfred Tennysons, each a genuine expression of himself if popular approval and encouragement tempted him to a certain over-emphasis of the less profound stratum in his nature. There is the melancholy, brooding poet, even hysterical at moments; the poet of the early *Confessions of a Second-Rate Sensitive Mind*, *The Two Voices*, of many sections of *In Memoriam*, and of the last poems so full of a passionate sincerity and melancholy. But there is the other Tennyson, primarily the artist pure and simple but in sympathy with his early Christian upbringing and anxious to render a good account of the talents entrusted to him, and only too sensitive to the voices of the critics and the reiterated demand that he should write great and edifying poetry, the sincere champion in his own doubting heart of Christian feeling and the Christian faith in God, Freedom, and Immortality. The simpler Christian in Alfred is dominant in the Vicar of Grasby in Lincolnshire, Charles Tennyson-Turner. The melancholy, questing Alfred is isolated in Frederick, from whom FitzGerald looked for something great when Alfred had given himself over too much to edification and the public: "You are now the only man I expect verse from. Such gloomy grand stuff as you write . . . we want some bits of strong, genuine imagination." Charles's poems took almost without exception the form of the Italian sonnet but with a fresh set of rhymes in the second quartet. In the final edition they numbered more than three hundred, which is somewhat excessive. The best are not the religious or theological but those on aspects of Nature in a minor Wordsworthian manner or on simple incidents as the best-known *Letty's Globe*. It is more difficult to assess the poetry of Frederick. His first volume, *Days and Hours*, is not of a kind to gain immediate recognition. The poems are thoughtful and original. One does not feel the influence of any other poet. The main themes are the different seasons and Nature treated in a very imaginative way: *The Birth of the Year*, *First of March*, *To April*, *Thirty-first of May*, etc. Each is made the occasion for a strain of thought always dignified and even noble; at times remote as in *A Dream of Spring*, the subject of which is a vision of one who loves him, though not of this world, but awaits him with certainty in another world:

> I am the spirit that hath onward led
>   Thy mortal steps, the being that shall be
>   Hereafter loved by thee, and only thee,
> The soul thy soul shall wed;
>
> Before the bases of the world were laid,
>   Or bloodless dust awoke unto the sun,
>   The secret spirit of the Highest One
> Knew all things He hath made;
>
> The thoughts of God were harmonies to be—
>   Music and light—the waters and the wind—
>   And souls ordained their perfect life to find
> In perfect sympathy;

and so on at considerable length, for Frederick never took to heart his brother's lesson of compression. But such a strain of thought is sincere in Frederick, somewhat of a mystic and later a Swedenborgian. Many of his short poems are fine; there are fine things too in his longer poems, interminable as they are and obscure in their general drift.

Chapter Thirty-Four

MID-VICTORIAN POETRY

(1) *Arnold, Clough, and Kingsley*

THE decay of faith and the spread of industrialism form the background of Mid-Victorian poetry. Not all these Mid-Victorians were full-time poets, like Tennyson and Browning; Arnold and Clough were public servants, Rossetti and Morris were artists; and their vocations left a mark on their poetry.

Matthew Arnold (1822–1888) was the son of Dr. Arnold of Rugby. He was a reformer like his father, and not in education only; with his European outlook he struck his finger on all the ailments that threatened England with anarchy. On these he preached to the nation at large in prose that all could understand, employing every weapon of debate, logic, wit, irony, and banter. His verse was addressed to a more select audience; its tone was habitually grave and often sad.

Arnold saw himself as one who stood alone on a naked beach from which the tide of faith had ebbed. In the Ages of Faith Christ had lived in the hearts of the faithful:

> Now he is dead! Far hence he lies
> In the lorn Syrian town;
> And on his grave, with shining eyes,
> The Syrian stars look down.

Yet Arnold's was a soul naturally Christian: when he outgrew the dogmas in which he had been too strictly reared, he still clung to what he regarded as the truth of Christianity, its exaltation of righteousness, self-renunciation, kindness, and purity. The spread of industrialism combined with the decay of faith to depreciate these Christian values, as men abandoned the kindly life of the country with its ancient pieties for the feverish competition of manufacturing towns.

What propped his mind in those bad days? Three things —Nature, Poetry, and Love. Arnold was a devout Wordsworthian, but his view of Nature was not Wordsworth's. He understood and felt Wordsworth's healing power; his visionary power he did not understand, never having known in himself that access of mind, those visitations from the living God, which Wordsworth enjoyed in moments of ecstasy. For Arnold the secret of Nature was not joy but peace, sometimes it seemed to him the peace of mere acquiescence; or if joy, only the joy of the stars as they perform their appointed shining. It was the steadfast self-sufficiency of Nature as she went about the business of her seasons that calmed and strengthened him. From high poetry he drew not only strength but joy. And at rare moments, when a loved hand is clasped in ours, a bolt is shot back in the breast, and we see again the hills where our life rose, and the dawn of a hope, that, as the river of Time draws to the ocean, peace may come to the soul of the voyager on its breast, as the night-wind brings upstream "murmurs and scents of the infinite sea".

Of love as a personal, disturbing factor in Arnold's life there are some, if veiled, indications in a few of his most poignant poems. He stood up better than his friend Clough to the stern discipline of the elder Arnold, but he felt its effect throughout his life:

> For rigorous teachers seized my youth,
> And purged its faith, and trimm'd its fire,
> Show'd me the high, white star of Truth,
> There bade me gaze, and there aspire.

However his religious doubts may have led him away from his early teaching, the moral influence was enduring. The Puritan in Arnold is even too obvious in his inability to do justice to French literature and character because of his dislike of what he calls 'lubricity'. But into his life came, if we may trust at all the group of lyrics entitled *Switzerland* (and some others which connect with that group), a love for one between whom and him lay the gulf of a different ethic, temperament, and experience. The best known of the group is the poem which opens with the vivid image of the loneliness of the human heart:

> Yes! in the sea of life enisled,
> With echoing straits between us thrown,
> Dotting the shoreless watery wild,
> We mortal millions live *alone*.
> The islands feel the enclasping flow,
> And then their endless bounds they know.

Human Life, not included in the group but evidently referring to the same experience, expresses in another poignant figure the same consciousness of a gulf that even love cannot cross:

> No! as the foaming swath
> Of torn-up water, on the main,
> Falls heavily away with long-drawn roar
> On either side the black deep-furrow'd path
> Cut by an onward-labouring vessel's prore,
> And never touches the ship-side again;
>
> Even so we leave behind,
> As, charter'd by some unknown Powers,
> We stem across the sea of life by night,
> The joys which were not for our use design'd;—
> The friends to whom we had no natural right,
> The homes that were not destined to be ours.

Arnold wrote some nobler poems, but none quite so poignant; and once one has detected the hidden experience it is difficult not to suspect its influence in what seem more purely imaginative creations, even it may be in that early imaginative poem which Tennyson envied him, *The Forsaken Merman.* If that very difficult poem, *The New Sirens,* has any discoverable meaning, it voices the conflict between Arnold's Puritan conscience and the appeal of pleasure, not the cruel pleasures associated with the name:

> Oh, your pardon!   The uncouthness
> Of that primal age is gone,
> And the skin of dazzling smoothness
> Screens not now a heart of stone;

but despite their more prevailing because more reasonable appeal,

> "Ah," you say, "the large appearance
> Of man's labour is but vain,
> And we plead as staunch adherence
> Due to pleasure as to pain,"

yet in the end leaving the same sense of emptiness:

> In the pines the thrush is waking—
> Lo, yon orient hill in flames!
> Scores of true love knots are breaking
> At divorce which it proclaims.
> When the lamps are paled at morning,
> Heart quits heart and hand quits hand.
> Cold in that unlovely dawning,
> Loveless, rayless, joyless you shall stand!

It is probably an intentionally obscure poem, but it suggests an Arnoldian version of the theme of Swinburne's prelude to the *Songs before Sunrise*, and it was at Swinburne's instance that it was reprinted.

The severe repression to which these poems bear witness must be borne in mind in considering Arnold's poetic output. His first volumes, *The Strayed Reveller* (1849) and *Empedocles on Etna* (1852), attracted little attention. It was the volume of 1853, the volume containing *Sohrab and Rustum* and *The Scholar Gipsy*, with the famous preface on poetry, which gave him the place among poets that he enjoyed with those for whom Tennyson and Browning had said their say, and who refused to be carried away by the intoxicating strains of Rossetti and Swinburne. But after 1867 Arnold wrote no more verse except an ode on Westminster Abbey evoked by the death of his friend Dean Stanley, and three little "croons, pathetic, sweet", on the deaths of his canary and his two dachshunds. It pleased him to make out that the poet in him had been killed by the Inspector of Schools; but that was not the first or the only repressive factor. Arnold was a poet with a clear view of what poetry should be; but his inhibitions were potent and his sense-endowment was not rich. His ear was uncertain. His eye preferred moonlight to sunlight. There is no lovelier scene in his poems than the moonlight scene in *Tristram and Iseult*:

> And far beyond the sparkling trees
> Of the castle park one sees
> The bare heaths spreading clear as day,
> Moor behind moor, far, far away,
> Into the heart of Brittany.

Less lovely, perhaps, but more sublime, more Arnoldian in its detachment, is the closing scene of *Sohrab and Rustum*:

> But the majestic river floated on
> Out of the mist and hum of that low land
> Into the frosty starlight, and there moved,
> Rejoicing, through the hush'd Chorasmian waste
> Under the solitary moon. . . .
>   . . . Till at last
> The long'd-for dash of waves is heard, and wide
> His luminous home of waters opens, bright
> And tranquil, from whose floor the new-bathed stars
> Emerge, and shine upon the Aral Sea.

In Wordsworth and Byron Arnold saw the two chief English poets of the nineteenth century, but he himself had neither the sixth sense which was Wordsworth's peculiar gift nor the abandonment of Byron: the 'Switzerland' lyrics reveal a nature that, if not absolutely master of passion, is certainly not its slave.   His habitual mood was resignation, and resignation does not sing.   Elegiac, not lyric, was the mode proper to his temperament.   For, if his poems lack or repress passion, they often breathe warm affection.   *Rugby Chapel, A Summer Night,* and *Thyrsis,* poems inspired by his love for his father, his brother, and the friend of his youth, are among the best and most characteristic things he ever wrote.

Though the vein of poetry in Arnold was not rich, it was pure; and he refined it further by the diligent study of the best models.   Homer and Sophocles, Milton, Goethe, Wordsworth, and Keats were more than influences on Arnold; they were models that he kept consciously before him: Goethe notably in the reflective poems in irregular blank verse—*The Youth of Man, The Buried Life, The Future,* and others; Keats perhaps only in *The Scholar Gipsy* and *Thyrsis,* and there mainly in the touches of "natural magic" and the stanzaic form, which recalls the structure of some of Keats's odes with interesting differences.   In Keats he saw a supreme artist rich in the sensuous endowment that he lacked himself, but he also divined the greater soul behind, as Carlyle failed to do.   Arnold's poetry is the poetry of a scholar and a critic.   He had learned from the Greeks that to be good a poem must have a good subject, must be beautiful not in patches but as a whole, orderly, lucid, and sane.   He disliked, though he had felt its charm, the insubstantiality (he comes near to calling it the inanity) of Shelley, and Tennyson's jewellery, and the eccentricity and obscurity of Browning.

Arnold's devotion to the Greeks was not all pure gain.   The pastoral note in *Thyrsis* is too slight to offend, is even an added grace; but the noble epic 'episode' of *Sohrab and Rustum* is too deliberately starred with Homeric similes; the poetic *nisus* of *Balder Dead* is too weak to carry forward its mass of mythological detail; and the Sophoclean tragedy of *Merope* is frigid to the point of being dead.   With all his Hellenising Arnold is not really a Greek, not so much of a Greek in spirit as his pagan master Goethe.   His wistful tone will not let us forget the Christian centuries that separate him from Sophocles.

And, alive as he was to the faults of the Romantic Revival, he was one of its children after all. His most poetic (we do not say his most characteristic) things, things like *The Neckan*, *The Forsaken Merman*, the description of the Oxford country in *The Scholar Gipsy*, or of the Alpine dawn in *Obermann Once More*, are essentially romantic. Classical and Romantic influences blend in the beautiful lines *To a Gipsy Child*, lines written in the manner of Wordsworth, but of the Wordsworth of *Laodamia*, Wordsworth writing in the manner of Virgil. In *A Summer Night*, perhaps the most perfect of all his poems, he has no thought of models, Classical or Romantic, but writes out of the fulness of a heart sorrowing for a brother's death.

Arnold once expressed the hope that his poetry might live because, though he had less poetic sentiment than Tennyson, less intellectual vigour and abundance than Browning, he had more of a fusion of the two than either. His modest hope has been fulfilled; no Victorian poet has worn better. And no prose critic of his country and his age has foretold more justly the trend of democracy, seen better the spirit which alone can give ethical value to the "new order", than the man who in his final message proclaimed as the watchword of a truly democratic society the words, "Shun greed and cultivate equality".

Thyrsis commemorates Arnold's friend, Arthur Hugh Clough (1819–1861), a product of Rugby and Balliol like himself. Clough too was a natural Christian fallen on an iron time. But he had not Arnold's resilience: at Rugby he took Dr. Arnold more seriously than his son did; at Oxford he was swept off his feet by the Tractarian Movement. Recovering, he set himself to wrestle in his own strength with the problems of modern life: *Dipsychus*, which records his struggle, is a kind of weak, Mid-Victorian *Faust*. The hero of *Amours de Voyage* is a doubter too, and a failure in love. The later *Mari Magno* shows Clough in happier mood after his own happy marriage. But the most readable of his long poems to-day is *The Bothie of Tober-na-Vuolich*, the story of an Oxford reading-party in the Highlands. The condition-of-England question provides a background; but the real interest of the poem does not lie there. Nor do its rough hexameters deserve Arnold's praise of them as Homeric; they are most effective in the mock-heroic passages which relieve the serious theme. The charm of the poem—and it still charms a fit audience—lies in the descriptions of the Highlands, and, above all, in its youthful, Oxonian spirit.

Clough had no lyric gift, and Swinburne, to whom poetry meant song, scoffed at him:

> There was a bad poet called Clough,
> Whom his friends found it useless to puff.

But Clough's lines, "Say not the struggle nought availeth", have cheered millions to whom Swinburne means nothing. Nor have we all forgotten *Peschiera* and *Qua Cursum Ventus*. Clough was greater than his poetry: he had not art enough, nor indeed inspiration enough, to be a great poet; but Arnold, who as good as told him so, also declared that no purer or more subtle spirit ever breathed—nor any, we may add, with a deeper love of truth.

Carlyle's teaching helped Clough to discard "Hebrew old clothes". It was the social, not the religious, side of that same teaching that appealed to Charles Kingsley (1819–1875). But Kingsley's answer to the condition-of-England question, his gospel of Christian Socialism, was delivered in prose; as a poet he is remembered only for a handful of lyrics—*The Three Fishers*, *The Sands of Dee*, *The Last Buccaneer*, "When all the world is young, lad"—simple, ballad-like pieces with the true popular ring. His long narrative *Andromeda* ought also to be remembered, at least by scholars, for its verse; Kingsley's hexameters are the best in English, much more 'Homeric' than Clough's or Longfellow's.

Chapter Thirty-Five

MID-VICTORIAN POETRY

(2) The Pre-Raphaelite Group

DANTE GABRIEL ROSSETTI (1828–1882) turned his
back on the religious and social problems that weighed so
heavy on Arnold and Clough.   He cared nothing for science,
philosophy, history, or politics.   Love and Beauty to him were
all in all.   His worship of them did not lift him with Plato to
the contemplation of the Idea of Beauty laid up in the heavenly
places, nor with Dante to the vision of the Divine Love that
moves the sun and the other stars.   It remained individual
and earthly, the love of a man for "one loveliest woman's form
and face".   He may say,

> Thy soul I know not from thy body, nor
> Thee from myself, neither our love from God,

but the God with whom their love is one is not the Christian
Deity.   *Ave* and *World's Worth* reveal Rossetti's understanding of the reverence of the Virgin and the mystery of the
Eucharist, but it is the understanding of an artist, a dramatic
poet, not of a believer.   Refusing to breathe the common air
of the world around him, unable to rise like his sister into the
purer ether of religion, he found the walls of the ivory tower
which he had made his House of Life slowly closing in on him
till they stifled him at the last.   It might have been otherwise
if his wife had lived and his home been filled with the laughter
of children.   Other elements in Rossetti's personal tragedy do
not concern the student of his poetry.   After his wife's death
in 1862 he wrote no more for years; the *Poems* published in
1870 were mostly written before she died.   His only other
published volumes were, in 1861 *The Early Italian Poets*,
afterwards named *Dante and his Circle*, a collection of translations of rare felicity; and *Ballads and Sonnets* in 1881.

Rossetti's poetry is an exotic in our English garden.   He
was three parts Italian by blood and half Italian by culture.
In boyhood he absorbed Coleridge and Keats; at nineteen he
discovered Browning, "and everything else fell into the background"; but he underwent a stricter discipline in his minute

study of the early Italian poets.   He was at home in Italy, not contemporary Italy, the Italy of Mazzini and Garibaldi and Cavour, but the Italy of the Middle Ages, a land of poets and painters in whose company he could forget the drab ugliness of industrial England.

Rossetti himself was a painter before he was a poet.   He was the master-mind of the pre-Raphaelite Brotherhood, whose aim it was to bring Art back to the truth of Nature.   Details impress themselves on minds sensitised by emotion; conversely, emotion may be conveyed, whether in painting or in poetry, by the faithful delineation of significant details.   *My Sister's Sleep* is a perfect example: significant details faithfully delineated, stroke on stroke, convey not only the visible scene but the feeling of the scene and the season—a quiet room on Christmas Eve where sleep passes into death.   *The Portrait* is equally perfect in the same pre-Raphaelite style.   In *The Blessed Damozel* there is the same clear painting of details, each for a moment in the focus of vision, "the clear-ranged unnumbered heads", all on a background of infinite space.   Later, Rossetti's colouring deepened, grew richer but less pure; his style, from being direct and, except for some choice archaisms, plain, turned into a kind of aureate diction, heavy with exotic Latinisms and compound adjectives in the manner of Keats. It is like a change from water-colour to oils.

For narrative he had another style, or other styles.   *A Last Confession* and *Jenny* are dramatic monologues, the former very much in Browning's manner.   These have modern subjects, and *Jenny* is unique in its expression of pity for a tragedy of real life.   His other narrative poems are all mediaeval in setting or tone, with the light of the Middle Ages refracted through a sombre, sensuous temperament.   One mediaeval form, the ballad, attracted him particularly.   Only in *Stratton Water* did he imitate the simple popular ballad.   *The White Ship* and *The King's Tragedy*, though in simple ballad diction, are really historical lays recited by eye-witnesses.   In *Troy Town*, *Eden Bower*, and more boldly in *Sister Helen* he used the ballad device of the refrain.   *Sister Helen* is a masterpiece in its artificial kind.   Helen, melting a waxen image of her false lover, recalls Virgil's Pharmaceutria; but the form is modelled on the ballad of *Edward*, both in its attack—

" Why do you melt your waxen man,
    Sister Helen?"—

"Why dois your brand sae drap wi' bluid,
Edward, Edward?"—

and in its evolution, the story not being told directly but inferred in mounting horror from the dialogue between brother and sister. All these poems, except *Stratton Water*, are pervaded with a sense of evil and doom; and the same is true of the mediaeval romances of *The Bride's Prelude* and *Rose Mary*. The stifling atmosphere of *The Bride's Prelude* is tainted with evil; evil spirits occupy the heart of the magic beryl in *Rose Mary*; the black magic of *Eden Bower* and *Sister Helen* is wrought by souls envenomed with hate.

Rossetti's cult of Love and Beauty finds its fullest, subtlest, and most sumptuous expression in the sonnet-sequence called *The House of Life*. It is not a true sequence; some of the sonnets are early, others late, and there are few links between them; each is the monument of a moment of emotion or passion, a station on the *via amoris* which leads from the birth of love to the rapture of supreme surrender and wedded bliss, then down life's darkening slope to desolation, to the acquiescence in which Death seems a child on the widowed lover's knee, and to the one hope with which the series ends. For Rossetti love is an ecstasy, sensuous yet not wholly of the senses; at times it has the comprehensiveness of a mystical religion, when the loved one seems not as herself alone but "as the meaning of all things that are". Yet the craving for possession is never wholly absent.

Rossetti was not a prophet; he was a highly intellectual, sophisticated artist, often less intent on meaning than on colour and sound. Even in the heart-felt *House of Life* his language is sophisticated to excess; in his other poems he drew his inspiration less from Nature, of which he knew little, than from art and poetry. Many of his sonnets are on works of art; in many of his poems we catch echoes or overtones from Bürger and the balladists, or from the meaningless melodies of Poe, or the magical suggestiveness of Coleridge and Keats, or from Browning or Dante. We are in a hothouse full of strange, forced blooms and heavy odours. It is an enchanted and enchanting place; but those who believe with Arnold that what the complaining millions of men want from poetry is something to animate and ennoble them are fain to escape from it into the open air. Two things more must, however, be said of Rossetti: he left an indelible mark on English poetic diction, both by the simplicity of his earlier and the sumptuousness of his later style; and he expressed the passion of wedded love, in rapture and in desolation, with an urgency of thought and feeling unsurpassed in English poetry.

William Morris (1834–1896) went to Oxford in 1851 meaning to take holy orders, but as he had no real interest in the Church and a vivid interest in Gothic architecture, his friendship with Burne-Jones deflected him easily from theology into art. By Rossetti's advice he turned from architecture to painting; then he took up handicraft, and revolutionised the whole art of house-furnishing in England. Personal experience as a master-workman combined with his study of Gothic to convince him that the excellence of mediaeval arts and crafts came from the joy that the workman found in his work, a joy unattainable under capitalist conditions of competitive mass-production. This conviction made him a revolutionary socialist. These three stages in Morris's career correspond roughly to three stages in the development of his poetry.

The Defence of Guinevere (1858) is mediaeval in subject and studiously pre-Raphaelite in style—it was dedicated to Rossetti. Morris wrote of the Middle Ages, their romantic dreams and brutal realities, as he found them in the pages of Malory and Froissart. His knights are not Victorian gentlemen, but fighters by trade, hardened in the Hundred Years' War, fighting for revenge or gold as often as for love or glory. Such we find them in *Shameful Death*, and *Sir Peter Harpdon's End*, and *The Haystack in the Floods*. Their loves are like their hates; Morris knew the bitter of romantic love as well as its sweet. Some of the lyrics have a boyish abandon very unlike Rossetti's sophistications, but a refrain like

> Two red roses across the moon

invited Calverley's parody of

> Butter and eggs and a pound of cheese.

Morris's long narrative poems belong to his busiest years as a master-workman. *The Life and Death of Jason* (1867) tells at full length the story that Apollonius and Euripides left half told. In *The Earthly Paradise* a band of aged Norse rovers light on a land peopled by men of Greek race; hosts and guests entertain each other with stories alternately Greek and mediaeval. Morris professes to bring no message of hope or consolation; he is "the idle singer of an empty day", singing only for the recreation of men

> meshed within this smoky web
> Of unrejoicing labour,

and all under the doom of death. (But may not the singer "animate and ennoble" who tells, like Homer's minstrel, of the glorious deeds of men?) As a story-teller in verse, Morris took Chaucer for his master. He has all Chaucer's discursiveness, but little of his verbal felicity and none of his sly humour; if he had a bluff humour of his own, he kept it out of his verse. The result is rather monotonous—a harping on the two strings of love and death. Morris is always the poet, and his strong visual imagination often lights up his narrative with clear pre-Raphaelitish pictures of things seen, such as this of reapers at lunch:

> While on the turf beside them lay
> The ashen-handled sickles grey,
> The matters of their cheer between:
> Slices of white cheese, specked with green,
> And green-striped onions and rye-bread,
> And summer apples faintly red,
> Even beneath the crimson skin;
> And yellow grapes, well ripe and thin,
> Plucked from the cottage gable-end.

But the stories themselves are apt to be prolix, and the reach-me-down epithets, expletives, and obvious rhymes betray a hasty and incurious hand. Morris did not think much of a 'chap' who could not compose an epic while he wove a tapestry: we hope that the texture of his tapestry was not so loose as that of his epic. These strictures apply to the stories in *The Earthly Paradise*, not to the beautiful pageants of the months that are intercalated between them; and among the stories they apply less to the mediaeval than to the Greek, and least of all to the Norse. It was a lucky day for Morris when he fell in love with the Icelandic sagas, and confirmed his passion by a trip to Iceland. His robust nature was more at home there than among the Greeks. *Sigurd the Volsung* (1876), founded on the *Volsunga Saga*, is the best of all his narrative poems. The story of Sigmund, Sigurd's father, which fills the first book, is superfluous, and at bottom repulsive; but Sigurd himself has

sparks of chivalry, and his story, for all its savagery, is dignified
by the ever-present sense of doom.   The poem is still too long
for all that happens in it; but the march of the narrative is
quickened by the trampling measure, Morris's own invention,
a line of six beats in rising rhythm with frequent anapaests
and extra mid-line syllables, perhaps as good a substitute for
the dactylic hexameter of Homer as our rude northern tongue
affords:

> Then I taught them the craft of metals, and the sailing of the
>   sea,
> And the taming of the horse-kind, and the yoke-beasts husbandry,
> And the building up of houses; and that race of men went by,
> And they said that Thor had taught them; and a smithying-carle
>   was I.
> Then I gave their maidens the needle and I bade them hold the
>   rock,
> And the shuttle-race gaped for them as they sat at the weaving-
>   stock.
> But by then these were waxen crones to sit dim-eyed by the
>   door,
> It was Freya had come among them to teach the weaving-lore.

The diction, it will be seen, is almost pure Saxon; at times it
threatens to become Anglo-Saxon.

Morris's revolutionary socialism found literary expression
chiefly in prose romances; but *Poems by the Way* (1891) contains some prophetic chants on the good time coming, when
capitalism shall be abolished, and dignity and freedom return
to the lives of the workers, who will inherit an earth beautified
by Nature and Art and ask no other paradise.

Some of Morris's best poems were based neither on legends
nor on dreams of the future.   In *Mother and Son* he found
inspiration where Wordsworth found it, in the primary human
affections and duties, and produced his masterpiece.

No poet except Byron broke upon English readers with
quite the same surprise, the same blend of admiration and
shocked feeling, as Algernon Charles Swinburne (1837–1909).
His blood was as blue as Byron's: his father was an admiral
belonging to an old Northumberland family, his mother the
daughter of the Earl of Ashburnham.   Like Byron's *Hours of
Idleness*, Swinburne's two dramas, *The Queen Mother* and
Rosamond (1860), passed unnoticed; but the publication of
Atalanta in Calydon (1865), followed by *Poems and Ballads*

(1866), evoked a blend of the admiration which attended *Childe Harold* and the indignation provoked by the first cantos of *Don Juan*. But there was nothing immature in the art either of the dramas or of the lyrical poems. Swinburne's art had passed through a long period of experiment and discipline. At Eton he had excelled in Latin, and still more in Greek, verse, and had composed a poem in the manner of Pope. At Oxford he competed for the Newdigate, and for another prize offered for a poem on Sir John Franklin; he won neither. But at Oxford he met D. G. Rossetti and William Morris, and, as was his way in all his friendships, became their enthusiastic admirer. Under their influence, especially Morris's, he wrote, as we now know from M. Lafourcade's study of the unpublished poems, a number of poems in the manner of those in Morris's *Defence of Guinevere*, poems that might have been included in that volume without discredit:

> The night grows very old; almost
>   One feels the morning's feet move on;
> One lily glimmers like a ghost
>   On the black water, *only one*.
> I thought she was not dying; feel
>   *How cold her naked feet are grown!*
> I dare not either sit or kneel;
>   The flesh is stiffened to the bone.

But this phase passed. Swinburne's taste was not for mediaeval poetry but for Greek and Elizabethan drama; and his diction shows throughout the influence of the English Bible. By the time of his first published poems he had attained to a style of his own; and in the choruses of *Atalanta* and in the *Poems and Ballads* was revealed as the greatest lyrical poet since Shelley.

Atalanta in Calydon is in form a Greek tragedy, and its style and lyrical rhythms have exercised a marked influence on the translations of Mr. Gilbert Murray. The anti-theistic strain of feeling which runs through the choruses, if it can find support in the questioning, or arraigning, of Apollo and the Gods, not in Euripides "the rationalist" alone, but in Aeschylus and Sophocles—Aeschylus, not Euripides, was Swinburne's favourite dramatist—was sharpened and intensified by a strain in the poet's own temperament, ultimately constitutional, which reacted on his poetry much as the consciousness of his lame foot did on that of Byron, and was reinforced in Swinburne by the work of the Marquis de Sade, to which he was introduced by Lord Houghton. But what constituted the appeal of the poem was not its spirit, which most readers accepted as part of the reproduction of Greek tragedy, but its form, the mastery of style touched with archaism and artifice, and above all the varied, exciting rhythms of the choruses, from the opening Spring song:

The hounds of Spring are on Winter's traces,

through that on the frustrated life of man:

Before the beginning of years,

that on love as the great disturber of human happiness:

For bitter thou wast from thy birth,
Aphrodite, a mother of strife,

and the fourth chorus which arraigns "the supreme evil, God", to the closing commos chanted by Meleager, Atalanta, Oeneus, and the Chorus.

If readers, with some exceptions, passed without comment the underlying motive of *Atalanta*, the issue of *Poems and Ballads* in the following year both confirmed their impression of the young poet's lyrical and metrical virtuosity and presented them with a quite definite challenge. Never since *Venus and Adonis*, *Hero and Leander*, and the *Songs and Sonets* of Donne had the passion of the senses been presented with such daring frankness; and with equal frankness, and but little dramatic disguise, the anti-theism of the earlier poem was chanted in the *Hymn of Proserpine* and other pieces. And never had the fundamental ballad measure, the metre of stress and unstress and substitution, been used with a like emphasis and variety.

To the outcry raised by *Poems and Ballads*, which led their first publisher to withdraw the volume, Swinburne replied with the not irrelevant plea that the poems were dramatic, not the expression of personal feeling but of conceivable, some of them, as the title suggests, historical, moods of feeling. But the sensuous strain was too fundamental to be overlooked, and some of the poems, e.g. *The Triumph of Time*, were frankly personal. One of the most delightful, *Itylus*, is a sheer flight of imagination in which one seems to hear the sustained stream of the nightingale's song and the swish of the swallow's wings throughout.

Swinburne's intense but limited sensibility had two poles—sensuous passion and hero-worship. Even in *Poems and Ballads* the latter found expression in the lovely lines on the death of Landor:

> I came as one whose thoughts half linger,
>   Half run before,
> The youngest to the oldest singer
>   That England bore,

as well as in the more *exalté* ode *To Victor Hugo*. It was in this direction, the expression in poetry of his rather abstract passion for liberty and his worship of great men, that he turned as the storm over his *Poems and Ballads* passed away. The *Song of Italy* (1867), evoked by his admiration for Mazzini, has the fault which had already shown itself in the preceding volume, the inability of the poet to know when to stop, to give to his sustained lyrics the sense of a beginning, middle, and end, the gradual quickening of the inspiring feeling and its gradual subsidence as the close approaches. Swinburne always sings at the top of his voice in soaring hyperboles and endless diffuseness. The *Song* was followed by the composition of a number of poems which, some of them published separately in advance, ultimately appeared in 1871 as *Songs Before Sunrise*. The sunrise was to have been the advent of an Italian Republic; its place was taken, to his disappointment and that of Mazzini, by the House of Savoy.

This is the fullest expression of the more ideal aspect of Swinburne's genius, his passion for liberty and Italy; and to some critics it is the best of his work. Swinburne's conception of liberty is in the highest degree abstract, identical with national independence and republican institutions. England is a country "free and not free", a "beacon-bright Republic far-off sighted". Before he died Swinburne had become a champion of the British Empire, and denounced both Irish Home Rulers and Transvaal Republicans.

There is in the *Songs Before Sunrise* all the mastery of phrase and rhythm of the earlier volume; but the strain is thinner and shriller. For the weight of sensuous feeling in the love poems there is hardly a sufficient weight and fulness of thought to compensate. The inspiring motive is too vague. The most interesting poems are the personal prelude in which the poet defends his own change of theme and mood, and those of which the subject is not Italian deliverance but the larger, if vaguer, theme of human advance from theism to a passionate humanism and the materialism of the scientific thought of the day, as that had been expounded by Tyndall before the British Association at Belfast: *Hertha* and *The Hymn of Man*.

With these volumes Swinburne had completed the whole range of his contribution to the thought of poetry.   He was to write many more poems, dramatic, lyrical, and narrative, and some good poetry, but the notes are all the same.   What he had begun on the theme of Mary Queen of Scots was completed in the lengthy *Bothwell* and in the closing *Mary Stuart*. He gave his version of the story of *Tristram of Lyonesse* and later of *Balin and Balan*, partly (one suspects) as a protest against Tennyson's tamer versions.   He hated the moralisations of the passionate old love-stories.   He wrote of the sea in such volumes as *Studies in Song* and *Songs of the Springtides*, of babies in roundels and other forms.   He composed a fine elegy on the death of Baudelaire, and many other occasional and political poems.   He wrote sonnets on all the Elizabethan dramatists, and such contemporaries as Carlyle and Newman. He added nothing that marked any important development in thought or form.

Christina Rossetti (1830–1894) was the younger of D. G. Rossetti's two sisters.   Her devotion to the Anglican communion must not make us forget her Italian blood.   It shows in her capacity for passion and her instinct for style, though the passion was rigidly repressed and the style so chastened that it looks like artlessness.   Her style, no doubt, owed much to her brother's early manner; but it was her pious mother and her sister Maria who moulded her character.   (Several of her most characteristic poems—*Goblin Market*, *Noble Sisters*, *The Lowest Room*—deal with contrasted pairs of sisters.)   Maria afterwards entered an Anglican nunnery.   But Nature never meant Christina for a nun.   She was in love with this kindly earth and its innocent creatures; and she was in love with love.   She was twice engaged to be married, and twice broke off her engagement on religious grounds.   But it was a broken heart that she brought to God: though she chose the Sacred before the Profane Love, the choice did not bring her happiness, nor even peace.   The peace that she should have found in believing was haunted by regrets for the joys she had forgone.   True, in her first *Christmas Carol* she sang of the Christ-child as simply and self-forgetfully as she sang of the winter rain. But the dominant note of her devotional pieces is heard not in that carol but in such a poem as *From House to Home*. The House, this kindly earth, is a pleasance of stately trees and singing-birds, with a heath around it full of small innocent creatures— lizards and frogs and moles and harmless hedgehogs. Then an angel beckons, and in a night her summer turns to snow; she sees before her a pale woman, mocked and tortured, but her hope is anchored in Heaven and a Heavenly hand pours sweetness into her bitter cup. Then on her sight there rises a vision of Home, the New Jerusalem of the Apocalypse and the *Paradiso*. But Home is far away, and meanwhile God's staff is a rod. So too in the wonderful "Passing Away" God promises that she shall hear Him call, "Arise, come away, My love, My sister, My spouse"; but while He tarries she must watch and pray.

As she watched and prayed in the narrow room of her strict creed, slowly dying, haunted by memories of hopes forgone and by bodings of death, sometimes thinking of the grave as a resting-place, sometimes seeing herself as a ghost shut out from the House she had loved, she still had two earthly consolations. She never quite lost her childlike delight in the kindly little things of earth, though it was the robin, not the lark, that cheered the winter of her year. And she never lost at all the joy which the artist finds in the practice of his art. Christina Rossetti was a born singer, and she cultivated her gift assiduously. She was the truest pre-Raphaelite of them all, as Mr. Lubbock says. Her brother and Morris deserted the creed of their youth; Swinburne never really held it; Christina Rossetti, except when she was mesmerised by Tennyson or carried away by her generous admiration for Mrs. Browning, kept the pre-Raphaelite faith to the last. And she was not only the truest pre-Raphaelite of them all; within her narrower range she was a better artist in words than any of them. Her brother's early work is wonderfully clear-cut, no doubt; but a keen eye can discern the chisel-marks; in Christina's they have all been worked out. In the best of the short lyrics which chant what we have called her childlike delight in the kindly little things of earth, lyrics such as *Spring Quiet*, *Winter Rain*, *A Chill*, *Child's Talk in April*, her patient art achieves a simplicity like that which came to Blake by nature.

Chapter Thirty-Six

MID-VICTORIAN POETRY

(3) *Patmore, Thomson, and other Minors*

COVENTRY PATMORE (1823–1896) had no childish faith to lose, for he was brought up without religion, until, at the age of eleven, or so he tells us, it suddenly struck him what a fine thing it would be if there was a God. So early did he display his gift for wilful thinking. Later, having willed a God, and convinced himself that he had identified his own will with God's, he found all things plain, and dismissed Science as an "agile ape".

Patmore's has been a curious fate. For some years his *Angel in the House* was the most popular poem in England. It describes a course of true love that runs smooth to happy Christian marriage. Felix is a handsome squire with £600 a year; Honoria, the Dean's daughter, a dear, good girl, has £3000 now and more in prospect. The story of their unruffled courtship, sung in sparkling quatrains to the tune of the Old Hundredth, appealed to all that was respectable and sentimental in England and America. Then the wind changed, and a generation intoxicated with Swinburne scoffed Patmore's domesticities and his psalm-tune off the field. Admirers and scoffers were both wide of the mark. The merit of the poem does not lie in its story. There is no reason of course why true lovers should not be prosperous, and Patmore was only following Wordsworth in poetising the common; but his realism, unsafeguarded by humour, makes him ridiculous when he means to be sprightly. *The Angel in the House* lives by its Preludes, with their intimate analysis of a lover's moods, their epigrams, sometimes trite but always polished, and their occasional felicities of phrase and profundities of feeling. Here is a cold dawn worthy of Rossetti:

> The moon shone yet, but weak and drear,
>   And seemed to watch, with bated breath,
> The landscape, all made sharp and clear
>   By stillness, as a face by death.

And here is a simile of the rejected lover that takes one's breath away:

> He wakes renewed from all his smart;
>   His only love, and she is wed!
>   His fondness comes about his heart
>   As milk comes when the babe is dead.

The Victories of Love is a sequel to *The Angel*, and shares the fate of most sequels. Honoria's rejected lover marries without love a humble, homely woman, who wins his heart at last by sheer goodness and devotion, loses two of her children, and dies. The pathos of her letters is too Dickensian for us.

Among Patmore's shorter poems, the early *Tamerton Church-Tower* has a storm which Ruskin thought the best storm in poetry: *Amelia*, Patmore's own favourite, tells how an elderly lover took his young betrothed to see her dead rival's grave— a situation inviting mockery, but treated by Patmore with disarming innocence.

In 1864 Patmore became a Roman Catholic, his first wife, who had held him back, having died two years before. In 1865 he married again, and a third time in 1881. Nine odes which he printed privately in 1868 attracted no attention, and it looked as if his star had set. But in 1877 *The Unknown Eros* revealed a new and greater Patmore. *The Unknown Eros* is a strange medley. The satirical odes are merely ludicrous in their rabid Toryism and spiritual arrogance; but such Nature-poems as *Winter* and *Wind and Wave*, whether symbolic or not, are delightful simply as Nature-poems; and there are four personal odes about his dead wife and his motherless children— *The Azalea, Departure, The Toys*, "*If I Were Dead*"—which are almost intolerably poignant: no one but Patmore could so have bared his heart. Most of the other odes are in a lofty vein of erotic mysticism, as far removed apparently in spirit from *The Angel in the House* as they certainly are in form. They are Pindaric odes, not lawless like Cowley's, but obeying laws which we feel but cannot formulate. Patmore's erotic, anthropomorphic mysticism is grounded in the text, "So God created man in his own image; in the image of God created He him; male and female created He them". The key to life, whether on earth or in Heaven, is sex:

> In the arithmetic of life
>   The smallest unit is a pair—

with the male character everywhere dominant. The hero of *The Angel* had declared, "I love God in her"; Christian marriage, always a sacrament in Patmore's eyes, is a rehearsal for the bliss of Heaven. In *The Unknown Eros* he converts this proposition, likening the desire of God for the soul of His choice to the desire of the bridegroom for the bride, and using the myth of Eros and Psyche to symbolise their spiritual dalliance. In *The Child's Purchase* he dared a like treatment of the Incarnation. In the odes these mysteries are veiled in poetry; the prose *Sponsa Dei*, in which the veil was lifted, he burned on a warning from Gerard Manley Hopkins—"That's telling secrets". Patmore's erotic mysticism, for which he found his warrant in the allegorical interpretation of the Song of Songs, has edified some; others agree with Newman in disliking his "mixing up amorousness with religion", what Housman more brutally called "his nasty mixture of piety and concupiscence". But if Housman said that, he also said, "Nobody admires his best poetry enough". When all deductions are made, Patmore remains a classic, if a minor classic, of the Mid-Victorian Age.

Over against this arrogant, uxorious mystic stands the dark figure of James Thomson the younger (1834–1882). ("B. V." he signed himself: "Bysshe Vanolis", in honour of his idols, Shelley and Novalis.) It was not doubt that weighed on Thomson's soul: it was despair. His father, who was in the Merchant Service, came to grief when he was about nine; his mother was already dead; so the boy was brought up in the Royal Caledonian Asylum, and at seventeen, much against his will, became an Army schoolmaster. While still in his teens he fell in love, once and for ever, with a girl of his own age; her sudden death broke his heart. In 1862 he was dismissed from the Army for some breach of regulations, and thereafter earned a precarious living, mostly by journalism. Bradlaugh, whom he had known in the Army, befriended him, and imbued him with his own harsh secularism. Penury, despair, insomnia, and drink brought him to his grave at forty-eight. These things must be borne in mind in judging of his poetry.

Thomson's fame rests mainly on *The City of Dreadful Night*, a nightmare vision, or series of visions, of a city of despair. The river of suicides flows through it, and over it hangs a horror of great darkness, with no blue heaven beyond. Tennyson had cried in his despair,

> What hope of answer or redress?
> Behind the veil! Behind the veil!

For Thomson there was nothing behind the veil—no God, no purpose, no future life; and the most lamentable cry that goes up from the hopeless ones is for this brief earthly life wasted and given in vain. "Hell is a city much like London", says Shelley; and Thomson's City of Dreadful Night is much like the London through whose streets the terror of insomnia drove him to wander in the darkness. The whole poem is scarcely sane; but its aching sincerity and the pressure of thought which packs its clanging stanzas make it dreadfully impressive.

But Thomson had other moods. *Sunday at Hampstead* and *Sunday up the River* are gay with the gaiety of Cockney week-enders snatching a brief holiday from shop or desk. Gay, and manly too: the best songs in them—"As we rush, as we rush in the train", "Give a man a horse he can ride", "Let my voice ring out over the earth", "The wine of Love is music"—have a brave, exultant note that contrasts strangely with the hopeless moan of *The City of Dreadful Night*. We do not know enough of Thomson's private life to connect his varying moods in poetry with changes in his actual circumstances. The two *Sundays* belong to the years 1863–1865; *The City of Dreadful Night* to 1870–1874; but any inference we might be tempted to draw from these dates is confounded when we find that the terrible *Insomnia* and the rapturous *He Heard Her Sing* were written in successive months not long before his death.

Unlike most English poets, Thomson was a man of the people. Not to speak of his raucous political verses, there are plebeian touches in the two *Sundays* that are not to all tastes. But his humble birth was not without advantages. He had his roots in the common earth. His philosophy, such as it is, was drawn from life, not books. Contemporary fashions in poetry did not much affect him. His Oriental tale of *Weddah and Om-el-Bonain* has echoes of Shelley, and the sombre interior *In the Room*, where the talk of the various pieces of furniture leads up to the corpse of the suicide on the bed, recalls the early Rossetti by its accumulation of significant details; but he is no mocking-bird; he speaks with his own voice, and his voice, though often too free and easy, at its best is singularly clear and true.

Patmore and Thomson each believed that he had a message for his generation. So too, very much so, did Philip James Bailey (1816–1902) and Sidney Dobell (1825–1874). Bailey's *Festus* and Dobell's *Balder* were philosophies in verse, which people took seriously till Aytoun exploded them with his burlesque *Firmilian*, and branded their authors, along with Alexander Smith (1830–1867), as the Spasmodic School. The epithet describes not inaptly their constant straining after notes above their compass. Dobell is remembered, not for his pretentious *Balder*, but for the haunting ballad called *Keith of Ravelston*. Smith has left nothing so quotable, though there are fine things in his *City Poems*, which anticipated Thomson by many years. There are said to be fine things too in *Festus*, —but we have not dredged its 50,000 lines to find them.

The amount of Mid-Victorian verse and its high average quality point to a wider diffusion of culture than England had ever enjoyed before. The middle classes, growing rich and leisured, were sending more of their sons to Oxford and Cambridge, those ancient nurseries of poetry. And the culture they acquired was more and more an English culture. The riches of the Romantic Revival were revealed to them in full. Their fathers had at last accepted Wordsworth and Coleridge; now Byron was dethroned, and his place taken by Shelley and Keats, followed presently by Tennyson and Browning. Gifted students of these poets acquired a considerable command of the technique of English verse, which they had so wonderfully developed and subtilised. Even the lesser Victorians are very competent versifiers. We shall pass the chief of them in rapid survey, dividing them for convenience into merrymakers, music-makers, and mocking-birds.

We must not overlook the merrymakers, for Thalia too is a Muse, and her voice is very welcome in that serious, sentimental age. First then comes Frederick Locker-Lampson, who carried on the tradition of *vers de société* which goes back through Praed to Prior. Next we have Charles Stuart Calverley (1831–1884), prince of parodists; an elegant scholar too, with a genius for versification—his translation of Theocritus is an English poem in its own right. His mantle fell on J. K. Stephen, and on the less well-known but not less brilliant R. F. Murray of St. Andrews, both, like Calverley himself, inheritors of unfulfilled renown. These were our University Wits. On a more popular level we have W. S. Gilbert (1836–1911), whose comic operas filled the sails of British Drama after they had hung in the doldrums for a century. The best of their songs are as fresh as ever, and the *Bab Ballads* can still amuse.

The Universities which gave us these Wits gave us also a

GG

group of scholar-poets, nurtured on the Classics. William (Johnson) Cory was the best artist among them; his *Ionica* joins classic grace to romantic wistfulness. F. W. H. Myers (1843–1901) is remembered to-day chiefly for his work in psychical research; his poetry recalls Wordsworth in its simplicity and its vein of mysticism; his *St. Paul*, if not great, means greatly. John Addington Symonds (1840–1892), the historian of the Italian Renaissance, illustrates the bookishness to which scholar-poets are prone, but had too much real sensibility to be dismissed as a mere mocking-bird.

These scholars were not great poets, but they wrote as well as it was given them to write, whereas Richard Watson Dixon (1832–1900) and Lord de Tabley (1835–1895) never seemed to get out all the poetry that was in them. Dixon must have been a rare spirit to attract Rossetti and Morris in his youth and Hopkins and Bridges in his age; but he began in a style so oddly obscure that it looks perverse, and afterwards was too busy to give his poetry the concentration that poetry like his demanded. Or perhaps he simply had not air and fire enough to make his verses clear. When they do run clear, in short lyrics like "The Feathers of the Willow" and *Fallen Rain*, he gets simple-seeming effects as good in their own way as Christina Rossetti's. Lord de Tabley missed greatness for a different reason: he was too easily disheartened. His Greek tragedies were blanketed by Swinburne's *Atalanta*; his dramatic monologues looked pale beside Browning's; so he abandoned poetry for twenty years, just when he should have been perfecting his art. De Tabley was a poet through and through; but he lacked energy and intensity, and knew no more than Swinburne when to stop—faults not redeemed by grandiloquences like

> Daedal with argent amethyst and tinged
> In avenues of the marmoreal dawn.

In the ode "Sire of the rising day" the strict form helped him to intensity on a theme that lay very near his heart: the President of the Immortals has his will of us in life; dead, we defy him:

> Strong are alone the dead.
> They need not bow the head,
> Or reach one hand in ineffectual prayer.
> Safe in their iron sleep
> What wrong shall make them weep,

What sting of human anguish reach them there?
They are gone safe beyond the strong one's reign.
Who shall decree against them any pain?

If de Tabley had always written like that, he would not be among the minors.

Two Irish poets, Sir Samuel Ferguson (1810–1886) and William Allingham (1824–1889), have been somewhat obscured by the superior lustre of the Sinn Feiners, though both have the true Celtic lilt. Ferguson is remembered in Eire for his services to Irish scholarship, elsewhere for his *Forging of the Anchor*, a superb piece of eloquence, full of energy and imagination and crashing rhythms of his own invention. Allingham too had a sweet pipe of his own; he never quite fulfilled his promise, but his fairy songs still delight children as much as Mr. de la Mare's. It is to a younger Irishman, Arthur O'Shaughnessy (1844–1881), that we owe the word 'music-makers'. He was a typical music-maker himself; he had not much to say, but no minor Mid-Victorian said his say more melodiously than the author of "We are the music-makers" and "I made a little garden, yea, For my new love". Sir Francis Doyle (1810–1888) was not much of a music-maker; it is their heroic spirit, not their form, that has kept his *Private of the Buffs* and *Wreck of the Birkenhead* alive. He was the soldier's poet before Kipling.

Scotland produced nothing memorable in Scots during these years, but in English George MacDonald has left one unforgotten stanza:

Alas, how easily things go wrong!
A sigh too much, or a kiss too long,
There follows a mist and a weeping rain,
And life is never the same again.

English dialect poetry, raised to the rank of literature by William Barnes, is represented in this period by Thomas Edward Brown (1830–1897), who spun yarns in the Manx dialect. He wrote other poems also in what Barnes called "common English". Brown was a natural mystic like Wordsworth, but he had a familiar, robustious way with things Divine that is not at all Wordsworthian.

Women wrote a great deal of minor verse in Mid-Victorian days, but surprisingly little of it has lived, except *The High Tide on the Coast of Lincolnshire* of Jean Ingelow (1830–1897).

Long-winded as it is, obvious in sentiment, and obnoxious to parody, it has a kind of native sweetness like an English meadow.

We need not linger on the mocking-birds, singers often tuneful enough, but singing borrowed tunes. Tennyson had said prophetically,

> Most can raise the flowers now,
> For all have got the seed,

and it was Tennyson whom most of them imitated. They are all forgotten now—Lord Lytton, Sir Edward Arnold, Sir Lewis Morris, Alfred Austin, and the rest—all forgotten, or remembered only with a smile—Morris as "Penbryn's bold bard", Austin as the man whom Lord Salisbury made Laureate because nobody else applied for the office. We pass from them to two much greater men, who by their length of days connect the nineteenth century with the twentieth, but both had their roots in this Mid-Victorian era—George Meredith and Thomas Hardy.

Chapter Thirty-Seven

MID-VICTORIAN POETRY

(4) *Meredith and Hardy*

GEORGE MEREDITH (1828–1909) was older than any of the pre-Raphaelite group, yet he seems to belong intellectually to a younger generation, not because he accepted the evolutionary hypothesis—they all did that—but because he went on to accept Darwin's theory of Natural Selection and to apply it in his novels and poems to the interpretation of modern life.

All Meredith's poems might be called, what he calls one section of them, *A Reading of Earth*. Whether his thought owed anything to Fechner we do not know, but the key to it is given in a line that Fechner might have taken for his motto:

Till we conceive her living we go distraught.

Conceive Earth dead: then we are strangers here, consoling ourselves with dreams of a Beyond that shall free us from her hollowness. But conceive her living, and the evolutionary process is seen as the path by which she mounts to view her just Lord through the eyes of her great venture, Man. The path, you say, is red with blood; but Nature red in tooth and claw does not horrify Meredith: he scorns the sentimentalism that whimpers over those that have fallen in the struggle for life. Struggle proves strength, and strength is Earth's first need, for from strength comes pure blood, and from pure blood brain, by which Man has mastered the brutes. But brain is not Earth's ultimate goal: she has not travailed for millions of years only to produce a cunning animal who uses his wits merely to gratify his senses, whose sole aim in life is "ventral ease". Earth's ultimate goal is Spirit. Meredith does not pass from the natural to the spiritual *per saltum*, as Huxley did; no, the spiritual is rooted in the natural. Earth disowns the ascetic and the sentimentalist, who sever their roots in the natural life, no less than the sensualist who rises no higher; but to those who serve her she lends her strength. In *Earth and a Wedded Woman* the "lone-laid wife" is fortified against the lure of the flesh by the glad sound of rain; in *A Faith on Trial* the newly-widowed poet is lifted above his private grief by the sight of a cherry-tree in blossom. Earth is not moved by our private griefs; she aids us only if we serve her purpose with no craving for possession. And her purpose is the betterment of the race.

This thought informs Meredith's treatment of the duel of sex in his novels and, among his poems, in *The Sage Enamoured* and *Fair Ladies in Revolt.* Civilised woman has brains and claims to use them. True marriage, marriage that promises fair offspring, is the marriage of minds, not a union brought about by mere passion crying

> As the birds do, so do we,
> Bill our mate and choose our tree;

or by cold prudence advising

> Mates are chosen market-wise;
> Coolest bargainer best buys.

Modern Love shadows forth the inner tragedy of his own first marriage, the union of two high-spirited, highly civilised beings, who do not grow together in love and understanding, but drift apart, yet hanker still for the dead days of youthful passion. Frustrated passion is the theme of most of the *Ballads and Poems of Tragic Life.*

Finally, in *Aneurin's Harp* and *Odes in Contribution to the Song of French History* Meredith dealt with the struggle for life between nations. He did not himself belong to the classes that govern England. He was the son of a Portsmouth tailor, had some Welsh and some Irish blood in his veins, and was educated for two years in Germany: birth, blood, and education all fitted him to view England with detachment. And he feared for her, feared that she might relapse into "ventral ease", drinking destruction in gold, and fall before a stronger Power, as France fell in 1870 because she had forgotten that strength "is of the plain root-virtues born".

Meredith's reading of Earth, set forth most cryptically in *The Woods of Westermain*, most intelligibly in *The Thrush in February*, and most thrillingly in *The Lark Ascending*, is not easy to grasp, and is not made easier by his over-rapid, over-pregnant, elliptical style, and his lordly treatment of English idiom. Even *The Day of the Daughter of Hades*, the song of her who escapes for a day from her sire's dark realm below to rejoice in the light and the goodness of Earth, even that superb poetic conception is marred in execution by the poet's determination to be vivid and pregnant at any cost. *Love in the Valley*, written before he felt burdened with a message, is comparatively free from these faults; so is the sincere, sombre *Ballad of Past Meridian*, the most perfect in form of all his poems:

> Last night returning from my twilight walk
> I met the grey mist Death, whose eyeless brow
> Was bent on me, and from his hand of chalk
> He reached me flowers as from a withered bough:
> O Death, what bitter nosegays givest thou!
>
> Death said, I gather, and pursued his way.
> Another stood by me, a shape in stone,
> Sword-hacked and iron-stained, with breasts of clay,
> And metal veins that sometimes fiery shone:
> O life, how naked and how hard when known!
>
> Life said, As thou hast carved me, such am I.
> Then memory, like the nightjar on the pine,
> And sightless hope, a woodlark in night sky,
> Joined notes of Death and Life till night's decline:
> Of Death, of Life, those inwound notes are mine.

Meredith was a remarkable metrist. He had even less care than Browning for verbal melody, but he had a strong sense of rhythm, and (what is rarer in English poets) of quantity. His use of monosyllabic feet was a fruitful innovation:

> Thicker crowd the shades as the grave East deepens
> Glowing, and with crimson a long cloud swells.
> Maiden still the morn is; and strange she is, and secret;
> Strange her eyes; her cheeks are cold as cold sea-shells.

Phaethon is a daring experiment in that rarest of Classical metres, the Galliambic, aiming, not without success, at an effect of precipitate speed:

> Then the flame-outsnorting horses were led forth: it was so
>   decreed.
> They were yoked before the glad youth by his sister-ancillaries.
> Swift the ripple ripples follow'd, as of aureate Helicon,
> Down their flanks, while they impatient pawed desire of the
>   distances,
> And the bit with fury champed. Oh! unimaginable delight!
> Unimagined speed and splendour in the circle of upper air!

Thomas Hardy (1840–1928) may be profitably considered after Meredith. Though he was not known for a poet till

Wessex Poems appeared in 1898, he began to write verse in the 1860's, when the impact of *The Origin of Species* was fresh, when Natural Science was mounting a grand assault on Orthodoxy, and Swinburne was thanking his gods that no life lives for ever. Darwin himself had regarded Natural Selection as compatible with Divine benevolence, and Meredith had seen it as a step in Earth's ascent to the sight of her just Lord; but to Hardy's soft heart the spectacle of the pain of the struggle for life obscured any vision of such an ulterior purpose. The poems that he wrote in the 1860's inveigh against the indifference of Nature, and "crass Casualty", and "dicing Time", the witherer of youth and beauty. In the novels to which he turned for thirty years his mood oscillates from ironically gay to grave, the grave steadily predominating, and itself oscillating from resignation to revolt, from which it falls back into something like despair. In some of them, and those the most characteristic, the thought recurs that in producing modern, civilised man Nature has overreached herself and created a being whose desires she cannot satisfy, for whom therefore, since no life lives for ever, there can be no satisfaction.

When he returned to poetry, resuming what to him was "a more instinctive kind of expression", the same thought, and thoughts akin to it, find more condensed, lyric utterance in *Wessex Poems* (1898) and *Poems of the Past and the Present* (1901). Sometimes he speaks of Nature, sometimes of the ultimate Power behind her, call it Doom or God. His attitude to Nature is touchingly filial; for him she is still Mother Nature, a loving mother; if she wounds the things she loves, the reason is that she is blind. But if Nature is still a Mother, God is no Heavenly Father. Has He simply forgotten this speck of a planet in the infinite multitude of His creations? Is He unfeeling? Or altogether unweeting? Or—this thought came later—is He nothing but a pious imagination, a mirage projected by man's hopes on to the blank sky of the Unknown?

Such were the thoughts that haunted Hardy in those years. 'Philosophy' we must not call them: Hardy disclaimed system; his poems, he said, were "unadjusted impressions", truthfully recorded, but not harmonised into a philosophy. So he said in 1901; but for the great work to which he now bent his mind he did find in Schopenhauer's doctrine of the Immanent Will a kind of system, a frame at least into which his habitual thoughts seemed to fit. *The Dynasts* is a vast epic-drama of the Napoleonic wars, in 130 scenes, with hundreds of human characters, and above them an over-world of Spirits—Spirits Ironic and Sinister, Spirits of the Years and the Pities—who comment on their doings in the manner of a Greek chorus.   At certain crises in the action a transparency comes over the visible scene, revealing the whole as the interior of an immense skull, a beating brain lit by phosphorescence, in which light the individual human agents, who deem themselves free, are seen to be mere nerve-centres or ganglia knit each to each by innumerable fibrils and all enmeshed in

> A fabric of excitement, web of rage,
> That permeates as one stuff the weltering whole.

The tragic fact is this, that the ganglia, the individual human agents, are conscious and sentient, but the brain as a whole, the Immanent Will, neither knows nor feels.   Yet the heart of man clings to the hope voiced by the Spirit of the Pities, the hope that as the result of the long tragedy of history the Dreaming God will at last awake, the Immanent Will become conscious, and "fashion all things fair".

Translated out of the language of vision, what is this but the hope that inspired the foundation of the League of Nations? After Versailles Hardy lost that hope; but presently he regained it, for in the preface to the poems of 1922 he repudiated the title of pessimist, declaring for a creed which he called "evolutionary meliorism".   Perhaps there had come to him again, borne maybe on the wings of music, some hint, some intimation, such as he had sung of years before in *The Darkling Thrush*:

> So little cause for carollings
>   Of such ecstatic sound
> Was written on terrestrial things
>   Afar or nigh around,
> That I could think there trembled through
>   His happy good-night air
> Some blessed Hope, whereof he knew
>   And I was unaware.

It would be pleasant to think that this blessed Hope cheered the old man to the end; but seemingly it was not so.   Near the close of his life it seems that his mood oscillated once more and swung back in the direction of despair, that the "evolutionary meliorist" had a vision of the evolutionary process reversed and mankind reeling back into barbarism, as if on the brink of the grave he saw looming up on the horizon the shadow of the catastrophe which now threatens to overwhelm civilisation.

After *The Dynasts* Hardy attempted nothing more on the grand scale, but in the twenty years of life that still remained to him he issued volume after volume of short poems, "lyrical, narratory, and reflective"—*Time's Laughingstocks* (1909), *Satires of Circumstance* (1914), *Moments of Vision* (1917), *Late Lyrics* (1922), *Human Shows* (1925). *Winter Words* (1928) appeared posthumously. He had not much to say that was new, but he played some interesting variations on his old tunes. Their dominant note is still the note of doom, and most of them are in a minor key. Most, but not all: Hardy had known happiness in love, and he found delight in music and the beauty of Art and Nature. "Moments of Vision" he called one of these later volumes, and the name might be used of them all; they are glimpses into life, too often into its little ironies, the pur-blind pranks played on men by "crass Casualty" and "dicing Time". "Dicing Time" is Hardy's phrase, but in truth he loads the dice himself: 'Casualty' in Hardy is generally hostile to human happiness, not neutral or friendly, as it may be in Shakespeare. As he aged his mind dwelt more and more on things and people departed, whose ghosts haunt the bleak present. Three groups of poems stand out from this general background. The Boer War inspired a group which contains two of his most imaginative efforts, *The Souls of the Slain* and *Drummer Hodge*:

> They throw in Drummer Hodge, to rest
>   Uncoffined—just as found:
> His landmark is a kopje-crest
>   That breaks the veldt around;
> And foreign constellations west
>   Each night above his mound.

The outbreak of war in 1914 touched him still more closely; it horrified him to think of Wessex boys, Teutonic in blood and speech, slaughtering and slaughtered by furious Teutons. But his faith in the victory of justice and the ancient sanctities of Earth rang true in *Men who March Away* and *In Time of the Breaking of Nations*:

> Only a man harrowing clods
>   In a slow silent walk
> With an old horse that stumbles and nods
>   Half asleep as they stalk.

Only thin smoke without flame
From the heaps of couch-grass;
Yet this will go onward the same
Though Dynasties pass.

Yonder a maid and her wight
Come whispering by:
War's annals will cloud into night
Ere their story die.

The third group is headed *Veteris vestigia flammae.* In "When I set out for Lyonesse" he had sung gladsomely of the wooing of his Cornish bride: these poems, written in 1912–1913, are elegies on her death. Of all Hardy's poems they are the most personal, sincere, and pure.

Hardy's father, like Carlyle's, was a master-mason in a small way, and it is of people like him, humble but not the humblest, that he writes with most understanding and sympathy. Natural piety, so weak in Meredith, was strong in Hardy. He loved his own kith and kin, and his native county of Dorset, which he knew every yard of, from the downs to the sea. Moreover, he had a strong historical sense: he knew, and felt, that the turf he trod covered the bones of generations of kindred Englishmen, and before them of Normans, Saxons, Romans, and Ancient Britons. It has been said that Hardy's spirit haunted the graveyard; we might say with equal truth that for him all that ancient province of Wessex was a graveyard.

His loyalty to Wessex affects his language. Not that, with few exceptions, he wrote poems in Wessex dialect like his old friend William Barnes; but he held the view that if Winchester had remained the political capital the Southern, not the East Midland, dialect would have become Standard English; and he exercised his freedom as a Wessex man, not only to use dialect words when he needed them, but to treat Standard English as a plastic medium, and coin uncouth new words from Saxon components not previously compounded. Perhaps, too, his long apprenticeship to prose dulled his sense of the prosiness of some of his vocabulary, just as his practice of what Dryden called "the other harmony of prose" made his verse sometimes a little out of tune. He attempted a great variety of metres and rhythms, some of them modelled on Browning, or Barnes, or on local ditties; but his simplest measures, such as those we have quoted, are his best; his more elaborate stanzas are often ill-balanced. Yet there is a kind of music, if a broken music, in almost all his poems, which we can catch if we listen carefully, just as, if we look carefully, we can share almost all his moments of vision, so feelingly are they seen and so honestly recorded.

Chapter Thirty-Eight

THE NINETIES

TO a younger reader becoming fully aware of his taste for poetry in the eighties of last century there were two major luminaries still in the heavens, if verging towards their declination. Browning died in 1889, Tennyson in 1892. Among such younger readers Browning stood at the moment rather higher in favour than his more widely acknowledged rival, if such a word is admissible. But there were other poets whose appeal was more insistent, indicated more clearly the direction in which they wished to move, the so-called pre-Raphaelite group with their doctrine of Art for Art's sake; a group whose influence was to be felt by poets so divergent as Kipling, and Wilde, and Yeats. And there were yet others for whom the influence of Wordsworth was transmitted, if modified, by the author of *Empedocles on Etna* (1852), whose collected poems had been issued in 1869 and whose death had preceded that of Browning by a year.

The *Lachrymae Musarum* in which William Watson bewailed the death of Tennyson attracted the attention of readers who had not remarked the *Wordsworth's Grave* of 1890; and in like manner the *Shorter Poems* of the same year awakened or quickened interest in the work of an older poet, Robert Bridges, already the author of a sonnet sequence, *The Growth of Love* (1876), and a poem, *Eros and Psyche* (1885), as well as a number of verse-dramas. Both poets were conscious and careful artists working in the classical tradition but with interesting differences of spirit and form. After a verse tale, *The Prince's Quest* (1880), quite in the manner of William Morris, Watson turned away from the drift of romantic modern poetry and revived, one might almost say, the ideal of the eighteenth century, "What oft was thought, but ne'er so well expressed". He shared Hazlitt's admiration of Akenside. His aim became to give expression in a large and felicitous manner, with careful attention to the fall of the accents and the correctness of the rhymes, to sentiments recognisable by and shared with large sections of the public—patriotism qualified by a sincere passion for justice, eulogy of other poets illumined and tempered by criticism, the dubious view of life and the ways of Providence which Arnold had made current, and Nature as Wordsworth and Tennyson had taught us to see her. On all these themes Watson declaimed in many different forms—ode, sonnet, lyric, epigram, all excellent in their way, if with no suggestion of a fresh, a subtler interpretation. Still, in the poetic eloquence of which Gray showed his mastery in the sister odes it would not be easy to indicate anything finer than the closing section of *The Father of the Forest*.

"What led me to poetry", Bridges has said, "was the inexhaustible satisfaction of form. . . . It was an art which I hoped to learn. I did not suppose that the poet's emotions were in any way better than mine, or mine than another's." But Bridges is less of the orator than Watson. It is not "what oft was thought" that he is intent on expressing, but what he himself felt of the value of love, of the thrilling experience that moments in the life of Nature can give: "The north wind came up yesternight", "The storm is over, the land hushed to rest", "In the golden glade the chestnuts are fallen all", of the joys and sorrows of human experience: *On a Dead Child*, or

> I never shall love the snow again
> Since Maurice died;

or again, for joy is more often his mood than sorrow, a tempered but deep joy:

> Then comes the happy moment: not a stir
> In any tree, no portent in the sky:
> The morn doth neither hasten nor defer,
> The morrow hath no name to call it by,
> But life and joy are one,—we know not why,—
> As though our very blood, long breathless lain,
> Had tasted of the breath of God again;

and in the same mood more simply realised:

> The idle life I lead
> Is like a pleasant sleep,
> Wherein I rest and heed
> The dreams that by me sweep;
> And still of all my dreams
> In turn so swiftly past,
> Each in its fancy seems
> A nobler than the last,

And every eve I say,
  Noting my step in bliss,
That I have known no day
  In all my life like this.

But the deepest source of joy is the sense of beauty.   A
delicate sense of beauty, an eager quest for beauty, a constant
meditation on the significance of beauty runs through all he
wrote.

Though as careful an artist as Watson, Bridges was less conservative, more willing, with his younger fellows, to experiment, but not in their direction of free verse.   He preferred
the more difficult path of endeavouring to restore our sense of
the quantity of syllables, longs and shorts.   The emancipation
of English metre from the monotonous eighteenth-century
pattern, effected largely by the influence of the restored interest
in the ballad, had emphasised stress as the essential element,
giving the utmost freedom of substitution in the foot:

'Tis the middle of night by the castle clock,
And the owls have awaken'd the crowing cock,
    Tu—whit—tu—whoo!

The heavier the stress laid on the stressed syllable, the more
easy it is to slur or pass rapidly over the intervening syllables,
and it is to this that the verse of Swinburne (himself a balladist)
owes its peculiar and intoxicating rhythm:

When the hounds of Spring are on Winter's traces,
  The mother of months in meadow and plain.

Bridges could secure subtle effects in a stressed line:

Whither, O splendid ship, thy white sails crowding,
  Leaning across the bosom of the urgent West,
That fearest nor sea rising, nor sky clouding,
  Whither away, fair rover, and what thy quest?

or

When men were all asleep the snow came flying,
  In large white flakes falling on the city brown,
Stealthily and perpetually settling and loosely lying,
  Hushing the latest traffic of the drowsy town.

It was when the classical metres, especially the elegiac combination of hexameter and pentameter, were composed with
stress for quantity that the effect was to a classically trained ear
intolerable:

Out of the golden remote wild west where the sea without shore is,
  Full of the sunset and sad if at all with the fulness of joy—

so Swinburne, and the stress on "joy" and "sad" is apt to become a thud. Bridges set himself to show that the element of quantity is still audible in English words. In the word "demonstrable" we are conscious that the long syllable is the central *unstressed* syllable. His own elegiacs run:

'Twas but vainly of old, Man, making Faith to approach thee
  Held an imagin'd scheme of providence in honour,

which, if read like Swinburne's, would require a stress on the last syllable of "honour". By most of us such classical lines are read as irregularly stressed lines and hardly recognised as metrical. In his *Testament of Beauty* (1929), his final vindication of his faith in beauty as the inspiring and guiding force in human progress, Bridges uses a loose alexandrine to be read with the more level accent of French verse which makes easier the recognition of the longs and shorts. The poem has been described as a parallel to the *Prelude*. A juster comparison would be with the *De Rerum Natura* of Lucretius; indeed Mr. Edward Thompson tells us that Bridges meant at first to call his poem *De Hominum Natura*. In both poems there is the same combination of poetic description and reflection with what is simply exposition in verse, exposition which we feel might have read better in the less obtrusive rhythms of prose. There is nothing in *The Testament of Beauty* to compare with the great passages in which Wordsworth recalls his early impressions of Nature or Lucretius denounces the fear of death. The fundamental reason is that it lacks their deeper strain of feeling.

If Bridges drew away more and more from the strongly stressed ballad metre to which Swinburne had given such varied and sonorous quality, it was just this rhythm which another poet was to use for very different themes and moods. The most startling volume of the early nineties was the *Barrack-Room Ballads* (1892) of Rudyard Kipling. They repelled some readers almost violently; but on the other hand they found a response immediate and unqualified among readers of every class and in every part of the Empire, to say nothing of other than British countries. His short stories doubtless contributed to this success, but stories and poems are much alike, and it was

the poetry as such, tone and measures, which delighted readers
not usually sensitive to literary form.   It is a form that can at
one extreme become amusing doggerel, if at the other subtle
and elaborate rhythms.   Kipling was a bold virtuoso in verse
and prose.   His earliest verses, *Departmental Ditties* (1886),
were clever journalism, at times in execrable taste (*The Post
that Fitted*).   But with the next volume Kipling's sense of the
romance inherent in his theme, the British Empire, what it had
meant in adventure, in valour and discipline, in self-abnegation
and sense of duty, grew steadily deeper and more serious even
as the dangers from within and without which were threatening
that Empire increased.   With his final settlement in England
his sense of the romantic element in English history and character took in the past, and found enhancement in the beauty
of English scenery.   Sir Francis Doyle (*Return of the Guards*,
1866) and Sir Henry Newbolt later (*Admirals All*, 1897) and
others touched some of the same notes, but in his sense of the
romantic element in English history, her soldiers of the old
army, her Tommy Atkinses, and their contacts with strange
peoples in remote lands, and his feeling for the charm of
southern English scenery, Kipling's closest affinity is with a
novelist and poet of a very different outlook on life and different
feeling for the rhythm of verse, Thomas Hardy.

    It was not from Bridges nor Watson nor Kipling that the
"nineties" acquired the associations which the word for a time
evoked; nor yet from such older men as Lang and Stevenson
and Henley, all accomplished versifiers whose principal work
was done in prose.   Lang's *Helen of Troy* (1882), his most
serious bid for a place among the poets, met with a reception
which profoundly disappointed him; and most of the verses
collected after his death from such volumes as *Grass of Parnassus* (1888) and *Ban and Arrière Ban* (1892) as well as from
miscellaneous sources are, when not light experiments in old
French and other forms, brief records of personal tastes and
moods; and it is when most personal that they are most poignant
and rememberable.   The same is true of Henley and Stevenson.   Lang and Stevenson were both Scots, aware of a conscience and a religious upbringing, and not averse from preaching.   Lang was the more Victorian and Tennysonian.   In *Helen
of Troy* he treats the story of Helen and Paris much as Tennyson
had done that of Tristram and Iseult in *The Last Tournament*.
But the personal note in one poem is a passionate one:

HH

Come to me in my dreams, and then,
Saith one, I shall be well again,
For then the night will more than pay
The hopeless longing of the day.

Nay, come not thou in dreams, my sweet!
With shadowy robes and silent feet,
And with the voice and with the eyes
That greet me in a soft surprise.

Last night, last night in dreams we met,
And how today shall I forget?
Or how remembering, restrain
Mine incommunicable pain?

Nay, where thy land and people are
Dwell thou remote, apart, afar,
Nor mingle with the shades that sweep
The melancholy ways of sleep.

But if, perchance, the shadows break—
If dreams depart, if men awake,
If face to face at last we see,
Be thine the voice to welcome me.

That is enough for one poet; but Lang has left many varieties of witty and charming verse.

Stevenson, whose life was a constant fight with disease and the prospect of an early death, put out to sea more boldly, dropped his Presbyterian moorings even before health and climate had driven him from Edinburgh:

The belching winter wind, the missile rain,
The rare and welcome silence of the snows,
The laggard morn, the haggard day, the night,
The grimy spell of the nocturnal town.

Some record of these troubled years is contained in the poems which were not issued till after his death, love-poems and poems, which are far from the optimistic strain of much of his later writing in poem and essay:

I have left all upon the shameful field,
    Honour and Hope, my God, and all but life;
Spurless, with sword reversed and dinted shield,
    Degraded and disgraced, I leave the strife.

Like other Scots the maturer Stevenson was not averse from preaching in verse and prose, apt to thump the pulpit when

determined to make us face life and death with courage and
hope:

> To make this earth our hermitage,
> A cheerful and a changeful page,
> God's bright and intricate device
> Of days and seasons doth suffice.

That is the strain of some of the best known poems, including
the well-known requiem "Under the wide and starry sky",
and the *Celestial Surgeon*; but some strike a deeper note: "God,
if this were all", and *The Woodman*, a vision of the endless
warfare which is life in all its forms, not unlike Meredith's
"Enter these enchanted woods" or similar glimpses in Hardy's
prose.   But the poems of most appeal are the records of the
exile's home-sickness: "In the highlands, in the country
places", "Do you remember, can we e'er forget", and others.

All the poets of this group were rather talkers than singers,
not unlike in that respect to Herrick and other poets of the
seventeenth century.   But Stevenson's Muse catches the lyric
cry once or twice: "Yet, O stricken heart, remember, O remember", "I will make you brooches, and toys for your delight".
A Child's Garden of Verses gives happy expression to memories
of his own guarded childhood.

Of the three Henley comes closest to a clever reporter or
journalist in verse: "London Types", "In Hospital", "London
Voluntaries".   Yeats turned away from him; Binyon could
find nothing in him good enough for the fifth volume of the
Golden Treasury.   Yet some of us recall from "Echoes" the
lovely lines:

> A late lark twitters from the quiet skies;
> And from the west,
> Where the sun, his day's work ended,
> Lingers as in content,
> There falls on the old gray city
> An influence luminous and serene,
> A shining peace.

But the poets who, with the later prose writings of Oscar Wilde
and the illustrations of Aubrey Beardsley, gave a peculiar
flavour to the name "the nineties" were a group of young men
for whom the most vital tradition was still that of the pre-
Raphaelites, poets and painters.   The link between the older
and this later group was just Wilde, not in virtue of his early
poems, full of echoes of Keats and Tennyson and Arnold and

Rossetti and Morris, but of these later things and the whole tenor of his cult of beauty, his discipleship to Pater, and the doctrine of burning with a hard, clear, gem-like flame. In one way or another this was the conscious or semi-conscious ideal of such poets as Lionel Johnson, Arthur Symons, Ernest Dowson, and, the most curious and self-conscious artist among them, the most responsive (while retaining his independence and aloofness) to all the reactions of the critical years through which he lived out his life to the full—William Butler Yeats (1865–1939). The early movement had been essentially one of escape from the modern world of machinery, industry, and banal morality. Morris sought it in the past, the world of Froissart and the French romances of the twelfth and thirteenth centuries, or again in the past of the Norse Sagas, heroic stories of war and love. Holman Hunt had dreamed of making more real by his pictures the world of early Christianity. Rossetti's world was that of the Italian poets of the *dolce stil nuovo*. Swinburne sought compensation for his thwarted instincts in the lusts and cruelties of pagan Rome. But there is another way of escape, one which leads to a world one may believe in just because it can be exposed to no scientific or historical investigation. It lies in the faith that the world of sense and intellect, of science, is a world of illusion behind which lies a fairer world, the laws of which are revealed, not by the scientific reason (Huxley and Tyndall repelled Yeats as Bacon and Locke had repelled Blake) but by the heart and imagination. This is the burden of Yeats's early poems from *The Wanderings of Oisin* (1889) to *The Wind among the Reeds* (1899):

> Beloved, gaze in thine own heart,
> The holy tree is growing there;
> From joy the holy branches start,
> And all the trembling flowers they bear.
>
> .   .   .   .
>
> Gaze no more in the bitter glass
> The demons, with their subtle guile,
> Lift up before us when they pass,
> Or only gaze a little while;
>
> .   .   .   .
>
> For all things turn to barrenness
> In the dim glass the demons hold,
> The glass of outer weariness,
> Made when God slept in times of old.
>
> .   .   .   .

Thy tender eyes grow all unkind:
Gaze no more in the bitter glass.

Blake had pointed Yeats in this direction; and Blake and Rossetti are the chief influences in this early poetry, if for the Christian world of the older poet, and the Italian background of the other, he substituted a Celtic world of his own imagination and old Irish legend. The mood of the love-poems is the intense, single-minded passion which Rossetti had revived, if Yeats is more like Petrarch inasmuch as his passion was an unfulfilled passion. In the world of Yeats's dreams and legends and strange beings of Celtic mythology, understood or misunderstood, for many readers no more than romantic-sounding names, lovers wander,

Murmuring softly, lip to lip,
Murmuring gently how far off are the unquiet lands.

Verse dramas were among his earliest works, the most notable *The Countess Cathleen* (1892), the performance of which evoked a protest from the Roman Catholic authorities, a help to the advertisement of Yeats's poetry; for a better example of the spirit of the period is *The Land of Heart's Desire*, that land beyond the world of sense and intellect to which the imagination and heart turn with, it may be, a fatal longing.

With *The Wind among the Reeds* (1899) and the collected *Poems 1899–1905* (1906) ended, one may fairly say, this early poetry of dream and music and longing. The Irish theatre and drama drew him into closer contact with his public and into the management of affairs. The result was that when he turned back to poetry in *The Green Helmet and other Poems* (1909–1912) it was in a mood of disillusionment that he reflected on his own dreams and poems, a mood at times of anger; and *Responsibilities* (1912–1914) is in the same key. In *Adam's Curse* of the 1906 volume he had given the clearest and loveliest expression to the Petrarchan lover's feelings and attitude:

We sat grown quiet at the name of love;
We saw the last embers of daylight die,
And in the trembling blue-green of the sky
A moon worn as if it had been a shell
Washed by time's waters as it rose and fell
About the stars and broke in days and years.

> I had a thought for no one but your ears:
> That you were beautiful, and that I strove
> To love you in the old high way of love;
> That it had all seemed happy and yet we had grown
> As weary-hearted as the hollow moon.

He now begins to suspect that he has sacrificed too much to the "old high way of love". He has awakened from a long dream of love and begins to think he has been a fool:

> Does the imagination dwell the most
> Upon a woman won or woman lost?
> If on the lost, admit you turned aside
> From a great labyrinth out of pride,
> Cowardice, some silly over-subtle thought,
> Or anything called conscience once;
> And that if memory recur, the sun's
> Under eclipse, and the day blotted out.

Compare with the dreamy melancholy tone of *Adam's Curse* the tone, passionate but a little scornful, of *The Mask*. Yet it is himself, not the lady, he blames. She remains a miracle:

> Although crowds gathered once if she but showed her face,
> And even old men's eyes grew dim, this hand alone,
> Like some last courtier at a gypsy camping place
> Babbling of fallen majesty, records what's gone.
>
> The lineaments, a heart that laughter has made sweet,
> These, these remain, but I record what's gone. A crowd
> Will gather, and not know it walks the very street
> Whereon a thing once walked that seemed a burning cloud.

And if a too reverent love were folly, what of his efforts to create a people's theatre and revive a national literature?

> What have I earned for all that work, I said,
> For all that I have done at my own charge?
> The daily spite of this unmannerly town,
> Where he who served the most is most defamed,
> The reputation of his life-time lost
> Between the night and morning.

The difference between Yeats's early and later poetry reminds one of the early and later poetry of Donne, but his has changed in the opposite direction, from the ideal to the real, the spiritual to the sensuous. Some of his later poems are almost defiantly bawdy. One is reminded on another side of Milton's disillusionments when he realised that his high dream of a reformed

England had all ended in smoke and he will arraign the weakness of human nature.   For all Yeats's dreams seemed to end in disappointment, his enthusiasm for Ireland and Parnell and Sinn Fein:

> Romantic Ireland's dead and gone,
> It's with O'Leary in the grave.

But the rebellion of 1916 and what followed awakened a deeper feeling:

> A terrible beauty is born.

Yet the direction which emancipated Ireland has taken is not his.   The old distrust of Democracy and its vulgarity, the admiration of Nietzsche as a counteractive, the recollection of his own aristocratic ancestors, Swift's doctrine of the right ordering of the State in the relation of ruler, advisers, and the many, all turned his mind, helped by the influence of Ezra Pound, in the direction of Fascism.   A strange philosophy of history and the gyrations of time took the place of his earlier dreams and gave us such poems as *Leda and the Swan, Gyrations, Sailing to Byzantium*, and *Byzantium*, which are claimed to be his best poems, perhaps for young readers, poets of to-morrow.   For older readers the poems of most appeal are those which express less enigmatic, more human moods,— memories of friends, wishes for his son and his daughters, moments of vision: *Friends, The Cold Heaven, The Wild Swans at Coole, Solomon to Sheba, Her Praise*.

Of Yeats's friends and fellow-members of the Rhymers' Club Ernest Dowson, Lionel Johnson, Richard le Gallienne, and Arthur Symons were the most outstanding poets.   Of Dowson and Johnson Yeats was to write later:

> You had to face your ends when young—
> 'Twas wine or women or some curse—
> But never made a poorer song
> That you might have a heavy purse,
> Nor gave loud service to a cause
> That you might have a troop of friends.
> You kept the Muses' sterner laws,
> And unrepenting faced your ends,
> And therefore earned the right—and yet
> Johnson and Dowson most I praise—
> To troop with them, the world forgot,
> And copy their proud steady gaze.

Their single-hearted devotion to their art produced a few fine lyrics and meditative poems in which the note of self-pity is audible. Dowson is the most purely lyrical, the author of one or two unique lyrics, delightful refrains on one or two recurring themes—love, and desire, and regret, with moments of *sagesse*, dreams of a better life: "They are not long, the weeping and the laughter", "Calm, sad, serene behind high convent walls",

> Exceeding sorrow
>   Consumeth my sad heart!
> Because to-morrow we must depart
> Now is exceeding sorrow all my part,

and, probably the best known, "Last night, ah, yesternight", with its refrain, "I have been faithful to thee, Cynara, in my fashion".

Lionel Johnson was pre-eminently the scholar, the young precocious scholar and wide reader, giving to books the hours of night stolen from sleep by his constitution:

> Dreams! Who loves dreams? Forget all grief!
> Find in sleep's nothingness relief?
> Better my dreams. Dear heavenly books!
> With kindly voices, winning looks,
> Enchant me with your spells of art,
> And draw me homeward to your heart:
> Till weariness and things unkind
> Seem but a vain and passing wind:
> Till the gray morning slowly creep
> Upward and rouse the birds from sleep;
> Till Oxford bells the silence break,
> And find me happier for your sake.

He was a Catholic and a loyal Irishman, but whatever his theme the meditative note prevails, at its most characteristic and effective in the rememberable lines on the statue of Charles at Charing Cross:

> Sombre and rich the skies;
> Great glooms, and starry plains.
> Gently the night wind sighs,
> Else a vast silence reigns.
>
> The splendid silence clings
> Around me, and around
> The saddest of all kings,
> Crowned and again discrowned.

Yeats did not share the weakness of some of his friends against

which they sought protection in the bosom of the Catholic
Church.   His proud spirit took its own way, more interested
in the Ireland of old Celtic myths, tales of Cuchulainn and Finn,
than the more obvious background of the Virgin and the
Saints.   It has been said by a recent writer that a South Irishman is either a Catholic or an anti-clerical.   But Catholic
poetry had its representatives in the nineties, not all of them
decadents.   Coventry Patmore had led the way in his *Unknown
Eros* (1878), reasserting in a lofty, not to say arrogant, tone the
appeal to the imagination of Catholic doctrine and discipline,
the high doctrine of the sublimation of sensuous (Eros) in
spiritual love, a passionate devotion to the Christ and the
Virgin Mother:

> Song and silence ever be
> All the grace life brings to me;
> Song of Mary, mighty Mother;
> Song of whom she bare, my Brother,
> Silence of an ecstasy
> When I found Him and no other.

So Johnson; and Dowson can write in the same strain in the
intervals of his celebration of "love as to a creature":

> Dark is the Church, save where the altar stands;
> Dressed like a bride, illustrious with light,
> Where an old priest exalts with trembling hands
> The one true solace of man's fallen plight.

But the chief Catholic poets of the nineties were Alice Meynell
—*Poems* (1893), *Later Poems* (1901)—and Francis Thompson
—*Poems* (1893), *Sister Songs* (1895), *New Poems* (1897). A
fine, even fastidious, critic, Mrs. Meynell is a poet of feeling at
once delicate and poignant.   One sonnet, *Renouncement*, which
has found its way into many anthologies, gives voice to the
conflict through which a deeply religious mind must pass in
one way or another.   Her poetry is not ascetically devout.
Love is a main theme in her earlier poems, as is the beauty
of Nature.   The devout poems came later, quietist but penetrating: *San Lorenzo's Mother*, *The Shepherdess*, *The Fold*, *Why
wilt thou chide?*, *I am the Way*, etc.

Francis Thompson is a more flamboyant poet.   Rescued
by the Meynells from a vagabond life in London not unlike
that of De Quincey, he poured into many of his poems a
blended gratitude, admiration, and love—*Love in Dian's Lap*,

nine irregularly cadenced poems on the indistinguishable
beauty of his lady's body and spirit.   In other long, elaborate
odes he celebrates the charm of her children, *Sister Songs*.   In
the *New Poems* (1897) the influence of Coventry Patmore
becomes dominant in odes on religious, mystical themes: *The
Mistress of Vision, The Dread of Height, From the Night of Foreboding, Any Saint*.   In other elaborate, not to say pompous,
odes he endeavours to combine Nature as he had learned to
feel about it from Shelley (on whom he wrote a very sympathetic essay) with Catholic doctrine and worship: *Ode to the
Setting Sun, Against Urania, An Anthem of Earth*.   By Reason
of Thy Law is a slightly different rendering of Patmore's
Remembered Grace.   But Thompson's diction is at the opposite
pole from Patmore's dignified, sinewy style.   It is thick-sown
with metaphor, and full of echoes of his reading of Crashaw
and Donne and Spenser and Shelley and Wordsworth and
Coleridge and Poe.   Through his poems too rings the note of
self-pity, and the poems which have taken the firmest hold of
readers of poetry for the sake of poetry are such comparatively
simple expressions of this central theme as *The Daisy* and *The
Poppy*, in which this personal note blends with another, his
love of children.   The same personal feeling pervades his best
known ode, *The Hound of Heaven*, and the last of his lyrics,
The Kingdom of God, in which, as in most of the later poems, his
diction grows simpler:

> The angels keep their ancient places:—
> Turn but a stone, and start a wing!
> 'Tis ye, 'tis your estrangèd faces,
> That miss the many-splendoured thing.
>
> But when so sad thou canst not sadder,
> Cry;—and upon thy so sore loss
> Shall shine the traffic of Jacob's ladder
> Pitched betwixt Heaven and Charing Cross.
>
> Yea, in the night, my Soul, my daughter,
> Cry,—clinging Heaven by the hems;
> And lo! Christ walking on the water
> Not of Genesareth but Thames!

In the year of *Barrack-Room Ballads* and *Lachrymae Musarum*
(1892) appeared a small volume which caught the eye of such
established critics as Saintsbury, Lang, and Symonds, *Granite
Dust*, by Ronald Campbell Macfie.   This early success was not

followed up till *New Poems* were published in 1904, and in the
crowd Macfie was overlooked.   His poetry is poetry in a sense
that a good deal of accomplished verse is not.   But from the
beginning the purer lyric note of *With a Gift of Roses*, *An
October Eve*, and others, was crossed by a strain of passionate
preaching not quite to the taste either of lovers of poetry pure
and simple or of more orthodox and Catholic poets.   *New
Poems* opened with the beautiful ode *If I were Sleep*, and it was
in the ode that Macfie specialised in his later years: *To the
Twentieth Century*, *Marischal College*, *The Titanic*, *In Memoriam:
John Davidson*.   That on Marischal College (on the opening
of the New Buildings by Edward VII) was a remarkable occasional poem, just because it transcended the occasional and
made its theme the mystery of scientific advance through hypo-
theses successively accepted with practical results and successively rejected, each in spite of shortcomings widening the vision
of our knowledge and of our ignorance.   Of Macfie's greatest
ode, *War*, something will be said later.   But we may be
permitted here to cite the short poem in which at the end
of his life he summed up the bitter experience of apparent
failure:

> When *I-who-am* meet face to face upon my way forlorn
> The happy *I-who-might-have-been*, the demi-god unborn,
> When he with all my dreams fulfilled meets me out-fought,
>   outworn,
> It is as sorrow meeting joy, as Midnight meeting Morn,
> When *I* meet *I-who-might-have-been*, the demi-god unborn.
>
> When *I-who-am* meet *I-who-was*, and in God's sight compare
> His promise with my failure, his laughter with my care,
> His harvest with my barrenness, his hope with my despair,
> Then blown as by a wind the flames of Hell upleap and flare,
> When *I-who-am* meet *I-who-was* and cringe and cower there.
>
> When *I-who-am* meet *I-who-was* and *I-who-might-have-been*,
> I heavy-hearted, haggard-eyed, they happy and serene,
> He upon Earth, and He in Heaven, and I in Hell between,
> Then crouch I in the flames as one who shameth to be seen,—
> When *I-who-am* meet *I-who-was* and *I-who-might-have-been*.
>
> When *I-who-am-was-might-have-been* meet *I-who-am-to-be*,
> Then mortal meets immortal love, and Time Eternity;
> Then in all failure and all pain the Hand of God I see—
> The Hand of God that evermore maketh and mouldeth me,—
> When *I-who-am-was-might-have-been* meet *I-who-am-to-be*.

There were not a few tragedies in the lives of the poets, for poetry is not a source of profit, at least to the poet. One of the saddest was that of John Davidson, whose death occasioned the ode referred to above. The *Fleet Street Eclogues* (1893) first attracted attention to his work, for he had already written plays. They were followed by *Ballads and Songs* (1894), a second series of *Fleet Street Eclogues* (1896), and *The Last Ballad* (1899). Like Macfie, Davidson was a Scot and a little of a spasmodic, apt when strongly moved and angry to over-spur his Pegasus and grow a little shrill. But it is neither such high-pitched ballads as *The Exodus from Houndsditch*, *The Ballad of a Nun*, and a *Ballad of Heaven*, nor yet his later *Testaments*, that will keep his work alive, but the sweeter strain of the poems of Nature such as *St. Mark's Eve* and others in *Holiday and Other Poems* (1906). *The Runnable Stag* is a delightful revel of rhythm and rhyme, Edgar Allan Poe with a difference,—a kind of poem which Mr. Masefield was to cultivate in *Reynard the Fox* and *Right Royal*.

"It has been observed", writes Johnson, "in all ages that the advantages of nature or of fortune have contributed very little to the promotion of happiness." Gray in the security of a College Fellowship was not apparently a happier man than Johnson struggling in London for a livelihood. If John Davidson's struggle ended tragically there is more of the joy of life in his poems than in a small volume issued in 1896 by another Fellow of Cambridge, *A Shropshire Lad*, by A. E. Housman. This was followed in 1922 by *Last Poems* in the same mood, and some have been printed since his death, including an early poem significant of all that was to follow, *Easter Hymn*:

> If in that Syrian garden, ages slain,
> You sleep, and know not you are dead in vain,
> Not even in dreams behold how dark and bright
> Ascends in smoke and fire, by day and night,
> The Hate you died to quench and could but fan,
> Sleep well and see no morning, son of man.
>
> But if, the grave rent and the stone rolled by,
> At the right hand of majesty on high
> You sit, and sitting so remember yet
> Your tears, your agony and bloody sweat,
> Your cross and passion and the life you gave,
> Bow hither out of heaven and see and save.

Housman's affinity as a poet is with Hardy if we judge by its main burden, his arraignment of a world in which the dice seem to be so heavily weighted against poor humanity. But there is a great difference in both tone and style. For Hardy's profound pity Housman substitutes a note of almost personal anger; and the classical scholar is more studious of the right word, the briefest expression of the dramatic moment, the telling allusion:

The Spartans on the sea-wet rock sat down and combed their hair.

The recurrent theme is so uniform that at times its expression seems hardly worth preservation, since it has already found sufficient, even happier, utterance.

In 1896 were issued privately forty-eight poems by Mary Coleridge, and in the following year a selection from these with a few not previously printed appeared as *Fancy's Guerdon*. A collected edition did not appear till 1907. Her poems also are short and epigrammatic lyrics, not so pointed as Housman's. They record experiences, some of them slight, others elusive or enigmatical. Occasionally the appeal is clear and searching.

If Kipling was the surprise of the early nineties, the greater surprise was the appearance of *Wessex Poems* in 1898. Of Thomas Hardy's poems something has been said already because, though published late, the earlier of the poems date as far back as the sixties. But their importance for the history of English poetry, their influence on later poets, was due in no small measure to their emergence just at this date. For if anything is clear from some reading of the poetry of the eighties and nineties, to go no further back, of poets such as Lang (a notable instance) and Stevenson and Gosse, and Wilde's earlier poems, and Henley and many others, it is that it was possible for an accomplished man of letters who was not essentially a poet to write excellent verses in a variety of moods and forms. These are the years of experiments in old French forms, Lang's *Ballades in Blue China*, Swinburne's *A Century of Roundels*, Henley's *Echoes* (that is of other poets). The question in many minds was, "Could we look for anything fresh in diction and verse which should yet be no mere experiment but the expression of a vein of sincere and original thought and feeling?" Kipling's was an experiment but of a rather special kind, used for a special purpose. Later Gerard Manley Hopkins was to excite attention, but the actual influence of Hopkins has of late been much exaggerated.   The greatest influence has been that of Hardy, alike in diction, verse, and mood.

In *Wessex Poems*, and the volumes which followed, the Romantic Movement comes quite definitely to its swan-song. It does so just because Hardy is so much at heart a romantic, a romantic in his lingering affection for the Faith he has perforce abandoned; so much the heir of the romantic poets that in Italy his strongest interests are the memory of Shelley's *Skylark*:

> The dust of the lark that Shelley heard
> And made immortal through times to be;

and the tomb of that poet and Keats by the pyramid of Cestius, who has hence derived his only interest for us:

> Say then, he lived and died
> That stones which bear his name
> Should mark through time where two immortal Shades abide:
> It is an ample fame.

In Hardy the romantic and the realist meet like a wave in its onset met by the powerful reflux of what has gone before.   For Hardy's poetry is the final expression of the disillusionment which had been at work ever since the sixteenth and seventeenth centuries.   It had begun with Copernicus and Newton, but it was with the appearance of Darwin's *Origin of Species* (1859) and *Descent of Man* (1871) that the process seemed completed, man assigned his humbler place among created beings. The greater Victorians, Tennyson and Browning, had fought against the implications of modern science.   Arnold and Meredith had striven in different ways to accept and accommodate.   The pre-Raphaelite poets had turned away to dream dreams, aware some of them that they were dreams:

> Dreamer of dreams, born out of my due time
> Why should I strive to set the crooked straight?
> Let it suffice me that my murmuring rhyme
> Beats with light wing against the ivory gate,
> Telling a tale not too importunate
> To those who in the sleepy region stay
> Lulled by the singer of an empty day.

Hardy as novelist and poet—for if Stevenson and Meredith were novelists who wrote some poems, Hardy was a poet who had written novels—faced the facts, for it was not the new philosophy alone which called all in doubt that troubled him: it was the support that this philosophy gave to or got from (whichever way you choose to look at it) the facts of experience, where

> Crass Casualty obstructs the sun and rain,
> And dicing Time for gladness casts a moan.

A. E. Housman was to strike a similar note, but his, as we have said, was an almost personal quarrel with Providence not inspired by the same sympathy with average humanity. Hardy's sympathy is neither self-pity nor personal anger. It is Crabbe's pity, especially for women, expressed in a less conventionalised diction and a more varied verse, for in language and metres or stanzas Hardy's closest affinity is with the interesting poet of Dorset writing in the Dorsetshire dialect, William Barnes, whose *Poems of Rural Life* appeared in 1844.

Chapter Thirty-Nine

TWENTIETH-CENTURY POETRY

(1) *The Pre-War Years, 1901–1914*

THE period on which we now enter begins and ends in war, and the war of 1914–1918 lies black across the middle of it. The Boer War, in which it begins, marked an epoch in our public life: it dispelled the dream of security which had lulled us since Waterloo, revealed that we had no friends in Europe, and that Germany hated us. Incident after incident evinced that hatred in the years which followed. But none of the poets except Doughty and Binyon showed any apprehension of the approaching storm. Meanwhile at home the Liberal victory of 1905 promised an era of peace, retrenchment, and reform; instead of which came the suffragist agitation, the Coal Strike of 1912, and unrest in Ireland boiling up to mutiny and rebellion. But of these things also poetry took no heed, withdrawing from public issues into a kind of pastoralism.

In fine, the new century inaugurated no revolution in English poetry. The decadent strain of the nineties died out, and so presently did the Imperialist strain, when Kipling settled down in England and beat his sword into a ploughshare. Otherwise the Victorian Age passed unbroken into the Edwardian. The great names of these fourteen years, and indeed of the next fourteen, were still those of Hardy, Bridges, and Yeats. Among younger poets Binyon had already shown himself the true heir of the great classical tradition; Mr. Sturge Moore was a classicist also, in a narrower sense; Mr. Masefield harked back to Crabbe and Chaucer, Mr. Gibson to Wordsworth; even in the highly original work of Mr. de la Mare one heard faint echoes of earlier dreamers. The Catholic tradition was continued by Mrs. Meynell, the pre-Raphaelite by Mr. Bottomley and Mrs. Annand Taylor; while both these traditions combined in the work of the two poetesses who called themselves conjointly "Michael Field".

Charles Montagu Doughty (1843–1926) stood alone, as kinless as Melchisedec, a Mid-Victorian by date, but in spirit an Elizabethan born out of due season. Doughty was a great man and wrote a great travel book in prose; but he doomed his verse to oblivion by his manhandling of the English language. *The Dawn in Britain* (1908) is spaciously conceived, but—

> If evil you, were I, O, my loved sons
> Of one . . . ! no more, (for immense dool so chokes
> A mother's throat,) queen Corwen couth say forth—

who is sufficient for 30,000 lines like these? In *The Cliffs* (1906) and *The Clouds* (1912) the modern theme of a German invasion abated Doughty's eccentricities a little; but they broke out again in *The Titans* (1916) and *Mansoul* (1920). Yet even in the lunar landscapes of these last poems we come on unexpected nooks of beauty, with vignettes as sharply done as anything in *Arabia Deserta*:

> Quarters the quiddering swallow, each flowery mead . . .

> Broods o'er those thymy eyots drowsy hum;
> Bourdon of glistering bees, in mails of gold.

> And hurl by booming dors, gross bee-fly kin;
> Broad girdled, diverse hewed, in their long pelts.

No English poet ever loved England more passionately than Doughty.

Of the other poets whom we have named, Laurence Binyon (1869–1943) began to write in the eighteen-nineties, the decade about which a wag exclaimed,

> Lo! how upon Parnassus' slopes they romp,
> The sons of Wat, Dow, David, John, and Thomp;

but its *fin de siècle* spirit left him untouched. His masters were Arnold and Bridges, his themes the beauty of Nature and the joy of youth, ever renewing in the aged world

> Freshness to feel the eternities around it,
> Sun, moon and stars, night and the sacred dew.

His *London Visions* (1896 and 1898) were visions of the human as well as the natural scene, its tragedies as well as its joys. The lyric impulse which informed his habitual mood of rapt contemplation demanded a larger utterance than the song afforded: he found it in the ode, which gives room not only for lyricism but for narrative and reflection. The *Odes* of 1901 contain some of his most perfect, if not his greatest, work: in *Tristram's End* he challenged comparison with Arnold and Swinburne, and was not discomfited. Then, the lyric impulse perhaps flagging, he turned, in *Penthesilea* and *The Death of Adam*, to straight narrative in stately blank verse reminiscent of *Sohrab and Rustum*. Thus much he had accomplished before 1914; but the better half of his poetic life still lay before him.

When Mr. Thomas Sturge Moore (b. 1870) issued *The Vine-dresser* in 1899, some of us thought it the most accomplished first poem that had ever appeared in English—too accomplished perhaps; a little more of what Coleridge called 'ebullience' might have held greater promise. Its theme was Greek; and the poems which followed it in the next few years—*The Centaur's Booty*, *The Rout of the Amazons*, *Pan's Prophecy*, *To Leda*, *Theseus*, *The Gazelles*—all but the last sought to revivify and reinterpret the myths and legends of Ancient Greece. Mr. Moore is a practising artist; all his life, like Keats, he has worshipped the mighty principle of beauty in all things. The beauty he worships is at once abstract and sensuous; he has rendered it with a plastic vigour that deserves more praise than it has received.

These two poets began to publish before 1900. With the new century new stars appeared; none of them was of the first magnitude, but, added to those already above the horizon, they made such a galaxy as has seldom been seen in English skies. Consider these names, to mention no others: Meredith, Swinburne, Hardy, Doughty, Bridges, Mrs. Meynell, Davidson, Housman, Thompson, Yeats, Kipling, "AE", Binyon, Sturge Moore, Davies, Synge, de la Mare, Bottomley, Mrs. Taylor, Gibson, Masefield, Abercrombie, Flecker, Lawrence, Brooke—all living and writing between 1900 and 1914. What other period of equal length can show such an assemblage of poets of all but the first rank?

Two poets arrived in 1902, as unlike as contemporaries could well be, Mr. Walter de la Mare (b. 1873) and Mr. John Masefield (b. 1878). Mr. de la Mare is lord of two domains, childhood and dreamland, domains which lie so near together that it is often hard to say of his verse how much is memory and how much imagination. He won children's hearts with his *Songs of Childhood* (1902) and the more substantial *Peacock Pie* of 1913. In these Songs of Innocence we see the world through the eyes of a wondering child, wise, humorous, imaginative, and strangely observant. It is on the whole a friendly world, where fairies and white naiads consort familiarly with bunnies, hares, and daddy-long-legs. But even before

Peacock Pie appeared, the *Poems* of 1906 and *The Listeners* of 1912 had shown that Mr. de la Mare's poetic field was more than a new and flowerier *Child's Garden of Verses*. The epitaph, "Here lies a most beautiful lady", is the loveliest thing of its kind in the language; but it is not so characteristic as the name-poem of *The Listeners*, with its exciting syncopated rhythms, clear imagery, and aura of mystery. Mr. de la Mare is a metrical genius; he can paint significant detail like Rossetti —*The Sleeper* rivals *My Sister's Sleep*; but what makes him unique is his uncanny power of conveying by mere suggestion a sense of "unknown modes of being" surrounding and permeating this visible life. A shadow looms dimly over *The Dwelling-Place*; but in *The Listeners* itself these unknown modes of being are not felt to be sinister; only they are unknown, not familiar fairies and naiads but phantom listeners, unheard and unseen; for which reason they inspire awe: awe, but not yet fear: that was to come after 1914.

Mr. Masefield spent a year of his youth at sea "in sail", and afterwards saw business life in New York. He made the most of both experiences; of the first in *Salt Water Ballads* (1902), fine fresh ditties with the tang of the sea in them and the swing of the chanty. For Mr. Masefield too is a metrist of genius; the ionics *a minore* of

> And a gréy míst on the séa's fáce, and a gréy dáwn breákíng

were new to English verse. In 1911 he took the British public by storm with *The Everlasting Mercy*, quickly followed by *The Widow in the Bye-Street, Dauber*, and *Daffodil Fields*. With these four poems Mr. Masefield poured new life into English narrative verse. No old far-off themes and stately diction for him, but common contemporary life in the raw, described in outspoken, almost brutal language—the conversion of a hardened ruffian, the hanging of a widow's son, a sailor who would be a painter, a *crime passionnel*. Dauber rounding the Horn "in sail" is done from the life. Crabbe too was a realist in verse, actually a more veracious, unsentimental realist than Mr. Masefield; but he had not Mr. Masefield's sensationalism in action and diction, nor the lyric pulse which beats through his verse even in narrative. These things, with his gift for story-telling and frontal attacks on the feelings, marked Mr. Masefield for the laurel.

The realism of Mr. Wilfrid Gibson (b. 1878) is different in

setting and tone. He began in the Tennysonian tradition; but in *Stonefolds* (1907), *Daily Bread* (1910), and *Borderland* (1914) he discarded that, and set himself to be the Wordsworth of his native Northumberland. The moving accident is not his trade; like Wordsworth and unlike Mr. Masefield, he eschews the sensational, content to tell plain tales of the joys and sorrows of his humble neighbours—miners, quarrymen, enginemen, shepherds, and "gangrel bodies". The dramatic form of these poems allows him to go even beyond Wordsworth in the direction of "language actually used by men". They are not dialect poems, like Barnes's, but here and there their English is enlivened with a racy dialect word. Mr. Gibson has not Mr. Masefield's lyric gift; his blank verse sometimes skirts the verge of prose; but at its best, as has been said, it has a noble plainness like granite. He is the most *substantial* of all the Edwardians. Yet he has a sense of mystery too, though he is no mystic: *Flannan Isle* communicates the authentic thrill of the unknown:

> Three men alive on Flannan Isle,
> Who thought on three men dead.

Among the Edwardian poets, as we shall call them, the three whom we have just named—Mr. de la Mare, Mr. Masefield, and Mr. Gibson—these three, with Binyon, seem to us the most likely to endure. The rest we must pass in briefer review. They are all true poets, who will be remembered for this poem or that, if not in their entirety. The oldest of them, Herbert Trench (1865–1923), will be remembered for "Come, let us make love deathless", rather than for his more ambitious flights in the wake of Meredith and Yeats. William Henry Davies (1870–1940) is a unique figure. No English poet, not even Clare, had less education. He was reared in the slums of Newport, and tramped the roads of England and America for years as a pedlar or a 'hobo'; yet this 'super-tramp', as he called himself, kept a kind of innocence, staring at Nature with the eyes of a happy child, and piping his joy in her like a bird—"the throstle with his note so true". Davies had no classical tradition behind him; but he had our Saxon vocabulary at command, and with it got such effects as this:

> A rainbow and a cuckoo's song
> May never come together again,
> May never come this side the tomb.

Few women poets survive from the Edwardian any more than from the Mid-Victorian age. Mrs. Meynell and "Michael Field" were really late-blooming Victorians. But of Edwardians, properly so called, two at least should not be forgotten—Charlotte Mew (1870-1926) and Mrs. Annand Taylor (b. 1876). Yeats included neither in his *Oxford Book of Modern Verse*, though Hardy thought Charlotte Mew the best woman poet of her time; and certainly her *Farmer's Bride* and *Rambling Sailor* contain very moving poems. The rich colouring of Mrs. Taylor's *Rose and Vine* (1907) shows the influence of Rossetti; in *The Hours of Fiammetta* she recaptured the subtle ardours of the Italian Renaissance; the rich sense-material of *The Dryad* is transfigured in the flame of her vivid Celtic spirit to a masterpiece of symbolism.

Mr. Gordon Bottomley (b. 1874) also showed the influence of Rossetti, and of Morris, in his *Poems of Thirty Years*, but it was in poetic drama that he found himself, as did Lascelles Abercrombie (1881-1938). Poetic drama in England, drama for the stage, not the closet, died with Dryden at the end of the seventeenth century. The eighteenth yielded nothing but Addison's frigid *Cato*. All the great Romantics and several of the great Victorians tried their hands at drama; but none of them, not even Browning, had dramatic gift and stagecraft enough to succeed on the boards. (The comparative success of Tennyson's *Becket* owed more to the actor-manager than to the poet.) When British drama began once more to attempt serious themes, as it did in the 1880's, it fell almost at once under the spell of Ibsen, which meant realism and prose. The credit of restoring poetic tragedy to the boards belongs to Stephen Phillips (1864-1915). Phillips was not a great poet, but his eloquence and command of stagecraft—he had been an actor—gave his blank-verse tragedies (*Paolo and Francesca, Herod*, and others) a great, if transient, vogue. But Phillips was a traditionalist; Mr. Bottomley and Abercrombie were innovators. Abercrombie aimed at a diction which should be at once poetic and modern. He was more interested, however, in ideas than in persons; his imposing *Sale of St. Thomas* lacks dramatic life. It was in staging that Mr. Bottomley innovated. He turned back instinctively to the choric origins of tragedy; relying for effect not on scenic illusion but on beauty of spoken word and rhythmic movement, he reduced the mechanical appliances of the modern stage to a simple pair of folding curtains, which in his latest *Lyric Plays* he replaced by a chorus. Mr. Bottomley is half Scottish; his *Lyric Plays* are almost all based on Scottish history or legend.

Mr. Hilaire Belloc (b. 1870), best known for his rewriting of English History from the Roman Catholic point of view, matched, if he did not outmatch, Kipling in his praise of Sussex; and some of his sonnets, epigrams, and 'cautionary' rhymes are not yet forgotten. His co-religionist, Gilbert Keith Chesterton (1874–1936), was not so good a poet, though his brave, booming voice made things like *Lepanto* sound uncommonly like poetry. The *Lyra Evangelistica* of the Rev. Arthur Shirley Cripps (b. 1869), with its pure seventeenth-century note, might have been better known in England had not its author spent his life as an Anglican missionary in Africa.

Unlike most poets, Mr. Ralph Hodgson (b. 1871) has written too little; but almost all he has written is memorable, above all the rapturous *Song of Honour* (modelled, too closely perhaps, on Smart's *Song to David*), and the sculpturesque *The Bull*. James Elroy Flecker (1884–1915) illustrated the influence of modern French poetry, which was to affect the technique of English verse considerably after the war. In the 1890's Arthur Symons had introduced us to the French symbolists; Flecker affiliated himself on an earlier school, the Parnassian school of Leconte de Lisle, exotic in subject, exquisite in finish, eschewing personal emotion, and aiming solely at the creation of beauty. Flecker's residence in the East, while it furnished him with exotic subjects, gave the Orientalism of his *Golden Journey to Samarkand*, and still more of his *Hassan*, a barbaric tone which is not to all tastes. But Flecker was a true poet: he had the singing voice. In the years immediately before the war, many eyes were turned on Rupert Brooke (1887–1915). Poet, wit, and scholar, what might so vivid a being not accomplish with his easy command of tuneful and pellucid verse? A dash of cynicism which he sometimes affected *pour épater les bourgeois* was set down to his youth. Indeed Brooke possessed the poetic temperament in its purest form, the form which Keats defined (and possessed), the capacity for enjoying sense-experience simply as experience, whatever its objects. He might have said with Keats that if he saw a chick below his window, he could become a chick "and peck about the gravel". With all these gifts, Brooke was in some danger of being spoiled; but the war saved him.

"AE", Synge, and Lawrence will be touched on in a later chapter.

Early in George V's reign, Mr. (now Sir) Edward Marsh, scenting a new spring of poetry in the air, brought out the first of a series of anthologies which he called "Georgian Poetry". The title was a misnomer to begin with: the chief contributors to his first volume were Edwardians.   They were not a coterie, nor even a school: what common denominator would cover poets so diverse as Mr. de la Mare and Mr. Gibson? Presently some of these contributors died and others dropped out, and their places were taken by less distinguished names.   Most of the new-comers were true poets; some of them—notably Mr. Blunden and Mrs. Shove—were original poets; and all of them were competent versifiers in traditional modes.   But they were content with small things; they did not emulate the lofty flights of the great Victorians; they saw Nature in her gentler, more domesticated, aspects, and saw her (in Blake's phrase) with, not through, the eye.   It was these new-comers surely whom Mr. Bullough had in mind when he called Georgian poetry "an Indian summer of romance"—a season, if we may so interpret him, of more light than heat.   Meanwhile a new generation was arising which scoffed at the sentiments of the Georgians as sentimentality, deriding their traditional metres as "old rhymes of an earlier day", and hunting for new techniques wherewith to express their modern sensibility.   In their mouths 'Georgian' became a term of contempt; but we, who enjoyed the Georgians, even the lesser Georgians, in their day, sometimes find ourselves wishing that their supplanters had more of their tunefulness and clarity.

Chapter Forty

TWENTIETH-CENTURY POETRY

(2) *The War Years, 1914–1918*

THE outbreak of war in 1914 stirred many young soldiers to poetry, not to glorify its pomp and circumstance, still less to write hymns of hate, but to express their new-found sense of the beauty and dearness of the homeland which they might never see again.   Much of this war-poetry, born as it was of a temporary mood of exaltation, was evanescent, like the poetry men make when they fall in love; but Mr. Robert Nichols and Mr. Robert Graves were born poets, and the former's *At the Wars* and the latter's *Rocky Acres* express the feeling we have tried to describe in language that is likely to endure.   These two survived to write much poetry after the war in other moods. Another true poet who survived the war was Mr. Maurice Baring.   But who can estimate what English poetry lost by the deaths of Charles Sorley, Wilfred Owen, Julian Grenfell, Francis Ledwidge, Rupert Brooke, and Edward Thomas, and who knows how many others, inheritors of unfulfilled renown? The extraordinary promise of Sorley's *Marlborough Poems* was cut short before he was twenty-one.   Grenfell, the English patrician, and Ledwidge, the Irish peasant, both turned to Nature for solace in the din of war, Grenfell with calm trust—

> The fighting man shall from the sun
> Take warmth, and life from the glowing earth;

Ledwidge with lingering looks cast back on the old days of peace—

> But it is lonely now in winter long,
> And, God, to hear the blackbird sing once more!

Brooke and Thomas, unlike these three, were already writers of established reputation.   Nothing in Brooke's life became him like the last few months of it.   He had outgrown the flippancies of youth but not its generous ardours when he died on active service at Scyros in the spring of 1915, leaving for epitaph the noble sonnet:

496

If I should die, think only this of me:
That there's some corner of a foreign field
That is for ever England.   There shall be
In that rich earth a richer dust concealed.

Edward Thomas (1878–1917) impressed all who met him by his character and his profound knowledge of, and feeling for, the English countryside, of which he wrote charmingly in prose.   Among those who met him was the American poet, Robert Frost, who was in England when the war began.   It was Mr. Frost's example and advice that led Thomas to try his hand at verse; but he was killed in action before he had quite mastered the new medium.   There is the stuff of poetry in all he wrote, but, as Emerson said of Thoreau's verses, "the thyme and marjoram are not yet honey".

The war revealed two remarkable poets in Mr. Siegfried Sassoon (b. 1886) and Wilfred Owen (1893–1918).   Mr. Sassoon entered it, no doubt, in the same exalted spirit as many other young soldiers; but as it went on exaltation succumbed to horror and indignation, to which he gave passionate utterance in verse.   Owen had written verse before the war with Gray, or Keats, or Tennyson for models; but it was his admiring friendship for Mr. Sassoon that made him a war-poet.   The waste of war afflicted him even more than its horrors; it moved him less to indignation than to pity.   The subject of his poems, he wrote, "is War, and the pity of War.   The poetry is in the pity."   His compassion extended to the foe.   In that arresting poem, *Strange Meeting*, he dreams that he has escaped out of the battle down some profound dark tunnel.   A stranger recognises him, and they talk together of

The pity of war, the pity war distilled.

At parting the stranger reveals himself:

I am the enemy you killed, my friend.
I knew you in this dark; for so you frowned
Yesterday through me as you jabbed and killed.

Owen's influence on the technique of post-war verse will be considered in the next chapter.

The war which touched these young poets to such different issues did not leave the older men unmoved.   Hardy's old heart was stirred, as we have seen, to write "Men who march away"; Bridges compiled *The Spirit of Man*, a wonderful anthology which has an even deeper significance in this war than it had in the last. Only Yeats remained unaffected: it was not Ireland's war! Most of the middle-aged poets were too deep in some sort of war-work to have much time for writing verse. Mr. Gibson served in the ranks, and recorded his experience of trench warfare in verse so plain that it sounds almost prosaic. Mr. Masefield's *1914* is a noble example of patriotic poetry; other memorials of his public service, his *Gallipoli* and *The Old Front Line*, are in prose. Mr. de la Mare used such little leisure as his war-work left him to issue a small volume of poems, which he called *Motley*. The mark of the war is stamped deep on the title-poem, in which the "simple happy mad" fool in motley shrinks aghast from the foul Satan-mad fool of War,

> Who rots in his own head.

It is stamped too on the accompanying piece named *Marionettes*, the title and temper of which recall, and are probably meant to recall, the supernal machinery of Hardy's *Dynasts*. For the rest, *Motley* contains some of Mr de la Mare's most delicate work. There are notes in it which were not heard, or were very faintly heard, in *The Listeners*; the unnamed shadow which loomed over *The Dwelling-Place* in *The Listeners* has a name now: it is Death. Yet the poet's last word is a prayer that when he is dust these loved and loving faces may please other men. But the poet on whom the war produced the most remarkable effect was Binyon. As a stretcher-bearer with the French armies he saw it at as close quarters almost as Mr. Gibson. The lyric fire, which seemed to us to have died down a little in his narrative poems, burned up again stronger than ever. His voice took on a deeper note; his verse broke into larger and more turbulent rhythms. He wrote, always in the same exalted strain, of the things he had seen with his own eyes in training or on service—of London defying the Zeppelins, guns sweeping round Stonehenge on parade, guns thundering at the front, the sower sowing behind the lines, Arras, Ypres, the patience of the French wounded, the lads in hospital blue. One stanza from his requiem *For the Fallen* went home to the nation's heart:

> They shall grow not old, as we that are left grow old:
> Age shall not weary them, nor the years condemn.
> At the going down of the sun and in the morning
> We will remember them.

The war-poets whom we have named were all, in a sense, romantics, and all except Wilfred Owen wrote in traditional measures. Meanwhile among the new generation a revolt was preparing against all the standards that had governed English poetry since the Romantic Revival. It was not wholly, nor even mainly, a literary revolution. We may describe it in the most general terms as a revolt against Humanism, against that anthropocentric view of life which had supplanted the theocentric conception of the Middle Ages. The leaders of the revolt maintained that Western Europe had taken the wrong turn at the Renaissance, which made Man, not God, the measure of all things, and had gone finally and fatally astray at the time of the French Revolution, when Rousseau cast adrift the last anchor that held men to the ancient faith, the doctrine, namely, of Original Sin. No layman put the case against Humanism more pungently than Thomas Ernest Hulme (1883–1917). Rousseau had proclaimed that man was naturally good and perfectible by his own efforts; on the contrary Hulme declared that man was by nature a poor, limited creature, who could be saved only by the grace of God. Hulme, as we have said, was a layman; but professional theologians, both Catholic and Protestant, were moving in the same direction. The Doctors of the Roman Church, having killed Modernism, were buttressing their perennial philosophy by a fresh study of St. Thomas Aquinas; while among the extreme Protestant sects this Neo-Thomism, as it was called, was balanced by a movement which may be called Neo-Calvinism, a reaffirmation of the fundamental principles held by the fathers of the Reformation. The theologians agreed with Hulme that man could be saved only by the grace of God; they added that he could be kept safe only by organised institutional religion. No doubt the war precipitated the revolt: its leaders could point to the state of Europe and say, "See what Humanism has brought us to!"

Romanticism was the child of Humanism; to attack the one was to attack the other. The Wordsworthian theory which had dominated English poetry for more than a century was assailed in its citadel. Wordsworth had defined poetry as "the spontaneous overflow of powerful emotions". "No", said the rebels. "Poetry is an art, not a dumping-ground for emotion." Hulme denounced the Romantic poets, even the best of them, as 'sloppy', always moaning or whining about something, always craving for the infinite, and wrapping up the truth in semi-religious veils of 'cosmic emotion'. The poetry of the future would be cheerful, dry, and sophisticated, and exceedingly exact in its choice of words, since poetry—so he put it—"is no more nor less than a mosaic of words".

These ideas did not come to full fruition till after the war; but the allied movement called Imagism belongs to this chapter, for it had run its course, in this country at least, before the war was over. The Imagists owed their name, we believe, to Mr. Ezra Pound; but we shall excuse ourselves from discussing that person who was never to our knowledge a British national. Imagism as a poetic creed was really based on an *obiter dictum* of Edgar Allan Poe's, which in its turn was derived from an *obiter dictum* of Coleridge's. Actually, Coleridge meant no more than that in a long poem like the *Iliad* all the parts could not be at the same high pitch of tension, from which Poe drew the conclusion that a long poem was a contradiction in terms, and that what we call a long poem is really a series of short poems linked by passages of prose. Up to a point the Imagist prospectus was unexceptionable; their insistence on precision, conciseness, and clarity was all to the good; but by limiting poetry to the image they condemned themselves to carving cherry-stones. Imagism was more an American than an English movement, though Hulme sponsored it, and wrote a few Imagist pieces himself, as also (more surprisingly) did D. H. Lawrence; but its chief practitioners in this country were "H. D." (Hilda Doolittle), her husband Mr. Richard Aldington, and Mr. F. S. Flint; and of these only "H. D." kept the faith for any length of time. Her models were the Greeks, and the best of her cameos are Greek in their clear-cut outline.

Two other phenomena fall to be noted in these war years, though rather as portents than achievements. 1916 saw the first issue of *Wheels*, one of those coterie anthologies which have been such a doubtful blessing to English poetry in our day. *Wheels* represented the poetry of the Left, in opposition to the orthodox *Georgian Poetry* of Mr Marsh. Its moving spirit was Miss Edith Sitwell, of whom we shall have more to say later. The other phenomenon was the publication in 1917 of *The Love Song of Alfred J. Prufrock*, by Mr. Thomas Stearns Eliot (b. 1888). Mr. Eliot, though born in Missouri, came of an old New England family, and had studied at Oxford and in Paris, where he came under the influence of the French

Symbolists, before settling in London. Later he acquired
British citizenship. *The Love Song of Alfred J. Prufrock* is the
maundering self-communion of a futile, middle-aged, middle-
class lover. Its evolution by free association, its studied banality
of phrase, and deliberately pedestrian rhythms were portentous
for English poetry, though their full significance was not
recognised till *The Waste Land* appeared in 1922.

Chapter Forty-One

TWENTIETH-CENTURY POETRY

(3) *Between the Wars, 1919–1939*

WE have reached the last lap of our long course. We enter on it with some trepidation, partly because Time has not yet sifted the wheat of recent poetry from the chaff, partly because we are not conscious of possessing that "modern sensibility" which the young poets arrogate to themselves and demand of their critics.

When the war ended in 1918, most of us hoped that we should emerge a better and stronger nation, "purged by its dreadful winnowing-fan". It was not to be. A year or two of elation and inflation was followed by a psychological and economic slump, in which the poets wandered confusedly, and are still wandering. Most of the older men kept the faith. Hardy, as we saw, despaired for a time, and perhaps fell back into despair at the last; but the rest clung to the belief that "the great soul of the world is just", and continued to write in that spirit. And for our part we are convinced that when the first post-war decade comes to be seen in true perspective Hardy's *Late Lyrics*, Yeats's *Tower*, Bridges's *Testament of Beauty*, with Binyon's two great odes, will stand out as its chief monuments in poetry. Of Hardy, Bridges, and Yeats enough has been said. *The Sirens* and *The Idols* are Binyon's greatest poems. Odes he calls them, but in scope and structure they are unlike any other English odes, even his own. They are symphonies in verse, each developing a theme in successive movements in different measures. The theme of *The Sirens* was originally suggested by the first transatlantic flight, made by Messrs. Brown and Alcock; then it expanded into a hymn to the spirit of adventure, which lures man on to conquer Nature and his fellow-men, to defy Space and the old opposition of Time, till he achieves the last conquest of all, to stand erect before utter calamity, and, having nothing, is free of all the Universe,

> And where light is, he enters unafraid.

The Idols of the second ode are those false gods whom man has projected out of his own terrors and superstitions and blind desires, before whom he lies in chains of his own forging, till at a vision of beauty in common things a spring of love wells up in his heart, and he sees them for the phantasms they are:

> The Idols fade.   The God abides.

For the next ten years Binyon gave most of his leisure to translating the *Divina Commedia* into terza rima, true Dantesque terza rima, with each tercet syntactically complete in itself. But his creative powers were only in abeyance; *The North Star* of 1941 showed that he was enjoying a second spring comparable to Tennyson's: the astringent effect of his long study of Dante can be felt in the firm structure of his *Mediterranean Verses*.

The post-war slump seemed to affect Mr. de la Mare for a little while; at least in *The Veil* (1921) he made a brief, and for him a strange, incursion into realism of the grimmest kind: the light which had illumined the lovely *Sleeper* was focused on the dreadful figures of the criminal in the dock, the drug-addict, the suicide.   In the other poems of *The Veil* and *The Fleeting* (1926) he returned to his proper domain, but subtler and more elusive than ever.   At times his heart misgave him as to what lay beyond the frontier, and he warned his proud imagination not to bend her sail to forbidden horizons.   That poem and two others in *The Veil* are definitely religious; but the prevailing tone of these later volumes is not one of faith, only of "poor mortal longingness".   In the years between the wars Mr. de la Mare compiled four remarkable anthologies: two of these, *Early One Morning* and *Behold This Dreamer*, prove that he is not only a great dreamer and lover of children but a profound student of dream- and child-psychology.   The last of his *Collected Poems* is a sustained argument for the value of the dream-life:

> And conscience less my mind indicts
> For idle days than dreamless nights.

For all his anthologising Mr. de la Mare has not lost his creative gift: *Bells and Grass* shows that he can still sing songs of childhood as he did forty years ago.

Mr. Masefield celebrated the return of peace to England with a long poem on fox-hunting, the typical sport of the England he loves.   *Reynard the Fox* is modelled on Chaucer's *Prologue*; the meet gives Mr. Masefield the same opportunity to bring English people of different ranks together as the Canterbury pilgrimage gave Chaucer. Mr. Masefield has not Chaucer's witty touch, nor his universality; his characters are more Trollopian than Chaucerian, recognisable contemporary English types, not the lineaments of universal human life. But as contemporary types they are very well done, and as a whole *Reynard the Fox* is the best sustained and the evenest in execution of all Mr. Masefield's long poems. In *Right Royal* he applied similar methods, not quite so successfully, to the other typical English sport of horse-racing. The little verse he has written since then has not added much to his fame as a poet; but *The Landworker* shows that he has not lost his power.

That other good Edwardian, Mr. Wilfrid Gibson, came home from the war to resume his old Wordsworthian rôle with the harsh, grim *Krindlesyke*, and to add lyric to his repertoire of narrative and drama. Others of the older poets, Georgians, Edwardians, even Victorians, continued to write in traditional measures, and gained many recruits. Ronald Macfie's long ode, *War*, is one of the most remarkable poems that the war produced, not so heavily weighted with thought as Binyon's odes, but more passionate, more rhetorical—a vivid description, from the detached but passionately sympathetic point of view of a pacifist, of what the war meant in the factories at home and in the fields of France, the whole in its beauty and its ugliness wrought into a philosophy of progress which looks back to the beginnings of the world as modern science conceives them and forward to a final fulfilment of the high aims for humanity of which prophets in all ages have dreamed, when the roar of guns will cease, and

> Only the embattled legions of the mind
> Spirit with spirit will in love contend
> To comprehend
> The soul behind
> Beauty and power—
> The love that sighs in every wind
> And breathes in every flower.

Some of the poets who were writing before 1919, *e.g.* Mr. Aldington, Mr. Graves, Mr. Turner, and perhaps Mr. Williams, came under modernist influence and will be touched on in that connection. Most of the Georgians, however, stuck to their Georgian colours: here we have space only for a few of them. John Freeman was not a professional man of letters, but a successful business man, for which reason perhaps the men of letters treated him with unusual indulgence. Freeman was not equal to sustained flights; his voice is muffled; and his variations on traditional measures often disappoint the ear; but he was a genuine poet in his modest way, sensitive to the beauty of the changing seasons—witness *Merrill's Garden*—a true lover of England and the English scene, especially its trees, and a man who remembered his own childhood. His poems, written, we are told, under the imminent shadow of death, have a muted wistfulness that we would not miss. No such indulgence was shown to Mr. Edward Shanks. This innocent Georgian became, with Mr. (now Sir) John Squire, the favourite butt of modernist satire. Granted that his sentiments are conventional and his measures traditional, the author of *A Lonely Place* deserved more discriminating treatment. Mr. Edmund Blunden is a more solid poet, so solid that some readers find him stodgy, and he himself has owned that his poetry "is not the fruit of facility". He has edited Clare, and Clare is the Nature-poet whom he most often recalls. He sees Nature much as Clare saw her, and records his impressions of the rivers and hamlets and woodlands of Sussex and Kent with the same patient fidelity. His inspiration has flagged of late; the flush of life has left his verse. Kent has another poet in the Hon. Victoria Sackville-West. She knows the "blue goodness of the Weald" as well as Kipling; its greenness too; but she also knows the "wet and weeping soil" that underlies it, and the hard, dirty toil that has gone to make its verdure. There is no false pastoralism about her pictures, nor yet the bitter realism of Crabbe: the land is a hard task-mistress, but a just one. *The Land* (1926) is a refreshing poem, more like Hesiod perhaps than Virgil, with something of the eighteenth century in its cool good sense. Her noble kinswoman, Lady Margaret Sackville, has written good poetry too since she cast off the spell of Swinburne. Few Nature-poems of recent years are more delicate in perception or more chaste in execution than those of the Rev. Andrew Young. Some of the recruits to traditionalism will be touched on later; meanwhile we must turn to the modernists.

The tap-root of the new crop of poetry which sprang up after or just before the Armistice was that revolt against Humanism and Romanticism which we described in the last chapter. Hulme supplied its philosophy, but its Boanerges

KK

was David Herbert Lawrence (1885–1930). Lawrence went beyond Hulme; he was in revolt not only against Western civilisation but against reason itself, calling on men to return to the life of instinct and "think with the blood". His own blood was hot enough; he fascinated the anaemic intellectuals of his day, till they called the years 1910 to 1930 "the age of Lawrence". It was chiefly as a novelist that he proclaimed his gospel of the flesh, but good judges believe that his poems will outlive his novels. Certainly the stricter form of verse spares us such rhapsodies as make *The Plumed Serpent* so tedious; and that he was a real poet no one will deny who remembers the lovely lines which tell how as a child he sat at his mother's feet while she played the piano. Lawrence excelled in describing states of mind that verge on the unconscious; but his unique gift was his physical imagination, an almost *animal* sympathy which enabled him, as it were, to enter into the experience of creatures other than man, to realise what it was for a tortoise to be a tortoise.

While this revolt was the tap-root of modernism in poetry, it drew sustenance from several other sources. First, and chiefly, from the new science, or half-science, of psychoanalysis, which at the time of the Armistice attained a wonderful vogue from the success with which it had been applied to the treatment of war neuroses. Freud had revealed the unsuspected extent to which the flow of thought is determined by forgotten memories and repressed instincts, mostly sexual. Novelists and biographers flocked after him, repeating formulae he had himself discarded; some poets were affected too. Mr. Graves succumbed to Freud for a time, and saw symbols, especially sexual symbols, in everything. Mr. Herbert Read was more eclectic in his psychology: when Freud failed him, he turned to Jung, and from Jung to Adler. We do not profess to follow the workings of Mr. Read's subconscious mind; he can write simply and interestingly about his boyhood in prose and about some of his war experiences in verse. Apart from specifically Freudian doctrines, psycho-analysis increased people's interest in the subconscious mind, and strengthened the tendency to substitute free association for logical or chronological sequence in poetry. Next to psychology, the science which most attracted the moderns was anthropology, which does for the mind of the race what psycho-analysis seeks to do for the mind of the individual. *The Golden Bough* provided a quarry in which Mr. Eliot and others dug assiduously.

Other more purely literary influences were at work, the most important perhaps being that of the French Symbolists, whom Gosse and Symons had introduced to British readers many years before. But these Victorian critics were concerned chiefly with what the Symbolists had to say; the moderns cared more for the way they said it. The Symbolists, like the Imagists, sought to purge poetry of all foreign matter, narrative or reflective, leaving a residuum of "pure poetry". But whereas the Imagists, aiming at clear, precise images, appealed almost exclusively to the eye, the aim of the Symbolists was to approximate poetry to music, in particular to the music of Wagner, using words as the musician uses notes, not to convey logical meaning, but by their associations and patterned sounds to induce or evoke in the reader a state of mind which M. l'Abbé Brémond likens to the mystic trance.

The Symbolists were French, the Imagists mostly American; but the modernists were also considerably influenced by certain English poets, notably by Hopkins, Owen, and Donne. Gerard Manley Hopkins falls to be considered here, for though he died in 1889 he was unknown to the general public, except for half a dozen pieces in an anthology, till Bridges published his poems in 1918. Hopkins (b. 1844) was bred an Anglican, but became a Roman Catholic in 1866, and two years later entered the Society of Jesus. He was acutely sensitive to natural beauty; such of his early poems as survive have all the sensuous opulence of the early Keats. For seven years after becoming a Jesuit he wrote nothing except a few occasional verses, submitting himself heart and soul to the discipline of his Order, and practising the Spiritual Exercises of its founder, that he might glorify God and save his own soul. In 1875, on a suggestion from his rector, he wrote *The Wreck of the Deutschland*, his longest and most difficult poem, telling of the deaths of five nuns who went down in that ship. Thereafter he sent a poem now and then to friends like Bridges and Dixon; but he published nothing, holding that literary fame should mean nothing to a priest. His last five years were spent in Dublin. Ill-health, nostalgia, and uncongenial work reduced him to a state of desolation, a feeling that God has forsaken him, which wrung from him some poignant personal sonnets. Before the end, however, he seems to have outsoared the shadow of that dark night of the soul; in what seems to be his last poem, strangely

KK*

entitled *That Nature is a Heraclitean Fire, and of the comfort of the Resurrection*, he sees all Nature consumed to ashes, and the soul alone left imperishable, an "immortal diamond". It has been said in varying tones of harshness that the poet in Hopkins was strangled by the priest. It was not so. Hopkins retained to the last his acute sensibility to the beauty of Nature, but he dedicated it, like his other powers, *ad majorem Dei gloriam.* Thus the famous *Windhover* seems at first to be simply a vivid description of the kestrel's flight, till we discover that the bird is a symbol, and observe that the sub-title of the poem is *To Christ our Lord.* Hopkins believed that the chief end of all things is to glorify God, and that everything glorified God by being its own perfect, unique, individual self. He held with Duns Scotus that form, not matter as Aquinas taught, was the principle of individuation. It is this inner form, uniqueness, or 'inscape' as he called it, that Hopkins constantly strives to express, and it is this endeavour that leads him to take such strange liberties with the English language. We may forgive his use of dialect words and invented words, but not his maltreatment of order and syntax—not such tmeses as "wind-lilylocks-laced", such contortions as

Commonweal

Little I reck ho! lacklevel in, if all had bread.

Moreover he discovered, or rediscovered—for he found that Langland and Skelton had been before him—a kind of purely accentual prosody, which he called "sprung rhythm". His admirers find it easier to imitate these oddities, which he himself was outgrowing, than to emulate the exquisite sensibility, quick imagination, and subtlety of his adoring, agonising spirit.

It was the same with Wilfred Owen. His imitators were attracted not so much by his grave compassion as by certain innovations, inner rhyme and 'pararhyme', by which he tried to give variety to his verse. By 'pararhyme' he meant an imperfect rhyme in which the consonants of the final syllables are the same but not the vowels:

It seemed that out of the battle I escaped
Down some profound dark tunnel, long since scooped
Through granite which Titanic wars had groined.
Yet also there encumbered sleepers groaned.

What his imitators mostly fail to observe is that the second vowel or diphthong in the pararhyme is regularly lower in pitch than the first, producing a subdued or baffled effect.

Interest in Donne had been stimulated by the publication of the Clarendon Press edition of his poems in 1912. People who were tired of Georgian smoothness and simplicity were attracted to Donne even by his harshness, which they probably exaggerated, still more by his intellectual energy, wit, and daring similitudes. Few of them perhaps understood the firm foothold that Donne had on a consistent, if antiquated, system of philosophy; certainly none of them achieved that magical fusion of wit and passion with which Donne at his best electrifies his readers. Among poets already known as such whom Donne influenced were Mr. Aldington, who from an Imagist turned a bitter metaphysical; Mr. Walter John Redfern Turner, once a romantic Georgian, whose metaphysical poems Yeats himself envied; and perhaps Mr. Charles Williams, whose poetry certainly became more metaphysical after the war, though whether this was due to Donne's influence or was the natural development of a contemplative and deeply religious mind we cannot say.

The modernists were in revolt not only against the spirit of Romantic poetry but against its forms. Years before, Bridges had declared that in English poetry rhymed verse and Miltonic blank verse were exhausted. He himself experimented, not very successfully, in quantitative measures; other poets, notably Mr. de la Mare, found out many inventions in the way of new stanzas and cadences; but all of them—Hopkins was as yet unknown—kept within the bounds of metre, which had always been recognised in English as the mark that distinguished verse from prose. But now Miss Amy Lowell, the leader of the American Imagists, proposed to discard metre for what she called "organic rhythm", which term she explained by reference to the give-and-take of the breath. To which it may be objected that in healthy people breathing, unless voluntarily controlled, is fairly regular, while other organic rhythms not subject to voluntary control, such as the heart-beat, are almost perfectly regular. And regular rhythm *is* metre. These bodily analogies, therefore, do not carry us far in the direction of distinguishing "organic rhythm" from metre. Moreover we have observed in Whitman, the father of modern "free verse", that the more truly poetic he is the more regular, *i.e.* the nearer to metre, do his rhythms become—

As toilsome I wandered Virginia's woods;

When lilacs last in the dooryard bloomed;

and that when he is most deeply moved, as he was by the murder of Lincoln, he falls not only into metre but into rhyme—

O Captain! my Captain! our fearful trip is done;
The ship has weathered every rack, the prize we sought is won.

In point of fact nearly all modernist verse of recent years is metrical, most of it falling into the irresistible iambic beat. Much of it, however, still discards rhyme and stanza, which frees it no doubt from the limitations that rhyme and stanza impose, but sacrifices the pleasure they afford, without, so far as we can perceive, providing any equivalent satisfaction to the ear.   In fine, "free verse", if both words be taken literally, is a contradiction in terms.   As Professor Phillimore once put it, "Free verse is like playing a game without rules.   But the rules make the game."   New poets may invent new games; but rules they must have.

To return from this excursus.   Most of the influences that we have mentioned—the new psychology, anthropology, symbolism, and metaphysics—met in the work of Mr. Eliot, and contributed not a little to its surprising success.   But Mr. Eliot can scarcely be counted the pioneer of English modernism. That honour may fairly be claimed by Miss Edith Sitwell.   Not that Miss Sitwell broke with tradition altogether; she is tolerant of metre, and even, in its place, of rhyme.   Her innovations took another direction.   She has told us that her senses are like those of primitive peoples, and are interchangeable. Which means that she enjoys, or suffers from, a rare form of synaesthesia; many people see sounds, Miss Sitwell hears colours.   She uses this gift to pierce down to the essence of things seen, which she renders in images, not in ambiguous symbols or loose metaphors.   Much of her work consists of experiments in the mental effect of assonance, dissonance, alliteration, and pause.   She expounds these "secrets of the kitchen", as Henry James called them, at some length; but only of *Aubade* does she explain the meaning, and that poem proves to be a description of a stupid country girl coming down in the morning to light the kitchen fire.   In other poems she seems to be playing with things salved from the wreck of the culture she was reared in.   As for modern civilisation, it is a thin matchboard flooring over a shallow hell.   In *Gold Coast Customs* she gazes into that hell, and draws on cannibal Ashanti for images of its rotting horror.   Not much here of what Arnold thought the complaining millions ask from poetry! Nevertheless, with her sharp perceptions, knowledge of dance-music, and feeling for what she calls 'texture', Miss Sitwell has taught us to see things we never saw before, and has helped to supple the rhythms and freshen the diction of English verse. Her brothers, Sir Osbert and Mr. Sacheverell Sitwell, share her virtuosity if not her peculiar sense-endowment.   Sir Osbert's post-war satires were rather ineffectual.   All post-war satire, even Mr. Sassoon's, was rather ineffectual.   *Facit indignatio versus*, no doubt; but indignation is only the propellent; the bullet should have a worth-while billet, and our post-war satirists all seemed to be either firing into the blue or potting at very small game.   We have his sister's assurance that Mr. Sacheverell Sitwell is one of the greatest poets that have been born in England these hundred and fifty years, in support of which claim she adduces his skill in assonance, dissonance, alliteration, and pause.   Tennyson too possessed these verbal arts, and groaned that he had nothing to say.   In *Agamemnon's Tomb* Mr. Sitwell has much to say of the degradation of death, and says it eloquently.   He does best, however, with a model, as in his variations on themes by Pope and other poets, or in his descriptions of pictures in *Canons of Giant Art*, where his visual imagination can weave arabesques over other men's creations.   Lacking this guidance, his most ambitious poem, *Dr. Donne and Gargantua*, which should have said something of good and evil, is a maze without a clue, if not without a plan.

In 1922 a new star became lord of the ascendant.   Mr. Eliot's *Waste Land* was hailed by the rising generation as a landmark in English poetry comparable to the *Lyrical Ballads*. Its vogue was due in part to causes which we have already mentioned; in part to what we regard as its chief faults—an abuse of private association and allusiveness which seven pages of notes were insufficient to elucidate; but no doubt its main attraction lay in the ironical fidelity with which it mirrored the prevalent mood of disillusionment, and its bold innovations in versification and style.   Its general intention is fairly plain; it is the voice of one crying in the wilderness of a Godless world.

The symbol of the Waste Land comes from the Grail legend: fertility will not return to it till the Holy Vessel is found.   But while this much is fairly clear, all attempts to explain the evolution of the poem in detail amount simply to guesses at the association of ideas in Mr. Eliot's mind.   Even if we guessed right, the discovery, though biographically interesting, would have no poetic value.   We know now that *The Ancient Mariner* was composed out of a tissue of forgotten memories linked by literary associations; but the knowledge has not affected our appreciation of the unity and beauty of the poem.   So it would be with *The Waste Land*.   In the final section the symbol of the thunder and the repeated DA, DAYADHVAM, DAMYATA—self-surrender, sympathy, self-control—point the way of escape from the wilderness.   But it was not till 1928 that Mr. Eliot defined his position, declaring himself a royalist in politics, classicist in literature, and Anglo-Catholic in religion; after that he grew more communicative.   *Ash Wednesday* (1930) is not an easy poem.   The old faults of private association and allusiveness are there—the first stanza implies a knowledge of a *ballata* of Guido Cavalcanti, a sonnet of Shakespeare, and the portion of the Book of Joel appointed to be read on Ash Wednesday; but the reader perseveres in the conviction that Mr. Eliot has something of value to say within the terms of a consistent, comprehensible dogma; and that if he is obscure it is mainly because he is striving to describe a rare and obscure experience, that dryness of the spirit which St. John of the Cross called the Dark Night of the Soul, a waste land from which there is no escape save by waiting patiently on God:

> Teach us to care and not to care.   Teach us to sit still.

When Mr. Eliot turned to drama in *The Rock, Murder in the Cathedral,* and *The Family Reunion,* he naturally became yet more communicative.   The choruses of *The Rock,* in which he calls on men to rebuild the Church, are mostly couched in plain Biblical language, and very impressive they are.   In his latest poems— *Burnt Norton, East Coker, The Dry Salvages,* and *Little Gidding* —he has relapsed into an obscurity which is hard to penetrate yet seems worth penetrating, since it arises in the main from the difficulty of the thoughts with which he is wrestling, thoughts of death and immortality, of heredity and personal identity, of the reality or the illusion of time.   For Mr. Eliot the Incarnation is the focal point alike of human history and of the life of the individual soul, at once an *opus operatum* and an act perpetually renewed, the point of intersection of time and eternity.   In *Little Gidding* he sees himself as one who stands "nel mezzo del cammin di nostra vita", looking before and after, and perceiving the need for a second regeneration, a purging of fire by fire, the fire of love, in which the fire and the rose are one.   In religion Mr. Eliot stands to-day where he stood in 1928, and some of those who admired only the bleak irony of his earlier poems now cast stones at him.

The years 1919–1929 were a confused and, except for Mr. Eliot and the older traditional poets, a barren decade.   Many of the young poets who should have carried on the great English tradition had fallen in the war.   As for the innovators, Mr. Eliot's early imitators, *servum pecus*, are all forgotten already, and when a new generation of real poets arose, men who had been too young to fight in 1918, though they owed much to Mr. Eliot in technique, their spirit was quite alien to his, and their eyes were turned in the opposite direction.   But before we discuss this new generation, commonly, though somewhat arbitrarily, represented by Messrs. Day Lewis, Auden, and Spender, let us glance for a moment at what was doing in Ireland and Scotland.

Most of the twentieth-century poets whom we have named so far were English by birth or adoption.   Meanwhile in Ireland a remarkable literary movement developed almost, if not quite, independent of English influence; in Scotland too there was a kind of renaissance, though on a smaller scale. The seeds of the Irish revival were sown in Mid-Victorian days by writers like Sir Samuel Ferguson; they flowered when Yeats returned to Ireland.   For such a revival Ireland possessed three major advantages—a native mythology which provided poets and dramatists with an unexhausted quarry of "storial matter", a national theatre which served as a common hearth on which the scattered embers of dramatic talent could be gathered together to keep each other aglow, and three men of conspicuous genius—Yeats himself, G. W. Russell ("AE"), and J. M. Synge.   Yeats's career has already been discussed. George William Russell (1867–1935) was a much less versatile and melodious poet than Yeats, but a purer mystic, never led astray by that will-o'-the-wisp, that hocus-pocus of evocation and incantation, which had such an attraction for Yeats.   There was no taint of magic in AE's mysticism; it was "a hard, austere, and lonely way", a discipline of thought and will, not an indulgence in dream and desire.   Still AE could dream too and wander with Yeats in the twilight of Irish mythology.   John Millington Synge (1871–1909) was the dramatist of the trio. Yeats's own plays were rather dramatic poems than dramas; but Synge was a born playwright.   His prose dramas do not concern us here; his few poems have the same picturesque idiom and ironical flavour.   These were the central figures in the movement; but round them gathered a cluster of poets astonishing to find in so small a country within so short a period.   Wilde, Trench, Lionel Johnson, and Ledwidge have already been mentioned in other connections; they do not really belong here, for though Irish in blood they were English in culture.   The Catholic tradition was continued by Katherine Tynan (Hinkson); but again we think of her rather as a Catholic than as an Irish writer.   (On the other hand Mr. Austin Clarke takes us back to a stratum of belief that crops out strangely here and there through the surface of Irish Catholicism, the worship of the Sidh, the old gods of pre-Christian Ireland.)   No recent Irish poets are more Irish, or, perhaps for that reason, more popular in Great Britain, than Mr. James Stephens and Mr. Padraic Colum.   The former is the more various genius, part Puck part Ariel, with a serious strain too which is neither, and never more himself than when he is translating from the Irish.   Which reminds us that besides poets writing in English, who alone concern us here, there exists in Ireland a school of poets who write in Erse and have a long bardic tradition behind them, from which they, and their English-writing brethren, have taken hints not only for subjects but for lyric forms and rhythms unfamiliar to British ears. Mr. Frank O'Connor has made elegant translations of some of these Irish poems. Lady Gerald Wellesley (Dorothy Wellesley), though English born, may be mentioned here on the strength of her Irish connection.   Yeats admired her metaphysical poems; for our part we like her best when she is most concrete, as when she writes about horses with the knowledge of a breeder and the imagination of a poet.   Dr. Oliver Gogarty and Mr. L. A. G. Strong are well-known novelists; they are also poets and wits: Dr. Gogarty's epigrams might have graced the Greek Anthology.   We have named those who to our limited knowledge seem the best of recent Irish poets; but there are others, among them Mr. F. R. Higgins, whom Yeats looked on as his destined successor.

Puir auld Scotland had none of Ireland's advantages for a revival of letters—no native mythology, no leader like Yeats, and little of the Sinn Fein passion that drove the Irish movement on.   Moreover she started from a lower level in the Victorian Age.   Scots vernacular literature under Victoria has been summarily dismissed as kailyard prose and Whistlebinkie verse.   One or two poets, like William Thom and Alexander Laing, struck the favourite Scottish notes of pathos and humour not unskilfully; but most of the vast Whistlebinkie collection had better have been left where it was found in the poet's corners of provincial papers.   It looks as if Burns had taken so heavy a crop off the ground that it needed a hundred years to recover.   Things mended a little towards the end of the century.   In the 1880's Stevenson wrote some accomplished Scots verse; but though Stevenson had a strong sentimental attachment to Lowland Scots—"dear to my heart as the peat reek"—he thought in English.   And the same may be said of Andrew Lang.   The most considerable of genuine Scots poets in Victorian days was J. Logie Robertson, "Hugh Haliburton", whose *Horace in Homespun* (1884) has much of the curious felicity that we noted in Ramsay's imitations of Horace. The new century saw a revival of interest in Scottish history, art, language, and literature.   The yield in verse was very considerable in quantity, and respectable, if seldom distinguished, in quality.   Nobody attempted anything big; most of them struck the familiar Scottish notes of humour, pathos, patriotism (deepened by the war), domesticity, and theology. Linguistically they fall into three classes.   First, and most numerous, are those who use the traditional literary Scots, the Scots (or Anglo-Scots) of Ramsay and Burns.   At the head of this class stands Miss Marion Angus.   She is the sweetest singer of them all, and has that touch of natural magic, and that tragic undertone which, rightly or wrongly, we associate with Celtic blood.   There was nothing Celtic about Walter Wingate; he had not much imagination, but he had humour, and (what is rarer in Scotsmen) he had wit, and a masterly command of diction and metre.   Regionalism has always played a part in Scottish poetry: John Buchan was best inspired by his Border streams, as Mrs. Violet Jacob is by the Braes of Angus and the Howe o' the Mearns.   The second class contains one member, Mr. Christopher Murray Grieve. Conceiving that a century of Whistlebinkie had left Scots unfit for high poetry, Mr. Grieve has ransacked the makars and the dictionary for material out of which to frame a new poetic diction for Scots. His critics scoff at his "synthetic Scots"; but there is really nothing absurd in attempting to do for Scots verse what Spenser did for English; *solvitur*—or *solvetur*—*ambulando*. Finally there is Dialect verse. Besides the traditional literary language there are in Scotland four distinct local dialects, still spoken by the common people. Of these the most distinctive and vigorous is Northern Scots, spoken between the Moray Firth and the Firth of Tay. In this dialect Dr. Charles Murray has written poems which for realism and vital force surpass anything Scots verse has done since Burns died. Dr. Murray owed his success first of course to his native genius, but after that to the fact that he wrote in a living speech which was his own mother-tongue. Another good dialect poet, Miss Mary Symon, also uses Northern Scots.

These Irish and Scottish poets were almost all traditionalists. Not so the new generation of English poets who began to arrive about 1930. Mr. Cecil Day Lewis, Mr. Wystan Hugh Auden, and Mr. Stephen Spender had all sat at Mr. Eliot's feet. But it was his technique they learned, not his doctrine. Mr. Eliot's eyes were turned to the garnered culture of the past; these young men looked to the future. They liked the shape of things as they were no better than he, but they meant to go through with it and make new poetry for a new and better world to be won by social revolution. They all were, or believed themselves to be, communists, though Mr. Spender wore his red with a difference. As it happened, they all began to write at the time when the blizzard of the great depression which blew up in America in 1929 first struck these shores. Mr. Auden looks round him and sees

> Smokeless chimneys, damaged bridges, rotting wharves and choked canals;

Mr. Spender's heart bleeds when he sees the unemployed men who loaf in the streets,

> And turn their empty pockets out,
> The cynical gesture of the poor.

Of these three poets Mr. Day Lewis has developed most consistently. In *Transition Poem* (1929) he was trying to find himself, to find what he would be at and whom he should address: the result is chaotic both in form and matter.   In *From Feathers to Iron* (1931) the prospect of fatherhood gives a direction to his life, a hope that will take shape on the day when he can say, "Unto us a child is born".   In *The Magnetic Mountain* (1933) this hope for himself spreads into a hope for mankind, and his style grows firmer and clearer.   Then came the Spanish War, and with the victory of Franco and the menace of Fascism lowering darker and darker over Europe the hope which had dawned in *The Magnetic Mountain* was overcast.   *Overtures to Death* strikes a tragic note, indignant and ominous, though not despairing.

Mr. Auden's career is less easy to summarise; he is so clever —too clever for a poet, we are tempted to say.   His *Orators* (1932) is a wilful gallimaufry of verse and prose, satire and objurgation, realism, fantasy, burlesque, and mere mystification, 'guying' his readers.   Still from *The Orators* and the *Poems* of 1930 one thing emerges clearly enough—the body politic is sick almost to death.   The disease is at once psychological and economic; he calls in Dr. Freud as well as Dr. Marx.   Capitalist civilisation is disintegrating, and the old school-tie will not save it.   We must have action, revolutionary action, if we want to live; if we don't, "we'd better start to die".   The tragedy of the Spanish War wiped the ironic smile from Mr. Auden's lips; *Spain* was written in deadly earnest, though even into its stern *Vae victis* his ingrained habit of irony obtrudes here and there.   Mr. Auden is now in America; where he is in politics we do not know.   As a poet he has influenced his younger contemporaries more than anyone except Mr. Eliot.   Since *Look, Stranger* (1936) he seems to have rested on his laurels; but he is still under forty, and with his unusual combination of gifts, lyric and satiric, he may yet prove himself *le Byron de nos jours*.

Anger and scorn enter largely into Mr. Auden's denunciation of the *status quo*; Mr. Stephen Spender (b. 1909) is moved rather by compassion, compassion for the workless men who idle in the streets and the children in slum schools who have never seen the sea.   The Spanish War gave his inherited Liberalism a more definitely socialistic direction—

> No man
> Shall hunger.   Men shall spend equally,
> Our goal which we compel.   Man shall be man—

a gospel, nevertheless, which recalls Maurice rather than Marx. Mr. Spender's early poems, like Mr. Lewis's, are too intro-spective, taking stock of his own soul. *The Still Centre* (1939) is much more objective, concrete, and intelligible; even the oldest lover of poetry can find satisfaction in *Port Bou* and the poem on the Greenland expedition. Mr. Spender has little of Mr. Auden's vivacity, and none of his humour; but he has real poetic sensibility, a good ear, and a strong lyric impulse, which would find more effective utterance if subjected to the discipline of the stanza.

These three are political poets; however hard we may find them in detail, we know in general what they would be at. Can we say as much of any of their contemporaries, even of Mr. Louis MacNeice, the ablest, certainly the robustest, of them all, a fine scholar, and a master alike of the old manner and the new? He is a friend of Mr. Auden's, but he does not share Mr. Auden's communism: on the contrary he is a rugged individualist, who views the contemporary scene with ironic detachment:

> The glass is falling hour by hour, the glass will fall for ever,
> But if you break the bloody glass you won't hold up the weather.

Only when he sees the individual menaced by totalitarianism, and freedom of thought crushed by "tight-lipped technocratic Conquistadores", his detachment gives way, and he bursts into a passionate *Epitaph for Liberal Poets*.

We have neither space nor knowledge enough to deal in detail with the other poets of the decade 1929–1939. They are too numerous and too near. Ever since Mr. Roberts's *New Signatures* in 1932 there has been a steady flow of anthologies, annuals, and poetry magazines. Much of it is coterie work, and every coterie puts forth a manifesto pro-claiming its view of the nature and purpose of poetry, till Mr. Eliot is provoked into saying, "Everyone talks of poetry, but no one gives us a poem". The most we can do is to note such tendencies as we have been able to distinguish in the themes and forms of recent verse.

The surrealists profess to record the automatism of the mind in such states as reverie, dream, trance, delirium, madness. Such records may have clinical value; poetic value they have none unless their content is coherent and significant enough for the waking mind to compose it into a work of art, something beautiful, amusing, awe-inspiring, or the like. Surrealism invaded English prose in the later work of James Joyce; fortunately, though sponsored by Mr. Read and expounded by Mr. Gascoyne, it has made little impression on English verse. The phenomenon reminds us, however, of a truth long recognised in a vague way, though its full significance was first revealed by the psycho-analysts, the affinity of poetry and dream, and generally the rôle of the subconscious in determining the flow of thought. Mr. Charles Madge's *The Pass* is a pure dream-poem, not a poem composed in a dream, like *Kubla Khan*, but a dream composed into a poem, like Wordsworth's dream of the mounted Bedouin. We do not ask of such poetry that it should convey a 'message'; it is enough if it present an image with such a hint of something behind as sets our own fancy working, moves us, and gives us pleasure. Pleasure—that is the test by which so many of the moderns fail. Mr. Edwin Muir's *The Riders* is not exactly a dream-poem, but it grew out of an image which presented itself spontaneously to the poet, already clothed in verse. With Mr. Dylan Thomas too the image comes first. When his barmy noddle's working prime—if one may quote Burns in such a connection—image after image boils up in it, to be fused and bent to his poetic purpose, though what that purpose is we can seldom discern through the tornado of wild and whirling words, violent metaphors, and Biblical allusions that envelops his fixed ideas about sex, and sin, and death. Still he is a poet; he thinks in images, and to the imagination he appeals. So do the Symbolists, though they work by suggestion rather than presentation, through the ear rather than the eye. Not so the Metaphysicals, whose conceits are engendered in the intellect. The poetry of Mr. Empson and Mr. Barker is too deep for us; or perhaps, as the ghillie said of a turbid stream, "It's no sae deep as it's drumlie". A good deal of modern poetry is auto-biographical; indeed Mr. Julian Symons lays it down that art to the artist is an autobiographical game—which is true in the sense that every artist holds his own mirror up to Nature. T he youngest of these coteries is the New Apocalypse. Their ai.n, according to Mr. Henry Treece, is to emancipate the individual man, in his whole nature, from mechanisation in every form, which emancipation may come by way of myth, imagination, and personal religion. As yet, however, they have produced no myths in verse that are recognisable as myths, and their prose stories are not distinguishable from the ordinary commercial article. Yet the value they set on the individual and on imagination and personal religion encourages the hope that here perhaps is the first flush of the dawn of a new Romantic Revival.

These poets all believe that if poetry is to live it must come to terms with the material conditions of modern life and the conclusions of modern science, make poetry not, or not only, of nightingales and sunsets but of air-liners and express trains, and take account of man's animal as well as his spiritual part. (By "modern science" they mean chiefly the new psychology: the stupendous revelations of modern physics have not yet penetrated into poetry.)

With this extension of the field of poetry goes an extension, or at least a change, in its vocabulary: poetic diction is banned in favour of language "such as men do use", even if it be technical or colloquial. In versification the passion for experiment seems to be abating. Free verse in its worst sense has almost disappeared; metre has reasserted itself, but not to the same extent stanza. Blank verse has been unstiffened; but no one except Miss Sitwell has invented many new rhythms. In rhyme, however, there have been some interesting experiments in the use of inner rhyme, assonance, and 'pararhyme' after the manner of Wilfred Owen: Mr. Day Lewis has some good examples.

Meanwhile the ranks of the traditionalists have received some notable recruits, none more notable than the South African poet, Mr. Roy Campbell, who struck a "lyre of savage thunder" in *The Flaming Terrapin* in 1924, then swooped on bookish poets in *The Georgiad*, then soared to occasional sublimity in *Adamastor* and *Mithraic Emblems*, his elemental force finding room and verge enough within the bounds of traditional metres. The Spanish War, which left so deep a mark on English poetry, made a crisis in Mr. Campbell's life also. Most English poets took the Republican side: Mr. Campbell fought for Franco; one of his most striking poems describes an air-combat in Spain. Another South African poet, less forceful than Mr. Campbell but worth noting, is Mr. William Plomer. Among British-born poets Mr. A. E. Coppard is well known for his short stories; he ought to be known also for the Caroline grace of his short poems. Something of the same grace, though of a sterner cast, is seen in the verse of Julian Bell, who fought and died for the Republican cause in Spain. Mr. Redwood Anderson's strange, mystical note recalls Mr. de la Mare; but he is no imitator. Mr. Rostrevor Hamilton, Mr. Frank Kendon, Mr. Laurence Whistler, to name no others, carry on the English tradition. Indeed the last ten years have yielded a remarkable crop of good, if not great, poetry, much of it produced by women. Of these Miss Ruth Pitter is probably the best known: in 1934 she won fame as a fabulist with the gay grotesqueries of *The Mad Lady's Garland*; but she has also written much fine serious verse. Miss Muriel Stuart does not write in Scots, but among women poets of Scottish birth she ranks next to Mrs. Taylor and Miss Angus. Another Scotswoman who has written some true and tender English verse is Miss Lilian Bowes-Lyon. Then there are Miss Stella Gibbons, Mrs. Sylvia Lynd, Mrs. Jan Struther, Miss Sylvia Townshend Warner, all accomplished and versatile writers in verse as well as prose; and others with whom we are less familiar.

The difference between the two schools, the traditional and the experimental, should not be exaggerated. Not a few poets can use either manner. Mrs. Charles Madge, for instance, though generally counted among the modernists, can also write simply and beautifully in traditional measures. Moreover the difference seems to be lessening. The traditionalists have something to learn in variety of subject-matter, vocabulary, and rhyme; and more to teach in the qualities that make poetry pleasurable—clarity, shapeliness, and melody. On the whole the traditionalists seem to be winning; in that fine anonymous anthology, *Fear No More*, which appeared in 1940, five poems in every seven are in rhyme. Perhaps we are approaching the confluence of the two streams.

We have traced the course of English poetry from its first known beginnings down to 1939. Further than that we do not care to go, having nothing of value to say of the poetry which the present war has so far produced. But looking beyond the present we make bold to apply to English poetry what Wordsworth wrote of British freedom:—

> It is not to be thought of that the Flood
> Of English song, which, to the open sea
> Of the world's praise, from dark antiquity
> Hath flowed, "with pomp of waters, unwithstood" . . .
> That this most famous stream in bogs and sands
> Should perish; and to evil and to good
> Be lost for ever.

A SELECT BIBLIOGRAPHY

This bibliography, like the book it belongs to, is intended primarily for the general reader. Accordingly, besides standard texts, we have tried, where possible, to name editions readily accessible to any lover of poetry.

CHAPTER I. (1) Except for some short pieces (notably *Finn, Waldere, Maldon,* the early Northumbrian poems and the lines on the Fasting Seasons) ed. in *The A.S. Minor Poems* by E. van K. Dobbie, N.Y. 1943, and *The Paris Psalter and the Meters of Boethius* ed. G. P. Krapp 1943, all A.S. poetry comes from four MSS. of the 10th or 11th century—the B.M. Cotton Vitellius Axv (*Beowulf* and *Judith*); the Exeter Book (*Widsith, Deor,* the dramatic lyrics, *Christ, Juliana, Guthlac, Phoenix, Riddles,* etc.) ed. G. P. Krapp and E. van K. Dobbie 1936; the (Bodleian) Junius MS. (*Genesis, Exodus, Daniel, Christ and Satan*) ed. G. P. Krapp 1931, and the Vercelli Book (*Andreas, Fates of the Apostles, Elene, Dream of the Rood*) ed. do. 1932.

 Beowulf and the Finn Fragment ed. A. J. Wyatt and R. W. Chambers, Camb. 1920; W. J. Sedgefield, Manchester 1925; F. Klaeber, 1936. *Runic and Heroic Poems* ed. B. Dickins, Camb. 1916. *Widsith* ed. R. W. Chambers, Camb. 1912. *A.S. and Norse Poems* (dramatic lyrics) ed. N. Kershaw, Camb. 1922. *The O.E. Riddles* ed. A. J. Wyatt, Boston 1912. *Andreas* ed. G. P. Krapp, Boston 1906. *Christ* ed. A. S. Cook, Boston 1900. *Elene, Phoenix* and *Physiologus* ed. do., New Haven 1919. *Judith* ed. do., Boston 1904. *Brunanburh* ed. A. Campbell 1930. *Gnomic Poetry in A.S.* ed. B. C. Cotton, N.Y. 1914. *Widsith, Waldere, Deor, Three Northumbrian Poems, Dream of the Rood,* and *Maldon* are in Methuen's O.E. Library.
 Translations:—*Beowulf* tr. D. H. Crawford (verse) (Medieval Lib.); tr. J. R. Clark Hill, rev. C. L. Wrenn (prose) 1940. *The Poems of Cynewulf* and *The Caedmon Poems* tr. C. W. Kennedy (prose) 1910 and 1916. *A.S. Poetry, Selected,* tr. R. K. Gordon (prose) (Everyman's Lib.). *A.S. Poetry: An Essay,* G. Bone (verse), Oxford 1943.

(2) *Epic and Romance,* W. P. Ker 1897; *The Dark Ages,* do., Edin. 1904; *Eng. Lit.: Mediaeval,* do. 1912. *The Heroic Age,* H. M. Chadwick, Camb. 1912. *The Oldest English Poetry,* C. W. Kennedy, N.Y. 1943. *Beowulf: An Introduction,* R. W. Chambers, Camb. 1932. *Beowulf and Epic Tradition,* W. W. Lawrence, Cambridge, Mass. 1928. *Beowulf and the Seventh Century,* R. Girvan 1935. *A.S. Christian Poetry,* A. J. Barnouw, The Hague 1914. *Cambridge Hist. of Eng. Lit.,* Vol. I.

CHAPTER II. (1) LAYAMON: *Brut* ed. Sir F. Madden (Soc. of Antiquaries) 1847. *The Bestiary,* see *An Old Miscellany containing a Bestiary* ed. R. Morris (E E T S) 1872. *The Ormulum* ed. R. Holt 2 vols. Oxfd. 1878. *Orison of Our Lady* (E E T S). *The Owl and the Nightingale* ed. J. Stevenson (Roxburghe Club) 1838; ed. J. E. Wells (Belles Lettres Series). *Chanson de Roland* tr. C. Scott Moncrieff 1919; also by J. Crossland (Medieval Lib.). For texts of the Romances see E E T S *passim.* *Cleanness, Patience* and *Pearl* ed. Sir I. Gollancz (Select Early English Poets), Oxfd.; *Pearl* ed. C. G. Osgood (Belles Lettres Series). *Gawain and the Green Knight* ed. R. Morris (E E T S) 1897. *Romance of the Rose,* see Chaucer for partial translation, and for translation of the whole by F. S. Ellis see Dent's Temple Classics. *Specimens of Early English* ed. R. Morris and W. W. Skeat, Oxfd. 1898. *Fourteenth Century Verse and Prose* ed. K. Sisam, Oxfd. 1921.

(2) *La Littérature française au Moyen-âge,* Gaston Paris, Paris 1890. *Histoire littéraire du Peuple anglais,* J. J. Jusserand, Vol. I Paris 1890 (English edn. 1915). *Cambridge History of English Literature,* Vol. I 1908. *English Literature from the Norman Conquest to Chaucer,* W. H. Schofield 1906. *English Literature, Mediaeval,* W. P. Ker (Home University Lib.). *The High History of the Holy Grail,* ed. S. Evans (Dent's Temple Classics). *The Author of the Pearl in the Light of his Theological Opinions,* Carleton Brown (Modern Language Association of America). *The Allegory of Love,* C. S. Lewis, Oxfd. 1938.

CHAPTER III. (1) GEOFFREY CHAUCER: *Works* ed. W. W. Skeat 7 vols. Oxfd. 1894–97; 1 vol. ed. do. (Oxford Poets); ed. A. W. Pollard, H. F. Heath, M. H. Liddell, and Sir W. McCormick (Globe); ed. with notes F. N. Robinson, Oxfd. 1934. JOHN GOWER: *Works* ed. G. C. Macaulay 4 vols. Oxfd. 1899–1902; Selections, ed. do. Oxfd. 1903; modernised selections by H. Morley 1889; see also *Fourteenth Century Verse and Prose* ed. K. Sisam, Oxfd. 1921. WILLIAM LANG-LAND: *Piers Plowman* ed. Skeat 2 vols. Oxfd. 1886; 1 vol. (Everyman's Lib.); modernised version by Skeat (Medieval Lib.); selections in Sisam's *Fourteenth Century Verse and Prose.*
(2) Dryden's *Preface* to his *Fables* (see DRYDEN); Blake's *Descriptive Catalogue* (see BLAKE); W. Hazlitt, *Collected Works* Vol. V; *Chaucer*, Sir A. W. Ward (E M L); *A Chaucer Primer*, A. W. Pollard 1903; *Essays on Medieval Literature*, W. P. Ker, 1908; *Chaucer*, E. Legouis, Paris 1910, Eng. tr. 1913; *Chaucer and his Poetry*, G. L. Kittredge, Cambridge, Mass. 1915; *Some New Light on Chaucer*, J. M. Manly, N.Y. 1926; *Geoffrey Chaucer*, J. L. Lowes 1934. For GOWER see *Essays on Medieval Literature*, W. P. Ker 1905.

CHAPTER IV. (1) J. LYDGATE: *Minor Poems* ed. J. O. Halliwell-Phillips 1840; *Falls of Princes*, etc. E E T S various editors. T. CHESTRE: *Sir Launfal*, tr. J. L. Weston, Boston 1914. For *The Cuckoo and the Nightingale, Flower and the Leaf, Assembly of Ladies, Court of Love* see Skeat's Chaucer Vol. VII. T. OCCLEVE: *Works* E E T S ed. F. J. Furnivall and Sir I. Gollancz 3 vols. 1892, 1897, 1925. S. HAWES: *Pastime of Pleasure* E E T S ed. W. E. Mead 1928. A. BARCLAY: *Ship of Fools*, English version, N.Y. 1928; *Eclogues* E E T S ed. B. White 1928. J. SKELTON: *Complete Poems* ed. P. Henderson 1930. *Ancient English Christmas Carols* ed. E. Rickert (Medieval Lib.). *English and Scottish Popular Ballads* ed. F. J. Child 5 vols. Boston 1882–85; also 1 vol. Boston 1904. *Townley Mysteries* E E T S ed. A. W. Pollard 1897; *York do.* E E T S ed. L. Toulmin-Smith 1885; *Chester do.* E E T S ed. H. Deimling and G. W. Mathews 1893–1916; *Coventry do.* ed. J. Halliwell 1841. *Castle of Perseverance* E E T S ed. F. J. Furnivall and A. W. Pollard 1914. *Everyman and Other Plays* ed. E. Rhys (Everyman's Lib.). H. MEDWALL: *Fulgens and Lucrece* ed. F. S. Boas and A. W. Reed, Oxfd. 1926; also in *Five Pre-Shakespearean Comedies*, F. S. Boas (World's Classics). J. HEYWOOD: *Dramatic Wgs.* ed. J. S. Farmer 1905. J. BALE: *Dramatic Wgs.* ed. do. 1907. *The Nutbrown Maid*, first in *Arnold's Chronicle* 1521 ed. F. Douce 1811, then in Percy's *Reliques*, q.v.
(2) *The Mediaeval Stage*, Sir E. K. Chambers, Oxfd. 1903. *Introd. to Child's* 1 vol. *Ballads*, G. Kittredge 1904. *The Dark Ages*, W. P. Ker, Edin. 1904; *Essays on Medieval Literature*, do. 1908. *English Miracle Plays, Moralities and Interludes*, A. W. Pollard, Oxfd. 1927. *European Balladry*, W. J. Entwistle, Oxfd. 1937. *John Skelton, Poet Laureate*, I. A. Gordon, Melbourne 1943.

CHAPTER V. (1) *Sir Tristram* ed. Scott 1804; S T S ed. G. P. MacNeill 1886. The *cantus* on Alexander III's death is in Wyntoun, *q.v.* JOHN BARBOUR: *The Brus* S T S ed. W. W. Skeat 1893–94; *The Buik of Alexander* S T S ed. R. L. Graeme Ritchie 4 vols. 1921–29. ANDREW OF WYNTOUN: *Chronykil* S T S ed. F. J. Amours 4 vols. 1902–9. HENRY THE MINSTREL: *Wallace* S T S ed. J. Moir 1889. For Scottish Romances see *Scottish Alliterative Poems* S T S ed. F. J. Amours 1897. For *Peblis* see Maitland MS. S T S ed. Sir W. A. Craigie 3 vols. 1919–20. For other *adespota* see Bannatyne MS. S T S ed. W. Tod Ritchie 4 vols. 1928–33. KING JAMES I.: *The Kingis Quair* ed. W. M. Mackenzie 1939. SIR RICHARD HOLLAND: *Book of the Howlat* ed. D. Laing, Edin. 1823. R. HENRYSON: *Poems* S T S ed. G. Gregory Smith, 3 vols. 1904–14; ed. H. Harvey Wood, Edin. 1933. W. DUNBAR: *Poems* ed. W. M. Mackenzie, Edin. 1932. GAVIN DOUGLAS: *Works*, ed. J. Small 4 vols. Edin. 1874. SIR DAVID LINDSAY: *Poems* S T S ed. D. Hamer, 1931. A. SCOTT: *Poems* S T S ed. J. Cranstoun 1896. A. MONTGOMERIE: *Poems* S T S ed. do. 1887, supplement ed. G. Stevenson 1910. A. HUME: *Poems* S T S ed. A. Lawson 1902. W. FOWLER: *Works* S T S ed. H. W. Meikle, J. Craigie and J. Purves 3 vols. 1914–40. *Gude and Godlie Ballatis* S T S ed. A. F. Mitchell 1897; selections ed. Iain Ross, Edin. 1939. For selections generally see W. M. Dixon's *Edinburgh*

Book of Scottish Verse 1910; M. M. Gray's *Scottish Poetry from Barbour to James VI* 1935.
(2) *Scottish Vernacular Literature*, T. F. Henderson 1898. *The Transition Period*, G. Gregory Smith, Edin. 1900; *Scottish Literature*, do. 1919. *Literary History of Scotland*, J. H. Millar 1903. *Essays on Medieval Literature*, W. P. Ker 1908.

CHAPTER VI. (1) SIR THOMAS WYATT: *Poems* ed. A. K. Foxwell 2 vols. 1913. HENRY HOWARD, EARL OF SURREY: *Poems* ed. F. M. Padelford, Seattle 1928; *Fourth Boke of Vergill* ed. H. Hartman, Oxfd. 1923. *Tottel's Miscellany* ed. H. E. Rollins 2 vols. Cambridge, Mass. 1928–29; also Arber's Reprints. *A Hundreth Sundrie Floures* ed. B. M. Ward 1926. *The Paradyse of Daynty Devises* ed. H. E. Rollins, Cambridge, Mass. 1927. *A Gorgious Gallery of Gallant Inventions* ed. do. 1926. *A Handfull of Pleasant Delites* ed. Arnold Kershaw 1926. GEORGE GASCOIGNE: *Works* ed. J. W. Cunliffe 2 vols. Camb. 1901–10. *Mirror for Magistrates* ed. L. B. Campbell, Camb. 1936. THOMAS SACKVILLE: *Works* ed. R. W. Sackville-West 1859. EARL OF OXFORD: *Poems* ed. A. B. Grosart 1872. For selections see *The Oxford Book of Sixteenth Century Verse*; for Sackville's *Induction* see *The English Parnassus* ed. W. M. Dixon and Sir Herbert Grierson, Oxfd. 1911.
(2) *The Italian Renaissance in England*, L. Einstein 1902. *Early Tudor Poetry*, J. M. Berdan, N.Y. 1920. *Sir Thomas Wyatt and some Collected Studies*, Sir E. K. Chambers 1933.

CHAPTER VII. (1) EDMUND SPENSER: *Poems* ed. J. C. Smith and E. de Selincourt 3 vols. Oxfd. 1909–10; 1 vol. ed. do. (Oxford Poets); ed. R. Morris (Globe). With notes—Variorum Edn. 8 vols. Baltimore 1932–; *Minor Poems* ed. W. L. Renwick 3 vols. 1928–30. SIR PHILIP SIDNEY: *Works* ed. A. Feuillerat 4 vols. (Cambridge English Classics); *Poems* ed. J. Drinkwater (Muses' Lib.). SIR WALTER RALEIGH: *Poems* ed. A. M. C. Latham 1929.
(2) *A Discourse of English Poetry*, W. Webbe 1586, reptd. in *Elizabethan Critical Essays* ed. G. Gregory Smith 2 vols. Oxfd. 1904; *Remarks on Spenser's Poetry*, J. Jortin 1734; *Observations on the F. Q.*, T. Warton 1754; *Lectures on the English Poets*, W. Hazlitt 1818; *Spenser*, R. W. Church (E M L); *Edmund Spenser*, E. Legouis, Paris, 1926; *E. S., An Essay on Renaissance Poetry*, W. L. Renwick 1925; art. 'Spenser' in *Ency. Brit.* 14th edn., J. C. Smith; arts. in *N. & Q.* Feb. and April 1932, W. H. Welply; *E. S.*, E. C. Davis, Camb. 1933. *Sidney*, E M L J. A. Symonds; Fulke Greville's *Life of Sidney* ed. Nowell Smith 1907. *Sir Walter Raleigh*, M. Waldman 1928.

CHAPTER VIII. (1) SIR JOHN HARINGTON: *Orlando Furioso in English Verse*, 1591. EDWARD FAIRFAX: *Godfrey of Buloigne, or The Recoverie of Jerusalem*. Done in English Heroicall Verse 1600, also by Richard Carew 1594. W. CHAMBERLAYNE: *Pharonnida* in *Caroline Poets*, Vol. I, ed. G. Saintsbury, Oxfd. 1905. C. MARLOWE: *Hero and Leander continued by George Chapman* in collected edns. of his works, see Chap. X, also in *Poems of Robert Greene, Christopher Marlowe and Ben Jonson* ed. R. Bell 1876. MICHAEL DRAYTON: *Poems*, ed. J. W. Hebel 5 vols. Oxfd. 1931–1941; *Select Poems of*, ed. A. H. Bullen 1883; *Minor Poems* ed. Cyril Brett, Oxfd. 1907; Chalmers' *British Poets* Vol. VI. JOHN MARSTON: see Chap. XII. FRANCIS BEAUMONT: *Salmacis* in Beaumont and Fletcher's *Works* in *Old Dramatists* Vol. II. THOMAS WATSON: *Poems* in Arber's Reprints. *Elizabethan Sonnets* with Introduction by Sir Sidney Lee (An English Garner, which has also sonnets of Sidney, Barnes, Lodge, Giles Fletcher, Constable, Daniel, P. Percy, Drayton, Spenser, and others). SAMUEL DANIEL: *Complete Works*, ed. A. B. Grosart 5 vols. 1885; *A Selection from the Poetry of Daniel and Drayton*, ed. H. C. Beeching 1899. For lyrics see *Elizabethan Lyrics*, ed. A. H. Bullen 1882, 1885 and his collections from Song Books, Dramatists, Romances and Prose Tracts 1887 to 1890. For pastoral songs see *England's Helicon* ed. do. 1887; ed. H. Macdonald (Everyman's Lib.). *English Madrigal Verse* ed. E. H. Fellowes, Oxfd. 1920. *Elizabethan Lyrics* ed. Norman Ault, Oxfd. 1925. *An English Garner*, ed. Ed. Arber 8 vols. 1877–96. *The Oxford Book of Sixteenth-Century Verse*.
(2) *The Later Renaissance*, J. Hannay, Edin. 1898 (*Periods of European Literature*).

From the Renaissance to the Civil War, J. Jusserand *op. cit.* Vol. II. *The Literature of Shakespeare's England*, E. C. Dunn 1936. *The French Influence in English Literature from the Accession of Elizabeth to the Restoration*, A. H. Upham, N.Y. 1911. *The French Renaissance in England*, Sir Sidney Lee, Oxfd. 1910.

CHAPTER IX. (1) G. WITHER: *The Poetry of*, ed. F. Sidgwick 2 vols. 1902. W. BROWNE: *Poetical Works* ed. G. Goodwin 2 vols (Muses' Lib.). G. and P. FLETCHER: *Poetical Works* ed. F. S. Boas, Camb. 1908. W. DRUMMOND: *Poetical Works* ed. L. E. Kastner 2 vols. Manchester 1913; ed. W. C. Ward 2 vols. (Muses' Lib.). JOHN DONNE: *Poems* ed. Sir H. J. C. Grierson 2 vols. Oxfd. 1912; 1 vol. ed. do. (Oxford Poets); ed. H. I'A. Fausset (Everyman's Lib.). BEN JONSON: *Poems* ed. B. H. Newdigate, Oxfd. 1936. Selections in Sir H. Grierson's *Metaphysical Lyrics and Poems of the 17th Century*, Oxfd. 1921, Norman Ault's *17th Century Lyrics* 1928, *The Oxford Book of 17th Century Verse*. (2) *The Poetical Works of George Wither*, Charles Lamb 1818. *Spenser, The School of the Fletchers, and Milton*, H. E. Cory, Berkeley 1912. *Introd.* to Muses' Lib., Browne, A. H. Bullen. *Drummond of Hawthornden*, D. Masson 1872. *Life of Donne*, Izaak Walton 1658. *Life and Letters of Donne*, Sir E. Gosse 2 vols. 1899. *Secentismo e Marinismo in Inghilterra*, Mario Praz, Florence 1925. *A Study of Ben Jonson*, A. C. Swinburne 1889; *Ben Jonson*, G. Gregory Smith E M L; *The Sacred Wood*, T. S. Eliot 1920.

CHAPTER X. (1) *Calisto and Meliboea* ed. W. W. Greg and F. Sidgwick 1908. NICHOLAS UDALL: *Ralph Roister Doister* ed. W. W. Greg 1935; also Arber's Reprints. *Gammer Gurton's Needle* ed. H. F. Brett-Smith, Oxfd. 1920. THOMAS NORTON and THOMAS SACKVILLE: *Gorboduc* ed. J. W. Cunliffe, Oxfd. 1912. THOMAS PRESTON: *Cambyses* reptd. in Hazlitt's Dodsley Vol. IV. JOHN LYLY: *Works* ed. R. W. Bond 3 vols. Oxfd. 1902. CHRISTOPHER MARLOWE: *Works and Life*, ed. R. H. Case, 6 vols. 1930–33. THOMAS KYD: *Works* ed. F. S. Boas, Oxfd. 1901. ROBERT GREENE: *Plays and Poems* ed. J. C. Collins 2 vols. Oxfd. 1905. GEORGE PEELE: *Works* ed. A. H. Bullen 2 vols. 1888. Select plays of Marlowe in Mermaid Series. (2) *Hist. of English Dramatic Lit.*, Sir A. W. Ward 3 vols. 1899. *Shakespeare's Predecessors*, J. A. Symonds 1900. *The Mediaeval Stage*, Sir E. K. Chambers 2 vols., Oxfd. 1903. *John Lyly*, J. Dover Wilson, Camb. 1905. *Sources of the Hamlet Tragedy*, J. Fitzgerald 1909. *The Tudor Drama*, C. F. T. Brooke 1912. *Shakespeare's Fellows*, G. B. Harrison 1923. *Date and Order of Peele's Plays*, H. M. Dowling in *N. & Q.* 11 and 18 March 1933. *Introd. to Tudor Drama*, F. S. Boas, Oxfd. 1933. *The tragicall history of Christopher Marlowe*, J. E. Bakeless 2 vols., Cambridge, Mass. 1942.

CHAPTER XI. (1) (*a*) Texts: *The Cambridge Shakespeare* ed. W. G. Clark and W. A. Wright 9 vols. Camb. 1862–66; 1 vol. ed. do. (Globe); ed. W. J. Craig (Oxford Poets); with life by B. H. Newdigate (Shakespeare Head Press). (*b*) With notes: *The New Variorum Shakespeare* ed. H. H. Furness and others, Philadelphia 1871–, 24 vols. publd.; *The New Cambridge Shakespeare* ed. Sir A. T. Quiller-Couch and J. Dover Wilson, Camb. 1921–, 17 vols. publd. Many other edns. Handy edns., one play to each vol.—*Arden, Temple, Yale*. (2) *Brief Lives*, J. Aubrey 1681. *Life*, N. Rowe 1709. Pope's *Preface* to his edn. 1725. Johnson's do. 1765. *Dramatic Character of Sir John Falstaff*, M. Morgann 1787. *Lectures on Shakespeare*, S. T. Coleridge 1808. *Characters of Shakespeare's Plays*, W. Hazlitt 1817. Goethe's *Wilhelm Meister* tr. T. Carlyle 1824. *Shakspere: His Mind and Art*, E. Dowden 1875. *A Study of Shakespeare*, A. C. Swinburne 1880. *Shakespeare*, Sir W. A. Raleigh (E M L). *Shakespearean Tragedy*, A. C. Bradley 1908. *Character Problems in Shakespeare's Plays*, L. Schücking, Eng. trans. 1922. *Shakespeare Truth and Tradition*, J. S. Smart 1928. *Prefaces to Shakespeare*, 3 series, H. Granville Barker 1927, '30, '37. *Shakespeare Studies*, E. E. Stoll, N.Y. 1927; *Art and Artifice in Shakespeare*, Camb. 1938. *William Shakespeare*, Sir E. K. Chambers 2 vols. Oxfd. 1930. *The Essential Shakespeare*, J. Dover Wilson, Camb. 1932; *The Fortunes of Falstaff*, Camb. 1943. *Shakespeare's Problem Comedies*, W. W. Lawrence, N.Y. 1931.

LL

(3) Aids to study: *A Shakespearean Grammar*, E. A. Abbot 1869. *Shakespeare-Lexicon*, A. Schmidt 2 vols. 1874. *Shakespeare's England*, 2 vols. Oxfd. 1916. *Shakespeare Glossary*, C. T. Onions,· Oxfd. 1922. *The Elizabethan Stage*, Sir E. K. Chambers 4 vols. Oxfd. 1922. *Companion to Shakespeare Studies* ed. H. Granville Barker and G. B. Harrison, Camb. 1934.

CHAPTER XII. (1) BEN JONSON: *Works* ed. W. Gifford 9 vols. 1875, also 1 vol. *n.d.*; ed. C. H. Herford and P. Simpson, Oxfd. 1928-, 6 vols. published. GEORGE CHAPMAN: *Plays* ed. T. M. Parrott, 2 vols. 1911. JOHN WEBSTER: *Works* ed. F. L. Lucas 4 vols. 1927. CYRIL TOURNEUR: *Works* ed. Allardyce Nicoll 1930. JOHN MARSTON: *Works* ed. A. H. Bullen 3 vols. 1887; *Plays* ed. H. Harvey Wood 3 vols. 1934-39. THOMAS MIDDLETON: *Works* ed. A. H. Bullen 8 vols. 1885-86. THOMAS HEYWOOD: *Dramatic Works* ed. R. H. Shepherd 6 vols. 1895-96. THOMAS DEKKER: *Dramatic Works* ed. do. 4 vols. 1873. F. BEAUMONT and J. FLETCHER: *Works* ed. A. Glover and A. R. Waller 10 vols. Camb. 1905-12. PHILIP MASSINGER: *Works* ed. F. Cunningham 1 vol. *n.d.* JOHN FORD: *Works* ed. W. Gifford 2 vols 1827, rev. A. Dyce 3 vols. 1867, rev. A. H. Bullen 3 vols. 1895. JAMES SHIRLEY: *Dramatic Works and Poems* ed. Gifford and Dyce 6 vols. 1833. Select plays of all these dramatists except Chapman and Marston in Mermaid Series.
(2) *A Study of Ben Jonson*, A. C. Swinburne 1889; *Jonson*, G. Gregory Smith (E M L). *Intro.* to Shepherd's Chapman, A. C. Swinburne. *John Webster and the Elizabethan Drama*, Rupert Brooke 1916. *Thomas Heywood*, A. M. Clark, Oxfd. 1931. *John Ford*, M. J. Sargeant, Oxfd. 1935.

CHAPTER XIII. (1) ROBERT HERRICK: *Poems* ed. A. W. Pollard with Preface by A. C. Swinburne 2 vols. (Muses' Lib.); ed. F. W. Moorman, Oxfd. 1915; ed. E. Rhys (Everyman's Lib.). THOMAS CAREW: *Poems* ed. A. Vincent (Muses' Lib.). SIR JOHN SUCKLING: *Poems* ed. A. H. Thomson 1910. RICHARD LOVELACE: *Poems* ed. C. H. Wilkinson, Oxfd. 1930. GEORGE HERBERT: *Works* ed. F. E. Hutchinson, Oxfd. 1941; *The Temple* ed. E. Thomas (Everyman's Lib.). RICHARD CRASHAW: *Poems English, Latin and Greek* ed. A. R. Waller, Camb. 1904; ed. L. C. Martin, Oxfd. 1927; also in Muses' Lib. HENRY VAUGHAN: *Works* ed. L. C. Martin 2 vols. Oxfd. 1910; ed. E. K. Chambers 2 vols. (Muses' Lib.) THOMAS TRAHERNE: *Poetical Works* ed. B. Dobell, 3rd ed. 1932. ANDREW MARVELL: *Poems and Letters* ed. H. M. Margoliouth, Oxfd. 1927; *Poems and Satires* ed. G. A. Aitken (Muses' Lib.). ABRAHAM COWLEY: *English Writings* ed. A. R. Waller 2 vols. Camb. 1905. *Caroline Poets* ed. G. Saintsbury 3 vols. Oxfd. 1905-21. For selections see *The Oxford Book of Seventeenth Century Verse*; also *Metaphysical Lyrics and Poems of the Seventeenth Century* ed. Sir H. J. C. Grierson, Oxfd. 1921.
(2) *The Age of Milton*, J. H. B. Masterman 1901. *The First Half of the Seventeenth Century*, Sir H. J. C. Grierson, Edin. 1906. *Cross Currents in the Literature of the Seventeenth Century*, do. 1929. *The Cavalier Spirit and its influence on the Life and Work of Richard Lovelace*, C. Hartman 1925. *The Seventeenth Century Background*, B. Willey, Camb. 1934. *T. Traherne*, G. I. Wade, Princeton 1944.

CHAPTER XIV. (1) *Poems* ed. W. A. Wright, Camb. 1903; Columbia edn. 2 vols. N.Y. 1930; 1 vol. ed. D. Masson (Globe); ed. H. C. Beeching (Oxford Poets). (2) Addison's *Spectator* no. 61 *et seq.* 1712; Johnson's *Lives of the Poets* 1779-80; *Life of J. M.*, D. Masson 6 vols. Camb. 1859-94; *Milton*, Mark Pattison (E M L); *Milton*, Sir W. A. Raleigh 1900; *Studies in Milton*, S. B. Liljgren 1919. *Milton*, Rose Macaulay 1934. *Milton and Wordsworth*, Sir H. J. C. Grierson, Camb. 1935. *Milton's Later Poems*, W. Menzies in Essays and Studies, 1938. *Preface to Paradise Lost*, C. S. Lewis 1942. *Milton, Man and Thinker*, D. Saurat 1944.

CHAPTER XV. (1) SAMUEL BUTLER: *Collected Works* ed. A. R. Waller and R. Lamar 3 vols. Camb. 1905-28. JOHN OLDHAM: *Poetical Works* ed. R. Bell 1854. SIR WILLIAM DAVENANT: *v. Select Works of the British Poets* ed. R. Southey 1831. SIR JOHN DENHAM: *Poetical Works* ed. T. H. Banks, New Haven 1928. EDMUND WALLER: *Poems* ed. G. Thorn Drury 2 vols. (Muses' Lib.). JOHN DRYDEN: *Works* ed. Sir Walter Scott rev. G. Saintsbury 18 vols. Edin. 1882-92; *Poetical Works* ed. W. D. Christie (Globe); ed. J. Sargeant (Oxford Poets); *Poems* (Selected) ed. B.

Dobree (Everyman's Lib.). NATHANIEL LEE: *Works* 3 vols. 1734. THOMAS
SOUTHERNE: *Works* 2 vols. 1713. NICHOLAS ROWE: *Works* (with Life by Dr.
Johnson) 2 vols. 1792. SIR CHARLES SEDLEY: *Poetical and Dramatic Works* ed.
V. de S. Pinto 2 vols. 1928. EARL OF DORSET: *v.* Johnson's Collection Vol. XI.
EARL OF ROCHESTER: *Collected Works* ed. John Hayward 1928. APHRA BEHN:
Works ed. M. Summers 6 vols. 1915. JOHN NORRIS: *Poems* ed. A. B. Grosart 1871.
THOMAS FLATMAN: *Poems and Songs* 1686. THOMAS OTWAY: *Works* ed. J. C.
Ghosh, Oxfd. 1934. *Seventeenth Century Lyrics* ed. N. Ault 1928. *Oxford Book of
Seventeenth Century Verse*. *Minor Poets of the Caroline Period* ed. G. Saintsbury
3 vols. Oxfd. 1905–21. *Minor Poets of the 17th Century* ed. R. G. Howarth
(Everyman's Lib.).
(2) Johnson's *Lives*. *Dryden*, G. Saintsbury (E M L). *Lectures on Dryden*, A. W.
Verrall, Camb. 1914. *Poetry of John Dryden*, M. Van Doren, N.Y. 1931. *Le
Public et les Hommes de Lettres en Angleterre (1660–1744)*, A. Beljame, Paris 1881.
The Age of Dryden, R. Garnett 1895. *The Augustan Ages*, O. Elton 1899. *Cross
Currents in English Literature of the XVIIth Century*, Sir H. J. C. Grierson 1929.
Seventeenth Century Background, Basil Willey 1934. (For Marvell and Cowley
v. Chapter XIII.)

CHAPTER XVI. (1) ALEXANDER POPE: *Works* ed. W. Elwin and W. J. Courthope
10 vols. 1871–89; *Poetical Works* ed. A. W. Ward (Globe); *Poems*, general editor
J. Butt 1939–; *Collected Poems* intr. E. Rhys (Everyman's Lib.). MATTHEW
PRIOR: *Writings* ed. A. R. Waller 2 vols. Camb. 1905–7. JOHN GAY: *Poetical
Works* ed. G. C. Faber (Oxford Poets); ed. J. Underhill 2 vols. (Muses' Lib.).
THOMAS PARNELL: *Poetical Works* ed. G. A. Aitken 1894. JOSEPH ADDISON: *Mis-
cellaneous Works* Vol. I. ed. A. C. Guthkelch 1914. JONATHAN SWIFT: *Poems*
ed. by W. E. Browning 2 vols. 1910; ed. H. Williams 3 vols. Oxfd. 1937. JOHN
ARBUTHNOT: *Life and Works* ed. G. A. Aitken, Oxfd. 1892. A. PHILIPS: *Poems* ed.
M. G. Segar, Oxfd. 1927. C. SMART: *Song to David* ed. P. Searle 1924; *Rejoice
in the Lamb*, ed. W. F. Stead 1945. TICKELL, GLOVER, WALSH, MALLET:
v. Collections by Johnson or Anderson or Chalmers. *Oxford Book of Eighteenth
Century Verse*. *Eighteenth Century Poetry, An Anthology*, W. J. Turner 1931.
Anthology of Augustan Poetry, F. T. Wood 1931. *Minor Poets of the Eighteenth
Century* ed. H. I'A. Fausset (Everyman's Lib.).
(2) Johnson's *Lives*. *Alexander Pope*, Sir Leslie Stephen (E M L). *Alexander Pope*,
Edith Sitwell 1930. *On the Poetry of Pope*, G. Tillotson, Oxfd. 1938. *Matthew
Prior*, L. G. W. Legg 1921. *Addison*, W. J. Courthope (E M L). *Jonathan Swift*,
Sir Leslie Stephen (E M L). *Swift*, C. Van Doren 1930. *Le Public et les Hommes de
Lettres en Angleterre (1660–1744)*, A. Beljame, Paris 1881. *The Age of Pope*, J.
Dennis 1894. *The Augustan Ages*, O. Elton, Edin. 1899. *Some Observations on
Eighteenth Century Poetry*, D. Nichol Smith, Oxfd. 1938. *Eighteenth Century
Background*, Basil Willey 1940.

CHAPTER XVII. (1) LADY WINCHELSEA: *Miscellany Poems 1713* ed. M. Reynolds,
Chicago 1903. JAMES THOMSON: *Poetical Works* ed. D. C. Tovey (Aldine) 2 vols.
1897; ed. J. L. Robertson (Oxford Poets); ed. H. D. Roberts 2 vols. (Muses' Lib.).
JOHN DYER: *Poems* ed. E. Thomas 1903. EDWARD YOUNG: *Poetical Works* ed. J.
Mitford 2 vols. 1866. Poetical Works of BEATTIE, BLAIR and FALCONER, ed. G.
Gilfillan, Edin. 1854. Poetical Works of ARMSTRONG, DYER and GREEN, ed.
do. Edin. 1858. MARK AKENSIDE: *Poems* ed. A. Dyce (Aldine) 1857 and 1894.
HENRY CAREY: *Poems* ed. F. T. Wood 1930. JOHN BYROM: *Poems* ed. Sir A. W.
Ward 2 vols. 1894–95. SAMUEL JOHNSON: *Poems* ed. T. M. Ward (Muses' Lib.);
ed. D. Nichol Smith and E. L. McAdam 1941. OLIVER GOLDSMITH: *Miscellane-
ous Works* ed. D. Masson (Globe); *Complete Poetical Works* ed. A. Dobson (Oxford
Poets); *Poems and Plays* intr. A. Dobson (Everyman's Lib.). The Three WARTONS
—A Selection ed. E. Partridge 1927. WILLIAM COLLINS: *Poems* ed. T. M. Ward
(Muses' Lib.); ed. E. Blunden 1929. THOMAS GRAY: *English Poems* ed. D. C.
Tovey, Camb. 1898; *Poetical Works of Gray and Collins* ed. A. L. Poole and C.
Stone, rev. L. Whibley and F. Page, Oxfd. 1937; *Poems and Letters* intr. J. Drink-
water (Everyman's Lib.). WILLIAM SHENSTONE: *Poetical Works*, ed. G. Gilfillan

Edin. 1854. THOMAS CHATTERTON: *Complete Poetical Works* ed. H. D. Roberts 2 vols. (Muses' Lib.). THOMAS PERCY: *Reliques of Ancient Poetry* ed. H. B. Wheatley 3 vols. 1876–77 and 1891; 2 vols. (Everyman's Lib.); *Bishop Percy's Folio MS.* ed. Sir I. Gollancz 4 vols. 1905. *Oxford Book of Eighteenth Century Verse. Minor Poets of the Eighteenth Century* ed. H. I'A. Fausset (Everyman's Lib.).
(2) Johnson's *Lives. The Age of Johnson*, T. Seccombe 1899. *James Thomson*, G. C. Macaulay (E M L). *Gray*, Sir E. Gosse (E M L). *Dr. Johnson and his Circle*, J. Bailey 1912. *Collins*, H. W. Garrod, Oxfd. 1928. *The Beginnings of the English Romantic Movement*, W. L. Phelps, Boston 1893. *A History of English Romanticism in the Eighteenth Century*, H. A. Beers, N.Y. 1899. *Eighteenth Century Background*, Basil Willey 1940. *Life of Thomas Chatterton*, E. H. W. Meyerstein 1930.

CHAPTER XVIII. (1) *Poems by William Cowper*, 2 vols. 1782–85, 1782–86, some copies with Preface by John Newton. *Poems of . . . A New Edition to which are now first added the Olney Hymns by William Cowper and Translations from Madame Guion*, 1806, 1808. *Poems, the early productions of W. Cowper, now first published. With anecdotes of the Poet collected from letters of Lady Hesketh*, ed. J. Croft 1825. *Complete Poetical Works* ed. H. S. Milford (Oxford Poets). *Poems* ed. H. I'Anson Fausset (Everyman's Lib.). C. CHURCHILL: *The Poetical Works of Charles Churchill.* With Memoir . . . by G. Gilfillan, Edin. 1855.
(2) *The Stricken Deer; or, The Life of Cowper*, Lord David Cecil 1929. *The Life of W. Cowper*, T. Wright, 2nd edn. 1921. *William Cowper, ou de la Poésie domestique*, Sainte-Beuve (Causeries de Lundi XI. pp. 132–65, 1856).

CHAPTER XIX. (1) *The Poetical Works of the Rev. George Crabbe with His Letters and Journal and His Life by His Son*, 8 vols. 1834 and later edns.; in one vol. 1847 to 1901. *Poems* ed. Sir A. W. Ward 3 vols. Camb. 1905, '6, '7. *Poetical Works* ed. A. J. Carlyle and R. M. Carlyle (Oxford Poets). *Oxford Book of Regency Verse.*
(2) *Crabbe*, A. Ainger (E M L). *Un Poète Réaliste Anglais*, R. Huchon, Paris 1906; trans. as *George Crabbe and his Times*, Frederick Clark 1907, with a bibliography. *Essays in English Literature 1780–1860*, G. Saintsbury 1890. *Hours in a Library*, Sir Leslie Stephen Vol. II 1892.

CHAPTER XX. (1) *Habbie Simson, Banishment of Poverty, Blythesome Wedding, Bonnie Heck* first in Watson's *Collection*, q.v. LADY GRIZEL BAILLIE: "Werena My Heart Licht" first in T.T. *Miscellany*, q.v.; "The Ewebuchting's Bonnie" first in *Edinburgh Magazine* of May 1818. LADY WARDLAW: *Hardyknute*, Edin. 1719; reptd. with additions of Ramsay in *Evergreen* and T.T. *Miscellany. Watson's Choice Collection* 1706, 1709, 1711; reptd. Glasgow 1869. ALLAN RAMSAY: *Poems* 3 vols. 1853; ed. C. Mackay 2 vols. 1866–68; *Evergreen* 2 vols. Edin. 1729, reptd. 2 vols. Glasgow 1876; *Tea-Table Miscellany* 3 vols. Edin. 1724–27, reptd. 2 vols. Glasgow 1876. ROBERT FERGUSSON: *Poems* 2 vols. Edin. 1771; ed. R. Ford, Paisley 1905; *Scots Poems* ed. Bruce Dickins, Edin. 1925. ALEX. ROSS: *Scottish Works* S T S ed. M. Wattie 1939. For the other songs named on pp. 265-66 see *The Edinburgh Book of Scottish Verse.*
(2) *Scottish Vernacular Literature*, T. F. Henderson 1898; *Lit. Hist. of Scotland*, J. H. Millar 1903; *Edinburgh Essays on Scots Lit.* Edin. 1935.

CHAPTER XXI. (1) ROBERT BURNS: *Complete Works* ed. Alexander Smith (Globe); *Poetical Works* ed. J. L. Robertson (Oxford Poets); *Poetry* ed. W. E. Henley and T. F. Henderson 4 vols. Edin. 1896–97; *Poems and Songs* (Everyman's Lib.).
(2) *Life*, J. G. Lockhart, Edin. 1829. *Burns*, T. Carlyle 1854. *Burns*, W. E. Henley, Edin, 1898. *Robert Burns*, T. F. Henderson 1904. *Life of Robert Burns*, F. B. Snyder, N.Y. 1932. *Robert Burns, His Personality, his Reputation and his Art*, do. 1936. *Robert Burns, la vie et les œuvres*, A. Angellier 2 vols. Paris 1893.

CHAPTER XXII. (1) J. W. VON GOETHE: *Sorrows of Werther*, Eng. trans. Bohn's Standard Library 1854. J. J. ROUSSEAU: *Nouvelle Héloïse* Eng. trans. 3 vols. 1810; *Du Contrat Social* trans. G. D. H. Cole (Everyman's Lib.); *Émile* trans. B. Foxley (do.). LAURENCE STERNE: *A Sentimental Journey* ed. G. Saintsbury (do). HENRY

BIBLIOGRAPHY

MACKENZIE: *The Man of Feeling* ed. H. Miles 1928. EDMUND BURKE: *Reflections on the Revolution in France* ed. F. W. Raffety (World's Classics). THOMAS PAINE: *Rights of Man* ed. G. J. Holyoake (Everyman's Lib.). WILLIAM GODWIN: *Political Justice* ed. H. S. Salt 1890; abridged edn. R. A. Preston 1926.
(2) *L'Ancien Régime*, A. de Tocqueville ed. G. W. Headlam, Oxfd. 1904. *History of English Thought in the 18th Century*, Sir Leslie Stephen 2 vols. 1876. *Cambridge Modern History*, Vol. VIII. *Shelley, Godwin and their Circle*, H. N. Brailsford (Home Univ. Lib.).

CHAPTER XXIII. (1) *The Poetical Works of William Blake* ed. J. Sampson, Oxfd. 1905, 1913. *The Writings of William Blake* ed. G. Keynes (Nonesuch) 3 vols. 1925. *Poetry and Prose of William Blake* do. 1927. *The Poems of William Blake* ed. W. B. Yeats (Muses' Lib.). *The Lyrical Poems of William Blake* ed. J. Sampson with Introduction by Sir W. A. Raleigh, Oxfd. 1905. *The Prophetic Writings of William Blake* ed. D. J. Sloss and J. P. R. Wallis 2 vols. Oxfd. 1926. *Selected Poems of William Blake* ed. L. Binyon 1931.
(2) *W. Blake*, A. C. Swinburne 1868, 'Golden Pine' edn. 1925. *The Life of William Blake*, by A. Gilchrist 1863, 1922; ed. R. Todd (Everyman's Lib.). *W. Blake*, P. Berger, Paris 1907, Eng. trans. 1914. *W. Blake*, O. Burdett 1926 (E M L). *An Introduction to the Study of Blake*, M. Plowman 1927. *W. Blake*, J. Middleton Murry. *Blake and Gray* in *The Background of English Literature*, Sir H. J. C. Grierson 1925, 1934.

CHAPTERS XXIV AND XXV. (1) (a) W. WORDSWORTH: *Poetical Works* ed. E. Dowden 7 vols. 1892–93; ed. N. C. Smith 3 vols. 1905; ed. E. de Selincourt to be completed by H. Darbishire, Oxfd. 1940–; 1 vol. ed. T. Hutchison (Oxford Poets); ed. J. Morley (Globe). (b) S. T. COLERIDGE: *Poetical Works* ed. J. Dykes Campbell (Globe); ed. E. H. Coleridge 2 vols. Oxfd. 1912, also 1 vol. same year.
(2) (a) *Biographia Literaria*, S. T. Coleridge (Everyman's Lib.); *Introduction to Golden Treasury Selections*, M. Arnold; *Wordsworth*, F. W. H. Myers (E M L); *La Jeunesse de W.*, E. Legouis, Paris, 1896; *Wordsworth*, Sir W. A. Raleigh 1904; *Oxford Lectures on Poetry*, A. C. Bradley, Oxfd. 1909; *Life*, G. M. Harper 2 vols. 1916, 1929; *Letters of W. and D. Wordsworth* ed. E. de Selincourt 6 vols. Oxfd. 1935–39; *The Later Wordsworth*, E. Batho, Camb. 1933; *A Study of Wordsworth*, J. C. Smith, Edin. 1944. (b) *Lectures on the English Poets*, W. Hazlitt (Everyman's Lib.); *Coleridge*, T. de Quincey, Edin. 1889; *Dissertations and Discussions*, J. S. Mill 1859; *Essays and Studies*, A. C. Swinburne 1875; *Appreciations*, W. H. Pater 1889; *Letters* ed. E. H. Coleridge 2 vols. 1895; *S. T. C.*, J. Dykes Campbell 1894, 1896; *The Road to Xanadu*, J. L. Lowes 1927, 1930; *S. T. C.*, Sir E. K. Chambers, Oxfd. 1938; *The Life of Coleridge, The Early Years*, L. Hanson 1938.

CHAPTER XXVI. (1) *Minstrelsy of the Scottish Border* ed. T. F. Henderson, 4 vols. 1918; *Poems* ed. J. G. Lockhart 1842; ed. J. Logie Robertson (Oxford Poets); ed. F. T. Palgrave (Globe); *Poems and Plays* ed. A. Lang 2 vols. (Everyman's Lib.).
(2) *Life*, J. G. Lockhart 10 vols. 1839, 5 vols. 1900; *Sir Walter Scott*, R. H. Hutton (E M L); *Scott*, G. Saintsbury 1897; *Scott and his Poetry*, A. E. Morgan 1912; *Sir W. S.*, John Buchan 1932; *Letters* ed. Sir H. J. C. Grierson 12 vols. 1932–37; *Sir W. S., Bart.*, do. 1938; *Survey of English Lit.* 1780–1830, O. Elton 2 vols. 1912.

CHAPTER XXVII. (1) *Works* 4 vols. 1826, 6 vols. 1829, 1831—the first in this country in which important poems were not suppressed. More complete edns. had appeared in Germany and France. *The Works of Lord Byron*, with his letters and journals and his life by Thomas Moore 17 vols. 1832–33. Reissued in Paris in 1835 with additions and with notes by Scott, Campbell and others and a life by Henry Lytton Bulwer. *Poetical Works* ed. Ernest Hartley Coleridge (the first seven vols. of *The Works of Lord Byron* ed. R. E. Prothero and E. H. Coleridge) 1898–1904. *The Poetical Works* ed. with memoir by E. H. Coleridge 1905. (Also in Oxford Poets.)
(2) *Byron*, J. Nichol (E M L). Preface to a *Selection from the Works of* . . . A. C. Swinburne 1866, reptd. in *Essays and Studies* 1875. *Byron* in *Essays in Criticism*,

M. Arnold, Second Series 1888. *A Survey of English Literature, 1780–1830*, O. Elton 1912. *Byron, Arnold and Swinburne* and *Byron and English Society* in *The Background of English Literature*, Sir H. J. C. Grierson 1925, 1934. *Byron in England*, S. C. Chew 1924.

CHAPTER XXVIII. (1) *The Complete Works* ed. R. Ingpen and W. E. Peck 10 vols. (Julian edn.) 1926–30. *Complete Poetical Works* ed. T. Hutchinson (Oxford Poets).
(2) *Shelley*, J. A. Symonds (E M L). *Essays in Criticism, Second Series*, M. Arnold 1888. *Oxford Lectures on Poetry*, A. C. Bradley, Oxfd. 1909. *A Miscellany*, do. 1929. *Shelley*, Francis Thompson 1909. *Shelley and the Unromantics*, Olwen Ward Campbell 1924. *Shelley et La France, Lyrisme anglais et Lyrisme français*, Henri Peyre, Paris.

CHAPTER XXIX. (1) *Complete Works* ed. H. Buxton Forman 5 vols. 1900–1901. *Poetical Works* ed. E. de Selincourt 1912. *The Poems . . . arranged for the first time in chronological order*, Sir Sidney Colvin 1924. *Poems* ed. G. Thorn Drury with introd. by Robert Bridges (Muses' Lib.). *Poetical Works* ed. H. Buxton Forman (Oxford Poets). *Letters* ed. M. Buxton Forman, 2nd edn. Oxfd. 1935.
(2) *De Johannis Keatsii vita et carminibus*, A. Angellier, Paris 1892. *On the Study of Celtic Literature*, M. Arnold 1867. *Keats*, Sir Sidney Colvin (E M L). *John Keats*, do. 1917. *Essays on Art*, J. W. Comyns Carr 1876. *Lectures on Poetry*, J. W. Mackail 1912. *John Keats*, A. Lowell 2 vols. Boston 1925. *Keats's Shakespeare*, C. F. E. Spurgeon, Oxfd. 1928. *Keats and Shakespeare*, J. Middleton Murry, Oxfd. 1925, and *Studies in Keats* 1930. *Keats*, H. W. Garrod, Oxfd. 1926. *Keats' Craftsmanship: A Study in Poetic Development*, M. R. Ridley, Oxfd. 1933.

CHAPTER XXX. (1) W. S. LANDOR: *Poetical Works* ed. S. Wheeler 3 vols. Oxfd. 1937. *Works* with Life by J. Forster 8 vols. 1876. R. SOUTHEY: *Poetical Works* 1850; *Poems* ed. Fitzgerald, Oxfd. 1909. S. ROGERS: *Poetical Works* ed. with a memoir by E. Bell 1875 (Aldine); *Poems* with steel engravings by Turner and Stothard 1834, with a memoir by S. Sharpe 1860, 1890 (Routledge's Pocket Library). T. MOORE: *Poetical Works* ed. A. D. Godley, Oxfd. 1910. T. CAMPBELL: *Complete Poetical Works* ed. with notes by J. L. Robertson, Oxfd. 1907. JAMES HOGG: *Works* Centenary edn. 1876. LEIGH HUNT: *Poetical Works* ed. Thornton Hunt 1860; ed. H. S. Milford (Oxford Poets). JOHN CLARE: *Poems* ed. J. W. Tibble 2 vols. 1935. T. L. BEDDOES: *Works* ed. H. W. Donner, Oxfd. 1935; *Poems* ed. R. Colles (Muses' Lib.); *Beddoes, An Anthology*, F. L. Lucas, Camb. 1932. GEORGE DARLEY: *Complete Poetical Works* ed. R. Colles 1908. C. J. WELLS: *Joseph and his Brethren* with introd. by A. C. Swinburne 1876 (World's Classics). THOMAS WADE: *Fifty Sonnets, The Contention of Death and Love, Helena* in *Literary Anecdotes of the XIXth Century*, Vol. I, W. R. Nicoll and T .J. Wise 1895. THOMAS HOOD: *Complete Poetical Works* ed. W. Jerrold, Oxfd. 1906. L. E. L.: *Collected Poems* 2 vols. 1873; *Life and Remains* ed. L. Blanchard 2 vols. 1841. FELICIA HEMANS: *Collected Works* 7 vols. 1839.
(2) *A Survey of English Literature*, O. Elton 2 vols. 1912. Chapters by Saintsbury in Vols. 11 and 12 of *Cambridge History of English Literature* 1914, 1915.

CHAPTER XXXI. (1) *Poems* ed. Hallam, Lord Tennyson, 9 vols. 1907–8; also 1 vol. pub. Macmillan (many reprints).
(2) *Alfred, Lord Tennyson, A Memoir by His Son*, 1897; *Tennyson*, Sir A. Lyall (E M L); *Commentary to Tennyson's In Memoriam*, A. C. Bradley 1920; *A.T., A Modern Portrait*, H. I'A. Fausset 1928; *A. T., Aspects of his Life, Character and Poetry*, H. Nicolson; *Essays Ancient and Modern*, T. S. Eliot 1936.

CHAPTER XXXII. (1) *Works* ed. Sir F. G. Kenyon, Centenary edn. 10 vols. 1912; ed. A. Birrell 2 vols. 1898.
(2) *Literary Studies*, W. Bagehot 1879; *Introd. to the Study of B.*, A. Symons 1886; *Handbook to the Works of B.*, A. Orr 1887; *B. as a Philosophical and Religious Teacher*, Sir H. Jones 1891; *R. B.*, C. H. Herford 1925; *Collected Essays*, W. P. Ker 1925; *Lyrical Poetry from Blake to Hardy*, Sir H. J. C. Grierson 1928; *Eight Victorian*

Poets, F. L. Lucas, Camb. 1930; *Letters of R. B. to E. B. B. 1845–46* 2 vols. N.Y. 1930; *B. and the XXth Century*, A. A. Brookington, Oxfd. 1932; *A Browning Handbook*, W. C. de Vane, N.Y. 1935.

CHAPTER XXXIII. (1) ELIZABETH BARRETT BROWNING: *Poetical Works* ed. Sir F. G. Kenyon 1897; do. (Oxford Poets); *Aurora Leigh* ed. A. C. Swinburne 1898; ed. H. B. Forman (Temple Classics). THOMAS BABINGTON MACAULAY: *Poems* (World's Classics). EMILY BRONTË: *Complete Poems* ed. C. W. Hatfield, N.Y. 1941. EBENEZER ELLIOTT: *Poetical Works* ed. E. Elliott 2 vols. 1876. JOHN KEBLE: *The Christian Year* in World's Classics and Everyman's Lib.; *The Christian ·Year, Lyra Innocentium and Other Poems* in Oxford Poets. JOHN HENRY NEWMAN: *Poems* (Oxford Standard Authors). EDWARD FITZGERALD: *Rubáiyát* in G T S (1st edn. with variations in 2nd, 3rd and 4th edns.); ed. C. Ganz and Sir E. D. Ross 1938; *Rubáiyát* and *Six Plays of Calderon* in Everyman's Lib. FREDERICK TENNYSON: *Shorter Poems* ed. C. B. L. Tennyson 1913. CHARLES TENNYSON-TURNER: *Collected Sonnets* (Preface by Hallam, Lord Tennyson) 1898. *Oxford Book of Victorian Verse*.

(2) *Edward FitzGerald*, A. C. Benson (E M L). *History of Nineteenth Century Literature* (1780–1900), G. Saintsbury 1901. *Literature of the Victorian Era*, H. Walker, Camb. 1910. *A Survey of English Literature 1830–1880*, O. Elton 2 vols. 1920.

CHAPTER XXXIV. (1) MATTHEW ARNOLD: *Poems*, 3 vols. 1895; 1 vol. (Globe). ARTHUR HUGH CLOUGH: *Poetical Works* with Memoir bv F. T. Palgrave (Muses' Lib.). CHARLES KINGSLEY: *Poems*, Collected edn. 2 vols. 1927; ed. E. Rhys (Everyman's Lib.).

(2) *Letters and Memoirs of C. Kingsley*, 2 vols. 1877, '78, '83. *Letters of M. Arnold to A. H. Clough* ed. H. F. Lowry 1932. *M. Arnold*, L. Trilling 1939. *The Poetry of M. A.*, C. B. Tinker and H. F. Lowry 1940.

CHAPTER XXXV. (1) D. G. ROSSETTI: *Collected Works* ed. W. M. Rossetti 1886. A. C. SWINBURNE: *Poems* 1904; *Tragedies* 1905–6; *Bonchurch Collected edn.* 20 vols. 1926–27; selections ed. by himself 1887; selections with introd. by L. Binyon (World's Classics). WILLIAM MORRIS: *Collected Works* ed. May Morris 24 vols. 1910–; *Prose and Poetry of W. M.* (Oxford Poets); *Earthly Paradise* ed. J. Drinkwater 3 vols. (Muses' Lib.). C. ROSSETTI: *Poetical Works* ed. W. M. Rossetti 1904.

(2) *D. G. Rossetti, His Family Letters with a Memoir* ed. W. M. Rossetti 2 vols. 1895; *Recollections of R.*, Hall Caine 1928; *The Pre-Raphaelite Tragedy*, W. Gaunt 1943. *Life of A. C. Swinburne*, Sir E. Gosse 1917; *La Jeunesse de S.*, G. Lafourcade 2 vols. Paris 1928; *S., A Literary Biography*, do. 1932. *Life of W. Morris*, J. W. Mackail 1899, 1932. *C. Rossetti*, Walter de la Mare in *Trans. Royal Soc. of Lit.* 1926; *C. Rossetti*, F. Shore, Camb. 1930. *Eight Victorian Poets*, F. L. Lucas, Camb. 1930.

CHAPTER XXXVI. (1) COVENTRY PATMORE: *Poems*, 9th collected edn. 2 vols. 1906; *The Angel in the House* ed. A. Meynell (Muses' Lib.). JAMES THOMSON: *The City of Dreadful Night and Other Poems* 1888. P. J. BAILEY: *Festus* 1839, 1845, 1864, 1880. S. DOBELL: *Balder* 1835, 1854. ALEX. SMITH: *Poetical Works* ed. W. Sinclair, Edin. 1909. F. LOCKER-LAMPSON: *London Lyrics* ed. A. Dobson 1904. C. S. CALVERLEY: *Verses and Flyleaves*, Camb. 1885. J. K. STEPHEN: *Lapsus Calami and Other Verses* 1886. R. F. MURRAY: *The Scarlet Gown*, St. Andrews 1891; *Poems* with Memoir by A. Lang 1894. SIR W. S. GILBERT: *Original Plays*, 4 Series 1896–1920; *Bab Ballads* 1869, 1874, 1898. W. (JOHNSON) CORY: *Ionica* 1858; *Ionica II* 1877; *with additional poems* ed. A. C. Benson 1891. F. W. H. MYERS: *Collected Poems* ed. E. Myers 1921. J. A. SYMONDS: *Miscellanies* 1885. R. W. DIXON: *Songs and Odes* ed. R. Bridges 1896; *A Selection* with Memoir by R. Bridges 1909. LORD DE TABLEY: *Collected Poems* 1903; *Selected Poems* ed. J. Drinkwater, Oxfd. 1924. SIR SAMUEL FERGUSON: *Poems* with introd. by A. P. Graves 1918. W. ALLINGHAM: *Works* 6 vols. 1890; *Poems* selected by H. Allingham (G T S). JEAN INGELOW: *Poems* 2 vols. 1893; 1 vol. (Muses' Lib.). WILLIAM BARNES: *Poems of Rural Life* 1844, '79, '83; *Select Poems* ed. T. Hardy, Oxfd. 1908. T. E. BROWN: *Poems* 1903; *Selected Poems* (G T S). For selections see *The Oxford Book of Victorian Verse*.

532 A CRITICAL HISTORY OF ENGLISH POETRY

(2) *Memoirs of Coventry Patmore*, B. Champneys 2 vols. 1900–01; *Life of C. P.*, Sir E. Gosse 1905. *Lit. of the Victorian Era*, H. Walker, Camb. 1910. *Life and Poetry of James Thomson*, J. E. Meeken, New Haven 1917.

CHAPTER XXXVII. (1) GEORGE MEREDITH: *Poetical Works* with notes by G. M. Trevelyan 1912. THOMAS HARDY: *The Dynasts* 1903–8; *Famous Tragedy of the Queen of Cornwall* 1923; *Collected Poems* 1932; *Selected Poems*, ed. G. M. Young 1940.
(2) (*a*) *New Studies*, E. Dowden 1895; *The Poetry and Philosophy of George Meredith*, G. M. Trevelyan 1906; *G. M.*, Sir James Barrie 1909; *Letters* ed. by his son 2 vols. 1912; *Figures of Several Centuries*, A. Symons 1916; *G. M.*, J. B. Priestley (E M L).
(*b*) *Thomas Hardy, A Critical Study*, L. Abercrombie 1922; *A Study of T.H.*, A. Symons 1927; *Early Life of T.H.*, F. E. Hardy 1928; *Later Years*, do. 1930; *T. H.*, E. Blunden (E M L); *The Art of T. H.*, Lionel Johnson 2nd ed. 1923.

CHAPTER XXXVIII. (1) SIR WILLIAM WATSON: *Poems (1878–1935)* 1936. ROBERT BRIDGES: *Poetical Works* (excluding the eight Dramas) 1936. RUDYARD KIPLING: *Verse, Inclusive Edition*, 1933. ANDREW LANG: *Poetical Works* ed. Mrs. Lang 4 vols. 1923. R. L. STEVENSON: *Poems* in *Collected Works*—Tusitala edn. Vols. XXII and XXIII 1923–24; Skerryvore edn. Vol. XX 1924–25. W. E. HENLEY: *Works* 5 vols. 1921. LIONEL JOHNSON: *Poetical Works* 1915. ARTHUR SYMONS: *Poems* in *Collected Works* Vols. I–III 1924. W. B. YEATS: *Collected Poems* 1933. FRANCIS THOMPSON: *Works* ed. W. Meynell 3 vols. 1913; *Collected Poetry* 1913. ALICE MEYNELL: *Poems, Complete Edition* 1923. A. E. HOUSMAN: *Collected Poems* 1939. RONALD C. MACFIE: *Collected Poems* 1929. RICHARD LE GALLIENNE and JOHN DAVIDSON: no collected edition.
(2) *The Eighteen-Nineties*, Holbrook Jackson 1913. *Robert Bridges*, E. Thompson 1944. *W. B . Yeats*, J. Hone 1942. *Introd. to A Choice of Kipling's Verse*, T. S. Eliot 1941.

CHAPTER XXXIX. (1) C. M. DOUGHTY: *Under Arms* 1900; *The Dawn in Britain* 6 vols. 1906; *Adam Cast Forth* 1908; *The Cliffs* 1909; *The Clouds* 1912; *The Titans* 1916; *Mansoul* 1922. LAURENCE BINYON: *Collected Poems* 2 vols. 1931; tr. of *Divina Commedia* 1932, 1938, 1943. T. STURGE MOORE: *Collected Poems* 4 vols. 1931–33. WALTER DE LA MARE: *Collected Poems* 1942. JOHN MASEFIELD: *Collected Poems* 1928. W. W. GIBSON: *Collected Poems* 1926. H. TRENCH: *Poems* 2 vols. 1918. W. H. DAVIES: *Poems* 1934. CHARLOTTE MEW: *The Farmer's Bride* 1916; *The Rambling Sailor* 1929. RACHEL ANNAND TAYLOR: *Poems* 1904; *Rose and Vine* 1908; *The Hours of Fiammetta* 1910. STEPHEN PHILLIPS: *Lyrics and Dramas* 1913; *Panama and Other Poems* 1915. LASCELLES ABERCROMBIE: *Poems* 1930. GORDON BOTTOMLEY: *Plays* 1920; *Gruach* 1921; *Poems of Thirty Years* 1925; *Lyric Plays* 1932. HILAIRE BELLOC: *Sonnets and Verse* 1938. G. K. CHESTERTON: *Collected Poems* 1927; *New and Collected Poems* 1929. REV. A. S. CRIPPS: *Africa Verses* 1929. RALPH HODGSON: *Poems* 1917. J. ELROY FLECKER: *Collected Poems* ed. Sir J. C. Squire 1916, 1923. RUPERT BROOKE: *Collected Poems* 1918; *Complete Poems* 1932. *Georgian Poetry* ed. Sir E. Marsh 5 vols. 1911–12, 1913–15, 1915–17, 1918–19, 1920–22. *Golden Treasury of Modern Lyrics*, ed. L. Binyon 1924.
(2) See Chapter XLI (2).

CHAPTER XL. (1) ROBERT NICHOLS: *Such Was My Singing* 1942. ROBERT GRAVES: *Collected Poems* 1938. MAURICE BARING: *Collected Poems* 1925, 1929; selected 1930. CHARLES H. SORLEY: *Marlborough and Other Poems*, Camb. 1916. JULIAN GRENFELL: see 'Soldier Poets' first series 1916. FRANCIS LEDWIDGE: *Collected Poems* 1945. EDWARD THOMAS: *Collected Poems* 1922. SIEGFRIED SASSOON: *Selected Poems* 1925; *Satirical Poems* 1926; *Nativity* 1927; *Road to Ruin* 1933; *Vigils* 1934: WILFRED OWEN: *Poems* ed. E. Blunden 1931. T. E. HULME: *Speculations* ed. Herbert Read 1924. 'H. D.': *Collected Poems* 1925. RICHARD ALDINGTON: *Poems* 1934. F. S. FLINT: *In the Net of the Stars* 1909; *Cadences* 1915; *Other World Cadences* 1920.
(2) See Chapter XLI (2).

CHAPTER XLI. (1) W. J. R. TURNER: *The Hunter* 1916; *The Dark Wind* 1920; *New Poems* 1928; *Songs and Incantations* 1934. CHAS. WILLIAMS: *Poems of Conformity* 1917. JOHN FREEMAN: *Collected Poems* 1928; *Last Poems* 1930. EDWARD SHANKS: *Collected Poems* 1926. EDMUND BLUNDEN: *Poems 1914–30*, 1930. V. SACKVILLE-WEST: *The Land* 1926; *Collected Poems* 1933. REV. A. YOUNG: *Collected Poems* 1936. D. H. LAWRENCE: *Collected Poems* 1932. HERBERT READ: *Poems 1915–1935*. G. M. HOPKINS: *Poems* 1918; with additions 1930. EDITH SITWELL: *Selected Poems* 1936. SIR O. SITWELL: *Collected Poems and Satires* 1931. SACHEVERELL SITWELL: *Collected Poems* 1936. T. S. ELIOT: *Collected Poems 1907–1935*, 1936. 'A.E.': *Collected Poems* 1913, 1926. J. M. SYNGE: *Poems and Translations*, Dublin, 1912. K. TYNAN (HINKSON): *Collected Poems* 1930. JAMES STEPHENS: *Collected Poems* 1926. PADRAIC COLUM: *Poems* 1932. DOROTHY WELLESLEY: *Poems of Ten Years* 1934. L. A. G. STRONG: *Selected Poems* 1931; *March Evening* 1932. For other recent Irish poets see Yeats's *Oxford Book of Modern Verse*. J. LOGIE ROBERTSON: *Horace in Homespun*, Edin. 1882. MARION ANGUS: *The Lilt*, Aberdeen 1927; *The Singin' Lass* 1929; *The Turn o' the Day* 1931. WALTER WINGATE: *Poems*, Glasgow 1919. JOHN BUCHAN: *Poems, Scots and English*, 1917. VIOLET JACOB: *Collected Poems*, Edin. 1944. C. M. GRIEVE: *Sangschaw* 1926; *Penny Wheep* 1926; *First Hymn to Lenin* 1931. CHAS. MURRAY: *Hamewith* 1909; *A Sough o' War* 1917; *In the Country Places* 1920. See further W. Robb's *Book of Twentieth Century Scots Verse*. C. DAY LEWIS: see text. W. H. AUDEN: *Poems* 1930, 1933; *The Dance of Death* 1933; *Look, Stranger* 1936. STEPHEN SPENDER: *Twenty Poems* 1930; *Poems* 1933; *The Still Centre* 1939. L. MACNEICE: *Blind Fireworks* 1929; *Poems* 1935. CHAS. MADGE: *Disappearing Castle* 1937. EDWIN MUIR: *First Poems* 1927; *Six Poems* 1932; *Journeys and Places* 1937. DYLAN THOMAS: *Eighteen Poems* 1934; *Twenty-five Poems* 1936. ROY CAMPBELL: *The Flaming Terrapin* 1924; *Adamastor* 1930; *The Georgiad* 1931; *Mithraic Emblems* 1932; *Flowering Reeds* 1933. W. C. F. PLOMER: *Family Tree* 1929; *Fivefold Screen* 1932. A. E. COPPARD: *Collected Poems* 1928; *Cherry Ripe* 1935. JULIAN BELL: see *Julian Bell: Essays, Poems and Letters* 1938. REDWOOD ANDERSON: *Babel* 1927; *The Vortex* 1928. RUTH PITTER: *Mad Lady's Garland* 1934; *A Trophy of Arms, Poems 1926–1935 n.d.* MURIEL STUART: *Selected Poems* 1927. LILIAN BOWES-LYON: *The White Hare* 1934; *Bright Feather Fading* 1936. KATHLEEN RAINE: *Stone and Flowers* 1943. Much recent poetry has not yet appeared in book form, but examples will be found in the following anthologies and periodicals: *New Signatures* ed. M. Roberts 1932; *The Faber Book of Modern Verse* ed. do. 1936; *Recent Poetry 1923–33* ed. Alida Monro 1933; *Poems of To-morrow* ed. Janet Adam Smith 1935; *The Year's Poetry* 1934, '35, '36, '37, '38; *Poems of Twenty Years* ed. M. Wollman 1938; *Fear No More* 1940; *New Verse* ed. G. Grigson; *New Writing, Folios of New Writing, New Writing and Daylight, Penguin New Writing*, all ed. John Lehmann.

(2) *New Paths on Helicon*, Sir H. Newbolt 1925; *A Survey of Modernist Poetry*, L. Riding and R. Graves 1927; *Aspects of Modern Poetry*, E. Sitwell 1934; *A Hope for Poetry*, C. Day Lewis 1934; *Letters of G. M. Hopkins* ed. C. C. Abbott 1935, 1938; *Contemporary British Lit.* T. B. Millett, J. M. Manly, and E. Rickert 3rd edn. 1939; *The Present Age*, Edwin Muir 1939; *Poetry and the Modern World*, D. Daiches, Chicago 1940; *The Trend of Modern Poetry*, G. Bullough 2nd edn. 1941; *G. M. Hopkins*, W. H. Gardner 1944.

INDEX

(Poems by known authors are not included)

Lovelace, Richard, 150
Lucan, 83
Lucretius, 186
Lydgate, John, 39, 40-41
Lyly, John, 103-104

Macaulay, Thomas Babington, 425-426
MacDonald, George, 459
Macfie, Ronald Campbell, 482-483, 504
Machiavelli, 346
MacNeice, Louis, 518
Macpherson, James, 227
Macrobius, 15
Madge, Charles, 519
Maldon, 5-6
Mallet, David, 208, 217
Malory, Sir Thomas, 39, 75
Mantuan (Baptista Mantuanus), 70, 87
Marie de France, 39
Marino, G. B., 94, 152
Marlowe, Christopher, 80, 104-105, 140
Marot, Clément, 68
Marston, John, 80, 88, 134
Martial, 95, 227
Marvell, Andrew, 155-156, 174
Masefield, John, 315, 488, 491, 503-504
Massinger, Philip, 137-138, 142-143
Mayne, John, 266
Medwall, Henry, 49
Meredith, George, 461-463
Merry Devil of Edmonton, The, 135
'Metaphysical' school, 98-99
Mew, Charlotte, 493
Meynell, Alice, 481
Michael Angelo, 292, 346
Mickle, W. J., 266
Middleton, Thomas, 134-135
Milton, John, 5, 11, 34, 71, 136, 146, 158-171, 183
Minot, Laurence, 9-10
Mirror for Magistrates, A, 41, 66
Miscellanies, Early Tudor, 64, 65
—, Elizabethan, 85-86
—, Commonwealth, 157
—, Restoration, 190
Molière, 132
Montaigne, 157
Montemayor, 86
Montgomerie, Alexander, 59, 60
Montrose, James Graham, Marquis of, 150, 263
Moore, Thomas, 392-393
Moore, Thomas Sturge, 488, 490
Morris, William, 445-447
Moschus, 364
Muir, Edwin, 519
Murray, Charles, 516
Murray, Robert Fuller, 457

Musaeus, 80
Myers, F. W. H., 458

Nairne, Lady, 395
Nash, Thomas, 86, 106, 107
Newman, John Henry, 392, 405, 430-431
New Signatures, 518
Nicholas of Guildford, 9
Nichols, Robert, 496
Niebuhr, 425
Nietzsche, 479
Norris, John, of Bemerton, 190
Nutbrown Maid, The, 42

Occleve, Thomas, 40, 41, 92
O'Connor, Frank, 514
Odes, Horatian, 95, 155, 157
—, Pindaric, 95, 156, 222, 226
Oldham, John, 175
"O lusty May, with Flora Queene", 59
Orison of Our Lady, 9
Ormulum, The, 9, 19
O'Shaughnessy, Arthur, 459
Oton de Granson, 25
Otway, Thomas, 188-189
Ovid, 25, 66, 80, 83, 111, 186, 191, 192, 194
Owen, Wilfred, 497, 508-509
Oxford, Earl of, 65

Painter, William, 102
Parnell, Thomas, 207
Pascal, 241
Pastorals, 41, 55, 69-71, 86-88, 91, 92-93, 162, 192-193, 194, 206, 208, 223-224
Patience, 14
Patmore, Coventry, 453-455
Pearl, The, 10, 14, 15
Peblis to the Play, 53
Peele, George, 106-107
Percy, Thomas, bishop, 228-230
Perizonius, 425
Persius, 80, 88, 186
Petrarch, 22, 27, 59, 62, 63, 67, 77, 82, 163, 346, 371, 385
Philips, Ambrose, 192, 207, 208
Phillips, Stephen, 493
Phoenix, The, 5
Pindar, 388-389
Pistil of Susane, 52
Pitter, Ruth, 521
Plato and Platonism, 76, 94, 97, 353, 363 n., 367
Plautus, 100, 110
Plomer, William, 520
Pope, Alexander, 191-202
Pope, Walter, 190
Praed, Winthrop Mackworth, 457
Preston, Thomas, 101, 107